Whitney Bienni

The 2014 Whitney Biennial was curated by Stuart Comer, Anthony Elms, and Michelle Grabner. They were assisted by Elisabeth Sherman, curatorial assistant; Mamie Tinkler, Biennial coordinator; and Martha Joseph, Biennial assistant.

Whitney Museum of American Art, New York
March 7–May 25, 2014

Sponsored in part by

BCBGMAXAZRIA

and

Deutsche Bank 

Major support is provided by

Sotheby's

Generous support is provided by The Brown Foundation, Inc.; The Keith Haring Foundation; Anne Cox Chambers; and an anonymous donor.

Additional support is provided by 2014 Biennial Committee Chairs: Beth Rudin DeWoody and Rebecca and Marty Eisenberg; 2014 Biennial Committee members: Philip Aarons and Shelley Fox Aarons, James Keith Brown and Eric Diefenbach, Barbara and Michael Gamson, Jill and Peter Kraus, Diane and Adam E. Max, and Carla Emil and Rich Silverstein; the Consulate General of the Federal Republic of Germany; the Cultural Services of the French Embassy in the U.S.; the Juliet Lea Hillman Simonds Foundation; and Judy and Archibald Cox, Jr.

Funding for the 2014 Biennial is also provided by endowments created by Melva Bucksbaum, Emily Fisher Landau, and Leonard A. Lauder.

Whitney Museum of American Art
945 Madison Avenue at 75th Street
New York, NY 10021
whitney.org

Distributed by Yale University Press
302 Temple Street
P.O. Box 209040
New Haven, CT 06520
yalebooks.com/art

Printed and bound in the United States
10 9 8 7 6 5 4 3 2 1

ISBN: 978-0-300-19687-0
ISSN: 1043-3260

This catalogue was produced by the publications department at the Whitney Museum of American Art, New York: Beth A. Huseman, director of publications; Beth Turk, associate editor; Anita Duquette, manager, rights and reproductions; and Jacob Horn, editorial assistant.

Managing editor: Beth Turk
Project manager: Donna Wingate
Manuscript editor: Karen Kelly
with Jason Best, Thea Hetzner, and Diana Stoll
Conversations editor: Deirdre O'Dwyer
Proofreader: Sam Franks
Catalogue design: Mark Owens, Life of the Mind, with Ghazaal Vojdani
Production: Sue Medlicott and Nerissa Dominguez Vales, The Production Department
Separations and printing: GHP, West Haven, CT

This book is typeset in Aldine 721 and Monotype Grotesque

Whitney Biennial 2014

Whitney Museum of American Art, New York
Distributed by Yale University Press, New Haven and London

Table of Contents

Foreword

To understand the Whitney Museum of American Art's decision to ask three individuals from outside the Museum to serve as curators for the current Biennial, two of whom are practicing artists and each of distinct geographical, occupational, generational, and theoretical perspectives, it is worth taking a moment to reflect upon the role of curators during more than eight decades of the exhibition. The first Whitney Biennial, in 1932, followed the democratic, artist-centric spirit of the annual exhibitions held from 1918 at the Whitney Studio Club, the antecedent of the Museum. Its purpose was as simple as it was idealistic and elusive (even at a time when the number of practicing American artists was far fewer than today): to survey the broadest possible cross section of American art, a representational sample of the diverse schools and style from all regions of the United States. While the Biennial was—and continues to be—an invitational exhibition, for decades the Museum sought to downplay the voice of the curators. Indeed, for more than thirty years, the Biennial catalogues did not even list the names of the curators who had organized the exhibition; the desire was always to foreground the art and the artists themselves. As with the role of an editor, the thinking went, the curator should be more or less invisible.

This ethos had its roots in the very conceptual foundation of the Museum, which originated as a "non-institutional" institution—an organization run by and for artists. The Museum's founder, Gertrude Vanderbilt Whitney, was, of course, an artist, as were three of the four original curators. The organizational structure of the Biennial was radical for its time: not only were artists invited to choose what artworks they wanted to show, they were often consulted as to how and where their work would be exhibited, a practice that continued until 1940—this in an era when such decisions were exclusively dictated by juries or other official arbiters of taste. Moreover, in the desire to encourage a market for American art, which did not exist at the time (now hard to believe), visitors were told that works were for purchase and artists' addresses were listed in the catalogues to facilitate potential sales.

To marvel at how different the Biennial was then is also to appreciate its dramatic evolution, and central to that has been a willingness (hesitant at times, but born of necessity) to rethink the role of the curator and to experiment with the curatorial process. That, of course, makes it sound far easier than it was. Even after the center of the art world arguably shifted to New York following World War II and American art secured its place on the international stage, the Whitney was still reluctant to depart too much from its artist-centric tradition. The Museum faced criticism for not exercising its editorial voice and critical expertise in its Biennials; it was not until the 1970s that the curators of the exhibition began to be identified in the catalogues, and that, perhaps, was simply in a desire for transparency, to openly acknowledge who was extending the invitations. But by the late twentieth century, a proper survey of contemporary American art had become impossible to attempt, certainly one as expansive as what had been mounted during the Museum's early years. As the role of the curators became more critical, the Museum explicitly took authorial responsibility for the point of view and content of the exhibition (which, in turn, led to another bout of criticisms, these based on charges of favoritism for particular artists and galleries). The process is never perfect—and that, in part, is what continues to give the Whitney Biennial its vitality. For the past couple decades, the Museum has sought to move beyond the tradition of selecting its team of curators for the Biennial from its own ranks, in the desire to bring outside voices to the table, to ensure that we were not just "talking to ourselves." Sometimes this has been in the form of advisors representing different views and geographical locations; other times, the Museum has included outside curators on the team itself, among them an art publisher, independent curators, as well as directors and curators from other museums and arts organizations.

For the 2014 Biennial, the Museum has taken this process of experimentation a step further, with two in-house curators acting in the role of advisors and three external curators asked to organize the exhibition. Each has been given a floor of the Museum, which will, in effect, create a compendium of three individual exhibitions, each with a distinct point of view. At first glance, this could not seem more diametrically opposed to the origins of the Biennial. And, of course, on the one hand, it is. Yet even if it has long been impossible to create what might be remotely considered a comprehensive survey of contemporary American art (limitations of space aside), the Whitney has not strayed from the centrality of art and artists at the core of the institution's founding, even as we respond to the ever changing dynamics that inform the contemporary moment in American art.

Foreword

In this, the first Biennial curated wholly by curators selected from outside the Museum, we have chosen three curators who have not been based in New York, affording views from outside the city's art scene. Stuart Comer, until very recently, has been living and working in London for the past decade; Anthony Elms, now based in Philadelphia, worked in Chicago for seven years; and Michelle Grabner has spent her entire career living and working in Wisconsin and Illinois. Both Grabner and Elms are working artists who are also established curators: Grabner founded and operates two exhibition spaces, the Suburban and the Poor Farm, and is also a professor at the School of the Art Institute of Chicago, while Elms serves as associate curator at the Institute of Contemporary Art at the University of Pennsylvania. Stuart Comer is the non-artist of the group, but in his curatorial practice, he is equally interested in a more fluid understanding of contemporary culture a stance reflected in his own career evolution as his position has morphed from curator of public events to curator of film at the Tate Modern and now to chief curator of media and performance art at the Museum of Modern Art.

To recognize the essential role of the curator, in this, an era of art defined by no rules and no schools, it not to argue for the primacy of the curator. Rather, by openly acknowledging their subjective positions and their reluctance to define, summarize, and systematize current artistic practices, these three curators, among the more astute observers/participants of the contemporary art scene, invite viewers to experience the selected art in a more pure, less filtered state—to explore, to question, to wonder, to suggest new paradigms and ways of thinking: visually, intellectually, perceptually, and viscerally. After all, this is what art is and should be about.

First and foremost, my great gratitude to these three curators. A Biennial is difficult enough to curate in eighteen months from within, even more doing so from a distance. And negotiating the limitations and inequality of gallery spaces, as represented by each floor of the Whitney's Marcel Breuer building, is no easy task. I also express my deepest thanks to Elisabeth Sussman, curator and Sondra Gilman Curator of Photography, and Jay Sanders, curator of performance, for serving as curatorial advisors to the 2014 Biennial; to the peerless Biennial team: senior curatorial assistant Elisabeth Sherman, Biennial coordinator Mamie Tinkler, and Biennial assistant Martha Joseph; as well as to the entire Whitney staff, who have once again shown their dedication to and enthusiasm for this demanding and rewarding project.

The 2014 Biennial's corporate sponsors—BCBGMAXAZRIA, Deutsche Bank, and Sotheby's—have long demonstrated their commitment to championing art that takes risks and pushes boundaries and I am grateful for their continued support of the Whitney and its signature exhibition. The generous contributions of the Brown Foundation, Inc., the Keith Haring Foundation, Anne Cox Chambers, and an anonymous donor were essential to the exhibition. My appreciation also goes to the 2014 Biennial Committee Chairs, Beth Rudin DeWoody and Rebecca and Marty Eisenberg, and committee members Philip Aarons and Shelley Fox Aarons, James Keith Brown and Eric Diefenbach, Barbara and Michael Gamson, Jill and Peter Kraus, Diane and Adam E. Max, and Carla Emil and Rich Silverstein. I am also grateful to the Consulate General of the Federal Republic of Germany, the Cultural Services of the French Embassy in the U.S., the Juliet Lea Hillman Simonds Foundation, and Judy and Archibald Cox Jr. for kindly recognizing the importance of this year's Biennial. In addition, I am deeply grateful to Melva Bucksbaum, Emily Fisher Landau, and Leonard A. Lauder for their longstanding devotion to the Whitney and their foresight in the creation of endowments for the Biennial. The steadfast commitment of these individuals and organizations has made the exhibition a reality.

Adam D. Weinberg
Alice Pratt Brown Director

Introduction

The invitation to co-curate the 2014 Biennial has been an exciting opportunity to talk with a wide range of artists; to give shape to the ever-changing discourse of contemporary art; and to rethink how American art is understood, articulated, and debated. While we are not co-curators in the traditional sense of working together to present a unified vision—we each have a floor of the Museum on which to present an exhibition—there are certainly moments of connection and areas of overlap within the building and also times where our individual approaches meet in other spaces. The amount of negotiation and discussion about everything from overarching conceptual ideas to schedules for screenings and performances among the three of us has been surprisingly large given that we were quite distinctly going our own ways. Perhaps one of the biggest surprises we encountered during the process was during discussions of one another's preliminary lists of artists and interests. At that point, it became clear that we were inspired by a number of the same artists, even as our lists grew in markedly disparate directions. Our common connections also extended to an engagement with writing; artists who have been practicing for decades (often without fanfare); the expansiveness of media; the enduring presence of those who are gone; resistance to traditions and labels; the double (if not triple and quadruple) roles of participants: artist/educator, author/artist, publisher/presenter, and so forth; and the way authorship, even for an individual maker, is often wildly complex, combinatory, and collaborative today. If there is any central point of cohesion, it may be the slipperiness of authorship that threads through each of our programs. But this is not surprising as it mirrors the ever-increasing speed of our digital world and the ease with which we pull, organize, and recombine the information we consume. In many ways, it has simply become inefficient to slow down and figure out who is responsible for a specific idea or action, opening up interesting areas of collaboration.

Staging a biennial in the context of a museum, particularly one dedicated to the art of a single country and located in one of the art world's major centers, distinguishes the Whitney's exhibition from the growing number of biennials and surveys being held around the world. We hope that our iteration of the Biennial will suggest the profoundly diverse and hybrid cultural identity of America today. The exhibition and this catalogue offer a rare chance to look broadly at different types of work and various modes of working that can be called contemporary American art. Some borders—formal, conceptual, geographic, temporal—get tested, but we can still see through the assembled projects and people how the breadth of art is expanding because it is the artists and makers themselves who are pushing boundaries by collaborating, using the materials of others, digging through archives, returning to supposedly forlorn materials, or refusing to neatly adhere to a medium or discipline.

We are honored to be part of the long and formidable history of the Whitney's Annuals and Biennials, many of which have been held in the Museum's Marcel Breuer–designed building on Madison Avenue. This sense of history was not lost on us, although as outside curators our relationship with both this signature exhibition and its longstanding home, the building itself, means something quite different than it does to staff curators, and we have organized this exhibition largely independent of discussions of it being the last in the building for the foreseeable future. Each of us has a point of view shaped as much by cities of our formation and work—Chicago, Detroit, London, Los Angeles, Milwaukee, and Philadelphia as well as New York. And we each came to the building carrying our own experiences of it and of the Whitney, from personal watershed to familiarity as cultural destination. As such, our collective interest in working with, or at moments against, the Breuer building was not one of nostalgia—saying goodbye—but rather of engaged newcomers, excited at the opportunity to work with this singular and distinctive setting. Moreover, both buildings, the Museum's current home and its new Renzo Piano–designed building downtown, served as inspiration for artists across our three exhibitions.

The design and organization of this catalogue is meant to parallel that of the exhibition. Each of us has a chapter which presents our thinking as curators and, more important, the artists we have invited to participate. Yet each chapter is quite different: Stuart's section pairs artists with critical discourse from a variety of writers, curators, and critics; Anthony's chapter enables the artists to speak for themselves, whether visually or linguistically, sometimes with a collaborator of their choosing; and Michelle's section features a series of conversations between artists and a diverse range of colleagues, friends, critics, and strangers. The textures that appear on the cover of this volume and in the interstitial spaces (the breaks between sections) come from rubbings of the surfaces of Breuer building—a motif meant to ground the reader of the wide-ranging content in the physical facts of the exhibition experience.

What attracted us most about the invitation to work on the Biennial was the chance to do what we love: talk and work with artists to publicly present their efforts. To that end, there are essentially three Biennials under one roof. And yet it is still one exhibition with one name. This is not an exhibition with three budgets, three opportunities to craft the structure for events, three screening rooms, three performance spaces, or three catalogues; it does not even divide perfectly into three floors. Together, we want the viewer to have a singular encounter with artists that is wide ranging, thoughtful, spirited, strident, as well as exciting and engaged. We invite you to locate in our collective efforts our unified desire to engage with the various concerns and questions we all must ask ourselves today.

Stuart Comer
Anthony Elms
Michelle Grabner

I. Stuart Comer

ESSAYS

ARTISTS

Shape-shifting
Stuart Comer

Over lunch, we discuss clouds and explosions. Surrounded by antique architectural maquettes built a century ago in the adjacent Carpenters' Guild, we compare notes about time spent in California and mutual friends in Beirut. This conversation in Paris, my first personal encounter with Etel Adnan, draws out the crux of what has impressed me in her books: a sharpened sense of matter and antimatter, of violence in the physical world, and the atmosphere of exile.

Adnan is best known as an acclaimed poet and essayist, and a defining voice in Arab-American literature. Her practice as a painter predates her work in literature, but she has gained wide attention for her paintings only recently. She is keenly attuned to the politics of language and abstraction. Raised in Beirut speaking Greek and Arabic at home, educated in French and English in Paris and California, she resisted writing in French during the Algerian War of Independence, turning instead to making abstract paintings. The Vietnam War provoked a return to language in solidarity with the poets' movement against the war, and she began to write poems again.

During this time, while teaching at a small Catholic college in San Rafael, California, she conceived a form in which her writing and painting—previously considered discrete practices—could coexist: the *leporellos*, a series of concertina-fold, scroll-like books in which the written word and drawn or painted forms find the space and rhythm to renegotiate their conventional roles. The perfect format for a nomadic artist, the *leporellos* are portable, mutable scores that record a life lived across charged topologies of war, love, and intellectual inquiry. The books literally unfold into what Adnan's partner, the artist and publisher Simone Fattal, calls "readings of poetry taking place in the parallel world of color and sensory perception."[1]

The fragmented, horizontal format of the *leporellos* finds an unexpected echo in *I See Infinite Distance Between Any Point and Another* (2012), a film by London-based artist collective The Otolith Group, shot primarily in Adnan's Paris apartment as she reads from her poem "The Sea" (2011). As Adnan concludes narrating her dark meditation on the mutations and movements of the ocean in the Anthropocene, the film cuts abruptly to a panning, aerial shot of the frozen Danube in Budapest as it begins to thaw. The genial sound of Adnan's aging, cosmopolitan voice is displaced by the ancient cacophony of one state of matter becoming another. Not unlike the streams of floating glyphs, lines, and letters in the *leporellos*, the chunks of ice become unbound but not wholly discreet from one another. The deafening sound is a language of its own, one without a conventional voice.

Adnan's work and the nomadic, cosmopolitan patterns of her life have formed something of a loose framework for this exhibition. At eighty-nine years old, Adnan has long been defined as either a writer or a visual artist, but she is both, and the two are fluidly interchangeable in her practice. In any one of her projects, symbols shift and mutate: a letter might become a glyph, which might become a painted brushstroke of a mountainside. Fundamentally, the equivalence between different forms in Adnan's work and the constant process of translation among those forms gives her work its dynamism, which is the result of a hybrid approach to art-making that Adnan has been exploring for decades now across several continents (and often outside the established art-world context).

1. Simone Fattal, "On Perception: Etel Adnan's Visual Art," in *Etel Adnan: Critical Essays on the Arab-American Writer and Artist*, Lisa Suhair Majaj and Amal Amireh, eds. (Jefferson, NC: McFarland, 2002), 89.

Artists increasingly make work whose hybridity is marked not only by the incorporation of multiple forms and media but processes in which these forms translate and morph into one another, a condition marked by what the writer Kevin Killian has termed: "the permeability of the image and the magnificent instability of the sign." [2] This exhibition seeks to reflect this tendency towards shape-shifting, whether through complex relationships between linguistic and visual forms; the development of two-dimensional scores, scripts, and patterns into three- or even four-dimensional actions and environments; challenging binary conventions of gender; or the intricacy of cosmopolitan, cross-national identities. Ideas about migration and movement apply here, as do those related to a position (geographic or otherwise) at a kind of periphery, off the mainland so to speak, the point at which dominant cultural forces may lose some of their inexorable thrust and crosscurrents come more strongly into play. The surfaces and spaces of the gallery respond in kind, playing multiple roles—from white cube to theater to cinema, and sometimes all of these at once.

2. Kevin Killian, "Kylie Minogue and the Ignorance of the West" (lecture, Kootenay School of Writing, Vancouver, BC, Canada, February 2002, archived and emended, http://www.asu.edu/pipercwcenter/how2journal/archive/online_archive/v2_1_2003/current/others/killian.htm).

Adnan's *leporellos*, to me, can be seen almost as a proto-screen, a kind of precursor to the laptops, smartphones, and tablets that increasingly dominate our lives, where the distinction between language and image continues to collapse and multiple surfaces and screens abut and fold into one another. Uri Aran also explores this terrain, particularly its haptic and topological possibilities, its ambiguities and disorienting effect. Dashiell Manley creates arenas of text, image, and form in which the "remake" of a film occurs not on celluloid but through a dense series of associations among media. Jacolby Satterwhite appropriates his mother's drawings and phrases, introducing them into vibrant, digitally animated landscapes in which his own body continues to "draw" in space through the gestures of voguing. Travis Jeppesen works as a writer, yet he also is critically engaged with the relationship between words and physical forms, the role of language as it takes on new visual and spatial concerns—the *inhabitation* of objects by writing, which positions itself within the work of art. The work of the editorial collective Triple Canopy also bridges a number of conversations that come out of the art world, out of literature, and out of numerous other fields of inquiry, linking word, image, archive, and live action at the threshold of the virtual and the real.

Semiotext(e), too, has generated an international community invested in reconsidering the relationships between theoretical and visual practice. Established by Sylvère Lotringer in 1974 as a means of introducing French theory to the New York art world, this pioneering publisher gradually migrated west to California. Chris Kraus and Hedi El Kholti joined Lotringer along the way, shifting the concerns of the press toward more feminist and queer perspectives. The twenty-three new titles that they have produced for the Biennial suggest a role for the exhibition and the art space as a forum for discursive knowledge production in which words and images find new ways to meet, to generate and contest meaning and ideas. The forty-year history of Semiotext(e) also suggests how the dissemination of critical ideas has evolved in a digital era of self-publishing and on-demand printing.

The late Channa Horwitz, a contemporary of Adnan, began her career before the "digital age" had taken hold, but her work has immediate relevance in the contemporary moment, when our collective migration online, and our further absorption into abstract political and economic systems, has been accompanied by a simultaneous counter-reaction, a strong desire to reconnect with live, physical action. In Horowitz's work, there's an almost obsessive approach to a set of symbolic geometries, patterns, and systems. These abstract scores are designed to be transformed into dance and live performance, translating the static, two-dimensional surface into forms defined by movement and space. This transformation of abstraction into a living, organic situation generates a physical connection to the image; it's also a challenge to the virtualization of experience. This challenge is taken up in diverse ways and across diverse media by artists ranging from Pauline Oliveros, whose series of text scores evinces the artist's interest in "deep listening" and a physical experience of sound that goes beyond the mere acoustic to a more haptic understanding of acoustic experience, or Kevin Beasley and Sergei Tcherepnin, both of whom employ sound to connect us to the object in space and to the architectural environment that surrounds us, rooting visual observation in a more complex sensorial network. The members of Sensory Ethnography Lab also create a physically intense experience through their use of film, transforming documentary practice and ethnographic observation through a political understanding of physical sensation.

Where to locate the "American" in a survey of contemporary American art, especially one with as much history behind it as the Whitney Biennial, is a question that has often challenged, even vexed, curators, and one whose answer sometimes emerges as a surprise. As an American who has spent much of the last thirteen years in the UK, the answer here seems to relate in important ways back to California, where I spent the previous decade. This, too, can be traced to Adnan, and to Horwitz and Oliveros, all of whose experiences living and working in California allowed them a significant degree of freedom from hegemonic cultural forces at play on the East Coast and specifically in New York. Key to the work of Semiotext(e) has been its move to California, bringing continental European intellectual traditions into closer dialogue with the Pacific Rim. In that sense, California becomes a kind of threshold or alternate entry point into questions that surround American identity, one that stands in contrast to what has long been regarded as the dominant (transatlantic) mode of exchange and has ever increasing relevance as the focal point of immigration to the United States continues to shift from the East Coast to California and the American Southwest. Fred Lonidier has produced an important body of work addressing the border area between San Diego and Tijuana. Julie Ault, whose Biennial project begins in the downtown New York of David Wojnarowicz and Martin Wong, takes an unexpected turn into the deserts, mountains, and plains of the American West. Ault and Lonidier join a range of artists who bring a perspective from what might be thought of as the American periphery, places that have experienced the full-force impact of American influence and even dominance and yet have embraced, rejected, subverted, or augmented that influence in myriad ways, in the process reflecting back alternative American identities that challenge core assumptions about what it means to be "American." Their work ranges from Ei Arakawa and Carissa Rodriguez's project addressing Hawaii, the Philippines, and alternative conceptions of "the Pacific paradise," to Radamés "Juni" Figueroa, who foregrounds the historic cultural and artistic connections between his native Puerto Rico as well as the Caribbean at large with New York.

In thinking of Adnan's career, it neither seems accurate to describe her as an artist and a writer, nor does it feel right to deploy the now-fashionable slash, as in "artist/writer"—establishing, as the words do, in their obstinate separateness, a binary that we may struggle to overcome linguistically but which, via lived experience, Adnan proves is eminently possible. And as I've alluded to here, I find myself gravitating toward artists like Adnan who are working with culture in a freer and more open-minded way—not fighting so much against traditionally established boundaries as ignoring them, unwilling to define themselves as image-makers or writers, painters or sculptors or filmmakers, but working in the interstices of categorical distinctions. Morgan Fisher, for example, better known as a filmmaker but whose paintings and architectural installations employ rigorously stringent structural systems that simultaneously open up a certain degree of uncertainty to invite questions about the structures that define us. Thus, I tread wary here in any discussion of "identity," American or otherwise. After all, in what has become the standard system of nomenclature by which to delineate certain boundaries within the vast American cultural landscape, binaries are implicitly set up as well; whatever comes before the hyphen in the construction " -American" is still somehow distinct from the American itself and a fixed identity is established. Whereas a generation ago identity politics were at the forefront of art discourse, today many artists, particularly those who came of age in the aftermath of the culture wars, appear not so concerned with demarcating group identities but with exploring the multiplicity of myriad shifting identities that form the individual. Witness Yve Laris Cohen's white slab wall and its migrations from the Breuer building to the future home of the Whitney, now under construction, by Renzo Piano. Within the context of both structures, the wall's identity shifts, and with each back-and-forth journey, it bears evidence of its migration. It is never the *same* wall at any given moment, nor is our experience of it. Any comprehensive notion of its "identity," like the performance itself, is a fiction, existing solely in the imagination. Miljohn Ruperto's new work in animation betrays an attraction to the slippery, bivalent image, producing images that resist identification and definition by dynamically switching between two gestalts.

As Richard Hawkins writes in this book about the work of Tony Greene during the late 1980s: "The atmosphere of the times, at least in the art world, when it took the time to address the AIDS crisis, was focused (frankly) on a very narrow interpretation of social engagement that hardly ever included anything as open-ended or negotiable as paintings. Anything else, unfortunately—particularly things as bound up as Tony's paintings were with desire and yearning and memorializing—were probably just seen as elitist. Or mealy mouthed. Or cynically detached. Or even homophobic or AIDS-phobic in their perceivably far-too-easy and far-too-romantic equations of gay desire and anything other than stand-up-for-your-rights advocacy." Perhaps it was because of the pitched, confrontational stance adopted by a previous generation of artists to carve out space in the art world and in art discourse for what, at the time, were distinguished as alternate points of view, highly politicized notions of gender, race, or queer identity, that today we have the breathing room to see the work of an artist like Greene freed from the imperatives of aligning it with one political agenda. And artists in general have a wider latitude to explore a more individual, subjective, nuanced connection to political or social engagement. Artists such as A. L. Steiner, Lisa Anne Auerbach, and Fred Lonidier are rethinking the role of direct political action in their work, often shifting the focus from group identification to one that examines the complexities of the individual's relationship to larger sociopolitical constructs. The same can be said for Zackary Drucker and Rhys Ernst, who, like Yve Laris Cohen, are transgender artists challenging the very logic of binary structures on a fundamental level and exploring the infinitely divisible space between the ones and zeros that typically comprise the makeup of our social codes.

I think it is also important as well to reflect on what is not in the exhibition, a gap that the presence of Tony Greene's work as well as the project by Julie Ault address but which perhaps is most fully apprehended as absence, the empty space that appears in the chronological register of the artists selected between the emerging generation, such as Drucker and Ernst, as well as Satterwhite, Laris Cohen, and Beasley, and an older one, including Adnan, Fisher, and Oliveros. Thirty years after the AIDS crisis began to ravage a generation of artists, this lacuna in our culture is worth considering now, both in terms of its historic and devastating impact and how the silence of a generation bears on contemporary art being made today.

The Sticking Point
Cynthia Carr

Last fall, I finally ended my boycott of the High Line, that tourist-clotted park built on a defunct rail line in west Chelsea. From there I could gaze out over the floodplain, home to so many New York galleries. As if this would help me to understand another, more metaphoric, landscape.

Back in days of yore (the 1980s), I was an arts columnist on a self-appointed mission to track the underground and the cutting edge. It wasn't hard, since I focused on performance art, which was then marginal by definition. Often I was the only so-called critic who actually showed up at 2 am in some burned-out rec room of a club to bear witness. Even after the East Village performance clubs (8BC, WOW, Limbo Lounge, etc.) began to close, the city had acres of uncolonized space. I could still find *Siegfried* staged in ABC No Rio's brick-strewn "backyard" and the Swamp Festival at a South Williamsburg hole-in-the-wall just a couple of blocks from where a friend had been shot in the arm. But, looking back over the columns I wrote, I see that by late 1989 I was struggling to find the vanguard. Now I realize that that was also about the time the whole culture got stuck.

I noticed it first in pop culture, where there was suddenly no new youth movement to cheer or belittle. And now there hasn't been one for thirty-five years! We went from beatniks (late fifties) to hippies (late sixties) to punks and rappers (late seventies) to nothing. We entered an age of recycling, with every past movement revived as an empty shell, a style drained of its original emotion. As that Rotten fella once suggested, "No future."

Think, for example, of last year's *Punk: Chaos to Couture* at the Metropolitan Museum of Art's Costume Institute. Admittedly, punk style started in a London boutique—when Malcolm McLaren put the Sex Pistols together to publicize Vivienne Westwood's strategically torn T-shirts. But then punk became real, and it was not about glamour. *Chaos to Couture*, however, featured designers who prettified punk's deliberate ugliness, neutralized the menace, and generally defied the core value: the wretched can do it. At least that's what I gleaned from the media. I admit to boycotting that show.

Meanwhile, in the art world, the needle on the culture gauge stopped moving forward as we arrived at postmodernism—and then? We looked around and noticed other cultural traditions with their own forward-moving trajectories. The world was wide and we had discovered it! (Again!) Multiculturalism raised long-overdue questions about who is included in art's discourse, but it was not an art movement. Then multiculturalism mutated into globalism—also not a movement. Relational aesthetics? Interesting—and sometimes you can get a dinner out of it—but that's a permutation of the art-in-everyday-life practice that started in the seventies. In the galleries this season, I've seen Minimalism, Expressionism, Conceptualism, Photorealism, and, among other things, a style we called postmodern in the eighties and have designated more recently as the Pictures Generation.

I guess it's time to discard that old culture gauge or to rethink it. I try to stay positive. In pop culture, this stasis could actually signify real rebellion and true anticapitalism, a refusal to invent a new style with new products every kid would have to buy. As for art, pluralism is the ultimate freedom, right?

What this pluralism signifies, however, is that modernism really did end, along with much of the structure that surrounded it: not just the isms turned wasms but also concepts like the avant-garde and bohemia. A whole generation has grown up seeing all that as mere history. Since modernism lasted for almost a hundred years, I see not a generation gap but a generation chasm, bigger perhaps than the difference between the analogue and the digital. So have core values changed? I can't remember the last time I heard anyone talk about refusing to sell out, for example. Does that mean that artists now *want* to sell out? I refuse to believe it. Cynicism about art and artists is the default position. I won't go there, even if there are a few who say, "If someone comes to my studio and likes something, I make five of them." Serious artists know the difference between making art and making product.

One of the urtexts from the era when the needle got stuck is Guy Debord's *Society of the Spectacle*. (My translation from the original French is dated 1977.) We still live in that society, though Debord died in 1994, way before everyone was walking down the street staring at a screen. "The spectacle is not a collection of images, but a social relation among people mediated by images." That's truer today than when he wrote it.

Spectacle always invites coverage. That's how I explain the ubiquity of art reporting in the *New York Times* Style section and the Sunday fashion supplement, *T.* As the season began this past September, for example, the Style section ran a droll piece titled "A Gallery Opens, Spewing Cash." Art-world luminaries, fashion bigwigs, rap stars, and Michael Ovitz had gathered to celebrate the opening of Galerie Perrotin and Paola Pivi's show of large, fluorescent-colored polar bears. A blue box reaching almost to the ceiling spit out dollars and coins, and afterward everyone adjourned to a thousand-person party that occupied all four floors of the Russian Tea Room. Here was that seemingly elitist and decadent slice of the art world so often parodied in Hollywood films and denounced by right-wing politicians out to defund the National Endowment for the Arts.

I know. I know. The rich and the fabulous have always been with us, and the art world has room for everyone. But the whole art ecosystem is different from the one I entered in the last century. There are more galleries and more artists now, but there is less affordable space and less of what we used to call alternative space, which often provided a path into the system for those starting their careers. In 1982, there were seventy-four of these organizations in New York City alone, according to *Alternative Art New York, 1965–1985*. A few remain (e.g., Artists Space and The Kitchen), but much of the nonprofit world was either damaged or destroyed during the culture war that began in 1989, just when the culture gauge got stuck. I can't devise a conspiracy theory that makes this more than a coincidence, but the irony about alternative space has always been its dependence on federal, state, and corporate monies. Now everyone's more beholden to the marketplace.

So artists have new problems related to . . . are we still calling it late capitalism? (Did we get stuck there, too?) The first and most obvious question is who can afford to move to New York anymore to pursue a painting or performance career? The art world reflects the rest of the culture with its income inequality. Everything is more corporate now, and more institutionalized. The big galleries even have franchises, and they are big in every way. Some of them could house elephants. Some have usurped the museum's role. I was certainly grateful for shows such as *Picasso and Marie-Thérèse: L'Amour Fou* at Gagosian and *Happenings: New York, 1958–1963* at Pace. They were expertly curated—and free. But I wonder if it's time to start worrying about the middle class, i.e., the midsize galleries that have always been the art scene's backbone. The *New York Times* ran a page-one story last summer about the centrality of art fairs to art business, reporting that on average 36 percent of all sales now happen there, not in galleries. Actually, this is not a new trend. (A painter friend described seeing her work go off to Miami, or Shanghai or wherever, some years back: "I'm just one more shoe in the shoe box.") However, the selling of art has become spectacle, too, and the fairs seem increasingly difficult for galleries to ignore, while participating in them is hugely expensive.

At last summer's Art Basel, one artist mounted what I interpreted as a critique of this trend, though it misfired and became a debacle. Tadashi Kawamata installed eighteen crude huts, like those built in Brazilian shantytowns, just outside the art fair's sleek silver buildings. *Favela Café* seemed to be an attempt to shame the fairgoers with a statement about "how the other more-than-half lives." But the project came off as aestheticized distress and allowed the affluent literally to go slumming. A hundred or so activists showed up to protest the piece and were teargassed by police. The next day, the café was back in business, selling what one blog described as "falafel at reassuringly exclusive prices."

Can there still be an art that engages with the real world in some meaningful way or an artist who reimagines his or her dot of space on the planet and works out from there? Of course, and here's one example: Theaster Gates, a Chicago-based artist, urban planner, and visionary, and a participant in the 2010 Biennial. A recent Gates show, *My Labor Is My Protest*, included his Civil Tapestries, which look like Minimalist paintings—brown, beige, and off-white strips laid side by side. It turns out these strips are decommissioned fire hoses, and anyone who lived through the civil rights years knows what a fire hose signifies: jets of water strong enough to knock protestors off their feet. Gates, who is African American, took something distressing, neutralized it, and reclaimed it. Much of Gates's practice is social, hard to summarize, and based around abandoned buildings he's bought and "reanimated" on Chicago's South Side. His emphasis on cross-cultural dialogue, "radical hospitality," and neighborhood transformation through the arts is unfashionably utopian. And it doesn't fit the spectacle model.

I know some artists prefer that. I know some assiduously work the margins, and I remain interested in that. By way of monitoring the art world's underbelly, I've subscribed for years to a LISTSERV called Nonsense NYC, "a discriminating resource for independent art, weird events, strange happenings, unique parties, and senseless culture in New York City." I think that's how I ended up, some years back, descending into a large tunnel via a manhole in the middle of a busy Brooklyn intersection. Something vaguely artistic was occurring down there, though I don't remember what. (Only my sense of trepidation remains vivid.) More recently, I've been pleased to discover via the LISTSERV that certain people are out there staging Euripides tragedies in their Bushwick backyards or organizing conventions for pillaging pirates—costumes mandatory. ("Be creative. Chop off a limb, and come with a wooden peg leg.")

Recently, the Nonsense list guided me to a gallery in South Williamsburg, now a neighborhood where one is unlikely to get shot in the arm. Several young artists had opened a show about the archiving of performance, as in, "Can a performance still resonate or have impact when you only see its documentation or script?" The eleven monitors in the front room featured fragments of a twenty-four-hour piece done the year before, and downstairs I found more monitors with video from the gallery's archive. What's relevant here, though, is that I walked out of there thinking about how much it must cost to rent that building. (The artists also live there.) And I lost count of how many monitors they had. Still, this was a show that encouraged thinking. Not a single chartreuse bear in sight! So I'm not going to name the space because they don't deserve to have any negativity about the current scene nailed to their door.

It just made me realize that I had found one alternative to alternative space. Those who can somehow get the money set up their own spaces, create websites, and start tweeting and tumblring. My (young) informants tell me that groups of artists who graduate from art school together sometimes move to New York and live together, forming "very rogue, very specific subtribes," and "you have to know where to find them to find them." You become a brand. You inhabit a niche but never a garret. Given how many can't afford to be in New York at all, even in a pack, the art world has become more diffuse than ever, with artists working all over the country and connecting via online platforms. This seems a logical extension of globalism: Croatia. Lebanon. Japan. Why not the South Side of Chicago? Can we stop downgrading the latter into the category of the local?

So many of the artists I once covered were self-taught. Now nearly everyone seems to have emerged from MFA programs where they've learned a certain language. They are able to discuss their critical strategies and topics like the politics of postdisciplinarity. I don't know that that's necessarily bad, though I've seen a whole lot o' highfalutin discourse gussy up a whole lot o' terrible art. A certain innocence is gone. Work that's grounded in politics or that smacks of romanticism has moved to the outlier position. Or maybe that's just the work that doesn't get written about.

I began my own art career writing about Tehching Hsieh and Linda Montano, who spent one year (1983–84) tied together with an eight-foot rope. There was such purity to that work. It could not be sold. Really, I didn't think ordeal art could ever be commodified, but I was wrong. It too crossed over, banalized on shows like *Fear Factor* and *Jackass* and turned into spectacle by the likes of David Blaine. Last summer, rapper and businessman Jay-Z made his foray into performance art, appropriating Marina Abramović's epic 2010 piece *The Artist Is Present*. For two and a half months, six days a week, seven hours a day, Abramović sat across from one spectator at a time in the atrium of the Museum of Modern Art. It was the purest realization of a goal she'd set decades ago for all her solo work—to establish an "energy dialogue" with her audience. Director Mark Romanek saw the HBO documentary about this piece and discussed it with

Jay-Z, noting that the rapper "regularly performs to 60,000 people at a time." So Romanek suggested, "'What about performing [for] one person at a time?' He absolutely loved it. He interrupted me and said, 'Hold on! I've got chills. That idea is perfect.' He thinks, like me, that the music video has had its era." They asked for—and got—Abramović's permission.

Last July at Pace Gallery, Jay-Z performed his song "Picasso Baby" for six hours, with breaks, to one artist or actor at a time while each sat on a bench in front of his small stage. Naturally it was necessary to delete the two major components of Abramović's piece, silence and stillness. Following a time-honored rap tradition, Jay-Z bragged, while most of those who started out on the bench got up and danced: "It ain't hard to tell / I'm the new Jean-Michel / Surrounded by Warhols . . . / Twin Bugattis outside the Art Basel / I just wanna live life colossal / Leonardo da Vinci flows / Riccardo Tisci Givenchy clothes." Jay-Z is apparently a serious collector, and last August he released, not a music video, but a "performance-art film" about eleven minutes long. Many artists participated and had a blast, but evidence of umbrage over this event soon began popping up on blogs. In one thread, for example, people debated who was using whom. Were the artists trying to get mainstream attention? Was Jay-Z trying to get art-world prestige?

Discussing the blurry boundary between art and entertainment could fill a hefty tome. I won't be writing that, but I will consider MoMA's *Rain Room* (2013) by rAndom International. Here was art for people who don't like art—well, not only for them. But I do see the piece as a populist move—this idea of rain that won't fall on you. Too many people are still intimidated by art museums, and this bit of magic got seventy-four thousand people through the door and into lines, on which they willingly waited for hours. I hope some return. Me? I boycotted.

A few years back, I began keeping a file on artists who were selling, giving away, or destroying all their possessions (up to and including family photos and art made by friends)—and referring to these depletions as art projects. These radical critiques of ownership actually worried me. I wanted to be the old fogy telling these young fogies that we can't boycott everything. Don't you at least need a winter coat? I haven't been aware of a new depletion project, though, since Hurricane Sandy destroyed so much art. Some lost their life's work. In the face of real calamity, dumping everything seems frivolous, just another form of excess. I know the art world can look asinine at times, and we have our egomaniacs, but as that Rotten guy also said, "Never mind the bollocks."

Etel Adnan

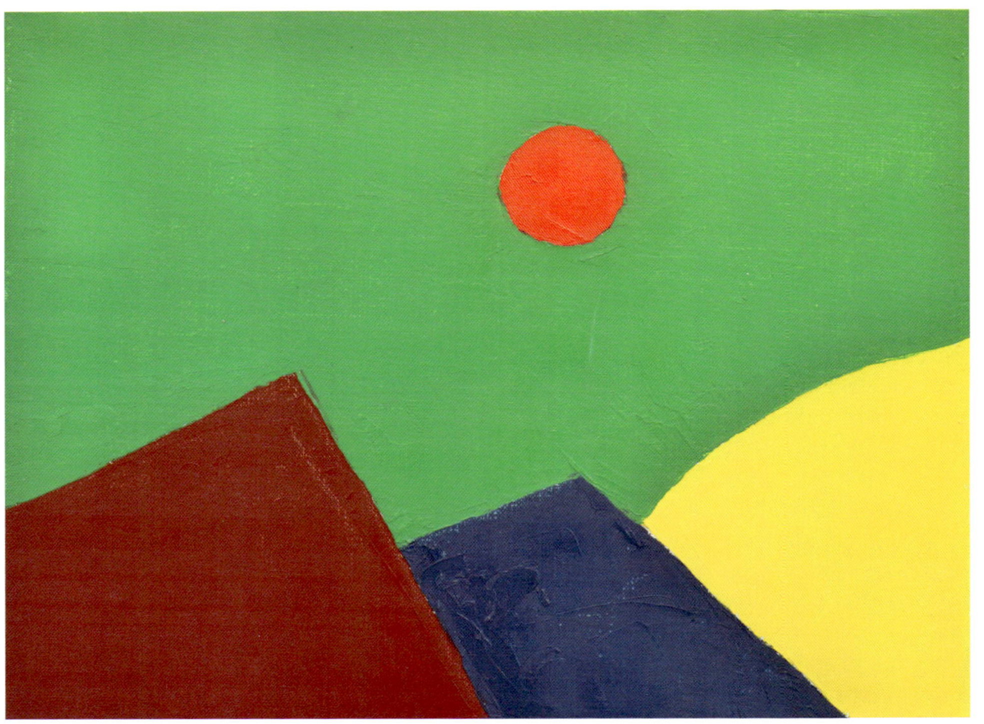

Untitled, 2012. Oil on canvas, 10 ⅝ × 13 ¾ in. (27 × 35 cm)

Born 1925 in Beirut, Lebanon

Lives in Sausalito, CA / Paris, France

Skies Streaked with Fire
Kaelen Wilson-Goldie

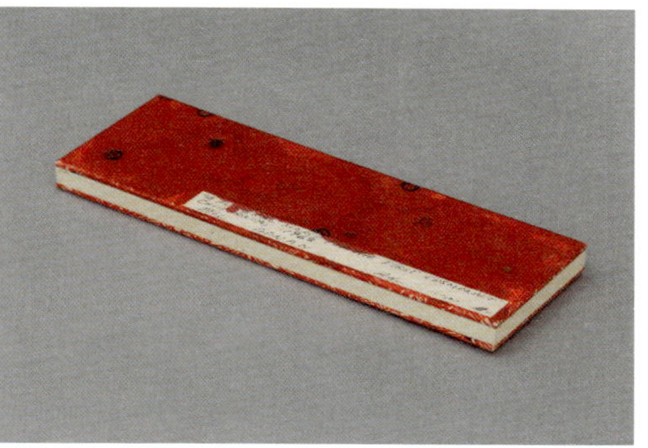

Cover of *Funeral March for the First Cosmonaut*, 1968. Ink and watercolor on paper 10 × 105 in. (25.4 × 266.7 cm)

"Mounir is on the phone. He is planning to make a film and wants me to write the scenario." So begins Etel Adnan's majestic and forceful novel *Sitt Marie-Rose*, about the abduction and murder of a woman who works as a teacher of deaf-mute children and an activist on behalf of Palestinian refugees. Set at the outset of Lebanon's long and gruesome civil war, the book is based on the real and well-known story of a Syrian émigré named Marie-Rose Boulos, a social worker, who, deemed a traitor to her faith, was kidnapped, tortured, and killed by members of a right-wing Christian militia in 1976.

Adnan's portrayal of a city imploding and a society tearing itself apart is so brutal in its language that one can easily forget that the story of Marie-Rose is wedged into another story about the making of a film. An unnamed narrator, a stand-in for Adnan, is enlisted to write the script. She wants to talk about the plight of Syrian laborers in Beirut, who are consumed by a city that is constantly being built, destroyed, and rebuilt on their backs. Mounir, the director and something of a dilettante, is more interested in hunting, heroism, and the primitive, untouched beauty of the rural Syrian landscape. For inspiration, he screens for a roomful of friends a selection of Super 8 films, which serve as evidence not only of the work in progress but also of his ideas adrift. "I see open expanses in the dust and wind," Adnan writes. "There is the color of swirling dust, and vast skies streaked with red fire." Woven throughout the novel are notes for a film that will never be made, a tangle of loose ends about hunters, game, guns, and birds falling from a bloodred sky.

Adnan seeks out a group of Syrian workers on a construction site. "I tell Mounir that there is nothing to be had here but the circles under the eyes, the bent backs, the sorrow, the infernal noise of the cement mixers, the sun that beats, and the rain that gnaws," she writes. "His film, decidedly, turns on nothing." Soon after the war begins, the workers are killed, struck down by fearful, xenophobic neighbors. Their deaths are not only pointless but also symptomatic of what Adnan calls the "mystic terror" and "ghetto instinct" that turn neighbor against neighbor in Beirut. Mounir and his gang soon abandon their film and take up arms, not for sport but for war. That the men who are introduced to readers as friends become the killers of Marie-Rose is just one of the novel's many remarkable twists. These men are part of the narrator's social milieu. They are not foreign, other, or unknown. They are not far. They are uncomfortably close.

As in so much of her work across a staggering range of disciplines and genres, from painting and poetry to novels, plays, essays, and unclassifiable prose works, Adnan doesn't allow for easy oppositions. She insists on complexities, complicities, and the incredible (often unspeakable) intimacies of violence. She steps into the space between dozens of binaries and proves that structure of thinking to be totally insufficient— not because humanity is doomed but because the

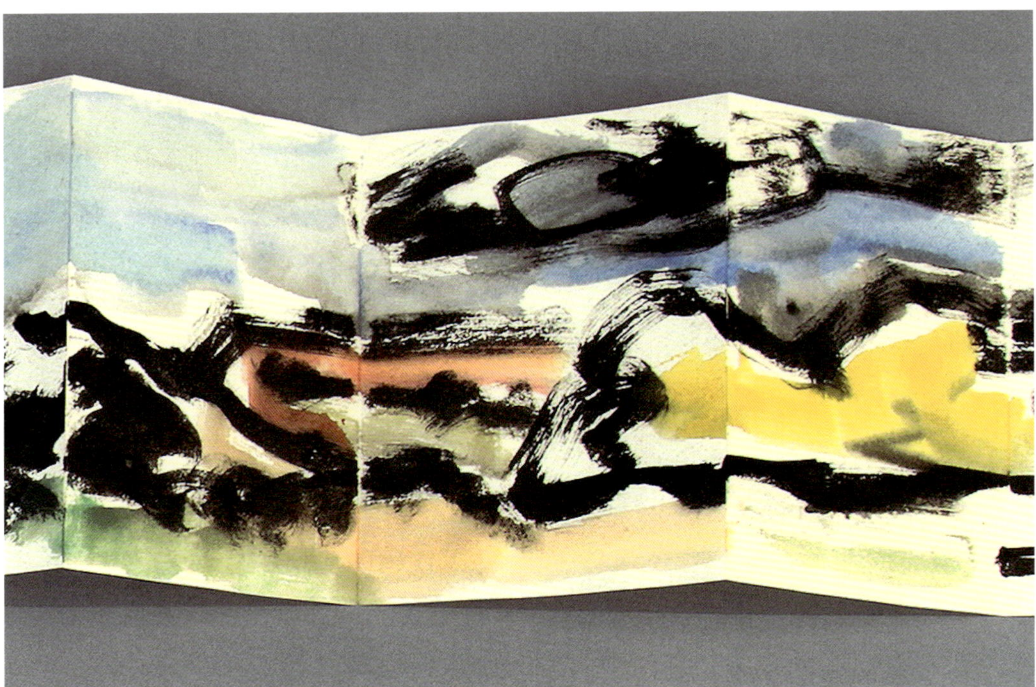

December From My Window, 1993 (detail). Ink and watercolor on paper, 7 ½ × 100 in. (19.1 × 254 cm)

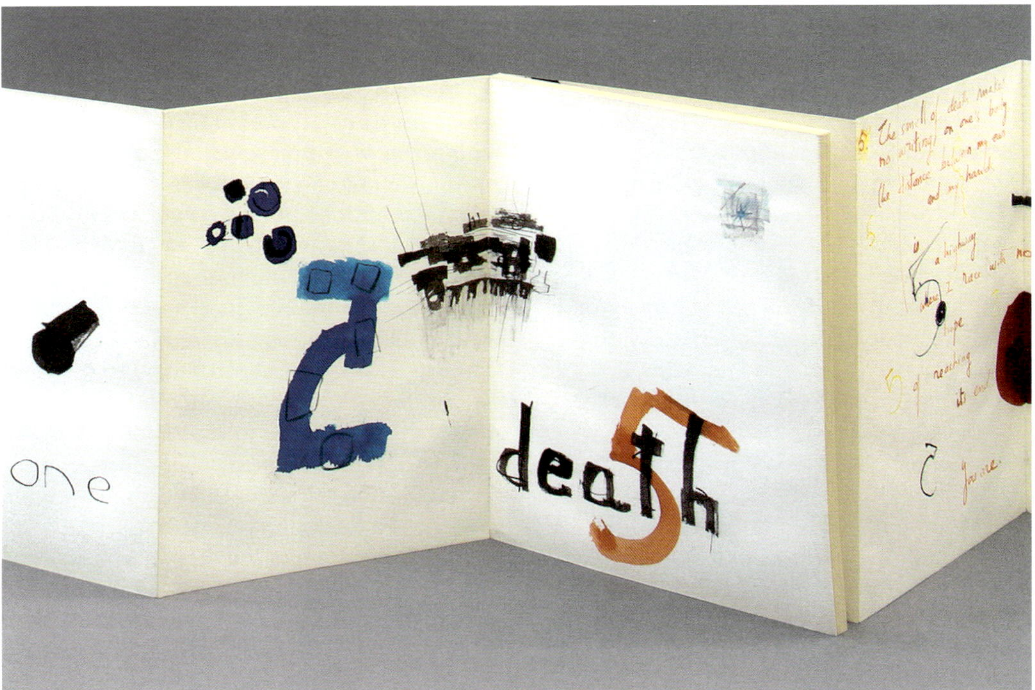

Five Senses for One Death, 1969. Ink and watercolor on paper, 11 × 255 in. (27.9 × 647.7 cm)

wonder of Adnan's world is that no one is exempt, beyond hope, or too far gone to be loved. There are no outsiders—to be blamed or otherwise—because there is no outside of this world, which Adnan adores, deeply, no matter its awful truths.

Adnan wrote *Sitt Marie-Rose* from a position of self-imposed exile in France. Born in Beirut in 1925, she left for the United States in the 1950s and stayed there for twenty years—studying, teaching philosophy, and painting. She returned to Lebanon in 1972 and became a journalist, working for a new, left-leaning, French-language newspaper called *Al-Safa*, which lasted only another two years, until the founding editor disappeared, most likely kidnapped and killed. Adnan moved to another French paper, *L'Orient-Le Jour*. When the civil war broke out and the fighting intensified, she left for Paris, where she wrote *Sitt Marie-Rose* in 1977, a year after Boulos's disappearance. After the book was published, Adnan returned to Beirut, only to find that she'd been banned from the newspaper and threatened with death. So she left once more for Paris, and, except for long but infrequent visits, she has not lived full-time in Lebanon since.

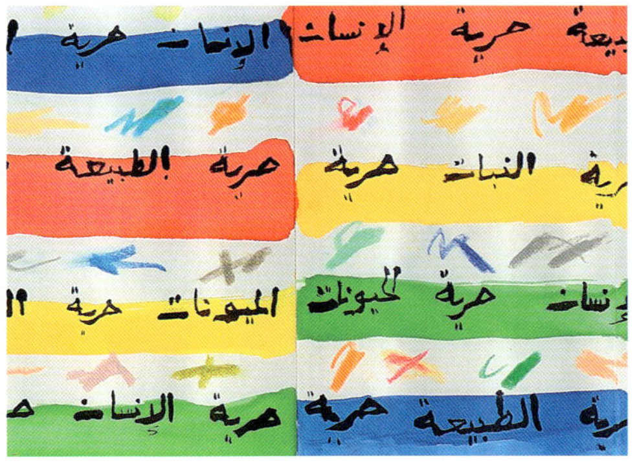

Human Freedom Animal Freedom Nature Freedom, 2011 (detail). Ink, color, and oil pastel on paper, 7 × 112 7/16 in. (17.8 × 285.6 cm)

Until two years ago, it was little known that before this period of compulsive returns, Adnan herself had been making films in addition to paintings and accordion-bound artists' books known as *leporellos*, during an extended stay in New York. Beirut and California, her mountain and her sea, remain the great subjects, the sources, firing Adnan's imagination, but New York and Paris occupy an equally interesting place in her oeuvre. They are neutral cities, the sites of practice and production, the places where Adnan seems to have learned how to look at a given landscape not without affection but dispassionately. Adnan's Super 8 films—shot from a midtown high-rise overlooking the East River—are meditative exercises in form, texture, and abstraction. Her New York *leporellos* likewise experiment with line, shape, and color. They convey none of the trial and frustration that characterize her other artist's books, in which she is clearly learning to write in Arabic by transcribing the poems of her friends and peers.

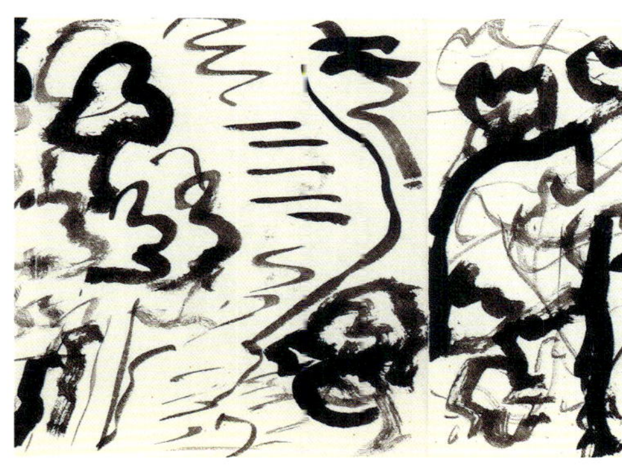

In the Forest, 2009 (detail). Sumi ink on Japanese cotton paper, 11 ¼ × 213 1/16 in. (28.5 × 541.1 cm)

It is often said that due to her complex heritage, Adnan grew up speaking Greek with her mother, Turkish with her father, French in the classroom, and Arabic on the street. But she writes primarily in English and, given the considerable chasm between classical Arabic and colloquial Lebanese, never wrote much in Arabic at all. Almost like pictograms, one does not so much read as scan these *leporellos*. They are whimsical studies in simple maps, urban forms, and architectural lines stripped down to the elements of a style.

The works Adnan made in New York in the 1960s carve out a kind of interlude, but an important one, for the *leporellos* and Super 8 films bring together the beauty of her paintings and the brutality of her prose. They are markers of her thinking, and they move curiously between states, with objects, moving images, and marks strung together like words. They re-create a sort of literary synesthesia. Like words placed in poems for their sound as much as their meaning, the New York books and films suggest how a sequence or a sentence might be felt as much as understood, which is a reminder of how *Sitt Marie-Rose* ends, in a devastating scene where the students of Marie-Rose feel the reverberations of bombs falling on Beirut from the ground beneath their feet. Having lost their teacher and sensing there is a kind of mad, relentless rhythm to this war, they rise and begin slowly, inexorably, to dance.

Ei Arakawa

Carissa Rodriguez

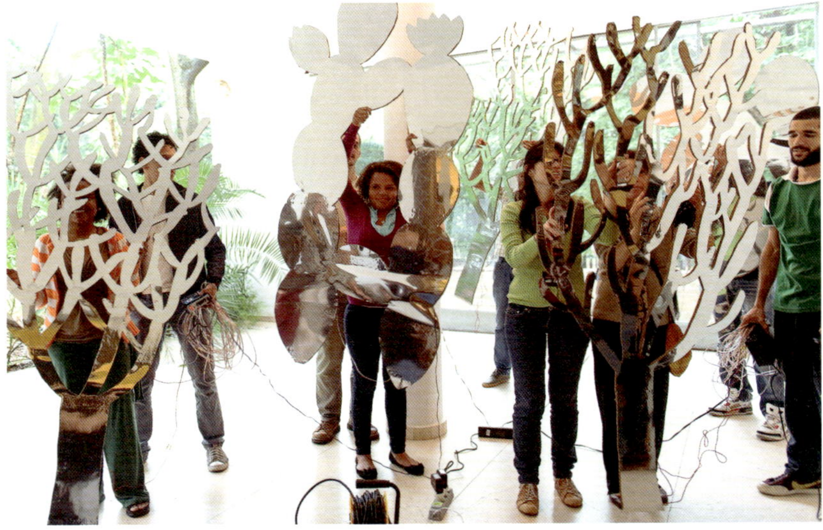

Sergei Tcherepnin with Ei Arakawa, *ARCHICACTUS (outgrow/autogrow)*, 2012. Performance (30th Bienal de São Paulo, October 20, 2012)

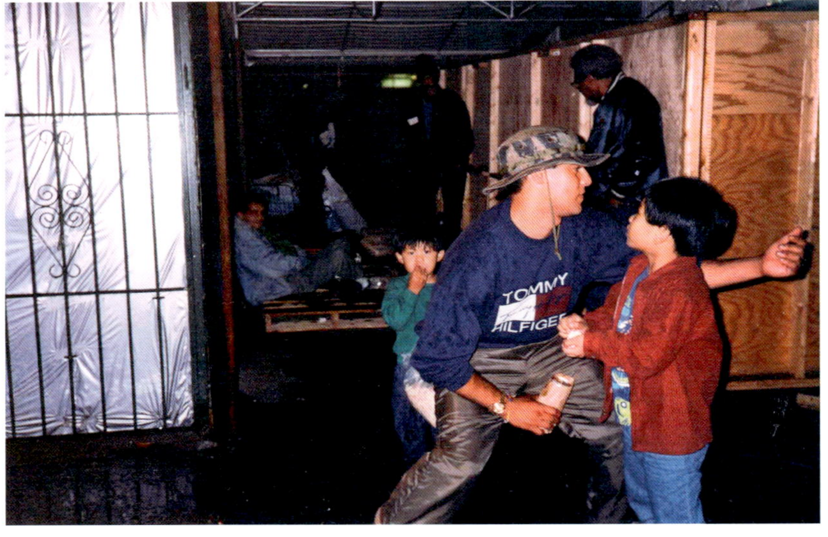

Carissa Rodriguez and Jodi Busby (b. 1967), *The Stand*, 1998–2000. An urban event, Lower East Side, New York

Born 1977 in
Fukushima, Japan
Lives in New York, NY

Born 1970 in
New York, NY
Lives in New York, NY

Ei Arakawa

Carissa Rodriguez

Critical Aloha
Negar Azimi

"Make a way out of no way."
—Barack Obama

We don't care if you're single or have a family or your race, gender, sexual orientation, disability or whatever—we're open to anyone and anything. So are you interested in getting away from everything—away from the government corruption, away from the societal expectations, off the grid and unplugged from the system?[1]

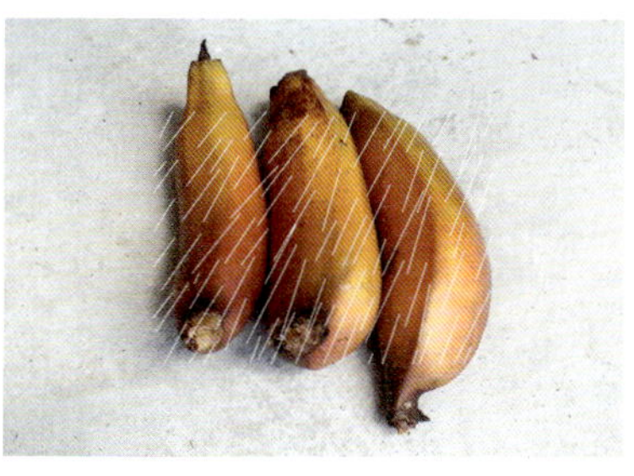

Ei Arakawa, *Weather & Cuban Banana*, 2013. Source image for Ei Arakawa and Carissa Rodriguez's project for the 2014 Whitney Biennial

On the Big Island of Hawai'i, there are legion "off-grid" communities, especially in the eastern-most district of Puna. According to experts on the subject, "many people in these areas seem to prefer the disconnected lifestyle. They say it reminds them of a Hawai'i from long ago."

In the so-called Hawaii episode of *The Brady Bunch*, Greg, Peter, and Bobby visit ancient burial caves in order to return what they believe is a bad-luck tiki idol.

This is a story not unrelated to the 1960s. This is a story about running away from California, Arizona, or New York City.

We intend to build our home out of earth bags but are more than open to anyone choosing their own style of building. If you don't know how, we'll work together. You can build a very nice, big house out of earth bags for as little as $500 to upwards of $5,000—still cheap either way. We would like to have gardens and fruit trees, as well as goats, chickens and fish. I also intend to grow and make my own herbal/natural remedies.

The word *aloha* is derived from proto-Polynesian. *Alo* signifies "presence," or "face," while *ha* means "breath of life."

Taking a shit in the garden.

I'm drinking rainwater.

There's something melancholy about this place.

We are very fun-loving, active, hard-working, open-minded and open-armed people. . . .
We wouldn't call ourselves religious, but we have beliefs alongside pagan/wicca and buddhism and are very connected to nature. We feel more at home out in the middle of the wilderness than we do in a house in the city.

Island = reset.

The gathering at the volcanic sauna was for women only. There was some inscrutable chanting and other confusing rituals. Massage, too. Clothing was optional.

Sometime around the middle of the nineteenth century, *aloha* entered colloquial English as "good-bye" but also "hello." It is said that Sean Penn's use of *aloha* in the movie *Fast Times at Ridgemont High* (1982) propelled the term to unprecedented visibility.

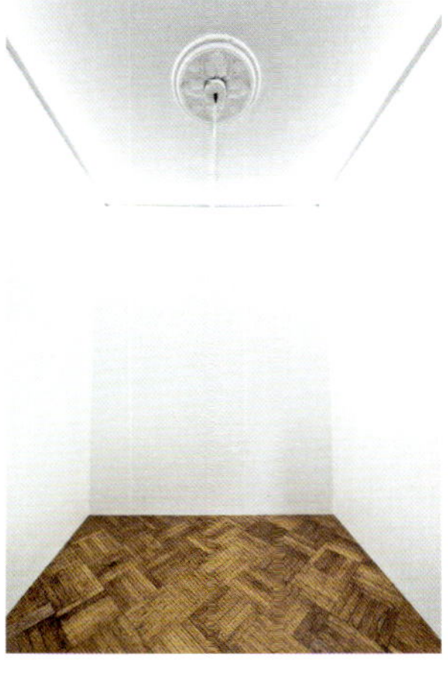

Carissa Rodriguez, *Anus Is The Night*, 2013 (detail). Drywall, steel framing studs, plaster, and paint, dimensions site specific (installation view, *La Collectionneuse*, Front Desk Apparatus, New York, May 6–October 7, 2013)

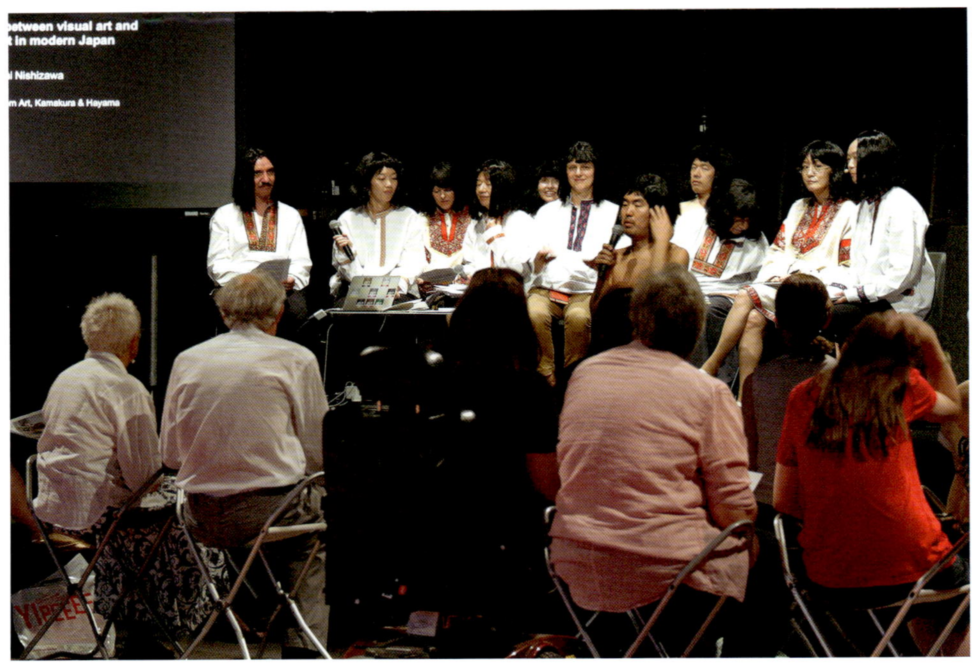

Ei Arakawa with Harumi Nishizawa (b. 1982) and Miwako Tezuka (b. 1971), *Joy of Life: Performance-Talk: The Relationship Between Visual Art and Performing Art in Modern Japan*, 2012. Performance (The Tanks, Tate Modern, London)

In the Japanese city of Iwaki, a former mining hub, there is a theme park devoted to the idea of Hawaii. Its name translates, roughly, to "Spa Resort Hawaiians." For the equivalent of thirty dollars, one can wade into hot springs, eat a Hawaiian-inspired meal, or see one of several ecstatic "hula-girl" shows.

The idea of Hawaii.

Born and raised in New York City, Carissa never had a tropical-island fantasy. Her practice has occasionally mined the banal bankruptcy of great ideas—from fashion to collecting art. She wonders, if the artist is an island, what does it mean to be a part of "this bigger continental thing?"

Born and raised in Japan, Ei is wary of being seduced. Very often, his work is invested in circumstances in which "the group" takes on a life of its own. Collaboration as risk. The exhibition as destination. The island as stage. *Watch out for bad weather!*

Struggling with unseriousness.

In the 1923 book *Suzanne and the Pacific* by Jean Giraudoux, the title character finds herself on a deserted island due to a violent storm. Unlike, say, Robinson Crusoe, Suzanne does not throw off the shackles of her own culture. She sticks to her bourgeois guns.

Carissa says: "I almost feel like I'm squatting . . . I'm trying to find a way in, to find meaning in it. I was thinking about the kind of contrast between a real kind of escape and a kind of false escape . . . we met people who were trying to live in an alternative way but then needed the internet to teach them how to do it."

offthegridsf.com, off-grid.net, offthegridpress.com, Facebook, Yelp.

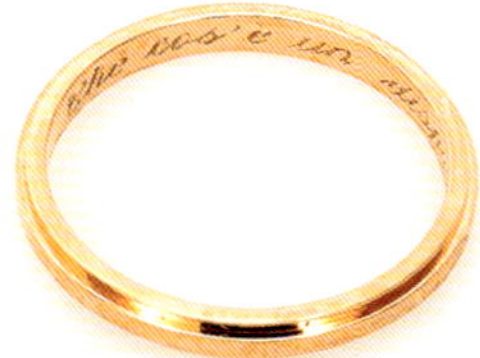

Carissa Rodriguez, *What Is An Apparatus?*, 2013 (detail). Cartier size 54 18-carat pink gold custom-engraved ring, jewel box, certificate, and carved marble surface. Engraving: *Che cos'è un dispositivo?* (installation view, *La Collectionneuse*, Front Desk Apparatus, New York, May 6–October 7, 2013)

Ei Arakawa

Gilles Deleuze says that *Robinson Crusoe* is the quintessential treatise on private property. In his 1953 essay "Desert Islands," Deleuze goes on to say that the unity of the deserted island and its inhabitant is not actual, but imaginary, "like the idea of looking behind the curtain when one is not behind it."

No one said anything about tiki bars.

Do you feel the same as we do about building a true community, getting back to the basics, and being able to focus on what truly matters in life? If so, get a hold of me! Let's make the vision of a thriving life into a reality!! (posted by butterflymama212@gmail.com)

Carissa Rodriguez

"We are here on this island in the middle of the Pacific in lieu of filing for divorce." Joan Didion might have written that.

Critical Aloha.

The Brady Bunch again. The boys are in for a surprise as, unbeknownst to them, they are shadowed by a mysterious man who will go to great lengths to prevent them from gleaning the deepest secrets of the caves. These caves hold secrets.

Ei sighs: "At this point, it's like Carissa and I are drifting, island to island."

1. Italicized passages are quotes from the website www.off-grid.net.

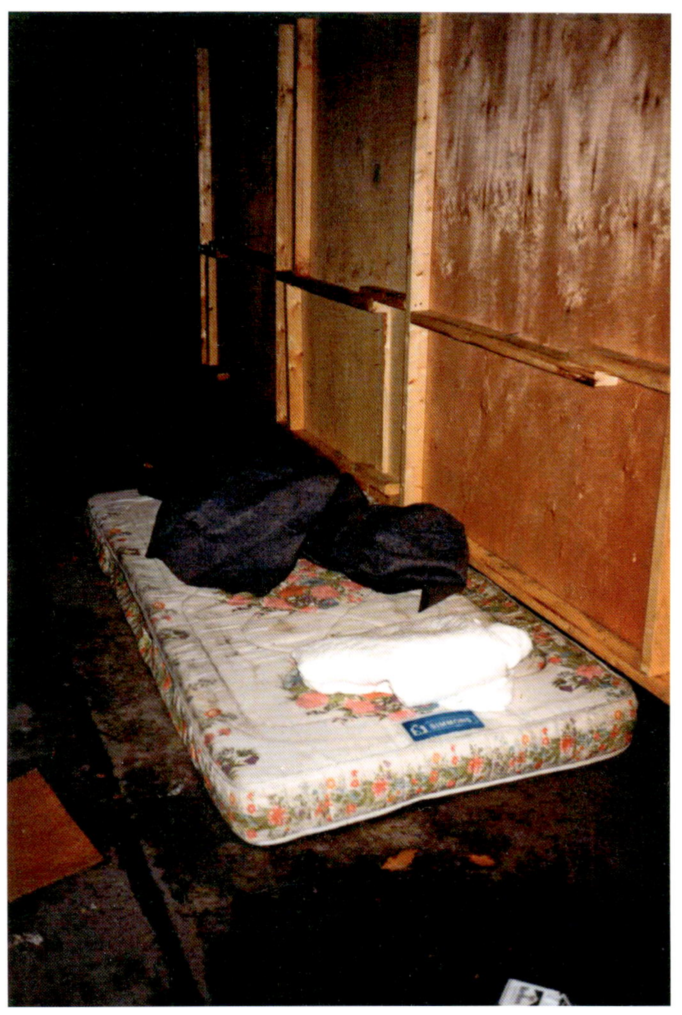

Carissa Rodriguez and Jodi Busby, *The Stand*, 1998–2000. An urban event, Lower East Side, New York

Uri Aran

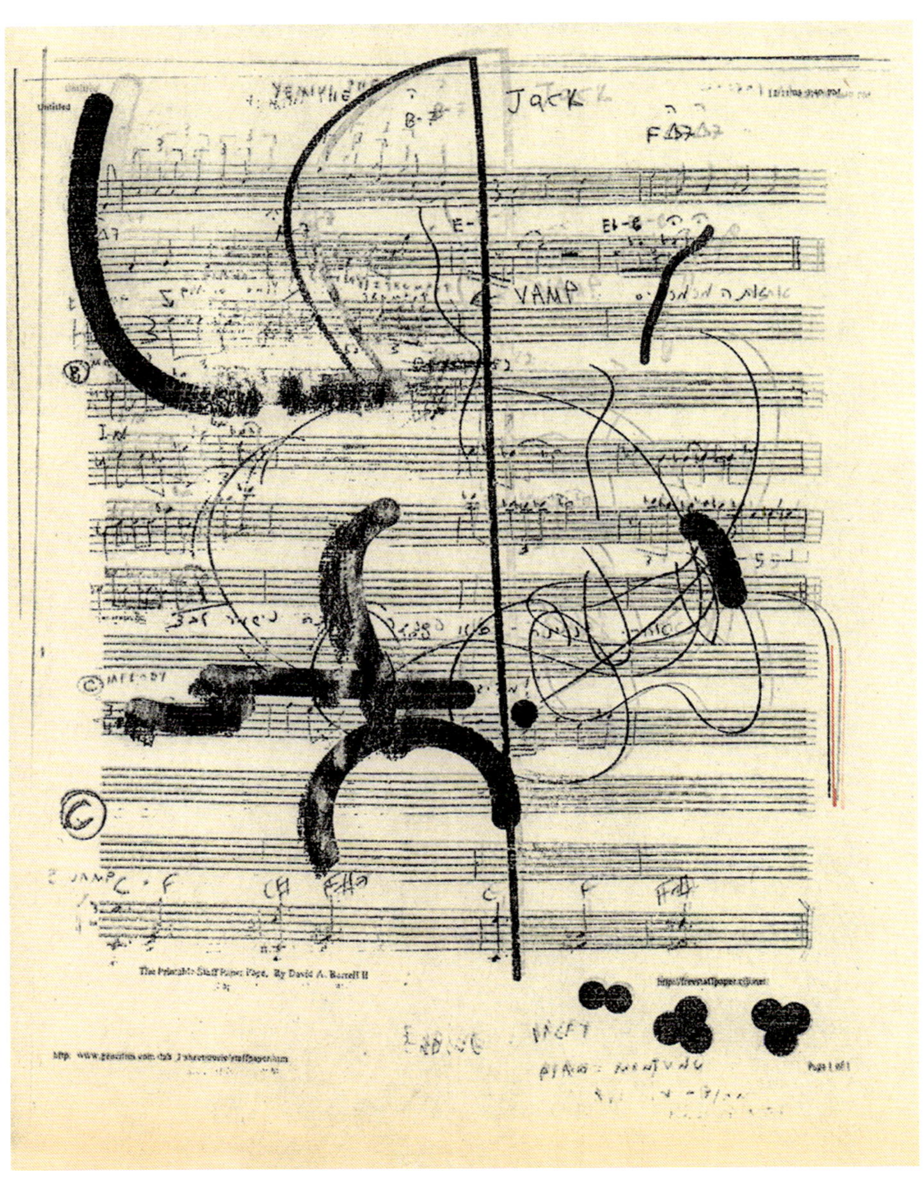

Untitled (For Dan), 2013. Mixed-media on paper, 8 ½ × 11 in. (21.6 × 27.9 cm)

Born 1977 in
Jerusalem, Israel

Lives in
New York, NY

Uri Aran

We Have Each Other
Fionn Meade

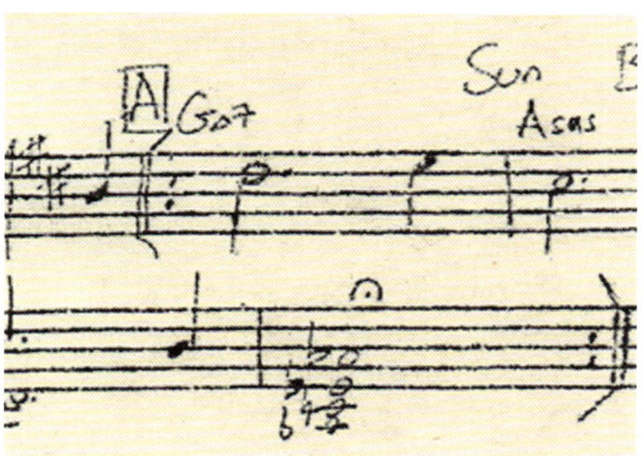

Untitled (For Dan), 2013 (detail). Mixed-media on paper, 8 ½ × 11 in. (21.6 × 27.9 cm)

Affect, gesture, and melodrama abound in Uri Aran's installations. The New York–based artist introduces story fragments and half characters into his sculpture, video, and drawing configurations, only then to obstruct any definitive catharsis of plot or identification. Aran's storyboard "personas"—which take form as everything from ID photos, pet imagery, toys, and consumer imagery to the artist's own snapshots—are displayed on sculptural supports (most often shelf-like pedestal structures and rough-hewn worktables), and are subject to rapid substitution patterns, following what the artist calls the "flat logic" of his idiosyncratic design. In these propulsive scenarios, Aran devises his characters' existences like a scriptwriter: plotting out every demise and rebirth and the emotive effect of each transition, revision, and step-by-step maneuver.

In Aran's 2012 solo exhibition at Gavin Brown's Enterprise in New York, for example, a passport photograph of an "uncle in jail" (and its scribbled caption) cropped up somewhat ominously here and there throughout the installation—occasionally trading places with an absurd image of a smiling dog or with a scaled-up or scaled-down photograph of a horse's head. Embedded like pieces on a game board, such human and animal metonyms do not cancel or wholly replace one another in Aran's landscape; rather, they become associative devices within a set of episodes that have no clear beginning or end. Adorned with linguistic labels describing modes of transportation and arrival—"by foot," "by car," "by bus," and so on—the works in the gallery show functioned as way stations for the estranging sentiments associated with having an "uncle in jail." Variously showing scenes of departure, or evoking loss, shame, or joy, Aran's sculptural tableaux were imbued with the echo of that oddly loaded phrase. A series of quick line drawings in the same installation—depicting a mouse, a horse, a shark, and a cat, and recalling Dieter Roth's comic draftsmanship—were superimposed over the image of a smiling pregnant woman, adding another level of protean transformation. Presented alongside worktables perforated with drill holes and holding configurations of everyday objects and cast-off studio materials—meticulously arranged, like mementos—Aran's images and sculptural topography offer an uncanny register of new life, confinement, and cultural displacement, all positioned among wood shavings and detritus.

Aran constructs a shape-shifting language with the most meager means, collecting an uneasy inventory of pathos, absence, and laughter. His spendthrift materials and halting linguistic repetitions work together to elicit a kind of sadness and nostalgia for the work's own materiality and imagery. Aran repeatedly goes over actions undertaken and sentimental iconographies, embracing and exhausting absurdity to the point of forcibly breaking it down into a new syntax.

While text often pins down an image—even a clichéd one—compelling it to perform as an illustration or a product, in Aran's work, images are forcefully *detoured* by language, in both spoken and written form. With their abrupt substitutions and transitions, his installations recall the process of learning a foreign language or studying a grammar primer. Social situations occur in medias res, repeated in various permutations and with different power relations, placing the viewer (now in the role of student) in the midst of the social fray. In his sculptural wall configuration *Dear Tenants (B)* (2013), for example, fragmented and partially effaced textual loose ends take on a foreboding and moralistic tone: close inspection

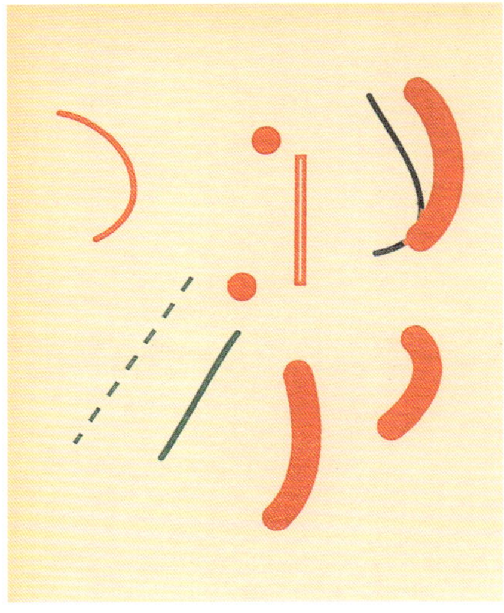

Untitled (For Dan), 2013. Mixed-media on paper, 8 ½ × 11 in. (21.6 × 27.9 cm)

of the stainless-steel backdrop, hung with images, objects, and a framed drawing, reveals handwritten phrases such as "We knew then & there" and "In the end, I guess, I learned such a great lesson." Scrawled out faintly, such pedantic phrases are obscured by scatological caricature drawings, making the caption-like textual elements seem to function as both mood enhancements and tutelary spirits within Aran's profiling universe.

There are potential plot turns and character situations implied throughout *Dear Tenants (B)*: two inkjet print-out images show a young woman taking a smartphone picture of her own pregnant belly; drugstore ID photos of anonymous young men lurk nearby; diminutive cutouts of happy dogs are countered with pictures of trusting, "smile-for-the-camera" human grins. Such socially awkward yet familiar images point to and mirror one another, like understudies in an existential crisis that is never completely enacted, only mapped out and obsessively, continuously rearranged.

The concepts of training and tutoring are also central to the video works that are so pivotal within Aran's endeavors, including his contributions to the recent Venice Biennale and his 2013 solo exhibition *Here, Here and Here* at Kunsthalle Zürich. In both presentations, the viewer was indirectly addressed by a directorial voice that is often audible in Aran's videos—and yet the viewer is notably and irrevocably excluded from any shareable meeting place or direct encounter with the quasi-narrator directing the action. In the video *Chimpanzee* (2013), for instance, a young woman speaks into a studio mic: "This was a special night, Dad dialed the phone and got our favorite pizza . . ."; and a young man and woman trade phrases: "I much prefer our downstairs neighbor on the first floor to our upstairs neighbor on the third floor"; "We have each other." Aran is seemingly just off camera, giving cues to the speakers, again placing the viewer in the position of estranged dialogue partner. Invoking what theorist Gilles Deleuze termed the "out-of-field" principle of cinema, namely that which "refers to what is neither seen nor understood, but is nevertheless perfectly present,"[1] Aran's videos conjure a coercive atmosphere of directives, compelling performers to repeat and vary their phrasing, while insinuating the viewer into a voyeuristic role. Everyday phrases and objects work off one another to create heightened moments of mimetic crisis, fear . . . and eventually pleasure. The viewer is in training here, being familiarized with scenes that evoke absence and emptiness, scenes that stay the same even as they change: deepened and yet made thinner and more artificial in their repetition.

Aran's frequent use of classical and jazz music to transition between scenes in his videos joins with the linguistic phrasing and image profiles of his characters to create a rhythm of metaphor, material, and identity. Though a comedic ambience of genre forms and familiar gags presides over the "poor cinema" that Aran's installations manage to animate and bring to life, his scenography is opened up throughout to a metaphysical doubt that rings and repeats long after the show is over.

1. Gilles Deleuze, *Cinema 1: The Movement-Image* (1983; repr., Minneapolis: University of Minnesota Press, 1986), 17.

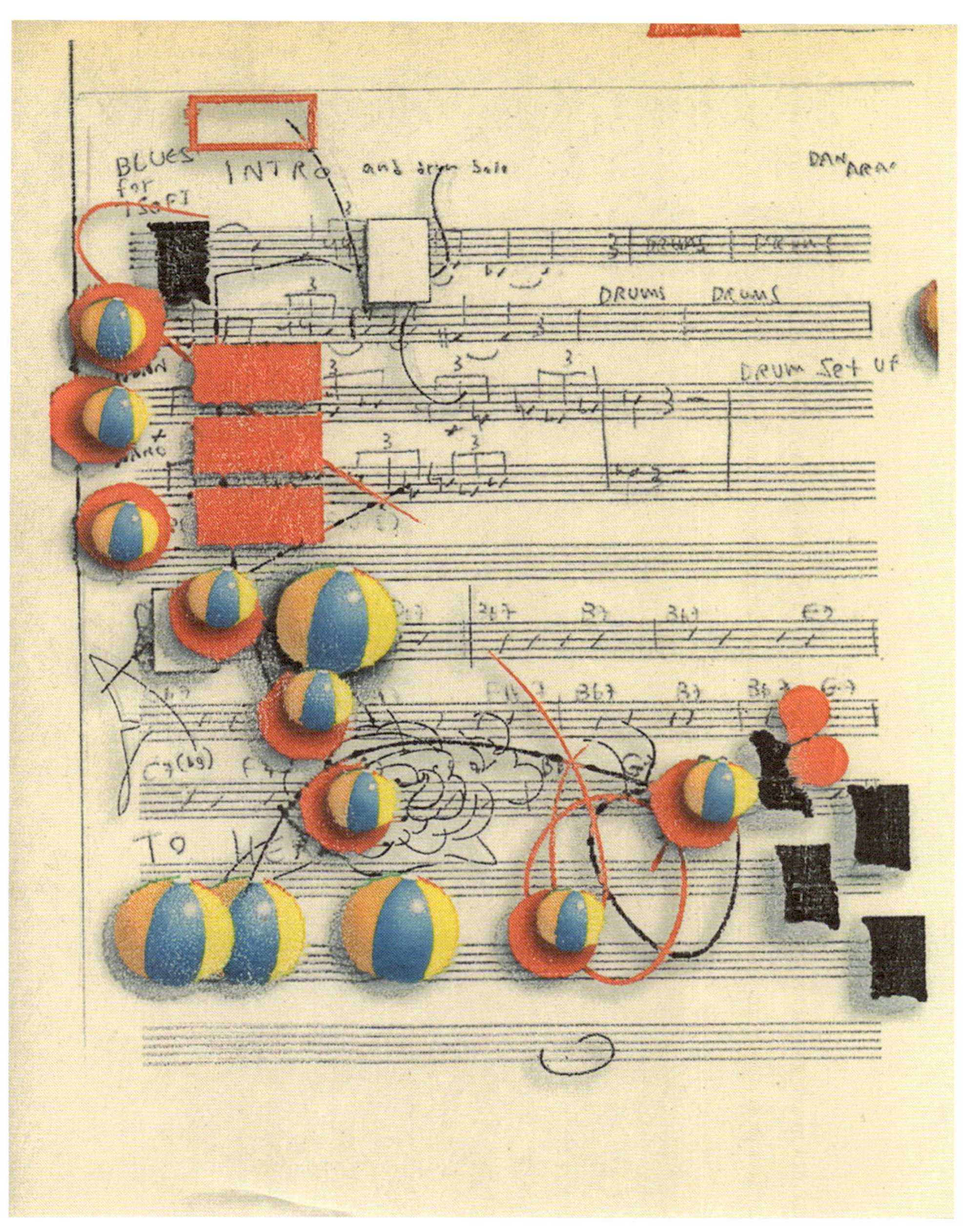

Untitled (For Dan), 2013. Mixed-media on paper, 8 ½ × 11 in. (21.6 × 27.9 cm)

Lisa Anne Auerbach

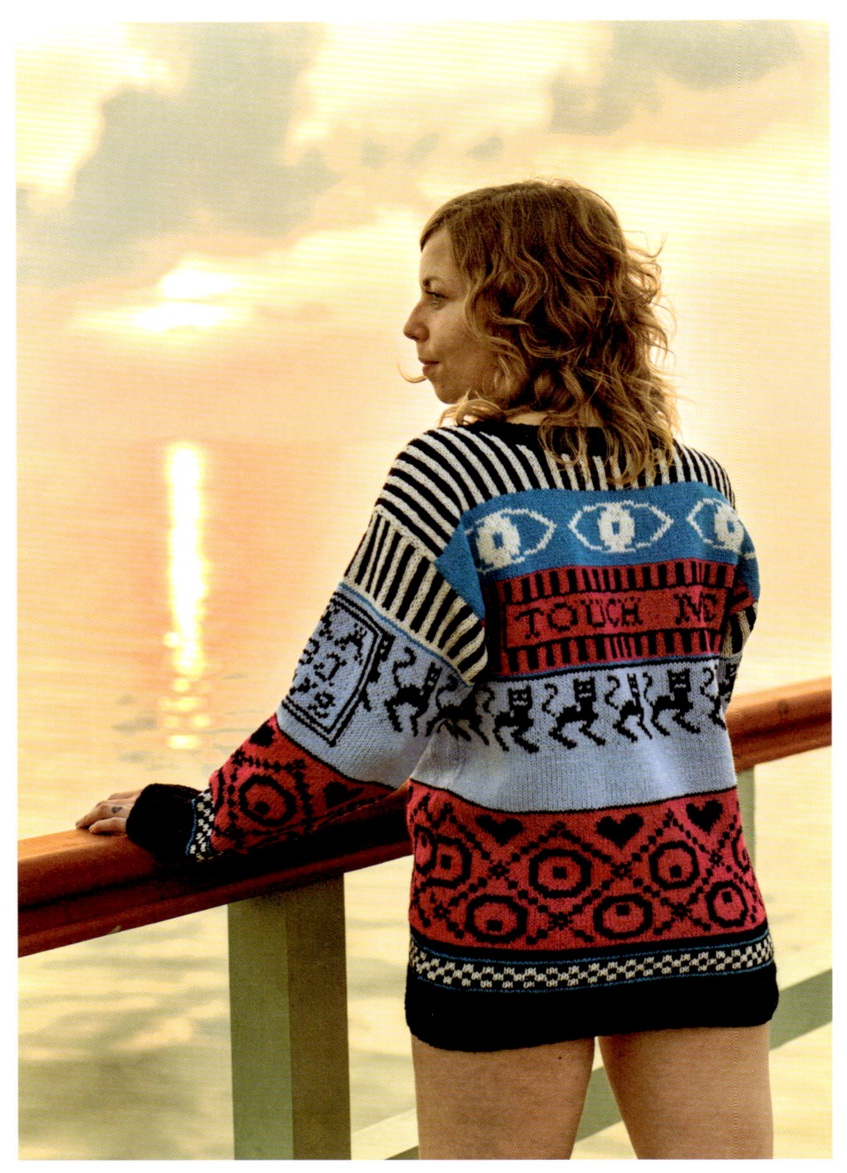

Touch Me, 2012. Wool, 21 × 31 in. (53.3 × 78.7 cm)

Born 1967 in
Ann Arbor, MI

Lives in
Los Angeles, CA

Lisa Anne Auerbach

Empress of Modest Propaganda

Mamie Tinkler

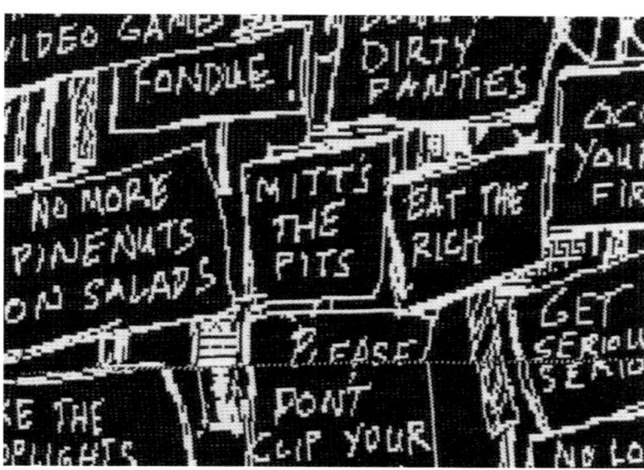

Strike First, 2012 (detail). Wool thread on linen, 63 × 80 in. (160 × 203.2 cm)

Lisa Anne Auerbach's art is situated at the strange juncture where social commentary and domesticity meet. At once deeply earnest and mordantly playful, her work presents a running chronicle of contemporary American life and some of its most intractable challenges: earning a living, feeding oneself, commuting, buying a home, and trying to be a decent person in a politically divided, economically skewed culture.

The aphorism "The personal is political" is the given condition of Auerbach's practice—a starting point for her career-long exploration of the narratives of everyday existence. Like a documentary photographer with a roving camera eye, she is a relentless observer of the exigencies, bureaucracies, and peculiarities of survival in contemporary life. Her work hints at utopian ideas, which is something of a paradox given its earthbound and contemporary nature. What if, she seems to want to know, we were all honest with one another?

Central to Auerbach's approach is the circulation of language in relation to physical bodies and objects. She has described herself as running "a modest publishing and propaganda empire," and her modes of distribution are various. Auerbach's texts are knitted into the weft of homemade sweaters, printed in zines and newsletters that the artist distributes, and trumpeted in the pages of a massive, 5-foot-tall journal the artist calls *American Megazine*. These alternative distribution systems call attention to Auerbach's role not just in authoring texts but also in (quite literally) *making* them.

The slogans emblazoned on Auerbach's sweaters are in turn diaristic and overtly radical. ("Everything I touch turns to sold / Steal this sweater off my back" says one; "What's all this talk about dying for revolution? / Live for it," says another.) They might compare to mottos on bumper stickers, except that these sweaters are intended to be worn on the body—effectuating a sensation of intense proximity to the art—and except for the painstaking labor that went into making them. The physicality of the work is paramount and heightens the subjective experience of reading. To look at the outsize issues of *American Megazine* (one features Auerbach's conversations with psychics around Los Angeles; another focuses on megachurches), viewers have to cluster around a pedestal while two performers turn the pages. This distinctly uncomfortable closeness—to the work, to other viewers—elicits conversation, exchange, and debate.

While Auerbach's slogans and signs are politically blunt, her humor infuses the work with subtlety, goofiness, mockery, and self-deprecation—sometimes all at once. One sweater, made in 2007, gives us a 9/11 knock-knock joke (it ends: "9/11 who?? I thought you said you'd never forget"): here, the artist pokes holes in nationalist sanctimony and provokes uncomfortable giggles. But her more poignant jokes are ones that we're not quite sure are being made, and that's where Auerbach's zines come in. *Saddlesore* and *BOOKSHELF*, among many others, document what might be called the minutiae of the artist's everyday life. Is she serious? Life, when examined at

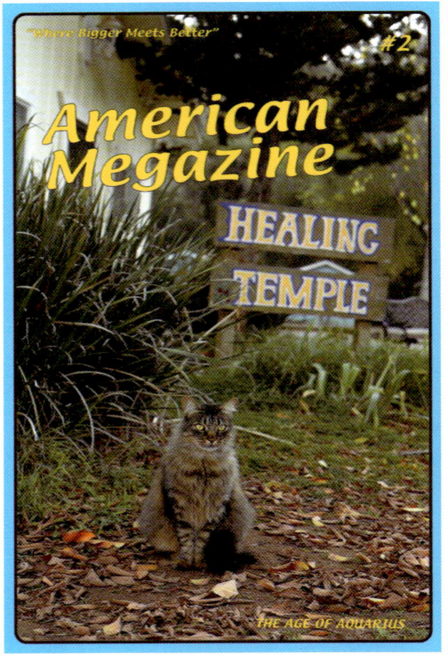

Cover of *American Megazine* #2, 2014

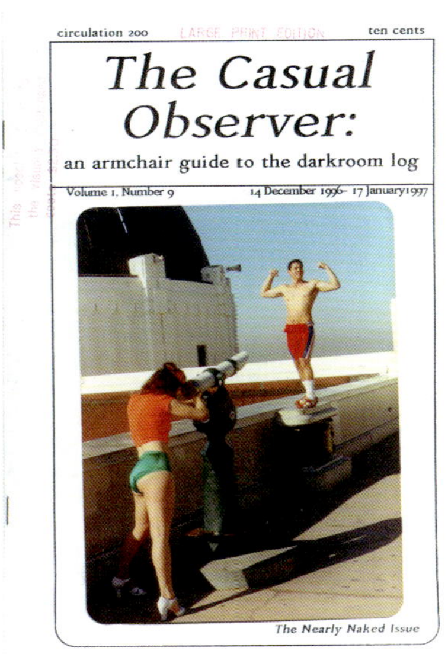

Cover of *The Casual Observer* (with Daniel Marlos) 1, no. 9, 1997

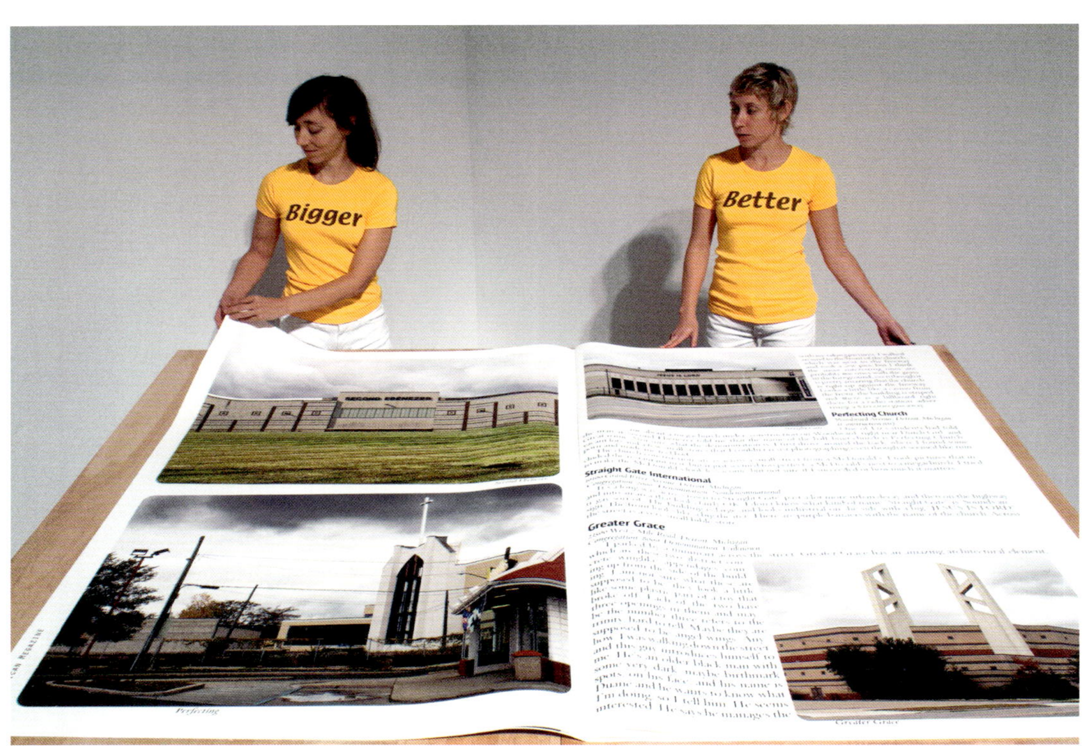

American Megazine #1, 2013 (installation view with mega-girls, Los Angeles Municipal Art Gallery). Ink on paper, 60 × 39 × ½ in. (152.4 × 99.1 × 1.3 cm)

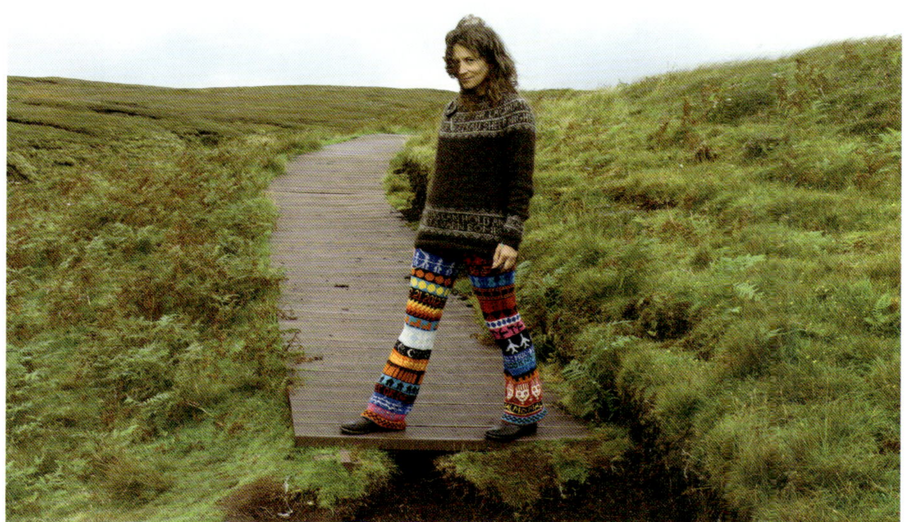

Telling it to the Sheep, Shetland, 2013. Photographic documentation of *Antisocial Practice Sweater and Journal Pants*, 2013 (detail). Wool, dimensions variable

the level of the tiny decisions that we constantly face—which books to throw away when you move? Is it okay not to bring a dish to a vegan potluck if you don't eat anything?—is hilarious, and sad, and sometimes sadly hilarious. Auerbach breaks existence down into its microscopic moments, until—like saying a word over and over until the familiar syllables don't make sense anymore—the whole exercise starts to seem absurd. What are we working so hard for, if these humble problems are the only ones we can ever hope to solve?

In her emphasis on work in all its many forms, Auerbach refutes an overwhelming trend toward aestheticizing domestic labor (from *Martha Stewart Living* to the Food Network). Though she utilizes technology as needed—digital cameras, an electronically controlled knitting machine, a giant Epson printer for the "megazines"—much of Auerbach's production is decidedly low-tech, not out of a Luddite sensibility or nostalgia for traditional ways of making but rather to acknowledge both the temporal and physical limitations of personhood. In an art world in which "poststudio" production is the norm, it is no longer redundant to describe an artist's work as DIY (a neologism that became necessary only when doing it yourself became the exception). Auerbach has always insisted that her art is not about the making, and yet labor-intensive, analogue processes are key to how her work functions. Handmade, small-scale production is not, for this artist, a quaint throwback or a feminist reclamation of craft; rather, it is her investment, her handiwork-made-visible (and in turn, a nod to other workers).

Auerbach has highlighted this distinction when discussing her sweaters. T-shirts, of course, regularly carry personal or political statements—but somehow, we rarely question the labor that went into making or designing the T-shirt, and we'd never assume that the wearer took any special care to fabricate it. T-shirts say "mass-produced." A sweater, by contrast, bears its origins in every stitch. Auerbach's labor brings us, the viewers, back into a relationship on a human scale. Our experience of viewing the sweater may not have a one-to-one relationship to Auerbach's making of it, but we can understand and project ourselves into the process of its creation.

Auerbach's zines hark back to a long history of amateur publishing by participants in dissident or marginal communities—feminists, punks, and obsessive fans. The rise of the blog has made zines less relevant, a less obvious tool for marginalized voices. But the zine-blog relationship is analogous to that between the sweater and the T-shirt. Auerbach's zines slow down conversation and allow one (quirky, silly, passionate) voice to be heard in full. Her work dodges the annoying contemporary phenomena of constant commentary, mediated debate, and sound bites. In the same way that a hand-knitted sweater will inevitably have irregularities, Auerbach's work, in its absolute physicality, is shot through with idiosyncrasies and particularities. She is not interested in a catchphrase that represents everyone, or even everyone like her. Her singular texts serve, somehow, as slogans for one person, and one person only.

Julie Ault

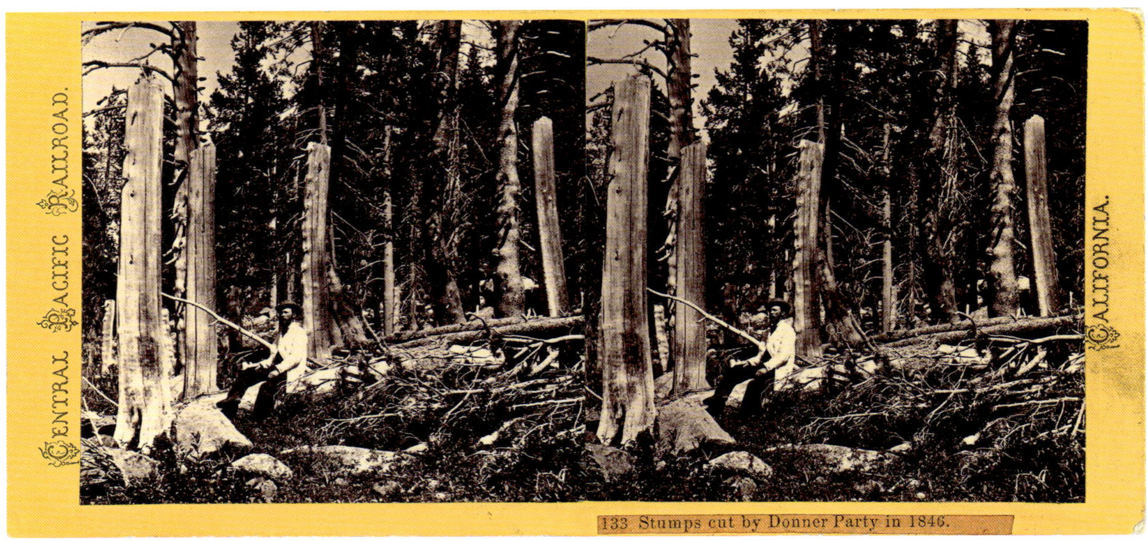

Alfred A. Hart (1816–1908), *Stumps cut by Donner Party*, c. 1868.
From the series "Central Pacific Railroad." Stereograph, 3 ¼ × 6 ¾ in. (8.3 × 17.1 cm).
Special Collections, University of Nevada–Reno Library

Afterlife: a constellation

Afterlife is a constellation of evidence and events that converse about disappearance and recollection. With various modalities, these artworks, artifacts, and texts activate and annotate the intricate relationship between archive and historical representation. In unison, *Afterlife* articulates a nexus of reference points, a cluster of concerns, a collection of contexts, and an amalgamated practice—artistic, curatorial, editorial, and archival.

A painting by Martin Wong
A photograph by David Wojnarowicz
A publication by Martin Beck
A sculpture by Robert Kinmont
A stereoscopic photograph by Alfred A. Hart
A text by Julie Ault
An apparition by Liberace
An excerpted passage by William Least Heat-Moon
An interview with Marvin Taylor
Documents and artifacts from the Downtown Collection at New York University
Two heliogravures by Danh Vo
Two paintings and a film by James Benning

Born 1957 in Boston, MA

Lives in Joshua Tree, CA / New York, NY

On Roniger Hill

Sundown: I am standing on Roniger Hill, and I am trying to see myself as if atop a giant map of the United States. If you draw two lines from the metropolitan corners of America, one from New York City southwest to San Diego and another from Miami northwest to Seattle, the intersection would fall a few miles from my position. I am on a flat-topped ridge 155 miles southeast of the geographic center of the contiguous states, 130 miles from the geodetic datum (the point from which all North American mapping originates), and about three miles from the precise middle of Chase County, Kansas. Were you to fold in half a three-foot-long map of the forty-eight states north to south then east to west, the creases would cross within an inch of where I stand, and you would see that Roniger Hill is nearly at the heart of the nation; but I think that is only incidental to my reason for being here. In truth, I don't much understand why I *am* here, but, whatever the answer, it's strong enough to pull me five hours by interstates from home, eight hours if I follow a route of good café food through the Missouri hills.

For years, outsiders have considered this prairie place barren, desolate, monotonous, a land of more nothing than almost any other place you might name, but I know I'm not here to explore vacuousness at the heart of America. I'm only in search of what *is* here, here in the middle of the Flint Hills of Kansas. I'm in quest of the land and what informs it, and I'm here because of shadows in me, loomings about threats to America that are alive here too, but

things I hope will show more clearly in the spareness of this county.

The Flint Hills: if you drive from the Atlantic Ocean to the Pacific by the most central yet least traveled national route, you set off on U.S. 50 from Ocean City, Maryland, pass before the Capitol, ride down Constitution Avenue, past the Declaration of Independence in the National Archives, past the Washington Monument and the Truman Balcony of the White House and the Zero Milestone it looks out upon, past the Lincoln Memorial, and then head into the countryside where the places are Hayfield, Virginia; Coolville, Ohio; Loogootee, Indiana; Flora, Illinois; Useful, Missouri; Dodge City, Kansas; the Royal Gorge of Colorado; Deseret, Utah; Eureka, Nevada; Placerville, California. You'll run out of route 50 only on the Embarcadero along San Francisco Bay, and behind will lie your course over four time zones, over the Alleghenies, along the northern edge of the broken Ozark Plateau, across the Rockies, over the Sierra Nevadas. At times you will have followed the routes of the Overland-Butterfield Stage, the Pony Express, the Oregon, Santa Fe, and California trails, and the Lincoln Highway; along the entire three thousand miles between Washington and San Francisco, you'll have seen only four other cities: Cincinnati, St. Louis, Kansas City, Sacramento. You will have closely paralleled the old "Main Street of America," highway 40, a road that has taken most of the cities and congestion and four-lane life, and, for half the trip, you will also have roughly paralleled route 66, the so-called Mother Road of the thirties. People write books about 40 and 66, but I know of nobody writing or singing about 50 (considering what fame can do, travelers of this transcontinental highway can be thankful Bobby Troup drove route 66). Yet, for at least the last couple of generations, the westering center of American population has followed 50, at times edging precisely along it like an aerialist on his wire. For the unhurried, this little-known highway is the best national road across the middle of the United States.

When an English woman, inspired by Isabella Bird's travels in nineteenth-century America, asked me last year how she might see the full dimension of the country, I said to drive highway 50 from ocean to ocean. If she begins in the East, I know the very mile where she will exclaim from behind her windshield that she has at last arrived in the American West. That spot is in Kansas in the Flint Hills in Chase County: if highway 50 is a belt across the midriff of America, then the Flint Hills make a buckle cinching East to West. From where I stand above what's left of the village of Bazaar, I can nearly see that stretch of road where the West begins. The traditional hundredth meridian be damned; at this latitude the West starts here, obviously, definitively. What's more, Chase County, Kansas, is the most easterly piece of the American Far West.

For twelve hundred miles, ever since driving smack through the morning shadow of the Washington Monument, my English traveler will pass from woodland to woodland — central Virginia looks much like central Missouri — but, several miles across the Kansas line, she'll begin to see fewer trees, see them thinning out and clustering in draws and valleys until she notices from the first rise of highway 50 in Chase County that, but for the wooded vales, the trees have nearly disappeared altogether. To encounter treelessness of such distance has often moved eastern travelers — and sometimes natives — more to discomfiture than rapture. Of the prairie, Willa Cather wrote in *My Ántonia: Between that earth and that sky I felt erased, blotted out.* The protection and sureties of the vertical woodland, walled like a home and enclosed like a refuge, are gone, and now the land, although more filled with cellulose than ever, is a world of air, space, apparent emptiness, near nothingness, where once the first travelers could walk for twelve hours and believe they had taken only a dozen steps. On a clear day of summer along this section of highway 50, the world changes in a few miles from green to blue, from shadows to nearly unbroken sunlight, from intermittent breezes to a wind blowing steadily as if out of the lungs of the universe.

The Flint Hills are the last remaining grand expanse of tallgrass prairie in America. On a geologic map, their shape something like a stone spear point, they cover most of the two-hundred-mile longitude of Kansas from Nebraska to Oklahoma, a stony upland twenty to eighty miles wide. At their western edge, the mixed-grass prairie begins and spreads a hundred or so miles to the shortgrass country of the high plains. On the eastern side, settlement and agriculture have all but obliterated the whilom tallgrass prairie so that it is hardly visible to anyone who would not seek it out on hands and knees; although the six million acres of the Flint Hills — also called the Bluestem Hills — were once a mere four percent of the American long-grass prairie, they are now nearly all of it. The grasses can grow to ten feet, high enough that red men once stood atop their horses to see twenty yards ahead; that wasn't common, but it occurred, and, even today in moist vales protected from development and cattle, I've found big bluestem and sloughgrass, the grandest of

the tallgrasses, eight feet high. In season, these and their relatives make the Flint Hills an immense pasturage nutritionally richer than the Bluegrass country of Kentucky. During the warm season, a big steer will gain two pounds a day, and the 120,000 beeves in the uplands will put on twenty-two million pounds.

Although the height of the Hills here is not remarkable, never rising more than three hundred feet from base to crest, their length and breadth would make them noteworthy even in places outside the somewhat level horizon of eastern Kansas, but, were they forested, my English traveler would hardly know she was crossing them. Because they belong to the open world of grasses, they dominate if not the sky then surely the horizon with their symmetrical and flattened tops, their trapezoidal slopes, and (at dawn and sunset) their shadows that can stretch unbrokenly and most visibly for a prairie mile.

These hills are largely limestones and shales distilled from the Permian seas that covered most of middle America off and on for fifty million years in the days when — had human beings and cities been around — a man could have paddled from Pittsburgh to Denver. Those seas were of such size that their sediments buried a mountain range with an eastern front once the equivalent to the New Mexico Rockies. Beneath Chase County, the great Nemaha Ridge, sometimes called the Kansas Mountains, lies about three thousand feet down, but its presence below the Flint Hills is coincidental: these tilted uplands are largely the result of erosion and not, like the Ridge or the Rockies, of upthrust. Still, today, the ancient Nemahas, as if gods buried alive, move their stone shoulders below and rattle the county atop its three fault zones, and, in time, the Flint Hills could split open and part like a biblical sea and the Nemahas may come again into the sun to throw the grassed slopes aside like so much surf.

Let this book page, appropriate as it is in shape and proportion, be Chase County. Lay your right hand across the page from right edge to left; tuck middle finger under palm and splay your other fingers wide so that your thumb points down, your little finger nearly upward: you have a configuration of the county watercourses, a manual topography of the place. Everything here has been and continues to be shaped by those four drainages: the South Fork of the Cottonwood River (thumb), the Cottonwood (index finger), Middle Creek (ring), Diamond Creek (little finger). Many more streams and brooks are here, but these four control the country, and where they have gone and are going and what they have done and are doing mark out where and what men have gone and done.

I am standing on Roniger Hill: I am facing west, dusk creeping up my back to absorb my thirty-foot shadow, the sun now a flattened crescent so dull I can look directly into it. The month is November, and, behind me, a nearly full moon will soon rise, and I am standing on this hill. I've been to this place before. Up here in the thirties Frank and George Roniger built three stone markers to honor Indian remains they unearthed atop the ridge. The Roniger brothers were bachelors, farmers, and collectors of stone artifacts from their fields lying below, and they believed this hill sacred to the people living around it in the time when Europeans were building cathedrals and sending children off to take holy cities from desert tribes. To me, this ridge is singular and, at night, almost unearthly, and I come here, in a friend's words, as *a two-bit mystic*, but I believe I've found my way onto the top by some old compass in the blood.

I've already said that what's left of Bazaar, Kansas, lies below. Lights in houses are coming on, but I can't make out the Ronigers' old brick home, and that's good because it's the nearest one, and when I come here I want Anglo civilization and its disruptions of the prairie contours far enough away so they soften and simplify into mere silhouettes. When the darkness is complete — before the moon blanches the valley — house lights will appear as campfires, and the hills can again assume their ancient aspect. Only the ponderous throb and roll of the Atchison, Topeka and Santa Fe Railroad, approaching now as it does about every half hour, breaks the illusion, an illusion that helps me see things here, to imagine how things have been. I've come into the county from that dreaming, and from it, finally, all my questions proceed, and, if things run true, I believe they will return to it.

I am standing on Roniger Hill to test the shape of what I'm going to write about this prairie place. For thirty months, maybe more, I've come and gone here and have found stories to tell, but, until last week, I had not discovered the way to tell them. My searches and researches, like my days, grew more randomly than otherwise, and every form I tried contorted them, and each time I began to press things into cohesion, I edged not so much toward fiction as toward distortion, when what I wanted was accuracy; even when I got a detail down accurately, I couldn't hook it to the next without concocting theories. It was connections that deviled me. I was hunting a fact or image and not a thesis to hold my details together,

and so I arrived at this question: should I just gather up items like creek pebbles into a bag and then let them tumble into their own pattern? Did I really want the reality of randomness? Answer: only if it would yield a landscape with figures, one that would unroll like a Chinese scroll painting or a bison-skin drawing where both beginnings and ends of an event are at once present in the conflated time of the American Indian. The least I hoped for was a topographic map of words that would open inch by inch to show its long miles.

Early, I aimed to write about a most spare landscape, seemingly poor for a reporter to poke into, one appearing thin and minimal in history and texture, a stark region recent American life had mostly gone past, a still point, a fastness an ascetic seeking a penitential corner might discover. Chase County fit. Then, a week ago, at home in the second-story room where I write, I laid over the floor the twenty-five U.S. Geological Survey maps that cover Chase County to the measure of an inch and a half to the mile, maps so detailed that barns and houses and windmills appear. On the carpet, the county was about seven feet by six, and I had to walk from the north border to read the scale at the south end. As I traipsed around this paper land, a shape came to me: while thirteen of the maps contain only narrow strips of Chase, the central twelve hold almost all of it, and their outlines form a kind of grid such as an archaeologist lays over ground he will excavate. Wasn't I a kind of digger of shards? Maybe a grid was the answer: arbitrary quadrangles that have nothing inherently to do with the land, little to do with history, and not much to do with my details. After all, since the National Survey of 1785, seventy percent of America lies under such a grid, a system of coordinates that has allowed wildness to be subdued. Would coordinates lead to connections? Were they themselves the only links we can truly understand? Could they lead into the dark loomings that draw me here?

Now: I am standing on Roniger Hill to test the grid. I'm not waiting for revelation, only watching to see whether my notions will crumble like these old, eroding slopes. Standing here, thinking of grids and what's under them, their depths and their light and darkness, I'm watching, and in an hour or so I'll lie down and sleep on this hill and let it and its old shadows work on me, let the dark have at my own shadows and assail my sleep. If my configuration is still alive by morning, then I'll go down off this ridge, and, one more time, begin walking over Chase County, Kansas, grid by topographic grid, digging, sifting, sorting, assembling shards, and my arbitrary course will be that of a Japanese reading a book: up to down, right to left.

So.

Sunrise: sometime last night just before I went into my sleeping bag, the south wind — the one that so blows here the Kansa Indians may have taken their name from it, South Wind People — eased to a brief stillness almost unnatural. (I once asked a countian when this Kansas wind would stop. He said, *Never.*) It seemed to sit on the land, on Roniger Hill, on me, pushing me down into a burden of sleep, leaning heavily as if to impress me into the prairie earth, and then, I don't know when, it rose once more and fetched up chilled bird calls from the south valley, dumped them over me as if from a pitcher of drawn well-water, poured them down, and I got up and rolled my bag, not hurrying before the lightning and murk of clouds coming on, hurrying only a little in the sparse raindrops. Then, as often happens in the Flint Hills, the morning shifted, rearranged itself, all the while getting cooler and clearer, and I went off up-county with a tool kit not of shovels and trowels but of imaginary lines and questions and loomings and the archaeologist's perpetual unease that time is running out before the obliteration hits. And that's how I started off my fourth term in Chase County, Kansas.

Again: let the book page represent this county in east-central Kansas. Divide it horizontally into thirds and split those vertically into quarters so you see twelve sections of a grid that looks like a muntin-bar window of a dozen lights. These are their names north to south, east to west: Saffordville, Gladstone, Thrall-Northwest, Fox Creek, Bazaar, Matfield Green, Hymer, Elmdale, Homestead, Elk, Cedar Point, Wonsevu.

To them attach this old Indian story: The white man asked, *Where is your nation?* The red man said, *My nation is the grass and rocks and the four-leggeds and the six-leggeds and the belly wrigglers and swimmers and the winds and all things that grow and don't grow.* The white man asked, *How big is it?* The other said, *My nation is where I am and my people where they are and the grandfathers and their grandfathers and all the grandmothers and all the stories told, and it is all the songs, and it is our dancing.* The white man asked, *But how many people are there?* The red man said, *That I do not know.*

The population of Chase County is 3,013 at the last counting (about what it was in 1873 when its remarkable courthouse was

built), and that's four persons to the square mile, roughly as many as in a Brooklyn apartment. Chase is thirty miles long north to south, twenty-six miles east to west on the south border and a mile shorter on the north. Five hundred twenty-six miles of county road run Chase, 403 of them gravel, seventy-six broken asphalt, forty-six dirt, and one concrete; except for lanes twisting down creek hollows, these roads follow the cardinal compass points along section lines. Three state and federal highways traverse it: Kansas 177 splits it longitudinally, U.S. 50 crosses near its middle before breaking off into a forty-five-degree angle, and Interstate 35 (the Kansas Turnpike) takes a similar angle to link Kansas City, a hundred miles northeast, with Wichita, thirty-five miles southwest. Chase countians use these cities, but more commonly they drive to Emporia, twenty-five miles east of county center.

Of a dozen settlements, three or four still can be called villages and two are towns — Cottonwood Falls, the county seat, and Strong City. Only in these, once linked by a horse trolley, can you buy gasoline *and* groceries. When citizens want a new car or the latest novel or a pair of spectacles, they must drive to Emporia in Lyon County. Chase no longer has a resident physician, dentist, or a pharmacist, but it does have six lawyers, six insurance and thirteen real estate agents. There is one high school, one middle school, two grammar schools, and sixty teachers; within seventy miles of its borders are a couple of dozen colleges and universities. Chase has eleven sites on the National Register of Historic Places (more per citizen than any other Kansas county), a single newspaper (the weekly *Leader-News*), one public library, sixty-six volunteer firemen, six filling stations, one sheriff and two deputies, one barber, and one traffic light (flashing). Also: a nine-hole golf course (sand "greens," players in coveralls, hazards of curious cattle pressed to the barbed-wire fences), an annual rodeo, an airfield (grass), a gun club (Friday night shoots), a movie house (piano still down front), a nursing home. And so on. Before the last world war there was more of almost everything except abandoned farmhouses and collapsing windmills.

You may see the county from one of the many transcontinental flights that pass right over it, or you may view it from an Amtrak window (no stops in the county), or you can get fired down the long, smoking bore of the turnpike that shoots across it. You may also see it from its graveled roads, dirt lanes, pasture tracks, or vestiges of historic trails, or from its couple of hundred miles of canoe-

18 CROSSINGS

navigable waters, and you can travel it by leg and butt — that is, by walking and reading. There's another means too: call it dreaming, where the less conscious mind can mouse about.

People passing through from other counties have sometimes found it a good spot to get thumped. A man from Marion, immediately west of here (now residing safely in Colorado), told me: *We used to call it Chasem County. The story there was chase 'em, catch 'em, kick 'em.* I add only that people in Cottonwood Falls will comment on the number of federal marshals shot down in Marion. But one thing is surely here: Chase County, Kansas, looks much the way visitors want rural western America to look. A college student, a Pennsylvanian working on a ranch near Matfield Green, said to me: *I can't believe this county. I can't believe it's still like this. I mean, it's so Americana.*

"On Roniger Hill" from *PRAIRYERTH: A DEEP MAP* by William Least Heat-Moon

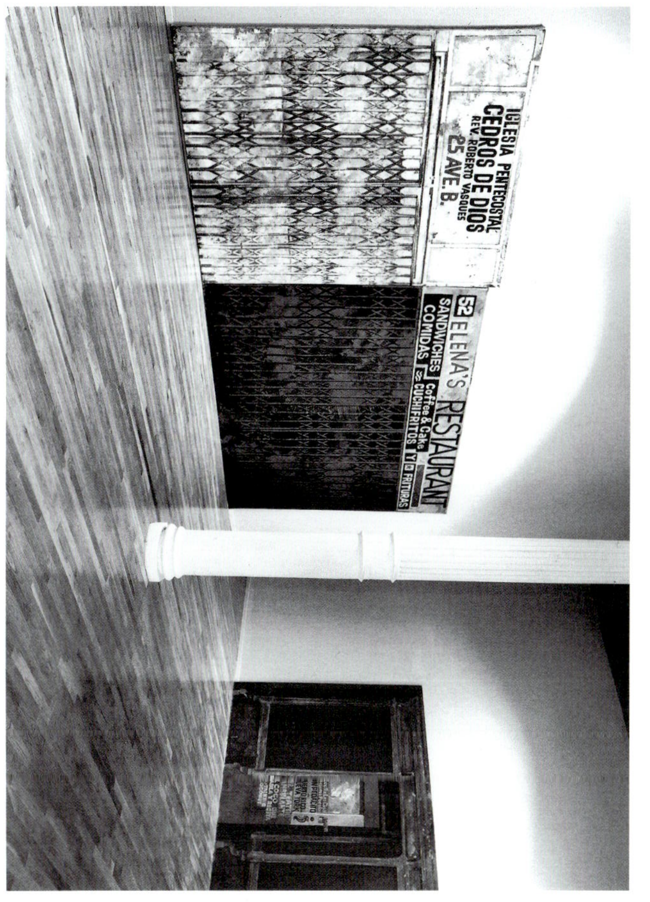

Martin Wong (1946–1999), *Pentacostal Church, Elena's Restaurant, and Untitled (Poetry Store)*, 1986 (installation view, Semaphore Gallery East, New York)

Kevin Beasley

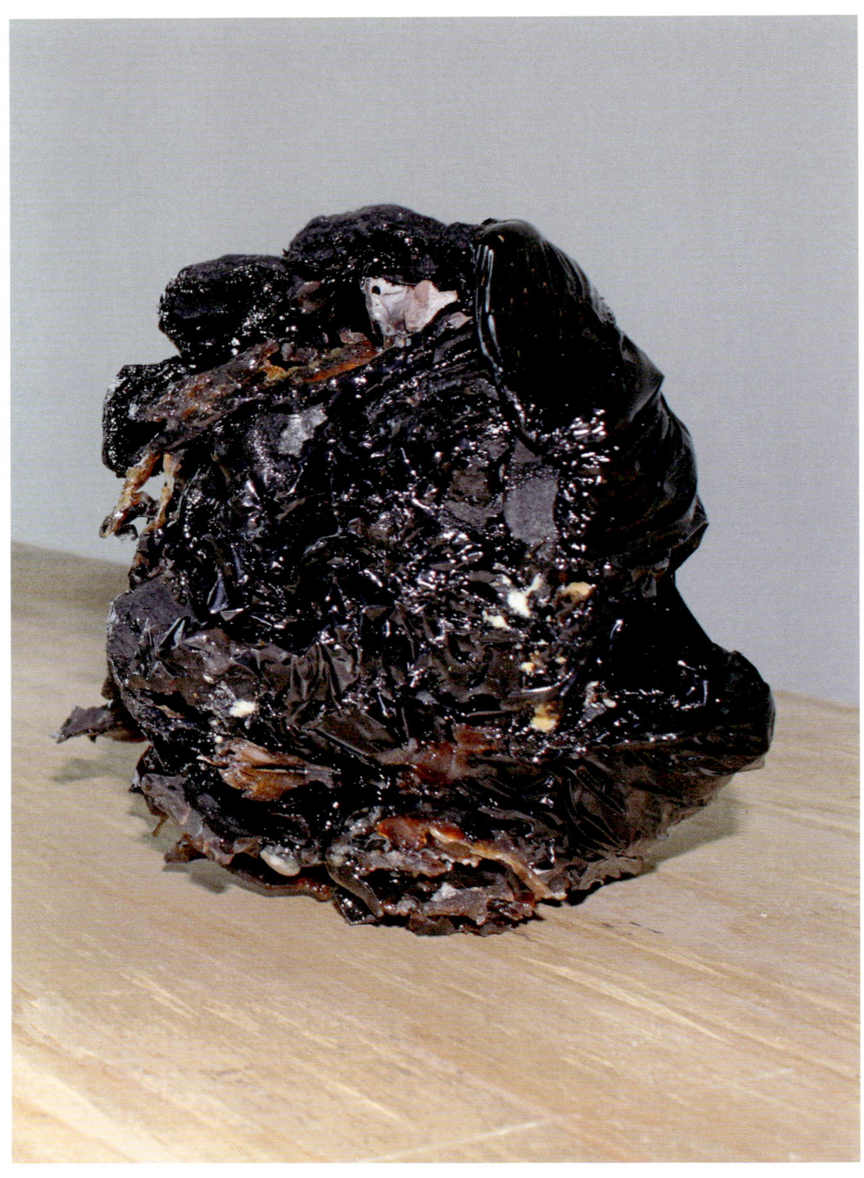

Untitled, 2011. Winter glove, latex, cast resin, peanuts, and polyurethane foam, 7 × 7 × 8 in. (17.8 × 20.3 cm)

Born 1985 in Lynchburg, VA

Lives in New York, NY

Hole: A Way In
Thomas J. Lax

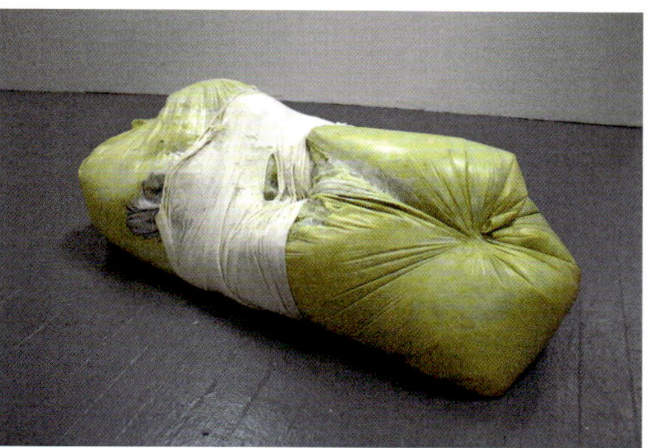

Untitled (Sack), 2012. Foam, resin, T-shirt, mattress cover, cotton, and thermal shirt, 51 × 23 × 16 in. (129.5 × 58.4 × 40.6 cm)

The white T-shirt—stretched taut over a transparent mattress cover, a thermal shirt, and poly urethane foam—bears an uncanny resemblance to its original function: the stitches and seams along the object's side would have once withheld an armpit from view. Stretched and removed from the body of its previous owner, the hole is one of *Untitled (Sack)*'s several allusions to the gaps and folds out of which the sculpture's contents seep through and reveal its holdings. The hardened resin that gives these extrusions their luster also makes the object look wet, as if it were recently produced or a point of entry or refusal. At 4 feet in length, *Untitled (Sack)* (2012) is anthropomorphic in scale, and its compressed form resembles a body bag. The shirt's threads construct a barrier between the unknown, bounded form beneath and the viewer; like the armpits it housed before, the shirt fails to fully withhold the found and used materials that it struggles to encase.

Kevin Beasley's sculptures shuffle between the thrown away and not yet formed, but they almost always relate in some way to abjection. Feminist cultural theorist Julia Kristeva has described the condition thus: "Apprehensive, desire turns aside; sickened, it rejects . . . But simultaneously, just the same, that impetus, that spasm, that leap is drawn toward an elsewhere as tempting as it is condemned. Unflaggingly, like an inescapable boomerang, a vortex of summons and repulsion places the one haunted by it literally beside himself."[1] Between subject and object, the abject is a frontier, a stray, an ambiguity: a state of abandon. Installed in direct relationship to their architectural container, often on the floor directly in the viewer's path, Beasley's objects make use of—and continue to look like—biological matter, geological debris, and organic waste. Their near life size renders them anthropomorphic, yet these are disconcertingly truncated, compressed forms. They are at once nonhuman and human-like—distinct from the viewer's body, yet threatening and dissolving that boundary all the while.

To make sculptures such as *Untitled (Sack)*, Beasley fills found and discarded clothing and objects with polyurethane foam made by combining a resin polymer catalyst with a reactant. He has a brief, half-hour window to give his materials shape and form—manipulating, wrapping, and binding the object before the foam solidifies. Beasley's intervention marks his objects: their form is an index of his very physical handling. His technique is itself a variation of the casting process—a basic tool of sculpture and industrial production alike. Beasley makes use of molds, including found objects such as shower caps and yoga balls, that allude to the body even if they cannot be recognized in their imprint. He also produces handmade molds whose shapes bear little representational function. His own body functions as a kind of mold as he wrestles and grapples with his materials. Although Beasley inserts himself into the chain of reproduction, constructing unique objects by hand and with

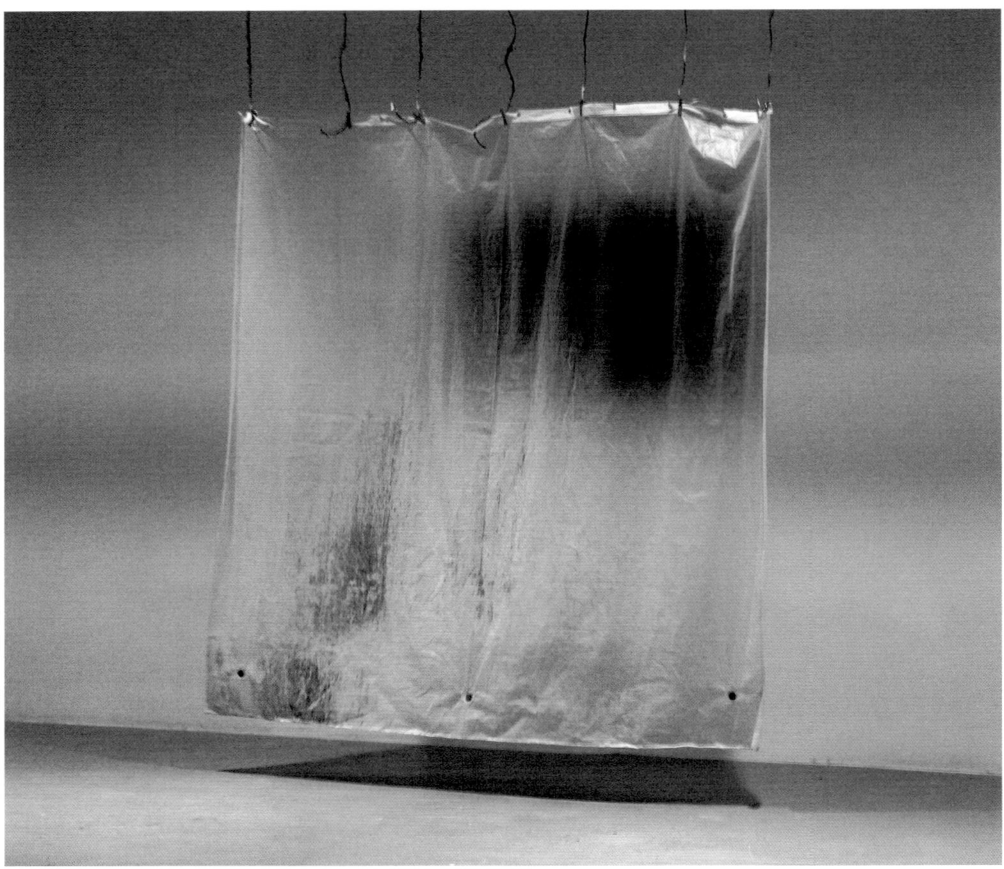

Untitled, 2012. Shower curtain, hair clips, twine, foam, and inkjet print, dimensions variable

his body, he does not relinquish references to industry and automation. Indeed, the chemicals he uses to fabricate his foam are industrially manufactured, produced, and sold. They fill the insides of any number of domestic products, like car seats and sofas; and as insulation, packaging, and soundproofing, they expedite the transportation of goods. Combining the industrial with the organic, the ready-made with the handmade, Beasley's foam not only mediates between the artist's laboring body and the imprints of his production, it makes visible the otherwise unseen links between commercial circulation and a consumer corpus.

Beasley explores an expansive language of sculpture and its "capacity for investing in the body as a receiver and safe for our experiences,"[2] which he extends to time as well as space. The artist's sonic experiences, like his objects, invite their respective viewers and listeners into relationships with one another. For his breakthrough *I Want My Spot Back* (2012), Beasley placed himself with three turntables in the center of the atrium of New York's Museum of Modern Art.[3] Over two days, he mixed and slowed down approximately forty a cappella tracks, all by deceased black male rappers prominent in the early to mid-1990s—the moment when hip-hop gained worldwide attention as a black-authored commodity.[4] Beasley improvised with extracts of the artists' voices, digitally manipulating their frequencies, volume, and equalization and playing the turntables by hand with his fingers. Miming the process by which producers make beats and DJs embellish and mix tracks, Beasley emphasized the audio's timbre and vibration over its content, even as he resuscitated the musicians' presence from their recorded voices. The artist and surrounding onlookers shared this experience with museum visitors unwittingly listening to the sometimes earsplitting sounds, as the subwoofers thundered throughout the building and their vibrations shook its architecture. Both elevating and reducing the original tracks, he transformed the music into a physical sensation.

The performance's phenomenological intervention relates structurally to Beasley's objects.

Evoking ubiquity and invisibility, interiority and enclosure, they bear perceptible, contradictory pressures on the body. The title of *I Want My Spot Back* directly references the Notorious B.I.G.'s posthumously released song "Tonight" (1999), but the work's overtones also made larger claims to time and space, institutional and urban. Occurring one week before the then year-old Occupy movement would turn its attention to the Superstorm Sandy relief effort, the performance's title and physical intervention cited a tale of two cities that has kept pace with an inequitable America. Beasley makes reference to particular and contingent bodies, eschewing illusion and pushing the materials he uses to the limits of their capacity. While his objects and time-based works evolve from experiences in specific places that happen to bear autobiographical relation to where he grew up, attended school, and currently lives (Lynchburg, Virginia; Detroit; New Haven, Connecticut; and New York), they refuse personal representation, save for the traces of their ongoing formation. Emerging from ready-made materials and everyday beats, the artist's materials are returned—assisted, remixed, and worked over—now rendered unfamiliar and ambiguous. Through a confusion of material and physical identity—corpse or trash, excess or lack—Beasley draws our attention to the kinds of dislocation, crisis, and doubt that habitually lie before us, quietly asking us to take notice even if we might again look away.

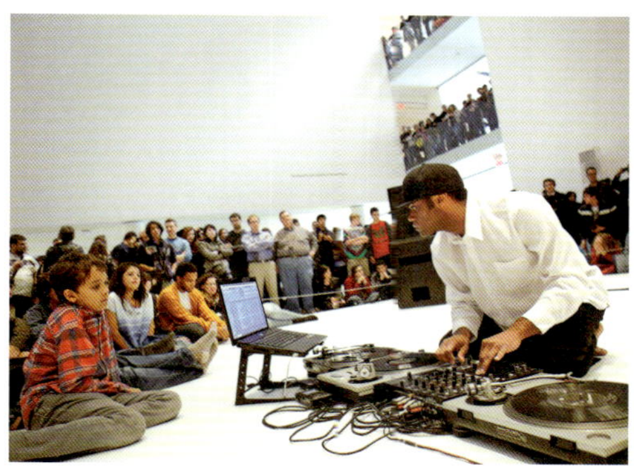

I Want My Spot Back, 2012 (installation view, *Some Sweet Day*, The Museum of Modern Art, New York, October 15–November 4, 2012)

1. Julia Kristeva, *Powers of Horror: An Essay on Abjection*, trans. Leon S. Roudiez (New York: Columbia University Press, 1982), 1.
2. Kevin Beasley, "WTF Is My Sculpture," unpublished artist statement.
3. *I Want My Spot Back* took place during the dance exhibition *Some sweet day*, organized by American artist Ralph Lemon (b. 1952) and curator Jenny Schlenzka. The work was previously performed at Lemon's invitation in the East Village's Danspace Project as part of the finale for American choreographer Ishmael Houston-Jones's (b. 1951) platform of experimental dance by black dance makers, *Parallels*. See Ralph Lemon and Melissa Perel, "Gimme Shelter | Infiltrating the MoMA Atrium, Part 1: An Interview with Ralph Lemon on the Curation of 'Some sweet day,' " http://blog.art21.org/2012/12/07/gimme-shelter-infiltrating-the-moma-atrium-part-1-an-interview-with-ralph-lemon-on-the-curation-of-some-sweet-day/#.UnHQ846hDzI (accessed October 30, 2013); and Danielle Goldman, "Judson Now Writer-in-Residence Danielle Goldman on Conversations Without Walls: Reflections on Some sweet day," http://www.danspaceproject.org/blog/?p=836 (accessed October 30, 2013).
4. An abbreviated list of the names and birth and death years of some of the artists whose songs Beasley appropriated demonstrates the truncation of their lives: Big L (1974–1999), Eazy E (1963–1995), Guru (1961–2010), the Notorious B.I.G. (1972–1997), Ol' Dirty Bastard (1968–2004), Tupac Shakur (1971–1996).

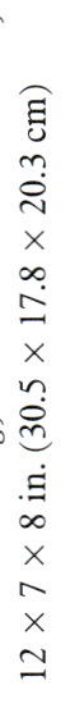

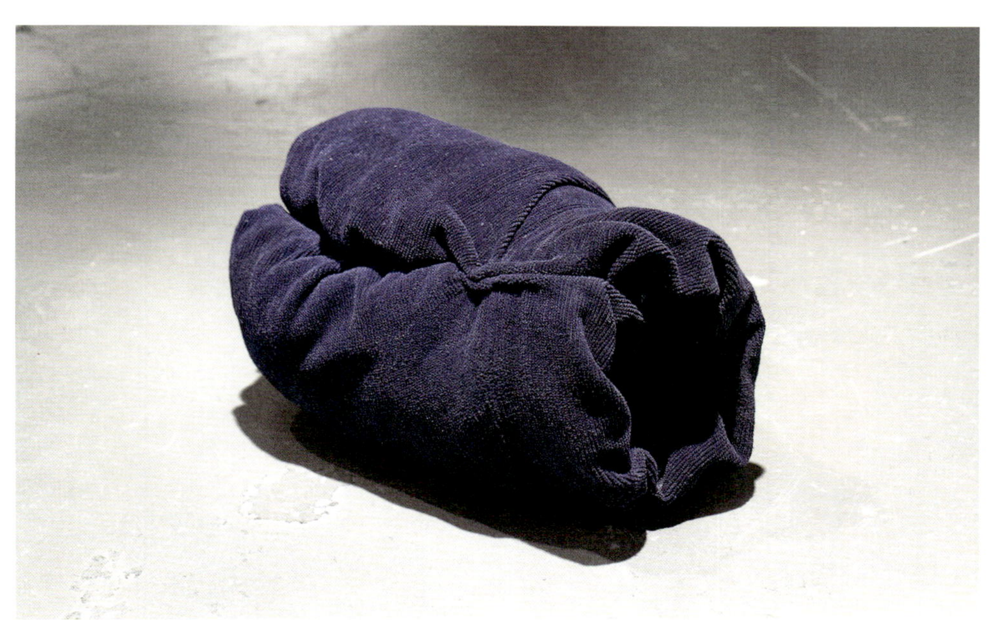

Your Awaited Evening, 2010. Bathrobe and latex, 12 × 7 × 8 in. (30.5 × 17.8 × 20.3 cm)

Andrew Bujalski

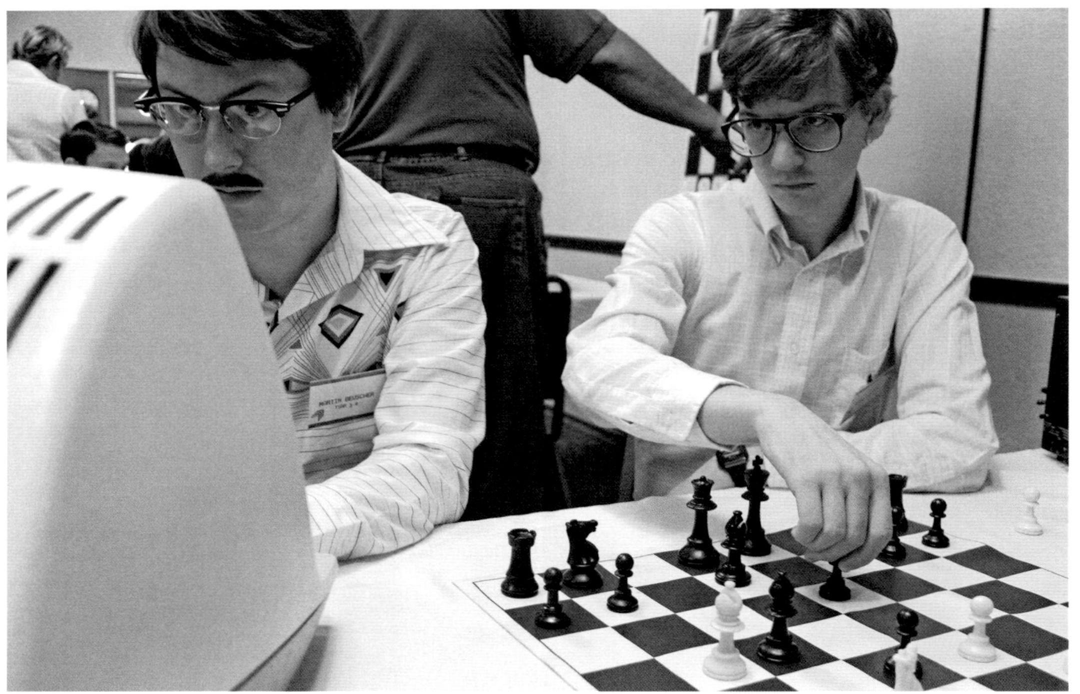

Still from *Computer Chess*, 2013. NTSC video, black-and-white, sound; 92 minutes

Born 1977 in Boston, MA

Lives in Austin, TX

An Analogue Romance
Amy Taubin

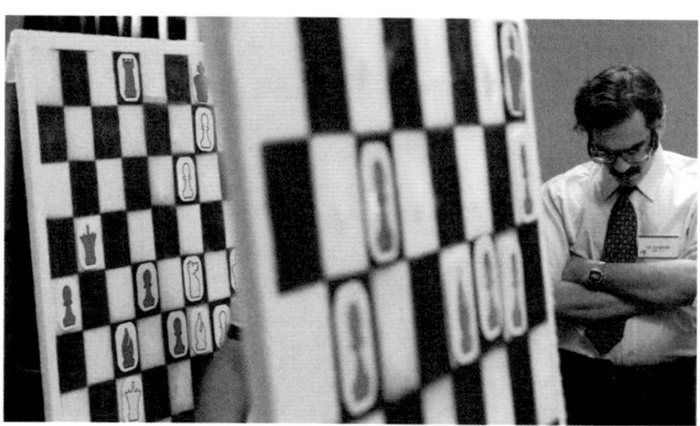

Still from *Computer Chess*, 2013

Computer Chess, Andrew Bujalski's oddly and utterly mesmerizing fourth feature, is the director-writer's first venture into history. Bujalski's previous features have been rigorously accurate, nearly ethnographic, contemporary comedies of manners, depicting his own cohort negotiating the liminal zone between graduating from college and settling into adult careers and relationships. Set in the recent past, roughly 1980 (although the analogue technology that is central to the subject and the production of the movie seems like an ancient relic), *Computer* Chess explores the early days of personal computers and the crude actuality of and wild fantasies around artificial intelligence.

Bujalski has cited two inspirations for this idiosyncratic movie. One is a book about chess trivia that he bought despite being merely a casual player. It contained references to tournaments in which computer played against computer, using software developed for the ultimate purpose of defeating a human being. The other was seeing an early video camera, the Sony AVC-3260, in Michael Almereyda's documentary *William Eggleston in the Real World* (2005). Almereyda included excerpts from Eggleston's 1974 video *Stranded in Canton*, for which the photographer used the Portapak, souped up with sophisticated lenses. Bujalski fell in love with the look of this early black-and-white video, especially the propensity of the camera to produce ghost images (trails of light that occur when the camera pans away from a bright object or light source). He and his cinematographer, Matthias Grunsky, who has shot all of Bujalski's features, also souped up their used AV-3260s by discarding the ½-inch analogue videotape recorders that came with the cameras (the entire rig was dubbed the Portapak) and replacing them with digital recorders, which at first seemed simple but turned out to introduce compatibility problems that proved expensive to fix in postproduction.

Bujalski has always been drawn to fragile and near-obsolete technology. In the decade when most of his moviemaking peers embraced video because it was cheaper and easier than film and didn't look much worse than sitcom TV, Bujalski shot and edited *Funny Ha Ha* (2002), *Mutual Appreciation* (2005), and *Beeswax* (2009) on 16 mm, thereby positioning himself in a history of American independent filmmaking from John Cassavetes to Richard Linklater, with Shirley Clarke and Jim Jarmusch in-between. He clearly had a romance with the grainy look of the stuff (and one suspects his characters would have had as well). The black-and-white video produced by the AVC-3260 and similar cameras of the 1970s somewhat resembled black-and-white 16 mm film. Although the video image had less definition and depth and the contrast ratio had only two possibilities—extremely high and extremely low—video noise had something of the texture of film grain. The analogue tube camera gives *Computer Chess* its future-past sci-fi tone, just as Chris Marker's black-and-white stills do in *La Jetée* (1962). The movie seems like something retrieved from a

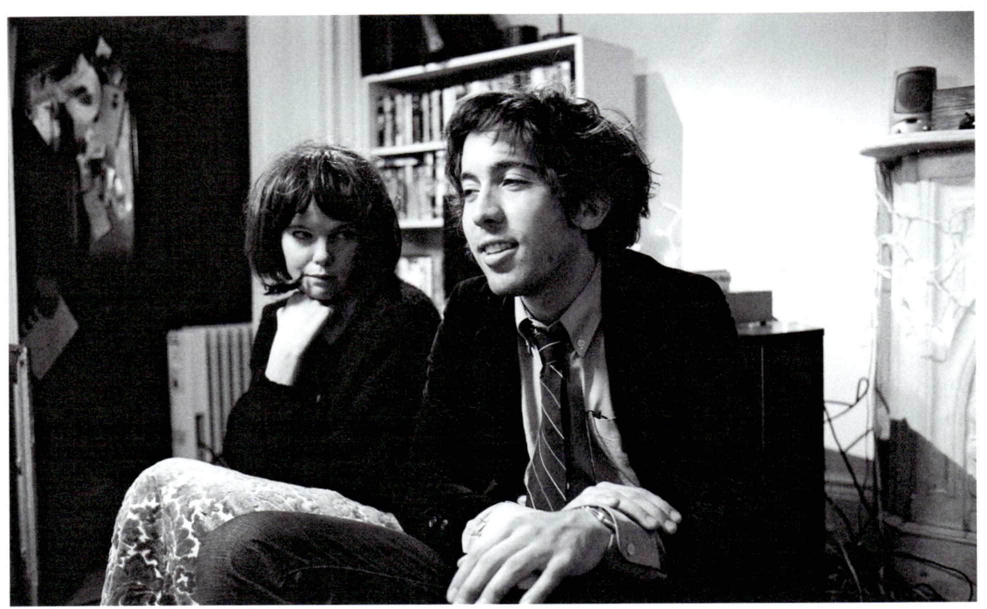

Still from *Mutual Appreciation*, 2005. 16mm film, black-and-white, sound; 109 minutes. Pictured: Pamela Corkey and Justin Rice

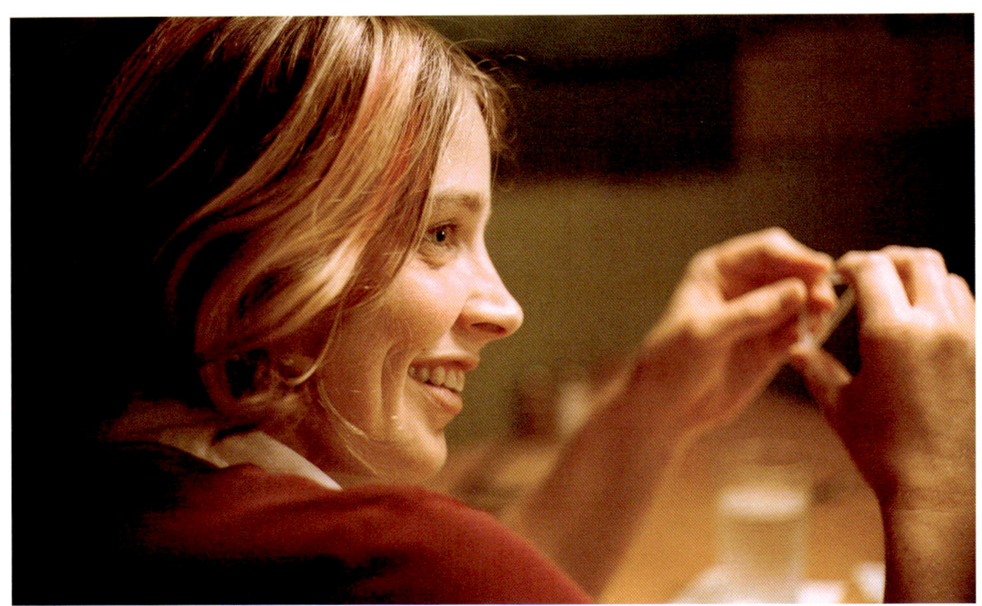

Still from *Beeswax*, 2009. Super 16mm film, color, sound; 100 minutes. Pictured: Tilly Hatcher

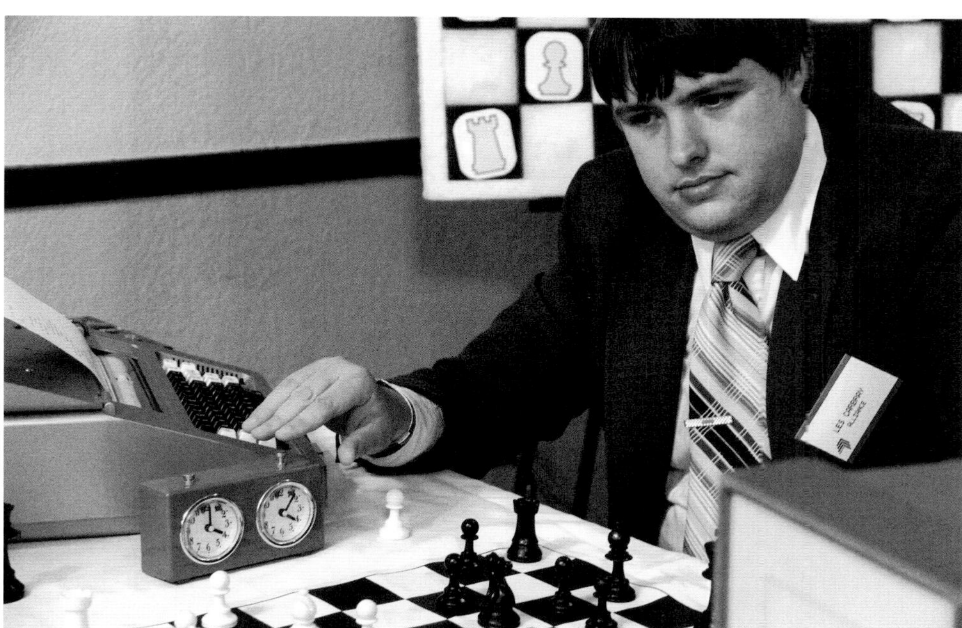

Still from *Computer Chess*, 2013

thirty-five-year-old time capsule, which, in terms of the speed of technological change over that period, is light years away.

The opening scenes suggest a documentary shot in an anonymous hotel, into which teams from hot university computer-science departments have dragged their tank-like PCs in order to compete in a computer chess tournament. As the bespectacled nerds (only one young woman among them) set up their equipment, we sense something of the excitement around artificial intelligence when its manifestations were laughably limited and painfully slow. But gradually the movie turns surreal as the camera follows participants into one another's rooms and eavesdrops on personal conversations. This is, after all, a convention, and even nerds have after-hours recreations, pot smoking and futile attempts at sexual dalliance ranking high on the list.

The narrative begins to focus on Peter Bishton (embodied by first-time actor Patrick Riester), an earnest young man whose devotion to computer chess is sabotaged by his sexual anxieties and his projection of his unconscious fears and desires on his surroundings. As the movie syncs more closely with Peter's subjectivity, the hotel becomes haunted by apparitions from Stanley Kubrick films: a room filled with ghostly cats; ominous hallways out of *The Shining* (1980), which, coincidentally or not, was released about the same year in which *Computer Chess* is set; and a computer that, like Hal in *2001: A Space Odyssey* (1968), begins to function on its own, posing questions about mind and soul, i.e., about the "ghost in the machine." Thus a crucial philosophical issue going back to Descartes is condensed, as if in a dream, with AI and the ghosting effect of black-and-white analogue video. If that were not enough, Peter comes terrifyingly face-to-face with a femme fatale in the form of a robot, like the one created by Thomas Edison even as he was inventing the apparatus of cinema. In her essay "On the Eve of the Future," Annette Michelson wrote: "The female body thus comes into focus as the very site of cinema's invention."[1] In *Computer Chess*, Bujalski rehearses and checks Edison's move.

(A longer version of this essay was published on Artforum.com, November 2013.)

1. Annette Michelson, "On the Eve of the Future: The Reasonable Facsimile and the Philosophical Toy," *October* 29 (Summer 1984): 20.

Lucien Castaing-Taylor

Véréna Paravel

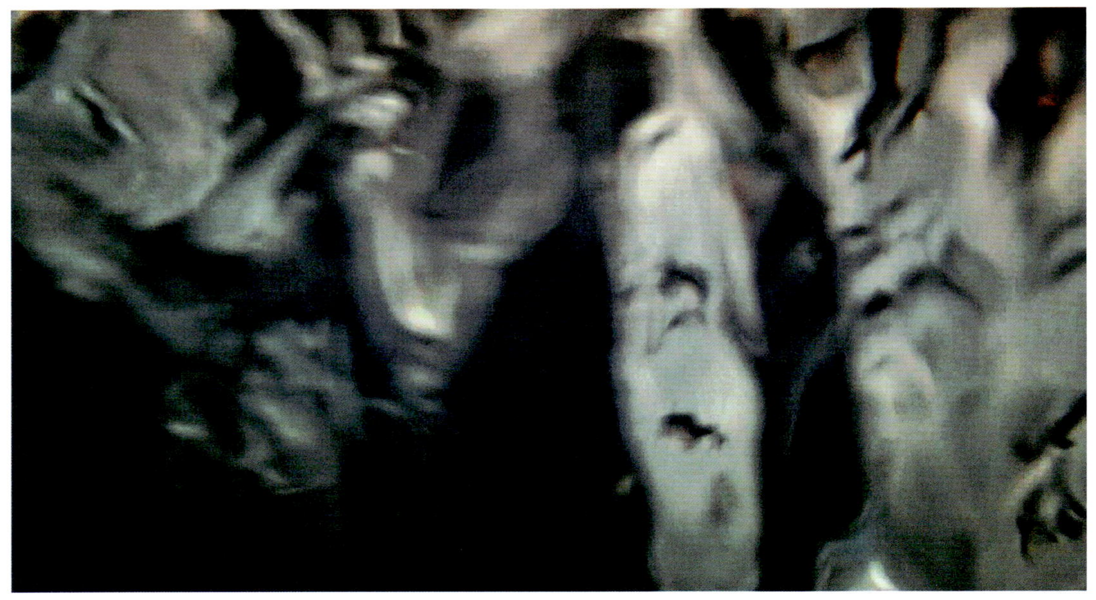

Lucien Castaing-Taylor and Véréna Paravel, *Spirits Still*, 2013.
Projected transparencies, dimensions variable

Born 1966 in Liverpool, United Kingdom
Lives in Boston, MA/ Paris, France

Born 1971 in Neuchâtel, Switzerland
Lives in Boston, MA/ Paris, France

Sensory Ethnography Lab

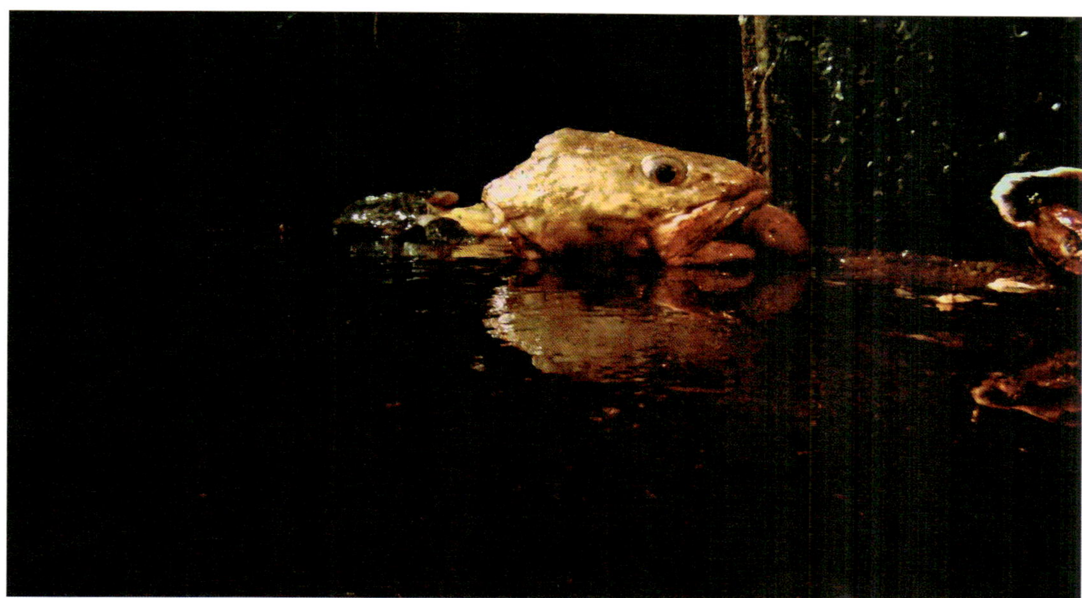

Lucien Castaing-Taylor and Véréna Paravel, still from *Leviathan*, 2012. DCP (Digital Cinema Package), color, sound; 87 minutes

Founded in 2006

Based at Harvard University, Cambridge, MA

We See into the Life of Things
Philip Hoare

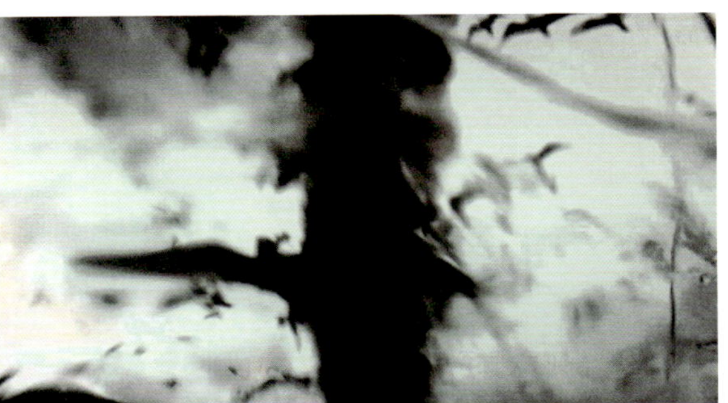

Lucien Castaing-Taylor and Véréna Paravel, *Spirits Still*, 2013. Projected transparencies, dimensions variable

> *. . . and simultaneously feeling that etherial thrill, the submerged savage beneath, in his death-gasp, kept his hammer frozen there; and so the bird of heaven, with archangelic shrieks, and his imperial beak thrust upwards, and his whole captive form folded in the flag of Ahab, went down with his ship, which, like Satan, would not sink to hell till she had dragged a living part of heaven along with her, and helmeted itself with it. Now small fowls flew screaming over the yet yawning gulf; a sullen white surf beat against its steep sides; then all collapsed, and the great shroud of the sea rolled on as it rolled five thousand years ago.*
>
> —Herman Melville, *Moby-Dick*, The Chase—Third Day

God has abandoned this place. It is the most intense otherworld imaginable. Out of the darkness, clanking chains and fraying nets are hauled out of roiling water by hooded figures like medieval torturers. Dawn slashes the unseen horizon; waves surge upward like watery cliffs. Our perspective swivels sickeningly.

This could be happening at any point in time. This ship might as well be tossing overboard dead slaves, the despised prophet Jonah, or nuclear waste. Our sins are rehearsed here, in puffs of shared cigarettes, eviscerated fish guts, the eerie cries of eddying gulls, "shrill as the shriek of the sea hawk."[1] Cartilage, metal, flesh, shell and bone clatter, and slump. Oil, salt, and sweat douse the decks. Via the fish-eye lenses of GoPro cameras, we descend to the level of those bug-eyed, benthic monsters, their whiskers stilled in the moment of death like nineteenth-century arrangements in oil or sliced up while still alive, piscatorial angels deprived of their wings by modern-day Brueghelian demons.

A man, identified only by his tattoos—like those that sailors once believed would ensure that their drowned bodies were brought home—showers in what looks like a plastic bag. A man dozes in front of a cable-TV show that entertains America by mirroring what he does out there for real. Any sophisticated sense of dominion and human hubris yields to the unremitting, unforgiving elements over which we have no control. At any point, the positions might be reversed: the hunter might find himself swapping places with his prey. "I am sleepy, and the oozy weeds about me twist."[2]

Here there are none of the normal parameters that determine our ordinary experience. Even the sky is upside down. Fulmars fly in the sea; flounder swim in the air. Starfish float like coral-colored confetti. A trapped shearwater scrabbles on deck, temporarily grounded; such procellariids were once seen as the souls of seamen condemned to sheer off over the seas; others thought they were demons, their discordant squawks the sound of infernal discontent.

An indeterminate heavy-metal track grinds out of the ether, sounding more like a séance with the Apocalypse. Guglielmo Marconi, who established a radio station on nearby Cape Cod, believed that his instruments might one day pick up the voices of long-dead sailors drowned in the ocean beyond. Serpentine line plays out from a pair of drums, tethering the depths to fine white linen and china plates in hushed dining rooms. Nature is ravished at our behest. It is hard to connect our civilization with that which feeds it. Men die here in order that we might dine on scallops or cod.

It's as hard to believe why anyone would elect for such duties as it is to understand why Yankee whalers, after spending five years at sea, might return to New Bedford owing money to the ship. These are the modern-day Ishmaels, Starbucks, Flasks, Queequegs, and Stubbs—men of New England and the rest of the world. Their occupations resemble more those of executioners or prisoners, institutionalized by the brutality they are expected to undertake for our benefit. It is as if these men, who inhabit the stained, saturated, careening images of Lucien Castaing-Taylor and Véréna Paravel's film *Leviathan*, are sentenced to the sea.

But they're regular guys—I've met them, in bars in New Bedford and on boats off Cape Cod—set apart from us only by their daily dallying with death, their own and that of their catch. Even now, New Bedford is set outside the normal flow of our contemporary life. Its wharves are ranged with accumulations of rust and rope; a modern-day fleet counterpoints the nearby national historical park, with its blocks of extravagant captains' houses, "harpooned and dragged up hither from the bottom of the sea."[3] While we spend our days bathed in the moon-glow of artificial screens, they roll and toil in a time beyond our knowing, in the dark on vessels that appear to be put together from a scrap yard and that may yet be dismantled by the swell. The sea is the enemy below, from which dollars must be dragged. At any moment, it will rise up to engulf them and us.

The recording angels of *Leviathan*'s endeavors in the ectoplasmic Atlantic document something heroic, happening even as we doze in our comfortable beds. The profits from this living nightmare, or just another day at sea, will pay the rent and tip the bartender. Meanwhile the ocean's skin, as Melville called it, is punctured and breached repeatedly, violently, only to close over the wounds we have inflicted.

1. Herman Melville, "Billy in the Darbies," in *Billy Budd, Sailor & Other Stories* (Harmondsworth, UK: Penguin, 1981), 403.
2. Ibid., 409.
3. Herman Melville, *Moby-Dick* (San Francisco: Arion Press, 1979), 34.

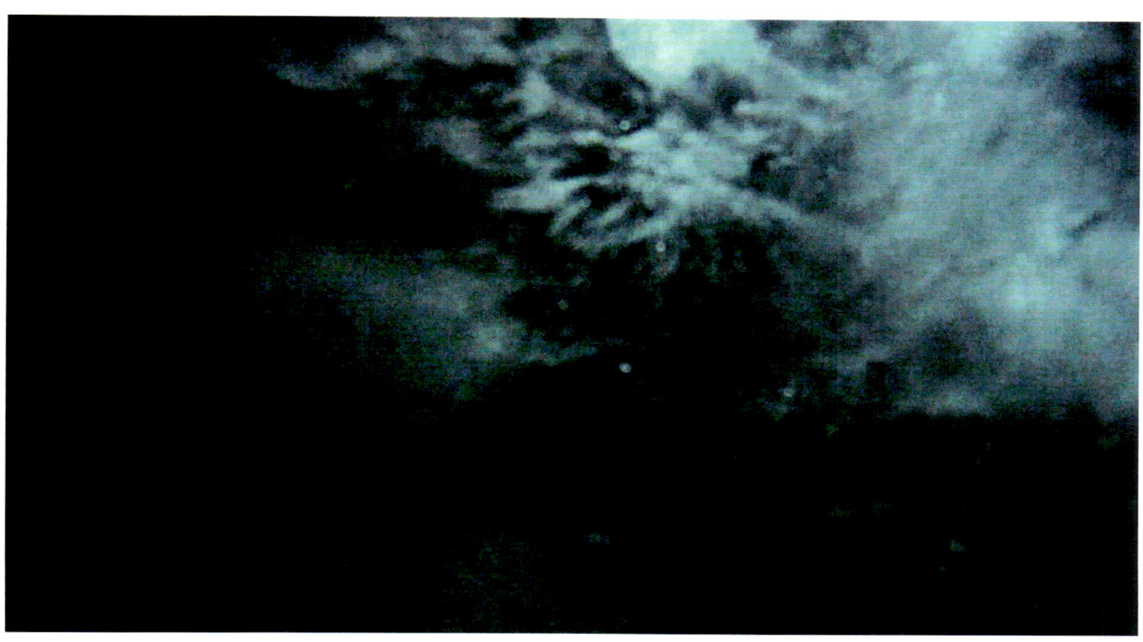

Lucien Castaing-Taylor and Véréna Paravel, *He Maketh a Path to Shine After Him; One Would Think the Deep to be Hoary*, 2013. High-definition video, color, silent; 360 minutes

The Sensory Ethnography Lab
Dennis Lim

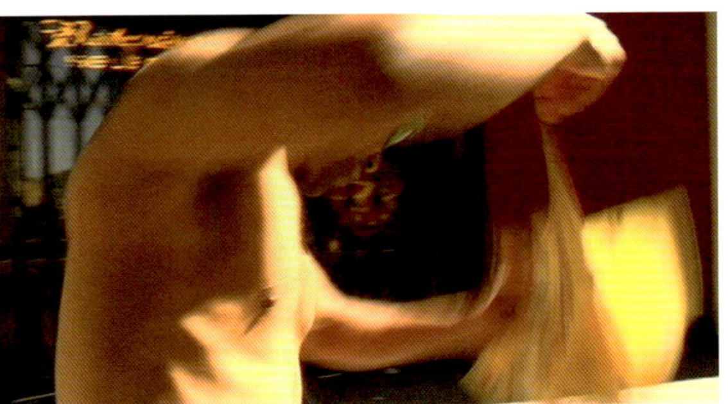

Véréna Paravel, *7 Queens*, 2009.
Video, color, sound; 22 minutes

In a mere seven years, the Sensory Ethnography Lab at Harvard University has gone from an unusually ambitious academic program to arguably the most vital incubator of experimental cinema in the United States today. To fully grasp the seismic effect of the SEL, situated at the intersection of cinema, art, and anthropology, it helps first to understand the parochial landscape into which it emerged.

Documentary these days, not least in the United States, is a largely informational genre, driven by issues or causes, by personalities behind or in front of the camera. The ethnographic film, traditionally the province of anthropologists investigating the cultures of others, is in some ways even more rigid, charged with analyzing data and advancing arguments. In both cases the emphasis is on content over form. What tends to get lost is the fundamental awareness that film, unlike a pamphlet or an academic paper, is ideally suited to capturing the flux of lived experience.

Lucien Castaing-Taylor, a filmmaker and anthropologist, established the SEL in 2006 as an intervention into this landscape, on the premise that documentary and art are not mutually exclusive and that the intensive fieldwork of anthropology could nourish both. In practice this means rejecting the laziest devices in the contemporary documentarian's tool kit: reductive story arcs, infantilizing voice-overs and talking heads, manipulative music cues. At the same time, it reconnects documentary to the work of such pioneers as Robert Flaherty and Jean Rouch, and indeed to the medium's eternal promise as an instrument for both capturing reality and heightening the senses. The aspirations of sensory ethnography—to experience the world, and to transmit some of the magnitude and multiplicity of that experience—are in essence what compelled Dziga Vertov to imagine the camera as an all-seeing, endlessly perfectible Kino-Eye and Pier Paolo Pasolini to describe cinema as a language that "writes reality with reality."

Besides teaching the main SEL class, often alongside an associate, Castaing-Taylor is also responsible for what is still the Lab's most widely seen film, *Sweetgrass* (2009), a collaboration with Ilisa Barbash, also an anthropologist and a curator of visual anthropology at the Peabody Museum at Harvard. This meditative chronicle of sheep ranchers at work in Montana's Absarkoa-Beartooth Mountains was filmed over the course of three summer pastures; from the two hundred hours of footage of grazing, shearing, lambing, and more, Castaing-Taylor also produced a suite of shorter, more structural videos—like the 20-minute *Hell Roaring Creek* (2010), in which a seemingly endless flock of sheep traverse a stream at dawn—which have been shown both in galleries and in theaters.

Documenting a way of life as it slips toward extinction, *Sweetgrass* is a work of salvage ethnography that remains ever wary of the trap of romantic nostalgia. (Only in its terse closing title does the film reveal that it was in fact chronicling the final days of the century-old practice of the Montana sheep drive.) *Sweetgrass* also encapsulates several recurring traits and concerns of SEL works. First, there is an emphasis on the rhythms and the meaning of labor, an awareness that work reveals plenty about how people relate to one another and to their surroundings. Second, while *Sweetgrass* maintains a more or less observational stance, there is none of the vaunted fly-on-the-wall detachment of cinema vérité—indeed, SEL films often enact an encounter, or at least acknowledge, a connection between filmmakers and subjects, whether by including interactions on camera or otherwise subtly acknowledging the presence of the filmmaker. Third, what anthropologists call "thick description" finds its analogue in an accumulation of sensory detail, which emerges not just from the alertness and patience of the camera but also from the richness and specificity of the film's soundscapes, generally recorded on location and crafted in postproduction by the sound artist Ernst Karel with an ear for the musicality of found sounds. (Karel's presence at the lab has ensured that most SEL films hear as attentively as they see.) And, finally, in contrast to the self-imposed strictures of most documentaries, SEL works engage promiscuously with multiple realms of cinematic art, employing the durational techniques and formalist compositions of the avant-garde and slyly alluding to all manner of film genres—in the case of *Sweetgrass*, the Western, the pastoral, and the nature film.

Bearing the imprimatur of Harvard—where it was set up as a collaboration between the Departments of Anthropology and of Visual and Environmental Studies—the SEL may appear to be part of the establishment. But Castaing-Taylor and his cohorts make a point of calling themselves amateurs. They come to filmmaking not from film school or the industry trenches but from other academic backgrounds and as such their approach is genuinely interdisciplinary.

Despite their shared interests and methods, the works of the SEL do not add up to a monolithic movement. The notion of a laboratory is central: students are not instructed to work in a particular manner but are encouraged continually to rethink their assumptions and positions, and to experiment and collaborate, as the numerous partnerships among filmmakers attest. In the best possible sense, these are filmmakers still finding their way, whose approaches have yet to harden into habit or dogma. The best works of SEL encapsulate the promise of sensory ethnography and of cinema itself—to describe and transcend the bounds of time and space.

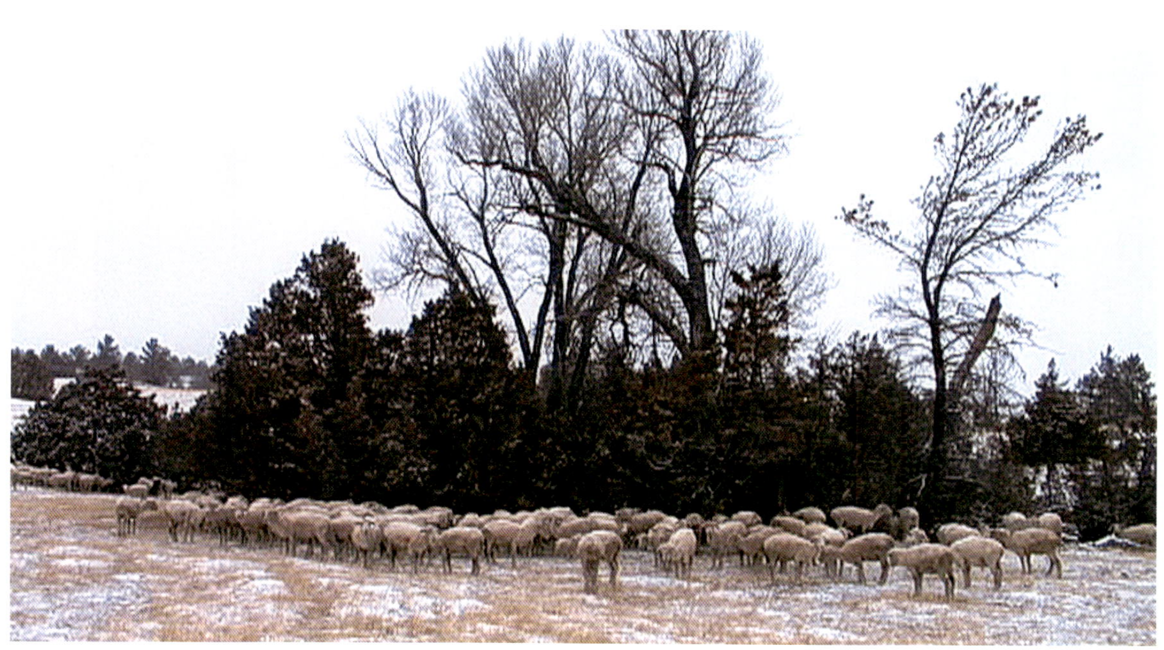

Lucien Castaing-Taylor, *Coom Biddy*, 2012. High-definition video, color, sound; 8 minutes

Zackary Drucker

Rhys Ernst

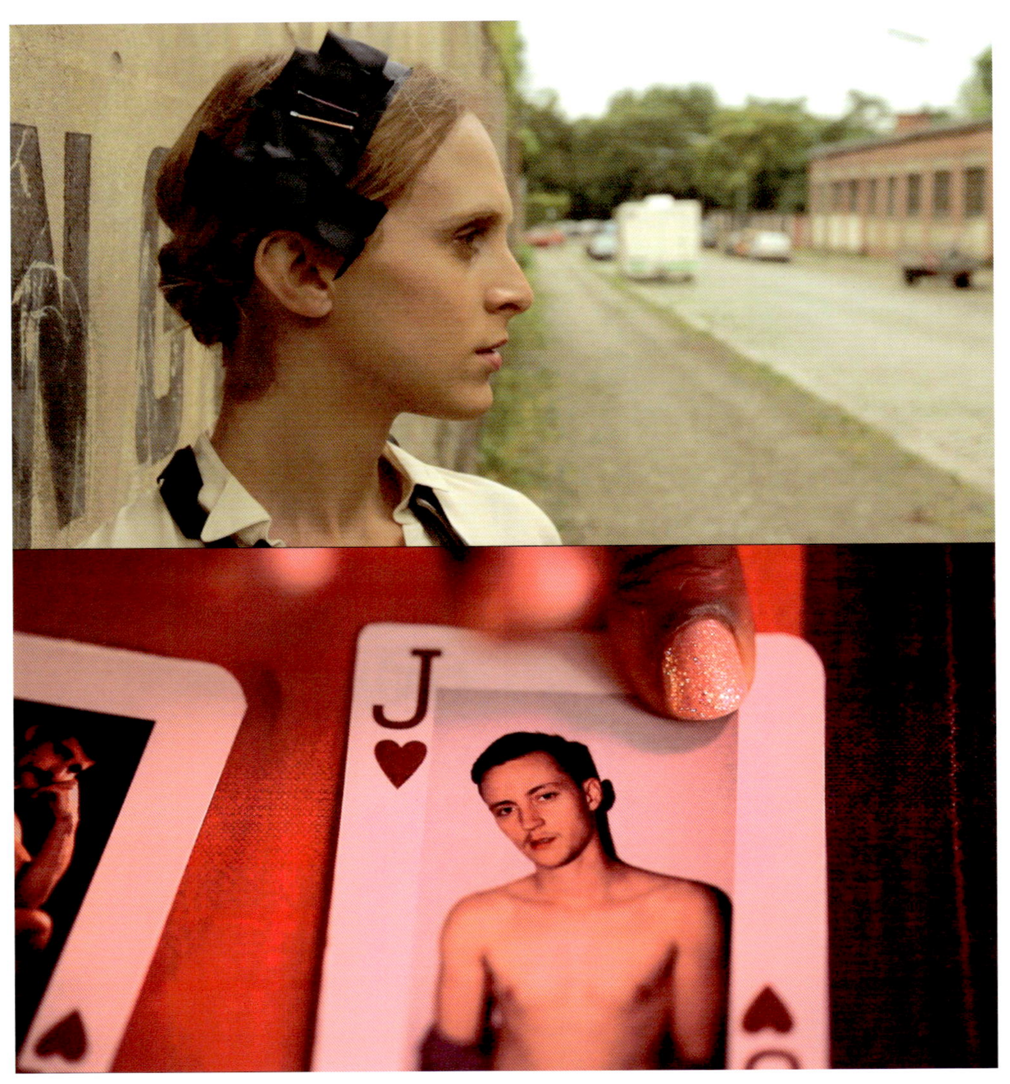

Stills from *She Gone Rogue*, 2012. High-definition video, color, sound; 23 minutes

Born 1983 in
Syracuse, NY
Lives in
Los Angeles, CA

Born 1982 in
Pomona, CA
Lives in
Los Angeles, CA

Zackary Drucker

Rhys Ernst

Kicking Holes in the Darkness
Kristine Stiles

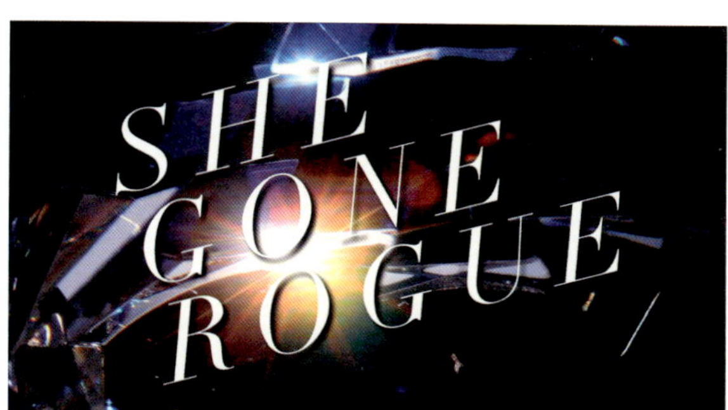

Still from *She Gone Rogue*, 2012

Seventeen minutes and thirty-five seconds into Rhys Ernst and Zackary Drucker's twenty-two-minute film *She Gone Rogue* (2012), the heroine of the narrative, Darling (played by Drucker), appears at a threshold, staring across its psychic abyss at her doppelgänger (also Drucker), who returns her gaze. The only figure in the scene who acknowledges the audience is the clown in a painting in the background, whose one fully alive dark eye fixes viewers with an interrogating look. This perceptive eye is the metonym for the performer known as Flawless Sabrina (a.k.a. Jack Doroshow), appearing here as "Mother Superior Flawless Sabrina." An open door divides the two Darlings for a moment, and then the Darling in the middle ground flees the scene, while the Darling in the foreground rushes through the open door under the omniscient eye of Mother, who, as Ernst puts it, embodies "the matriarchal lineage of trans-women who have passed a legacy down of the expanding and multiplying self."[1] A principal theme of *She Gone Rogue* is the timeless quest to recover and permit the multiplicity of the self, which unfolds in various forms—ego, persona, psyche, spirit, and mind—and coalesces in endlessly shifting identities. The two Darlings personify this theme in the urgency and immediacy of their mutual identification. This instant summarizes the broader connotations of the film and provides a key to its narrative, dense with social, political, feminist, and queer meanings, and with psychoanalytic implications.

The film functions as a kind of rejoinder, from two artists at the forefront of the "trans-cinema" field, to a question that gender theorist Judith Butler posed in the preface to her 1990 book *Gender Trouble: Feminism and the Subversion of Identity*: "What happens to the subject and to the stability of gender categories when the epistemic regime of presumptive heterosexuality is unmasked as that which produces and reifies these ostensible categories of ontology?"[2] Later in the same volume, Butler suggests: "The task is not whether to repeat, but how to repeat or, indeed, to repeat and, through a radical proliferation of gender, to *displace* the very gender norms that enable the repetition itself."[3] She adds: "If identities were no longer fixed as the premise of political syllogism, and politics no longer understood as a set of practices derived from the alleged interests that belong to a set of ready-made subjects, a new configuration of politics would surely emerge from the ruins of the old."[4] Butler closes her book with a final question: "What other local strategies for engaging the 'unnatural' might lead to the denaturalization of gender as such?"[5]

Throughout *She Gone Rogue*, and especially in the instant described above, Drucker and Ernst accomplish this task of denaturalizing gender. Moreover, they arrive at several of the "strategies" sought by Butler: for example, using cinematic editing and scenography to construct convoluted narrative structures that undermine linear, time-based storytelling; setting action in disassembled dream spaces that render the characters' mental states fragmentary and indiscernible; and presenting a gamut of identities and genders in overlapping segments that refer to tropes of sexuality as both hegemonic and counterhegemonic. Hegemony in this film is conveyed voyeuristically, in a pastiche of love and longing—at once genuine and parodied—glimpsed through the glass of a cabin window at twilight, the romantic glow of candlelight accentuating the faces of the couple sitting across from each other, engrossed in conversation. Counterhegemonic constructions are organized in a raucous cacophony of objects and images; claustrophobic assemblages and painted portraits; the physical vibration (at one point) of the set itself; transitions of locale; and exhibitionistic presentations of gender self-interpretation and self-determination.

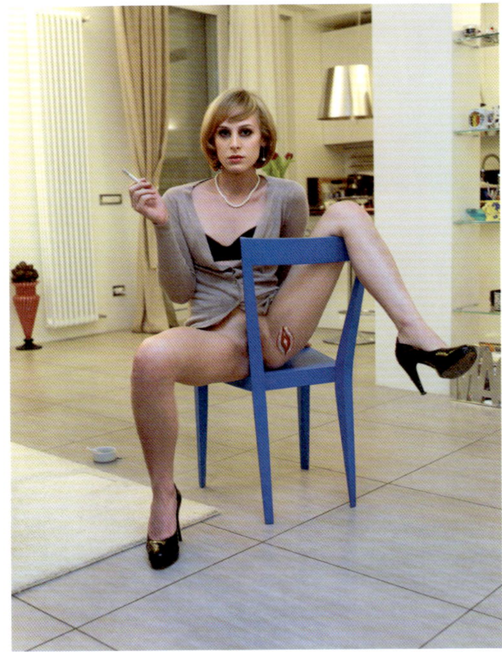

Zackary Drucker and Manuel Vason (b. 1974), *Don't Look at Me Like That*, Collaboration #3, Milan, 2010. Duratrans on LED light box, 36 × 24 in. (91.4 × 61 cm)

In other contexts preceding *She Gone Rogue*, Drucker and Ernst have revealed a wicked sense of humor, marshaled to undermine the insidious, specious reasoning that leads to suppressive political and social consequences. A 2010 photograph of Drucker by Manuel Vason evinces the complex wisdom in this humor: seated on a blue chair in a domestic setting, smoking a cigarette, Drucker splays her legs, exposing a *vagina dentata*—with actual teeth—located on her upper thigh, not far from the expected anatomical location. Gorgeous in her best string of pearls, Drucker gazes candidly into the camera lens and calmly instructs: "Don't look at me like that." The video for *She Gone Rogue*'s Kickstarter campaign is a lampoon of a TV cooking show, in which Ernst plays a mustached sous chef, whipping up "transformational reductions" in the form of plastic confetti. Drucker chops up false eyelashes and mixes in sparkly stones as she tells viewers about the film and flirts suggestively: "Make sure your oven is preheated to 400 degrees, and you are ready for action." After asking for donations to the project, Drucker promises the viewer "a slice," prompting the deadpan Ernst to brandish a giant, phallic knife. Such images are not camp but outright satire, directed at prescribed phallocentric and feminized categories, duties, and behaviors.

By refusing to be what they are not, Drucker and Ernst overturn the supposed normativity of heterosexuality, configuring their own social politics. A group of photographs showing the evolution of their relationship makes this point vividly. These pictures testify to the process of expansive "multiplication" that both artists have undergone: rejecting regimes of gender, denying dicta of state and organized religion, and repudiating any attempt by institutions or individuals to control their bodies/beings. The photographs reveal how, alone and together, Ernst and Drucker have transitioned through the liminal space between genders, dismantling the political imperatives of gender mandates. Drucker describes these images as "authentic diaristic documents . . . of our moments together, from two androgynous bodies transitioning to falling in love, companionship, partnership, and play, and then to images of us alone."[6] Although she insists that they are "straight-up family snapshots,"[7] these exquisite photographs achieve a singular force through framing, lighting, and setting, all of which aid in visually presenting the warp of emotion in this relationship. The portraits depict the moods of the artists—which range from desirous, playful, and searching to contemplative, skeptical, and lonely. Each photograph, with its Vermeer-esque, intimate lighting, offers a portal into a life that was once private and protected, and is now made public. Yet Ernst and Drucker also confound this

Zackary Drucker

Rhys Ernst

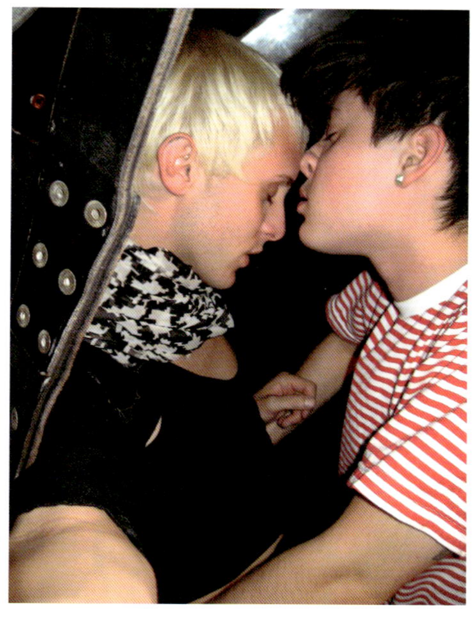

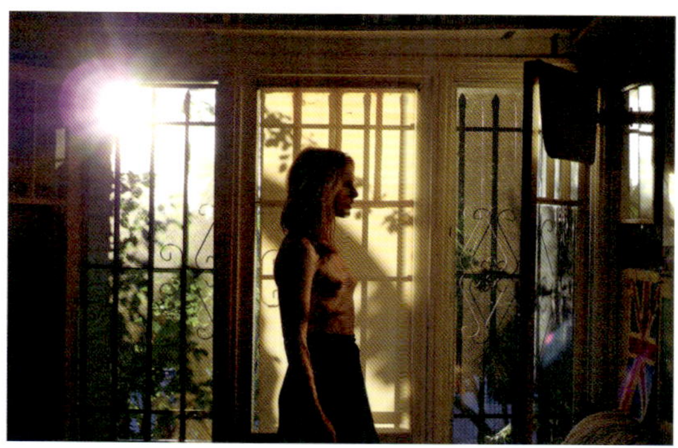

Zackary Drucker and Rhys Ernst, from the *Relationship* series, 2008–13.
Chromogenic prints, dimensions variable

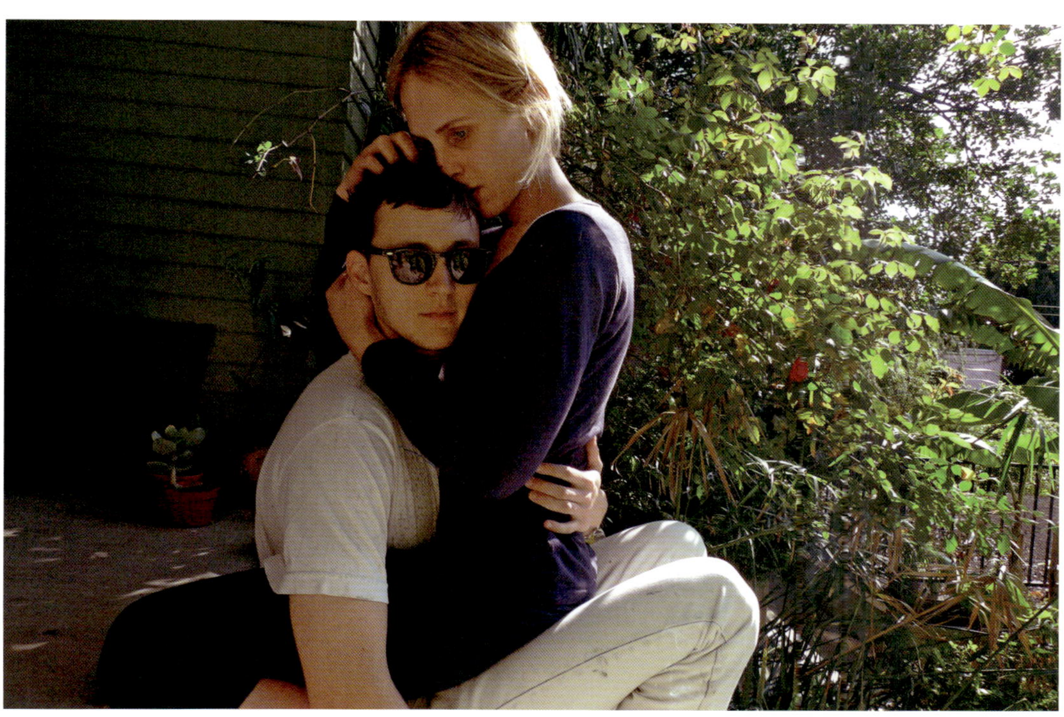

privileged view by being self-consciously performative, staging themselves in the images as the personas they may be, but also as they wish to be seen. Autobiography here is both fact and fiction. These arresting photographic works express "a lie that tells the truth" (to borrow Picasso's famous observation about the capacity of art). Whatever the future of their relationship, Drucker and Ernst produce art resonant with rare strength, integrity, and subversive power.

She Gone Rogue shares formal and conceptual strategies with the films of Todd Haynes (whom Ernst admires) and draws on similarly diverse sources, including "European art-film, punk, grunge, glam, underground [and] mainstream, pop art, and pulp fiction."[8] A subplot of the film is the semiautobiographical tale of star-crossed lovers, predicted by the Whoreacle of Delphi (played by Vaginal Davis, a self-

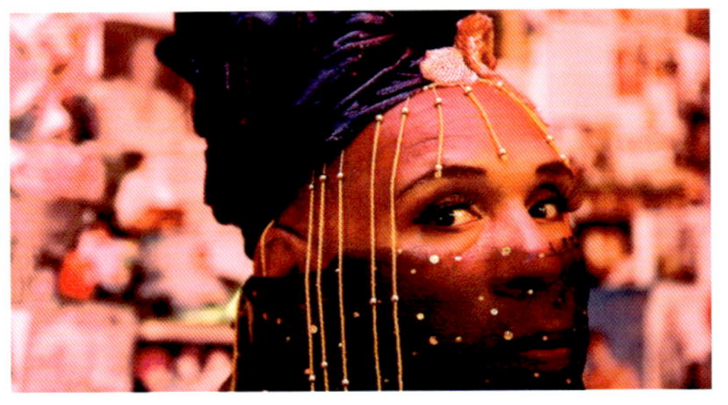

Still from *She Gone Rogue*, 2012

identified "gender-queer," whose chosen name is an homage to Angela Davis). Darling visits the Whoreacle, where she is attacked and molested in the bathroom. After escaping, she meets with the Whoreacle, who is reading a deck of tarot cards embellished with erotic imagery. "You will find your true, deepest love, a little tiny diminutive man," the Whoreacle predicts (describing Ernst). "This is the man of your dreams. You will have a wonderful time together in this beautiful afterlife. You know the ending of this story already . . . You were possessed before you were a possession." Drucker's imagination is overcome.

In its nonlinear schema, the film does not begin with this scene, but with an end point, after the lovers have separated, as we surmise through fragments of a letter: "I just need some space [for] a while. I'm sorry." The apparently unexpected departure of her lover leads Darling to visit and care for her ailing Aunt Holly (Holly Woodlawn), who is an important emotional touchstone throughout the film. The note from her lover also sends Darling down a "rabbit hole" in the wall of the home owned by the artist Ron Athey (the actual Los Angeles abode of Drucker and Ernst). She peers through the open hole in the wall into a shed and beyond to a forest, and then

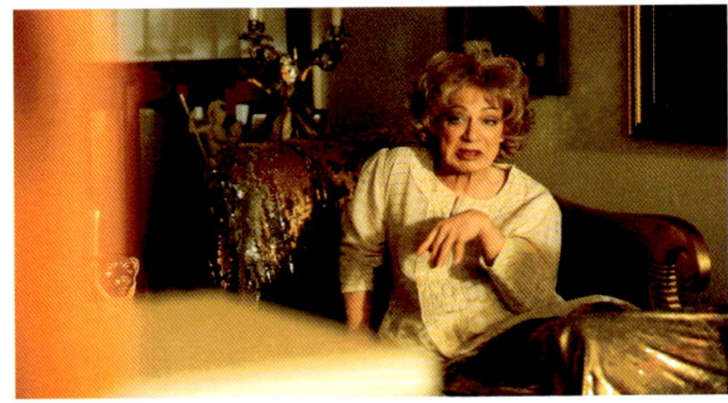

Still from *She Gone Rogue*, 2012

enters a surreal world—from which it is unclear whether she will ever return. She is beckoned by the other Darling, who whispers: "A mirror facing a mirror. Follow me into a mirror, Darling"; and ominously: "Here, kitty kitty kitty . . . Where are you going? You are me, in one direction; and I am you, in another direction. Your body is a dead end. You don't even know which way you're traveling."

Running through the forest, Darling ends up at the home of her parents (played by Drucker's actual parents). As the three of them share a meal, her father sings a children's song, low and gentle, yet menacing: "Animal crackers in my soup. / Lions and tigers loop-de-loop. / Gosh, oh gee, won't we have fun / Swallowing animals one by one." The quest continues to Berlin, where the two Darlings move about and spy on each other

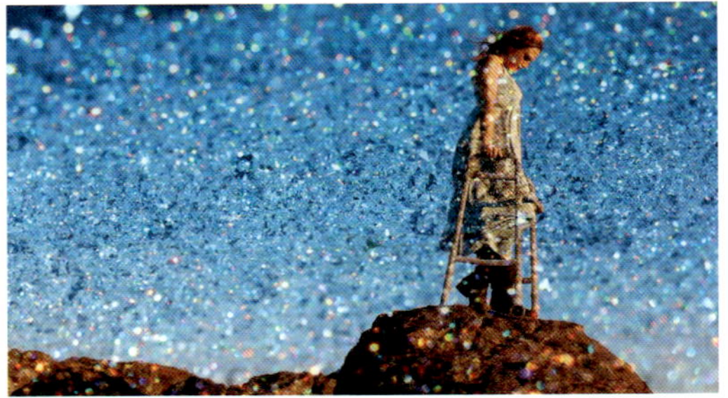

Still from *She Gone Rogue*, 2012

(a sequence that pays homage to Maya Deren's 1943 film *Meshes of the Afternoon*). Next, Darling arrives at the New York apartment of Mother Superior Flawless Sabrina, where—against a spectacular backdrop of masks, windup toys, makeup, and walls covered with paintings featuring the all-seeing eyes of Flawless—everything

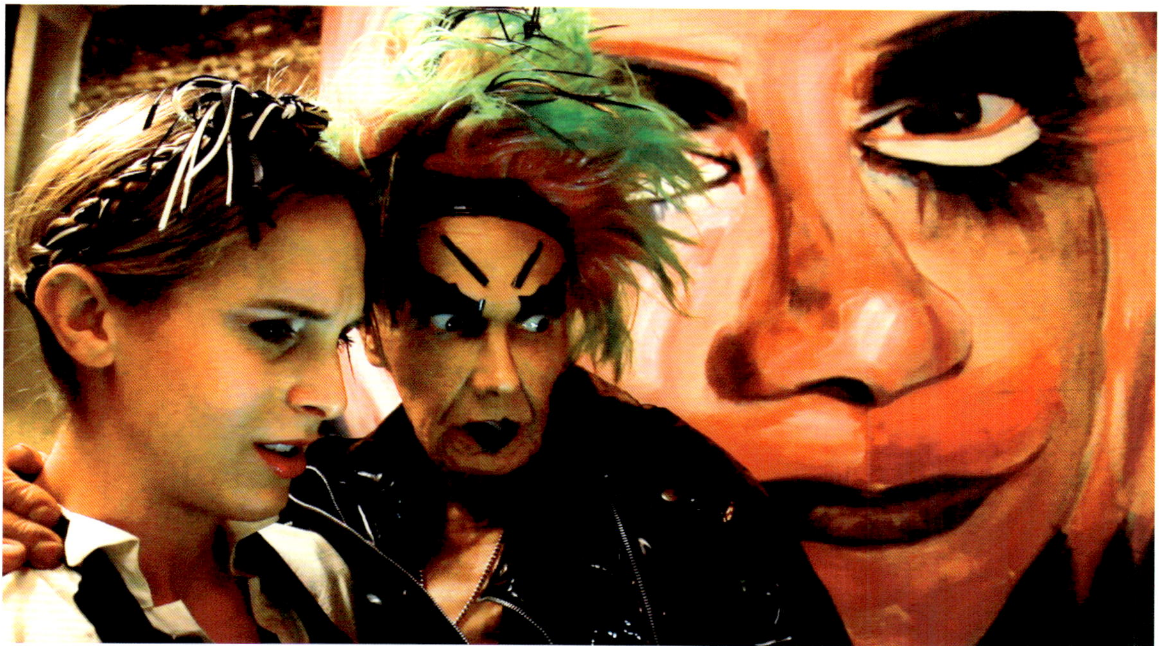

Still from *She Gone Rogue*, 2012

comes undone. Here, the refrain "She gone rogue" repeats, increasing in volume, until the sudden arrival at the door of the other Darling, and the confrontation described at the start of this essay: the adumbrated, psychological culmination of the film.

Close scrutiny of a still of this moment in *She Gone Rogue* reveals that Darling is gazing not, in fact, at her double through an open door but at herself, seen in a mirror. Thus Drucker and Ernst establish an opposition with the "other" at the door and at the same time with the "self" in the mirror. In this instant, they seem to fuse the mirror stage theorized by Jacques Lacan—when the infant first recognizes itself in a mirror and imagines itself as an autonomous "Ideal-I"—with the "I" that is perceived later in life, imbricated in what Lacan terms "socially elaborated situations." Lacan describes this dichotomy as one that "decisively tips the whole of human knowledge into mediatization through the desire of the other, constitutes its objects in an abstract equivalence by the co-operation of others, and turns the I into that apparatus for which every instinctual thrust constitutes a danger."[9]

While *She Gone Rogue* might relate to such Lacanian concepts, its content also invokes the conundrum explored by Ovid in the story of the nymph Echo's love for the vain Narcissus. Smitten with his own reflection in a pool of water, Narcissus rejects Echo, saying: "May I die before what's mine is yours." She responds with pathos: "What's mine is yours."[10] Drucker and Ernst's film traps and sequesters an elusive moment of psychic conflict, implying that in transitional states, and in negotiations with another, an individual wants, and must try, to "go rogue," daring to deviate from the chokehold of norms and standards long enough—an instant is enough—to risk discovery of an undifferentiated self/other.

The title of this essay derives from a sentence spoken by Flawless Sabrina, in Zackary Drucker's 2011 film *At Least You Know You Exist*. Flawless, how true it is that "kicking holes in the darkness is a very good hobby."

1. Rhys Ernst, Skype conversation with the author, September 29, 2013.
2. Judith Butler, *Gender Trouble: Feminism and the Subversion of Identity* (London: Routledge, 1990), viii.
3. Ibid., 148–49 (emphasis in the original).
4. Ibid., 149.
5. Ibid.
6. Drucker, Skype conversation with the author, September 29, 2013.
7. Drucker, email to the author, October 7, 2013.
8. James Morrison, introduction to *The Cinema of Todd Haynes*, ed. Morrison (London: WallFlower Press, 2007), 1–2.
9. Jacques Lacan, "The Mirror Stage" (1949), in Lacan, *Écrits: A Selection*, trans. Alan Sheridan (New York: Norton, 1977), 5.
10. Ovid, *Metamorphoses*, trans. A. D. Melville (New York: Oxford University Press, 1998), 61–66.

Radamés "Juni" Figueroa

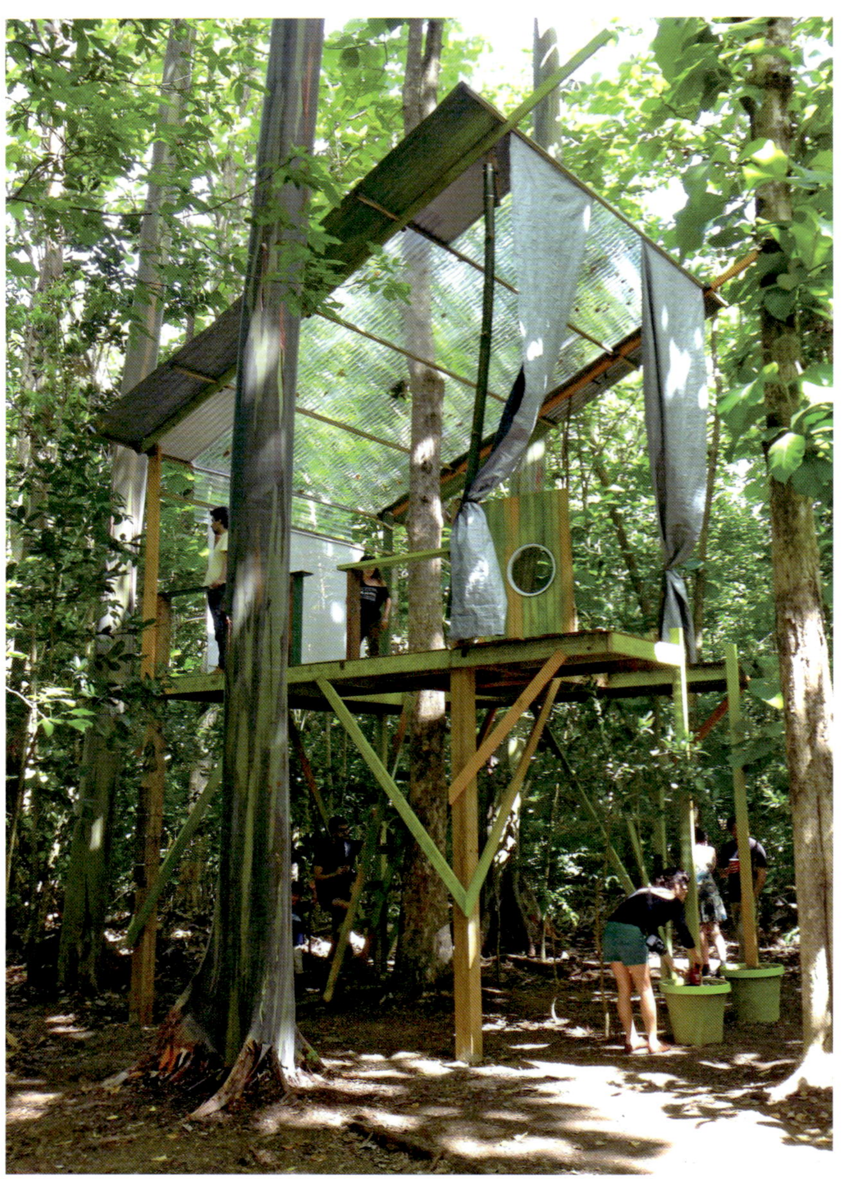

All images: *Tree House–Casa Club*, 2013 (installation view, Naguabo, Puerto Rico). Wood, plastic tarp, bamboo, zinc iron, corrugated plastic, glass windows, and paint, 299 3/16 × 192 15/16 × 192 15/16 in. (760 × 490 × 490 cm)

Born 1982 in Bayamón, PR

Lives in San Juan, PR

Sin Salsa No Hay Paraíso (Without Salsa There's No Paradise): A Conversation with Radamés "Juni" Figueroa

Pablo León de la Barra

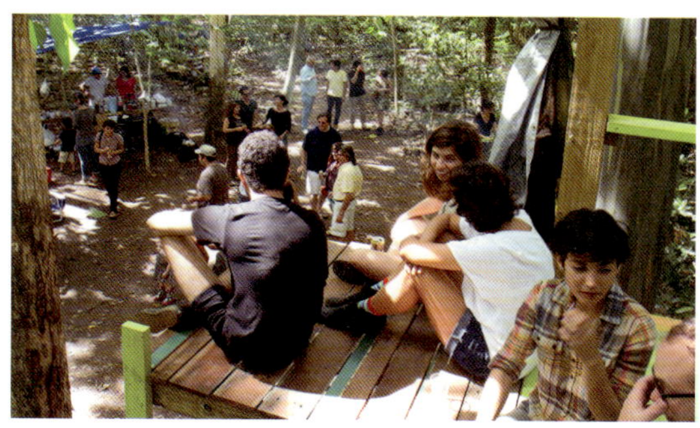

Pablo León de la Barra: Over the past five years, you have worked on a series of public artworks—from your tropical bus stops (2008–9) to animal print–painted rooftops in La Perla, Puerto Rico (2009). Can you explain this transition from painting to public space?

Radamés "Juni" Figueroa: Painting is a medium without limits, but I try not to become a slave to any medium. Public spaces open a wide range of inspiring possibilities. I love transforming my experiences and projecting my lifestyle into my artwork, creating environments and designing experiences within the context of art.

PLB: You have been exploring the concept of the "tropical readymade." Can you describe how this idea has developed over the years?

RJF: The tropical readymades are the result of living on a wonderful island that is also somewhat wild. I grew up between the mountains and the city, and with so many interesting things in my surroundings, I don't have to go far to find inspiration and a connection between art and nature. I started to grow plants in my sneakers and inside footballs, and so developed the tropical readymade.

PLB: There's a long tradition of using plants within exhibition spaces; Brazilian artist Hélio Oiticica and Marcel Broodthaers included plants in their installations, and museums have used plants as decoration. Can you tell me more about your interest in incorporating plants and vegetation-based environments into your art and in bringing art to vegetation?

RJF: In Puerto Rico we live between the beach and the forest, surrounded by dense vegetation. Those influences are always present when I'm producing work: the sensations produced by the climate, the flora and fauna. Addressing such sensations enables me to speak of where I come from without addressing the political in a literal way. Like Oiticica, I like creating environments in which bodies interact with the work. I speak of my experiences through the work, and what I know best is life next to the sea, the heat, the music, and a relaxed aesthetic. I adored participating in the 2011 Gran Bienal Tropical, which took place in the jungle, because the artworks and the vegetation were in direct dialogue.

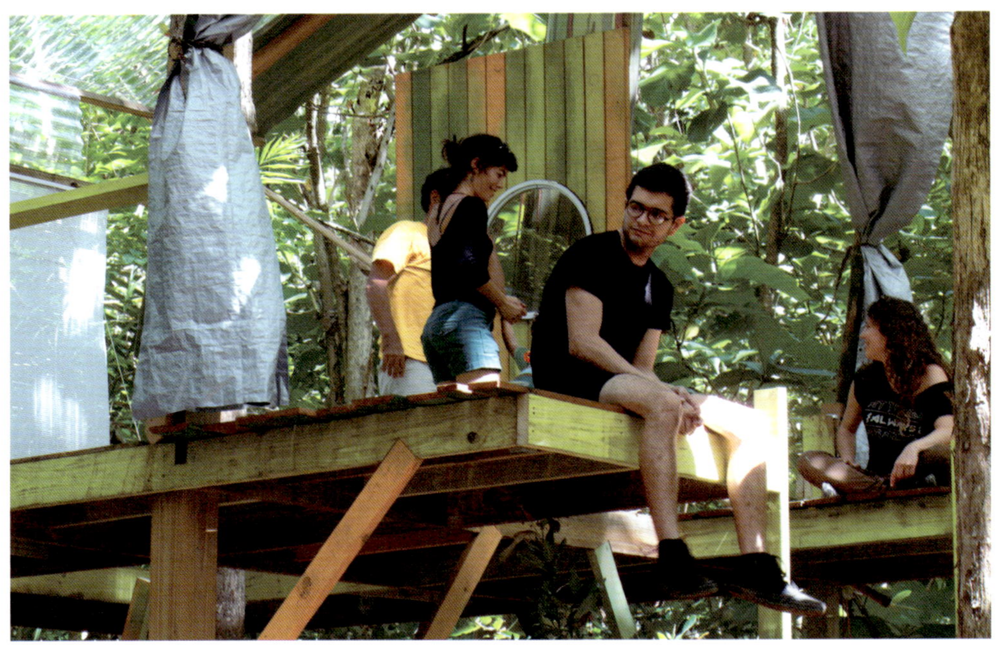

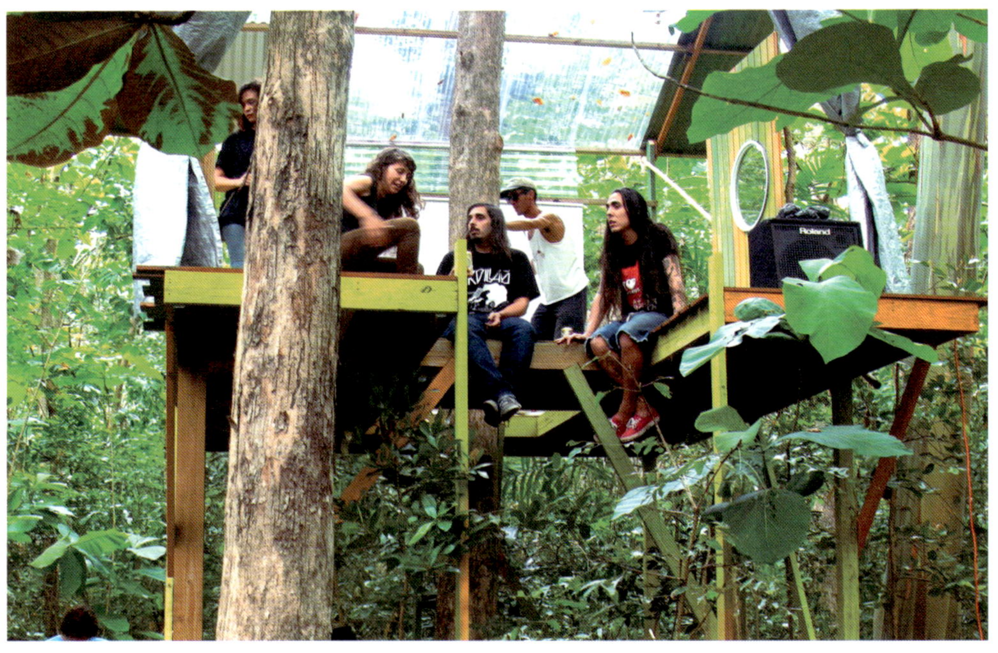
Roland

PLB: Your *Never Ending Tropical Fountains* (2010–) are columns of tropical fruits overflowing with liquor and fruit juices that promise a never-ending happiness but also the inevitable hangover. They evoke the concept developed in the late 1960s by Oiticica of *crelazer* (creleisure), a uniquely tropical possibility of creating through leisure. Can you talk about the relationship in your work between the idea of paradise and the sometimes not so easy reality of life in the tropics?

RJF: Living in the tropics is not easy, but neither is living a city. I prefer to focus on the positive aspects of life—enjoying peaceful nights at the beach sharing ideas, food, and drinks with good friends. I believe in Oiticica's idea of *crelazer*, that leisure and creativity are tied together. A lot of my ideas come from being on the street, at the beach, or at a bar; in my studio I connect these experiences with reading, research, and picture references to develop my projects.

PLB: Your father and your grandfather ran bars in Puerto Rico. Music, especially salsa but also punk rock, is important in your work. Can you tell us about this relationship?

RJF: I pretty much grew up in a bar owned by my grandparents. My father also had a bar. Both had jukeboxes playing salsa records all day. I would sing the songs to customers for money. Salsa music from the 1970s and 1980s was the real deal—hard life, drugs, and broken hearts! The *salseros*, like the punks, spoke of their lives. They lived every moment to the maximum, without apologies. That is the relationship between punks and the great salsa musicians: they knew no limits and produced great work under hard circumstances; they were faithful to their lifestyle. From them, I've learned how to create from whatever we have at hand.

PLB: For Beta-Local's independent-study program in San Juan, you built a giant functional sculpture—a tree house made of reclaimed construction materials from a eucalyptus forest. Can you tell me more about that project and how you activated the tree house with different activities?

RJF: I created the *Tree House—Casa Club* (2013) as part of my residency at La Práctica at Beta-Local. I collected materials throughout San Juan for nine months; once I had enough, I transported them to the middle of the Naguabo forest, where I stayed for two weeks, building the structure with friends. We used materials readily available in the forest, such as stones and water from a nearby river for the cement mix. I wanted *Tree House* to function as an experimental platform for all kinds of activities, to invite people to immerse themselves in the forest, to walk its paths and to rest from the noise of the city.

PLB: On December 11, 2009, you posted on Facebook, "Let's dream of houses on trees, coconut fountains and gardens with sound speakers. Let's do a party for tropical dreamers, a party where there's *limbers* (Puerto Rican icey) of *pitorro* (. . . moonshine rum aged with fruit . . .), *parcha* (passion fruit) and tamarind." This was something of a premonition, since you have been making coconut fountains, tropical gardens, and tree houses. What would you like to do next? What other dreams do you have?

RJF: At the time, I had those desires to create situations that celebrated life, and slowly many of these desires have become a reality. Now I am most interested in maintaining a good working rhythm and enjoying what I produce. I have always wanted to have a business of my own, whether it is a bar or a bookstore with a coffee shop. I would also like to produce music, among other things . . .

Translated by Karenin Biaggi Velázquez and Pablo León de la Barra.

Morgan Fisher

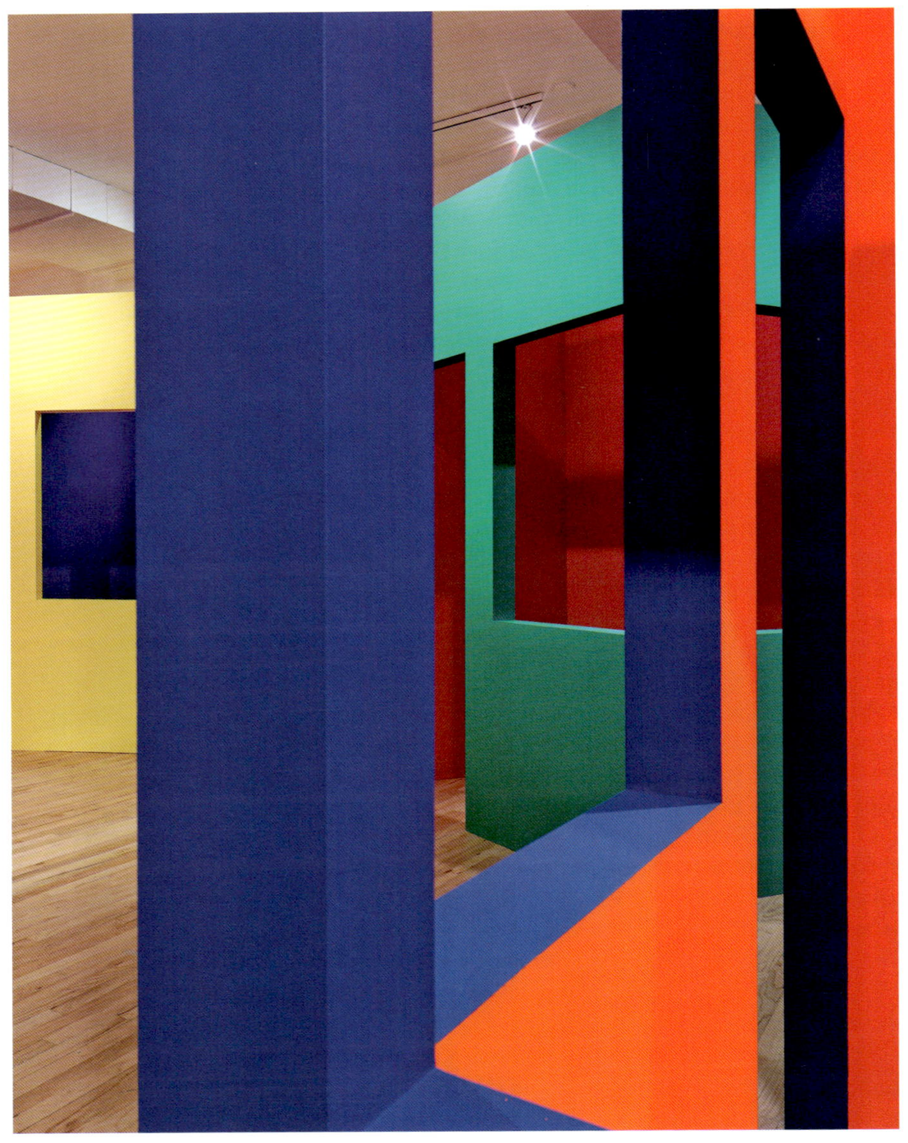

Six Variations on the Security Room (partial view), 2012. Acrylic on drywall, six rooms; 120 × 86 ½ × 58 ½ in. (304.8 × 219.7 × 148.6 cm) each; overall diameter of the work, approx. 374 in. (950 cm)

Born 1942 in Washington, DC

Lives in Santa Monica, CA

Morgan Fisher

Ro(Ro(Room)om)om

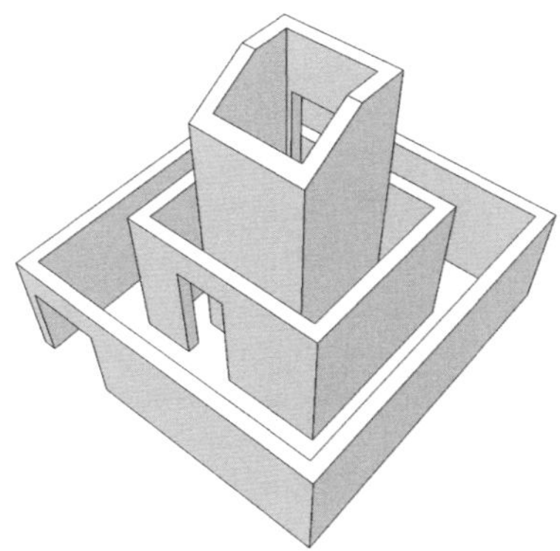

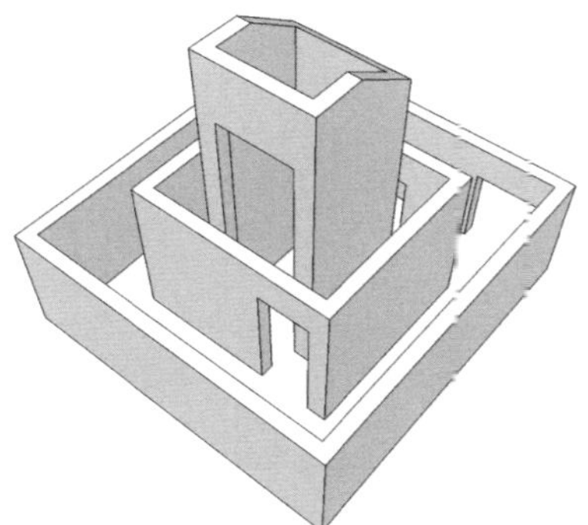

Proposal drawings for *Ro(Ro(Room)om)om*, 2014.
Unfinished drywall, 105 × 114 ¼ × 124 1/16 in.
(266.7 × 290.2 × 315.1 cm)

Ro(Ro(Room)om)om extends my interest in making work that in one way or another is determined by architecture. The reason for this or that aspect of the work comes not from me but from facts, actual or prospective, of architecture in relation to which the work is shown. Relying on architecture to make work is a way to avoid composition, which, because the artist invents it, is ultimately arbitrary. The alternative to work the artist makes up is work determined by sources outside of the artist, which accordingly the artist can cite.

My work has been against composition from the beginning, when I was making films. Architecture was able to play a part when I started making paintings and, more recently, sculpture. In several instances, architecture determined the size of a painting, its shape, and where it could be hung. Of course I made the decision that the architecture would do this, but at least this move, as I will call it, expressed my wish that the work come from sources outside of me. I didn't make it up; its origins were already there in the world, available to make decisions for me. The work deriving from architecture moved from painting strictly speaking toward the sculptural in 2011, when I made *Sixteen Walls*, a work that exactly reproduced at full scale a wall with multiple faces, the original of which was elsewhere in the city where the exhibition was held.

The direct antecedent of *Ro(Ro(Room)om)om* is *Six Variations on the Security Room*, made for a show at the Aspen Art Museum in 2012. The museum was building a new building, and it occurred to me that I could make full-scale mock-ups that reproduced certain details in the new building—for example, a group of walls—and then make paintings for them. I could show new paintings in the new building before it existed. I spent a long time looking at the plans but could not find suitable walls because, apart from having to choose the walls (an act of composition), I could not find walls that would make the paintings in a way that walls elsewhere hadn't already done.

I considered simply reproducing parts of the architecture as it would exist in the new building, but I would have to choose the parts and decide how to place them in relation to one another, both compositional decisions. The solution that finally came to me was to choose one room and multiply it, in effect turning the room into a module. Work based on a module is—as we know from the great Minimalist work of the 1960s—inherently against composition. One room multiplied how many times? I had previously done work based on the color wheel, which has six colors, so the answer was six identical rooms, all to be painted according to the color wheel. Which room? It had to be small enough that its six repetitions would fit in the exhibition space while still leaving room between them for circulation. The answer was the security room, a small room near the loading dock barely big enough for its occupant, who directly surveys comings and goings and also watches the monitors from security cameras in the galleries.

When Stuart Comer invited me to take part in the Biennial, he pointed out that the relation between the Whitney Museum of American Art and its new building under construction paralleled the relation between the Aspen Art Museum and its new building under construction when I had my show. I took the hint, but I didn't want to do again what I had done before. So, no array of modules, no complementary colors. I was getting worried when I realized that, unlike the earlier work, in which all the elements were at full size (that is, all at the same scale), there could be rooms at different scales. (Rooms at full scale would present problems. To keep the size of the work within reasonable limits, the rooms would have to be small and so of a similar kind, closets or closet-like, such as electrical rooms and other spaces for utilities. And rooms at full scale would have made the work too close to Bruce Nauman's works with rooms and passageways and to the labyrinths of Robert Morris, all explicitly scaled to the human body.)

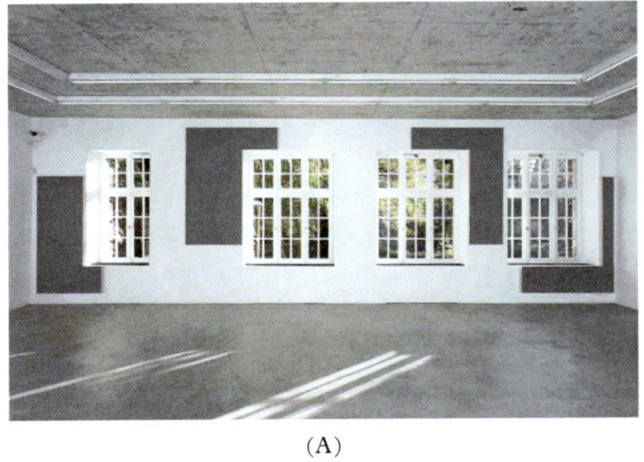

(A)

There were four questions: how many rooms, what scales, how to relate the rooms to one another, and which rooms? The answer to the first was the easiest: three, because that's the smallest quantity that makes a group.

The scales were easy too. I couldn't make them up. The answer was obvious scales in obvious relations: one room at actual scale, one room at half scale, one room at quarter scale. This halving and halving again is a simple geometric progression, a means known since antiquity for creating systematic differences between quantities, and that by definition is not a compositional procedure. And this set of relations progressively shrank the rooms, making it possible to include larger rooms with a wider range of functions that would better represent the new building.

How to organize the rooms? It couldn't be a matter of putting this room here and that room there to make a pleasing arrangement; that's composition. The rooms' being at different scales led to the idea, embodied in the title, of their nesting one within another, easily achieved if the rooms are all the same shape, as most rooms are, and roughly the same proportions. I would claim that nesting suggests itself, that it is self-organizing and, in any case, not compositional. Nested rectangular rooms would loosely resemble a concentric figure, the device that Frank Stella used in some of his early paintings. As Rosalind Krauss tells us in *The Optical Unconscious*, modernist painting allows the concentric figure, because, like the few other devices she names, it precludes the relation between figure and ground and so precludes the occasion for composition. The rooms' nesting one within another further enacts the condensing of space that is already present in the progressive shrinking of the rooms. What's more, on the principle of metonymy, in which a part of something stands for the whole, the concentric arrangement causes the building to contain itself, not once but twice, in effect concentrating and so intensifying its representation.

The remaining question was which rooms. I had to think first about size, but, to the extent that size allowed, rooms with a range of functions would best represent the museum, synopsize it. For the size of the work to be kept within reasonable limits, the room at actual size had to be the smallest in the building and the innermost in the work. That room is a closet in the curatorial offices on the seventh floor, a space so small that, as many closets are, it is not entered.

A room at the other end of this range is one that is big and open to the public: an exhibition space. But all the exhibition spaces in the new building are enormous, and their proportions would not suit. The exception is the gallery on the first floor, the smallest in the museum and, also exceptionally, open free of charge. Its proportions are similar enough to those of the closet, and at one-quarter scale it would not take up an inordinate amount of space. This room is the outer room in the work.

I needed to find a room with roughly the same proportions as these two that at half scale would fit between them. In the new building there are many rooms of many sizes and many proportions, but I found only two that would fit. Of the two candidates, the copier room on the third floor divides the space between the inner and outer rooms more evenly. And it goes without saying that the rooms in the work have the same orientation with respect to each other that they do in the building.

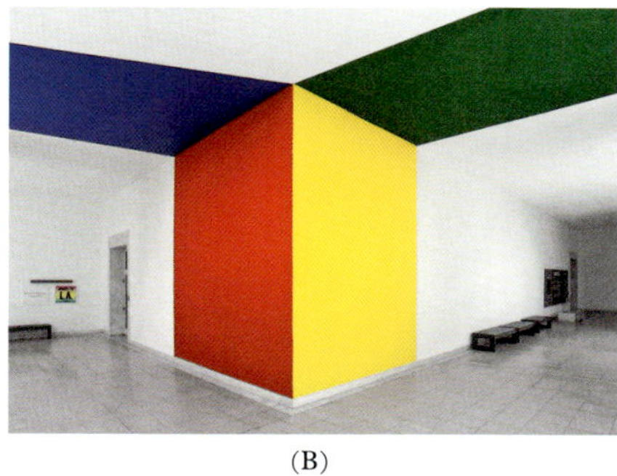

(B)

The adjustments for scale are not just in the horizontal but also in the vertical. The scaling leads us to expect that the middle room will be half the height of the inner room and the outer room half the height of the middle room. This would be so if all the actual rooms were the same height, but they are not. The different heights of the rooms in the work, adjusted for scale, are exactly those in the new building.

The different scales produce gradients of several kinds. A gradient implies change, something radically different from the equal emphasis produced by works based on the module and having instead the form of composition: minor and major centers of interest in a painting, rising intensity in music, and rising action in theater and film.

The outer room, the gallery, is used the most, and mostly by the public, and is on the first floor. The middle room, the copier room, is the next most used, but only by staff, and is on the third floor. The inner room, the closet, is used by the fewest of all, and is on the seventh floor. So these gradients rise together in elevation and to fewer and more exclusive users. Consonant with the rising gradient, the scales move from smaller to larger, and the rooms become taller, suggesting a ziggurat, a form of pyramid.

A pyramid culminates in its apex, its highest point that as such suggests the highest in the abstract. And an apex expresses in architectural form the equivalent of the climax, the moment of peak action in temporal works—music, theater, and film—that are organized by principles of composition, as almost all are, toward which the work moves and in which it culminates.

Despite seeming to be forms of composition, the gradients in *Ro(Ro(Room)om)om* expressing ascent are the result of chance (in the locations and functions of the rooms) and a mathematical operation, both inherently against composition. To remind us that this is so, the room that the work culminates in is a tiny closet that even though it is in the curatorial offices is still a humble and utilitarian space, occupied by no one, and so an anticlimax.

Further, a gradient that moves in the opposite direction is the relative size of the viewer, who in relation to the sequence of rooms shrinks. Relative to the scale of the outer room, the viewer is four times life-size, relative to the middle room twice life-size, and relative to the inner room life-size. The viewer is biggest relative to the one space that is open to the public, the space closest to the viewer and furthest from the exclusivity and privilege that, however comically, the closet represents. But even if in relation to the closet viewers are one-quarter their initial size, they are nonetheless life-size and so ultimately are undiminished.

The foundation of the work is the exact dimensions of rooms in the new building. The work is no more than a diagram of those dimensions, scaled as necessary, and for that purpose unfinished drywall is all that is necessary.

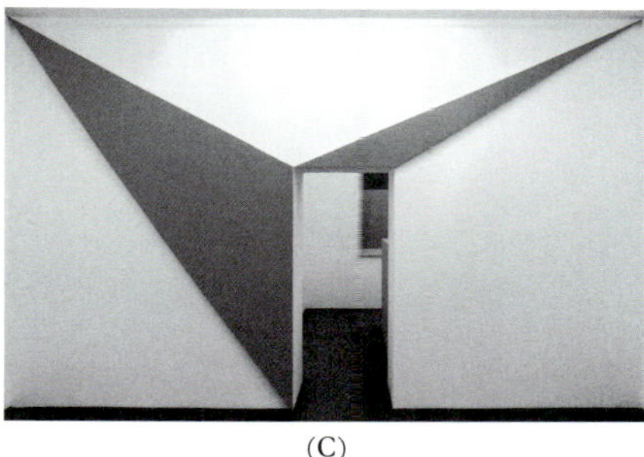

(C)

Ro(Ro(Room)om)om is the result of submitting one already existing source, or model, to another: three rooms in the new building that by chance—by more than chance, by luck—were the right size and shape to arrange themselves in an obvious way, submitted to a simple case of a simple mathematical operation. So *Ro(Ro(Room)om)om* is the result not of invention—of making something up—but of discovery.

A. The window paintings from the *Door and Window Paintings* (six paintings that are one work), 2002. Acrylic spray paint on canvas, mounted on panel; dimensions variable (the tallest painting is 83 ½ in. [212.1 cm] high; the widest painting is 64 ⅜ in. [163.6 cm] wide)

B. *Blue Green Red Yellow* (partial view), 2012. Acrylic on stucco, site-specific; height, 208 ½ in. (529.6 cm); total width on the wall, 309 ½ in. (786.1 cm) (the width of the red plus the width of the yellow); overall dimensions of the work, 208 ½ × 474 ⅛ × 187 ⅛ in. (529.6 × 1,204.3 × 475.9 cm)

C. *Edge and Corner Painting, Edge and Corner Painting* (two paintings from a group of five, each with the same title), 2005. Acrylic spray paint on canvas, mounted on panel; right-hand painting, 31 ⅛ × 78 ½ in. (79.1 × 199.4 cm)

Tony Greene

Curated by Richard Hawkins and Catherine Opie

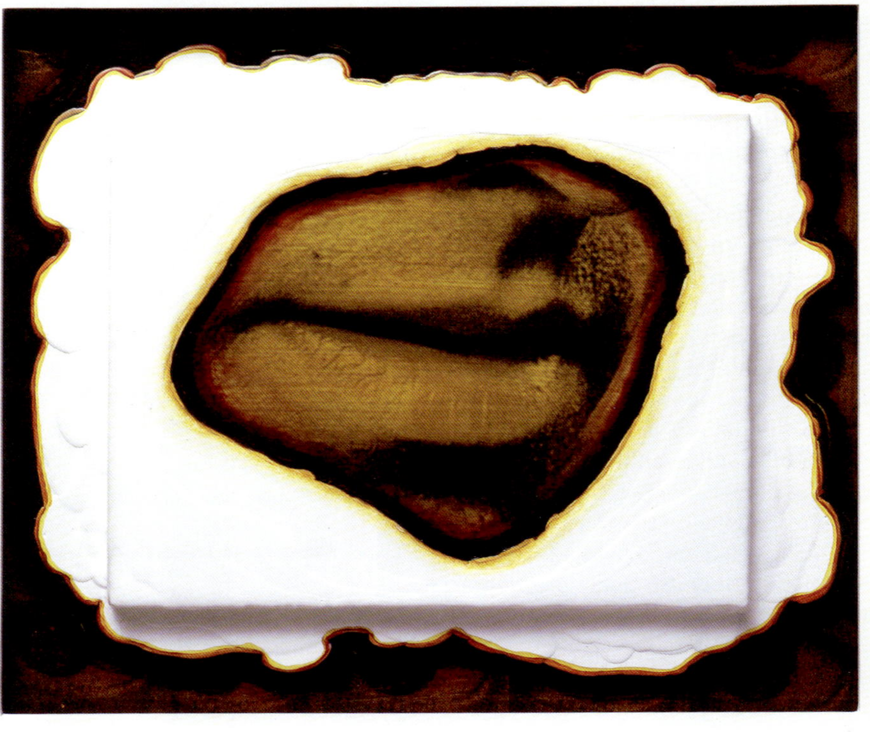

Untitled (yellow pour), 1990. Mixed media, 15 ½ × 16 ¼ in. (39.4 × 41.3 cm). Collection Ray Morales, from the estate of Norm Mac Neil

Born 1955 in San Francisco, CA

Died 1990 in Los Angeles, CA

Tony Greene

Letter to a Young Friend
Richard Hawkins

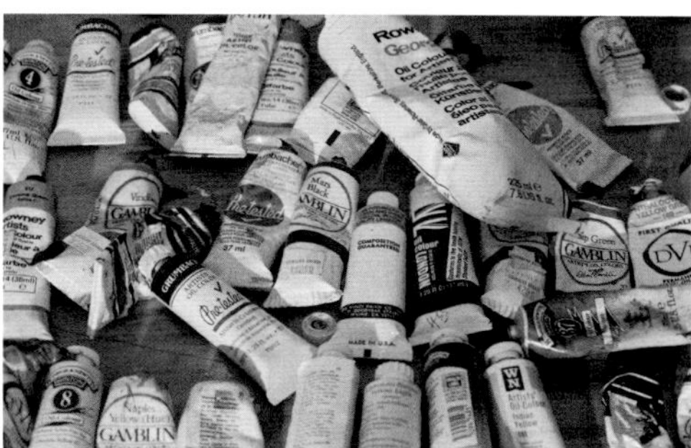

Catherine Opie (b. 1961), *Untitled #2 (Tony's Studio)*, 1990. Pigmented inkjet print, 12 × 12 in. (30.5 × 30.5 cm)

Since you've been kind enough to ask, my dear, here are my thoughts on why, despite the fact that you didn't live through the period in which they were made, you seem to like Tony Greene's paintings so much. I'm sorry if I sound so irritated in some parts, but, well, you know me by now.

On the Influence of the California Institute of the Arts: The works shown in the Whitney mostly date from only a year after Tony graduated from CalArts. Tony was incredibly influenced by his education there and thrived on the level of engagement and criticality for which the school is known. And, though I might like to find some against-all-odds dauntlessness in Tony for making paintings in the face of our school's very anti-painting discourse, it's not entirely true—no one at CalArts ever really insisted that students not make paintings. The "antiaesthetic" was the tone of the times, not just in Valencia but everywhere in the art world, and though no one on the faculty pooh-poohed painting in particular, students did seem to get some kind of message from the energetic responses to things that were *not* paintings, things seemingly less burdened by commerce, class privilege, and histories of all-male mastery and groundless transcendence. It was an unsaid directive that could somehow be expressed like this: were one to decide to make a painting at CalArts during that time, one might want to have an awfully good reason for doing so.

But, then again, Tony's paintings are not paintings in the strictest or purest sense of the term anyway. They're embellished and oil-glazed appropriated photographs, often with some kind of text on them—so I can certainly advise you (if you didn't already know) that appropriated photo plus text was a very, very, VERY 1980s CalArts thing to do.

Are the paintings underrated? Not at all, at least not at the time. Tony had a career the rest of us admired in the two short years from 1988 to 1990. On his CV, I count nineteen shows, in New York, Los Angeles, San Francisco, and even Atlanta and Sheboygan. At least four of those were solo presentations. Certainly the AIDS tragedies bound and corralled us but, at least in Los Angeles, our crowd also included New Narrative fiction writers and the pierced-and-tattooed scene surrounding Club Fuck. Somehow, queer theory was birthing itself and every little nonprofit space, and even a lot of commercial galleries were doing things around identity, desire, and sexuality. It was the rise of the Queers with a capital *Q*, and Tony's work was near the front. (Queer Nation, by the way, didn't officially start until 1990.)

Don't ask me why Tony's paintings have been in storage since 1993—if that's what you meant. I'm sure I don't know.

Dioramas: The taxidermied animals in Tony's paintings, especially big-racked bucks staring back, stately and regal . . . or handsome little fawns darting away into the underbrush, were the rare subjects for which Tony used his own photos rather than appropriated ones. I believe they were all taken at the Kimball Natural History Museum in San Francisco, and if you were to interpret the noble glare in a buck's expression as cruisey, I'm pretty sure you wouldn't be wrong: the museum is

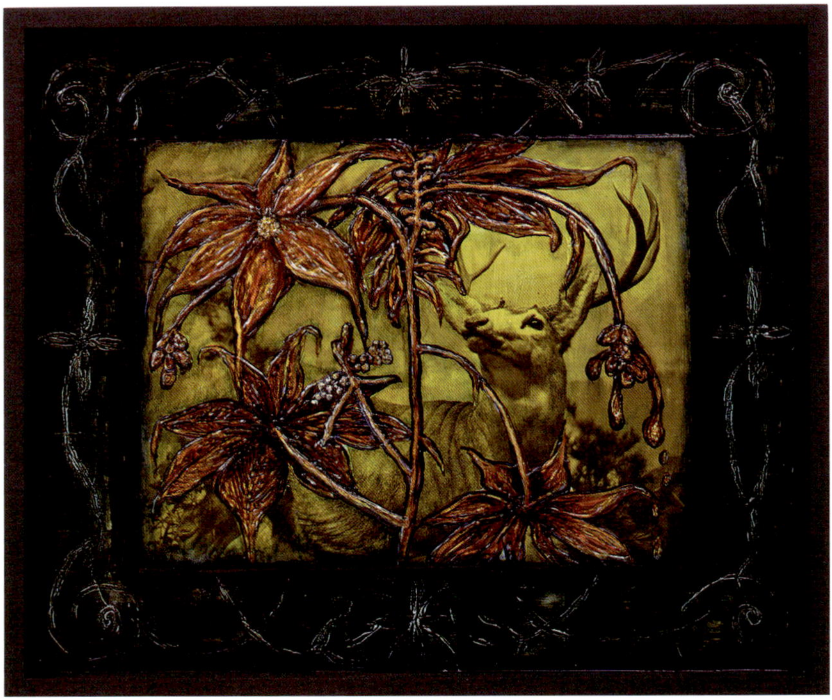

His Puerile Gestures, 1989. Mixed media, 25 ½ × 29 ¾ in. (64.8 × 75.6 cm). Collection Ray Morales, from the estate of Norm Mac Neil

right in the middle of the zenith of all gay cruising spots, Golden Gate Park. And if you were to say that there's some really romantic notion about a very noble and august portrayal of an endangered species in those paintings, I'd laugh and tell you that you'd have to ask Tony. (Hint: Yep.)

Why vintage photos? The history of pen-pal ads in the back of muscle mags, Bob Mizer's "subjective character analysis" codes, and that strange not-out-but-incredibly-cultured-queen world of *After Dark* magazine had yet to be anything worth theorizing when Tony started using physique-period images. But you could gather as much from little articles in contemporary issues of *Honcho* or *Mandate* or, once you discovered The Magazine in San Francisco or Physique Memorabilia in New York, you could delve into those rich little pre-*Advocate* pink-sheet histories yourself. This relatively untheorized story of how our fore-fuck-buddies had fantasized and actualized and kept their foolings-around hidden from the cops and the public eye became very important to Tony.

But I think he was also interested in how the leather community was initially birthed not by a single organized group or specific gathering place but, rather, by Tom of Finland drawings and AMG biker-boy photos proliferating and being distributed hand-to-hand and through the mail. You found them, got turned on by them, dressed up like them yourself, and then went out and made yourself a hot, sticky leather world where one had never existed before—all through the power of these images of totally made-up men.

I think, looking back, there's a dynamic in there that was important to Tony: it just takes one artist to sit down, ignore what the cultural mandates of the time are, and just focus on his own desires and fantasies. Eventually brand-new and much sexier worlds are built.

Are the paintings decadent or are they modernist? I don't know that the paintings are either, but if they are then it's probably some miraculous synergy between very old-school interior-designy kinds of things . . . but from a sex-club point of view. I know the 1970s San Francisco bathhouse scene was a crucial reference that Tony wanted in the work. It just somehow eventually got combined with this dreamworld of his: of officer's lounges and gentlemen's clubs, coffered ceilings, cracked-leather cabin chairs, ruddy old portraits stained with decades of cigar smoke, brandy dripping from the mustache tips of a distinguished old salt-'n'-pepper admiral Daddy (on whose lap you're hopefully sitting)... Somewhere between all those allusions lies the ultimate context Tony imagined for his paintings.

Tony's literary influences certainly figure into what you might be calling decadent. If there's a connecting thread, it's his interest in Melville, Huysmans, Proust, Gide, Genet, Denton Welch, and John Rechy, as well as contemporary writers like Robert Gluck, Gary Indiana, and Dennis Cooper—all male narrators with focused and oftentimes fetishizing descriptions of the male body. That, or at least some preference among a few of the above, for setting things in dark entangling interiors was certainly at play, but otherwise it's the canon that you'd read if you wanted to turn yourself into a contemporary gay dandy. I'm quite sure Tony would've identified with that. Two contemporary flashpoints in visual art are important here, though. Ross Bleckner's death-toll paintings (*8,122+ as of January 1986* [1985–86] and *16,301+ as of January 1987* [1987]) were highly influential to Tony in almost every way: the memorializing urn motifs, the arcane lettering, the varnish-like glazing, the buttery impasto . . . everything, especially the overall tenebristic doomfulness.

But if you remember that the Whitney retrospective of Robert Mapplethorpe opened in July 1988, you can look into the progression of Tony's work and see that it changed almost immediately. I don't think Mapplethorpe's 1970s collages were so well-known before then, but their unapologetic outness, their use of vintage porn, and especially their frame-within-a-frame format had a direct effect on Tony's practice.

Again, I don't know if that's decadence or modernism. Maybe you just mean *dark*. But what kind of paintings come from listening to glam-era Bowie and Eno, Dark Wave, Coil, and the Smiths? (I specifically remember Tony humming "This Charming Man," by the way.) Some of us have just always been gleefully more wrapped up in the darker, more lyrical side of things—AIDS or no AIDS. (And, having revealed that, if you happen to see a similarity between Tony's torso paintings and the first Smiths album cover . . . it's not for no reason.)

Activism and the Arts: Having been only an infant in 1990, you, of course, wouldn't know what these times were like except through history books. And were you to read those and come up with the idea that most of the works being made that addressed or commented on the crisis were either bold publicly engaged slogans—direct, with a sense of raging irony—or elegant and generous proto-Relational-Aesthetics, redirected readymades, then you wouldn't be totally wrong. The atmosphere of the times, at least in the art world, when it took the time to address the AIDS crisis, was focused (frankly) on a very narrow

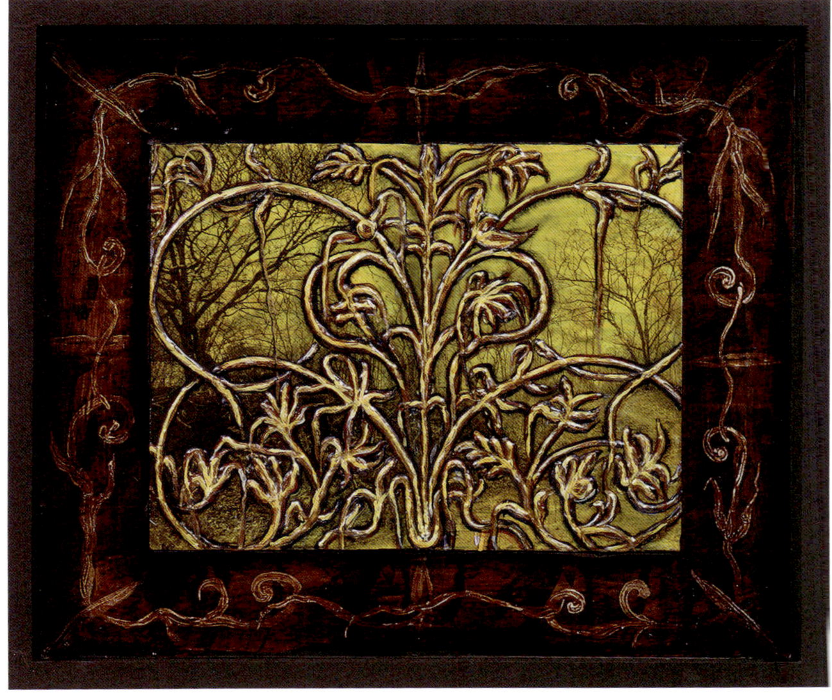

Opinion of Silence, 1989. Mixed media, 18 ½ × 21 ½ in. (47 × 54.6 cm). Collection Ray Morales, from the estate of Norm Mac Neil

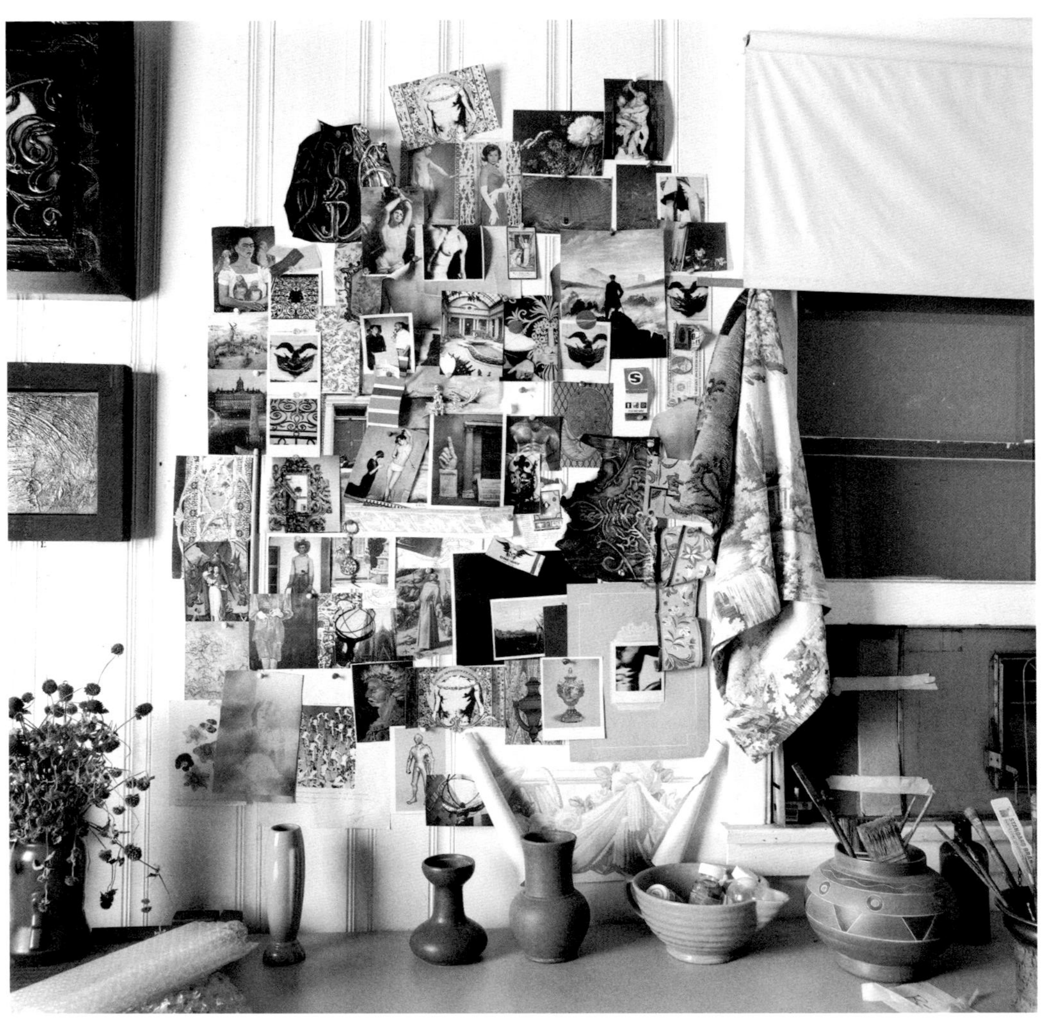

Catherine Opie, *Untitled #1 (Tony's Studio)*, 1990. Pigmented inkjet print, 12 × 12 in. (30.5 × 30.5 cm)

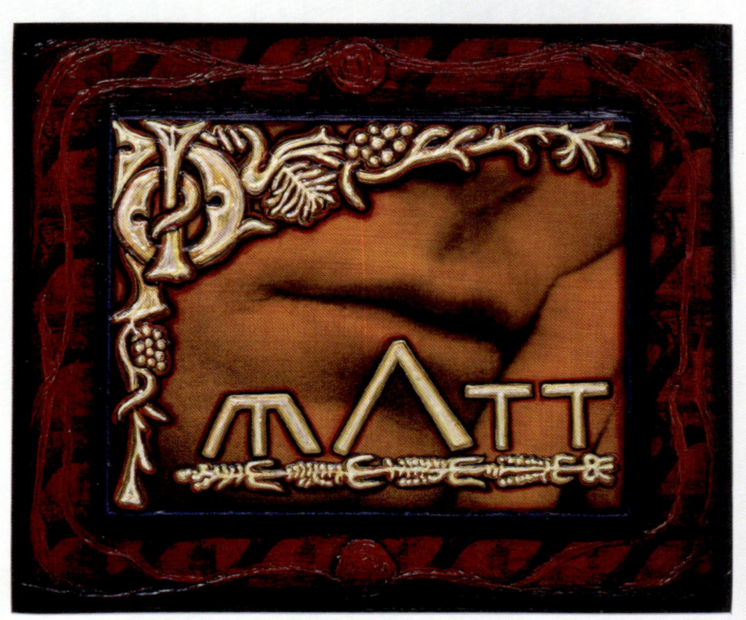

Untitled (Matt), 1990. Mixed media, 19 ½ × 22 ½ in. (49.5 × 57.2 cm).
Collection of Monica Majoli

interpretation of social engagement that hardly ever included anything as open-ended or negotiable as paintings. Anything else, unfortunately—particularly things as bound up as Tony's paintings were with desire and yearning and memorializing—was probably just seen as elitist. Or mealy mouthed. Or cynically detached. Or even homophobic or AIDS-phobic in their perceivably far-too-easy and far-too-romantic equations of gay desire and anything other than stand-up-for-your-rights advocacy.

The recent reappearance of Martin Wong's paintings, certainly, is a step in the right direction. But, still today, if a museum does something on the period or something that incorporates the crisis, you might see General Idea's wallpaper (but that too was problematic, see pages 102 to 104 of *AIDS Demo Graphics*) but you'll rarely see anything other than Gran Fury or Felix Gonzalez-Torres. The bitterest parts of me see this as an insidious exclusion, but it's probably just an oversight in the historical record. I'm sending you a copy of Gary Indiana's *Horse Crazy*. It's an excellent antidote.

Why these paintings now? Well, you tell me. I'm tired of being defensive and irritated by the lack of attention these amazing paintings of Tony's have received over the last twenty years. I'm still caught up in the loss of Tony and the arguments of the period in which they were made, but you're the one who came over, stood in the front of the painting of Tony's that I have in my dining room, and told me you were caught somewhere between slobberingly jerking off and feeling a really, really deep sob coming on. They're paintings that have the remarkable ability to do exactly that. They're seductive and horny, glitzy and sensuous, and full of seriously dark, sexy venom and profoundly honorific mourning. They're love letters to really hot lost guys and to the dim after-hours situations in which you might once have found them—except that they're these lush, glisteningly dark and wondrous paintings.

They transcend and enrich their original context—which is important, obviously—in a way that paintings made during wartime seldom do.

More information can be found at the working archive for Tony Greene's estate: grainofhisskin.tumblr.com. There are a lot of people for Cathy and me to thank: Judie Bamber, Monica Majoli, Millie Wilson, and Doug Ischar for being supportive during my own initial research phase of rearchiving Tony's work; Marcel Alcalá and Jeffrey Ono for acting as research assistants; and Heather Rasmussen for helping us curate and lay out the Biennial presentation.

Thanks also to the Peter Norton Family Foundation for generously housing many of Tony's works over these many years. Special thanks go to Ray Morales, who quietly, diligently, and insightfully watched over and preserved the works from the Norm MacNeil Trust of Tony Greene's estate. It's primarily because of, first, Norm's and, then, Ray's efforts that we're able to present such excellent examples of Tony's paintings today.

Channa Horwitz

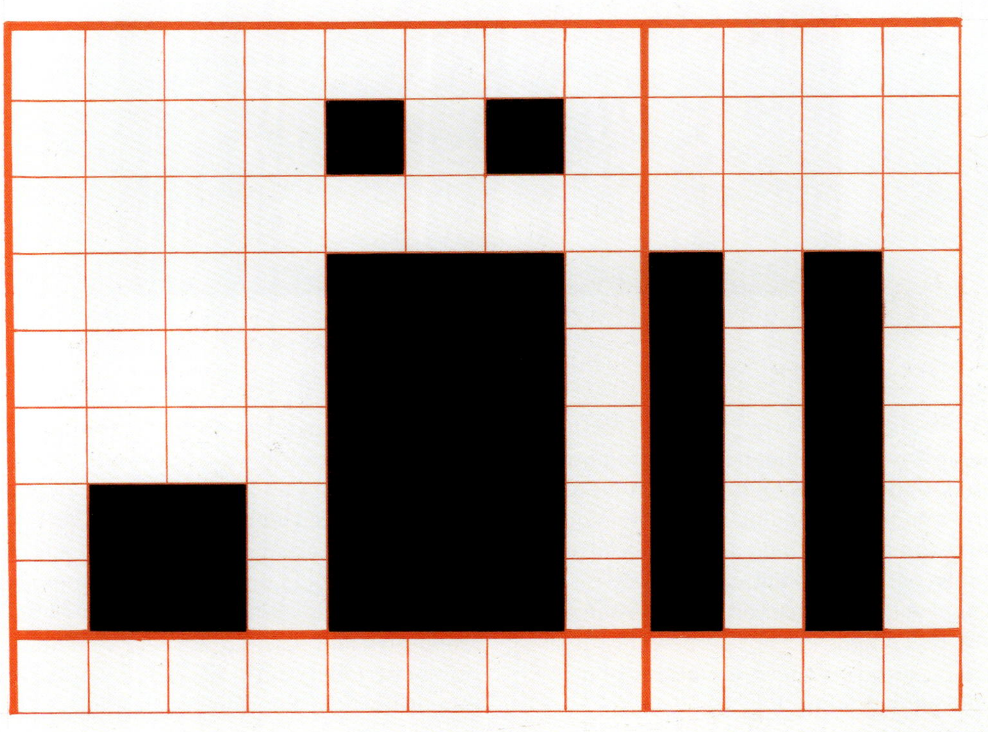

Language Series Three, 1964. Gouache on paper, 14 × 16 in. (35.6 × 40.6 cm)

Born 1932 in
Los Angeles, CA

Died 2013 in
Los Angeles, CA

Channa Horwitz

At the Still Point, There the Dance Is

Catherine Wood

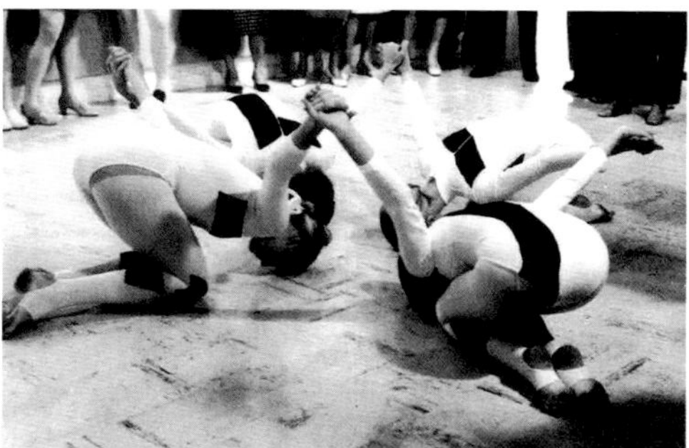

At the Tone the Time will be, 1969. Performance (Orlando Gallery, Encino, CA)

The late Channa Horwitz's 1964 series of drawings titled Window Shades depicts architectural interiors inhabited, in the artist's imagination, by a fictitious couple named Mr. and Mrs. McGillicutty. In these rooms—all similarly rendered with fabric swatches and stencils, showing a window and a shade—Horwitz seems to have been particularly fascinated by the changing position of the window blind, and how its lowering and raising alters the image. Critic Chris Kraus, who has written at length about Horwitz, observes that the "cute conceit" of this series would soon be superseded by the rigor and pure geometries of the artist's subsequent work.[1] But these fabricated scenes, with their partially obscured intimacy, also seem to anticipate the curious magnetism of the abstract grid drawings that would be the focus of much of Horwitz's career.

In the same year during which she created the Window Shades, Horwitz embarked on her Language series (1964–2005), using grids and graphs to explore patterns and movement. By the late 1960s, she had developed a system of composition she termed *Sonakinatography* (a term synthesizing *sound*, *motion*, and *notation*): working with graph paper, the artist drew black-and-white and colored squares, circles, and lines in ink to build complex matrices of sequential pattern. The figures 1 through 8 are the foci of the notation principle she created in these drawings, which visualize time, rhythm, and movement as graphic "beats." (The use of the number 8 was originally determined by the ready-made graph paper—with eight squares to the square inch—and by the idea of the eight corners of a cube.)

Horwitz's meticulously crafted, repetitive patterns evoke an image of the artist sequestered in her studio in the Hidden Hills enclave of Los Angeles, working through seconds, minutes, hours, as an intricate daily practice. At one level, the drawings serve as evidence of her labor: they are finely woven tapestries of time spent. On another level, they represent a basis in temporality that is outside of what might be termed the "love hours" of their making.[2] Resembling mathematical diagrams, computer punch cards, or sewing patterns, Horwitz's drawings are modern hieroglyphs that compress the expansive dramas and effects of movement, music, and gesture into silent two-dimensionality. From the flat surface of her picture plane—as from a graphic rendering of a cube—the observer can infer a third and even a fourth dimension.

Activity is folded into the construction of Horwitz's drawings and held there. They demand activity, also, from the viewer, in order to read them, to follow their patterns and progressions. But although Horwitz's conception was that her drawings, in their open simplicity, could somehow contain *everything*, and although she often gave her score drawings to other artists to interpret, it is not necessary to see that movement, sound, or gesture enacted literally. The drawings possess an extraordinary self-sufficiency: they neither vie for attention nor attempt to entertain. They could be maps for new, abstract temporal territories, or diagrams of disturbances radiating among the air's atoms and wavelengths. Yet in mood, these cryptic images persist with the resistant, almost

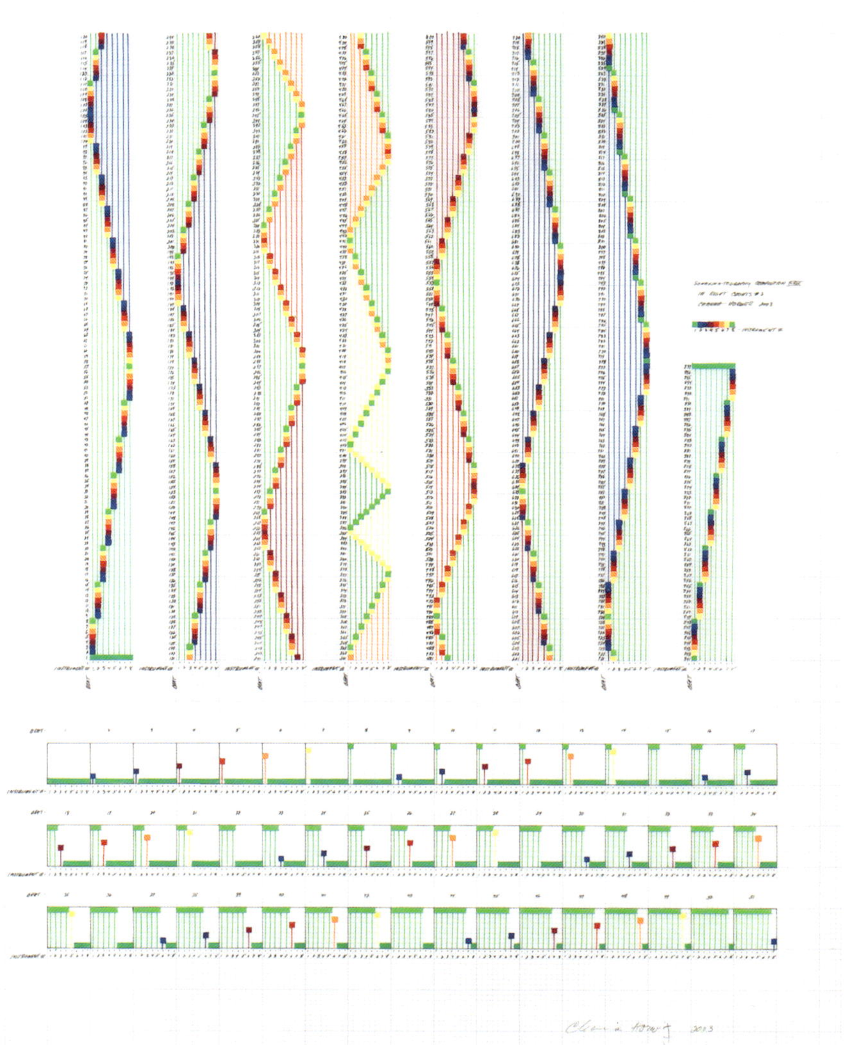

Sonakinatography Composition XVIII in Eight Counts #2, 2003. Casein on Mylar, 34 ½ × 28 in. (87.6 × 71.1 cm)

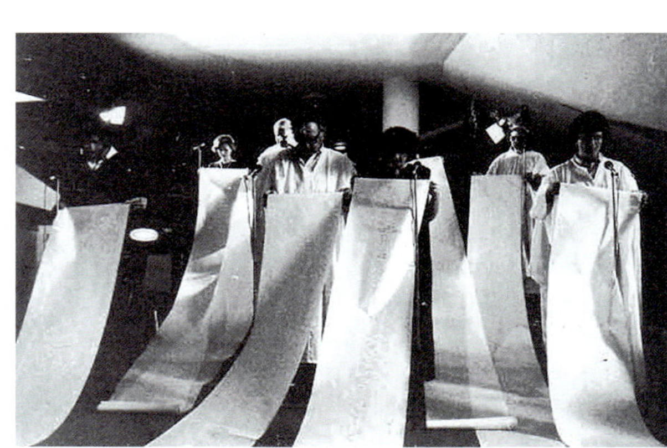

Poem/Opera, The Divided Person (Based on Sonakinatography Composition III), 1978. Performance (Bologna, Italy)

deliberately exclusive quality of strangers' rooms glimpsed from the street at night, rooms lit to expose the mystery of their interiors, but into which—tantalizingly—the viewer can never enter.

Although Horwitz's drawings thus communicate autonomously, the relationship between them and actual performance is significant, too. In some of her early assemblage paintings, Horwitz simply drew attention to the changes in light throughout a day: in the early 1960s, for example, she affixed a small box to the canvas and painted its gray shadow, while also allowing for the play of actual cast shadows on its surface plane. In her 1968 series of kinetic sculptures called Breathers, air is pumped in and out of balloonlike structures that operate like lungs, in sequences designated by the artist. (A "concert" of several Breathers was at one point conceived; Horwitz made small graph-paper drawings that plotted out the compositional breathing patterns and time sequences for the project, which was never performed.)

Initially, these drawings were strictly functional, in that they were clearly kinetic-object related. But as the drawings developed, Horwitz made them increasingly independent of any literal application as scores. In a 1978 performance, presented at the Palazzo della Cultura e dei Congressi in Bologna, dancers wearing black-and-white geometrically patterned costumes moved according to Horwitz's established graphic rules of circles and lines. After a 1978 performance of her *Poem Opera*, a work for eight vocalists (restaged as part of New York's High Line Art Performance program in 2012), Horwitz began to give drawings to performers to use as scores, without prescribing how they were to be interpreted.

Horwitz's drawings were again used as a score for choreographic interpretation in 2012's *Moments: A History of Performance in 10 Acts* at the Zentrum für Kunst und Medientechnologie (ZKM) in Karlsruhe, Germany—an exploration of ten pioneers of performance, curated by Boris Charmatz, Sigrid Gareis, and Georg Schöllhammer. The show included performances in which a rendering of Horwitz's drawn grid was taped onto the floor, a graphic-numeric structure activated by Charmatz and colleagues: standing within the floor grid, they performed sequenced gestures based on the other works featured in the exhibition. In this context, Horwitz's drawing thus served as a juncture where the radical origins of those performance works (which now exist only in the form of static objects, videos, or documentary photography) met with action, in the present tense. Through Horwitz's drawing—and other works on display by Marina Abramović, Anna Halprin, Reinhild Hoffmann, Adrian Piper, Yvonne Rainer, and others—Charmatz and his collaborators transposed the entire contents of a complex historical show into a performed primary code, as though exposing its live DNA.

Horwitz's arena in which to act is a world away from Abstract Expressionism. Her work's *presentness* is not suspended outside of time; rather, past, present, and future are manifested simultaneously as a singular image.

Horwitz's Sonakinatographies and other drawings have a significant place in relation to the work of other artists: they resonate with the compositional strategies of her contemporaries Sol LeWitt and Agnes Martin, and also with the abstracted notation scores of elder choreographers such as Mary Wigman and Rudolf Laban. They also make sense today, as works that represent the notion of the *time-based* as a stasis. In the past decade, the relationships among image, object, and action in art have been increasingly complicated through the pervasiveness of lens-based technologies. Images are often understood as modes of translation or communication, rather than as ends in themselves. Horwitz's works occupy a unique place in this evolving territory, because they reject and at the same time embrace their own potential as conduits. They go beyond the question of performance and its material trace as instruction or documentation. Her works are end points, registers of the passage of time, and potential beginnings, simultaneously. They are, a priori, enough.

The title of this essay derives from T. S. Eliot's poem "Burnt Norton," published in 1936.

1. See Chris Kraus, Channa *Horwitz: Full Circle, 1964–2005* (Los Angeles: Solway-Jones, 2005), 6.
2. See Mike Kelley's 1987 assemblage *More Love Hours Than Can Ever Be Repaid.*

Travis Jeppesen

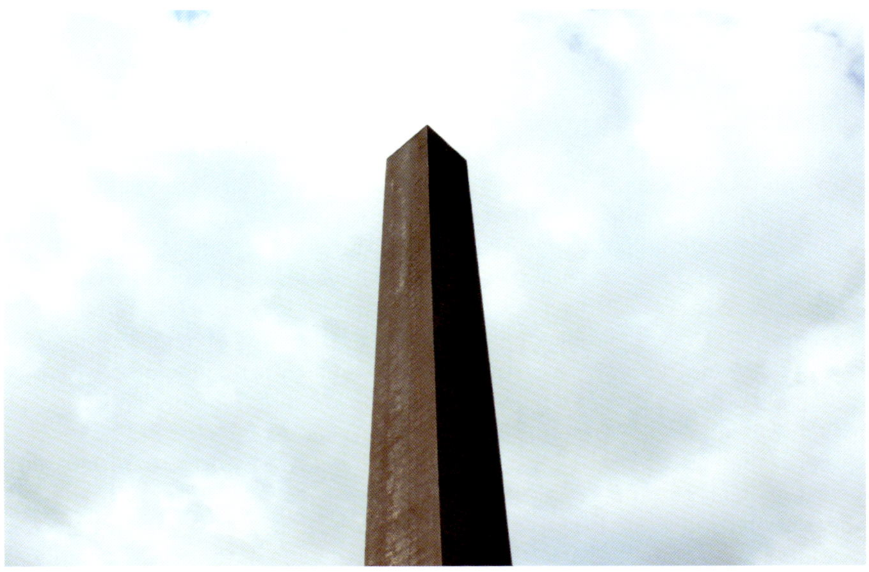

Sky Object, 2013

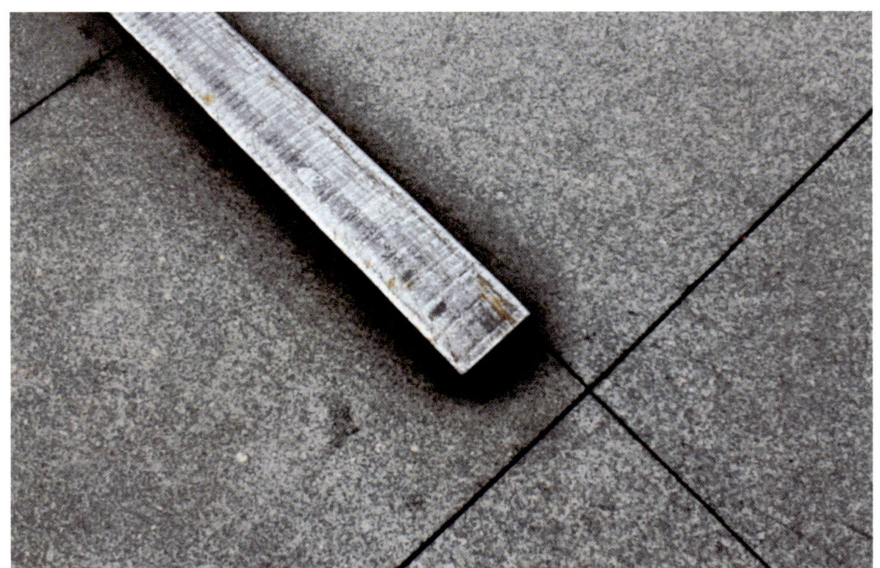

Ground Object, 2013

Born 1979 in
Fort Lauderdale, FL

Lives in London, United
Kingdom / Berlin, Germany

Travis Jeppesen

The Object

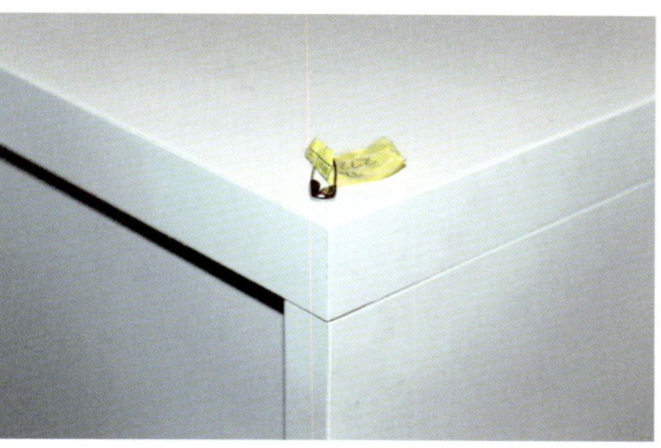

Sharp Object, 2013

He wonders how he will ever begin to write about the object. A bit like writing in the dark . . . The object is there in front of him, and yet isn't. Both at the same time. How can that be, that state of simultaneity. Oh very simple: it isn't. He drinks all his thoughts up, visits his feelings. No, not there. Feeling a place to run away from. Objects have no feelings . . . but could they? A question of investiture. So shitty to be left to wonder. Leave the wonderment at the beginning (i.e., "He wonders how . . . "), let's not get back there, not yet at least, too soon. Must move forward. The object contend with it. Let this moment be defined by it. Rather: let the object, its thingness, contaminate this temporal structure, he thinks, and thereby give rise to the formation of a moment. The beauty of a moment is that it passes a delightful turd. The turd is an object, but it is not the object he is now contending with. Contend with the non-turdness of the current object. In the moment. The moment of running away. Running away from feeling. The moment he finds himself facing the object, seated before it, forcing his thoughts to coalesce into something—words. Words the physical manifestation of something: the object. The object's bluntness. Not a copy, not a simulacrum, for that is not something *his* words could ever be. His words, he thinks, he knows, are always something else, even when they purport to represent, to critically engage with, the object and its thingness, what it purportedly *is* outside of all possible and potential representation. And yet he—not subject (for he recognizes the imperative to momentarily suspend his own agency in order to engage with the task to be elucidated henceforth), but another object, an*other* possible thing that things outside its particulate thingness—is not, in a sense, there. Not in the sense in which the object (the originary object, made originary by our writing of his writing of it, naturally) is there. The thing is, the goal he has set himself (his manic delirium, his sense of physicality, his manifestation of doom—his own private version thereof—through his manifestation of time, his awareness of spatiotemporal limitation) is to get *beyond* both facile representation but also and even mostly that "critical engagement" that the majority dismiss as the only possibility of *interacting* (he hates this word) with the object, and to enter into a state that would actually enable him to *inhabit* the object. And this, through writing. And for him, this writing, this striving-for-inhabiting, resonates with his current concern, to get beyond all the materiality—the thingness, the objectness—of writing—to contend with writing's failed project of transmitting meaning.

How do I *write myself into* the object? he asks himself.

(Always a failure, then, every instance of writing, and yet how to overcome.)

Describe the object in its thingness.

He goes over, in his mind, all the pathways through which one might approach the object, positioned as it currently is, in the room, on the floor, at the center of the black cloth, not far from where he rests his feet. It is a kind of hunger, this desired transformation, transmutation, transubstantiation, but then no, that's not it, for then what would the writing be, shit? Is it: to find a way to put the writing *inside* the object? No, but to make it (the writing) come *out of* it (the object)—and vice versa.

No eating, no shitting, he says aloud.

To inhabit means some encoding. Break that code to reseal it. That's what the process will look like. The thing things itself thingingly, he quotes Heidegger. A certain bluntness of proprieties yes that will do. Nietzsche lost his mind, Heidegger found it, gave it back in hideous form: an object of a subject called loss. He steps outside—*to get some air*, he thinks. Fat man in a wig comes pattering down the cobblestones, waving a book over his head. It is Leibniz. Eat my monads, scum! he screams.

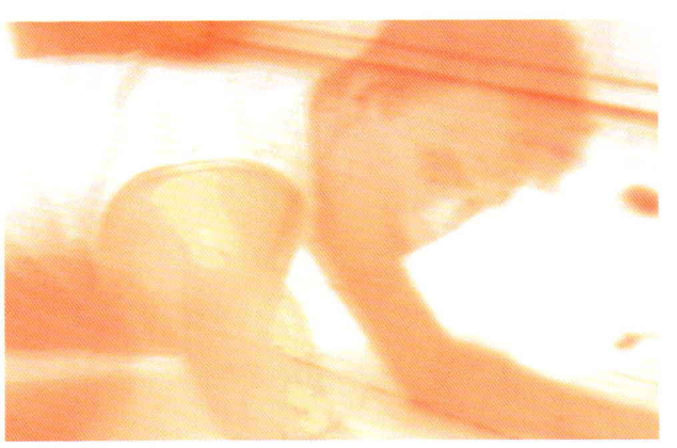

Transparent Object, 2013

He slams the door in the philosopher's face, runs back in to the object. *Into* the object, he would like, but he can't have. The object wills, for certain, but not beyond itself, that is certain also. My thingness not for you to take, it seems to call out . . . or was that Leibniz out there, tormenting him. That book he was waving over his head, what was it. Go have a look. A glance through the window . . . but Leibniz is gone, you'll never know what book it was now. Perhaps

it is better that way. Can substance be defeated? He knows: Desire to attain a state of total selflessness through the act, and yet this risks reducing writing to a sort of gratuitous masturbation. Cancel the second part of last thought. For this stab at conceptualization here is, admittedly, a means of propping up—propagating—excess.

The majority.

He initially wanted to call it "object-oriented criticism," until he realized—not just that he had the terminology wrong—but that his misuse of the word *criticism* would only serve to confuse this invisible majority *for whom he was writing against*. For this—this obviating the decision-making process via the thereness of the object—is to be an *act* of writing: a writing to come. No, *criticism*, *critique*, too specific the terminology; he favors the *openness*, the *activeness*—the *act*ness—of writing.

He is against control. He remembers reading a blurb on the jacket of the first edition of Barthelme's novel, *The Dead Father*. Something like, "Well gee, folks, it might look wild and crazy, but its redemption as a work of art is that it is all actually tightly controlled by the author, that makes him a genius, by my validating authority as a critic . . ." Why, he remembers thinking, would control ever be regarded as a positive value in writing?

And of course, the answer to that is quite simple: We live in a society of total control, so it is only natural, from a psychological standpoint, that they seek out forms of (what they perceive to be) control in art, and that *authorial exercise* (as opposed to insane or otherworldly *channeling*) be the defining characteristic of genius for that invisible majority.

Thus, in writing the object (never writing *of* the object): Deny all perimeters.

The object and its mysterious anti-nature, he thinks. Object considered as manifestation of mind no that's wrong.

Object and world, okay: he thinks that's something he can do. Hesitating to proclaim it in these terms, but since so many mispronouncements have already polluted the stratosphere, perhaps his will serve as a cleansing agent. (Or else risk collapsing the unity of the entire multiverse by further polluting. A risk taken every time one opens one's mouth and squeaks.) It is

a question of domains.

Treat myself to a fresh shirt, he decides.

Travis Jeppesen

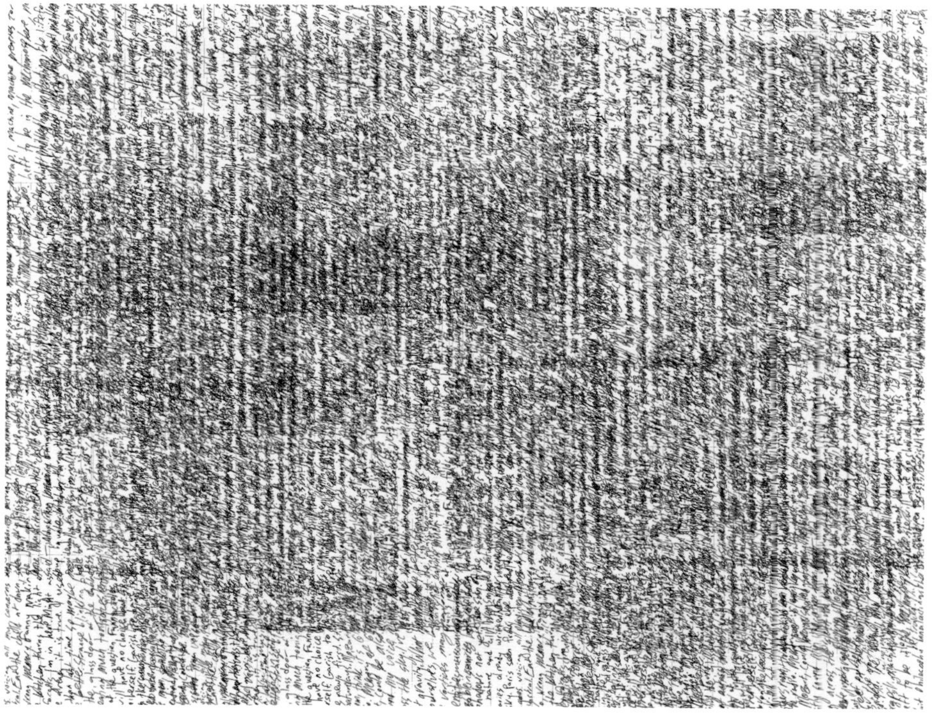

Untitled Painting, 2013

When we *write the object* (and here, the definitionality of what's being said matters, for we are not channeling classical exchanges of phenomenological wankery) we transiterate the resonant hallway of psychology to verify the made (constructed) status of objectitude (in its pure sense) and effectively emerge from this processual act as producers of a reality. He sees this as a completely viable anarcho-individualism that resists the fetishization of edges that gives the object its definitional status in our limited perceptuo-tactile exchange field therewith, and thus unleashes the animality that resides within the object's previously controlled essence. And within that animality resides a will . . .

Once the object is written—and liberated thus—we may begin to speak of objectity, he reasons. Now, objectity goes beyond mere thingness in its necessitude to claim a spectral identity. Identity, in their way of thinking of it, always comes with an I. Expend your shit logic across the evening sky. Objectity neologistically combines the object with identity, but also reality, to lay claim to a *scape* that evades the perceptual diminutive that typically derogatorizes the object in the field of the major Them. The object, then, *is* vision, it is a surface filled with ego eyes. Its constructedness matters less than the way it goes about reconceiving our own willed surfaces.

But of course, he reasons, this object thus edified will most certainly clash and cocirculate concurrently with others' edification of the object. And so the route becomes shortwinded, a show flourish—it is meant to be, in its measureless metonymity. No metaphoricity. Chains of difference overflowing, gather them up if you want into assorted cycles. Play god by defeating yesteryear. The answer, he suddenly conjectures, to Husserl dodging the intersubjectivity bullet: Everyone produces their own reality through their reciprocal arrangement of object-perceiving. Thus, in concept production, each concept is only designated for use by its original creator/inhabitor. Use exhaustibility. There are limits to this applicability: Why I Am So Unpopular. All these different realities clashing into one another. And the sparks caused by the interaction. No more human/nonhuman divisions, a rebirth of agency. All this, through the writing. He closes his eyes and sees thick blobs of text on paper. Pen rolls out of hand. From across the galaxy, the room, the object stares at him and sighs.

Yve Laris Cohen

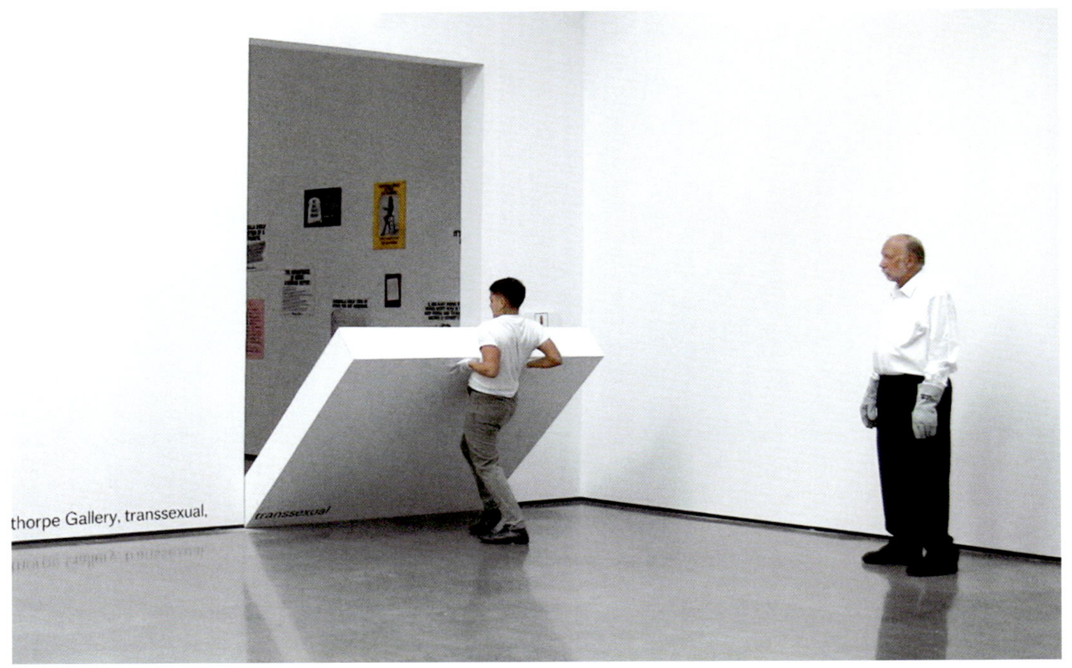

opening from *Landing Field: Vito Acconci and Yve Laris Cohen*, 2013. Performance
(Hessel Museum of Art, Center for Curatorial Studies, Bard College, April 20, 2013)

Born 1985 in
San Diego, CA

Lives in
Brooklyn, NY

CUTTING INTO THE NEW BUILDING
I talked to Stuart about this last week and I'm going to try to make the case for it here. Penetrating one of the new building's walls feels increasingly important, and I would like for it to remain on the table in our negotiations with the new building team. I'd like for the moveable wall's function—as portable didactic material that signals the supposed location of the artwork—to be as symmetrical as possible with respect to the two Whitney buildings. And, as heavy-handed as it is, I'm compelled by the regressive gesture of moving backward at a construction site—of literally destabilizing an incipient structure. Of interrupting a wall with a wall before it's become a wall. Because the holes in both buildings will be just big enough to accommodate the wall slab with a snug fit, the slab will likely collect wall material—scuffs and gypsum dustings—from each building over time. The wall slab will be a palimpsest that literally cross-pollinates the two buildings as it carries and deposits the wall particles, on its wall self, back and forth throughout the exhibition's two months. This mark-making and -taking process disperses the unidirectional force of the institution's downtown migration. The whole project is getting at this dispersal, yes. But the wall slab is the envoy that can literalize this aim.

ARTWORK INSURANCE
I've changed my mind about the wall's classification varying from performance to performance. I've returned to my original idea of the wall traveling southwest as art and northeast as prop. There's plenty of room for slippage and irregularity in this project in other arenas; I'd like the wall's spatiotemporal-financial path to remain consistent across the performances. Thus the number of times the wall is reinsured as an artwork corresponds directly to the number of performances. The performance itself will be the reverse-alchemic agent that changes the wall's status. By the end of the evening the wall slab has depreciated, and it reenters the Breuer building as an impostor. Once it's back in place on the third floor, I'll go through the paperwork with the registrar to get it reinsured as an artwork, sometime before the subsequent performance. Whether the wall is reinsured as art once it returns to the Breuer building following the final performance is a key question I haven't resolved yet. I might not know the answer until May.

ANACHRONISM
Is it possible to either hasten or retard the construction timeline for the new building's theater, beginning as soon as this month? What are the consequences of either scenario? Still excited by the idea of the theater being anachronistic. Even if this part of the project isn't explicitly made known, I think it could be subtly felt.

OSHA REGULATIONS AND FIRE CODES
I want to make a performance that can only happen in that theater while it is still an active construction site. I'm curious about the moment where the theater becomes a theater—when OSHA regulations governing permitted materials and human activity shift from those designated for construction sites to those reserved for theaters. For example, raw wood that hasn't been treated with flame retardant is forbidden in a theater, whereas it abounds on a construction site. I know fall protection is involved in both sets of regulations, but I expect the tie-off requirements and height limits are different for each context. OSHA regulations also reveal and shape who is considered a worker, since those rules are created to protect employees—not audience members or museum visitors or patrons or anyone else. Fire codes, on the other hand, protect audiences. If the Whitney were to hire me as a performer, would I be considered a worker on the Turner construction site, or are Turner employees the only ones subject to OSHA regs? I know that OSHA theater regulations, while stringent, are not explicitly laid out and designated as such. One of my roommates, a technical director for an uptown dance company, tells me that theaters have some agency in asserting which rules apply, and this depends on all sorts of architectural conditions such as the size of the house, and so forth. This is where it gets interesting and tricky, as theaters already interpret and reroute construction-site OSHA regs to apply to them (if I'm understanding this all correctly). The performance isn't sitting neatly between two discrete sets of mutually exclusive rules, as I'd initially thought. I still want this idea of the almost-theater and its accompanying legal loopholes to choreograph the performance, but

I'm thinking about it no longer being the sole impetus (see RUMOR AND DELAY).

TICKETING

What is the existing process by which a member of the public, unknown to the Whitney, can gain access to the new building site? Who signs off on their legitimacy? Could the performance supplant this process? That is, could I be the person to say Yes, I want this person in the audience, and then they're cool? Or could anyone who emailed to RSVP or bought a ticket be automatically cool? This area is still murky for me, until we know all the max occupancies and figure out audience size. I'm still interested in curating my audiences—doing internet searches on people who request a spot and giving the thumbs-up or -down or wait-listing. This only makes sense if the audience is very small—under 20 people or so—and at this point I'm less excited by this dimension of the project than others. I'd rather the wall's shifting classification be the administrative headache. What is very important, however, is how the exchange of money, or lack thereof, affects the status of the building. My roommate seems to think that once audience members pay to see a performance, wherever the performance is happening could be considered a theater when it comes to both OSHA requirements and fire codes—that monetary exchange can actualize a theater. I need to research this.

PUBLICITY

I mentioned to Stuart one idea for publicizing the performance: all the information would be on the wall slab only—found nowhere in exhibition materials or online. For me, this move isn't about hiding or denying the public that information but rather solidifying the wall's role as the docent for the project. This is also consistent with some of my past work. The performance dates and times, as well as instructions for RSVPing, would be printed along with Stuart's and Education's text, the title of the work, and potentially a materials list. I'll likely include performance information on the wall even if we decide to publicize the performances elsewhere. If there's some sort of performance calendar for the entire exhibition, I don't think I'd be opposed to being listed—mainly because I want to assert that I'm making performance and wouldn't want to shy away from a group identification around performance. I'd definitely want to be listed if there were a dance calendar. I'm not sure, though; my gut is also telling me to be hardcore and analogue.

RUMOR AND DELAY

Matthew Lyons and I have just started a conversation about possibly producing my work in The Kitchen's theater in the near future. I've begun to think about a potential relationship between that project and my biennial work. One idea involves doing "the same" performance for both sites, but the new Whitney building's incompletion will preclude some elements of the performance while the Kitchen theater's subjection to OSHA theater regs will inhibit others. Thus, the "full" performance can never be realized—we only see the pre- and post-theater versions, and the fantasy performance exists somewhere near the onset of the theater's becoming. A vanishing point. I want to tread lightly here, in case I want to leak a rumor about the connection between the two performances at a later date rather than announcing it in a press release or starting the gossip now. But this would be a way to both breach the temporal parameters of the exhibition and allow greater access to the work. Once people caught wind that I was doing the performance "again" at The Kitchen, they could wait and then have unfettered access to it there. Ostensibly.

CATALOGUE IMAGE(S)

I just got my hands on the original DV tape with footage from the CCS Bard performance that spawned the wall slab. I'll import it into Final Cut in the next couple days. I'm looking to pull a still image that gives some context for the slab—letting readers know that it's vestigial, at the very least. I've been working with a version of the footage that was compressed improperly; the video is squished and has interlace issues, but if you take a look at the attached stills you'll get the idea. I prefer the image with the wall falling into my arms.

Yve Laris Cohen

DANCE
Just a reminder that this project involves dance and is dance.

Fred Lonidier

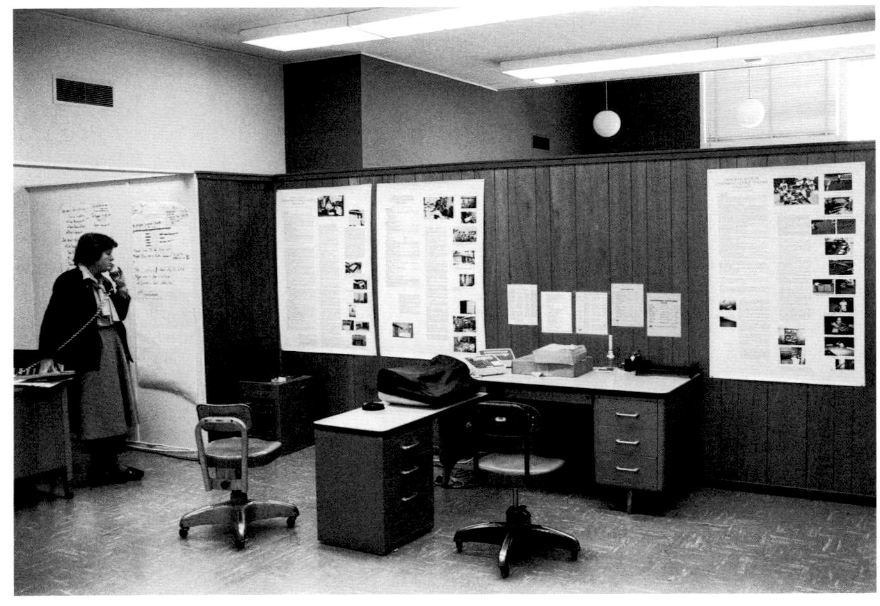

L. A. Public Workers Point to Some Problems. . . , 1979 (installation view, San Francisco Federation of Teachers, Local 61, 1980). Eleven photograph-and-text panels, 60 × 54 in. (152.4 × 137.2 cm)

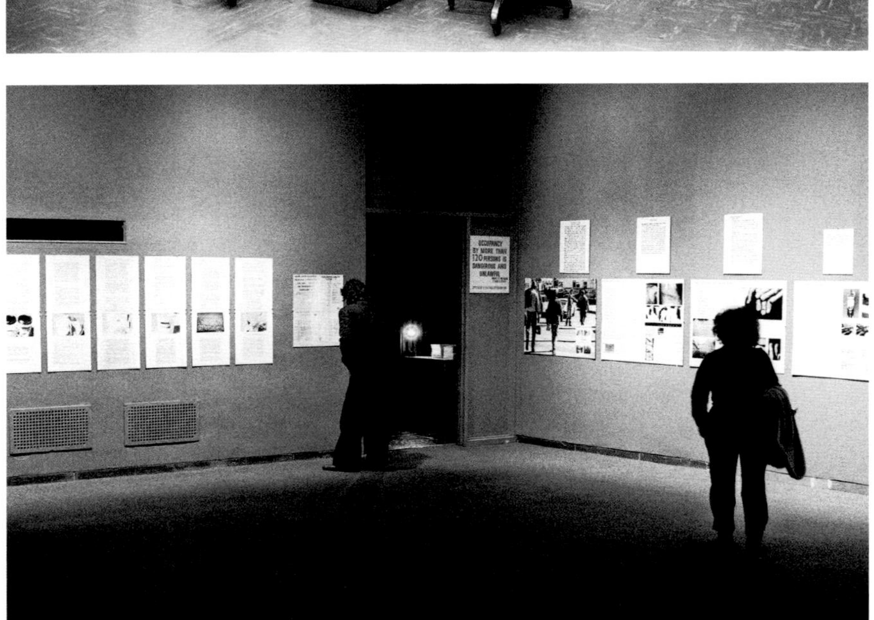

Health and Safety Game, 1976 (installation view, *The Health and Safety Game: Fictions Based on Fact*, Whitney Museum of American Art, New York, 1977). Fifteen photo-and-text panels, dimensions variable, and video, black-and-white, sound/silent; 20 minutes

Born 1942 in Lakeview, OR

Lives in San Diego, CA

Fred Lonidier: Conceptual Artist in the Labor Movement, or Vice Versa

Egija Inzule

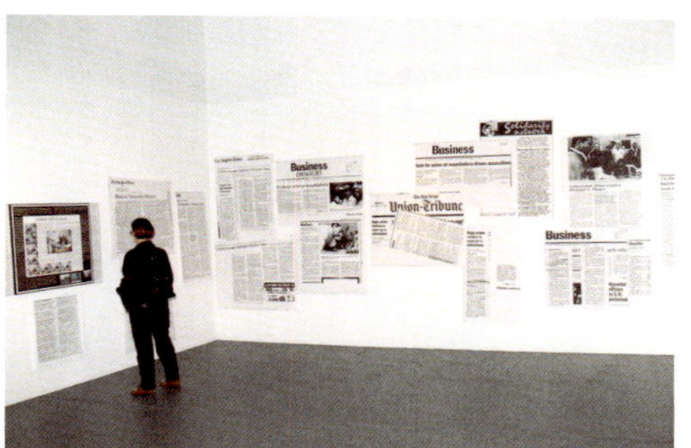

N.A.F.T.A. (Not A Fair Trade For All), Getting The Correct Picture: A monolingual, trade union descendent of Swedish immigrants and Cajuns goes across the border of the United States of America and the United States of Mexico, 1997–2008 (installation view, *Revolution: Agustin Casasola & Fred Lonidier*, Centro Cultural de la Raza, San Diego, November 12–28, 1999)

As a graduate student in the Department of Visual Arts at the University of California San Diego in 1970, Fred Lonidier was involved in the racial, sexual, and gender emancipation movements that grew up around the massive student-led mobilization against the Vietnam War. San Diego was the site of a U.S. military-industrial complex, and the university was a key center of antiwar activism. The school's faculty included Herbert Marcuse, who taught philosophy, and Fredric Jameson; Jean-Pierre Gorin, a former member of the Dziga Vertov Group, concerned with the relation between activism and art making—articulated by their famous declaration that they were "politically making films" rather than "making political films"—joined the faculty in 1975. This was the context in which David Antin invited Lonidier to join the "young faculty" of the visual-arts department, where he would be a professor for more than thirty years.[1] Here, together with photographer Phel Steinmetz, Lonidier developed a practice of photography notable for its political and sociological perspective and its focus on the labor movement as a lens through which to analyze the conditions of late capitalism from a radical left position.

Lonidier had been strongly involved in antiwar activism before he came to San Diego. He had refused military service during the Vietnam War, instead joining the Peace Corps and serving in the Philippines. He had not yet completed his two-year contract when he was classified as 1-A, conscripted, and brought back to the United States. Lonidier publicly criticized the politics of the Peace Corps, which he called an "expendable political gimmick."[2] In 1974, he would critically review his time as a volunteer in his video *CONFESSIONS of the PEACE CORPS: a slide lecture on U.S. foreign policy Confessed by returned volunteer*.[3] This self-reflexivity and examination of the grounds of his own involvement have remained integral dimensions of his practice.

It was not until he reached San Diego, however, that, in collaboration with Steinmetz and then-graduate students Martha Rosler and Allan Sekula (the so-called San Diego group), Lonidier evolved his artistic method of critically and sociologically examining specific social relationships through documentary photography. In panels that combined photographs and text, he used critical discourse analysis to reconsider means of representation and propose alternative tools of documentation. Adapting Bertolt Brecht's concept of the constructed nature of representation, the group's dialectical technique employed text and image informed by fieldwork and engaged investigation, all of which gave way to a form of complex realism. Sekula's essay "Dismantling Modernism, Reinventing Documentary" (1978), which enunciated this approach, became a kind of manifesto for the group; an early version of that text accompanied a 1976 exhibition of works by Lonidier and Steinmetz at the Long Beach Museum of Art, California. This exhibition included Lonidier's

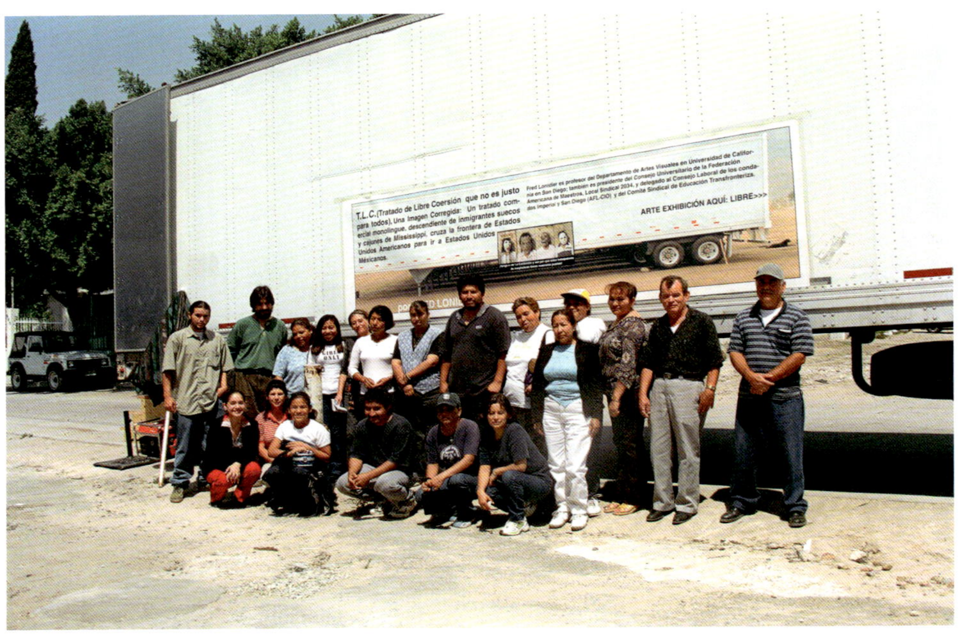

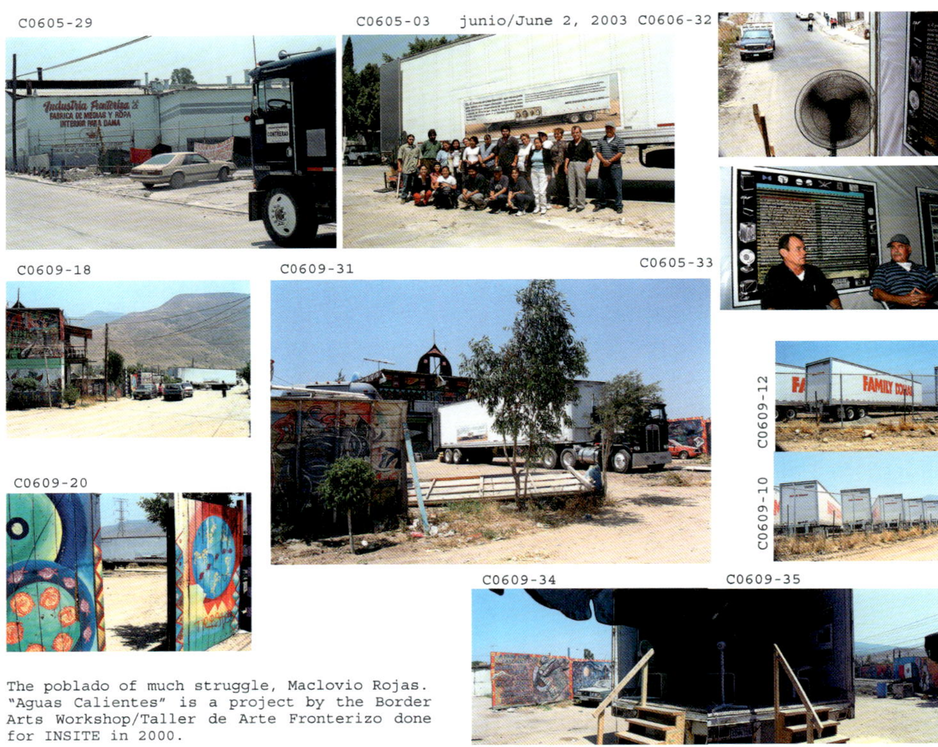

Top: Industria Fronteriza workers and supporters in May 2003 standing in front of Fred Lonidier's *N.A.F.T.A. Truck* in Tijuana, Mexico.
Bottom: images from the folder "N.A.F.T.A. . . Returns to Tijuana." All images from *N.A.F.T.A. #16 A/B* "'N.A.F.T.A. . . ' Returns to Tijuana," / "'T.L.C. . . ' Regresa a Tijuana," 2005. Two photographic panels, 32 × 124 in. (81.3 × 315 cm) each.
And from *#17 Mobile Transborder Labor Archive*, 2005. Archive box with inkjet prints and texts, 14 × 18 × 11 in. (35.6 × 45.7 × 27.9 cm).
Produced for the Transborder Mobile Archive, part of *inSite_05*, San Diego and Tijuana, August 26–November 13, 2005

Health and Safety Game (1976), the best known of his so-called labor works, and his first installation "for, by, and about class struggle through organized labor," as the artist has described his practice.[4]

Based on his fieldwork, Lonidier's labor works (1976–) are presented as case studies of workers he has interviewed.[5] *Health and Safety Game* focuses on occupational injuries and diseases where the latter is often long-term to manifest years after being sustained and often long after any available medical coverage had lapsed. Lonidier's documentary images, supplemented by X-rays and other medical information that may seem marginal but is of critical importance to his arguments, expose gaps in the health-care system, thus making the limits of the capitalistic economic order tangible. Following what he has described as a "general leftist strategy," the artist's analysis reveals that the only real solution lies in systemic change.[6] These labor works also address the increasing inability of American unions to protect their own interests. A member of the University Council—American Federation of Teachers Local 2034, Lonidier has criticized what he sees as a growing consumerist orientation in the American labor movement since World War II; through his analysis, he has attempted to push the movement in a more socialist direction.

Though Lonidier describes himself as mainly a "photo-text installation" artist, the site-specific character of his installations in the context of the labor movement is an essential element of his work. He typically shows his photo-text panels in union offices and community centers, relating their educational and socially and self-critical form to the specific public being addressed, an approach that also recalls strategies of such conceptual artists as Hans Haacke.

In contrast to the primarily informational aspect expressed by his artworks when they appear in union spaces, in art spaces these works function as documentations of their own potential—a potential derived from their presence in the labor unions and other local Southern Californian social organizations.

Works like *Health and Safety Game*, *L.A. Public Workers Point To Some Problems . . .* (1979), and *I Like Everything Nothing But Union* (1983) hang on the walls as a background to meetings, in entranceways, next to copy machines, and in other more or less inconspicuous but well frequented places. Since the works installed in these spaces are present for longer periods of time than possible in art-specific contexts, union members are able to view them over and over again. Lonidier's practice is deeply intertwined with his understanding of socially critical art as inseparable from work by organizations pursuing similar radical goals. In his dual position as artist and labor activist, he creates his own opportunities to present and discuss his works in these engaged contexts while simultaneously maintaining their specific potential as artworks.

His recent complex of works *N.A.F.T.A. . . (Not a Fair Trade for All) (. . .)* (1997–2008) documents the struggles of workers in the maquiladoras of Baja California, Mexico, and the organizations that help them unionize independently to avoid being held hostage to so-called protected contracts. In addition to his activities as a labor union activist, Lonidier initiated *Labor Link TV*, a series that offers a platform for the local labor movement and which has been broadcast on public-access channels of three television stations since 1988.

Translated by Nathan Aglaster.

1. In 2013, Fred Lonidier was named professor emeritus at the University of California, San Diego. He still lives in San Diego today.
2. Lonidier, quoted in "Peace Corps Volunteers Being Drafted," *Pittsburgh Press*, November 23, 1966, 5.
3. Since being exhibited in *Through the Lens of the Male Fetish for Fun and Profit* (June 2–August 15, 2013, Silberkuppe, Berlin), the video work is accessible online in its full length.
4. Lonidier, conversation with the author, San Diego, September 2013.
5. Lonidier's body of work demonstrates a differentiated approach to photography. For example, from 1967 to 1968, he was an active member of Draft Resistance Seattle, photographing the demonstrations and everyday activities of the movement. At the same time, he also documented the trial of Seattle Black Panther Party members Aaron Dixon, Larry Gossett, and Carl Miller. These photographs might only become part of an artwork, however, when contextualized with text and a specific subject matter. See the University of Washington, antiwar and radical-history project http://depts.Washington.edu/antiwar/ (Accessed December 8, 2013). Besides the labor works, there were other works, such as *29 Arrests* (1972), made in the context of the antiwar movement and meant to examine the power structures of photography from the viewpoint of "politics of realism" as subsequently discussed by Martha Rosler in her essay "In, Around, and Afterthoughts (On Documentary Photography)" (1981). Lonidier's photo work *The Girl Watcher Lens* (1972) criticizes photography from a feminist perspective and exposes a self-critical view from the perspective of the "male gaze," although these terms were introduced only later, particularly in Laura Mulvey's essay "Visual Pleasure and Narrative Cinema" (1975).
6. See Fred Lonidier, "Working with Unions II," in *Democratic Communications in the Information Age*, ed. Janet Wasko and Vincent Mosco (Toronto: Garamond Press, 1992).

Dashiell Manley

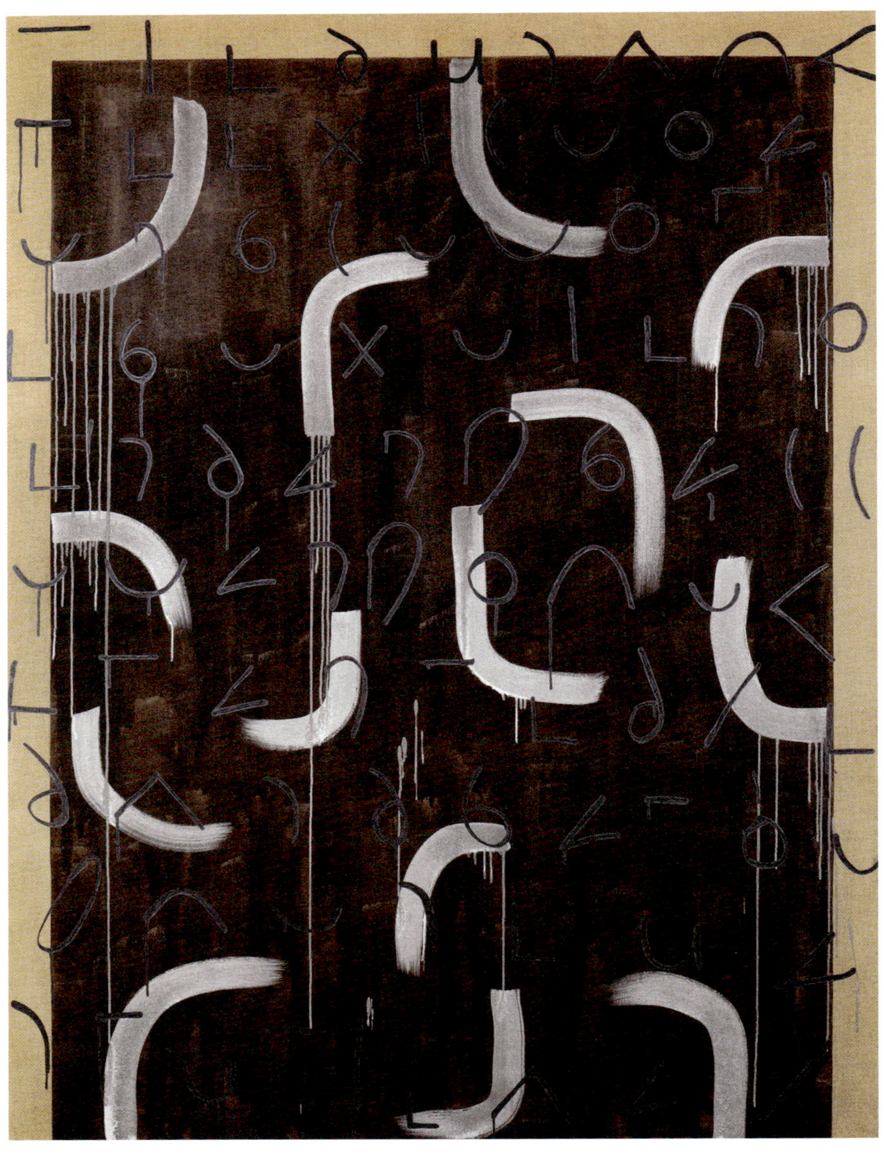

Scene 3 Version C #4, 2013 (detail). Gouache, ink, watercolor, linen, wood, acrylic sheet, lighting gels, paper, tape, and steel, 73 × 96 ½ in. (184.2 × 245.1 cm)

Born 1983 in Fontana, CA

Lives in Los Angeles, CA

Dashiell Manley

(Re)make, (Re)state, (Re)work
Elisabeth Sherman

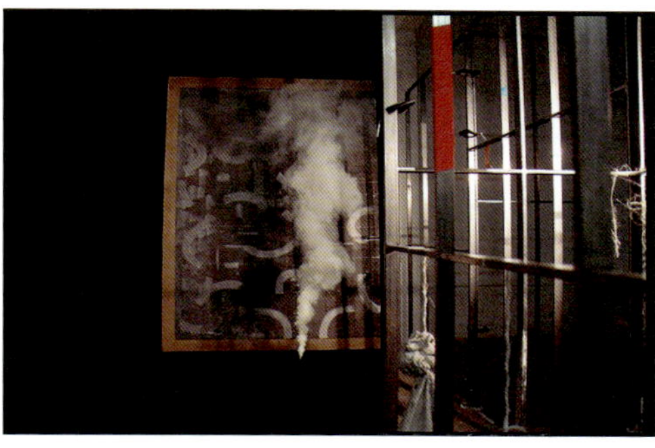

Still from *The Great Train Robbery (Scene 3)*, 2013. Two-channel video projection (JPEG files transferred to digital video), color, silent; 8:35 minutes

The Great Train Robbery, a silent film made in 1903, provides the source material for Dash Manley's ongoing multipart installation and video project of the same name. The 10-minute Western follows two robbers as they hijack a train, killing and stealing along the way, only for good to triumph in a final shootout as the townspeople vanquish the bandits. Manley's interpretation focuses exclusively on the film's third scene: the criminals break into the mail car, shoot the clerk, and explode a bomb at his feet.

Stills from *The Great Train Robbery (Scene 3)*, 2013. Two-channel video projection (JPEG files transferred to digital video), color, silent; 8:35 minutes

In moving from his source material to the final work, Manley transitions fluidly across and between media, complicating the definitions of these established categories of artistic production. He begins with a painting on stretched canvas that acts as both a backdrop for and a map of his movements in the video. Each of the five paintings is coordinated with a specific action from scene three of *The Great Train Robbery*, which he performs repeatedly on camera as the painting stands behind him. A second video channel documents Manley writing instructions for the accompanying gesture on the canvas in an abstracted variant of an early twentieth-century shorthand. This accretion of marks is captured through stop-motion animation. The resulting two-channel video is a disjointed amalgamation of imagery as Manley acts out the four motions while the illegible symbols directing the action accumulate.

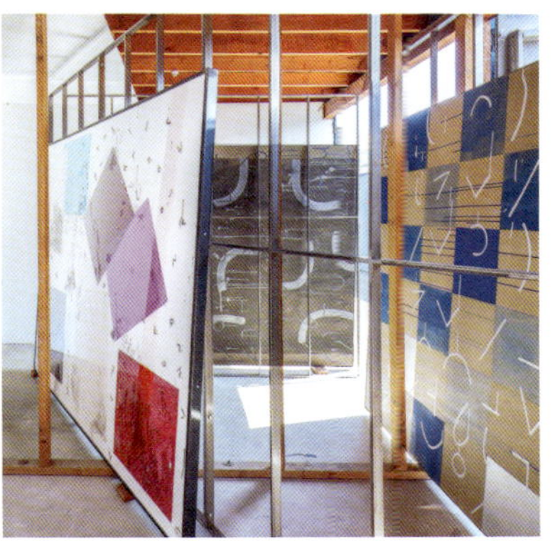

The Great Train Robbery (Scene 3 Version C), 2013 (installation view). Gouache, ink, watercolor, linen, wood, acrylic sheet, lighting gels, paper, tape, and steel, five units: three units, 72 ½ × 96 ½ × 2 in. (184.2 × 245.1 × 5.1 cm) each; two units, 73 x 96 ½ × 2 in. (185.4 × 245.1 × 5.1 cm); 102 × 288 × 120 in. (259 × 731.5 × 304.8 cm) overall

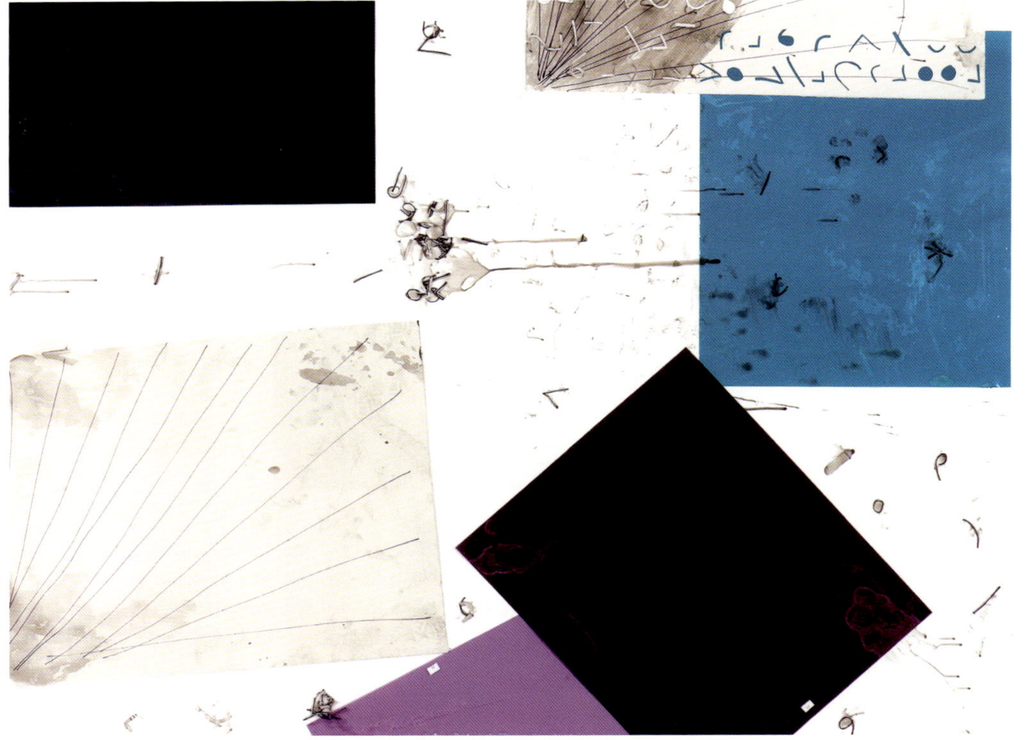

Scene 3 Version C #3, 2013 (detail). Gouache, ink, watercolor, linen, wood, acrylic sheet, lighting gels, paper, tape, and steel, 72 ½ × 96 ½ in. (184.2 × 245.1 cm)

Once the filming of the video is complete, Manley affixes the detritus of the process—lighting gels, plexiglass sheets, drawings, and props—to the verso of the corresponding painting, transforming the two-dimensional surface into a three-dimensional object. The artist then props these against the labyrinth of open structures that define and construct the space of his installation. Through a few moves and an incredibly sparse foundational vocabulary, Manley stitches together the typically disparate practices of video, painting, sculpture, installation, drawing, and collage. The boundaries of each become slippery, less definite, and radically less relevant.

The repetitive actions played out in the video and on the paintings are mirrored in the overall structure of the project: Manley has remade the third scene three times, which he notates as versions *A*, *B*, and *C*. He intends to eventually re-create all of the scenes in the original film, three times over. As with the oral traditions of storytelling or as in the recent glut of Hollywood remakes of superhero blockbusters, with each retelling of this simple story, variations occur and accumulate, and the new tale moves a step farther away from the source.

Made thrice over, out of order and across long periods of time, Manley's final version of *The Great Train Robbery*, with all of the scenes stitched back together, will be fragmented yet hold within it some record of the years encompassing its creation. In much the same way that the original film was cutting-edge for its time, utilizing brand-new technology and techniques, Manley uses (at present) current video-recording and video-editing technologies. Technology changes rapidly, however, more rapidly than he can complete this project, and just as the cinematic space of the 1903 film looks obviously false and practically humorous to today's audiences, so will Manley's videos acquire the patina of the past, and the viewer's perception of them will adjust accordingly.

The rapid obsolescence of technology is a popular subject for many contemporary media artists; much of this work employs outdated technologies to invoke a nostalgic reverie that often supersedes the intended subject matter, while in other artworks the nostalgia *is* the subject matter. Manley deftly avoids such pitfalls. Instead, he tracks this change as it transforms his own art, allowing the work to be contemporaneous at its inception and then to age inexorably in real time.

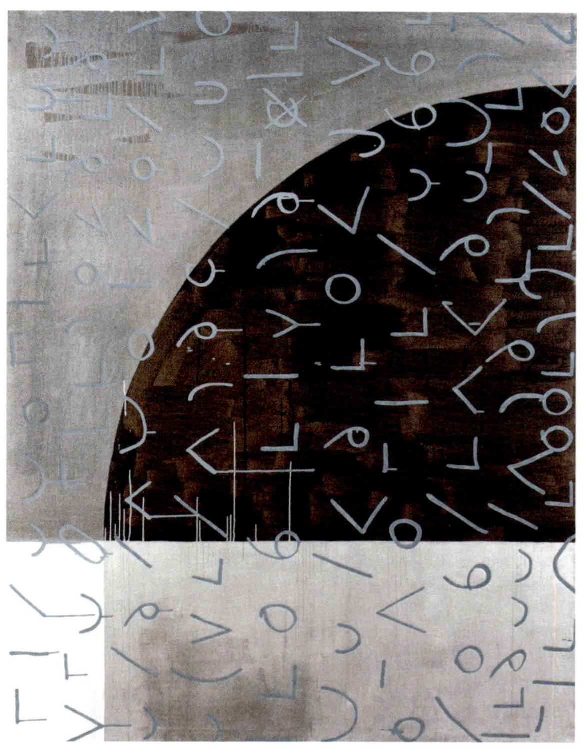

Scene 3 Version C #3, 2013 (detail). Gouache, ink, watercolor, linen, wood, acrylic sheet, lighting gels, paper, tape, and steel, 72 ½ × 96 ½ in. (184.2 × 245.1 cm)

The Great Train Robbery (Scene 3, Versions A, B and C) is not only steeped in the history and current trends of the film industry, it is informed by the landscape of the industry of filmmaking. Like works by many great Los Angeles–based artists before him, Manley's work reflects the inconstant, flimsy quality of the sprawling, studio-dotted metropolis. The wall studs that define the limits of his installation trace porous boundaries that are never filled in. When the paintings/objects are leaned against the beams, they again become film sets just as the artist used them in the making of his video, but here on display for the viewer to wander through. More than just rickety backdrops, they recall the industrial complex of the film industry, where everything is constantly being broken down, rebuilt, and broken down again, always standing at the ready to be transformed into something new. Under Manley's guidance, the instability becomes a virtue, a chance for reinvention.

Language is central to Manley's concerns. By disassembling footage from the original film, in which ideas are communicated speechlessly through grand, dramatic gestures, he creates the building blocks of a new grammar. These elements—which also include marks, physical space, cinematic space, and painted surfaces—are repeated, and recombined, and, like a dialect, take on their own inferences and context within the tightly built system, allowing for interpretation and further recombination. While their signification as a language is essential, precise comprehension is not. His "shorthand," derived from a professional idiom that was arcane a century ago, has been further removed from legibility by its reduction to simplified, disconnected shapes that read as much like hieroglyphs as like elements of an abstract painting. Each of the vocabularies in which he operates merges incongruent modes of communication into a new, symbolic whole.

In the tradition of experimental filmmaking, Manley's *The Great Train Robbery (Scene 3, Versions A, B and C)* expands on what has come before, allowing those tropes to encompass other artistic disciplines. The result is a whole whose parts speak the same language yet remain slightly out of sync with one another. Aligning himself with artists such as Wallace Berman (1926–1976)—whose unfinished, unstable masterpiece *Aleph* (1956–66) was a decade-long project steeped in language, symbol, and collage—Manley allows contemporary viewers to enter into the instability, find their own way through the symbolic language, and participate in the disjunctions between legible and illegible, past and present.

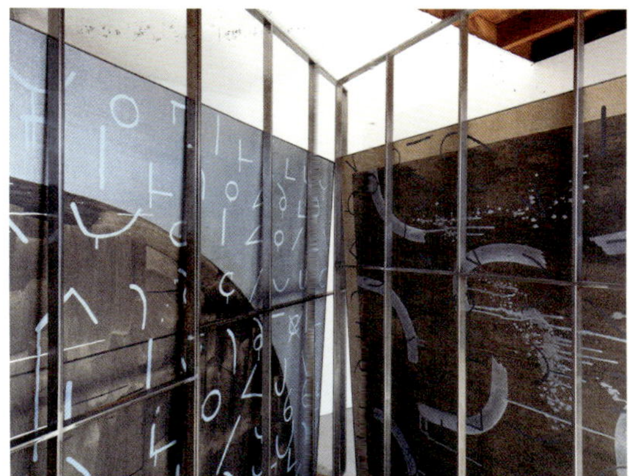

The Great Train Robbery (Scene 3 Version C), 2013 (installation view, storage facility, Los Angeles)

Keith Mayerson

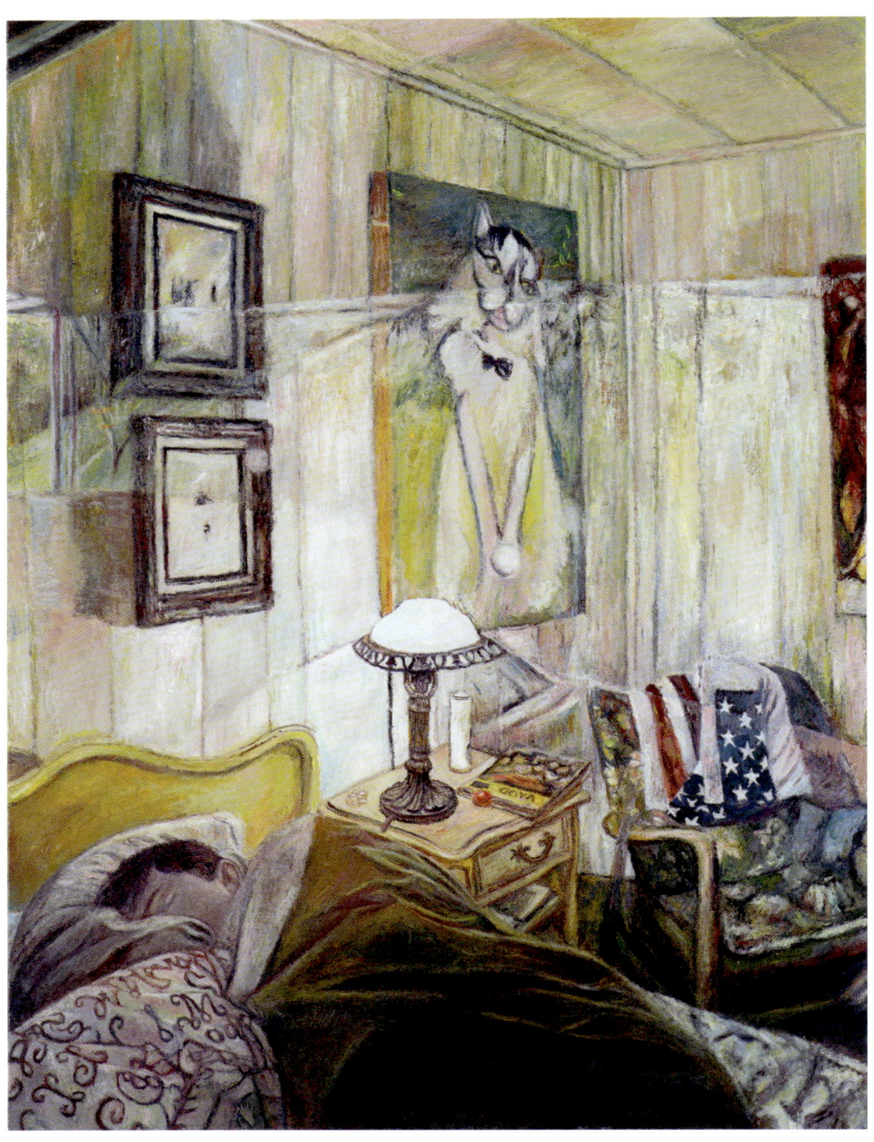

Sleeper, 2011. Oil on linen, 48 × 36 in. (121.9 × 91.4 cm). Private Collection

Born 1966 in
Cincinnati, OH

Lives in
New York, NY

Keith Mayerson

The NeoIntegrity Manifesto—My American Dream

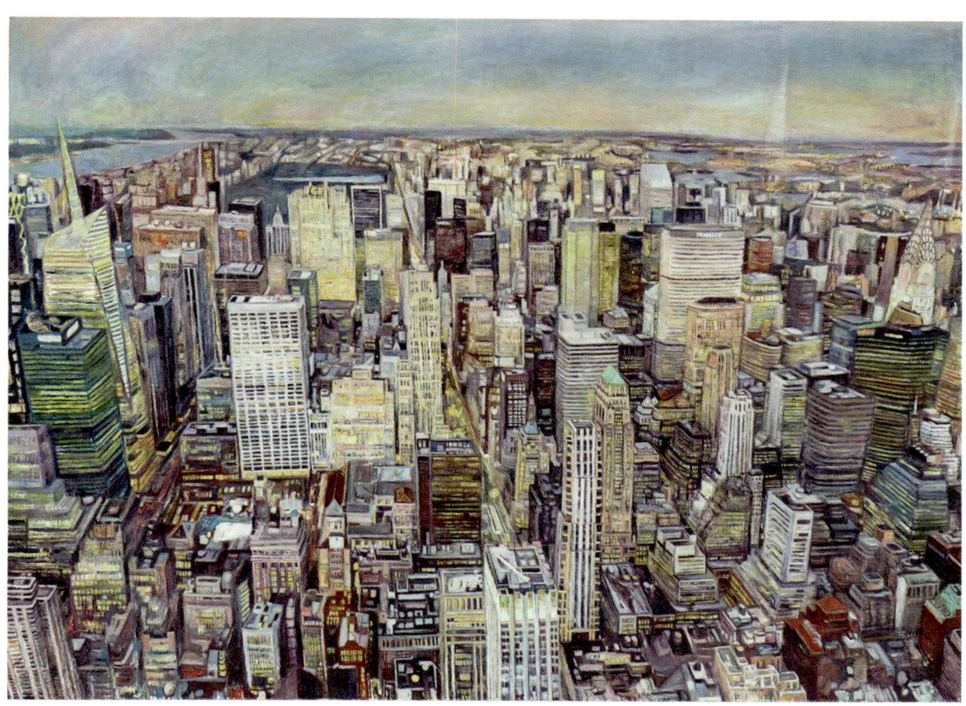

View from Empire, 2013. Oil on linen, 52 × 70 in. (132.1 × 177.8 cm)

Art is language, and language is power. A primary concept in semiotic theory is the Saussurean sign: the word that represents the object (the "signifier"), as opposed to the object itself (the "signified"). Art arises when a work reveals the arbitrary relationship between signifier and signified. At its best, perhaps, art provokes the sublime when you, as the viewer of the work, become the object—that is, when you recognize yourself as a being within a larger world. Art becomes spiritual when it "wakes us up" and shows us that we can commiserate with one another and then come together as a unit, or as a community, to make the world a better place. Art, whether a Mondrian painting or a Cady Noland installation, is most powerful when it triggers you to think about your thoughts, to become conscious of your consciousness, or to reflect on the world. There's something about the ineffability—the mystery, the stuff you can't put into language—that ultimately is the life force of any art, whether it's post-postmodern, postmodern, modern, or the work of the Old Masters.

In the hubris of my youth, inspired by the experience in 1990 of seeing one of the first Mike Kelley shows with stuffed animals on blankets at Metro Pictures, I wanted to start an art movement called NeoIntegrity. In a late-night fit of insomnia in 1993, I wrote the following two manifestos, which I have tried to follow—in my work, in my teaching, in my shows (and curated exhibitions), and in my life.

I. Stuart Comer

The NeoIntegrity Manifesto

1. Art should reflect the artist who made it and the culture in which it is produced.
2. Art is aesthetic, and, whether ugly, beautiful, or sublime, it should be interesting to look at and/or think about.
3. Art is not necessarily commodity, and commodity is not the reason to produce or appreciate art.
4. Art is about ideas, the progression of ideas, the agency of the artist to have ideas, and the artist's ability to communicate his ideas to the world—because agency and ideas are important and are what art is.
5. Art communicates via its own internal language and in the language the viewer brings to it. But this language is not entirely textual, and the work, in being an aesthetic object (or image, idea, film, comic, performance, etc.), communicates in such a way as to be transcendent, beyond language, and beyond traditional constructs of textually based ideology. The work of art is therefore a deep form of communication between artist and viewer and encourages the possibility of the sublime.
6. Art is, rather than tells; it is about itself; it shows itself to be about what it is rather than illustrating what it isn't.
7. Art is important because it reminds us that we are human, and ultimately that is its function.

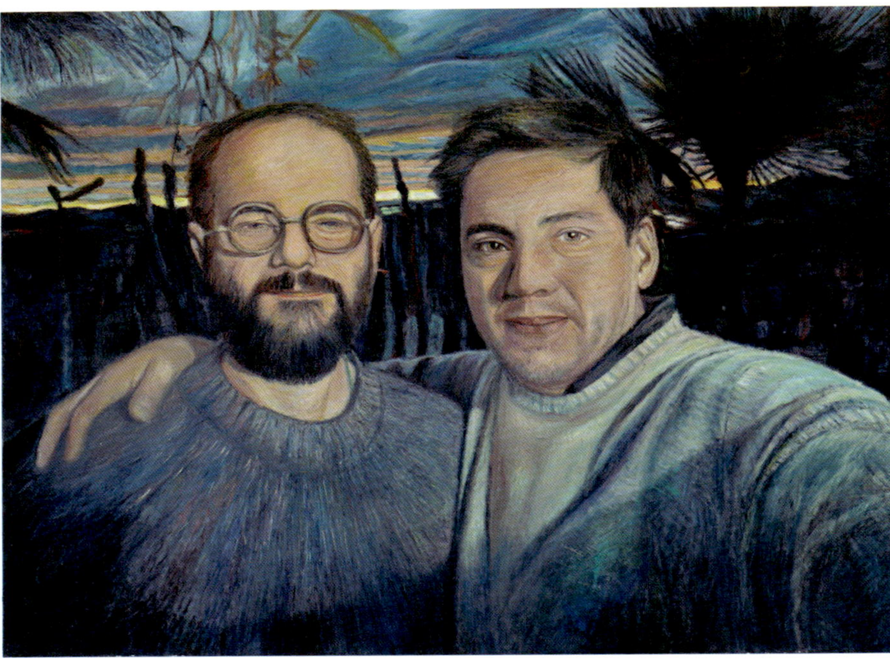

Husbands (Andrew and I), 2011. Oil on linen, 36 × 48 in. (91.4 × 121.9 cm)

The NeoIntegrity Manifesto of Painting

1. Painting can and should be sublime, in that it should generate images that produce tangible realities from the conscious and unconscious mind of the artist, trigger cognitive reactions in the viewer via form and light and color, and transcend language and received ways of looking at things. While ideological, painting should be the most direct form of communication between humans.
2. Painting should be alive—have a life of its own. In transgressing the hand, wit, and intentions of the artist, its arrangements of form, light, color, and space can create unique optical worlds. Paintings should cause an ineffable schism between belief and reality that makes them appear to breathe with life.
3. Paintings can be windows onto other worlds and windows into the soul, and can capture unlike any other medium a dream space/time. Artists cannot hope to fully control the meanings, interpretations, or events described by their own hands, as driven simultaneously by their conscious and unconscious minds.
4. Painting should be experienced: a good painting cannot be successfully reproduced or explained. Indeed, the only reason painting is important in the age of corporate commodity culture is that it has an aura that cannot be contained—it is the result of a peculiar human-made alchemy that comes closest to re-creating the soul.

Keith Mayerson

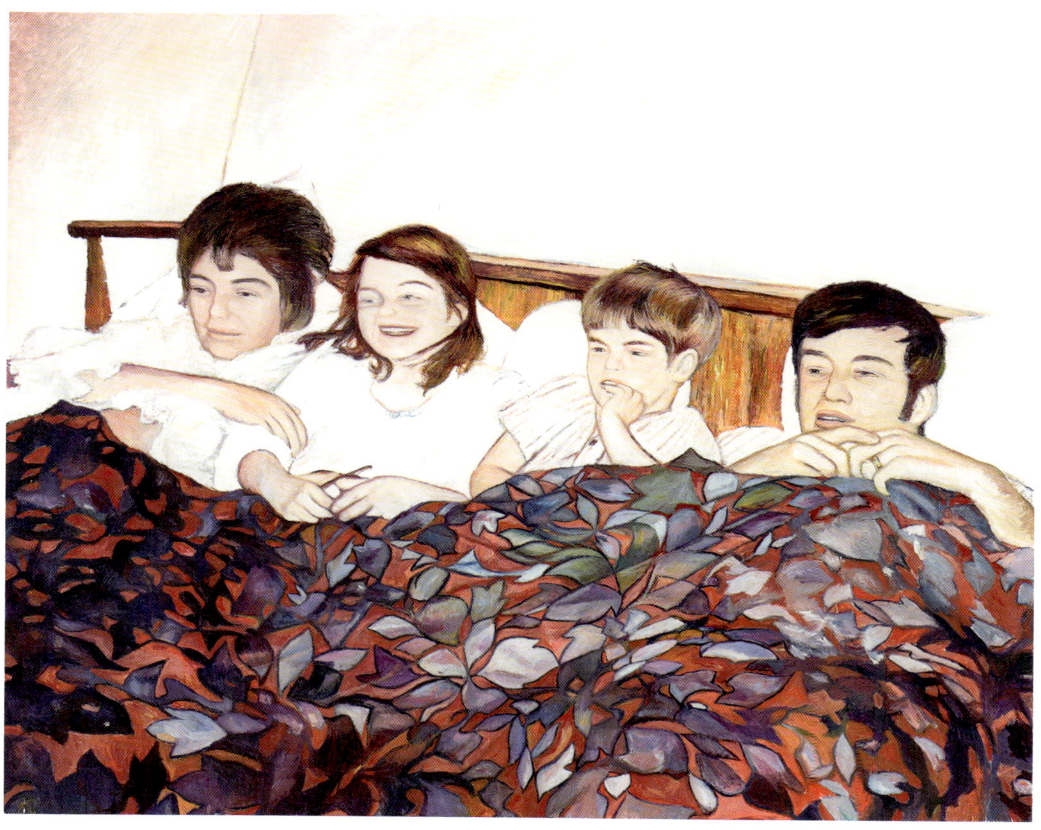

My Family, 2013. Oil on linen, 56 × 70 in. (142.2 × 177.8 cm)

My exhibitions often comprise installations of images that construct nonlinear narratives. The allegorical content of my work relates to the world yet, along with its formal elements, nurtures a transcendent and sublime experience. The viewer, who reads the installations like a prose poem or a comic strip, observes each individual image, and then in her mind ultimately assembles them all into a narrative of her own interpretation, thus completing the work.

My American Dream is a nonlinear-narrative series of paintings about the United States and one's place as an individual within it. It engages not just elegiac feelings for the twentieth century and national power; it also suggests that personal agency can help to define and strengthen this country. My imagery includes portraits of influential leaders and cultural icons from both past and present, events from recent history, and notable milestones from my own life. Hung salon style, the installation's dream-like imagery is representational (derived from appropriated imagery and photos that I have taken or directed) and abstract ("iconscapes" that have emerged from my subconscious). The work's narrative strategies are variously inspired by avant-garde theater, film, poetry, comics, and concept albums (such as the Beatles's *Sgt. Pepper's*, the Beach Boys's *Pet Sounds*, Brian Wilson's *Smile*, and John Lennon's recordings with Yoko Ono). Its formal strategies are modeled on works by Manet, Monet, and many Old Masters and modernists whose paintings were political and personal—as well as painterly, warm, and transcendent. *My American Dream* intimately recounts my journey as an artist into the twenty-first century and renders a contemporary portrait of the United States in challenging times. I paint from my heart and mind romantic images that not only hold deep significance to me but also extend into issues that are shaping both our world right now and our views of history. In these works, I hope to render the America of the moment: a country that is diversely and ideologically beloved yet hard to define, a country with a social and political landscape that is in a state of constant sublime transformation.

Bjarne Melgaard

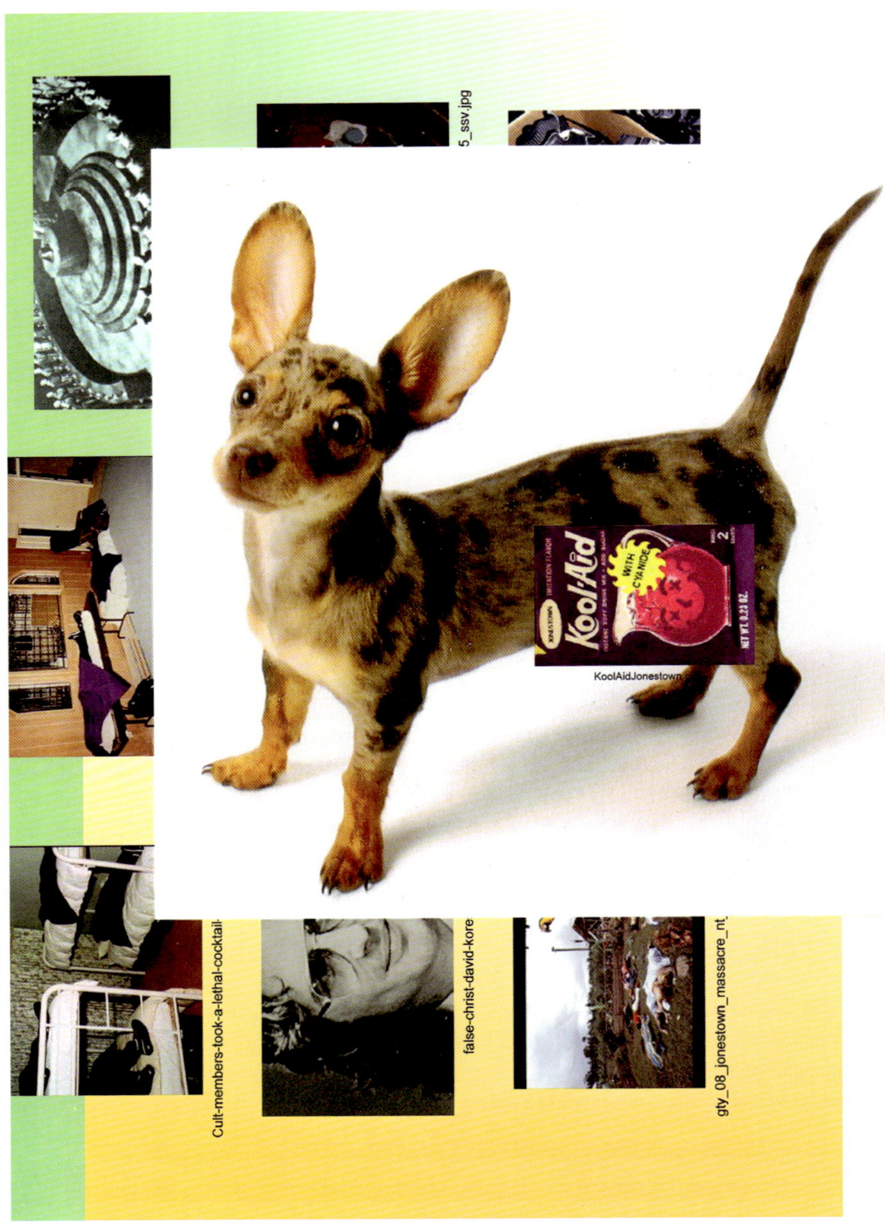

Bjarne Melgaard, 2013. All visual content produced by the artist; text excerpts from Travis Jeppesen's *The Suiciders*, 2013

Born 1967 in Sydney, Australia

Lives in New York, NY

Did motorcycle man fall off yet? I want to see the pink sparks that shoot up when his leather jacket slides across the highway. You know how much it costs to get another one? If every individual were to practice their own version of democracy, we wouldn't live in one. Where we're going, there's a female dictator who makes all the rules.

Matthew has a third testicle. Adam has a pet spider. Lukas has so many friends. I still want to go to the zoo. We will invade something instead.

800px-badung_puputan_1906=resized.jpg

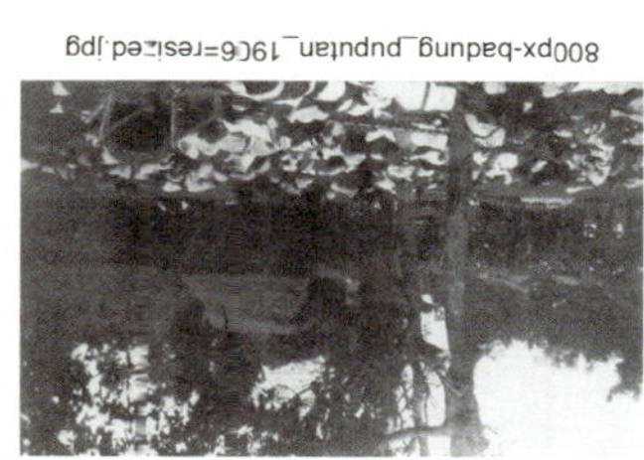

300px-Mountcarmelfire04-19-93-1.jpg

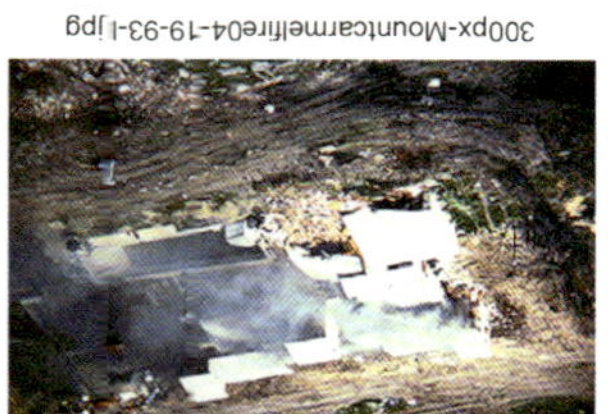

Lukas left school too. One day all the kids made fun of him. It's because he overslept, just grabbed the first t-shirt he could find, laying next to his bed. The t-shirt turned out to be a cum rag. The other kids saw the splatterments and laughed. He was so embarrassed, he set the school on fire and ran away.

Thankfully it hasn't even begun.

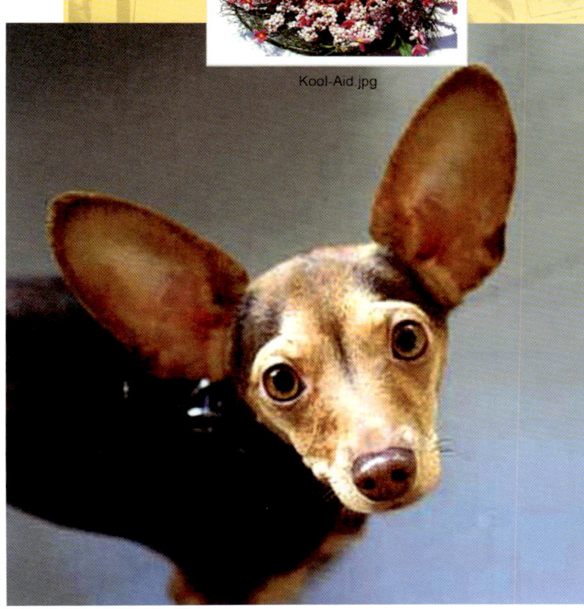

Kool-Aid.jpg

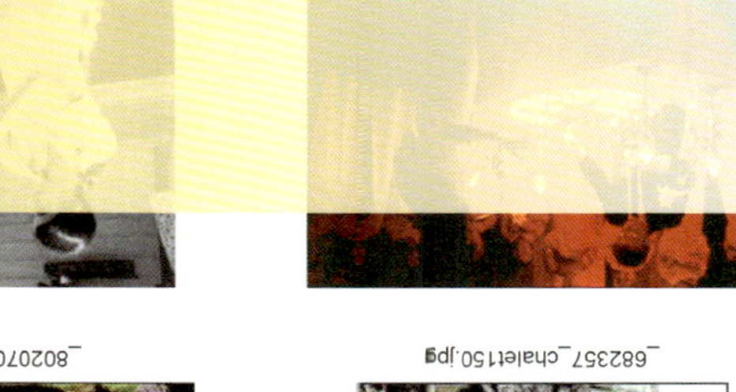

_802070_s

_682357_chalet150.jpg

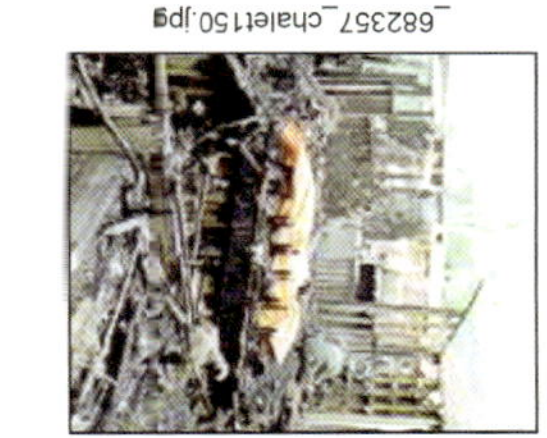

The whore wears a t-shirt advertising a popular beach resort and a white denim miniskirt with numerous stains of a questionable nature. She wants to offer us something. She gives us a smile that has no teeth. She's a teenager just like us, so we let her in the car.

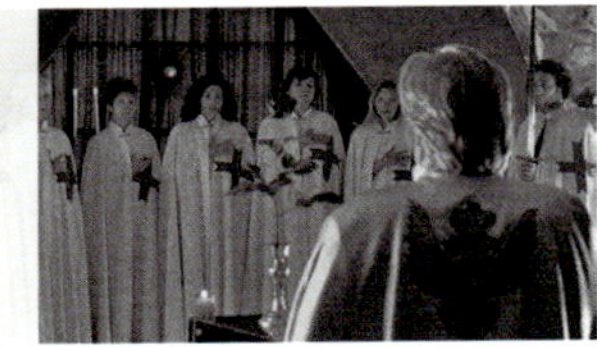
Order-of-the-Solar.png

They were all just dolls, you decide, those angelic people that satisfied your lightbulb yearnings. Now it gets dark and the ride gets faster. It's all black and yellow, the way the road works when you shout down at the asphalt. Lukas screams for five minutes without inhaling once, his face leaning out the window the entire time. The whore recites a poem.We're bringing Adam back to the zoo he escaped from. It's because of the mustaches he's drawing, we don't like them. Oh shut the fuck up Lukas just drive the car. You need to get us there before the sun turns purple and my skin begins to melt. You're an asshole, Matthew, nuclear meltdown is such a last century notion. A mercy blackout is better than getting a blowjob from the mustached stallion.

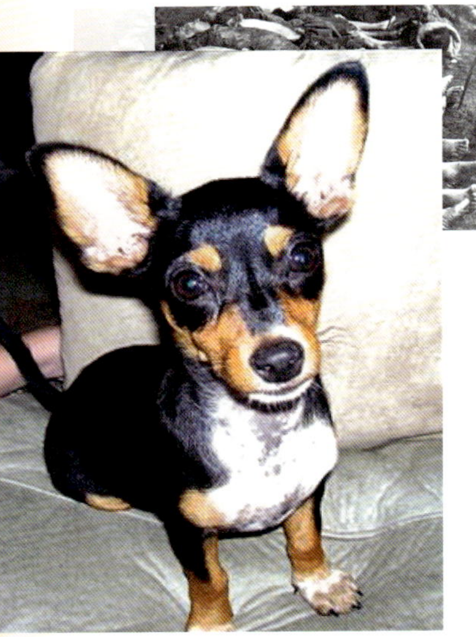

Have we found Jesus H. Christ yet? I think he flew into your brain, you nimwit. I would have definitely noticed, had that happened! I don't think you would. You're so tired these days. I dropped out of high school because of the insinuations. A lot of institutional settings make my breasts hurt.

Get out of my car, shouted Zach, pulled over. We don't have to pay for that either because we took you farther than you've ever been. Wouldn't have gone nowhere, just standing back there all black and sacred. Please, she protested, let me just tell you a story. I know you'll like it. They drove off. She told it anyway, even though there was no one there.

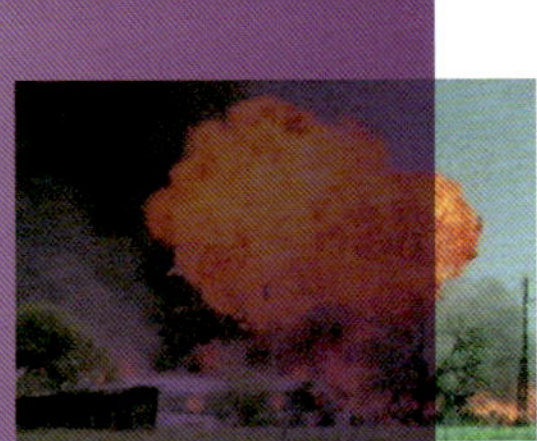
waco-fire.jpg

They drove on, or at least they pretended like they were driving. I drifted off into a place I'm not allowed to tell you about, less you get the wrong idea about this blue plastic garbage bag I'm always wearing on my head. The only thing that woke me was the sound of the telephone ringing – a sound that I always confuse with the dull hum of running water. Some people never get a chance to pray.

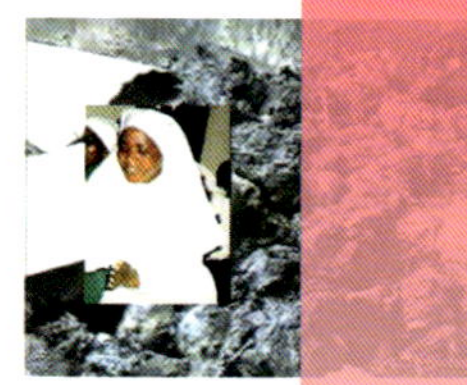

ten-commandments.jpg

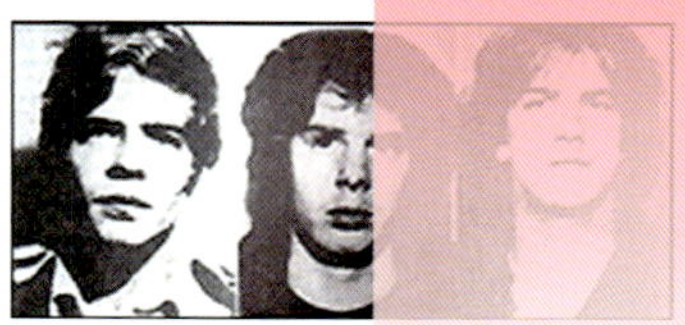

tumblr_lzutgasdpg1qop4kpo1_400.jpg

TXWACdavidian1_miller.jpg

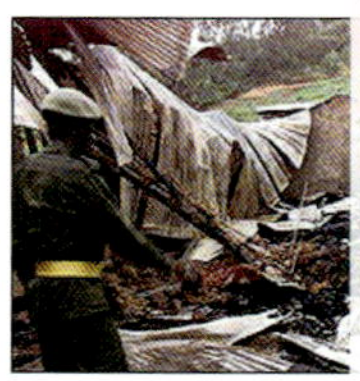

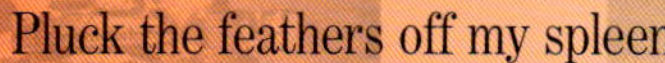

uganda-1.jpg

Strawberries on her teeth

They drove on, or at least they pretended like they were driving. I drifted off into a place I'm not allowed to tell you about, less you get the wrong idea about this blue plastic garbage bag I'm always wearing on my head. The only thing that woke me was the sound of the telephone ringing – a sound that I always confuse with the dull hum of running water. Some people never get a chance to pray.

Grapevines for sweety

That's not a parrot, that's a black crow. Get that black crow away from this vehicle. I don't wanna ride the lightning tonight. Is the sky trying to tell us something? Lukas takes out a metal pipe, jams it in his ear. Scream that one more time, into this pipe. I want to feel the words vibrate against my skull. I did what he told me. It's like pornography, he says.

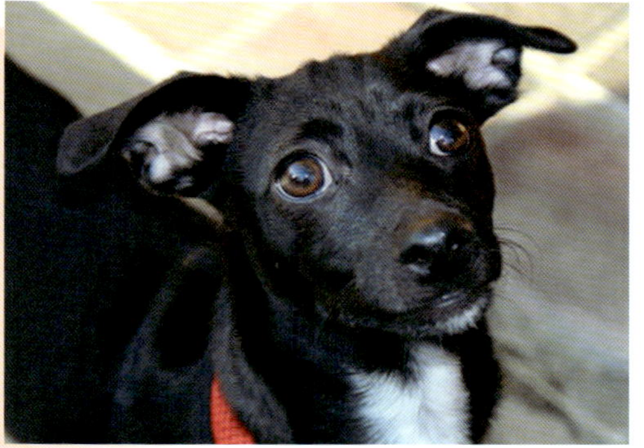

Pluck the feathers off my spleen

The whore smoked a cigarette and led a discourse around tragedy. At one point, Zach mistook Lukas's boner for the driving stick and shifted into the wrong gear. We all lurched forward, Matthew even further into whore's anal cavity, and crashed through a fast food restaurant that really had no business being there in the first place. In the back seat, we found a new animal – half-chicken and half-crab, it waddled into Adam's orifice and sang a beautiful melody:

Oh that was so beauteous, the whore had eyes. Please let me just freshen up before you tear me apart any further, I want to look good when my maker divorces me.

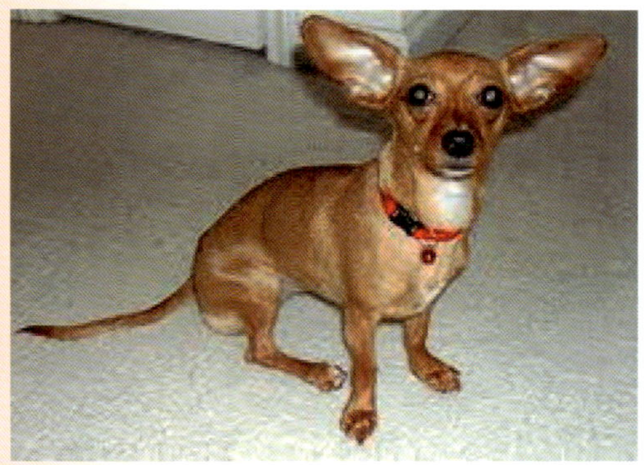

Ken Okiishi

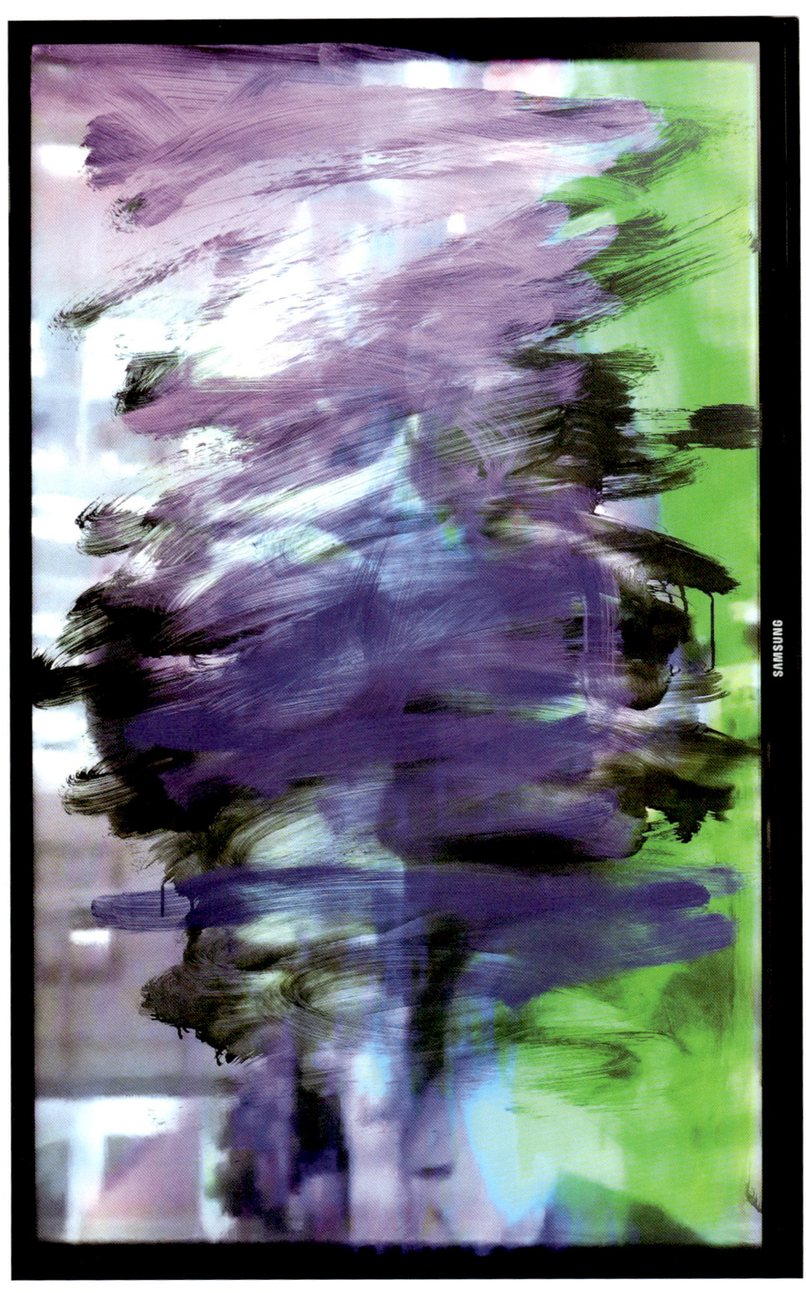

gesture/data, 2013. Oil on flat-screen television and video transferred to USB flash drive, color, sound; 35 5/16 × 21 × 3 11/16 in. (89.7 × 53.3 × 9.4 cm)

Born 1978 in Ames, IA

Lives in New York, NY/ Berlin, Germany

Ken Okiishi

Painting and Screen Otherwise
Michael Sanchez

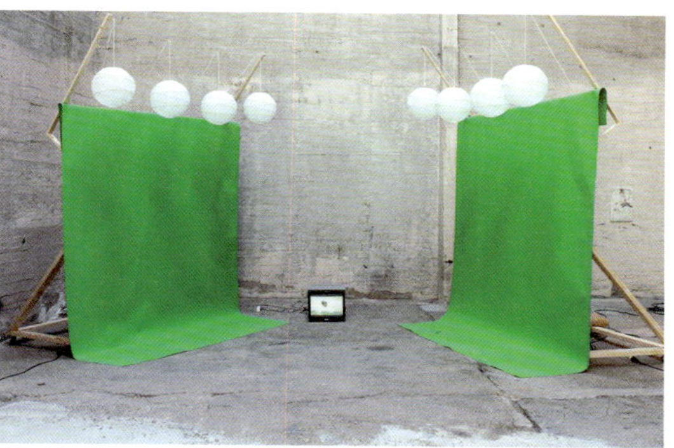

parapluis/paraplyer/'nobody can tell the why of it'/1857/oslo/2011, 2011 (installation view, *Nobody Can Tell the Why of It*, 1857, Oslo, May 27–August 14, 2011). Digital video, production monitors, paper; wood; wheels; lamps; sandbags; and speakers; dimensions variable

Although painting has always accommodated the technical requirements of different media of distribution, from tapestries to engravings to photographs, the ascendant medium now is the IPS screen produced in various forms by Apple and its competitors. While historical attempts to distribute art through new media like television met with only limited success, the distribution of painting through the touch-screen interface is today largely a fait accompli.

While this shift from print to blog and feed began some time ago, the complex accommodations and counteractions of art in relation to it have only recently become visible. Painting, for example, underwent a series of mutations at about the turn of the current decade. At that time, browsing through one of the major art aggregators would have revealed a profusion of abstract, monochrome, and pattern paintings flowing through the channels of the art market, frequently in diminutive styles and formats. This is, I believe, the result of several factors. A market disproportionately concentrated on young artists demanded that these artists make small, investible works. Compounding this fact were the ways in which the market converged with the portable media technology that gained momentum at the same time.

Since the technology presents images of paintings both in a grid of thumbnails and as high-resolution images, the most successful paintings work equally well in both of these scales. The scalability of monochromes and pattern paintings make them the most strategic forms: their scalar flexibility means that they can be viewed in any size, from thumbnail to wallpaper. They are low-information forms, which means that they function well as thumbnails. But they also accommodate large-scale viewing through both their all-over informational structure and their incorporation of subtle textural and relief effects that can only be appreciated in high-resolution, pleasantly offsetting the flatness of the touch screen.

Even the new gestural vocabulary that portable devices taught the population at about this time—tiny swipes and taps—migrated into painting. The work of the painter G. is paradigmatic here. His work is made of newspapers affixed to canvas, from which is torn a continuous gestural script of short U-shaped gestures and dots. The paintings come in different sizes but always with the same scalable motif and always in a vertical format, mirroring the default vertical orientation of the phone. The newspapers reverse-remediate the screens onto which they are distributed. Like all old media distributed through a newer medium, they provide a therapeutic visual effect. Their gray tones counteract the brightness of the screens; the layered effect of newspaper on newspaper counteracts their flatness. By staging installation shots with a gray cat roaming around his paintings, G. draws an explicit parallel between the experience of viewing his work and viewing photos of cats online (an activity that accounts for an enormous percentage of internet traffic). Paintings as cats: gray, modest, friendly, and in styles designed to trigger the instant affective response that keeps the image in circulation; images of paintings to be petted like cats as the fingers of the viewer scroll from one gray image to the next.

In G.'s work, painting and its screen image fuse. Again, the reasons for this are both economic and media-historical. As galleries began to use tablets not only to show their inventory to collectors physically visiting their sites but also to sell works solely on the basis of JPEGs, it has become increasingly necessary that the painting and the JPEG look exactly like each other. Assuming that works are purchased solely for investment purposes on the basis of JPEGs, it is not difficult to imagine an instance in which even their buyer never sees them in person and sends them straight into storage.

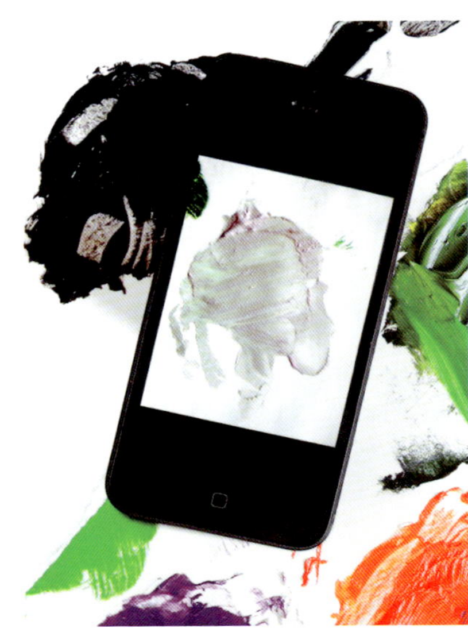
The artist's palette

Indeed, for certain segments of the market, it seems likely that rising urban rents and the new ubiquity of internet distribution may transform the gallery in dramatic ways. At this point it is not difficult to imagine a world in which the gallery becomes the off-site digital photo studio of a more flexibly engaged advisor. Video walkthroughs of gallery shows are already becoming more common, perhaps presaging the rise of virtual-reality exhibition views in conjunction with image aggregators. We may soon find ourselves in a situation where *no one* involved in the transaction views an artwork in person. From an artist's offsite fabrication facility to an advisor's photo studio to a collector's storage unit, the object withdraws entirely from human eyes.

This is still largely hypothetical. Within the very actual distribution logic of painting since the turn of the decade, however, painting is already made to look as much like its screen image as possible. But in order to pull off this trick, it cannot be materially identical to the screen. Painting must be separate from it in order to be mediated by it: to appear properly *on* a screen, painting cannot already *be* a screen.

In a series of works on view at the Biennial, O.'s crucial move is to conflate these two, fusing painting and screen on the level of a chemical bond. This conflation unleashes a whole series of paradoxes. Whereas a painting usually generates a single image, an infinite number of images can be taken of these screen-painting hybrids. No one JPEG can capture them. Yet their status as unique objects that must be seen in person is achieved precisely by the fact that they are painted onto their medium of distribution. And even this move, perverse as it is, is complicated by the fact that O. retroactively displaces the IPS touchscreen back onto the HDTV, mimicking painting's mimicking of touch-sensitive gestures on a surface that cannot respond to them.

Within an art media system currently tooled for scrolling image distribution, painting that literally takes the form of a screen poses a problem. Although video footage can be taken of these works and distributed through platforms like Vine, the interaction of the paint with the screen beneath is almost impossible to capture on another screen, particularly for a viewer habituated to platforms that privilege the still JPEG. Oscillating between the painted marks on the surface and the video beneath, the eye perceives the moving video as pure information, aggregates of shapes and color, rather than as people or objects. The paint changes both in relation to its backlighting and frontlighting, the screen-like fluorescent lights of the gallery complemented by warm spotlights designed to activate the effects of the paint (aptly named "interference").

The emphasis that these works place on irreproducible visual experience registers the current anxiety about a certain distribution logic that renders a visit to the gallery or museum superfluous. As such, they are products of this liminal media-historical moment, circulating in two convergent but fundamentally incommensurate systems. The oddness of these objects results from how, in moving through these systems, they rearrange their terms.

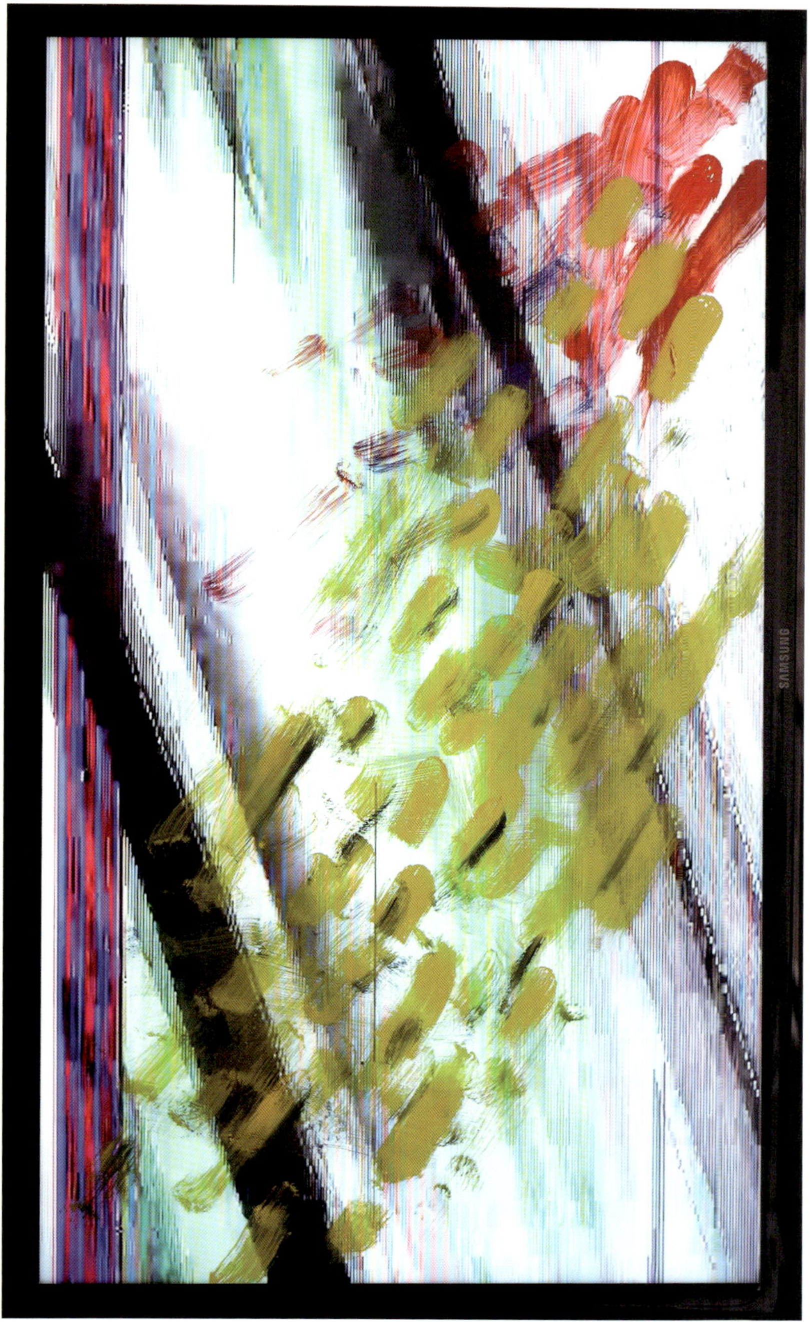

gesture/data, 2013 (detail). Oil on two flat-screen televisions and video transferred to USB flash drive, color, sound; 35 5/16 × 21 × 3 11/16 in. (89.7 × 53.3 × 9.4 cm) each. Collection of Pedro Barbosa

Pauline Oliveros

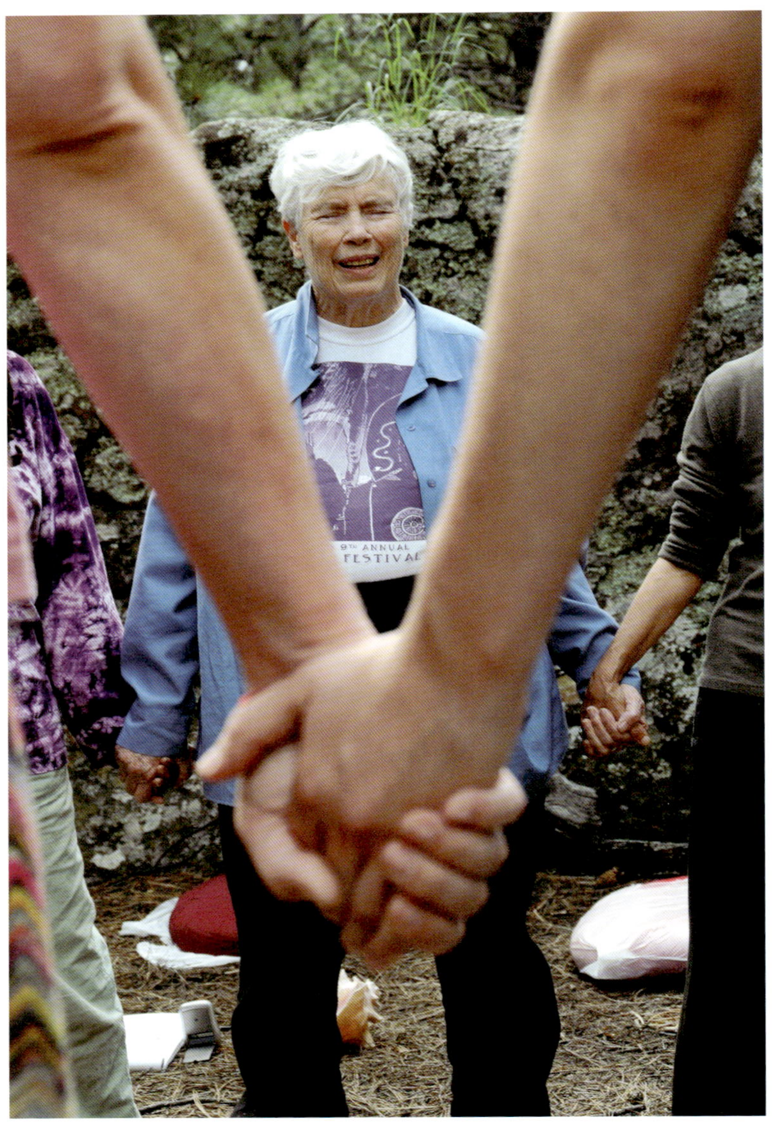

Oliveros directs Zena's Circle at Rose Mountain, New Mexico, August 2006

Born 1932 in Houston, TX

Lives in Kingston, NY

Pauline Oliveros: Pure Noise

Louise Gray

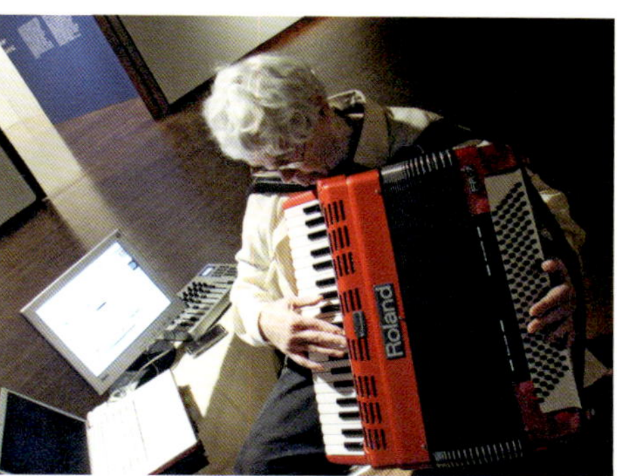

Oliveros performing "Pauline's Solo," Krannert Art Museum, University of Illinois at Urbana-Champaign, 2009

In Pauline Oliveros's interviews with Martha Mockus for the 2008 book *Sounding Out: Pauline Oliveros and Lesbian Musicality*,[1] the artist and composer recounts an early childhood memory, of hours spent listening to her grandfather's crystal-radio set. The young Oliveros mused on the rhythmic possibilities of the dot-dot-dashes generated by the set's Morse-code key, the static between radio stations, and the sounds records made as the windup mechanism of a record player slowed. From these elements were germinated the twin interests of Oliveros's life: music and technology.

Born in 1932 and raised in Houston, Oliveros is an accordionist by training, but her early exposure to music technologies—tapes, computers, and, more recently, digital modes—has been fundamental in shaping the way she works. Her initial contact with sound equipment came in the form of a Sears Roebuck wire recorder—a present from her mother in 1947—and then, in 1953, she acquired a Silvertone magnetic-tape recorder. These machines, with their possibilities of reordering sonic events, suggested to Oliveros radical new possibilities for composition—as well as a method by which narratives of gender and sexuality could be liberated.

After studying music at the University of Houston, Oliveros transferred to San Francisco State College and later joined the influential San Francisco Tape Music Center, founded in 1961 by composers Morton Subotnick and Ramon Sender and engaging many other significant composers, including Terry Riley, Steve Reich, and La Monte Young. When the center subsequently moved to Mills College, in Oakland, Oliveros became its director.

Her Silvertone recorder was pressed into action for Oliveros's first tape work, *Time Perspectives* (1960), a four-channel, labor-intensive composition that involved hundreds of yards of spooled audiotape and four speakers at its premiere at the San Francisco Conservatory of Music on December 18, 1961. For Oliveros, this composition marked not only a departure from conventionally notated scores but also a new approach to performance, as the physical interaction with the instrument (in this case, a manipulated tape recorder) and the importance of improvisation came into focus.

Just how extensively Oliveros was reshaping sound during this period is evidenced by *Bye Bye Butterfly* (1965), a two-channel tape work revising Puccini's 1904 opera *Madama Butterfly*. The work began by chance when Oliveros selected a record in her studio that turned out to be the aria from *Madama Butterfly*. Using a turntable, two oscillators, and a tape delay—her own ad-hoc system—Oliveros re-edited and re-presented the aria in an immediate and improvisational way. In the process she dispensed with the titular character's self-sacrificing heterosexuality (in Oliveros's version of the story, Butterfly's female friends are present, while her feckless lover, Lieutenant Pinkerton, is not), rejecting the opera's Orientalist fantasies. This kind of playful energizing of art through

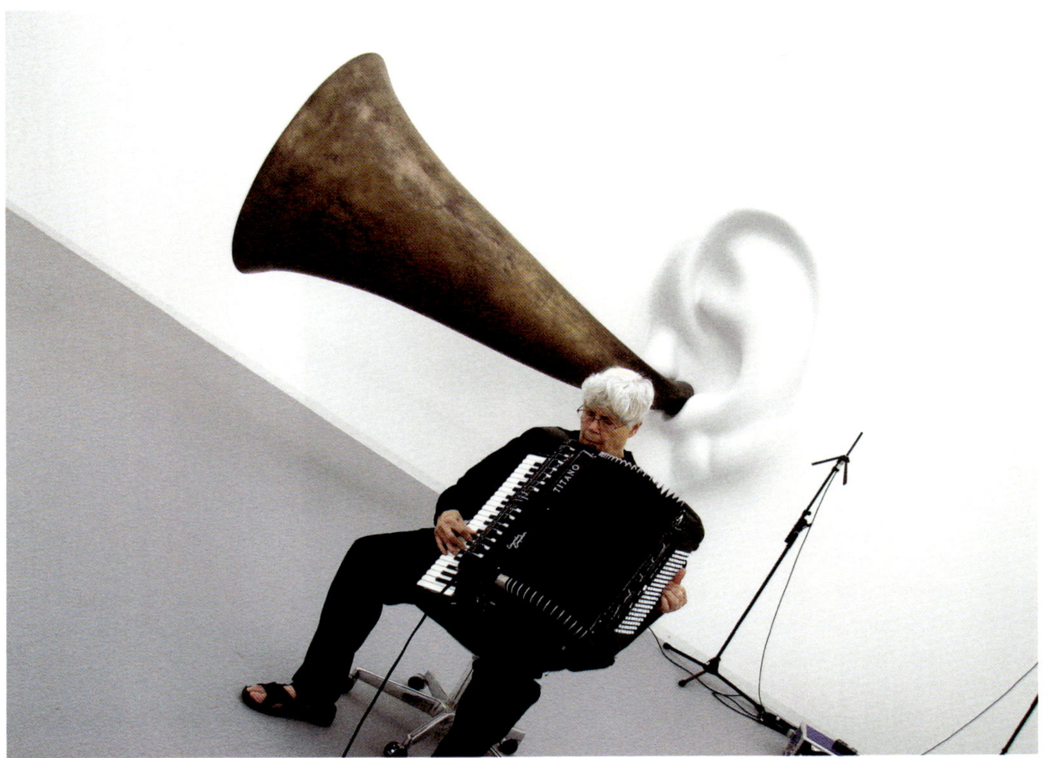

Oliveros performing "Pauline's Solo" with John Baldessari's *Beethoven's Trumpet (With Ear) Opus # 133* (2007) at Kunstverein Bonn, Germany, 2007

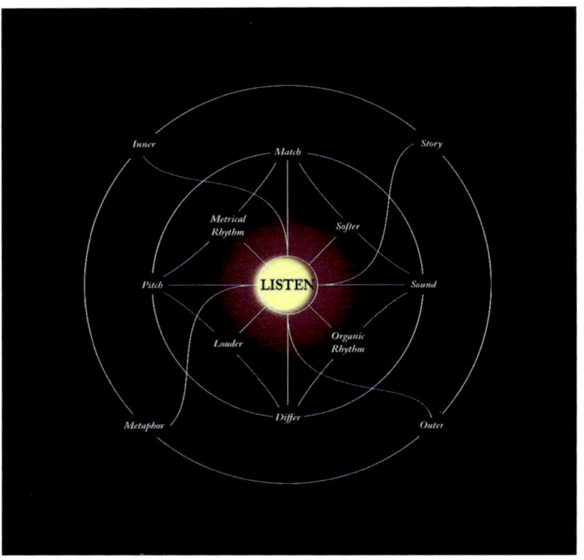

Nico Bovoso, art based on the score for *Wind Horse Mandala* (1990), used for the cover of Oliveros's *Anthology of Text Scores*, edited by Samuel Golter (Deep Listening Institute, 2013)

political consciousness-raising has remained central to many of Oliveros's endeavors over the years.

While teaching at the University of California, San Diego, in the late 1960s, she formed the ♀ Ensemble with a group of women—mostly graduate students, not all of them musicians—to explore the possibilities of sonic improvisatory work. With such composers as Annea Lockwood, Ruth Anderson, and Doris Hays, Oliveros has been instrumental in creating a solid and autonomous place for women in contemporary music—and in developing an audience and a market devoted specifically to female composers.

Collaboration is at the heart of Oliveros's work. In 1965 she initiated what she calls the Expanded Instrument System (EIS), a way of working that has taken her from acoustic and analogue modes to the digital and cyber technologies of recent years. Still in existence, the EIS program involves joining forces with other musicians and software engineers. The importance of cooperation to Oliveros is also manifest in a process that she calls deep listening: an acute and intensive experience that involves both mental and somatic attention, in tandem with an awareness of one's own persona in relation to those of others.

Although Oliveros coined the term *deep listening* in 1988 (her Deep Listening Band and Deep Listening Institute followed), the practice stretches back to some of her earliest endeavors, such as Sonic Meditations, a series of twenty-five instructional works begun in the late 1960s. With titles such as *Teach Yourself to Fly*, *Energy Changes*, and *Pure Noise*, these meditations started as a series of exercises for the ♀ Ensemble. More intimate than a set of Fluxus instructions, the meditations were eventually collated and published in 1974, dedicated to Amelia Earhart and the ♀ Ensemble. Other composers have certainly influenced the concept of deep listening as well, especially John Cage, whose revolutionary "silent" work, *4'33"* (1952), underlines the importance of listening as a way of constructing and framing a work of art. It also seems likely that Oliveros's training in the martial disciplines of tai chi and karate (she holds a black belt in the latter) played a role in these meditative approaches.

Oliveros's understanding of humanity's place within a universe of sound is crucial to her vision. "I am interested in the sensual nature of sound, its power of release and change," she wrote in 1995.[2] Nowhere is this more dramatically expressed than in her 1970 work *To Valerie Solanas and Marilyn Monroe in Recognition of Their Desperation*——. Named for the author of the *SCUM Manifesto*, infamous also for attempting to kill Andy Warhol in 1967, and for the iconic movie star who committed suicide in 1962, *To Valerie Solanas . . .* is a work for small ensemble or large orchestra, with rules that prevent the hierarchy of one voice or group of musicians over any other.

This sounding and listening—composer Suzanne Cusick calls it a "continuous circulation of power"[3]—implies social and political consequences. These can be as intimate as an audience humming together—as in her 1980 *MMM (Lullaby for Daisy Pauline, born September 19, 1979)*[4]—or as vital as realizing one's own role in merging the boundaries among performer, performance, and listener. Listening exercises by artists and crowds in the recent Occupy movement owe a debt to Oliveros's listening meditations, for whatever else sound is—compositional, tonal, or structured—it is also profoundly social. Indeed, Oliveros's emphasis on the communal has influenced and invigorated many younger artists. Using *To Valerie Solanas . . .* as their starting point, artists Pauline Boudry and Renate Lorenz created in 2013 an installation and film of the same title, following Oliveros's lead—as a lesbian feminist—in seeking a queer space in art.

Sound, Oliveros points out, is the first of our senses to develop and the last of our senses to leave us: to live within sound is a fundamental part of being human. Indeed, to see Oliveros perform on her digital accordion, drawing out the bellows of her instrument in a wide arc of movement, is to understand the motif of breath as the basis of sound.

1. Martha Mockus, *Sounding Out: Pauline Oliveros and Lesbian Musicality* (New York: Routledge, 2008).
2. Pauline Oliveros, "Acoustic and Virtual Space as a Dynamic Element of Music," *Leonardo Music Journal* 5 (1995): 19.
3. Suzanne G. Cusick, "On a Lesbian Relationship with Music: A Serious Effort Not to Think Straight," in *Queering the Pitch: The New Gay and Lesbian Musicology*, ed. Philip Brett, Elizabeth Wood, and Gary C. Thomas (New York: Routledge, 1994), 76. Cited in Mockus, 10.
4. Critic Tom Johnson wrote about his experiences listening to Oliveros's *MMM* in the *Village Voice*, June 23, 1980. His columns are collected in *The Voice of New Music, New York City, 1972–1982* (Eindhoven, Netherlands: Het Apollohuis, 1989), see 443–44.

Miljohn Ruperto

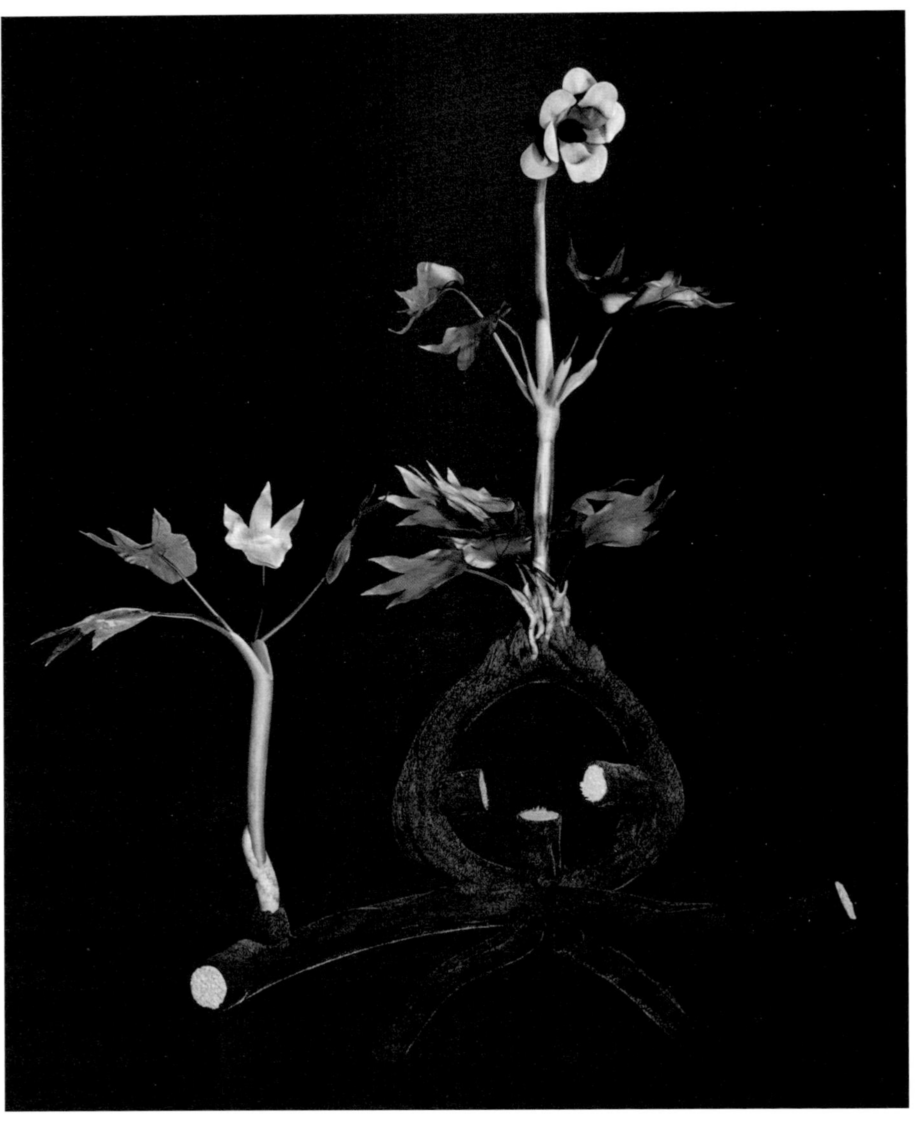

Miljohn Ruperto and Ulrik Heltoft (b. 1973), "Specimen 52r Podzim" from *Voynich Botanical Studies*, 2012– . Gelatin silver print, 19 11/16 × 15 3/4 in. (50 × 40 cm)

Born 1971 in
Manila, The Philippines

Lives in
Los Angeles, CA

Miljohn Ruperto

Re:Animation

Esther Leslie

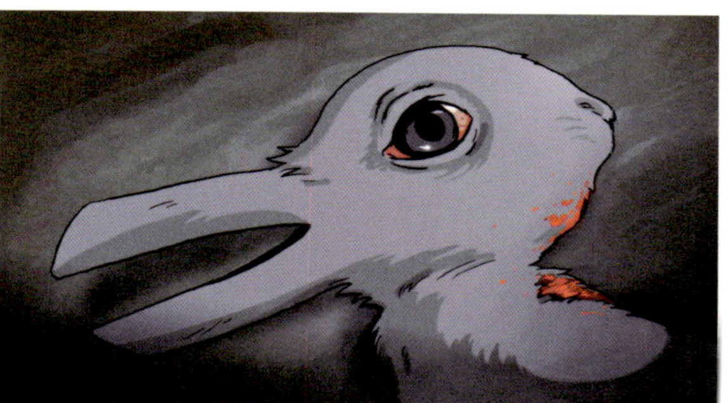

Janus, 2014. Digital image. Illustration by Aimée de Jongh (b. 1988)

In 2012, Russian scientists reported that they had managed to germinate the little arctic flowers of the species *Silene stenophylla* from seeds buried thirty-two thousand years ago by an Ice Age rodent in the permafrost of Siberia. The seeds, surrounded by the bones of woolly mammoths and bisons, had been frozen more than a hundred meters belowground. Once flowered, the ancient plant's petals were subtly different from the modern-day narrow-leafed campion, like a drawing that has been altered just a little. The frost shelters an archive. As global warming thaws it, the possibility of de-extinction emerges. At work in this process is reanimation. It is not animation—the input of life where it never existed before—which lends vivacity to a flat and/or inert model or image. Rather, it gives back life to what once had it. To reanimate—a notion that originated in European letters at the beginning of the 1600s—means to restore life or consciousness, to make alive again. It was reanimation that Antonie van Leeuwenhoek aspired to when he swept the dust from a roof's gutter in 1702 and added water to it. Within a few moments, he saw through his microscope animalcules coming to life, unfurling their desiccated bodies and swimming around their glass container.[1]

Ulrik Heltoft and Miljohn Ruperto's *Voynich Botanical Studies* both animates and reanimates. It rouses plants into life, as it constitutes three-dimensional forms, digitally constructing them, replete with textures promiscuously borrowed from various kingdoms of matter. These plants born out of light and liquid crystal are then photographed as handsome specimens, luminous and tangible. They receive more substantiality in this act of attention than they possessed hitherto, when they languished mysteriously in the fifteenth-century codex known as the Voynich Manuscript, alongside an impenetrable text in an indecipherable language. Heltoft and Ruperto have likely resurrected old plants illustrated in this manuscript that have only possibly existed. In addition to the plants, the manuscript itself is reanimated in their procedure. Accessed anew, the forms contained within it are laid out robustly, as if they're claiming a right to exist on their own terms, shedding the uncrackable code that only makes them more opaque. Reanimated plants and books: there are affinities between these two. Plants and printed items share matter and form. Paper and inks are vegetal. And both have leaves.

For Johann Wolfgang von Goethe, the botanist and poet, the leaf is the key to the plant code. He had an inkling of this code in 1784, when he wrote to a friend that he was now deciphering the "book of nature," letter by letter.[2] In 1790, he declared that all parts of a plant are leaves articulating themselves in different forms. What are called stamens or calyxes are transformed folia; the pod is a single, folded leaf with its edges grown together; husks consist of leaves grown over one another; compound capsules are several leaves united around a central point with their inner sides open toward one another and their edges joined. From cotyledon to petal, all is leaf in a variety of forms. The leaf that is the plant is mutable, self-transforming, and animate—or, as Goethe put it, metamorphosing. The leaf is a kind of artwork, morphing and modeling. Aesthetic botany of this kind witnesses an animating force coursing through nature as its forms proliferate. Goethe took the leaf of endless forms back to its origin, seeking the "primal plant," the first leaf, a prototype out of which will unfurl, shifting minutely in form, all the plants that are yet to come. When Goethe theorized and drew the incremental phases of plant morphology, he was developing the cultural form that would become animation.

This notion of the primal plant is adapted in the idea of primal forms or phenomena—the building blocks of style, as adopted by the cataloguer of plant life Karl Blossfeldt. His photographic album *Urformen der Kunst* (Primal Forms of Art, 1928)—homes in on leaves, flowers, buds, and stems, seeking future forms in the original articulations of nature.[3] Under Blossfeldt's camera's eye, the plant becomes a resource from which all forms spring—forms of life, objects, and artworks. In a review of Blossfeldt's photo album, Walter Benjamin names some of the forms that humans will imitate over time, though they will only know this is what they have done once their imaging technologies make the plants' intricacies more visible: ancient columns in horse willow, a Gothic bishop's staff in the ostrich fern, a rose window in saxifrage blossom, and totem poles in tenfold enlargements of chestnut and maple shoots.[4] Blossfeldt's stagings animate his plants in curious ways, rendering them prototypes of human inventions.

Heltoft and Ruperto's plant forms are as much reconstructions of what may once have been (reanimations) as constructions of what may never have existed outside their image form in the manuscript (animations). The images reanimate plants that have or might have been in an act of de-extinction that conquers the passage of time. Looking forward, like Blossfeldt, the images open up nature by anticipating a gamut of forms, an animated realm of possible future structures or ones detectable in the present. Everything that will come to exist in the future, plants and artworks, is, in a sense, an animated transposition of the primal leaf—including the practical and strange hybrids of genetic modification.

Animation and reanimation is at work in Ruperto's *Janus*, too. Janus, the god of beginnings and transitions, looks backward and forward across time and borderlines. The wreathed image stitches the past to the future, as a duck-rabbit creature oscillates between life and death. When it dies, it loops back into life again. The cartoon on which *Janus* is based was originally published in a German humor magazine in October 1892, which was the same month and year in which the first hand-drawn, hand-colored moving animated pictures, by Émile Reynaud, were shown, in Paris in the Cabinet Fantastique at the Musée Grévin. Simultaneously, visual research into perception discovered that the viewing eye wobbles constantly in small, jerky movements—saccades—punctuated by stops, or fixations. In 1892, this stop-start movement of the eye met the technological principle of the various forms of animation developed in looping optical entertainments, from the zoetrope to the praxinoscope to the zoopraxiscope to the kinetoscope and all the rest, all based on stillness animated into life. Backward and forward, around and around, the slides shift, the disks and the strips spin in a repeating movement. In *Janus*, the eye participates in the work of transitioning from animation to reanimation, from life to death to life. The duck-rabbit figure amplifies the eyes' saccades and fixations as they fail to rest on any one view. The animation of the jerking eye meets the reanimation of the duck-rabbit. Images and indeterminate forms live and live again.

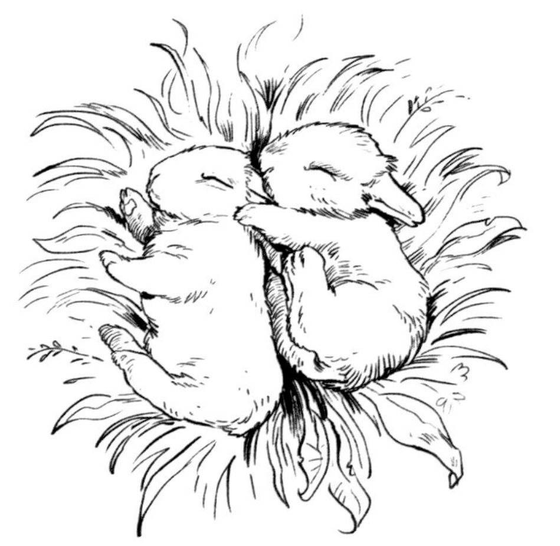

Duck-rabbit early ideas for *Janus*, 2014. Illustration by Aimée de Jongh

1. See D. Keilin, "The Leeuwenhoek Lecture: The Problem of Anabiosis or Latent Life: History and Current Concept," in *Proceedings of the Royal Society of London: Series B, Biological Sciences* 150, no. 939 (17 March 1959), 151.
2. J. W. Goethe, introduction to *The Metamorphosis of Plants* (Cambridge, MA: MIT Press, 2009), vii.
3. Karl Blossfeldt, *Urformen der Kunst* (Berlin: Ernst Wasmuth, 1928).
4. Walter Benjamin, *Selected Writings: 1927–1930* (Cambridge, MA: Harvard University Press, 2005), 156.

Miljohn Ruperto

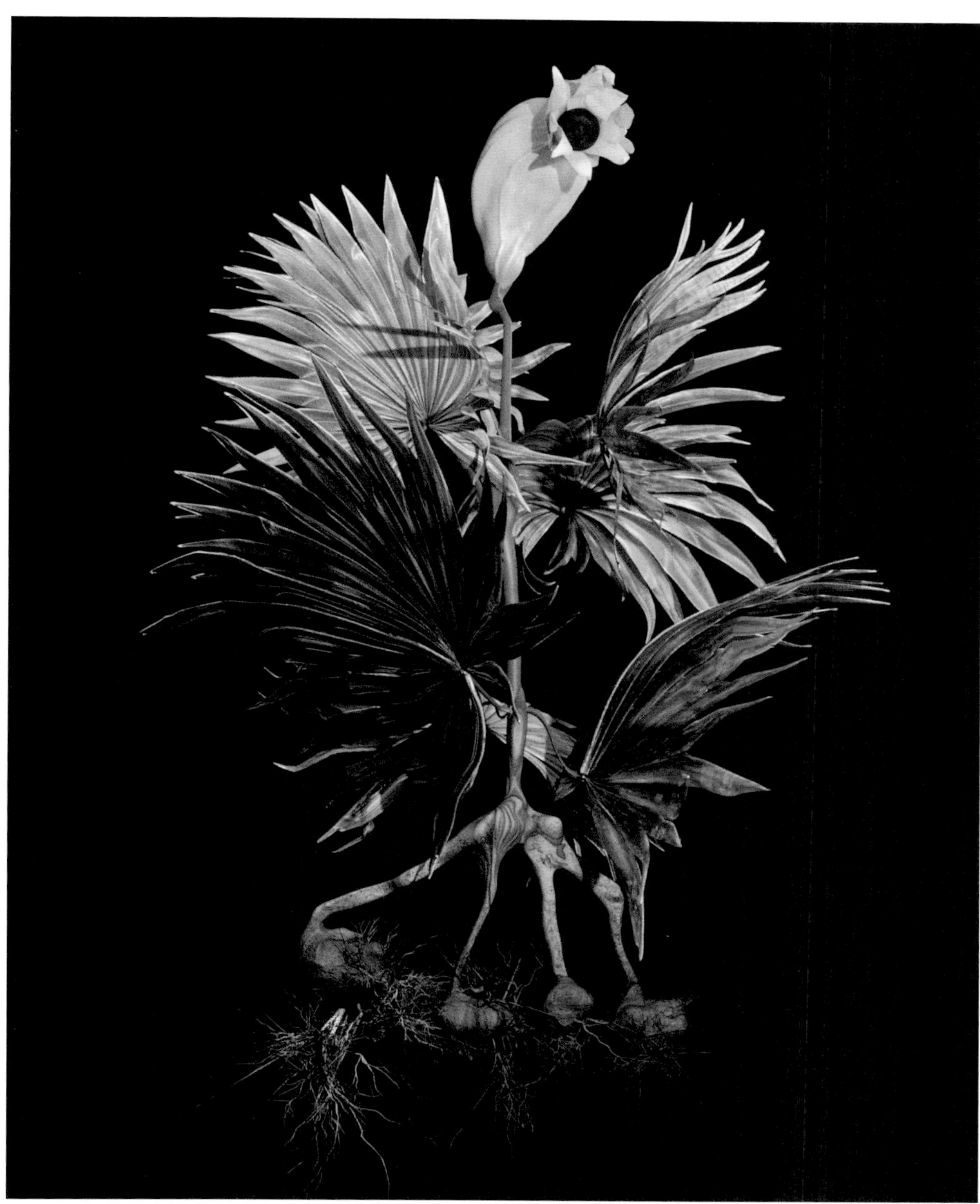

Miljohn Ruperto and Ulrik Heltoft, “Specimen 56v Jaro” from *Voynich Botanical Studies*, 2012–. Gelatin silver print, 19 11/16 × 15 3/4 in. (50 × 40 cm)

Jacolby Satterwhite

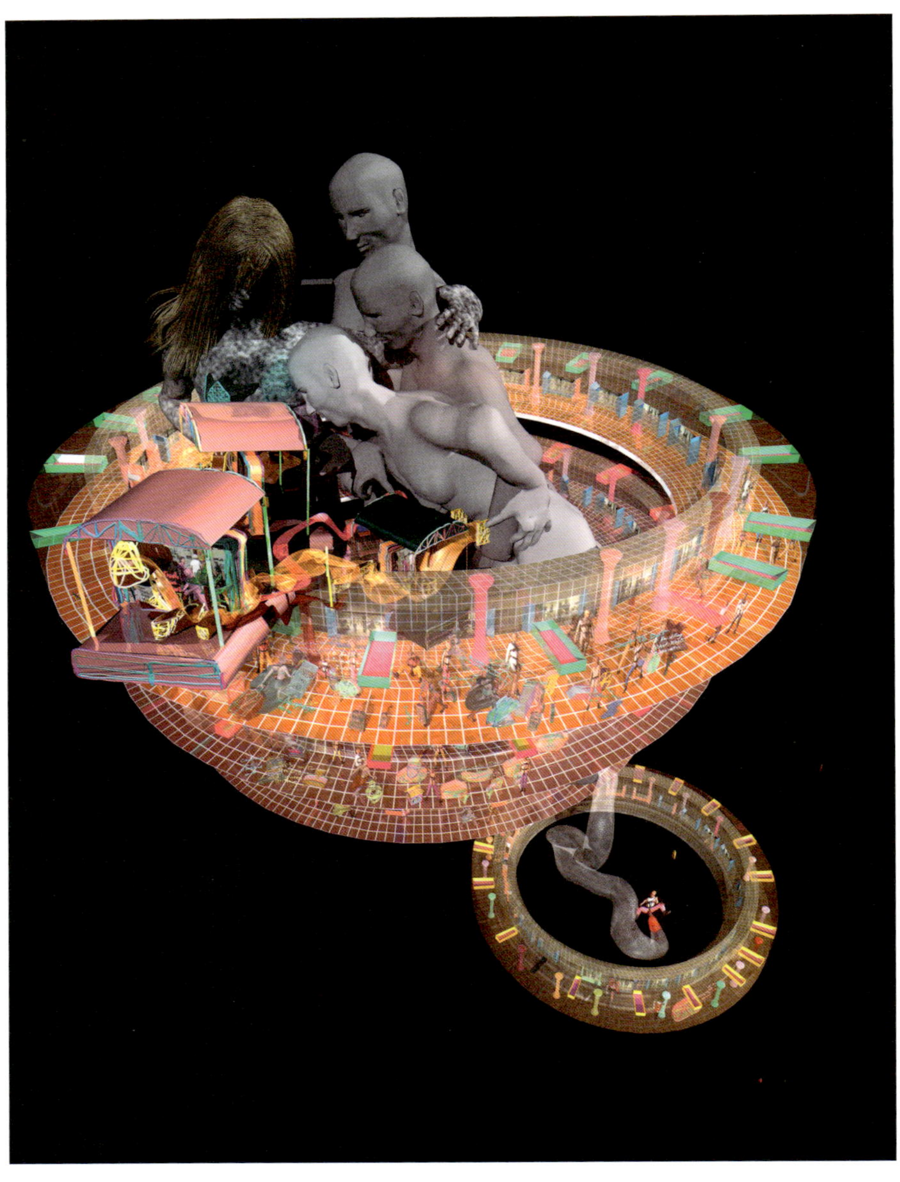

"Subway," still from the high-definition digital video *Reifying Desire 6*, 2014. Chromogenic print, 80 × 59 in. (203.2 × 149.9 cm)

Born 1986 in Columbia, SC

Lives in New York, NY

Jacolby Satterwhite

A Multitude of Dimensions
Naomi Beckwith

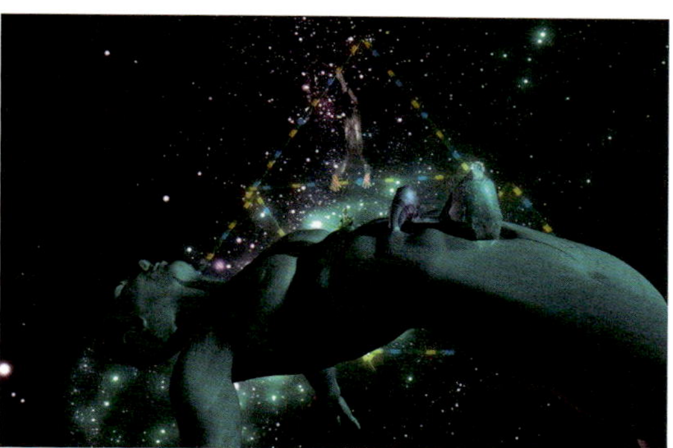

"Maternity," still from the high-definition digital video *Reifying Desire 6*, 2014. Chromogenic print, 53 × 30 in. (134.6 × 76.2 cm)

When asked about the origins of voguing—a vocabulary of stylized dance gestures and poses that he often references in his performances—Jacolby Satterwhite responds that they lie in the sixteenth century. Such temporal overreaching may seem strange considering voguing's popular roots in New York's late-twentieth-century ballroom club scene. Yet Satterwhite's observation acknowledges a direct line of descent linking this dance form, as well as the very idea of "the pose," to portraiture, a five-hundred–year tradition of self-fashioning and performativity. This correlation exemplifies what he calls his "hybrid thinking," connecting multiple, seemingly disparate sources of visual, historical, and cultural information—from dance and art history to family memorabilia and medical imagery. He synthesizes these into performance and video works whose allusions are as broad and uncanny as his ability to make his agglomerations appear seamless.

Take, for instance, Satterwhite's 2012 video work *Reifying Desire 3*, a filmic collage of surreal scenes embedded one inside another. Situated in the placeless ether of cyberspace, the computer-generated video opens with a group of nude, totemic characters who together refigure Caravaggio's shadowy *The Incredulity of Saint Thomas* (c. 1602). At the same time, the tableau also stages a kind of erotic insemination scene that unfolds onto another scene, in which an infinite number of Satterwhites, multiplied like a mass of Fritz Langian workers and dressed in identical space-age bodysuits, perform a series of ritualistic moves around a central Satterwhite. As the point of view shifts to hover above the dancing figures, we see another nude male character manipulating a set of hand-drawn objects comprising some sort of mechanical bellows that seem to be an energy source for the entire complex. The artist has borrowed those implements from a body of thousands of drawings that Satterwhite's mother made over several years and that have provided an endless source of imagery and a working iconography for the artist. This video is a wholly constructed fantasy world, yet within it he has remixed elements from pop culture, memory, and family history to create a nonnarrative, speculative space. Satterwhite is one of many visual artists in recent years who has found working with and inventing narratives conceptually fruitful.

While *Reifying Desire 3* depicts a fully invented cyberspace world, many of Satterwhite's performances take place in the analogue, physical world. In a series of compelling videos, he documents guerrilla actions in which he is clad in a futuristic patterned bodysuit and performs a series of supple movements taken from voguing, martial arts, and choreographer William Forsythe's angular dance techniques. The multichannel video *Model It* (2010) depicts Satterwhite on New York's Madison Avenue, acting as an alien, hyperkinetic counterpoint to the mass-marketed images of luxury and high fashion surrounding him. *Forest Nymph* (2010) places the

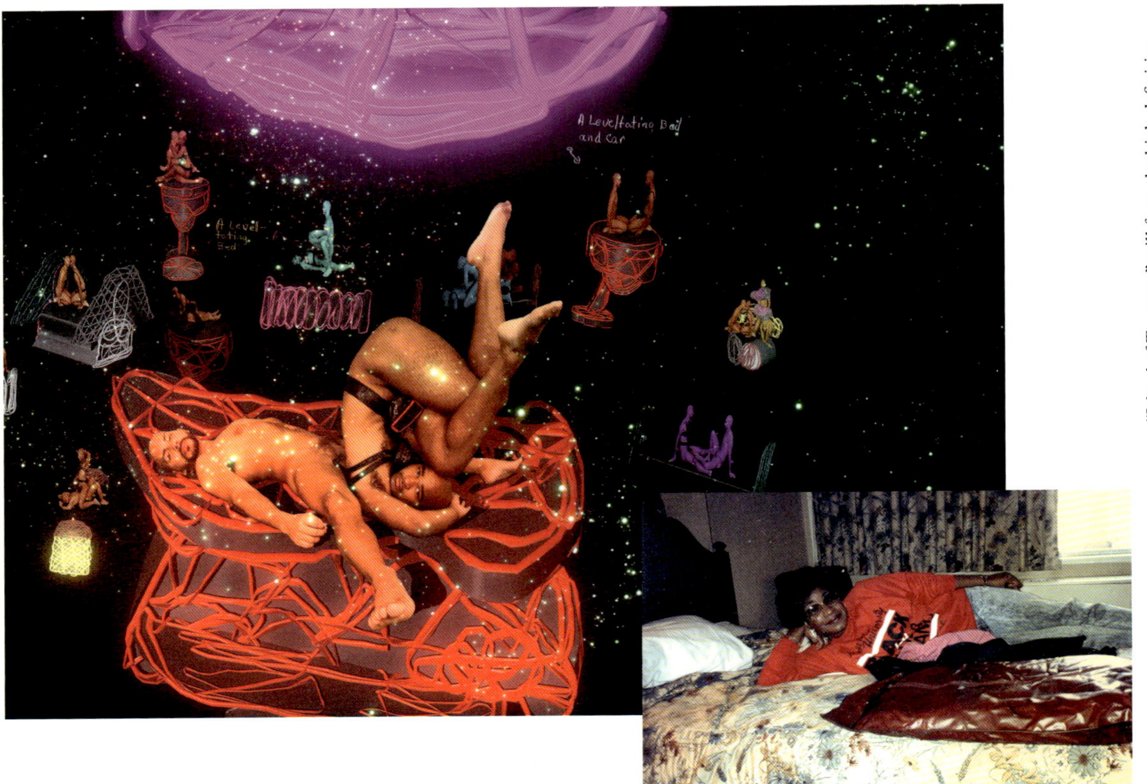

"Island of Treasure," still from the high-definition digital video *Reifying Desire 6*, 2014. Chromogenic print, 53 × 30 in. (134.6 × 76.2 cm)

Patricia Satterwhite on Levitating Bed

artist in a wooded landscape where he whips his head back and forth, swinging a long, thick braid reminiscent of a medieval flail as defense against digitally added fireballs. As live performances, his actions are inscrutable to the happenstance viewer, yet as videos—accompanied by house music and animations—their logic becomes clearer. In fact, the postproduction additions are visual manifestations of the things Satterwhite imagines as he performs; thus the videos reveal the inner workings of the artist's imagination. In many ways, Satterwhite's actions recall Adrian Piper's *Aretha Franklin Catalysis* performances (1971–72), in which Piper dances in public to the "Respect" anthem, but the music is playing only in her own head.

Piper's and Satterwhite's performances depict the moment when the artist enters an altered state of consciousness, inhabiting an internal world that is subjectively tangible and coherent but appearing lunatic or alien to observers. These artworks blur the line between insanity and intentionality—a personal concern for Satterwhite—while poetically embodying the sense of otherness that comes with being in an alienating or traumatizing environment.

When asked about the modeling in his digital videos or prints, Satterwhite says he wants the works to exist in four dimensions. Modern physics defines the fourth dimension as time, but the artist proposes an alternative way of perceiving Euclidean three-dimensional space and objects: a constantly evolving spatial awareness that integrates an object and its environment with the viewer's changing perspective. This is not a speculative notion for Satterwhite; rather, it feels absolutely possible to someone raised in a digital culture. An erstwhile gamer and programmer, Satterwhite is as comfortable in digital space as in its physical counterpart. He easily navigates and produces cinematographic clips characterized by shifting, floating points of view and swings from a macrocosmic pan to a microscopic focus—as in *Reifying Desire 5* (2013), which reveals an entirely plausible scene-within-a-scene at perfectly believable human scale.

Of course, Satterwhite is not the first artist who has attempted to defy time and geometry: it was the dream of the Cubists to puncture the two-dimensional plane over a century ago. In that aspiration, Satterwhite sees an attempt to converge seemingly incongruent dualities:

interior and exterior, three-dimensional and two-dimensional, the public sphere and the private realm. For instance, he considers Pablo Picasso's *Les Demoiselles d'Avignon* (1907) a testament to the artist's obsession with prostitutes, women who convert a private act into public commerce. Satterwhite interprets Cubism's aesthetic and formal inventions as derivatives of the movement's conceptual preoccupations; these mirror his own use of space as a conceptual realization of his concerns with the inner workings of the mind and its outward expressions.

While much of Satterwhite's work originates from a kind of introspection, lately he's begun to enlist the public as coconspirators in his explorations. A new project, *Grey* (2013–), documents visitors to his studio who are invited to respond to or interpret objects from his *Matriarch's Rhapsody Codex* (2012). The "codex" is a digital database of images and texts taken from the thousands of designs for QVC-style domestic products and instructions for living that were invented, but unrealized, by the artist's mother. Over the course of a year, Satterwhite faithfully transcribed her drawings, even reproducing her handwriting, and has incorporated their formal elements into his two-dimensional works, patterns for his bodysuits, and animations for videos such as the Reifying series. *Matriarch's Rhapsody Codex* is a tool with which Satterwhite can mine an archive of family photographs, videos, and memories to trace the real-life origins of some of his mother's imaginary products while simultaneously using the texts and forms as a vocabulary for building his artworks.

By inviting "the public" to engage with Mrs. Satterwhite's creative impulses, Satterwhite is effectively asking participants to find an entry point into someone else's mind. What results are playful scenes of creative movement and miming, theatrical acts that are also powerful exercises in empathy. In this empathic space that Satterwhite crafts with his visitors, he clues them in to his own practice of improvisational movement as a method of temporal displacement—to be elsewhere and present at the same time; to remix personal memory and a *longue durée* of art history and pop culture onto his performing body.

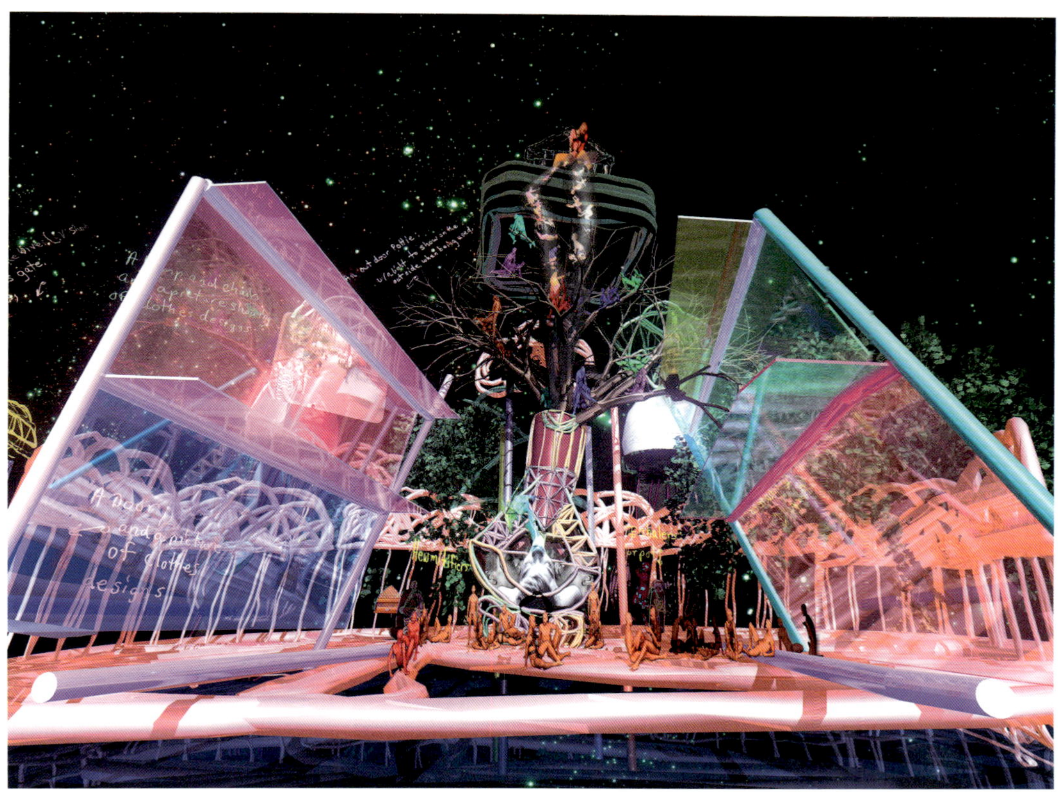

"Real Housewives," still from the high-definition digital video *Reifying Desire 6*, 2014. Chromogenic print, 53 × 30 in. (134.6 × 76.2 cm)

Semiotext(e)

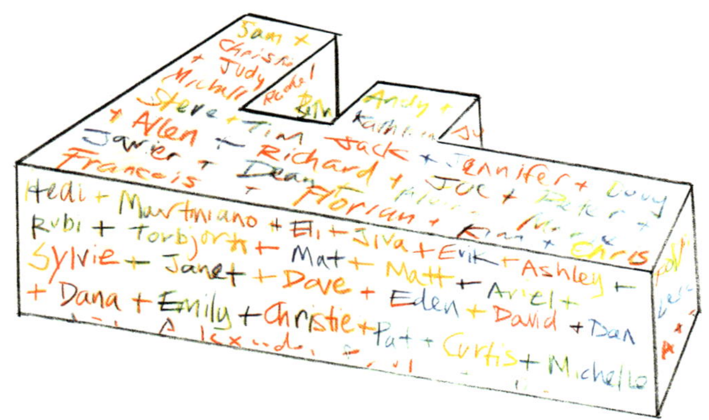

DELEUZE from A to Z

Sunday, April 29th

F as in Friendship

film Screening organized by

Semiotext(e)

at the

Mandrake Bar 2692 S La Cienega Blvd L.A. at 8:30 p.m

Paul Gellman, *F as in Friendship*, 2007. Lithograph, 22 × 15 in. (55.9 × 38.1 cm)

Founded in 1974

Based in Los Angeles, CA, since 2000

SOMEWHERE IN THE UNFINISHED: The History of Semiotext(e) Part 2, Los Angeles

It's not just you and me, it was people moving around doing their things and I was just trying to do mine and it didn't matter if it went anywhere or not. It was a feeling of energy and presence and there was a point. You don't always have to make a point—

—Sylvère Lotringer, from "The History of Semiotext(e)," by Chris Kraus and Lotringer, in *Hatred of Capitalism: A Semiotext(e) Reader* (2001)

Summer 2000: Hedi El Kholti, Sylvère Lotringer, Chris Kraus, Shannon Durbin, Ann Shelton, Giovanni Intra, and Mark von Schlegell gather on the shores of Lake Gregory in Crestline, California, during the July 4 weekend. Sylvère, Hedi, and Giovanni are working together on *More & Less 3*, a journal edited by Sylvère as part of his Critical Publications class at the Art Center College of Design in Pasadena. The magazine is already a year past its projected publication date. Other projects—most notably *Burroughs Live*, Lotringer's collection of interviews with William S. Burroughs—are in flux.

Founded by Lotringer, initially as a journal, in 1974, best known for its introduction of French theory to U.S. readers and its position "between high theory and art and life in America" (according to Avital Ronell), Semiotext(e) is about to end its nineteen-year association with Jim Fleming's Autonomedia, and begin a new business arrangement with the MIT Press. Up to this point, Semiotext(e)'s design and production have been handled exclusively by Fleming; it is completely unclear who will do these things after the separation. On the beach that afternoon, Chris hands out sections of the 846-page *Burroughs Live* galleys for everyone to proofread. Hedi, art director of *More & Less*, thinks: *This is crazy! English is my second language! I'm not a proofreader.* He will finish the layout of *Burroughs Live* (begun by Tim Koh) and will go on to design all subsequent Semiotext(e) titles.

2001: Semiotext(e) celebrates its move to the MIT Press and to Los Angeles with *Hatred of Capitalism*, its first and to date only anthology. Dedicated to "the end of an era," the book appears two weeks after the attacks of September 11. In *Bookforum*, Robert Glück sums it up best: "*Hatred of Capitalism* proposes a certain kind of freedom, which may involve unlearning as much as learning, dying as much as living—and which is characterized by an enlarged and even exalted sense of the possible."

2002–3: Shuttling between New York City, upstate New York, and Los Angeles, Sylvère and Chris discuss plans for how Semiotext(e) can continue beyond the success and institutionalization of French theory. Now that university presses are publishing philosophers that Semiotext(e) brought to American attention—Jean Baudrillard, Michel Foucault, Félix Guattari, Paul Virilio, and so on—why continue to do it? Our editorial efforts are voluntary. Started in 1991, Chris Kraus's Native Agents first-person-centered new fiction series concludes with Jane DeLynn's *Leash*. Sylvère reactivates friendships made while preparing the 1980 "Autonomia" issue of the *Semiotext(e)* journal in Italy, and recognizes the start of an "Italian theory" wave in the United States, which includes such figures as Antonio Negri, Christian Marazzi, Paolo Virno, Franco "Bifo" Berardi, and Maurizio Lazzarato. Semiotext(e) will subsequently publish works by each of these authors. December 17, 2002: RIP Giovanni Intra.

2004: Expected to adhere to the MIT Press's reasonable but rigid production schedules, Sylvère and Chris sense that they're out of their depth and consider abandoning the whole Semiotext(e) project. They never set out to be professional publishers. Morocco-born Hedi El Kholti, cofounder of the now-defunct Dilettante Press, becomes increasingly involved in all aspects of Semiotext(e). Hedi feels an equal affinity for Semiotext(e)'s literature and theory, and a new plan emerges. He sees an opportunity to expand the antibourgeois queer theory that Semiotext(e) had begun to advance two decades earlier (with the 1981 "Polysexuality" issue of the journal). Hedi, Sylvère, and Chris decide to work jointly as co-editors, with Hedi serving also as Semiotext(e)'s managing editor.

2005: Enjoying a new synergy, Semiotext(e) rents an office near MacArthur Park and hires artist Goody-B. Wiseman as its first paid associate. Writer Robert Dewhurst becomes its first intern. Several titles from Semiotext(e)'s Foreign Agents series are reissued with covers by contemporary artists; the new selection is called History of the Present. Native Agents publishes science-fiction novels by Mark von Schlegell and Maurice Dantec, and the "group novel" *Reena Spaulings* by the collective Bernadette Corporation. Marc Lowenthal joins the MIT Press and becomes Semiotext(e)'s liaison and ally. That winter, Sylvère invites Baudrillard to New York to give lectures at the New School and at the Jack Tilton Gallery. Hedi, Sylvère, and Chris meet to discuss future projects, including Pierre Guyotat's *Coma*, to be translated by Noura Wedell. Plans are made for Hedi, working with Marion Scemama, to finish Sylvère's long-pending interview project, *David Wojnarowicz: A Definitive History of Five or Six Years on the Lower East Side*, co-edited by Giancarlo Ambrosino, Justin Cavin, and Chris Kraus.

2006: Semiotext(e) publishes eight books, including Chris Kraus's *Torpor* and *David Wojnarowicz*, launched with events in Los Angeles and New York. Artist Mim Goodman produces the first Semiotext(e) website. Michael Silverblatt invites various Semiotext(e) writers onto his *Bookworm* show on National Public Radio. Andrew Berardini joins Semiotext(e) as an editorial associate, and Nick Zurko interns. Sylvère spends a semester in Baja California, where he plans to reside part-time after leaving Columbia University. The Deleuze A–Z film series, organized by Hedi and artist Marie Jager, is inaugurated November 12 at the Mandrake Bar in Culver City. Beginning with "A as in Animal," this occasional series will continue into 2009, screening rarely seen short films linked to Deleuze's interviews with journalist Claire Parnet. Posters are designed by artists Pauline Stella Sanchez, Eli Langer, Erick Bluhm, Jason Yates, and others. A core group of thirty or forty people attend most of the screenings.

2007: Semiotext(e) publishes thirteen books, including Tony Duvert's *The Good Sex Illustrated*, translated by Bruce Benderson, and Veronica Gonzalez Peña's *twin time: or, how death befell me*. On his blog, Dennis Cooper names *The Good Sex* as one of his ten favorite books of the year, calling it "spectacularly brilliant, beautiful, and wicked." March 6, 2007: RIP Jean Baudrillard.

2008: Semiotext(e) publishes eleven books, including *Correspondence: The Foundation of the Situationist International (June 1957–August 1960)* by Guy Debord, and *All the King's Horses* by Michèle Bernstein, translated by John Kelsey. Publication of Debord's correspondence feels both timeless and timely: the gallery scene and art world that it describes could be our own. Likewise, Bernstein's faux-confessional novel seems wholly contemporary. At a launch party for the two books at New York's Greene Naftali gallery (in January 2009), a Debord film is screened, and Eileen Myles and Chris Kraus give a dramatic reading from Bernstein's novel, as "Genevieve" and "Gilles." Joshua Clover will describe *All the King's Horses* in the *Nation* as "absolutely modern, boring as the surface of administered life. Within that infinitely flat moment, a secret adventure lurks almost in plain sight." Throughout the winter, Hedi works with Matt Fishbeck to create the "Holy Shit" issue of *Fake/Real*, a French zine. As Hedi writes in the introduction, "Everything falls into place magically if you try." These activities segue into the production of *Animal Shelter*, an occasional journal produced by Semiotext(e), with contributions by Ariana Reines, William E. Jones, Masha Tupitsyn, Sarah Lehrer-Graiwer, Paul Gellman, Erik Morse, Rachel Detroit, and others. Nondigital, nonhierarchical, the magazine functions as an intellectual diary, a snapshot of the present.

Chris and Hedi decide to continue the revisionist history of the 1980s (begun with Sylvère's Wojnarowicz project) by publishing archival books by Penny Arcade and Gary Indiana, two artists who are very important to us. Hedi travels to Penny Arcade's New York loft to gather images; Sarah Wang transcribes three of Arcade's performances as theater scripts.

That summer, during a trip home to Morocco, Hedi meets writer Abdellah Taïa. After a reading by Taïa in Casablanca, they walk around the city talking for most of the night. Hedi and Sylvère decide to option *The Coming Insurrection*, by the anonymous group known as the Invisible Committee, originally published in France by La Fabrique in 2007. Four months later, members of the Invisible Committee, accused of being terrorists, are arrested when riot police raid their homes and offices in the village of Tarnac, in central France.

On December 7, *Animal Shelter* is launched at the Mandrake Bar, with readings by Jennifer Doyle, Sarah Wang, Chris Kraus, and Paul Gellman, and with a screening of Lionel Soukaz and Guy Hocquenghem's *Royal Opera*, a late-1970s night stroll into Paris's most notorious cruising spots. August 2008: RIP Tony Duvert.

2009: Semiotext(e) publishes fourteen books, including Peter Sloterdijk's *Terror from the Air*; Eileen Myles's *The Importance of Being Iceland*; Abdellah Taïa's *Salvation Army*; Franco Berardi's *The Soul at Work*; and Penny Arcade's *Bad Reputation*. A semi-spontaneous "unofficial book signing" for *The Coming Insurrection* takes place in New York at the Union Square Barnes & Noble on June 14. Conceived as a prank, the event turns into a small occupation. As one friend recalls:

It was fun. We crowded the book signing area at Barnes & Noble, and when they tried to stop it, the crowd (maybe 100?) shouted down the security guards, who backed off. So we occupied the store much longer than we expected. A charismatic anarchist guy did all the talking, very crazy and animated, screaming about New York being a wasteland, about communism, etc., then the police came and we left, slowly, reading from the book all the way down four escalators.

Colin Moynihan's sympathetic report on the event appears in the next day's *New York Times*. Three weeks later, Glenn Beck denounces *The Coming Insurrection* on Fox News as "the most evil book in America," a diatribe he will continue throughout the summer. The book becomes the number-one nonfiction seller on Amazon.com. Semiotext(e) hosts a short U.S. tour for Taïa to promote *Salvation Army*, and cohosts a "Morocco" evening at Light Industry in honor of him and the publication *Bidoun*.

2010: Semiotext(e) publishes ten books, including Tiqqun's *Introduction to Civil War* and Tony Duvert's *Diary of an Innocent*. Semiotext(e) joins Facebook.

2011: Semiotext(e) publishes eight books, including *The Words and the Land* by Shlomo Sand; *Atta* by Jarett Kobek; *Halsted Plays Himself* by William E. Jones; and *Bubbles* by Peter Sloterdijk, the first volume of his massive trilogy, *Spheres*. Semiotext(e) makes its largest investment to date in this work; Sylvère believes that *Spheres* is the first attempt to reinterpret Western culture in term of space instead of time. Hedi and writer-translator Noura Wedell accompany Abdellah Taïa and Pierre Guyotat on a U.S. reading tour (Noura will later describe the experience in the third issue of *Animal Shelter*). Occupy Wall Street begins on September 17.

2012: Semiotext(e) publishes ten books, including *The Femicide Machine* by Sergio González Rodríguez, *Heroines* by Kate Zambreno, and *The Making of the Indebted Man* by Maurizio Lazzarato; and copresents "The City Machine and Its Streets," a symposium on Mexican politics and culture organized by Chris Kraus with González Rodríguez.

July 29, 2012: RIP Chris Marker, contributor to the "Oasis" issue of *Semiotext(e)*. August 28, 2012: R.I.P. Shulamith Firestone, author of *Airless Spaces* (Semiotext(e)/ Native Agents, 1998). September 16, 2012: RIP Mim Goodman.

2013: Semiotext(e) publishes nine books, including *Under the Sign of [sic]: Sturtevant's Volte-Face* by Bruce Hainley; *Returning to Reims* by Didier Eribon; *The Suiciders* by Travis Jeppesen; and *Schizo-Culture: The Event, The Book*, edited by Sylvère Lotringer and David Morris. A conference on Chris Kraus takes place at the Royal College of Art in London, and another on David Rattray at St. Mark's Poetry Project in New York. *Salvation Army*, a film version of Abdellah Taïa's book, premieres at the Venice Film Festival. On May 2, Assata Shakur, coauthor of Semiotext(e)'s *Still Black, Still Strong* (1993), is added to the FBI's Ten Most Wanted list. The reward for her capture is raised to two million dollars.

* * *

Asked to produce this text to accompany our contribution to the Biennial, we reflect on what distinguishes us from other independent presses. Our amateurishness? We don't have a real staff. We're dilettantes, foreigners. All of us would, in some sense, rather be doing something else. The books we publish arise from circumstances in our own lives. Which isn't to say we just publish our friends—but we do feel a loyalty to the writers we publish. They form a kind of community with us, even though they may not all love, or like, or even know each other. None of our books are ever remaindered. Our timing has never come from the market.

We were carrying the message, day and night for about ten years. That's about as long as you get. The houses are open and all you need is about three of you to go everywhere and make these gauzy invisible strings between people. It just makes sense that so many of us had time during the day and would stand in one another's kitchen. Smoking and talking and watching our faces change in the light.

—Eileen Myles,
Inferno (OR Books, 2008)

A. L. Steiner

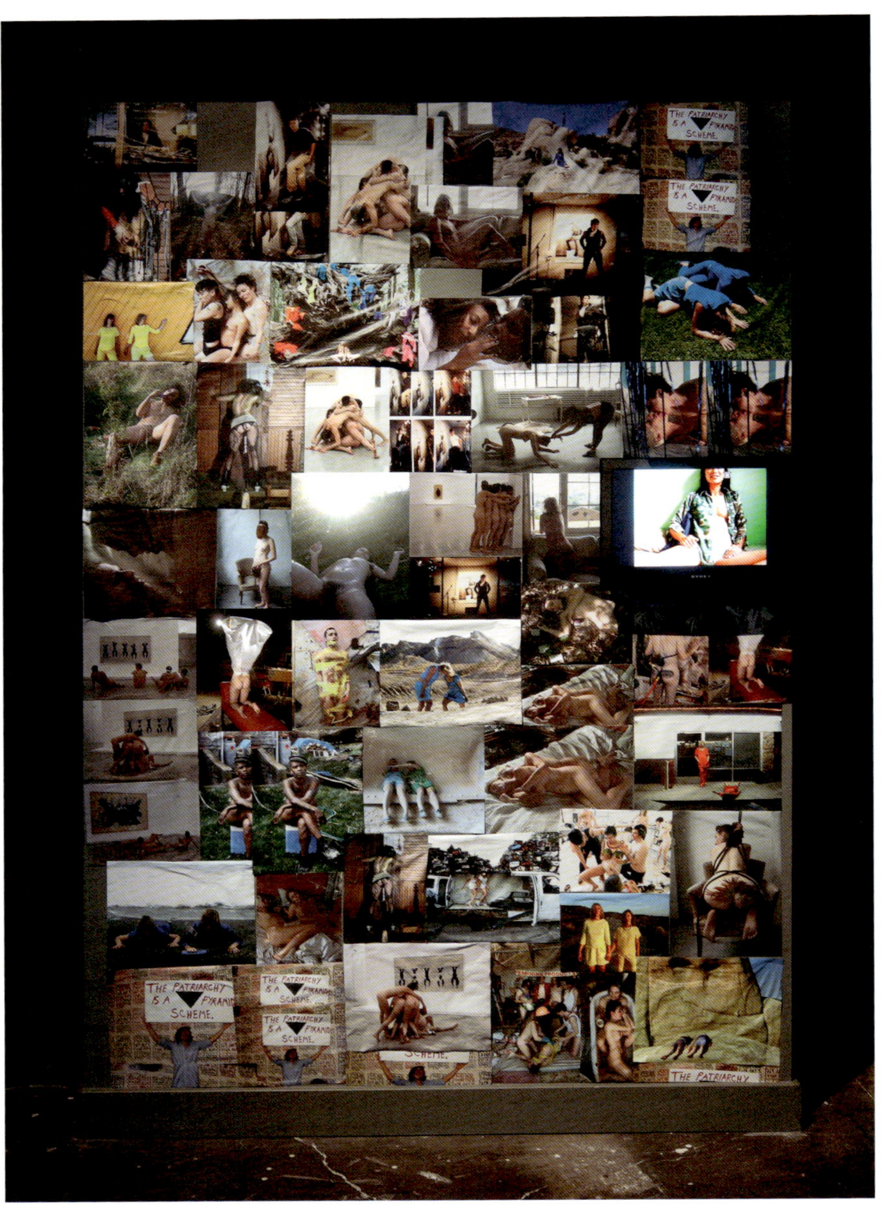

Still Video Still, 2013 (installation view, *Feelings and How To Destroy Them*, Portland Institute for Contemporary Art at Pacific Northwest College of Art Feldman Gallery, Oregon, September 5–October 27, 2013). Chromogenic prints and color photocopies, 69 × 100 in. (175.3 × 254 cm)

Born 1967 in Miami, FL

Lives in Los Angeles, CA

Malik Gaines + A. L. Steiner: A Conversation in the Midst of World Annihilation

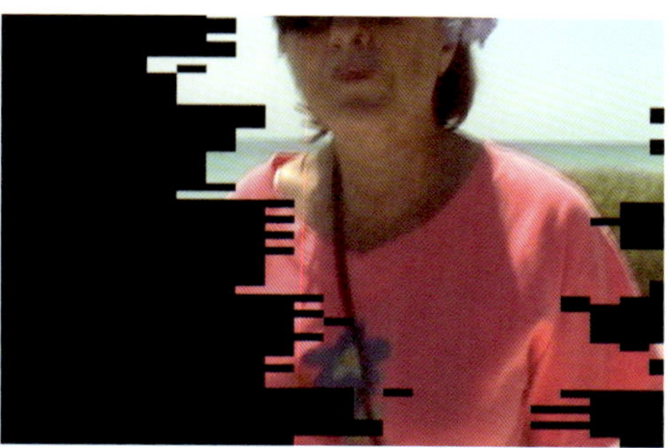

"Untitled (Berenice)," still from *More Real Than Reality Itself*, 2014. Multichannel digital video, color, sound

A. L. Steiner has consistently turned a subjective gaze toward political and social relationships. Whether in photography, performance, video, or arts activism, Steiner's contributions are characterized by an assured insistence that art forms are as complex as social forms and can be at once didactic, fun, beautiful, titillating, empowering, and melancholic.

Malik Gaines: The working title of your new video, which is still in progress, contains some irony: *More Real Than Reality Itself*. It reminds us that reality is a genre, realism is a style, and "the real" is a theory or, even more colloquially, an attitude or a mood.

A. L. Steiner: Yes—though I don't know if the video's final title will be *More Real Than Reality Itself* or *kkkrapitalist co-optation of revolution is the new disruption, or how my voice falters at the beauty of yours*.

MG: The piece presents a mundane contemporary reality where various radical histories are remembered and misremembered (dismembered?). You serve as both an interlocutor, who frames the questions about past and present, and a sexual citizen who playfully activates the distance in between. For many of us who have worked on, written about, and reimagined a radical history preceding our own—those of us who are too young for the discursive 1960s and 1970s but recall real glimpses of that time from our childhood imaginations—that distance is a space we have played around in. Never do we find this history reconstructed intact; the problem is always a matter of distance from imagination to experience. This distance seems to be embodied in one way by your sister, featured in the video, who was circumstantially involved in a notorious political group in the early seventies and who now appears to be anything but notorious or political. This is different from someone like Ericka Huggins, a former leader of a radical organization who was a well-known political prisoner, whose husband was assassinated while still a youth, and who continues to conduct activism. Huggins, whom you also interview, represents that distance by filling it with potent content, a living legacy. Your sister, who was apparently an inadvertent agent to begin with, presents a kind of amnesiac disavowal. Both are extraordinary. It's an ambivalent history, holding both of these examples along with the others you depict. Could we call this ambivalence queer?

ALS: It's incisive to try and frame ambivalence within this picture. I feel my own struggle—against paralysis brought on by empathic consciousness; against invisibility mandated by compulsory heteronormativity; against the requisite silence of female- and queer-identified bodies until called upon; against ineffectiveness, the erasure of any systems opposed to capitalist realism. It is queer, maybe the kind of queer that isn't "liberated" queer. Maybe it's the ambivalence of wondering if liberation is possible, how some can envision that generate that, how we find each other, and then what happens. These women grew up in a

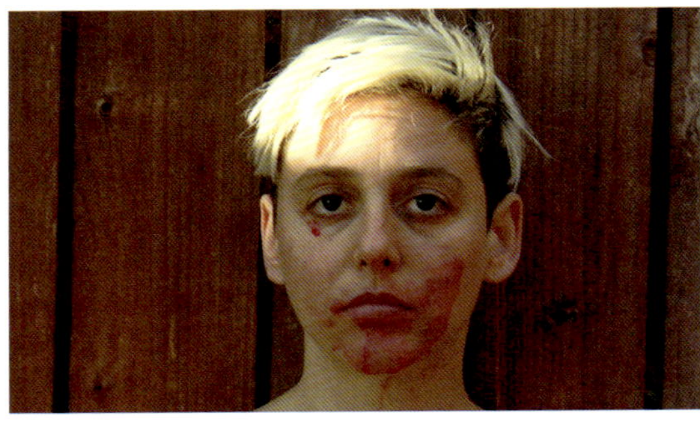

Untitled (Rachel) from *More Real Than Reality Itself*, 2014. Chromogenic print

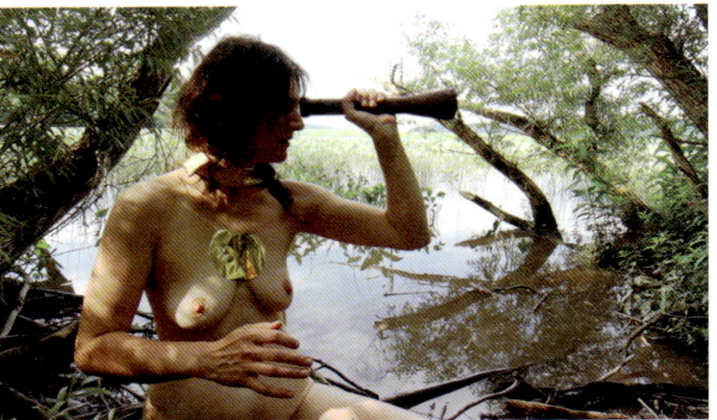

Untitled (Melissa/Chicks on Speed) from *More Real Than Reality Itself*, 2014. Chromogenic print

self-reflexive era—there was a collective consciousness regarding the provocation, shaping, and activation of change. We are in states of ontological anesthetization, a naturalized realism, which asserts that things are the way they are. We're not making choices—they're being made for us. How do we access consciousness in this state—in our actions, our choices, our behaviors? The people I've collaborated with on this piece have all survived somehow, each very differently. I'm not sure how their stories and legacies will end.

MG: In some ways, these are problems of difference, which serves both as an ordering mechanism and as an opportunity for this kind of queer ambivalence, a multiply sensitive kind of attention. One historical critique of realism, from Brecht and others, is that it's a mode that presents each relationship as inevitable, unchangeable, and so movingly true, or, as you've said, that "things are the way they are." The capitalist realism you're describing rallies class differences alongside other orders of difference; capitalism aligns with heteronormativity, for example, to portray the ideal "rightness" of each, as reflected in the other, forming a singular, powerful force. A queer sensibility breaks up the unity of that force: queer ambivalence troubles singularity; queer sex confounds the norm. As a critical mode, maybe it's a kind of consciousness, or self-consciousness, or, in the terms of that era, a raised consciousness?

ALS: How do we respond to a complete and totalizing doctrine of violence that we're communally perpetuating against our own humanity? Some form of higher consciousness is probably our only hope. Most Americans, even those in positions of power, don't consciously recognize what is patriarchal, supremacist, and misogynist. The term *heteronormativity* is not yet taught or included in our popular dictionaries—we don't freely utilize syntax that would more accurately describe how our minds and bodies participate within current sociopolitical and socioeconomic systems. Ericka Huggins talks about that in our interview. It's clearly unknown if, how, and when we as a species will access that particular form of knowledge. As universal sage Dr. Laurie Weeks notes in the piece, "Bees . . . don't have tiny wallets or safety deposit boxes . . ." You know?

MG: I want to ask you more about the distribution of violence: its rituals and spectacles, its technical uses, its proper and improper locations. One of the legacies of radicalism that concerns us is an array of violent tactics: the armed revolt, the destructive attack on private property and/or state property, and the rebellious suicide. These seem so far away, as do extrajudicial assassinations and other public state terrors; those seem to have moved away from Chicago, Los Angeles, Philadelphia, and out into "the world" or deep into our private prisons. The system works. The American violence you mention is highly ordered: spectacular here, invisible there, with proper distances in-between. And for artists who are concerned with power and representation and histories of political expression, the distance might be melancholic; I want to imagine the locations of violence but don't want to be there in them. As an of-color gay guy, I feel like I've spent my life carefully avoiding violence. Of course, there is a famous history of nonviolent protest. But part of your project pays attention to radicals who

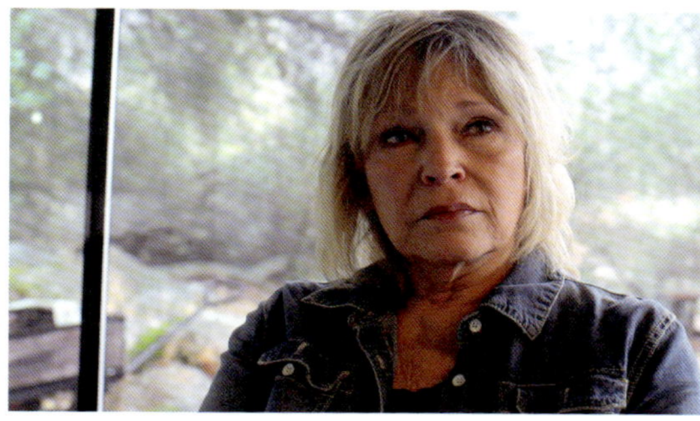

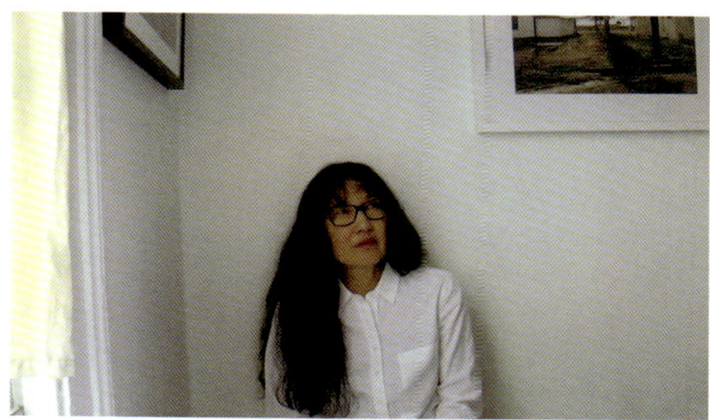

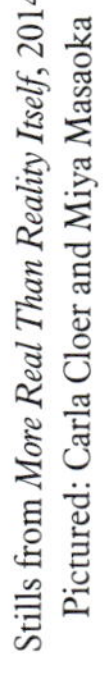

Stills from *More Real Than Reality Itself*, 2014. Pictured: Carla Cloer and Miya Masaoka

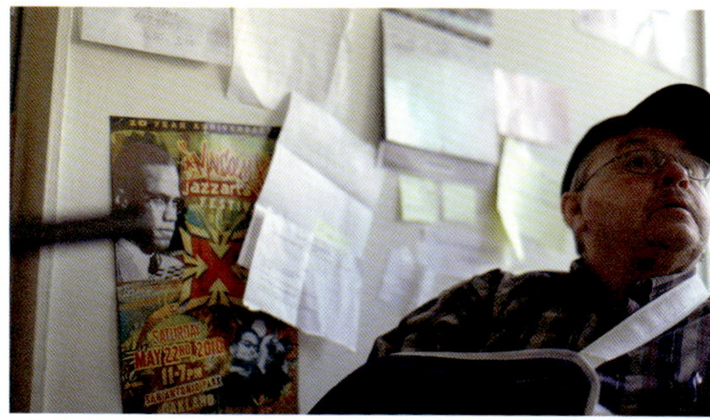

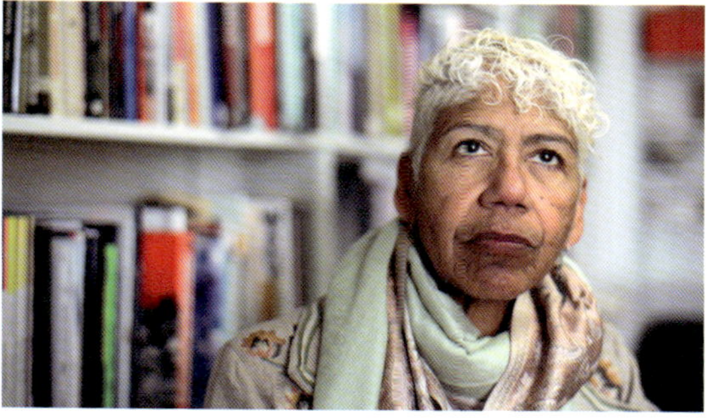

Stills from *More Real Than Reality Itself*, 2014. Pictured: Bo Brown and Ericka Huggins

differentiated themselves from that history. And one wonders, what happens to that violent revolutionary energy?

ALS: One of the subjects, Carla Cloer, wonders aloud whether tactics of the saboteur are now necessary, even though she's never participated in nonviolent protest, arrest, or sabotage. She's worked as a self-taught environmental conservationist and activist within a system she sees as failing—failing in its own ability to stop or change and failing its subjects. Miya Misoaka, whose family lost everything except what they could fit in two suitcases after being forced into an internment camp in California during World War II, infiltrated autoworker unions as a young organizer in the 1970s in order to confront corruption, racism, classist ideologies, and xenophobia. Rita Bo Brown, a cofounder of the revolutionary George Jackson Brigade, served seven years in prison for bank robbery. The debate regarding pacifism, nonviolence, and violence as multiplicities of strategies, rather than binaries, is ongoing. Peter Gelderloos recently published *The Failure of Nonviolence*; David France's *How to Survive a Plague* was nominated for an Academy Award; Jason Osder's documentary about Philadelphia-based black liberation and naturalist group MOVE, *Let the Fire Burn*, was released in 2013 to great acclaim; and there's talk of an Angela Davis biopic that several renowned entertainers are vying for. There's a fascination with protest and resistance from the 1960s to the 1990s within arts communities, where theatrical/spectacle-based strategies of interaction are quite common. Stefano Harney and Fred Moten's book *The Undercommons* is on my mind a lot right now. This strange, romantic idealism suppresses the very real and necessary power of activism against institutional violence. I see my projects somewhat in this vein—to what end am I making these "fine-art" works that mollify the institution and pacify a larger community? My voice is heard by a few in these prized and privileged spaces—spaces rife with the residue of violence and exploitation, "historical residues, collective residues," as theorist Ann Cvetkovich has stated—where my action is cauterized, insular, disciplined.

MG: Which is where sexuality returns, to play an important role in your work. Even when a context threatens to overly condition political content, there you and your cohort are, sometimes nude or sexually engaged, reminding us that we begin with bodies capable of creating pleasure, cultural transgressions, and affective solidarities. It's a long path from sex to revolution, but it's a starting point that should be remembered and enjoyed.

Sergei Tcherepnin

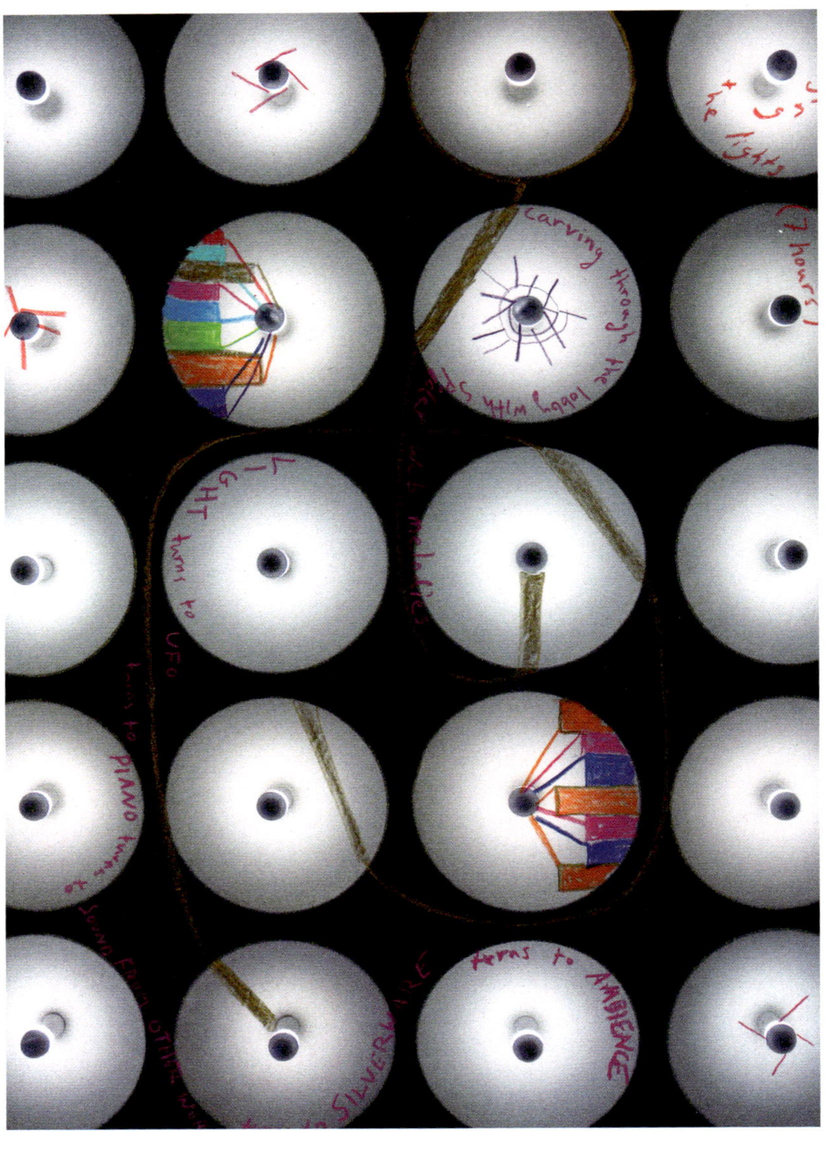

Photograph of the lights in the Whitney Museum Lobby with artist's notations, 2013. Source material for Sergei Tcherepnin's installation for the 2014 Whitney Biennial

Born 1981 in Watertown, MA

Lives in New York, NY

Note to Sergei
Bill Dietz

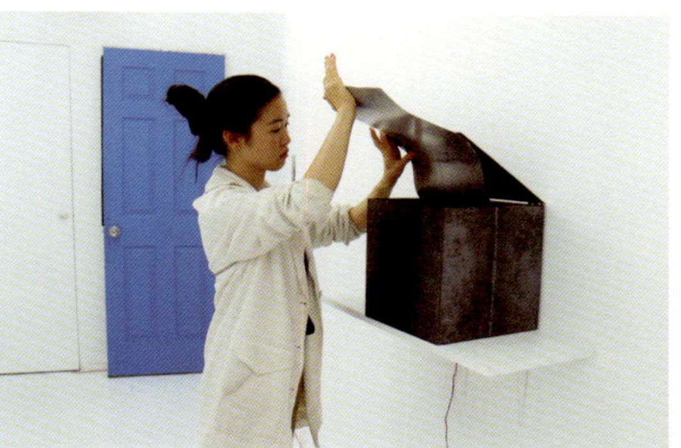

Pied Piper Box 3, 2012. Steel, zinc, brass, and transducer with wall-mounted shelf, dimensions variable

Dear Sergei,

Somewhere there's a photo of you and your brother as kids, smiling next to John Cage. Were you just posing for the picture, or was something actually funny? Do you think it'd still be funny today?

There's something in John Cage's Jerry-Lewis-meets-a-giggly-Dalai-Lama sense of humor that I've often found a bit suspect. His idolizations of Marcel Duchamp and Erik Satie are more than a bit quizzical: the bawdy, caustic character of *L.H.O.O.Q.* (1919) and *Relâche* (1924) is worlds away from Cage's "sunny disposition."[1] When he refuses to hear the historical avant-garde's razor-sharp irony and violent disgust for the bourgeoisie in his earnestly affirmative appropriations of it, Cage seems to be doing Peter Bürger's work for him. Satie writes,

> I see [*Furniture Music*] as melodious, as masking the clatter of knives and forks without drowning it completely, without imposing itself. It would fill up the awkward silences that occasionally descend on guests. It would spare them the usual banalities.[2]

And Cage writes,

> Why is it necessary to give the sounds of knives and forks consideration? Satie says so. And he is right . . . It is evidently a question of bringing one's intended actions into relation with the ambient unintended ones.[3]

Cage's signature guru grin is a method; Satie's upturned lip is a trap.

So, Sergei, are your pieces funny? And, if they're not, do they wink at us? Flirt with us? Cruise us?

The Pied Piper, who so often appears in your work in "the shortest short shorts the world has ever seen" (as Marina Rosenfeld once put it), is certainly amused when speaking of "furniture music." "Furniture music" in the very literal sense you offer it (transduction) means that every object is imagined as a potential *vibrator*. And what could be more opposed to the self-institutionalizing aspirations of sound art—its misguided aspirations to the status of inert object (museal furniture)? The Pied Piper represents a certain ironized participation: not just moralistically revealing that participation is promiscuous (inviting anonymous intimacy) but also offering an eminently specific, even composed, form of participation *after* that unabashed admission. The zinc tongues of your Piper Boxes are ready to play.[4] Objects are no longer sculptures but are instead relational, temporal transmitters.

In all fairness to Cage, there's a period during which his unfunny explicitness made him unavoidable. His rethinking of composition in works from his silent piece, *4'33"* (1952), to those of the mid-1960s straddles the line between expanding the material purview of the work ("anything can be music") and instrumentalizing the work in order to "indetermine" given situations. Works with no audible material whatsoever, such as his

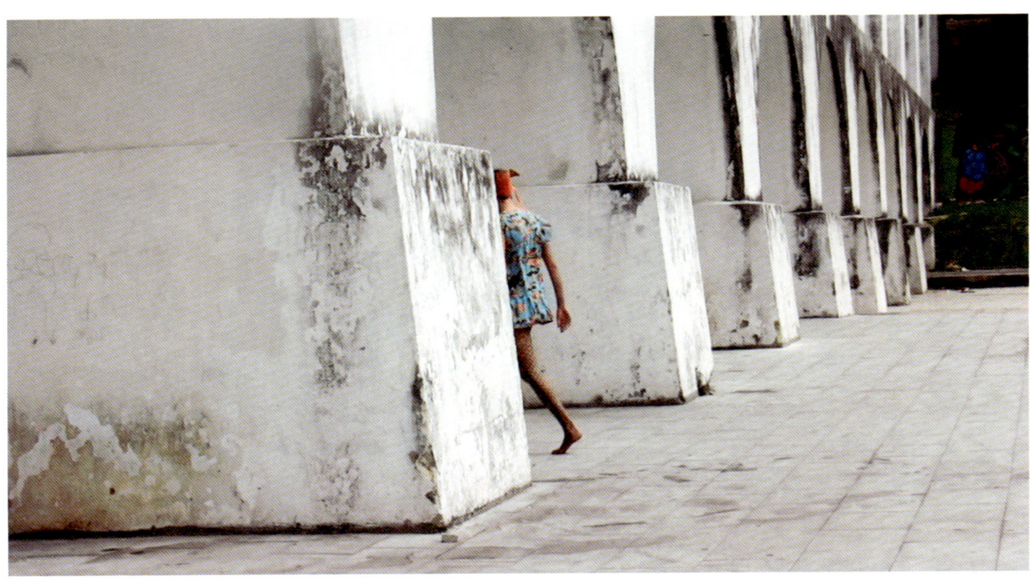

Still from *Pied Piper Playing Under the Aqueduct*, 2013.
High-definition video, color, sound; 7 minutes

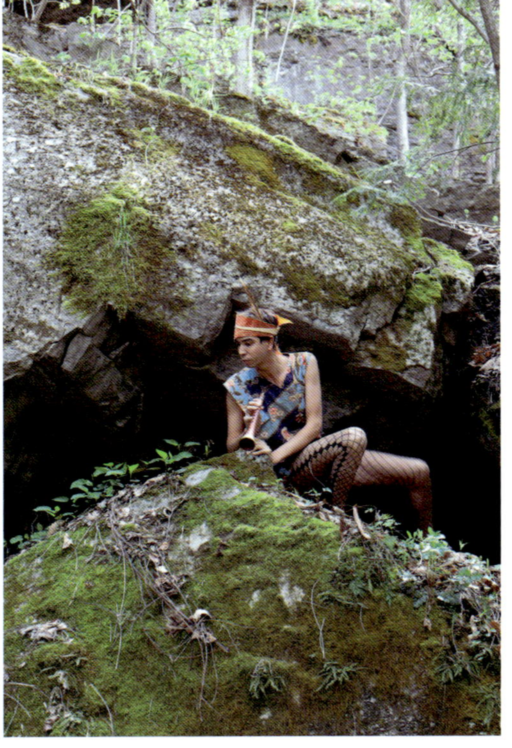

Piper's Revenge, 2012. Inkjet print, 4 × 6 in. (10.2 × 15.2 cm)

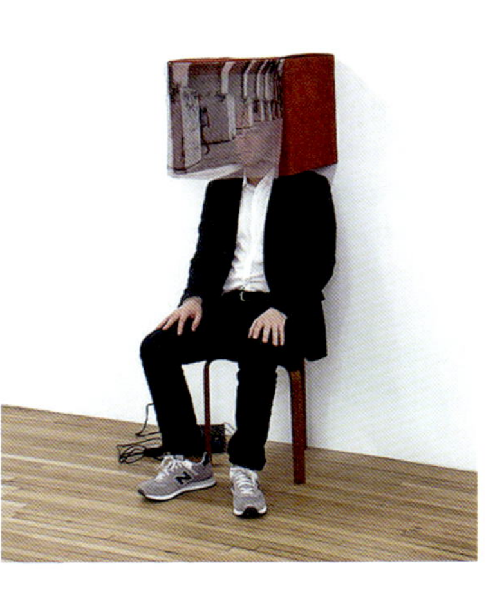

Ear Tone Box (Pied Piper Disappears), 2013. Microsuede, wood, zinc, silk, transducers, amplifier, and iPod, 16 × 16 × 18 in. (40.6 × 40.6 × 45.7 cm)

Variations series (1958–67), offer methods for indeterminately generating structures equally mappable onto sequences of sounds and orderings of everyday life. Maryanne Amacher decisively actualized this extended mode of composition in her response to Cage's 1937 essay "The Future of Music: Credo." If the young Cage's call for an "all-sound" music strengthened the institution of art by fortifying its potential for ubiquitous aestheticization, Amacher's call for an "all-time" music counteracts the Cagean trajectory's neo-avant-garde tendencies.[5] She writes,

> It will no longer be necessary to produce music as uninterrupted sound, to have it continue nonstop, as in the past . . . Music might sound for ten minutes, followed by a long span of silence, say an hour or two, and then maybe three minutes of sound. In any given twenty-four hours, for example, there can appear many wonderful musical surprises.[6]

Here, she calls for anything but an extension of *concertante* attention (sitting silently and listening to increasingly sporadic sound occurrences); instead, she proposes that the function of the musical work is to catalyze an indeterminate dynamic of modes of attention and distraction. Music, in its varying and unpredictable presence, might then break through and into everyday life.

Insofar as furniture represents a physical manifestation of petrified functions, a return to "furniture music," after Amacher, suggests a reversal of emphasis: not music as, or in, a state of furniture (the dead end of sound art), but furniture (as an infrastructure of social architecture) in a state of music. It's one thing to imagine a household embracing the "wonderful musical surprises" of all-time music and quite another to imagine a home with one of your Ear Tone Boxes next to the television. Would that be your revisionist addition to Gregori Warchavchik's 1928 Casa Modernista?[7]

Piper's Cave (2013) conjures a site not unlike the amorously appropriated urban spaces evoked in *Pied Piper Playing under the Aqueduct* (2013).[8] Likewise, the oscillatory architectural flux of your 2011 collaboration with Woody Sullender at Issue Project Room suggests that *any* fixed notion of "household" is inadequate. From the everyday objects incorporated in your first exhibition at Audio Visual Arts to the ugly mass-produced furniture in your show at Karma International, from the windows you outfitted at the Guggenheim Museum[9] to the lighting array in the Whitney's lobby, to the bodies of audience members under the docks on Fire Island,[10] your transductions have announced a vibratory form of relationality in which materialities commune as propagational media—that is, as excitable matter. Isn't this what the title *Be a speaker. So be it . . .* (2011)[11] means—that "taking" the transduced signal engenders what Leo Bersani calls the "extensibility of sameness"?[12] *Piper's Cave*, a built space, is furniture for a social scene yet to come. Your bench at Murray Guy, with its peristaltic grumblings, may buy us a first drink, but before we know it we're sitting in an acephalic machine more exotic than any darkroom's architecture.

After all, what's laughter but a body-borne transmission of vibration?

1. John Cage himself characterized his disposition as sunny. See, for example, Cage, foreword to *A Year from Monday: New Lectures and Writings* (1963; Middletown, CT: Wesleyan University Press, 1969), x.
2. Erik Satie, quoted in Alan Gillmor, *Erik Satie* (New York: Norton, 1992), 232.
3. John Cage, "Erik Satie," in *Silence: Lectures and Writings* (Middletown, CT: Wesleyan University Press, 1961), 80.
4. Sergei Tcherepnin's Pied Piper Boxes were included in his exhibition *Pied Piper Part I* at Audio Visual Arts, New York, May 17– July 1, 2012.
5. Even David Tudor's 1964 *Fluorescent Sound* for the lighting array of Stockholm's Moderna Museet is no exception. In an 1988 interview with Teddy Hultberg (available online at http://davidtudor.org/Articles/hultberg.html, accessed October 31, 2013), Tudor's remark that, "One day I was in the room when someone was turning on the fluorescent lights and they didn't know which to turn on and all of a sudden there was the most beautiful music," suggests that the work falls well within the "all-sound" rubric.
6. Maryanne Amacher, in a text she referred to as "The Future of Music II," published as a part of "Cage's Influence: A Panel Discussion," in *Writings through John Cage's Music, Poetry, and Art*, ed. David W. Bernstein and Christopher Hatch (Chicago: University of Chicago Press, 2001), 186.
7. This refers to Tcherepnin's contribution to the 30th Bienal de São Paulo, 2012.
8. *Piper's Cave* was included in the exhibition *Pied Piper, Part II: Ringing Rocks*, at Murray Guy's booth at Art Basel, 2013. *Pied Piper Playing under the Aqueduct* was included in the exhibition *Ear Tone Box*, Murray Guy, March 5–April 20, 2013.
9. Tcherepnin's *Between the Concert and the Wall* (2012) was included in the series Stillspotting NYC, organized by the Guggenheim Museum in 2012.
10. Tcherepnin participated in the 2013 Fire Island Pines Performance Series.
11. *Be a speaker. So be it...* (2011) is a collaboration between Ei Arakawa, Gela Patashuri, and Tcherepnin, which was presented in 2011 by The Showroom, London; Bétonsalon, Paris; and CAC Brétigny, Paris.
12. Leo Bersani, "Sociality and Sexuality," in *Is the Rectum a Grave? and Other Essays* (Chicago: University of Chicago Press, 2010), 118.

Triple Canopy

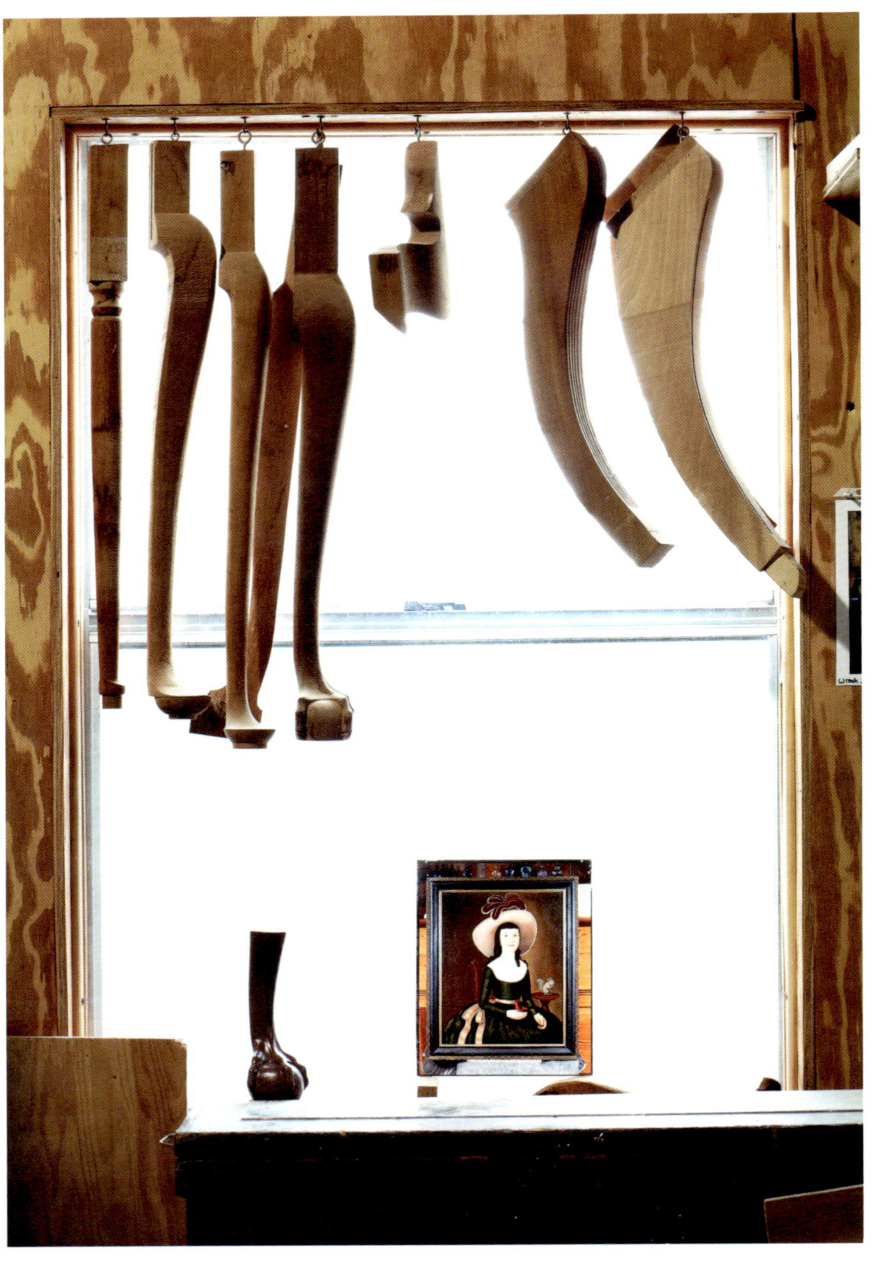

All photographs from the series *Pointing Machines (Chestertown, Maryland)*, 2013

Founded in 2007

Based in Brooklyn, NY

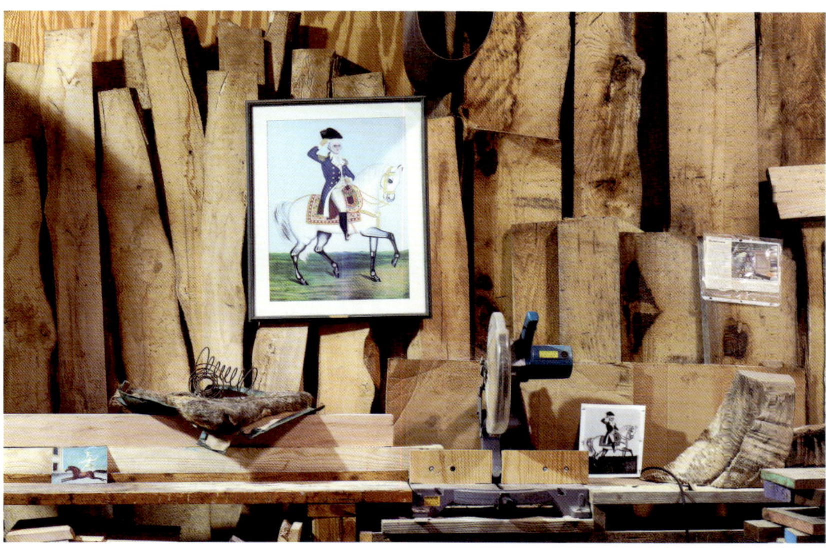

POINTING MACHINES

The Visit: We receive a text message from an unknown number—inviting us to "visit the present." At first, we wonder if we are being disparaged, since we consider ourselves very much of the moment. Puzzled, we weigh various potential interpretations. What are the characteristics of the present age? This is a matter not simply of listing smartphones, Intergovernmental Panel on Climate Change assessments, definitive personae, and hallmark conflicts but also of establishing a fundamental idea of an epoch. We begin to feel ridiculous and curse the invitation, yet also feel—who knows why—*compelled*. We accept. Anyway, we've lately spent too much time feeding words to machines (an activity that was to figure prominently on our list).

We are directed to the gleaming lobby of a Manhattan office complex. We watch workers —young and old, dressed for AutoCAD and FileMaker—swipe their cards and caress their phones; they seem to have organized themselves, organized the world, into a reliable repertoire of manual gestures.

We are reminded of a story written in 1850 by Edgar Allan Poe, "The Sphinx." Two gentlemen flee New York City during an outbreak of cholera to hole up in a cottage on the Hudson River. Very little happens, until one morning when the narrator looks out the window and sees a "living monster of hideous conformation"—covered with black fur, a massive crystal horn protruding from its head, a white skull outlined on its chest—charging toward him. The narrator loses consciousness. On waking, he is informed that he was only looking at a moth, "the genus Sphinx," that had become trapped in a spider's web.

This is what it is like when distance collapses. There is a terror in the dandy's reduced field of vision that we, sequestered in a noiselessly ascending elevator, seem to share: Everything is near, and nothing that is not near can be perceived.

A Show: We enter an auditorium. It's a relief to settle into cushioned folding chairs under dim lights.

We recall that in Poe's time it was the telegraph that promised, or threatened, to annihilate the interval between sender and receiver and level differences between original and copy by converting the book into code. That age—characterized by the inscrutable speed and complexity of financial exchange, the circulation of texts copied and cobbled together by both heedless and purposeful printers (for profit, for the public sphere), a crisis of authorship, the First Transcontinental Railroad—recalls our own.

Does this ability to recognize in the past an approximation of the present alleviate our anxiety? Now as then, we can say that the original accrues value while the copy creates value. But can we say that we are free, democratically so, to do what we like within the narrowing distance between goods and information about these goods?

The screen before us flashes to life:

A Slide: We see ourselves in a twentieth-century American museum. We hesitate beneath suspended concrete-grid ceilings and can't help but dwell on the sluggishness of the sculptures and paintings. There is a reason, beyond the immaculate architecture, climate control, and careful displays, that we are pleased to be in the museum. We are sympathetic to the modeling of images, objects, ideas, and experiences that occurs here, to the ceaseless accumulation of records, and to the tensions that ensue. On the one hand: the promotion and repetition of orderly stratification, division, and classification, the consolidation of value in unique objects. On the other: the replication of artworks via photography, facsimile, press release, catalogue entry, forgery, or conversion into code—all of which may distort or diminish the singularity of the original, even while granting it a special status. We wonder how we might marshal such opposing forces as we attempt to reproduce and, in some sense, possess these artworks—whether in print, online, or as three-dimensional scans converted into computer-aided design files to be widely distributed, modified, and materialized. We consider and compare possible strategies and formats for representation, conversion, and translation, and we weigh their varying degrees of information loss, addition, and modulation.

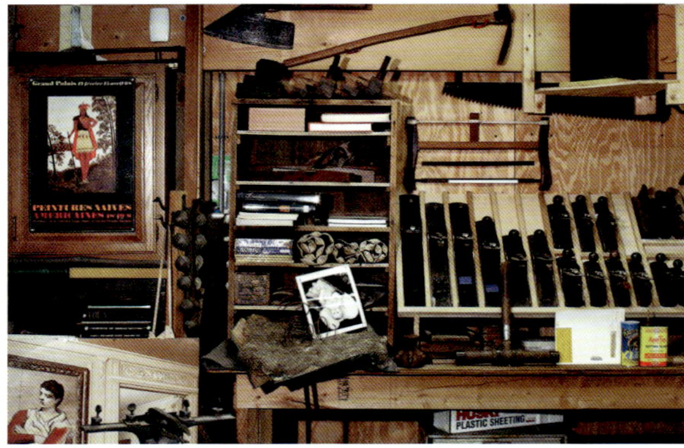

A Slide about Language: We see a page of a novel but not an original page or a scan of a credible edition on Google Books. Rather it is from an e-book, its text formatted to accommodate proliferating mobile devices. An animation of the page turning on the screen. Then: expressive language. The alphabet (we are English speakers) with its familiar associated phonemes. A peal of thunder introduces the postlapsarian world in *Finnegan's Wake*, "Bbababadalgharaghtakamminarronnkonnbronntonnerronntuonnthunntrovarrhounawnskawntoohoohoordenenthurnuk."

We have for some time been trying to figure out how we can write and speak alongside, or against, the highly accurate and undeniably impressive forms of presence rooted in digital scripts and interfaces. We have fixated on anachronism.

A Slide about Legacy: We see a contemporary factory floor dominated by neat, plastic enclosures: 3-D printers being tested and boxed, shipped to medical research facilities, department of defense contractors, and wealthy hobbyists. Technicians in white lab coats, whom we regard with a mix of awe and contempt, perform adjustments; they are skilled, advanced, and potentially rendering millions obsolete.

All the same, there is undeniably a fascination for the applications of this technology, and we ourselves have recently been marveling at the plan of the Egyptian Supreme Council of Antiquities to create a perfect replica of Tutankhamun's tomb. A company called Factum Arte ("dedicated to ... the production of works that redefine the relationship between two and three dimensions") is measuring a hundred million points within each square meter of the pharaoh's final resting place, employing laser scanners to convert the texture and colors into code. The resulting copy will provide visitors with a more complete encounter that includes touch. Almost no one will ever have to enter the tomb again—until the copy begins to deteriorate and the original must be scanned again, though perhaps a copy of the first copy is preferable; each preserves something of value.

A Slide about Historical Painting: We see ourselves again, this time in a private home that also seems to be another museum. In the image, we are seated as we are now, except in Queen Anne walnut side chairs, near cabriole-leg zomnos, lacquered escritoires, and an extraordinary fruitwood bench. There are so many paintings of George Washington here: Washington in snow-white breeches with blooming cheeks, Washington claiming dominion over peaked cherry trees, and Washington dangling gilded symbols of the Masonic order from his waistcoat. All are seemingly made from the same template, yet none are derivative.

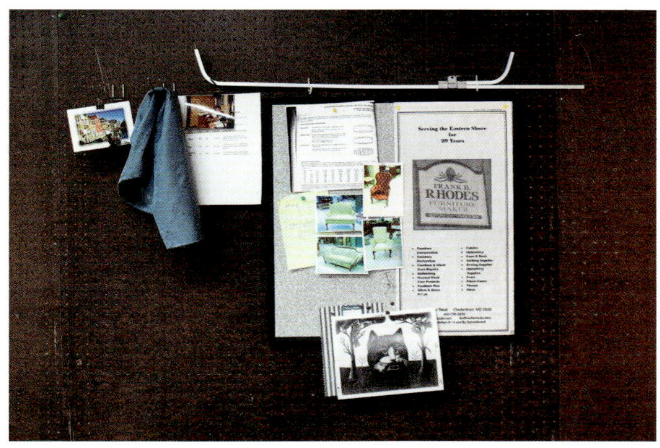

Now we see ourselves online, conducting image-based searches for these paintings: "Calder-style mobiles," "best Saarinen knock-offs," "Jasper Johns upload image Zazzle posters." We see Ionic molding, roses pompon wallpaper, and an anonymous portrait of a lusterless young girl, her torso cinched into a satin bodice. We are reading that copyright originated in the eighteenth-century distinction between reproducing a book (mindless) and reproducing a machine (edifying). Some believe the pointing machine, which plots the surface of a sculpture to facilitate the creation of copies, was invented to service the hunger for Greek statuary among the elites of conquering Rome; others believe that this special apparatus wasn't developed until the Renaissance, when there arose a great demand for reproductions of classical sculpture. "A work of art, since it is an object, may be copied and re-casted," Immanuel Kant pronounced in 1785, "and the copies thus made of it may be publicly circulated without requiring the consent of the author of the original or of those whom the latter used as the executors of his ideas." To Kant, the separation of the writer's identity from the written work—via reprinting, amalgamating, bowdlerizing, anthologizing, and appropriating—threatened public reason, and so the pirate must assume authorship.

We are seeing this house-museum recreated as a showroom, as an archive, as an interior-design layout, as a chart of the divagating paths taken by each object—painting, commodity, decoration, holding, auction item, Ektachrome slide, and eBay purchase—and as something we can take with us. We see ourselves step outside, onto the deck, ignite an e-cigarette, and take in the flatness of Maryland. *Plaster*: The slide show ends. We are immersed in a convincing approximation of natural light streaming into the atrium of a museum that brims with plaster casts, obviously historical, potentially futuristic. An impassive Apollo Belvedere regards the coiled figure of the Discobolus; the Apoxyomenos scrapes sweat and dust from his skin; Laocoön and sons pry miserably at determined serpents. Crowded together are the Capitoline Venus, the Venus de Medici, the Venus de Milo, and Michelangelo's Slaves. Diana Chasseresse selects an arrow as a young stag leaps behind her dimpled knee. Another version of the present, within the present: we reach for our phones in order to capture it find a new message from the unknown number: "This is how order is made and unmade."

Triple Canopy's contribution to the Whitney Biennial is *Pointing Machines*, an issue of its magazine devoted to the relationship between contemporary forms of reproduction, value, and language. This collective endeavor assumes the form of an installation and public programs within the museum as well as online and print publications, and includes collaborations with several artists and writers.

The essay and photographs in these pages were produced by Triple Canopy editors Lucy Ives, Alexander Provan, Peter J. Russo, and Hannah Whitaker. The photographs depict arrangements of reproductions of artworks and objects related to the Garbisch collection of American naïve art, and were taken in the wood shop and antique furniture showroom of Frank Rhodes, grandson of Colonel Edgar William and Bernice Chrysler Garbisch, in Chestertown, Maryland.

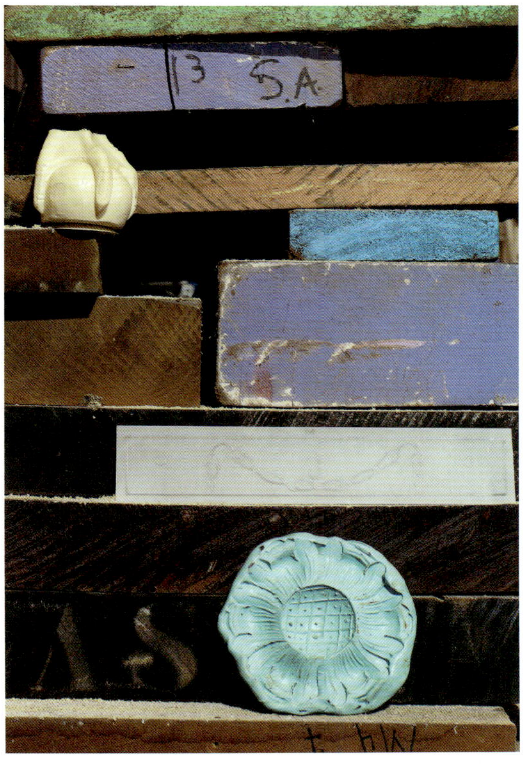

II. Anthony Elms

ESSAY

ARTISTS

"Sentences sometimes are impediments." *Anthony Elms*

Recurring dream/fear: on the audio guide, amid the static of scratchy celluloid, Laurence Olivier begins a stentorian introduction: "This is the tragedy of a man who could not make up his mind."[1] The quiet and the quite, the indirect and the indiscreet, the concatenated and the conflicted, the iridescent and the inscribed, the paused and the perfumed are all at hand, searching for footholds in an increasingly cluttered public sphere that no longer feels public. For it is no longer a sphere *for* the *collective* but is instead a sphere *of collections*, archives of private spheres splayed out for surveillance over a substrate of phantom value relations.

All quotes in section titles come from my converstaions with the artists.

1. Laurence Olivier, in *Hamlet*, directed by Laurence Olivier (1948; London: Two Cities Film).

I. "Shtick—A very good New York word."

If the Whitney Biennial is a snapshot of American art at this moment, and if any intimate encounter with American art at this historical moment must be mediated (as all intimacies these days are), then 945 Madison is as well-disposed a mediation as any. Marcel Breuer's building will serve as a medium-format device for capturing twenty-four scenes of America.

> Every time I try to think of the United States of America I get the cold sweats. I can't even look at a weather map anymore—it's too big. That's part of the reason I moved to Manhattan. I wanted to move to an island off the coast of America.[2]

Even though I haven't exactly moved to Manhattan, I concur with Spalding Gray, and 945 Madison Avenue is one of the more beautiful perches off the coast of America. As such, it offers a range of behaviors to ape, but site-specificity is not what appeals, in part because site-specificity, despite many claims, doesn't exist. It is simply a collectively agreed-to lie told to dress in a hybrid veneer, one part business casual to two parts critical engagement and a dash of somehow studious design. Years ago, artist Stephen Prina tried to recast the terms from site-specificity to system-specificity: bringing personal traits to bear on the spaces and settings we encounter.[3] In this vein, consider, then, Mark Wigley's contention that "architecture is more than simply an agent of any particular theory. It is theory's condition of possibility."[4]

Breuer's architecture makes possible a theory that is cribbed from a couple of concerns. One is from Susan Howe: "I believed in an American aesthetic of uncertainty that could represent beauty in syllables so scarce and rushed they would appear to expand though they lay half-smothered in local history."[5] This dovetails nicely into a peculiar phrase from Breuer's notes on his approach to building the Whitney Museum of American Art at 945 Madison Avenue: "What should a museum look like, a museum in Manhattan? Surely it should work, it should fulfill its requirements."[6] Engaging Howe under the dutiful ethic of Breuer's building, the theory goes: the selection of artists is required to expansively fulfill Breuer's museum in Manhattan in rushed and scarce syllables that sound deep uncertainties.

2. Spalding Gray, *Swimming to Cambodia*, directed by Jonathan Demme (1987; New York: The Swimming Company).

3. See for one example, Stephen Prina, "We Represent Ourselves to the World: Institutional Narrativity," in *The Lectures 1992*, ed. Oswaldo Costa, Barbera van Kooij, and Robin Resch (Rotterdam: Witte de With, 1993), 61–73.

4. Mark Wigley, *White Walls, Designer Dresses: The Fashioning of Modern Architecture* (Cambridge, MA: MIT Press, 1995), 20.

5. Susan Howe, "Personal Narrative," in *Souls of the Labadie Tract* (New York: New Directions, 2007), 16.

6. Marcel Breuer, "The Architect's Approach," notes on the Whitney Museum of American Art, Whitney Museum of American Art archives.

> Contemporary culture has chosen to celebrate individuals and to market their image. Architects wear their buildings the way film stars wear their gowns and politicians their rhetoric. Like politicians, star architects have agendas that are often fundamentally apolitical—founded on the abstract currency of image and the aura of innovation.[7]

7. Jill Stoner, *Toward a Minor Architecture* (Cambridge, MA: MIT Press, 2012), 73.

Jill Stoner's concrete fact is somewhat ill fitting in relation to 945 Madison Avenue, even if it does accurately sidle up to the outlines of Breuer's blunt, forward pose. First, the concept of a "star architect" was only a nascent, if malignant, tumor when Breuer planned this building. Second, Breuer wasn't apolitical, and if he wore 945 Madison Avenue, it was less as a gown than as gruff workwear. He unapologetically fortified the museum against the threat of the "abstract currency of images," declaring that 945 Madison Avenue "should not look like a business or office building, nor should it look like a place of light entertainment."[8] In effect, the building brutally turns away from business as usual in a way no new museum building (maybe even *any* large-scale building) ever will again.

8. Breuer, "The Architect's Approach."

Peculiar, for example, how 945 Madison Avenue articulates the term *public space*. Its personality is inconsistent, contradictory if quite staid. Aloof, also a suspected narcissist, it does not approach you first: you cross a dry moat to enter its resolute interior. The entrance hall, though modest in scale, feigns a grand embrace with its stern walls and emphatic lighting rhythm, which betrays the building's primary politics: it is enough to set the stage, find the proper aperture, and set the lighting to excel. Its dimensions are deceiving, and its surfaces are anachronistic. Through submarine-like ports, views onto neighboring buildings become compressed—alien otherworldly. Engaging points of view rather than one-track noblesse drift, 945 Madison Avenue's brutish concrete, granite, and slate are remarkably imprinted and cleaved, embellished with enough surface detail to ravish in even the shadowy pockets. There are deficiencies in the spaces, and the points of compromise become visible fissures. It's puzzling to figure out, for example, how to incorporate performance of nearly any scale in this building; as there is almost no back of house to Breuer. Not to mention, in order to have space for education, a sci-fi shipping crate has been docked in the dry moat. Stubborn surfaces tire knees, arches, hips (ask the guards). All considered, "Anywhere else it would be too much drama to handle, but this is the Upper East Side."[9] Nine forty-five Madison Avenue is a strong setting for artists to do what they do. I've always been astonished by 945 Madison Avenue. In tune with "we who 'love to be astonished.'"[10]

9. Press release, *Gossip Girl*, season 6, CBS Paramount, 2012.

10. Lyn Hejinian, *My Life* (Los Angeles: Green Integer, 2002), 10.

This half-smothered.

II. "Elizabeth Bowen wrote a phrase, 'It's the haunted that haunt,' which sets up a nice sense of lineage."

What can be said about the twenty-four artists and groups gathered? Given the sprawl, assembling an overview of American art these days is a fool's errand. And on the other hand, if I'm not accused of nepotism I've done something wrong. To paraphrase a position declared by musician Mayo Thompson: I try for timeliness, while reserving the right to ask my own dumb questions. It is always preferable to make time rather than to mark time. The twenty-four assembled artists and groups strike me as a "we who 'love to be astonished,'" and putting them together is a way to answer Breuer's question, "What should a museum look like, a museum in Manhattan?" with my astonishment.

A museum in Manhattan should tangibly and viably include poetry. It should give room to feelings with, not simply understandings of, the immediate, urban surroundings. Spirited voices, unreliable narrators who test relationships between histories of the present and the future should chart paths through the museum. These leaky and rejiggered histories must engage magick spells, ghosts, difficult personalities, cackles, collage rips, itinerant wanderings, certain crass rejoinders, idiomatic languages, propositions to refashion language, recastings of indignities, attempts to find ways to live for those now gone, materials imbued with the tension of class, compositions rendered as cleaving pattern, objects seemingly dropped by folksy aliens, and songs sung blue.[11] These half-smothered moments of astonishing uncertainty and scarcity should unsettle the geometry of moments spent in useful tension with this museum's strong-willed spaces.

These selected artists are not in the normal sense the chosen few. This was not my aim. A curator simply needs to listen to artists and and be an advocate for what astonishes. The worst would be to try to answer some shapely concern, and art history is far down the to-do list. Any attempt to report on my astonishment is roundabout at best. In honor of this delay, I overstep: many of the clauses, phrases, adjectives, and concerns that pepper this essay have been culled from conversations and encounters with the selected artists. For faint justification, I appeal to Wayne Koestenbaum's preemptive rejoinder disguised as an ethics: "The highest respect we can accord a work of art may be to say nothing about it."[12]

11. A museum in Manhattan must also try not to use the word *artwork* or the phrase *work of art*. Detest the fact that we define it as *work* for someone to agree to let a gesture attain value.

12. Wayne Koestenbaum, "Frank O'Hara's Excitement," in *My 1980s and Other Essays* (New York: Farrar, Straus and Giroux, 2013), 74.

This haunted tension.

III. "What's wrong with capitalism is we're all like Rihanna."

In an exhibition, all distances—temporal, spatial, political, social, and affective—should register. Distances, in flux and relative in any encounter with objects, establish prismatic details that must be maneuvered. Any curator should, at the very least, try to measure some of these distances in their narration of and refraction of object relations. It is the device of aphorism that allows this curator to navigate.

A functional definition of *aphorisms*: concise phrases of general truths; truths in pennyweights. An aphorism, more importantly, should be considered a statement of principle. Aphoristic thought recurs at important junctures in both spiritual and philosophical query (consider, for example, the works of Georg Christoph Lichtenberg, Blaise Pascal, François de La Rochefoucauld, Friedrich Nietzsche, Dorothy Parker, Ludwig Wittgenstein, Ad Reinhardt, Andy Warhol, and Miss Manners). The concept of aphorism is at least as old as Pythagoras, and likely older.

Someone—who remembers who?—once defined *aphorism* as a thought with its horizon removed. Without a horizon, no sense of overview is possible; it is confounded. The aphorism keeps our view truncated, stilted, and defined, even as it extends the world. Aphoristic thought does not follow Jorge Luis Borges's map, which, drawn at a scale of one to one, covers and becomes the terrain; instead, it takes us for a trolley ride on a microscaled tangle of track that promises to get us there. Each aphorism is an escape scenario at the ever ready.

The image-rich poetic device of aphorism relies on a distinctly visual prompt that endows singular objects with fugitive intelligence. "When a book and a head collide and a hollow sound is heard, must it always have come from the book?"[13] At that moment—*bonk!*—the scene outside our trolley window resembles the world,

13. Georg Christoph Lichtenberg, *The Waste Books* (New York: Penguin, 1990), 54.

different. The distances have been made malleable. Wayne Koestenbaum reminds me of the lowest goal for any exhibition:

> Sometimes it's important *not* to stand back from a painting. Sometimes it's important *not* to take in the big picture. Sometimes it's important to refuse everything but what Deleuze and Guatarri call "close vision," a vision that prevents the imperial crudities of historizing. . . . I advocate keeping art dispersed in its little villages, and refusing to plow art down with large boulevards that oversimplify the twists of history and that prevent individual barricades of resistance from flourishing.[14]

14. Wayne Koestenbaum, "The Inner Life of the Palette Knife," in *My 1980s and Other Essays*, 251.

I don't mean to dispute that real changes need to happen at the macro level, rather I'm placing a bet on attending closely and in person to the materials and ethics of objects (and object relations). To know what can be held in the hand might be small enough to stave off a larger disregard of distractions. (The next revised standard English thesaurus will clearly label *discovery* an oversize synonym for *light entertainment*.) Socially engaged practice? Social space is so fraught with materiality that the rooted uncertainty of objects is often taken for granted. For hours now the time for practice has passed, material to build striking heights from the forsaken depths of this sunset of empires. Where's my extension?

> I see that I've never told you how I listen to music—I gently rest my hand on the record player and my hand vibrates, sending waves through my whole body: and so I listen to the electricity of the vibrations, the last substratum of reality's realm, and the world trembles inside my hands.[15]

15. Clarice Lispector, *Água Viva* (New York: New Directions, 2012), 5.

This principle.

IV. "I like my magic with extension cords and space heaters."

> The obtuse meaning, soliciting the viewer's passionate attention, seemed, on the surface, trivial—a mere crease, a speck, like a trace of lipstick traveling too far outside the outline of the lip. The obtuse meaning—"obtuse" is a term of praise—gratified [Roland] Barthes because it carried no allegory, no symbolism, no ideology. It unprogrammatically titillated.[16]

16. Wayne Koestenbaum "In Defense of Nuance," foreword to Roland Barthes, *A Lover's Discourse: Fragments* (New York; Hill and Wang, 2010), x.

Trail Koestenbaum on Barthes with Breuer on Breuer:

> It should not look like a business or office building, nor should it look like a place of light entertainment. Its form and material should have identity and weight in the neighborhood of 50-story skyscrapers, of mile-long bridges, in the midst of the dynamic jungle of our colorful city. It should be an independent and self-relying unit, exposed to history, and at the same time it should have visual connection to the street.[17]

17. Breuer, "The Architect's Approach."

Perhaps Breuer would have accepted "unprogrammatically titillating" as a zippier rewrite of "It should be an independent and self-relying unit, exposed to history, and at the same time it should have visual connection to the street." There is a kind of critical distance built between Barthes and Breuer, but not the old kind. Famously, Fredric Jameson said modernity's critical distance imploded with the onset of postmodern subjectivity, submerged amid forces social, cultural, and economic. Dispassionate adjudication was lost. Some hacks are optimistic. John Kelsey: "If the old critical distance is lost, then we need to invent new distances, or learn to deal with loss of distance."[18] Echo remains in public play because critical distance is also necessary to balance, acoustically, direct projection and resonant echo.

18. John Kelsey, "The Hack," in *Canvases and Careers Today: Criticism and Its Markets*, ed. Daniel Birnbaum and Isabelle Graw (Berlin: Sternberg Press, 2008), 66.

"Lipstick traveling too far outside the outline of the lip"? Without doubt, I'll accept "obtuse meaning" when erotics based in the specificities of objects and settings and bodies cannot be ignored. Art that has not yet with certainty been ideologically or sexually or temporally fixed with a clear historical or individually directed desire. Let's cast this trivial distraction as critical distance.

"It should be an independent and self-relying unit, exposed to history, and at the same time it should have visual connection to the street"? Reverberant public space is necessary to survival. Note how distances, which are extended through varied distribution mechanisms (across technologies, formats, economies, and individuals), can generate more expansive narratives—geographically, temporally, and subjectively.

This exposure.

V. "It squeaks but it runs fine . . . just like my art."

Contingency cannot be anticipated. It just happens like a mambo lizard voguing to noise music. It is hard to imagine not wanting a Biennial to engage critically contingent perspectives, and it's just as hard to anticipate whether I will indeed construct a palpable sense of contingency at 945 Madison Avenue. Maybe this is why the ifs, hows, whens, thens, thoughs, and sinces of some distinct ways of making "unprogrammatically titillate."

These are casual contingencies, really. How does one ensure that the off topic, passed over, and passé are noticed?

> If this were a novel, on the first page it would have begun and on the last it would be done, but something or someone always comes along.[19]

19. Lyn Hejinian, *Saga/Circus* (Richmond, CA: Omnidawn Publishing, 2008), 85.

This delay.

VI. "Bill Cosby . . . uh . . . Bill Clinton, I always mix-up my B.C.s."

In this business, we know, you're nobody until you're talked about. It's togetherness. Several years ago, I hosted a lecture by ghost hunter and musician Michael Esposito, who said, "We like recordings more than we like to listen."[20] This aphoristic proclamation strikes me as being as devastatingly true today as it did that evening. Esposito was explaining why many ghost hunters are able to locate ghost voices only on playback of site recordings. These spirit disturbances go unnoticed on site, while back in the studio the recordings prove revelatory. A skeptic will simply dismiss these findings as static figments from the imaginations of those looking too hard; they will claim that the voices are nothing more than

20. Michael Esposito, lecture, Gallery 400 at the University of Illinois at Chicago, November 3, 2009, in connection to the exhibition *Alex Halsted and David Moré: Gnathonemus Petersii*, October 13–November 21, 2009.

recording interferences. Regardless, listening to and for voices is wearying compared to pushing a button, playing back a file, and finding patterns that fetch the familiar, understood, and classified.

Listening and *hearing* are not synonyms. At a gallery dinner on a certain coast, one guest overheard another guest speaking to one guest's loved one, this other guest guessing, quite self-assuredly, that a guest from the other coast must only be interested in art that is self-expressive, rather than artwork that speaks to the canon. Now who the hell would ever sign up to be art-historical canon fodder without the promise of expressing themselves? Besides, as Fredric Jameson pointed out,

> It seems important to make this into a two-way street and to insist on the need to explore the ways in which a specific biographical pathology—itself necessarily a historical phenomenon and a social face, by virtue of its very existence as an unconscious symptom—constitutes under certain circumstances a recording apparatus for a unique historical content that it can alone disclose and bring to objective expression.[21]

21. Fredric Jameson, *The Seeds of Time* (New York: Columbia University Press, 1994), 121.

Yes. Invest in voices that make you listen with eyes and hands. To electric histories. To syntax. Even pantomime. For example, Hejinian's "The sea said shoorash, but irregularly—I want to be very precise although it is impossible to spell these sounds—and occasionally it boomed."[22] Multiple and conflicting voices sometimes trip the tongue of a solitary speaker, with a "specific biographical pathology." What happens when a speaker disregards precision and breezes through fractured or multiple voices in a single act? The listener must swim a convoluted distance.

22. Hejinian, My *Life*, 85.

> Voice is always shared; in a sense, it's sharing itself. A voice begins with the entrenchment of a singular being. Later, with its speech, that being will remake its ties to the world, give sense to its own entrenchment.[23]

23. Jean-Luc Nancy, "Vox Clamans in Deserto," in *Multiple Arts: The Muses II* (Stanford, CA: Stanford University Press, 2006), 41.

This irregularity.

VII. "The more I think about it, the more I feel this is the way to do it. (If we are to do it.)"

Marcel Proust registered a lament:

> I had just noticed, in fact, that I had spent twenty-five minutes, that they had perhaps forgotten about me, in this room about which, despite the long wait, the most I could have said was that it was huge, greenish in color, and contained a handful of portraits. The need to talk prevents one not only from listening but from noticing anything, and in this case the absence of any description of external surroundings is description enough of an internal state.[24]

24. Marcel Proust, *The Guermantes Way* (New York: Penguin Classics, 2002), 550.

Over the past fifteen or so years, I couldn't possibly count the number of exhibitions, events, essays, press releases, and pieces that shared or riffed on the Situationist phrase, "On the passage of a few people through a rather brief moment in time." Exposed during the many returns to this phrase is description enough of an inner state, proving, once and for all, that time is not passing, and it's certainly not slipping, slipping, slipping into the future. Rather, time is coagulating and clogging and wrinkling and folding, slumping, delaying, bleeding.

"Isn't that a nineties concern?" "Seems seventies." "The most exciting new, nothing like it." "Where's the next discovery?" All cycle and response. I'm interested in cynicisms that are willing to cry—a "shoorash" that praises irregularity rather than cadences from now to next.

> This "at the one and same time" is the very matter of time, what time comprises. Time comprises a two-way journey, backs and forths, comings and goings, goings and comings; equally, however, it comprises broken journeys, goings that no longer come back but keep on going to infinity, journeys that double back on themselves in a loop that is no less infinite, albeit in a different sort of way. It comprises all the advances and withdrawals, the starts and renewals, the continuous flows and sudden splutters, the jumps, gaits, speeds, and rhythms of its movement. Through all this, it is time *itself*, utterly singular, always the same. Yet this "same" is nothing but the continual movement and change of all times at all times.
>
> And always there is this movement, this transport, passage, transfer, overstepping, journey, trajectory, displacement.[25]

25. Jean-Luc Nancy, "The Soun-Gui Experience," in *Multiple Arts: The Muses II*, 207–8.

The exhaustive order of Jean-Luc Nancy's litany is crucial. Each "transport, passage, transfer, overstepping, journey, trajectory, [and] displacement" opens a pocket of space. Stoner's assertion that, "space is the agency and theater of action."[26] Space is time. It embraces a kind of contingency gleaned from and multiplied in distinct, measurable blocks of time: in publications and performances and recordings and paintings and sculptures and videos and collages and photographs and transmissions and readings and objects.

26. Stoner, 59.

> But there's something funny about taking something time-related, extracting the time from it, and leaving us the three-dimensional product. You know, there's a big difference between shit and shitting. A huge difference. One could sum up the world on that note, you know?[27]

27. Gary Indiana, "Wiretap: A Walk through the Whitney, or What We Really Say When We Talk about Art," *Artforum* 32, no. 7 (March 1994), 113.

At this moment, am I shitting or shit? I hope both. I expect both from any exhibition. And hopefully the assembled artists once together will be dated and forward-looking and distinctively present, with a time-stamped identification and not a time-bound identity. Mallarmé detected something like this:

> Discarded dance-programmes and faded flowers, concert-programmes or dinner menus: they compose, there is no doubt, a literature all of their own, immortal with the immortality of a week or two.[28]

28. Stéphane Mallarmé, in P. N. Furbank and Alex Cain, *Mallarmé on Fashion: A Translation of the Fashion Magazine La Dernière Mode with Commentary* (New York: Berg, 2004), 32.

It has taken a length, a "shoorash," to know what it is. I've returned on many occasions to a statement by the artist and writer John Miller regarding the cultural value of artworks. It's a bit like a mission statement. Miller made this comment in a discussion with writer Maria Fusco about independently produced publications: "We tend to presume (and as an artist I'm inclined to presume) that the relevance of art should be long range. [That] if anything, it should become more relevant as time goes by and, therefore, qualify to be preserved. That may not be the case."[29]

As a curator I've no reason to presume. Many publications and artists and performances and recordings and paintings and sculptures and videos and collages and photographs and transmissions and readings and objects are and will continue to be cast aside as irrelevant by major archives or be simply lost. And, per Miller's assessment, they do not qualify; after all, an archive's business is in the long range narrative of business at hand. I'd add to this fact that the qualifications are always in negotiation, during which the sheer numbers of physical objects or traces out there guarantees irrelevance and marginalization. All who have not qualified for preservation still do claim a space, however compromised, private, uncomfortable, prickly, or imperfect, and are ready for close viewing.

Because "residue approximates vulnerability and fatigue, manufacturing material from form, welcoming that which had been omitted,"[30] there is a loping backwardness to the emotions and behaviors and desires when the hand and eyes reach for residue. It is an intimate and somewhat quiet, private space, even when a public din bleeds through the walls next door. And the assembled, as César Aira suggests, "considered the prospect at leisure, in a gentle, affectionate, futile way, since it was one of those things that is only a matter of time (which are the things that make time matter)."[31]

In this space of affection, navigate the inappropriately cared-for and tossed-aside particulars. For filmmaker Chris Marker, who was surely in Proust's green room—recording "all times" with a close view, "considering prospects at leisure in a gentle, affectionate, futile way," with all the "immortality of a week or two," reminded: "Moments to remember are just like other moments."[32]

This displacement.

29. John Miller, "Publish/Public: John Miller and Maria Fusco in Discussion," in *Put About: A Critical Anthology on Independent Publishing*, ed. Maria Fusco with Ian Hunt (New York: Book Works, 2004), 154.

30. Maria Fusco, *With A Bao A Qu Reading When Attitudes Become Form* (Los Angeles: New Documents, 2013), 121.

31. César Aira, *Ghosts* (New York: New Directions, 2009), 92.

32. Chris Marker, *La Jetée* (1962; Neuilly-sur-Seine, France: Argos Films).

WHITNEY MUSEUM OF AMERICAN ART
22 WEST 54th ST. • NEW YORK 19 • PLAZA 7-2277
Communicate with EDWARD BRYANT, Associate Curator

THE ARCHITECT'S APPROACH TO THE DESIGN OF THE WHITNEY MUSEUM

by

Marcel Breuer

In the designing of the project and after establishing its workings and its program we have faced the first and most important problem: What should a museum look like, a museum in Manhattan? Surely it should work, it should fulfill its requirements. But what is its relationship to the New York landscape? What does it express? What is its architectural message?

It is easier to say first what it should not look like. It should not look like a business or office building, nor should it look like a place of light entertainment. Its form and its material should have identity and weight in the neighborhood of 50-story sky-scrapers, of mile-long bridges, in the midst of the dynamic jungle of our colorful city. It should be an independent and self-relying unit, exposed to history, and at the same time it should have visual connection to the street. It should transform the vitality of the street into the sincerity and profundity of art.

The sketch of the project shows a sunken sculpture court between the sidewalk and the building, spanned by the entrance bridge; it shows the glass front of the lobby facing Madison Avenue, and the sculpture gallery which provides contact with the street and with the passersby. While the inverted pyramid of the building mass calls attention to the museum and to its special dedication, the mass is surfaced with a most durable, retiring, and serene material: a warm grey granite which is rather dark and has a mild play of reflection of the surroundings. The building, reaching out high over the sculpture yard, does not stop the daylight or the West sun; it receives the visitor before he actually enters the interior of the building. One sees the sunken yard and its sculptures from the sidewalk and the entrance bridge. Also, one sees the lobby and the sculpture gallery through the glass walls.

(more)

To emphasize the completeness of the architectural form, the granite facades on both streets are separated from the neighboring fronts: an attempt to solve the inherent problem of a corner building, which otherwise could easily look like a quarter-section of something. The project transforms the building into a unit, an element, a nucleus, and lends it a direction towards Madison Avenue. The overall granite facing, homogeneous, extending out and over towards Madison Avenue, reaching down into the sunken garden with openings which grow out of the surface, with the modulation of the Madison Avenue gap between it and the neighboring buildings, with the granite parapet along the sidewalk and with the structural concrete form of the bridge -- all this is an attempt to form the building itself as a sculpture. However, a sculpture with

Our purpose was
would focus visitors'
flexibility of spaces.
rectangular and unclut
columns or beams and p
floor-to-ceiling panel
interchangeability, in
are light grey, the co
slate floors another r

The floor area ne
This makes top lighted
that daylight would be
buildings opposite. W
ing and would reduce g
ing has controlled mec
trolled, adjustable li

We recognize that
element of a museum, a
rather serious research

adequacy of the lighting in a full sized mock-up before final installation.

Windows have lost their justification of existence in this building; only a very few remain, and only to establish a contact with the outside. These few openings, free from the strict requirements of ventilation and lighting, can now be formed and located in a less inhibited fashion, as a contrast to the strength of the main building lines.

It seems that large open gallery spaces with interchangeable partitions have to be watched, otherwise the general impression will be too clinical. To avoid this danger we suggest for the galleries rather unsophisticated close-to-earth materials: roughly textured concrete ceilings, split slate floors, walls covered with canvas and painted flat. Furthermore, the design includes a number of smaller, non-interchangeable rooms of definite decoration and furnishings. Painting and sculpture can be shown here in surroundings similar to a home or office.

While the average gallery height is 12' 9" clear, the top gallery height is 17' 6". This is in consideration of the increasing size of contemporary painting. The sculpture gallery is double story high, according to the wishes of a number of artists I talked with about this.

A maximum number of offices and the conference room have natural light. They are visually connected to roof terraces by means of glass walls. High parapet walls lend these areas complete privacy, and an atmosphere of concentration, indoors and outdoors.

###

102765

Academy Records

Matt Hanner

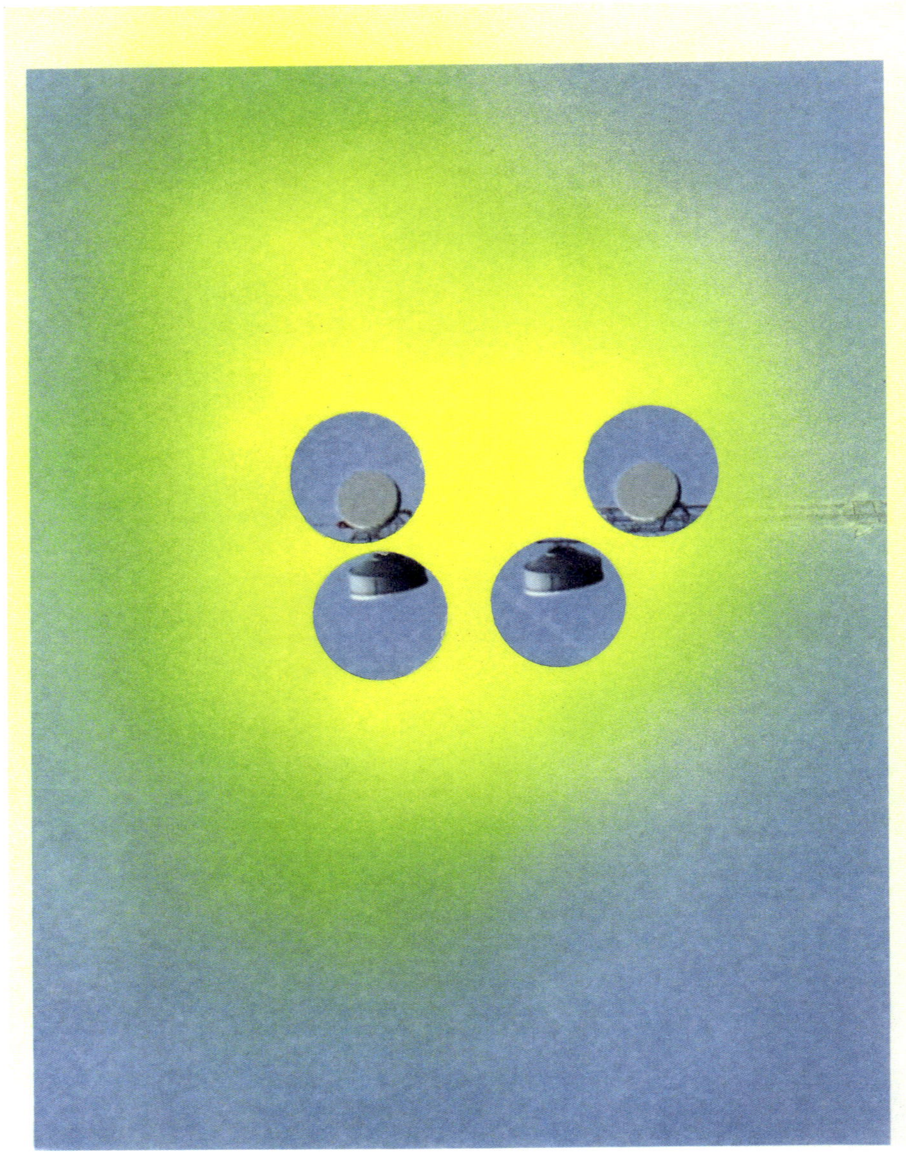

Matt Hanner, *Untitled (RZO series)*, c. 2011. Enamel on inkjet print, 8 ½ × 11 in. (21.6 × 27.9 cm). Collection of Erika V. Hanner

Founded in 2000
Based in Chicago, IL

Born 1971 in Columbus, OH
Died 2011 in Porter, IN

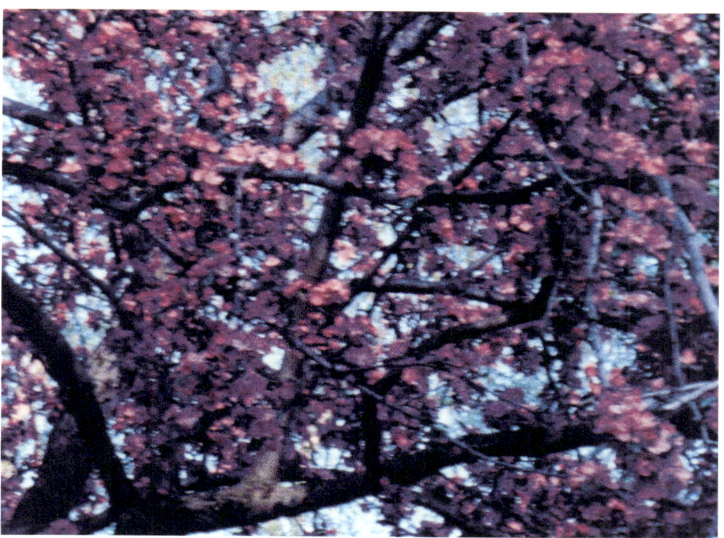

Academy Records, still from *The Bower*, 2011–13. 16mm film, color, silent; approx. 1:30 minutes, looped

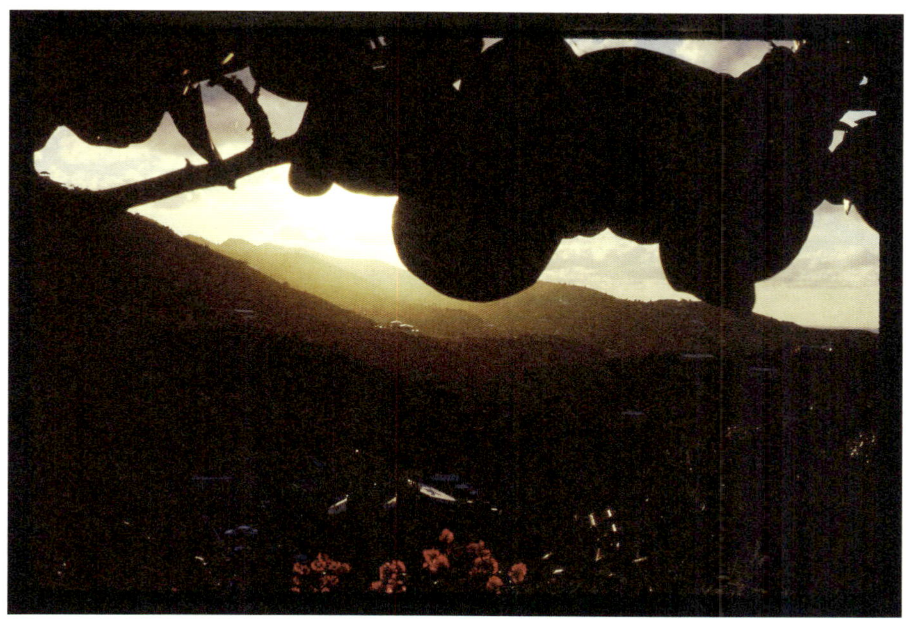

Matt Hanner, *Untitled (5/02 series)*, c. 2002. 35mm slide. Collection of Erika V. Hanner

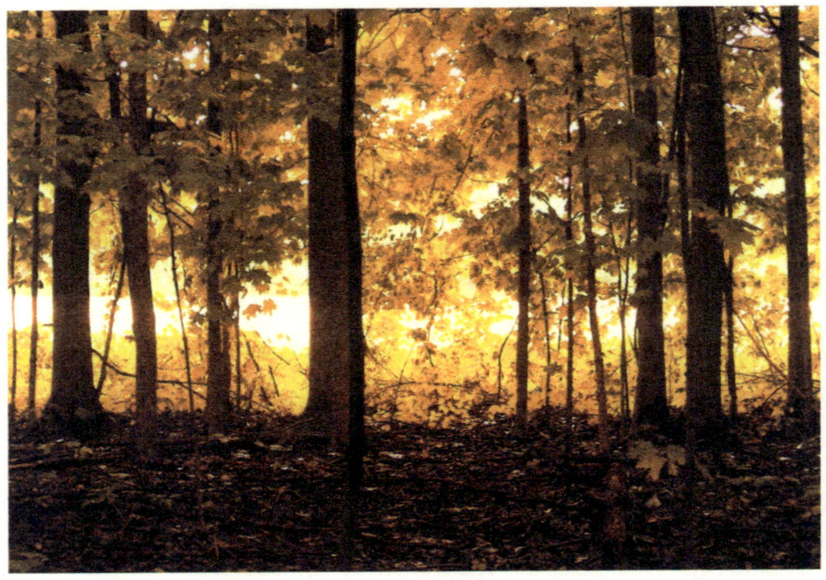

Matt Hanner, *Untitled (postcard series)*, c. 2011. Inkjet print, 4 × 6 in. (10.2 × 15.2 cm). Collection of Erika V. Hanner

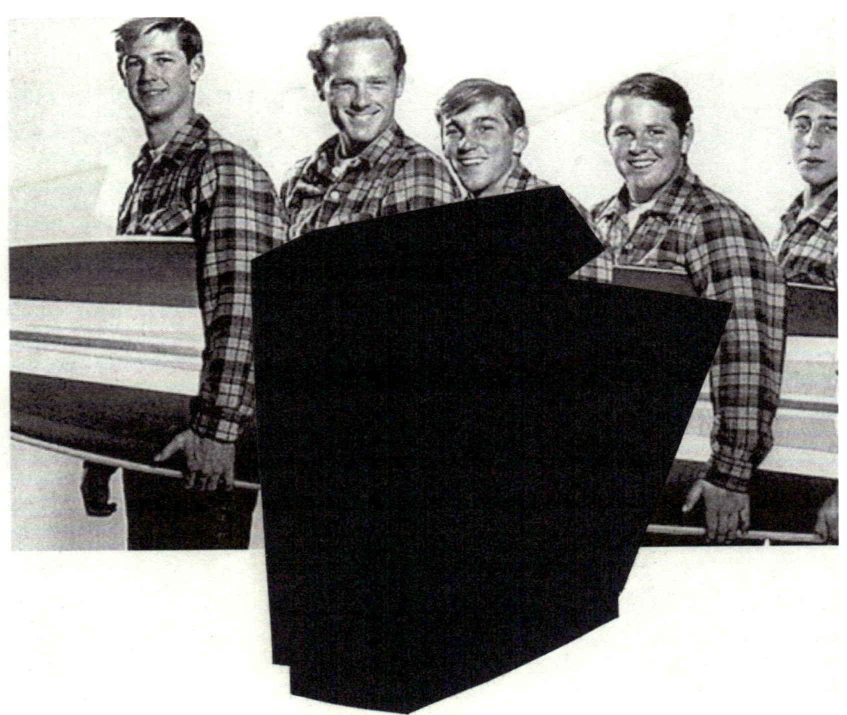

Academy Records, *Good Vibrations: Phantom Jukebox (The Conqueror Worm)*, 2013. Collage, 8 ½ × 11 in. (21.6 × 27.9 cm)

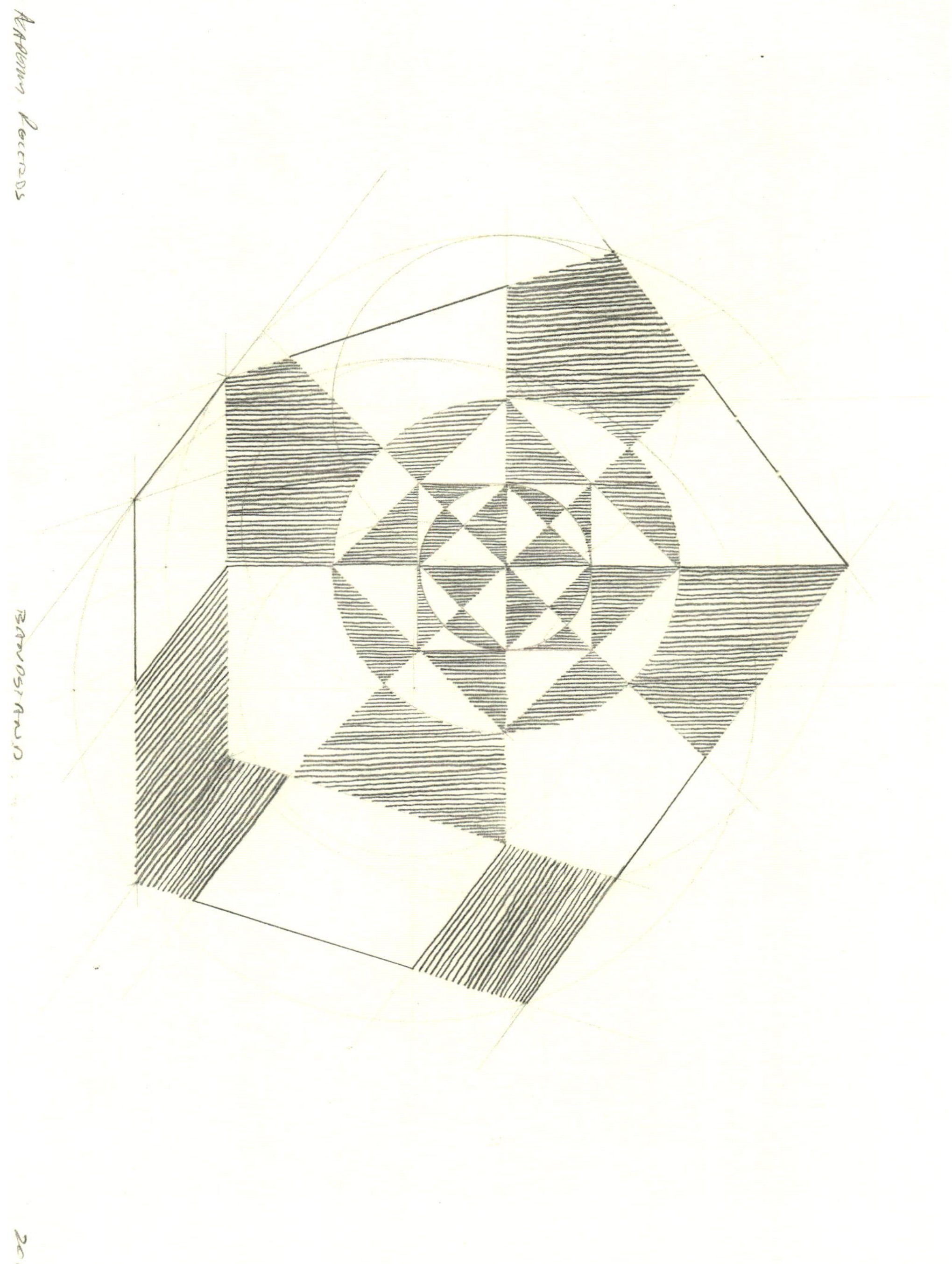

Academy Records, *Bandstand*, 2013. Graphite pencil on paper, 9 × 11 in. (22.9 × 27.9 cm)

Terry Adkins

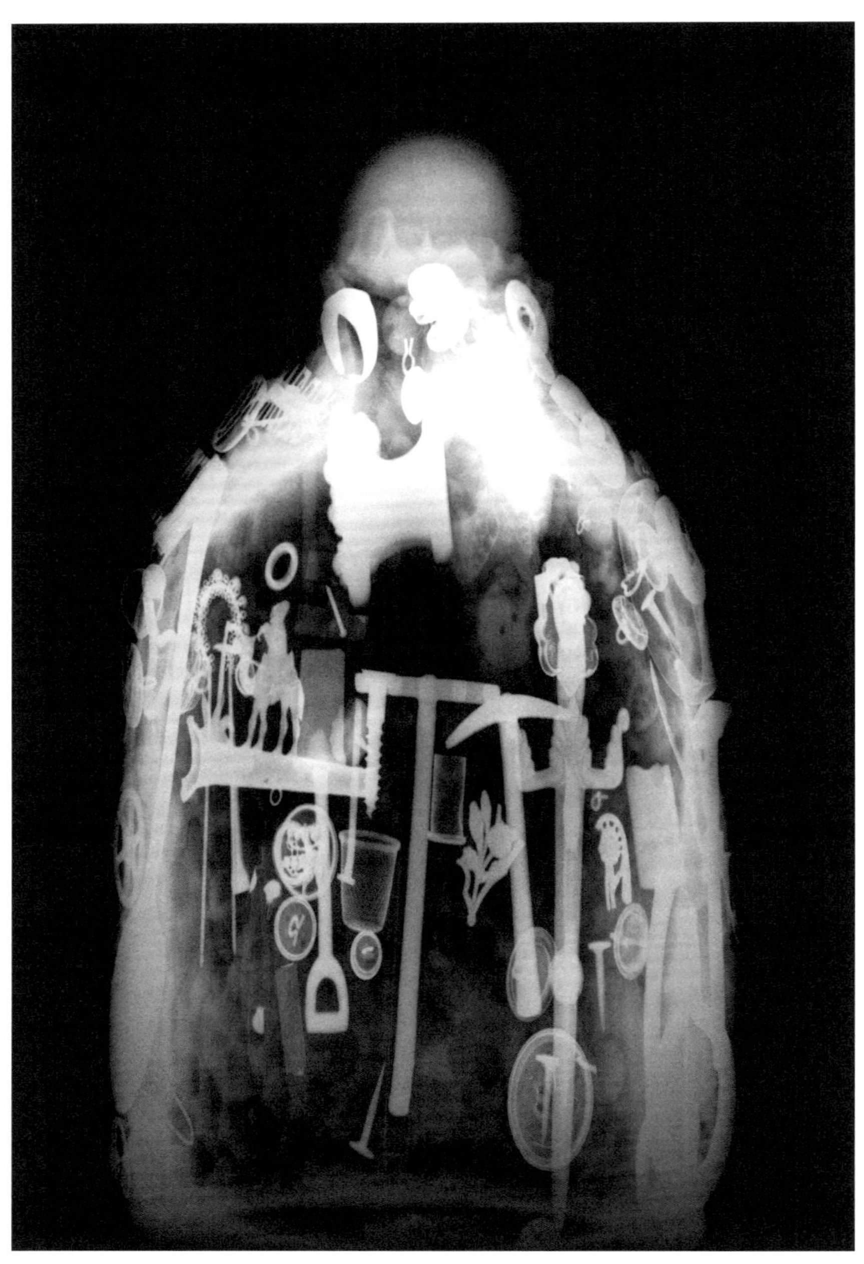

Ars Apollinare, 2012. Pigmented inkjet print, 72 × 48 in. (182.9 × 121.9 cm)

Born 1953 in Washington, DC

Lives in Brooklyn, NY/ Philadelphia, PA

Terry Adkins

Ars Memoriae

Ars Memoriae is an ongoing series of X-ray photographs taken of memory jugs from my own collection. The amassed density of their aggregate surfaces initially drew me to them. Their forms, built through accretion and sourced in attributes of power adapted from Congolese origins, embody the absorption and modification of ancestral beliefs about burial rites and the afterlife by black communities across the United States and Canada. Memorial vessels first appeared in early nineteenth-century cemeteries as enigmatic grave markers but have since come to be utilized as urn-like domestic shrines. They are characterized by an incongruous, muscular assemblage of everyday articles, including jewelry, keys, glass vials, mirrors, crystals, toys, hardware, combs, thimbles, seashells, pipes, watches, scissors, and other utilitarian objects, that were vitally associated with the deceased and were gathered to provide divine support for eternity. Conjured references to time, water, smoke, and light reoccur in the various combinations of employed materials.

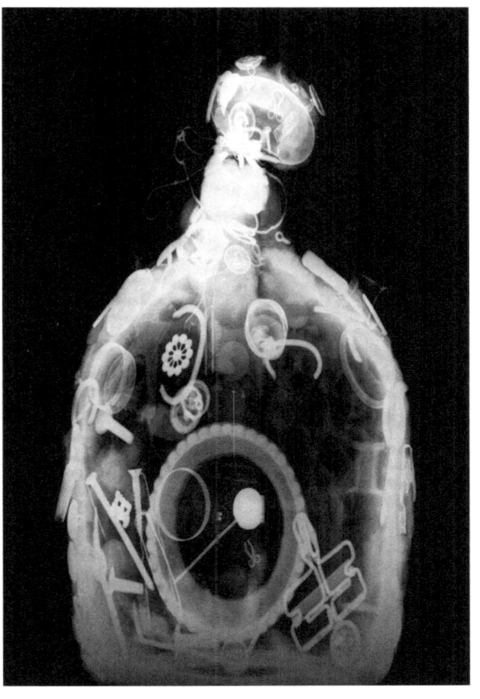

Ars Ravenna, 2012. Pigmented inkjet print, 72 × 48 in. (182.9 × 121.9 cm)

Exposing these vehicles of subtle force to electromagnetic radiation visually dematerializes them, reveals the spectral nature of their becoming, and discloses the quixotic instincts of their anonymous authors. Printed at human scale, the ensuing photographs are meant to impart a sense of the corporeal and to unveil the transcendental aspects of their funerary geneses. The *Ars Memoriae* project is also influenced by a canon of mnemonic devices and techniques that originated among the ancient Egyptians and was orally passed down through the Pythagoreans. The philosopher, mathematician, and cosmologist Giordano Bruno (1548–1600) later codified these procedures for his followers, who used them to organize memory impressions, improve recall, and assist in the recombination and invention of ideas. The encrusted memory jug tradition intrigues me because it stands at the juncture of creative imagination and commemorative custom. It is gratifying to behold and to retrace the work of nameless hands that engaged in an art triggered by purpose and rooted in necessity.

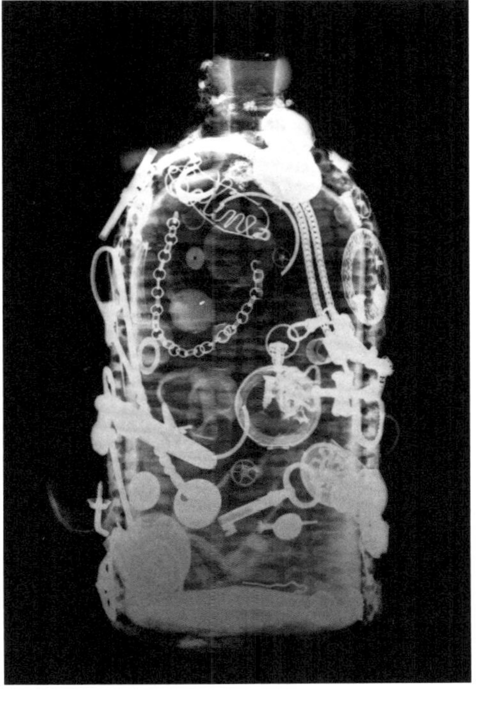

Ars Norfolk, 2012. Pigmented inkjet print, 72 × 48 in. (182.9 × 121.9 cm)

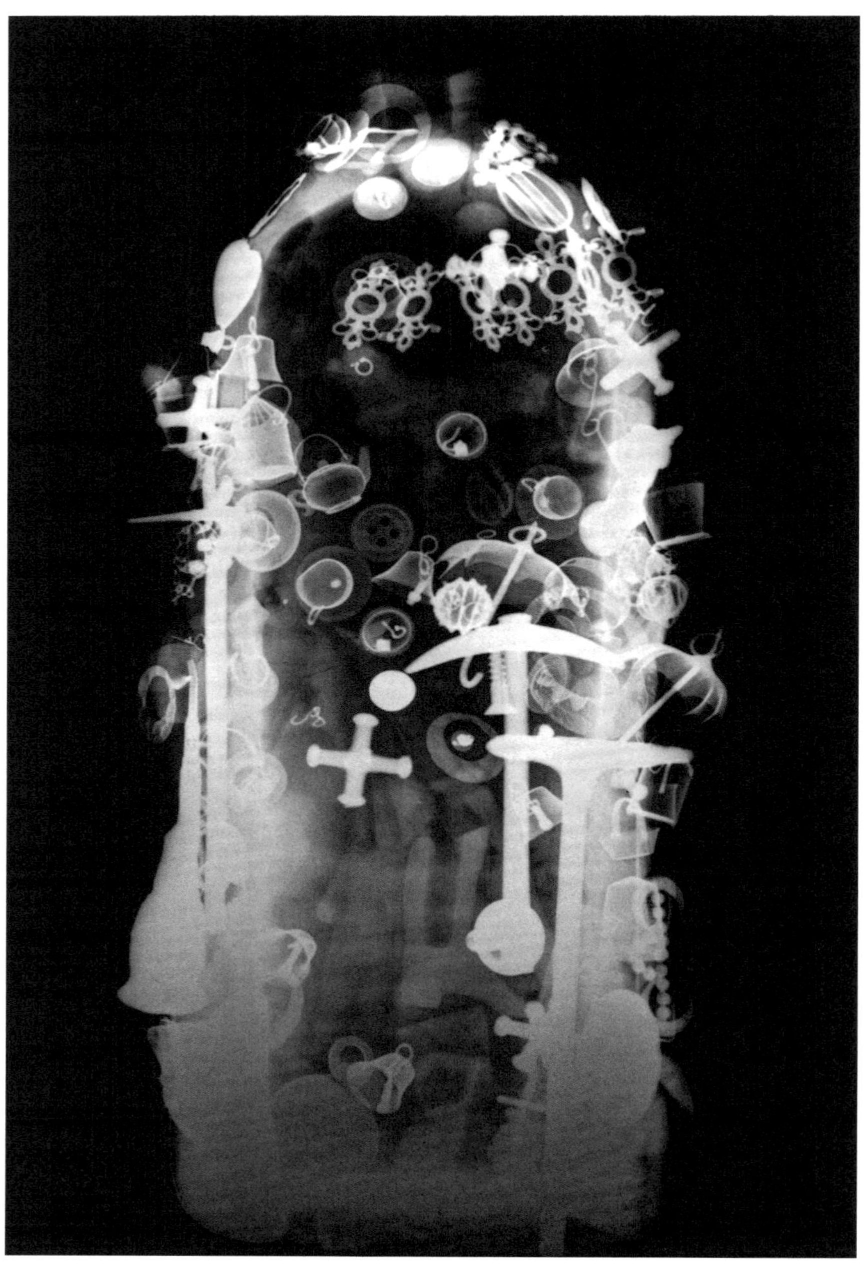

Ars Alexandria, 2012. Pigmented inkjet print, 72 × 48 in. (182.9 × 121.9 cm)

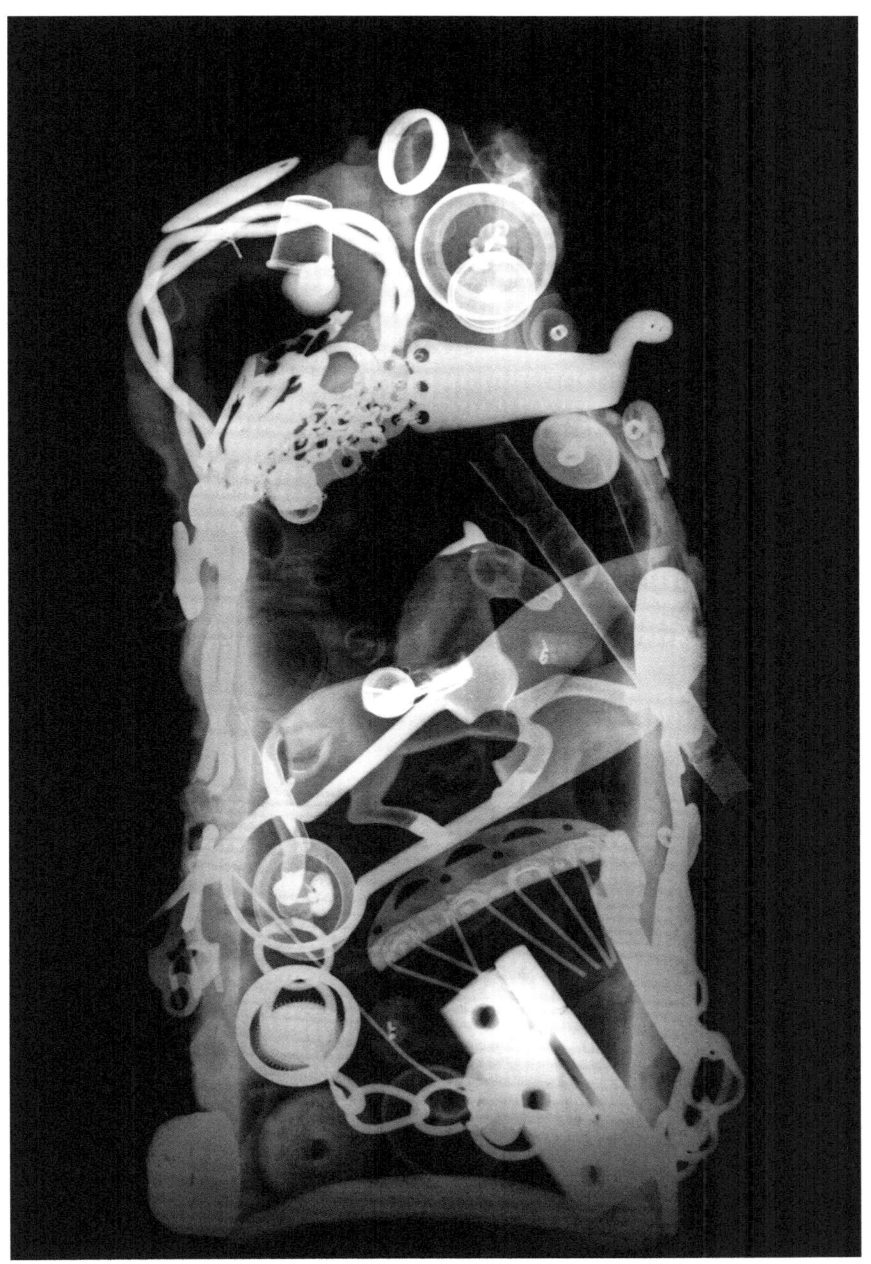

Ars Upperville, 2012. Pigmented inkjet print, 72 × 48 in. (182.9 × 121.9 cm)

Robert Ashley

Alex Waterman

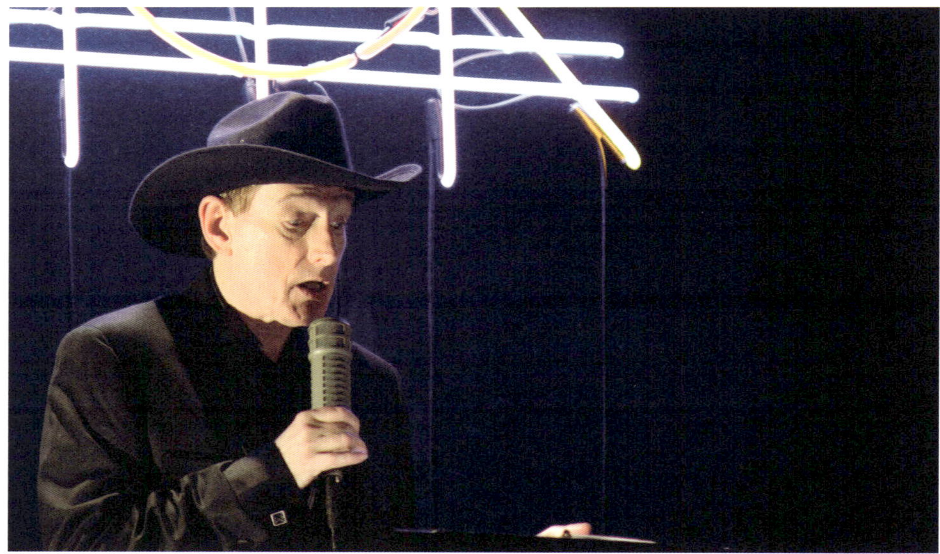

Performance of "El Parque," from *Vidas Perfectas*, Irondale Theater, Brooklyn, NY, December 2011. Pictured: Ned Sublette as "R," a.k.a. Raoul de Noget

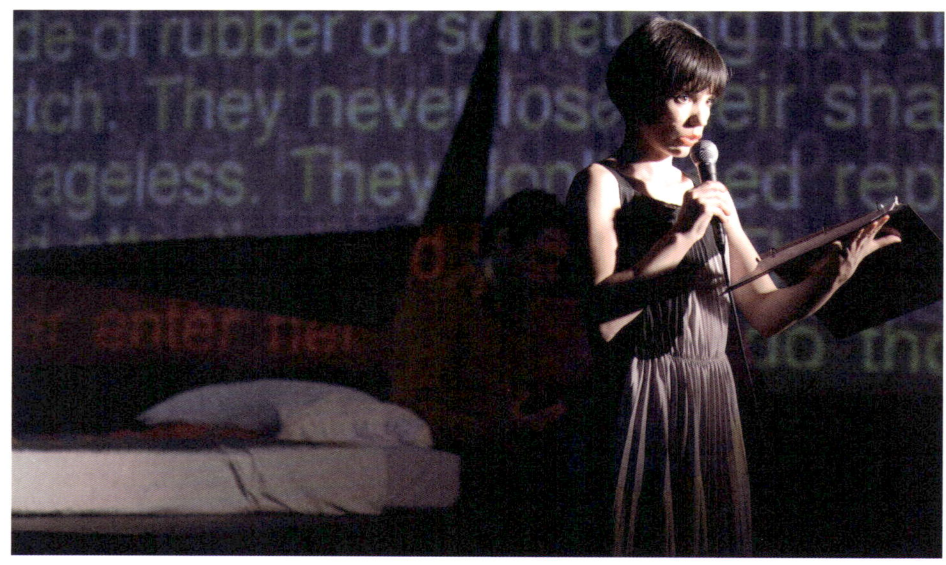

Performance of "El Parque," from *Vidas Perfectas*, Irondale Theater, Brooklyn, NY, December 2011. Pictured: Elisa Santiago and Abraham Gomez-Delgado

Born 1930 in
Ann Arbor, MI
Lives in New York, NY

Born 1975 in
Portsmouth, VA
Lives in New York, NY

Robert Ashley

Alex Waterman

Robert Ashley & Alex Waterman Present Three Selected Works from the Span of Ashley's Sixty-Year Career

CRASH

Crash (2014) is premiering at the 2014 Whitney Biennial. Written for six voices and incorporating light and video installation work by Alex Waterman and David Moodey, this opera is played in six short acts and features vocalists Gelsey Bell, Amirtha Kidambi, Brian McCorkle, Paul Pinto, Dave Ruder, and Aliza Simons.

Crash is about a man—unidentified, but clearly an older man. We learn about his attitudes and his prejudices, and his history as a member of a certain economic and social class. The music in the opera is entirely vocal. The singers take turns performing as the three distinct vocal characters over six acts, highlighting the unique qualities of each of their voices. Those not singing in character perform parts in a vocal "orchestra," accompanying the three soloists. Throughout the opera there are three simultaneous, but not synchronized, projections of photographs depicting vast, beautiful landscapes. With no other visual distractions, this creates an ideal space for meditation and for listening.

VIDAS PERFECTAS

Vidas Perfectas (2011–14) is a new Spanish-language production of Ashley's cult hit *Perfect Lives*, an opera for television that developed through live performances beginning in the late 1970s, and was first broadcast in 1984 on Channel Four in England. *Vidas Perfectas* stars Ned Sublette as Raoul de Noget and Elio Villafranca as Buddy; Elisa Santiago and Raul de Nieves play a range of other characters. Peter Gordon, the musical producer of *Perfect Lives*, returns as the musical force behind the sound of the new opera. *Vidas Perfectas* will be filmed in installments, over a two-week period during the course of the Biennial, in front of a live television audience. "*Perfect Lives*," says Ashley, "uses a musical form of storytelling—as opposed to evening-news style, or soap-opera style, or movie style. Here we use music to tell the story."

In *Vidas Perfectas*, Raoul de Noget ("no-zhay") and his friend Buddy, the "World's Greatest Piano Player," have come to a small town close to the border between Mexico and Los Estados Unidos, to entertain at Las Vidas Perfectas Lounge. Raoul, a Cuban, grew up north of the border, and Buddy (also Cuban) grew up on the other side of the border. As one of the characters in the opera describes Buddy after they become known in town: "There's no doubt that the Mexican is in it. The doubt is if he's Mexican."

Raoul and Buddy fall in with two locals, a man known as D (the "Captain of the Football Team") and his sister, Isolde. Together they conspire to commit the "perfect crime," a metaphor for something philosophical: to remove a large amount of money from the bank, for one day only, and let the whole world know that it is missing—a crime if they are caught, art if they are not. A couple of innocents, Ed and Gwyn, head for the border with D and his friend Dwayne, to elope and get married. They are, without knowing it, carrying the money (from the bank) in the trunk of their car. According to the plan, the missing money will be discovered to be back in the bank the next day.

Among the colorful characters that journey through the opera's seven episodes are a loving pair of unnamed old people from the Home for Old People; the sheriff and his wife (Will and Ida), who finally unravel the mystery of the crime; and Isolde, who watches the celebration of the changing of the light at sundown—amid a picnic of her neighbors—and who knows that the perfect crime has been successful.

266 Bowery
New York, NY 10002
October 6, 1974
phone: 431-3594

Ms. Marcia Tucker
Whitney Museum of American Art
Madison Avenue and 75th
New York, NY 10021

Dear Ms. Tucker;

I would like to be included in the Whitney Annual performing "The Trial of Anne Opie Wehrer and Unknown Accomplices for Crimes Against Humanity.

From 1967 on - the documentation of a life, concieved by Robert Ashley.

Beginning as a spectacular theater piece (1967-69) with 100 questions asked of me on tape by Robert Ashley, with four cross examinators on stage, slides of scrapbook material, film excerpts(Manupelli, Warhol, ist NY Theater Rally etc.) Ray Charles music, on the spot video and polaroid photos, prede3ded by an actual ONCE piece - a combat dance - all a part of the history of Anne Wehrer.

Redesigned as a solo piece (1970) with taped questions answered by me from a sculpture set. A plexiglass box with a chair and table and a TV monitors throughout the museum with projected visual material.

Performed (1974) as music for the Merce Cunningham Dance Company as a day to day direct answer to questions from Robert Ashley. Video taped by Mary Lucier. 2 performances.

Performed (1974) as an intimate living room conversation with Ashley at the Kitchen. 2 performances and one 6 hour performance at York University, Toronto.

Proposed for the Whitney - in it's museum form as a living sculpture. The 100 questions would be taped and answered as they are today - quite a change from the earlier enclosed tape. The performance would take place in a 4' x 8' x 7' plexiglass box, with a table a chair and a TV monitor. Other monitors would be placed throughout the museum. The video of each days performance (4 hours) would be shown when I was not present.

The piece would be the "talking" of a book to be published at the conclusion of the performances, including visual materials from all performances.

This would be the perfect realization of myself as sculpture, literature and art. I would love to perform and document the piece in this way.

Thank you for your consideration.

Sincerely,

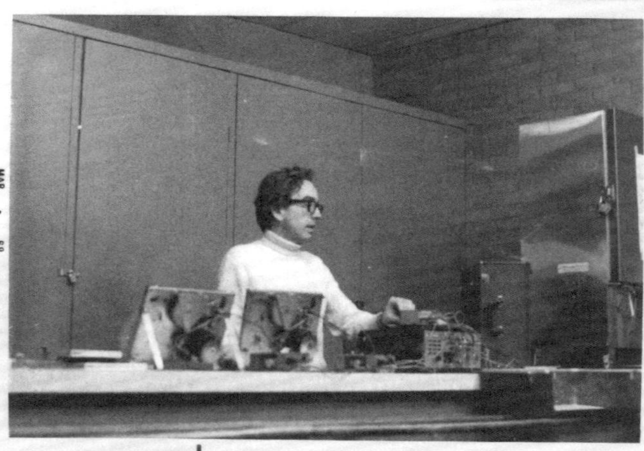

Letter from Anne Wehrer to Marcia Tucker, October 6, 1974
photograph: *The Trial of Anne Opie Wehrer and Unknown Accomplices for Crimes against Humanity*, 1968

THE TRIAL OF ANNE OPIE WEHRER AND UNKNOWN ACCOMPLICES FOR CRIMES AGAINST HUMANITY

Robert Ashley's *The Trial of Anne Opie Wehrer and Unknown Accomplices for Crimes against Humanity* was composed in 1968. It was originally writen for the ONCE Group—a collective of artists associated with the annual ONCE Festival of new music and performance—active in Ann Arbor, Michigan, from 1961 to 1969. The first production featured Anne Wehrer as herself, accompanied by members of the ONCE group. The performance at the Whitney Museum of American Art realizes Anne Wehrer's dream of presenting this work at the museum—and it comes almost exactly forty years after Anne wrote a letter to curator Marcia Tucker about the piece (see illustration). Ashley recalls Anne Wehrer, the inspiration for the opera:

> Anne Wehrer, who died in 2007, was a motivating force behind the ONCE Group. She had one of the most beautiful speaking voices I have ever heard: a lilting Virginia accent with a large pitch range and a huge variety of stresses. Moreover, she was generously voluble. (Once, after I had known her for some time, we started talking at lunch and she told me stories continuously for fourteen hours, with me saying "Uh-huh" about every fifteen seconds.) She seemed to remember every detail of everything that ever happened to her in her remarkable life. Her generosity (and the good luck that goes with generosity) caused her to come into contact, and usually to become friends, with everybody—from Frank Sinatra to Robert Rauschenberg to Andy Warhol and many other artists and art patrons, as well as a host of politicians, criminals, radicals, and all sorts of other admirers. And she just gives it away.
>
> The idea of making music with "characters" started with my work with the ONCE Group. It was a peculiar beginning, in that I was not working with opera singers, but with real people: these were simply friends doing musical things. This was clearly an unusual approach to "opera," and it culminated with *The Trial of Anne Opie Wehrer and Unknown Accomplices for Crimes against Humanity*.

In the staging of the piece, Anne is upstage, center, three-quarters turned away, with a closed-circuit video camera watching her middle body (her hands in particular, as she lights a cigarette or pours herself a drink); other cameras show the audience documents from her life: family photographs, legal documents, letters, and so on. During the performance, she answers a litany of questions posed by a pair of men, who sit downstage. A pair of women are designated as Anne's "proxies," sometimes answering questions on her behalf. At any time Anne might interrupt her own storytelling to answer a question directly or to enlarge on the details furnished by her proxies. She speaks at length—embellishing with anecdotes and gossip—telling the story of her extraordinary life.

Michel Auder

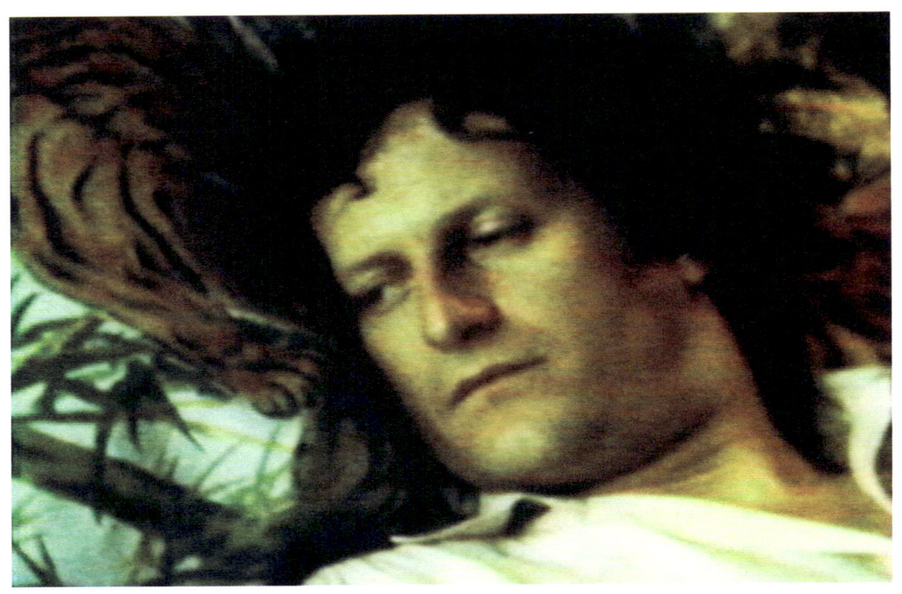

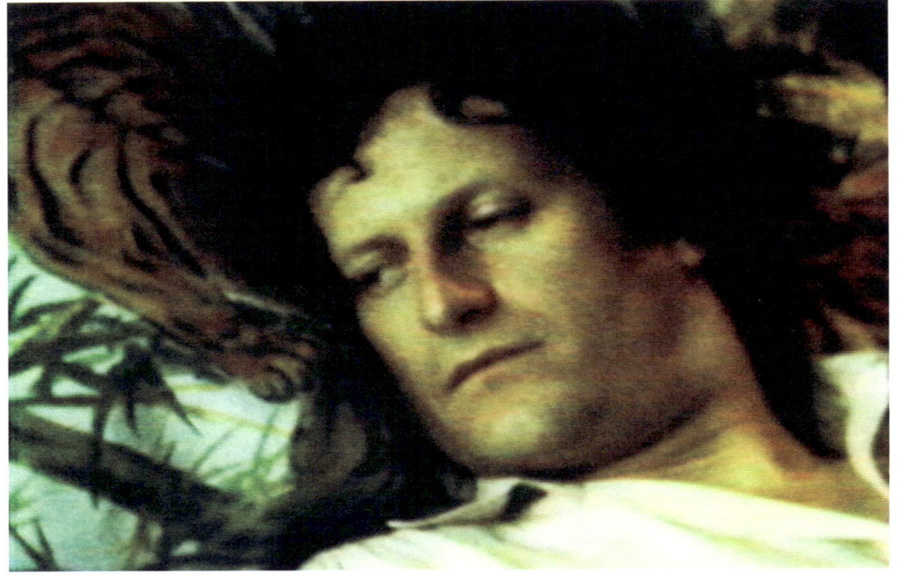

Stills from *48 Hours in 8 minutes—*, 1978. Super 8 film transferred to digital video, color, silent; 8:26 minutes

Born 1945 in Soissons, France

Lives in Brooklyn, NY

Physiques of Capture

Kate Levant

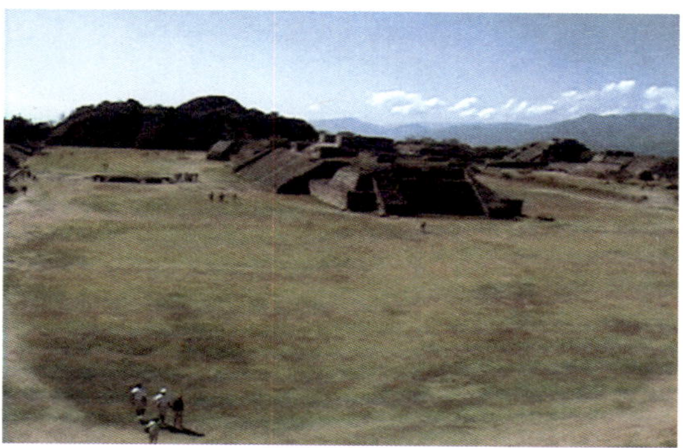

Still from *My First Pipe of Opium since 1973 - Mexico 2004*, 2004. Digital video, color, sound; 7:39 minutes

Vapor on a mountaintop surrounds the scene and is simultaneously the substance of the scene. Birds circle through it, assuming mutual movements along with this vapor mist. A hawk appears. A signal. The hunt. (*Do You Love Me?* [2011].) He watches the event evolve. This watching, this going forth of vision, is primal. He watches to acquire the motion occurring before him. He watches to capture it. And as his attraction draws him, from a distance, nearer, a resonance develops within his acquiring gaze, becoming a provocation to enter the mutual movements seen . . . Something like visual intercourse ensues.

Within these liminal contours of influence and compromise, Michel Auder has generated a life's work purposed to possess the passage and relapse of captivation. He's been doing this for decades—decades that have produced an archive to which Auder returns continually, to relapse and become captivated over and over again. Recording provides the means by which he traces and suspends the plays of these lapsing revolutions. A moment may be held captive within the recording medium and simultaneously be abandoned to disappear through the passes of life unbound. The medium receiving these traces both contains and lubricates such synthetic splits. The medium is Auder's essential accomplice.

Laying in bed for forty-eight hours with his camera upon him recording—this assumes the form of a portrait contained within the clasp of *48 Hours in 8 Minutes—Silent* (1978), and here we gain a cue. To find the essence in the process of fabricating it . . . watching and wondering, lying, laughing, and writing and watching and breathing, chitchatting and sleeping and touching and eating and looking, drinking and switching and sweating and leaving, all backdropped by his bedsheets of tigers snarling in the palms . . . Auder concentrates a motile resolution of the event to expose the composition of a moment's essence through its depiction—a picture in time, manipulated. While this discreet cut retains Auder's ceremonial gaze within the hours of its recording, what was captured yields as time advances onward.

The behaviors Auder is drawn to capture maintain pulse within his footage yet sneak like phantoms beyond the confines of their default origins. Through the medium, Auder is able to articulate the boundaries within which a being (a person, a place, a thing—regardless) exerts its life force to contend with time. And, while recording formats these passages into sequential, advancing frames, what appears in the footage is not achieved by way of detached mastery over some specimen observance. Auder's sensuality circulates through all of his footage, as he guides the recording along the contours of his intrigue. One feels that he handles video's capacities at the medium's threshold to capture exactly that which intrigues him in a subject. In this way, the visuals retained are essential evidence of Auder's attraction through the medium, negotiations expressed in an analogue physique.

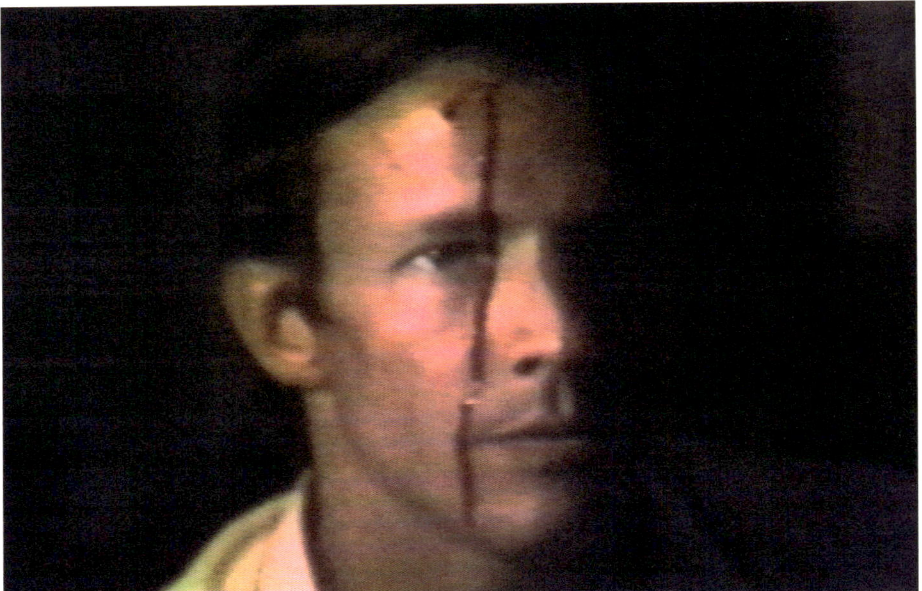

Still from *Made for Denise*, 1977. Betamax transferred to digital video, color, sound; 3:05 minutes

While an inhuman grain cooled through the primary stages of video's resolution—appearing as though its images were not watched enough, the recording equipment was not handled enough, or a human sensibility had not imposed enough on the technology's ability to receive all that occurred before its lens—Auder thrusts video out of its awkward adolescence into an initiation or rite of passage through his own life, arousing the medium's capacity to access the nature of his own captivation. He has turned his cameras on for hours and hours and hours, to watch along with him. And video has endured leisurely afternoons late into the night under water, under covers, across rooftops, across TV screens.

Even as Auder returns his video gaze back on the screens of pedestrian television—a domain in which video itself is in resolute command—his presence as captor never dissolves into the glitchy grain of video's resolution. Against the spectacle exposure of 1984's Olympic events, Auder contorts the athletic conduct to recede, eerie and strange. In *The Games: Olympic Variations* (1984), bodies compete through their televisual image into Auder's grasp of their performance. "Look at the action again!" an announcer calls out. Auder responds in lapsing musculatures. One runner's fingernails on the track cuts to a diver cycling perversely under the surface of the pool, interrupted by a repeating close-up of pronounced exhaustion cut to the sound of quivering string instruments. Attention is diverted, from competition between distinct athletic bodies, to their cropped parts blending into an ensemble pulse.

Television released these images live to mass audiences; however, once recaptured by Auder, the extracts gained a capacity to shift along axes fragmented and perpendicular to the sequential order by which they appeared on-screen. As editor, Auder recomposes how we read the significance of moments' potential fragilities and vitalities against the grain of their initial roles in the world from which they arise. Moments rise and fall against a priori rank. An event in time, sometimes decades after treading through the current of its instant, is subject to a kind of revolving vector crisis.

Regarding the arrangement of this year's Whitney Biennial presentation, Auder notes: "'Museum Heads' and 'Shopping Heads' . . . will be adding new footage to 'Museum Heads' . . . 'Shopping Heads' remains the same . . . 'Heads of the Town' no audio . . . will be adding new cuts and remove a few nonmoving images in the original version . . . 'UNTITLED (I was looking back to see if you were looking back at me to see me looking back at you).'" It's all here.

Michel Auder, like tides continuously variable, keeps busy. Recognizing his practice as merely intuitive would be an injustice to the work. Where have we witnessed an intuition so intimately receptive to the anachronistic movements through which life passes the substance of meaning before us? Maybe it is by way of mastery.

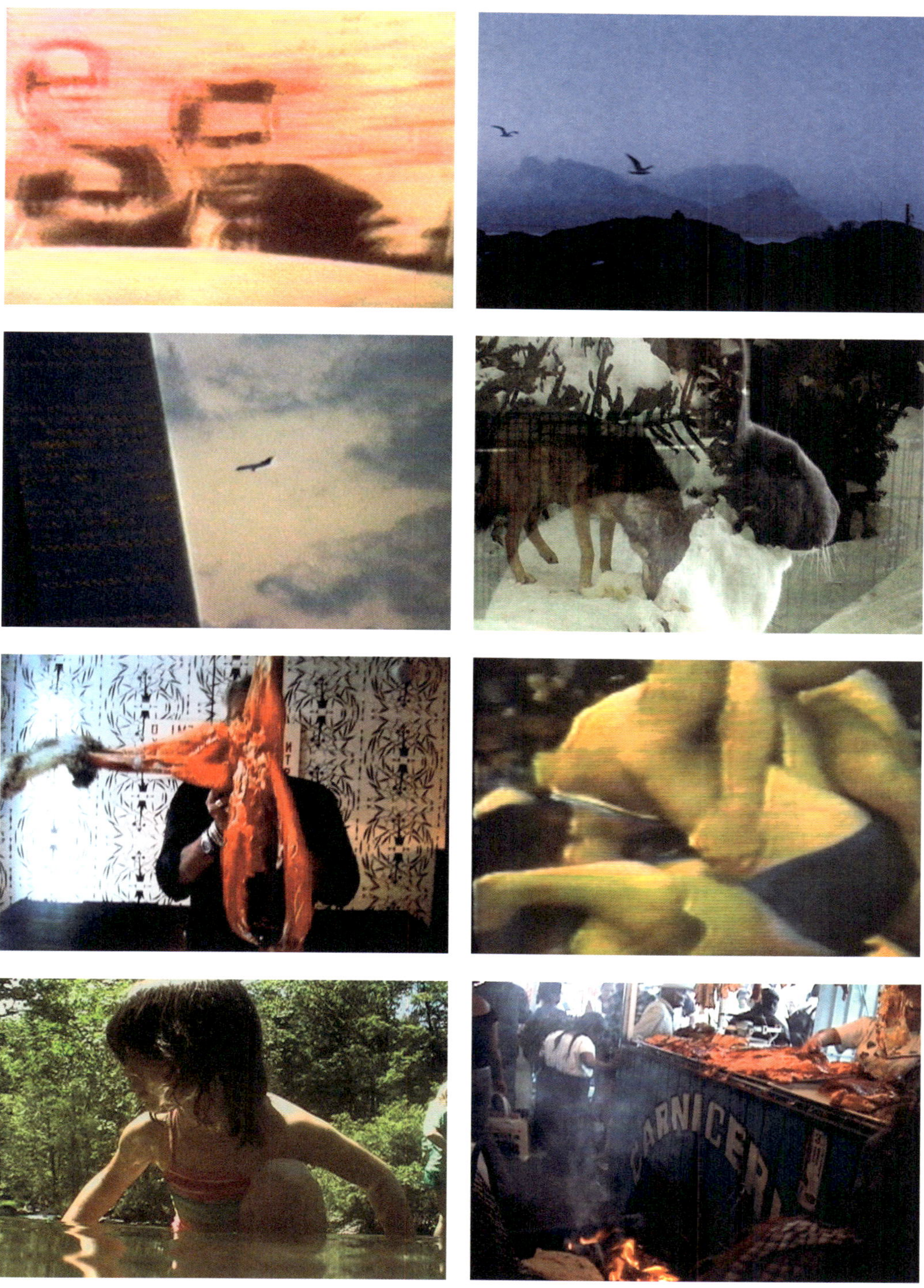

Stills from (top to bottom, left to right): *1981 Regan*, 1981 (edited 2009). Betamax transferred to digital video, color, sound; 4:22 minutes; *Apocalypse Later*, 2013. MiniDV transferred to digital video, color, sound; 5:13 minutes; *The Town*, 1999. Betamax transferred to digital video, color, sound; 5:11 minutes; *Narcolepsy*, 2010. Betamax, MiniDV, and phone video transferred to high-definition digital video, color, sound; 21:55 minutes; *Endless Column*, 2011. Phone video transferred to high-definition digital video, color, sound; 18:21 minutes; *The Games: Olympic Variations*, 1984. Betamax transferred to digital video, color, sound; 21:36 minutes; *Do You Love Me?*, 2013. Betamax, MiniDV, and phone video transferred to high-definition digital video, color, sound; 10:38 minutes; *My First Pipe of Opium since 1973-Mexico 2004*, 2004

Elijah Burgher

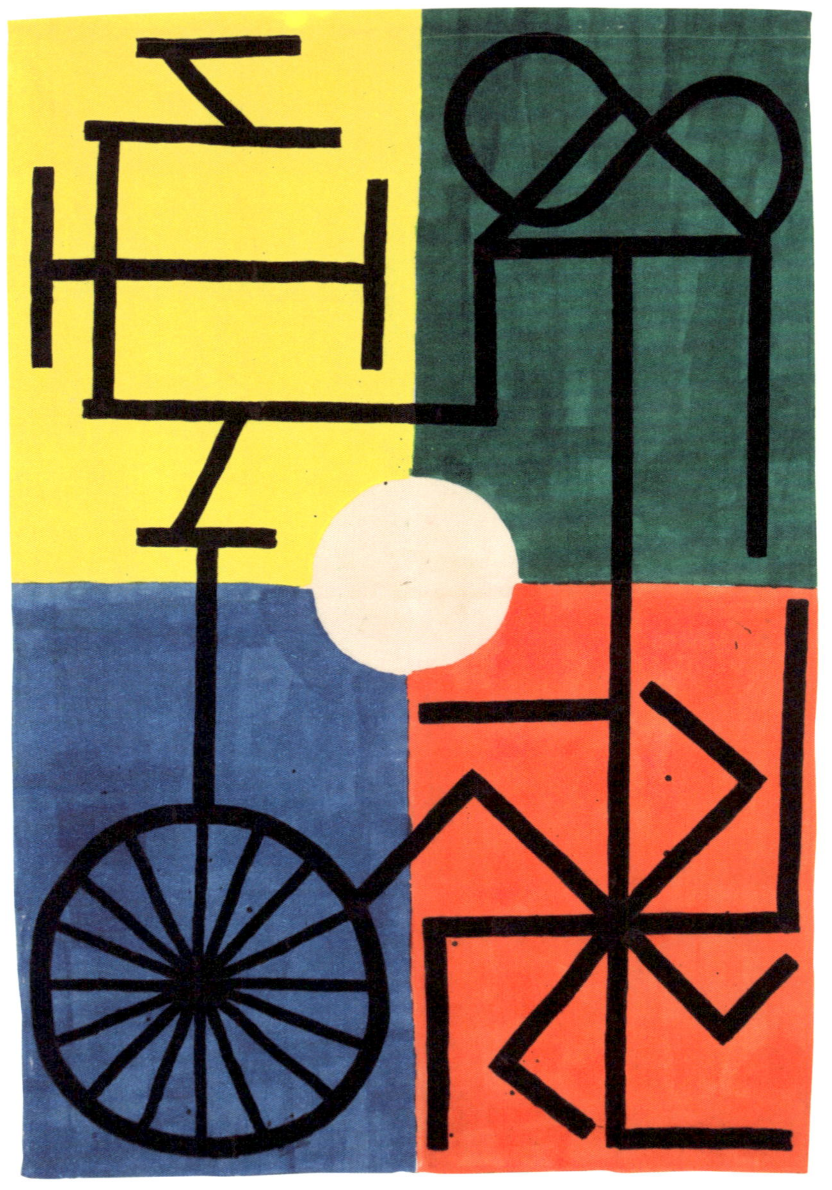

A Machine to Catch Ghosts, 2013. Acrylic on canvas drop cloth, 72 × 108 in. (182.9 × 274.3 cm)

Born 1978 in Kingston, NY

Lives in Chicago, IL

Elijah Burgher

A Boner for Death

To a teenager in the 1990s, homosexuality seemed like a death sentence. My constant adolescent erection was like a compass that pointed the way to my AIDS-related demise. A sympathetic high-school art teacher gave me a mix tape of Bronski Beat and Communards songs, which I tossed in the garbage after a single listen. I simply didn't want to feel good about it.

When I was twenty or twenty-one, I encountered an essay by Jean Genet in which he posits a unity between same-sex desire and the death drive, and it made me . . . *feel good.*

Genet argued—reactively to the dominant culture, perhaps—that if heterosexual love's ultimate consequence is reproduction, the bringing of new life into the world, then homosexuality is against life, an orientation toward death. It isn't difficult to find other examples of artists and thinkers making a similar connection: Samuel R. Delany in *Hogg* (1995), Leo Bersani in "Is the Rectum a Grave?" (1987), Pierre Guyotat in *Eden Eden Eden* (1970), and Dennis Cooper in nearly anything he ever had a hand in producing. Genet, William S. Burroughs, and the postindustrial band Coil were and remain my personal lodestars in this regard. I was exposed to all three in high school or shortly thereafter, disavowed them while sipping neomodernist Kool-Aid in grad school, and rediscovered them in my late twenties when I was truly setting out to make pictures and seeking counsel in this precarious endeavor.

The first track on the cassette my art teacher gave me was "Smalltown Boy," a melancholy but sprightly New Wave tune about gay migration to urban locales. In the music video, Jimmy Somerville, taunted by homophobic classmates, sings, "Run away, run away, run away," and he eventually does to find comrades in the big city. Now compare Bronski Beat's gay-power anthem with Soft Cell's "Tainted Love," suspending for a moment the latter's associations with VH1 programs about the eighties and DJ playlists for weddings. Marc Almond and Soft Cell's songs were a lot darker than they're usually credited as being, and their big hit is no exception. If the "Smalltown Boy" runs away to the city to find others, "Tainted Love" shows him a year or two later, now as a bar back or "dancer" whose hopes of romantic love are dashed on the cold, cruel reality of anonymous promiscuity and the general urban alienation that characterize life in the gay ghetto. Now raise the specter of AIDS, and the point really drives home. Coil did exactly that when they covered Soft Cell's hit, slowing it to a dirge, a monotonous croak substituting for Almond's theater-school yelp. Almond even makes a cameo in the video as the angel of death, visiting a victim of the plague in his hospital bed.

In 2004, I receive my MFA, a degree toward which I bear a gloomy sense of irony. John (also Jhon or Jhonn, as he preferred) Balance, Coil's lead singer, has just passed away. His death drive, expressed as mad lust for alcohol and other mind-altering substances, drove him over the edge of a banister in his home in England and onto his head, a fall resulting in injuries from which he perished within hours. I listen to the band's first record, *Scatology*, originally released in 1984, on repeat. Bush Jr. is in office. The cocktail has transformed AIDS into a manageable chronic illness by this point, but the president is a sufficient substitute for haunting the social and cultural landscape as a figure of death and mass destruction.

Scatology is a concept record about excrement and all things anal. But the band is not only being aggressive about their presentation of homosexual desire. Their interest in the anus and its products is also alchemical: shit turned into gold. Sonically, they transform rudimentary noise and samples into cathartic trance music. On the cover, an inverted cross frames a pair of beautiful bare buttocks—an update of Man Ray's *Monument à D.A.F. de Sade* (1933).

I am fixated on an Aztec sculpture of the god of death, Mictlantecuhtli, in the museum of the Templo Mayor in Mexico City, which traveled to the Field Museum in Chicago in 2008. Representing the chaos of decay into which we all eventually descend, the ceramic sculpture stands as tall as a human, with a large, grinning round head, its dome gridded with holes into which plugs of curly hair were once inserted. Mictlantecuhtli leans forward, his arms up and bent at the elbows, and hands palms out at chest level. His ass thrusts back either like he's about to squat or like he's begging to get fucked from behind. My interest in this sculpture increases as friends die, and I seek. . .what?

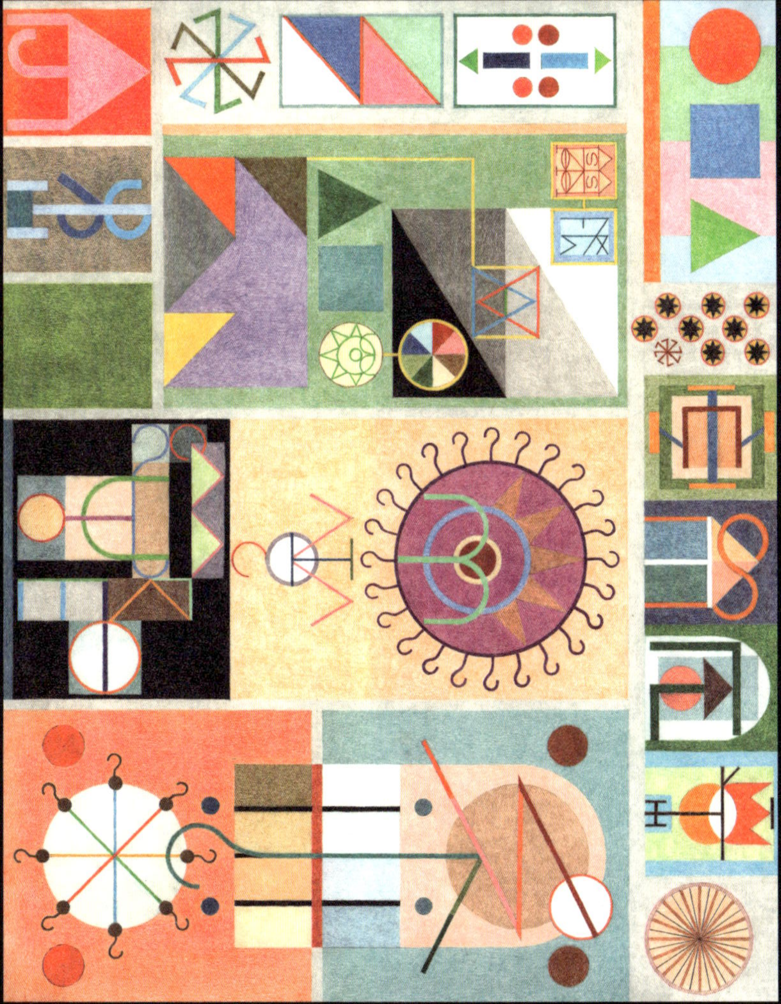

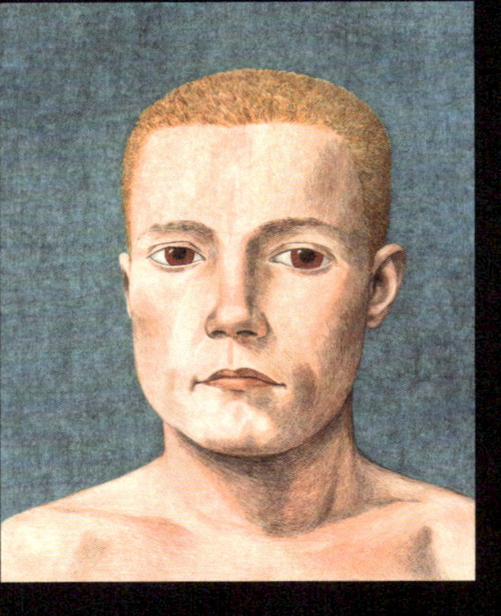

Lucifer, 2013. Colored pencil on paper, 24 × 19 in. (61.0 × 48.2 cm). Private Collection

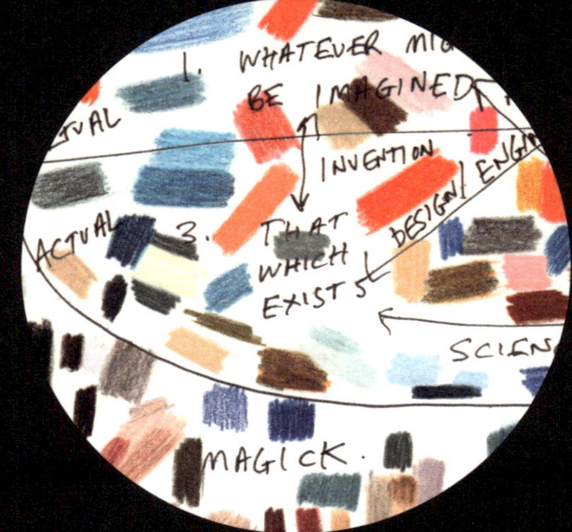

Final Theory (for Steve Reinke), 2013 (detail). Colored pencil on paper, 11 × 14 in. (27.9 × 35.6 cm)

Excremental Philosophy Illustrated, Vol. 1, 2013. Colored pencil on paper, 19 × 24 in. (48.2 × 61.0 cm)

An object of meditation in this gruesome and sexed-up personification of death, I suppose. William Pisarri, Mark Aguhar, and Tom Daws, may you all rest in peace.

When I begin reading Burroughs in earnest, I start with *The Wild Boys: A Book of the Dead* (1971). Although he and Brion Gysin might have had Cubism in mind when they invented the cut-up technique, I think the method's effects are as much temporal as spatial. The cut-up is a time machine in addition to being a teleportation device. It slices up and shuffles two or more discrete pieces of space-time into one another. I fantasize about time machines. For me, it'd likely be a coin toss between going to New York City in the late 1970s and going to Germany in the early 1930s. Burroughs's novels cause me to experience deep sadness for lost time, both moments in my personal past and historical moments to which I'll never have real access. In Burroughs's classic cut-up novels, memories of his St. Louis childhood, paranoid fantasies of intergalactic conspiracy, pornographic imaginings, and text appropriated from other sources are ground into word and image dust, fragments strung together by ellipses or hyphens. The most finely chopped passages are unpleasant and difficult to read. When I do so, I feel like I am swimming against the blasting current of time, and my subjectivity is coming undone.

My fantasy of traveling to Weimar Germany is largely based on the anarcho-communist Daniel Guérin's memoir of his adventures in that country during the years leading up to Hitler's seizure of power. A young communist, Guérin dutifully reports on the antifascist proletarians in their day-to-day resistance to the outbreak of brown shirts and swastikas. He also describes, however, chance meetings with vagabond youths, *Wandervögel* who have strayed from their official hiking clubs and created gangs of their own. These *Wild-Cliques*, or wild gangs bereft of a worldview (or confused by too many competing ones), drew on popular, escapist fiction about Germany's Teutonic past and America's Wild West to construct new identities for themselves and to improvise social groupings. They adorned themselves with runes and edelweiss while taking on names like Winnetou. I should quote Guérin at length here, because my synopsis inadequately portrays both the author's erotic awe and the motley mythologies with which these youths concocted their new selves. My point here, though, is that when major ideologies—or "Big Pictures," as Burroughs called them—fail to make sense of a contradictory, crumbling reality, we are left to remake our selves with whatever resources are closest to hand.

For the past couple of years, I have been collaborating with my friend Steve Reinke on a now-aborted video, pitting a symbol I invented (or, at least, named), the "Anal Swastika," against a meme from one of his text drawings, "Genital Holocaust." The pretext of our unfinished monster was a mutual interest in both the aesthetics of transgression and the cultural and psychological impact of the AIDS epidemic. The project foundered, I think, on a philosophical and aesthetic conflict, best summarized by countering the Anal Swastika's conception as a new myth with Genital Holocaust's status as an ironic provocation. The latter is a placeholder for meaning; the former purports to brim over with the stuff. We failed to find a middle ground between too little meaning and way, way too much. It might also be the case that I did not properly divine the meaning of my own symbol, that its power yet eludes me.

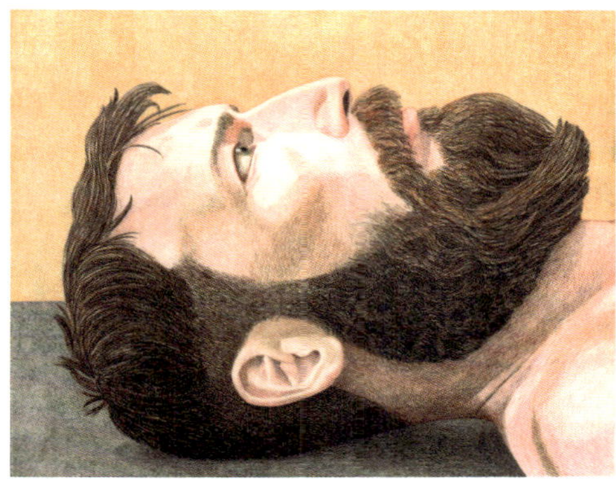

Portrait of Jhon Balance as Talisman Against Suicide, 2013. Colored pencil on paper, 19 × 24 in. (48.2 × 61.0 cm)

Again, 2004: I lost a green notebook that served double duty as a sketchbook and a diary. After John Balance died, a recording of one of Coil's last live shows is released, *And the Ambulance Died in His Arms*. I immediately ordered the CD online. On one of the tracks, "A Slip in the Marylebone Road," Balance speak-sings about losing a green notebook. I decided to experience the coincidence as a sign, although the meaning was unclear to me. It still is, but I tightly hang on to the correspondence, like a protective charm. My boyfriend at the time told me that he sometimes felt as if Balance were attempting to possess him while we are having sex. I believed him.

Jimmie Durham

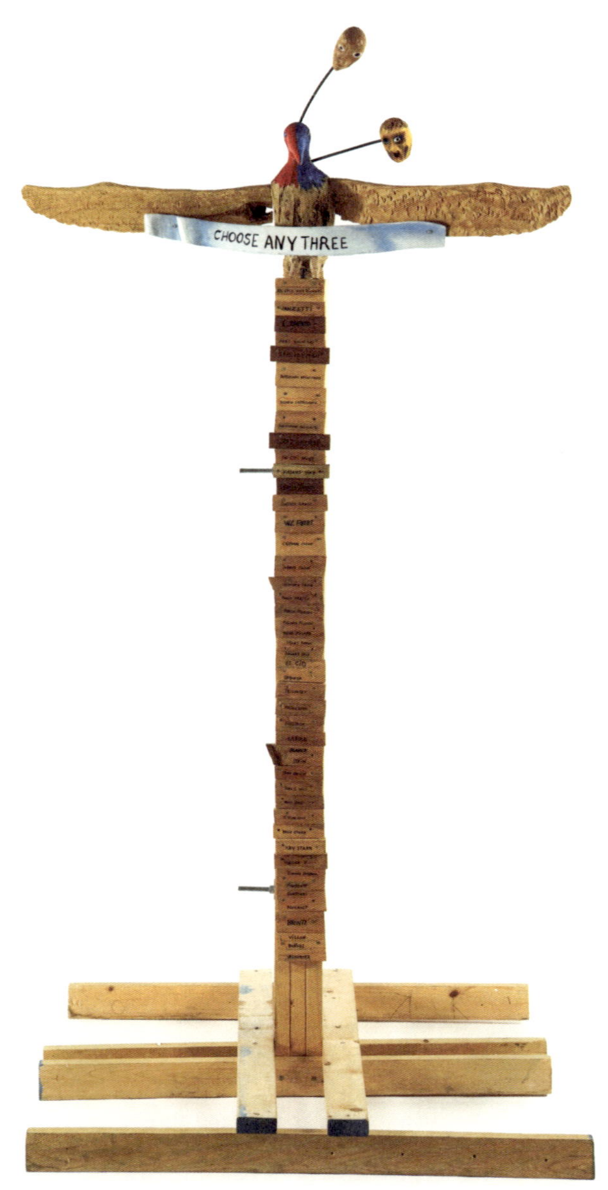

Choose Any Three, 1989. Carved and painted wood, metal, and glass, 99 3/16 × 49 3/16 × 48 in. (251.9 × 124.9 × 121.9 cm)

Born 1940
Washington, AR

Lives in
Berlin, Germany

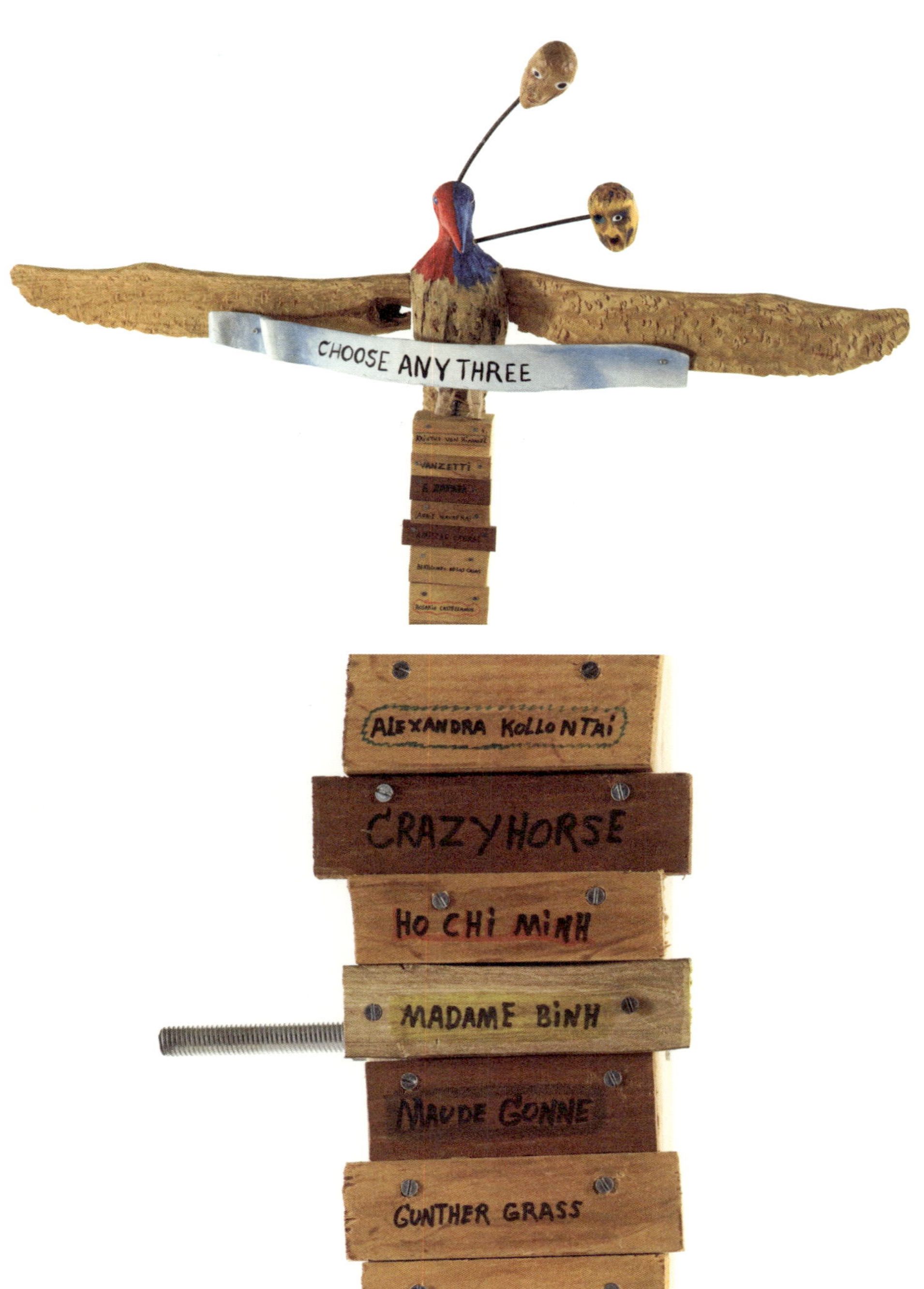

Choose Any Three, 1989 (detail)

Choose Any Three, 1989 (detail)

Joseph Grigely

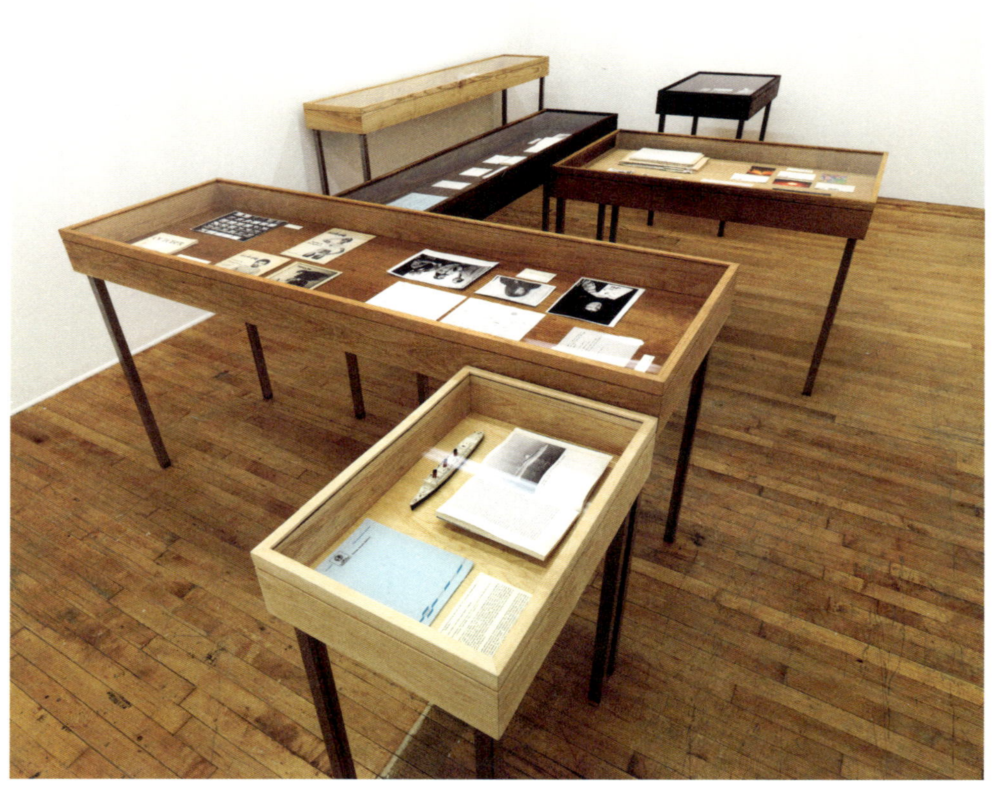

Joseph Grigely, *The Gregory Battcock Archive*, 2009–14 (installation view, Rowley Kennerk Gallery, Chicago, 2010)

Born 1956 in
East Longmeadow, MA

Lives in
Chicago, IL

Joseph Grigely

The Gregory Battcock Archive 2009–2014

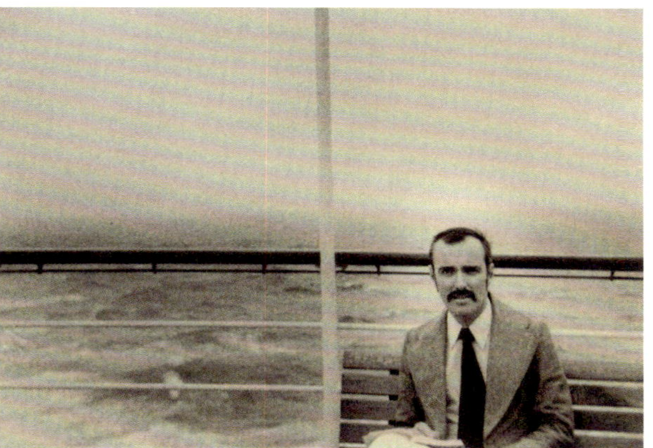

Gregory Battcock en route to Leningrad on the *Mikhail Lermontov*, 1973. Unknown photographer. The Gregory Battcock Archive

THE DISCOVERY OF GREGORY BATTCOCK'S ARCHIVE

Gregory Battcock came into my life in the fall of 1992, when, quite literally, I stumbled over him.

Having just spent a beautiful week hiking in the White Mountains, I returned to my studio in Jersey City. The studio was inside a former cigarette factory near the Hudson riverfront that took up an entire square block. In the late 1980s, the vast empty floors of the building had been divided and rented out to artists. For years, one floor—roughly 20,000 square feet—was occupied by a moving and storage company called Shalom. Occasionally people who had belongings stored at Shalom would divorce, lose their jobs, or die, and their accounts would lapse. At that point, Shalom would usually sell their furniture and household goods and discard any personal possessions. Things like clothes and family photographs could often be found littering the ground around their dumpster.

While I was hiking in the White Mountains, Shalom was evicted from the building. When they moved out, they left behind a ruin of unimaginable proportions—so many lives, once carefully packed in boxes, now haphazardly spilled out across the floor or were crammed into overfull dumpsters. The artists in the building salvaged the things they could, and what remained was the debris of uncountable lives.

Walking through the remains was unsettling. As a friend and I explored the space, we found an area with a lot of books and papers kicked across the floor. Many of the books were signed on the flyleaf with a big, loopy signature, "Ron Whyte"—a name that didn't ring a bell for me. But mixed in with Ron Whyte's books were some books that were inscribed with a name I did know, Gregory Battcock. Battcock had edited a well-known anthology on Minimalism—he also edited *Arts Magazine* for a while. As we sifted through the papers, we found photographs, correspondence, travel notebooks, and hundreds of copies of underground newspapers in which Battcock had published his essays. We hastily gathered what we could—enough to fill six or seven big cardboard boxes.

With some research, we learned that Whyte was a playwright who had been the arts editor for the *Soho Weekly News*. He had lived in an apartment immediately next door to Battcock on West 99th Street. Battcock, to our surprise, had been murdered in Puerto Rico in 1980—his body was found on the balcony of his San Juan condo on Christmas Day, with 102 stab wounds. We donated the bulk of the material to the Archives of American Art in Washington, DC. I kept some duplicate material and made copies of other materials, thinking that some day I would write about Battcock.

For almost two decades, this small archive sat in a box in my studio, until a few years ago, when I finally retrieved it and started to pursue answers to various questions—mostly the question of what could be learned about Battcock from the otherwise unpublished underside of his life that had been strewn across the fourth floor of a warehouse in Jersey City.

BATTCOCK

The first enigma was this: how did Battcock's and Whyte's papers end up in Jersey City? A student of mine, Maureen Burns, found the answer in the shape of a person still living on West 99th Street: the Reverend Paul William Bradley, who first worked alongside Whyte as an assistant and later, as his partner, shared apartment 3A with him. Battcock, who lived next door in 3B, stipulated in his will that the bulk of his literary estate should go to Whyte. But for reasons still unclear, Battcock's mother had the will invalidated and claimed most of Battcock's possessions—including his paintings by Andy Warhol, Malcolm Morley, and Christo; his wine cellar; and anything else she could turn into cash. She left behind the papers and some books, which Whyte and Bradley collected and put into storage. Nine years later, Whyte died after complications from surgery. Bradley explained the situation: "After Ron died suddenly in 1989, I had some financial hard times for a while and wasn't able to keep up with the payments on the storage in Jersey City, and the materials eventually were abandoned."[1] After the salvaged material was donated to the Archives of American Art, Bradley solidified the Smithsonian's holdings by giving the archives additional Battcock manuscripts and related materials that he had retained in his apartment.

Battcock's background was not without its share of twists and turns. Before he became an art critic whose prescience provided us with incisive anthologies on Minimalism, Idea art, and Performance art and books like *Why Art*, Battcock had been a painter. He held a Rome Prize Fellowship in 1958–59, and in the early 1960s he had several exhibitions in New York, including shows at the Schainen Stern Gallery and the Hudson River Museum. He had a studio in Hell's Kitchen, and his painting activities began to overlap with his emerging work as a critic starting around 1965, when he wrote about Warhol's films for *Film Culture*, and in 1967, when he wrote art reviews for the *Westside News*. By 1968, he was writing weekly reviews for the *New York Free Press* and monthly reviews for *Arts Magazine*.

Then, in January 1969, an exhibition organized by Seth Siegelaub titled *O Objects O Painters O Sculptures . . .* changed things for good for Battcock. "Anyone who doesn't go needs his head examined because this is perhaps the first exhibit this season that really goes someplace and offers something a little bit new and something that really matters," he wrote in the January 23 issue of the *New York Free Press*. "Another thing about this show," he continued, "is that perhaps it isn't art and maybe it's art criticism, which would be something I've suspected all along, that the painter and the sculptor have been moving further and further away from art and in the end perhaps all that would remain is art criticism."[2]

Battcock's review was titled "Painting is Obsolete."

Published the same year as Joseph Kosuth's "Art After Philosophy," Battcock's review was his first effort to address art's critical self-reflexivity. It also testified to a personally transformative moment: evolving as a critic and mindful of criticism's history, he went on to invert the direction of art's move toward criticism and turn criticism, if not into art, into something it had not been before. As a critic, his strength was in discovering ideological movements, and from emergent tendencies of his time—Minimalism, Performance art, and Conceptual art—he produced essays and anthologies that were part of the leading edge of these movements. His reviews and essays in *Gay* and the *New York Review of Sex* unmade and remade the genre of "criticism" in a way that made mainstream criticism seem as staid as it seemed unambitious.

Around the time of his review "Painting is Obsolete," Battcock took his own advice and quit painting. He enlisted his college friend George Walsh to help him dismantle his studio in Hell's Kitchen. As they emptied the studio and lined up the paintings for the trash truck, Battcock mentioned that Warhol had stopped by earlier in the day to take a painting. Walsh asked Battcock if he could have one, too. "You choose," Walsh recalls Battcock saying to him. "I can't," Walsh replied, "Do you have one you particularly like?"

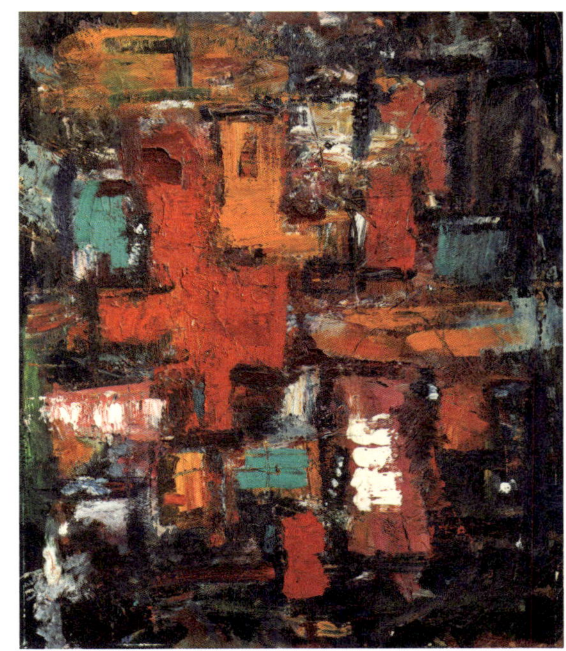

Gregory Battcock, *Untitled*, n.d. Oil on canvas board, 24 × 20 in. (61 × 50.8 cm). Collection of George Walsh

The painting Battcock particularly liked is 24 inches high and 20 inches wide, painted—that is to say, brushed, splattered, and raked—with oil paint on canvas-covered board. Like most of Battcock's work at the time, it is abstract and expressionist without being Abstract Expressionist. The painting reveals a sense of Euro-American modernism that fits neatly into the aesthetic paradigms of modular architecture and interiors of the time, like those of Eames and Knoll. The verso of the painting does not reveal a title, but it does conveniently indicate which end is the top and which is the bottom. "It's the only painting in which I feel that I came near to accomplishing what I wanted to do," Battcock told Walsh, as they finished their task.

George Walsh took the painting home with him to London, where it hung unframed for a decade in his sitting room, supported on the back by a single adhesive plastic hook. In 1981, he moved to Chicago, and the painting moved with him. By then, the 1970s, Battcock, and Battcock's unsolved murder, were all in the past.

THE ARCHIVE

Battcock counted among his many friends and acquaintances Jill Johnston, Andy Warhol, Lawrence Weiner, David Bourdon, Nam June Paik, Douglas Davis, and Seth Siegelaub (who proposed that Battcock collaborate with him on a book about the business of the art world). He was a meticulous correspondent who kept carbon copies of his letters and notes. He also kept a diary of his cruising activities in the woodsy stretches of Riverside Park off West 99th Street. Both in private and in public, Battcock was unafraid to say what he believed; he took obvious pleasure in instigating conflict with institutional authority, whether it was with the Museum of Modern Art, the Catholic Church, or his local post office.

The archive itself is expansive; it includes published material (Battcock's books and tear sheets of his essays and reviews, including those published under pseudonyms), photographs (some by Bourdon and Jimmy De Sana), and a range of international correspondence. With his neighbor Whyte, who assisted and collaborated on various writing projects, he traded late-night notes slipped back and forth under their apartment doors. Some of his correspondence is related to business—arrangements for lectures and travel, for example—but at every turn, Battcock's tone is anything but decorous. When the French critic Pierre Restany visited his class at William Patterson College, Battcock wrote to a friend: "Today Pierre Restany gave his Rio Negro lecture and film. Awful. He was drunk. The students fell asleep." This is typical of Battcock—he wrote not just about art but also about its margins: the parties, the galleries, and the gossip. While he had a Ph.D. in art education from New York University, Battcock was rarely so serious as when he was on the surface frivolous—as he was in many of his columns and in essays he published in his short-lived, self-published magazine, *Trylon & Perisphere*. In his notebooks, he was constantly scheming and planning and plotting and finding in every moment something worth writing down—he could find on a margarine package in a grocery store a comment that would serve as an introduction to an exhibition review. Battcock was an avowed aficionado of travel by ocean liners, which he described as "the last examples of transportation vehicles with personalities."[3] For Battcock, "art" was not just about what appeared in the galleries—it was also about how we move through everyday life. The archive also contains unpublished book proposals, including a murder mystery, a novel about the art world in the 1970s, and a book of essays initially published in *Gay*, as well

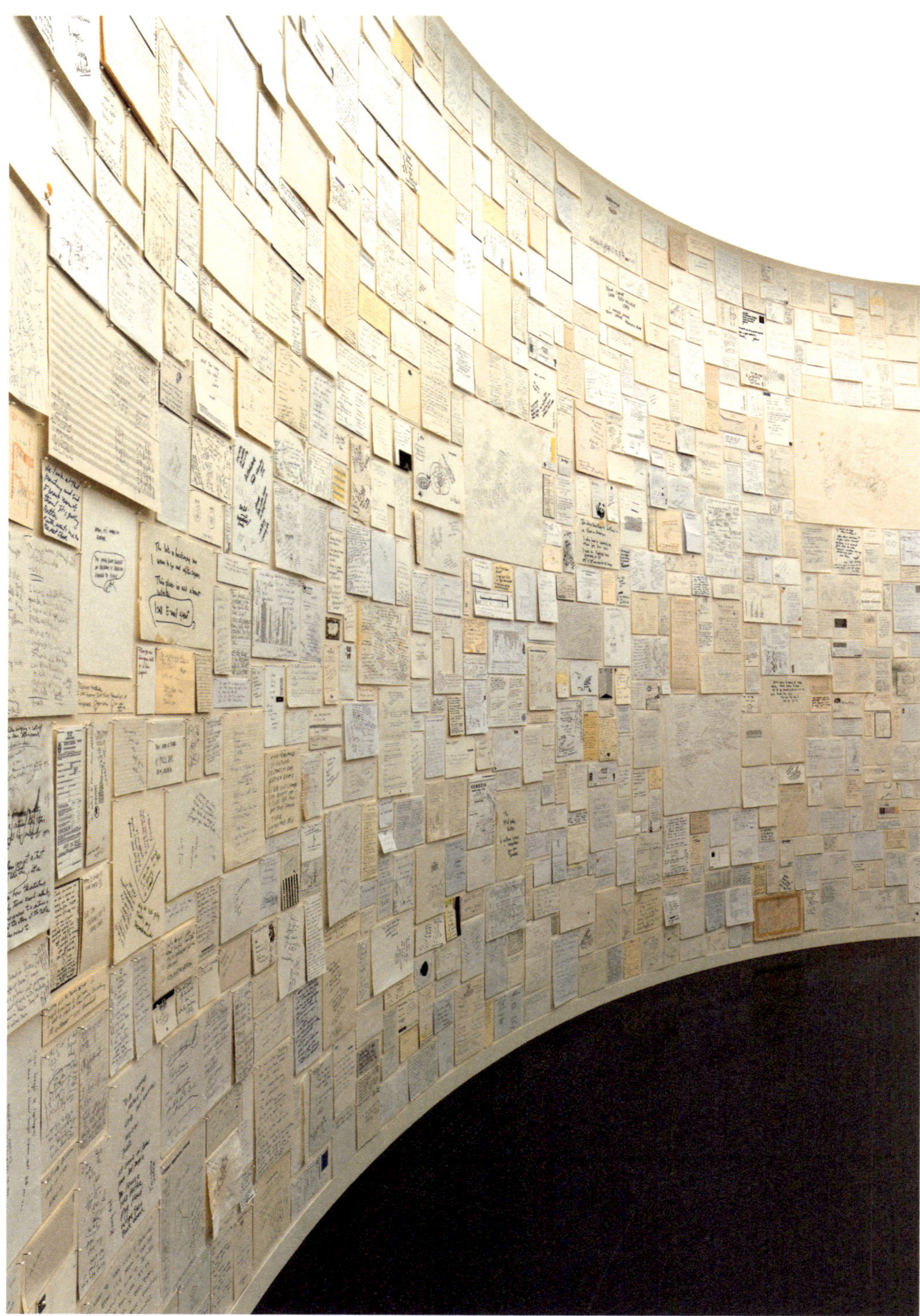

Joseph Grigely, *White Noise*, 2000 (installation view, *Erre, variations labyrinthiques*, Centre Pompidou-Metz, France, 2011). Oval-shaped room, inscribed conversations, and pins, 360 × 216 × 168 in. (914.4 × 548.6 × 426.7 cm)

an unrealized exhibition proposal on wall paintings and the wall: "The fact that paintings have a back side that is there and that is a condition of painting is a virtually unexplored phenomenon," Battcock wrote with foresight that was decidedly ahead of its time.[4]

ARCHIVES AS ART

The display of *The Gregory Battcock Archive* as an artwork has its beginnings in a body of art I developed in the 1990s and early 2000s called Conversations with the Hearing. Like the Conversations, *The Gregory Battcock Archive* uses the grid as an organizational structure to present an archive of physical documents as a form of storytelling. The vitrines in the exhibition are each made from a different hardwood, each is a different shape and different height, and they are composed as an irregular modular sculpture. A document is both a material artifact and a node within a network of human relations. We both draw and draw out Battcock from those relations—the artists he talked with, the critics he argued with, the meals he shared, the students he taught, and the tricks with whom he had sex—they are all here, some with names, some with pseudonyms (even Battcock had a pseudonym, Braniff Livingston). Battcock's archive encompasses a cross section of the art world in the 1970s—it is not just about art, art criticism, and art institutions but also about their place in a post-Stonewall New York. As a painter, teacher, critic, and traveler, Battcock was a consummate shape-shifter who left us with fragments of his daily life and his work, and from these fragments we can construct a portrait that is revealing in its incompleteness.

ACKNOWLEDGMENTS

Research on Battcock was supported in part by a Smithsonian Artist Research Fellowship. I am also grateful to the following people for their assistance: Paul William Bradley, George Walsh, Patricia Blackmon, Maureen Burns, Josh Rios, Danny Floyd, Rowley Kennerk, and Amy Vogel.

1. Paul William Bradley, email to the author, November 2, 2009.
2. Gregory Battcock, "Painting is Obsolete," *New York Free Press*, January 23, 1969, 7.
3. Gregory Battcock, "Ocean Liners: The Way They Were," *Art in America* 68, no. 6 (Summer 1980): 142–47.
4. Gregory Battcock, "Wall Paintings and the Wall," *Arts Magazine* 45, no. 3 (December 1970–January 1971): 24–26.

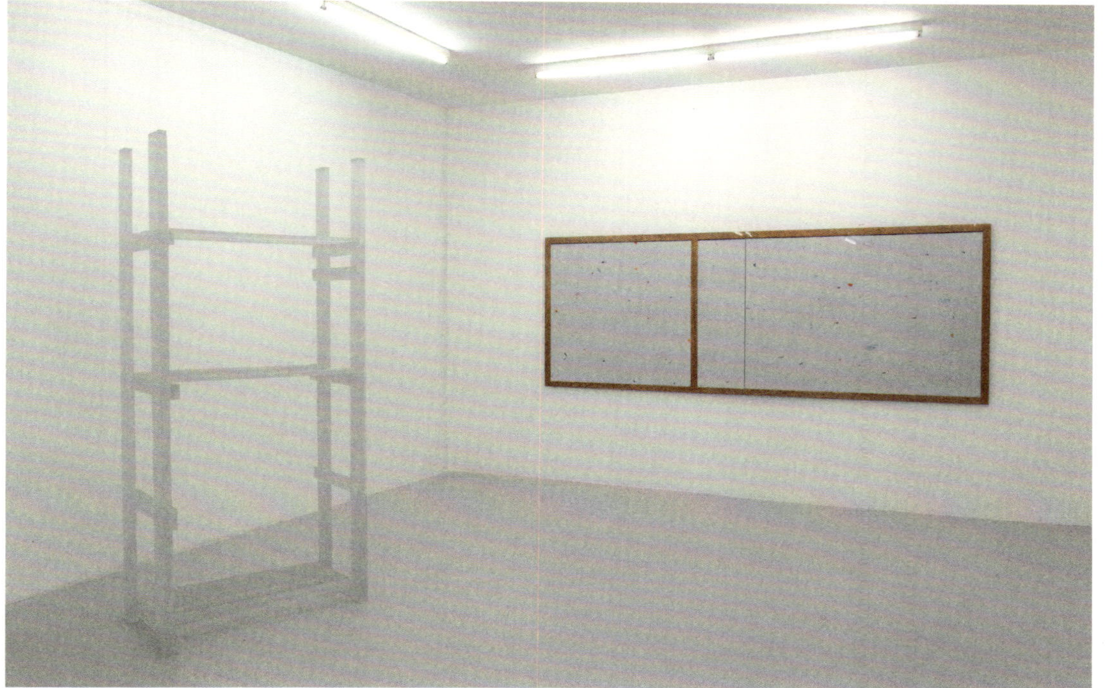

Joseph Grigely and Amy Vogel (b. 1968), *Storage Rack*, 2012. Polyurethane, 84 ¼ × 24 × 36 in. (214 × 61 × 91.4 cm) (left); Joseph Grigely, *Bulletin Board II*, 2012. Pigment print, 48 × 126 in. (121.9 × 320 cm) (right). Installation view, Air de Paris, Paris, 2012

Miguel Gutierrez

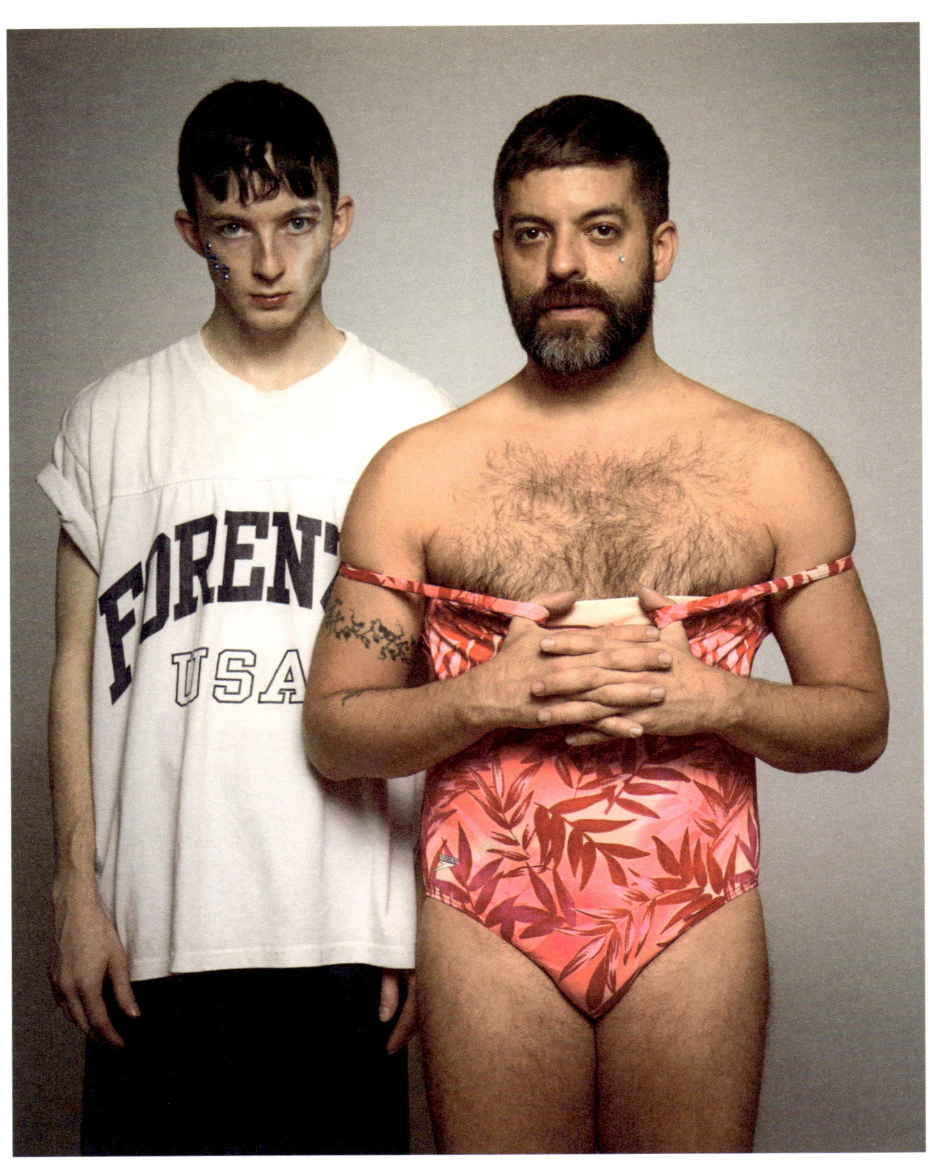

Age and Beauty Part 1: Mid-Career Artist/Suicide Note or &:-/, 2014. From left to right: Mickey Mahar and Miguel Gutierrez

Born 1971 in Flushing, NY

Lives in Brooklyn, NY

Miguel Gutierrez

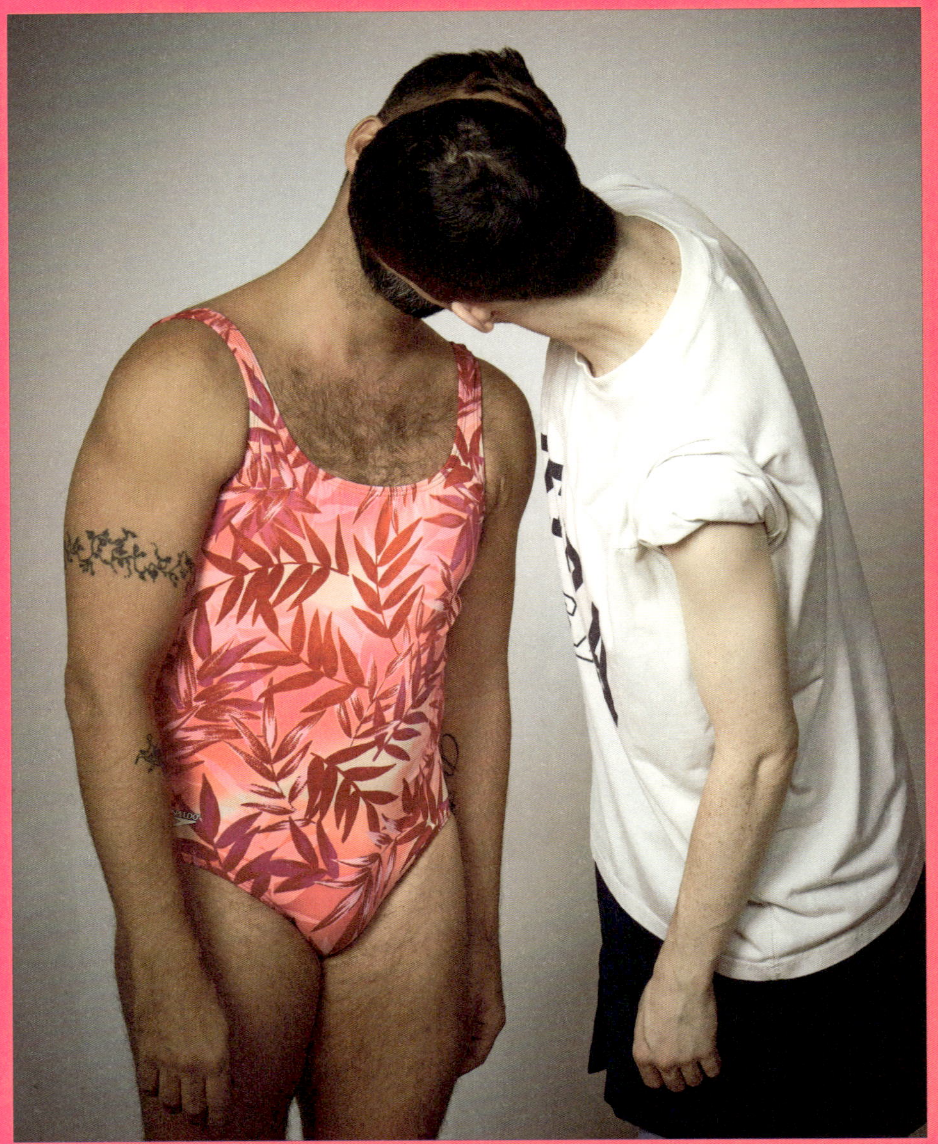

Age and Beauty Part 1: Mid-Career Artist/Suicide Note or &:-/, 2014. From left to right: Mickey Mahar and Miguel Gutierrez

WE ARETHE DANCERS
WE ARETHE DANCERS
WE ARETHE DANCER
WE ARETHE DANCERRRSS
WE ARETHE DANCERRRSSSS
WE ARETHE DANCERSSSSSSS
WE ARETHE DANC E ^^^\\/__
WE ARETHE DANCERS
WE ARETHE DANCERS
I AM BEAUTIFUL
WE ARE BEAUTIFUL
I AM BEAUTIFUL
AND WE ARE BEAUTIFUL
I AM BEAUTIFUL AND
WE ARE BEAUTIFULLL
WE ARETHE DANCERS
WE ARETHE DANCERS
WE ARE ↑THE DANCEUW9
WE ARETHE DAAANSEEURS
WE ARE!THE DA A A T N S E U R S.
I DON'T WANNA HURT MY VOICE SAYING IT BUT WE ARETHE DANSEURS.
I DON'T WANNA HURT YOUR EARS SAYING IT BUT WE ARETHE DAAAANSERS
I don't wanna kill your heart by naming it but we are the ones saying it
we ARETHE DANCERS WE
ARETHE DAAANCERS
WE ARETHE DANCERS WE
ARETHE DANCERS
WE ARETHE DANCERS
WE ARETHE DAAAN S I RSSS
WE ARETHE DANSIRS
WE ARETHE DAANNSIRS WE
ARETHE DANCERS
WE ARETHE / DANSIRSSSSURRS
DANSURRRS WE
ARETHE DANCIRSSS
WE ARETHE DANCERS
THE DAAANSIRRRSS WE
ARETHE DANSIRS
WE ARETHE DANCERS

Susan Howe

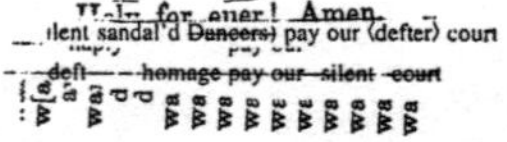

From *Tom Tit Tot*, 2013. Letterpress prints, 12 × 9 in. (30.5 × 22.9 cm) each

Born 1937 in Boston, MA

Lives in Guilford, CT

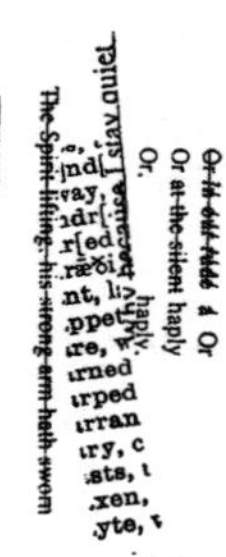
Or
Or at the silent haply
Or,
haply.
I stay quiet
nd
vay,
dr
ed
nt,
ppet
re,
rned
rped
rran
ry, c
sts,
xen,
yte,
The Spirit lifting, his strong arm hath sworn

a mere nitwit, who wasted precious parchment
WOODSLIPPERCOUNTERCLATTER
WOODSLIPPERCOUNTERCLATTER
WOODSLIPPERCOUNTERCLATTER

n certain Shrouds that
ne and were gone. He lean
though to meditate on wo

Secret Paintin

Gary Indiana

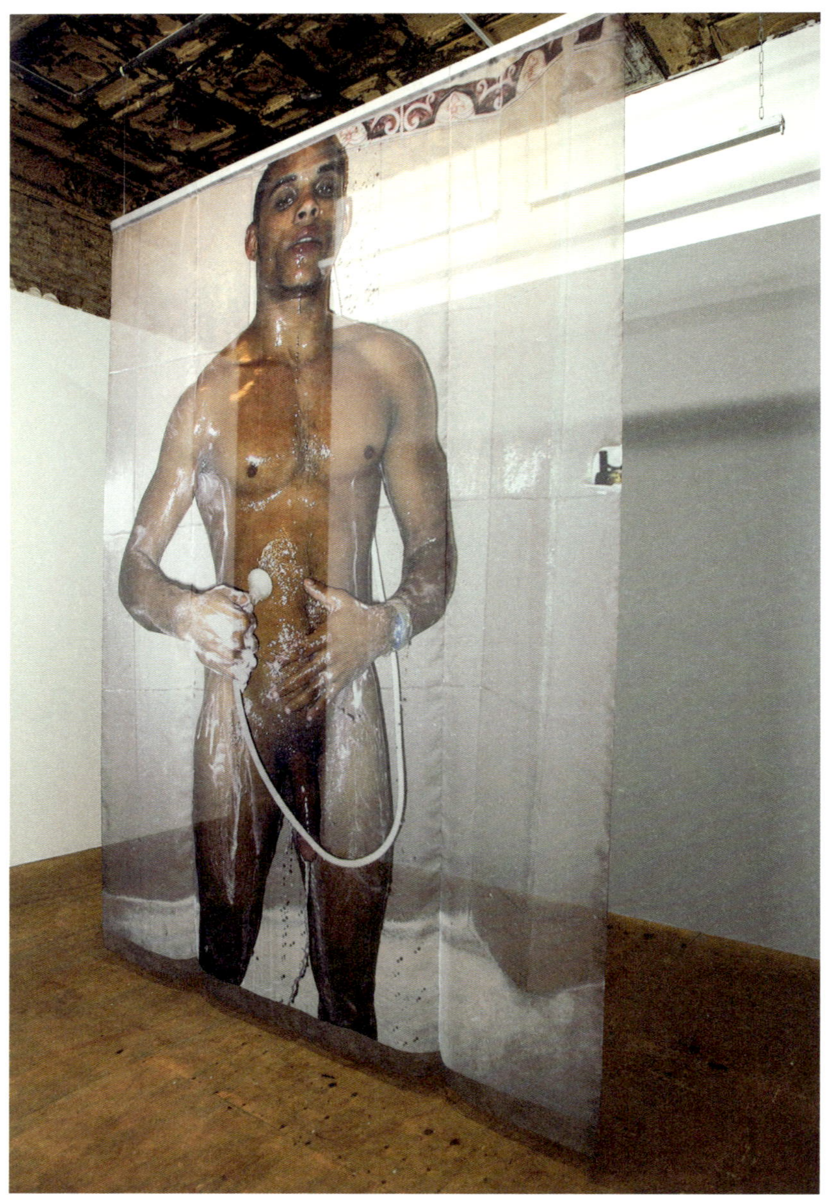

Untitled (Abdul, Havana), 2000–12. Dye on silk, 128 × 96 ⅔ in. (325.1 × 245.4 cm)

Born 1950 in Derry, NH

Lives in New York, NY/ Los Angeles, CA

Gary Indiana

I, Terrorist

You live in Massachusetts, or New Orleans. Or Tucson, or Santa Barbara.

Last week you threw away a Crock-Pot your mom gave you for Christmas twenty years ago.

Now you're watching CNN. A discomforting thought wriggles into your mind. What if some terrorist, or some lunatic mistaken for a terrorist, or a terrorist who is a lunatic, as so many are, fished that Crock-Pot out of the garbage and made a bomb from it? Could Mom's thoughtful Xmas gift mutate hideously into your freakiest nightmare? Can you be charged in that situation as an accessory, or conspirator, or an accessory to a conspirator, in a terrorist plot, or a lunatic plot, if your household trash is recycled as an explosive device by someone you don't even know?

Many innocent people languish right now in an American concentration camp in Guantánamo, Cuba, detained for years on even flimsier non-evidence than chance proximity to an inanimate object, on the whim of a shadow government both supersecretive and brazenly public about its ability to do anything it wishes to anybody on Earth.

Catholics, Jews, Buddhists: expiation in the driver's seat. One way or other, Catholic sins must be scrubbed and pardoned, or there goes the kingdom of heaven. Despite how disgusting you are, confession spares you the fires of hell. You may wait half of eternity to join God in his splendor, but he's holding a table for you, and one day he'll honor your reservation. Buddhists avoid bad karma by performing good works, to return postmortem as higher beings instead of carrots. Jews behave well, the schmucks, because it's the right thing to do.

In some countries trial defendants are found innocent, in others not guilty. I don't know any place where both verdicts are available, though they're not the same thing. "Not guilty" means reasonable doubt. You might have done it, you could have, probably you did, but congratulations, you got away with it. "Innocent" sounds like you definitely didn't do it, and just being called innocent turns your skin as blushing fresh as a twelve-year-old's, you cunning little criminal bastard.

Irony is not your friend. I am not even sure that any of this is irony. I don't know about you, but I can't listen anymore. Not to them, not to any of it. It's all the same thing, over and over. Proud and staunch. Tough in a crisis. Back from the brink. Better and stronger. When we care, nobody cares like we care. Our friends have always known exactly where we stand. Future generations are bound to thank us. Make no mistake. Our purpose is clear. We were just sitting down to eat the children, won't you join us? Actually, I do know about you.

All the wealth to very few of the very few, corresponding ruin of most of the terribly many, has countless, obvious, deleterious effects. But also more elusive ones, not at all obvious, erratically traveling through the society's nervous system. Their toxicity condenses exponentially, like mercury or Strontium-90 rising through the food chain, from plankton or prairie grass to mother's milk. However far certain poisons travel from their point of origin, they ultimately cause horrific violence when they come to a full stop.

It has never happened, not once since slaves built the pyramids, that the quantities of wealth the really wealthy have now existed in the same social order with the kind of misery we have now, without producing murder. In a mass society, mass murder. It's unlikely that any mass murderer thinks brutalist capitalism installed his compulsion to kill as many people as possible—his mind is full of God, or pussy, or what he envisions as an ideal shade of pink for the finish on a vintage Corvette—but then he doesn't have to think about it, since he incarnates it at the moment when he plans his first massacre at the local mall, movie theater, high school, or fast-food restaurant. Which he understands, in a nebulous way, to also be his last massacre, with himself his final victim.

May you, if it is the correct word, be spared the irony of life imprisonment for trashing a cookware item your mom gave you long ago for Bon Noël. Could you be in serious trouble?

You tell me and we'll both know. The charges against Dzhokhar Tsarnaev in the Boston Marathon bombing refer to a small kitchen appliance as a "weapon of mass destruction," a flight of contagious semantic hyperbole scattered across the media spectrum during the unexpected ratings bonanza of the Boston Marathon. The promiscuous use of terms like *weapon of mass destruction* has the obvious intention, and the effect, of demolishing all sense of proportion from the perception of events like the Boston bombings. This linguistic travesty is itself an act of terror, conflating the explosion of an improvised, homemade device with the detonation of a nuclear warhead—a Strangeloveian extreme of the Gulliver effect, wherein acts of violence are measured according to which populations they happen to, rather than levels of actual physical destruction. The latter, in Boston, were comparable to those of a drone-aircraft strike or a suicide bomber in a street bazaar. Not nothing, quite a lot something, really. But not much at all if you are seriously trying to make it sound like Hiroshima, or the firebombing of Dresden.

In a state of perpetual war, where no tangible enemy exists, the entire planet serves as the theater of conflict's available playing area. The dehumanizing terms of the Gulliver effect become the defining code of a police state. Any people anywhere—on a single city block, for example—can be parsed into citizens and "enemy combatants" instantaneously, according to the needs of an interminable melodrama with a script subject to hourly rewrites. In this state of things, the observed distinction between "us" and "them" follows the basic principle of slapstick: If you step in front of a bus and get killed, that's comedy. If I slip on a banana peel, that's tragedy.

Those aren't the only distinctions being passed through the mangle of absurdity. If two exploding pressure cookers that kill three people and maim several dozen others constitute weapons of mass destruction, the invasion of Iraq was justified because Saddam Hussein had access to a Sears catalogue.

Do we really, always, want everything both ways? Ecology for us, let the others take our garbage? If that's how it is, be careful what you put in the garbage, because it might come back and bite you in the ass.

Opportunistic edicts that the surviving suspect, a naturalized American citizen, should be declared an "enemy combatant" (and, à la Emma Goldman in 1919, stripped of his civil rights) issued from the darkling cave of sniveling bitterness and toxic self-pity where John McCain, much given to wearing the flag like a diaper while feeding his few remaining threads of respectability to the grotto campfire, has festered since his electoral rejection in 2008, joined at the lip to cavemate Lindsey Graham, Strom Thurmond's spiritual heir—each discerning, no doubt, the other's bizarre visions of a brighter world in the flickering shadows cast by the dying embers.

There was, too, a consensus among Halloween masks on chat TV that, even if he was a citizen, an obviously evil, obviously guilty individual like this one, being hazily connected to Chechnya, or Islam, or that fuzzy area near the bottom on maps of Russia, didn't deserve to have his Miranda warning read to him, if and when he regained consciousness.

There were predictable effusions of ugly feeling on Twitter and Facebook, from a global peanut gallery of borderline personalities, among them an Albany state senator named Greg Ball, whose signature tweet referred to the younger Tsarnaev brother as "scum bag #2," followed by the twittering question, "Who wouldn't use torture on this punk to save more lives?"—apparently confident that the kind of people who would vote Greg Ball into the state senate would also feel comfortable torturing a nineteen-year-old with multiple gunshot injuries who was, as far as anyone knew at the time, bleeding out in a local emergency room.

The violent fantasies ubiquitously aired on talk radio and twittered on social media reflected an energized, uninhibited atavism among the unassuagably angry, the incurably stupid, and the relentlessly patriotic, if these can be considered three separate categories rather than just one. Added to serial misreporting of "breaking news" gleaned from "reliable sources," which panned out as vaporous rumor, the misidentification, by various media (Reddit, the *New York Post*, John King on CNN, Fox affiliate KDFW in Dallas-Ft. Worth), of, variously, a "dark-skinned man," a Saudi marathon onlooker, a Revere High School varsity track star, a missing Brown University student, and the actress Zooey Deschanel as "suspects"—and, from the outset, the deft channeling of public hysteria into an urgent clamor for increased aerial and satellite surveillance, CCTV cameras on every city block, and arbitrary searches in the guise of "emergency exceptions" to constitutional restraints on law enforcement, exceptions that would allow, and inevitably normalize, the practice of shutting down an entire city to facilitate the capture of people suspected of crimes.

These fantasies reflected an unstable social pathology, an epidemic mixture of panic disorder, xenophobia, servile authority worship, and infantile narcissism, all of which easily accounted for 95 percent of "democratized" media commentary—the schoolyard insults, effusions of replacement envy, magical thinking, terminal self-revelation, and other indications of drastically impoverished inner lives commonly shared on reader threads dangling from news and opinion stories—as well as the standard onrush of cretinizing tabloid headlines, adventitious *New Yorker* think pieces, earnest *HuffPost* celebrity blogs, condescending liberal boiler plate in *Salon* and *Slate*, and the flatulent, valedictory musings of *Times* columnists and all-purpose cable personalities.

There appeared, almost as comic relief, an easily discernible, hysterically repressed undercurrent of sexual anxiety and category confusion in the coverage of the story's penultimate hours, as legible photographs of Dzhokhar Tsarnaev, and accounts of his incongruous backstory, emerged from the shadows, revealing a Diesel model waiting to happen, who until very recently had seemed the kind of agreeably birdbrained, laid-back stoner vast numbers of people usually perceive as an ideal zipless fuck. Squaring this realization with the requisite murderous outrage and histrionic collective mourning over the deaths of strangers was a novel challenge for a public trained to judge things by appearances, by people employed to manipulate it with images of things to judge.

Now, voyager. Your appliance problem. It could conceivably happen that your fingerprints on your mother's Crock-Pot, or your signature on an expired warranty card, could land you in custody. It could also happen that some creepy neighbor, who remembers vividly seeing you toss your Crock-Pot into the nonrecycle garbage bin, feels impelled by the same feeling of civic arousal that inspired so many virtuous citizens of the Third Reich to report the presence of Jews in the neighbor's attic. Thank god, as William Burroughs put it, for a country where nobody's allowed to mind his own business.

If an adroit government agency with no congressional oversight and conspiracy on the brain wishes to claim suspicion that you have ties to other Crock-Pots, or know someone who knows someone who knows someone who knows about some extraneous facet of a dubious satanic plot being hatched in some faraway country where a whole seething population of bloody-minded barbarians spends every waking minute hating America for its freedoms and fucking goats, your life as you know it could fly right out the window before anyone informs you that you have a right to remain silent, a right to an attorney, that anything you say can and will be held against you—and not just in a court of law, since whoever detains you will leak it to the press and convict you in the court of public opinion.

Maybe you know your Miranda rights, but some unfortunate Americans don't, or forget them in the chaos of being arrested. In extreme situations, many people become disoriented and verbally incontinent. Miranda was put in the law in part to protect such people from incriminating themselves. Dzhokhar Tsarnaev, in near-fatal gunshot trauma from several hundred rounds fired on his hiding place by the Boston police, without provocation (let me add that I know all about the Boston police, firsthand, and if they're the noble figures we heard about 24-7 for weeks after the marathon bombing, I am Marie of Romania) spilled for several hours until a judge read him his rights, at which point he immediately wised up and clammed up. As you would too, if you happened to be him—and, further to your Crock-Pot dilemma, as you also would if you happened not to be, and found yourself accused of being him, or associated with him because he went digging in your trash.

All the sound advice in the world may fail you, of course. Unless you have money and media access, the clandestine services and the police will probably do whatever they want with you, and deny it with deafening indignation if anyone ever calls them out about it. Our prison system is full of people who were Mirandized while unconscious, Mirandized by some agent whispering Miranda warnings under his breath on a different floor of the building, Mirandized while being pounded on the skull with a nightstick or zapped with 50,000 volts from a Taser, Mirandized in English when the only language they understood was Spanish or Chinese or Urdu.

One last tip. Next time you do your spring cleaning, why not donate that useless Crock-Pot from Mom to the Goodwill? You might also donate unwanted microwave ovens, pressure cookers, toasters, space heaters, hair driers, broken juicers, TV sets, battery-operated toys, dildos, cell phones, Game Boys, Xboxes, Sony PlayStations, and similar items cluttering up the home. These seemingly innocuous objects could easily fall into the wrong hands, and a simple act of trash disposal could blow up in your face. Or somebody else's face. Let the Goodwill take the rap for it.

Carol Jackson

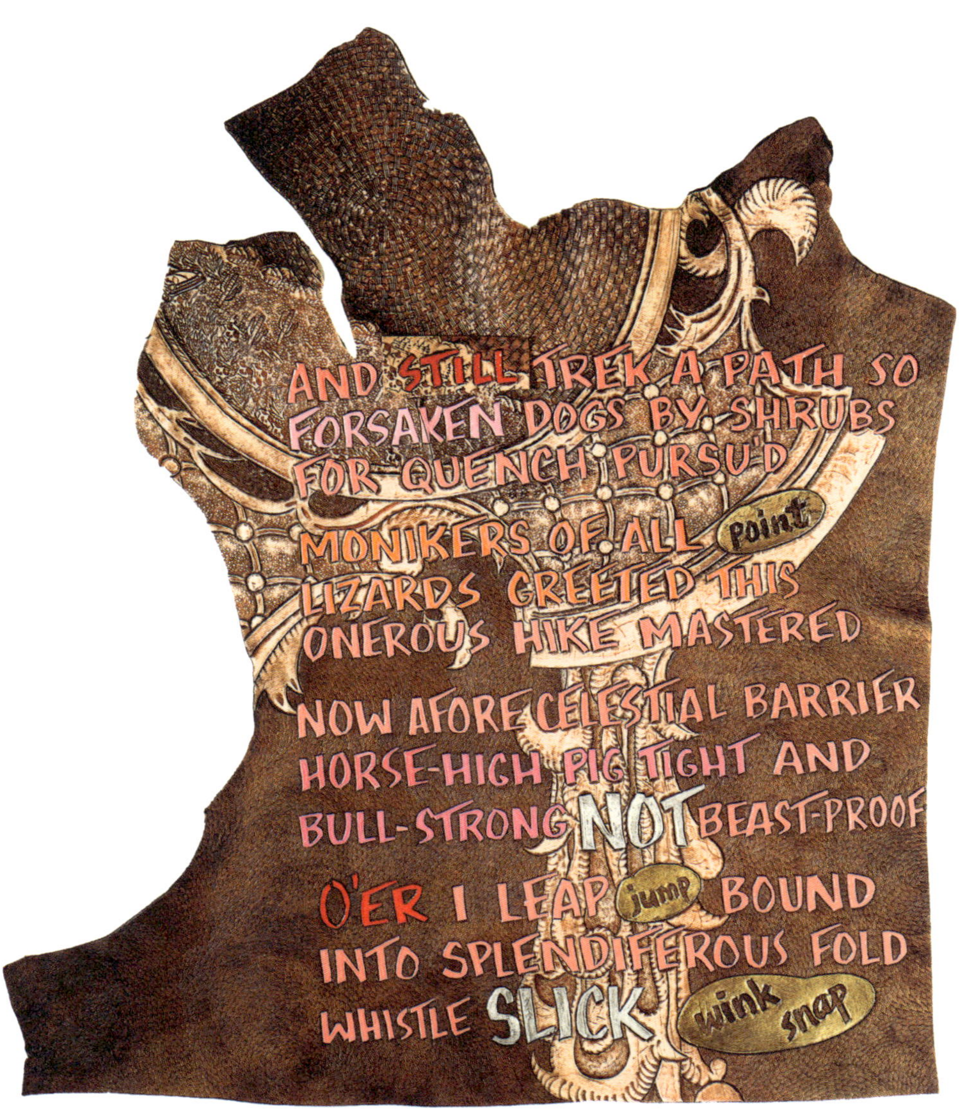

Cue Cards for Satan 4/1, 2013. Leather, enamel, and acrylic, 30 × 25 in. (91.4 × 167.6 cm)

Born 1962 in
Los Angeles, CA

Lives in
Chicago, IL

Carol Jackson

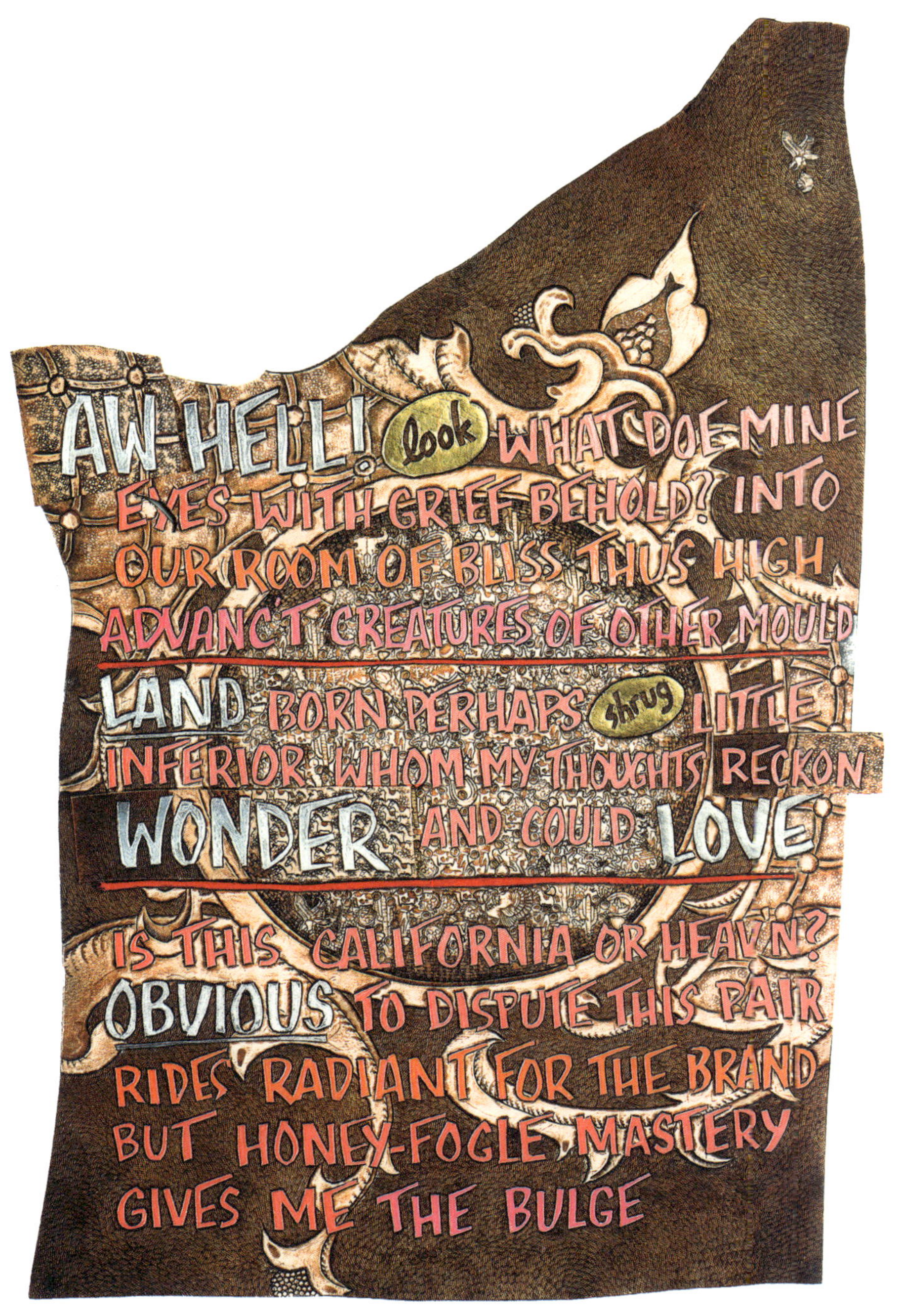

Cue Cards for Satan 4/2, 2013. Leather, enamel, and acrylic, 30 × 19 in. (91.4 × 167.6 cm)

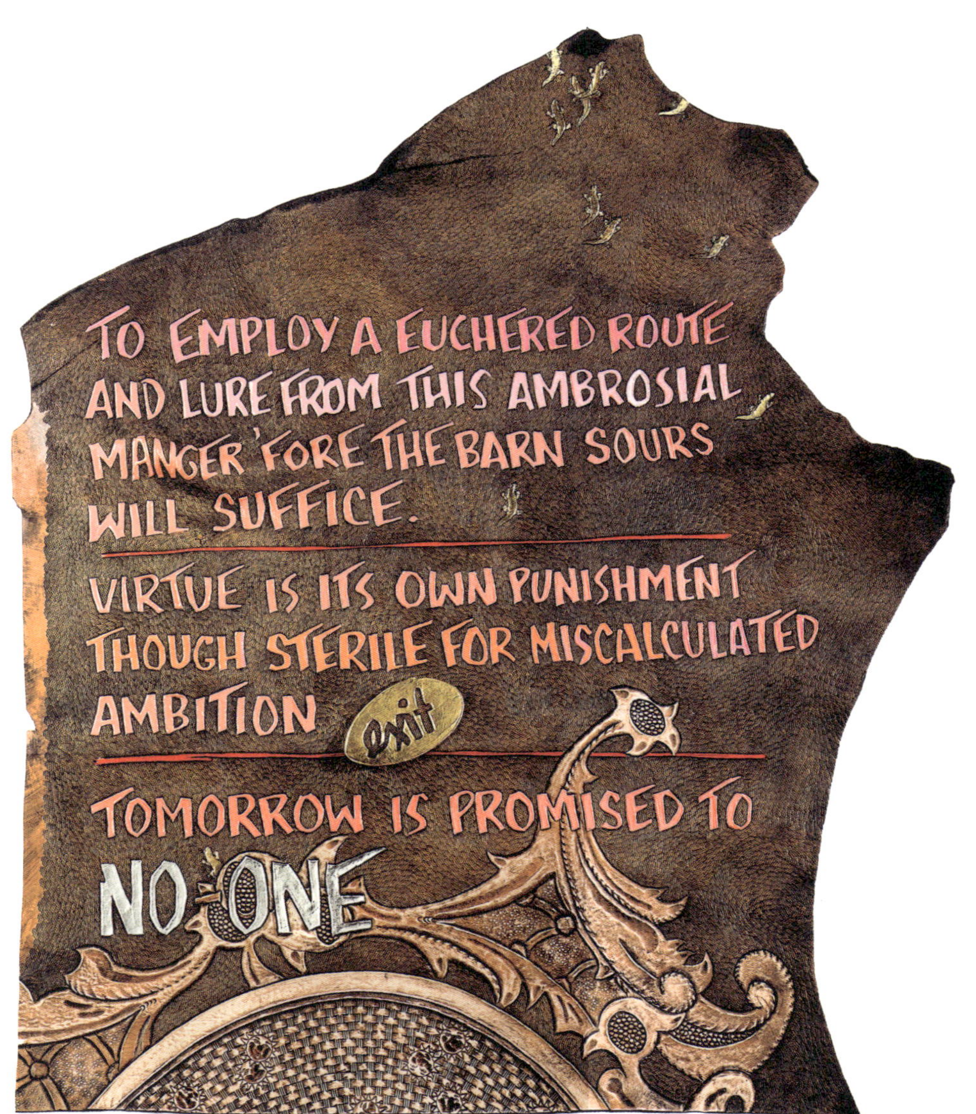

Cue Cards for Satan 4/3, 2013. Leather, enamel, and acrylic, 31 × 25 in. (91.4 × 167.6 cm)

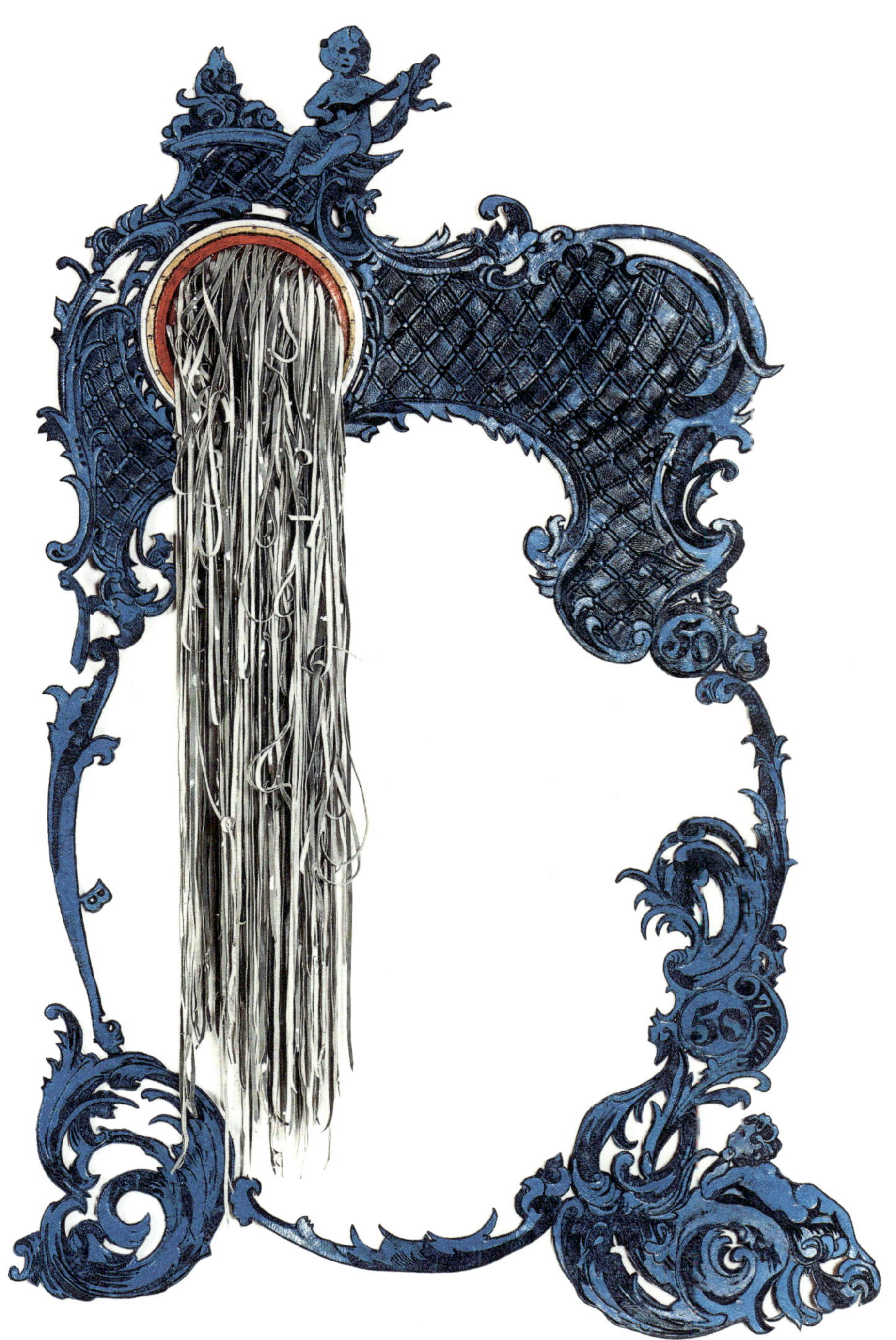

Artist's rendering for *BLEHH*, 2011. Leather, enamel, brass, and acrylic, 82 × 52 × 5 in. (208.3 × 132.1 × 12.7 cm)

Angie Keefer

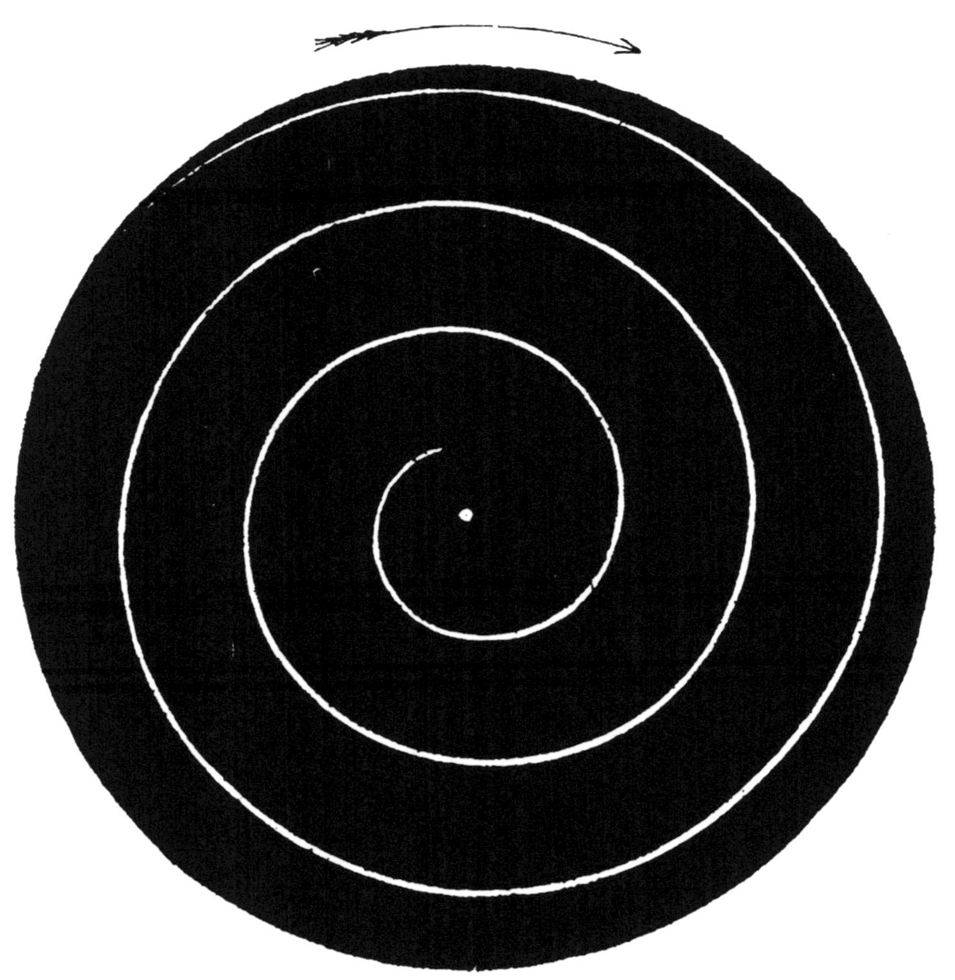

Plateau's spiral, 1849

Born 1977 in Huntsville, AL

Lives in Hudson, NY

Angie Keefer

Futures

One of the first concepts I learned as a kid in art class was "value," as in the difference between any two tones on a scale from light to dark. The definition combined the vocabulary of hearing (tone) with that of touch (scale) with that of optics (light), connecting aural, haptic, and visual senses. Value was fundamental for observation, and for reflection. Form could not be discerned, or created, without invoking this source. Our job, as amateurs of the oil pastel, was to forget about drawing edges where we thought they belonged, and focus instead on fields, surfaces, relationships. Understand value, we were told. How things begin and end will take care of itself.

Not long ago, I discovered "Where Do We Go from Here?," a brief polemic Marcel Duchamp delivered a few years before his death. Where do we go from here? It's the sort of question people ask on the tail end of a crisis, after the dust has settled, before the world keeps turning. The "here" Duchamp plotted then was the surface of the retina, which, in his assessment, had been colonized during the preceding century by a succession of isms, from the realism of Courbet and Manet through Abstract Expressionism and whatever others in between. Here, the profound work of artists "to bring to light startling new values which are and will always be the basis of artistic revolutions" had been neglected in favor of inconsequential debates over trivial distinctions between "representative" and "non-representative" forms. Stripped of its moral function to illuminate new values and unduly burdened by popular demand for "aesthetic satisfaction," art had become "a 'commodity' . . . a commonplace product like soap and securities." The "enormous output" of artists therefore amounted to the "enormous dilution" of artistic value—runaway inflation set off by a flood of counterfeit currency.

Duchamp made this speech during a symposium at the Philadelphia Museum College of Art in spring 1961. He was seventy-three years old. The United States was in the midst of what would turn out to be the longest economic boom in its history. The first of the postwar babies, who had grown up in this period of stability and affluence, were rounding the corner to adulthood and would soon be heading off to college—and art school—in record numbers. Meanwhile, Jim Crow laws were still in effect across the South, and military involvement in Vietnam was escalating. A disaffected fringe had already begun to protest what they saw as a blithe consensus mentality. Allen Ginsberg reported their non-strategy as early as 1955: "the best minds" of his generation "threw potato salad at CCNY lecturers on Dadaism," but the Beats' antics didn't inspire mass dissent. Plenitude was the pride and the anesthetic of the newly endowed middle classes. Duchamp concluded his talk by charting a course for tomorrow's young artists through a "revolution on the ascetic level," to occur at the edges of a "world blinded by economic fireworks." Where do we go from here? he had asked. "Underground"—literally out of sight—was his answer.

Ascetic derives from the ancient Greek word for "monk," as in hermit, as in *asketes*, which derives from the verb *askein*, meaning "to exercise." *Askein* referred to athletic exercise in the sense of a rigorous and disciplined regimen to condition the body and mind. Today, the English word *ascetic* usually just means "self-abnegating." An ascetic is someone who refuses sensual pleasure, often in pursuit of spiritual or philosophical ideals. The word's connection to a body is connection to a body denied.

Recently, a friend of mine married the sister of a Buddhist monk. The monk had given up money and possessions and was living in a monastery, so he wasn't able to attend the wedding. Instead, he sent a message by way of a relative, who read it aloud over a shoddy public-address system during the postceremony meal: "Lower your expectations." This sounded like sage advice for the new couple, albeit an unusual recommendation to make during their wedding celebration. Expect less of each other, and you are less likely to be disappointed by all the ways you will inevitably disappoint each other. But a few days after the fizz settled, I heard it differently: "Lower your expectations" means, "Experience is what you don't expect." And that means, "Pay attention."

I met with Duchamp's remains three and a half decades after his call for an ascetic revolution, while I was living an ostensibly monkish existence during another apparent economic boom that would turn out to be one in a series of enormous market bubbles. At the time, I was attending an expensive college by way of financial aid that included some scholarships, but otherwise consisted of government-subsidized loans, work-study, and easy credit—not in that order. The operations department of the university art museum advertised one of the highest-paying jobs on campus. I talked my way into the position, then spent nineteen hours a week there for the next two years, changing lightbulbs, installing exhibitions, and preparing artworks from the collection for loan to other institutions.

Before college, I had attended public schools, including one dedicated to the arts, which had been founded in 1968 by a handful of recent MFA graduates, the sort of people who would've had Duchamp on their radar. The idea was a little like *Fame*, if *Fame* had been set in central Alabama, instead of a metropolitan hub on the global cultural circuit, which is to say, it wasn't much like *Fame* at all, except that students committed to an extended class day to develop a concentration in their respective artistic fields. I passed an inordinate percentage of late-adolescent leisure hours poring over the school library's collection of *Artforum*, vicariously acquainting myself with contemporary art's greatest hits. At eighteen, my fix on Duchamp was accordingly half-toned and two-dimensional.

That changed a few weeks into my first semester in college and the museum job, when I wound up underground, in the basement woodshop beneath the exhibition galleries, alone with one of his readymades—the snow shovel—*In Advance of the Broken Arm*. I was to outfit a shipping crate in made-to-measure foam so as to safely send the shovel somewhere. While this was not an especially interesting job in terms of the labor involved, three long afternoons with *In Advance of the Broken Arm* did expand the scope of my mental Duchamp to encompass the patently obvious: what had registered primarily as a disembodied idea, transmitted through images and texts in books and magazines, was indeed a thing. No "as-if" attached to the task of packing it. I was not performing an absurd and rather boring piece of theater. I was working for an hourly wage. And all of this was supposed to be somewhat beside the point.

Don't get me wrong; I've read the transcript. Duchamp's readymades clearly articulate the enunciative paradigm diagrammed by historian Thierry de Duve—that the statement "This is a work of art," uttered (or otherwise demonstrated) in the proper circumstances (say, art institutions like museums, galleries, and magazines) among anointed subjects (artists and other assorted audiences), confers onto the work the status of art, and that this status is henceforth the work's only essential quality. The ritual makes the totem. Specifics are relatively irrelevant. Anything will stand (though some things will be easier to sell). Granted. So, why doesn't the road simply end there behind the curtain, with all of us exposed as the sham wizard we are?

If you focus for a little while on something moving steadily in one direction, like a waterfall or a rotating spiral, then shift your gaze to something stationary, that immobile thing will briefly appear to move. Aristotle first reported the phenomenon, noting after watching a river that "things really at rest are then seen moving." Lucretius caught it three hundred years later, adding that things really at rest are then seen moving in the opposite direction. Neither philosopher's account created much of a stir in his day. Ptolemy left Aristotle's version out of his *Optics*; others cribbed from Ptolemy, and the idea disappeared from thought for almost two millennia, until the nineteenth century, when it reemerged in northern Scotland as the "waterfall illusion," and in several other, unrelated accounts, often German in origin, sometimes occasioned by the movement of trains.

The perceptual experience of the motion aftereffect is paradoxical. Stationary objects seem to move without changing position. Though the effect is known to involve multiple stages of analysis in different parts of the brain, it is not yet well understood, and the question remains as to why this "misperception of the world" has survived biological adaptation.

Joseph Plateau, a Belgian physicist, studied the illusion in the mid-1800s. He developed a special device for the purpose, a black disk, with a thin white spiral line drawn from the center to the outer edge, that could be rotated at various speeds. If an observer were to stare at the moving disk, then look away, whatever she looked at next—Plateau's head, for example—would appear to grow or to shrink depending on the direction of rotation. The disk, which other scientists frequently employed over the next half century, came to be known as Plateau's spiral. By the time he described the motion aftereffect in 1849, Plateau himself was blind. His wife acted as his reader and secretary. His sister, an artist, drew his illustrations. (These last details are beside the point, too.)

Since Plateau's time, the field of neuroscience has matured. According to current research into the minute workings of the brain, information processing occurs at a cellular level, and cells adapt to persistent stimulation. When you look at a static object, its horizontal contours stimulate detectors in your visual cortex for downward and upward movement, but since both directional sensors are equally stimulated, they cancel each other out, and the object appears static. However, if you look at something moving in one direction, perhaps downward, as in the case of a waterfall, for example, cells consistently stimulated by the ongoing motion will become fatigued and therefore less reactive. When you shift focus from the waterfall to a static object, cells that sense an opposite motion will be newly stimulated, and their signals won't be effectively counterbalanced. The object will appear to rise. That is, cells develop expectations, and these expectations inflect perception. At least, this is the theory.

The motion aftereffect is an awkward reminder that thoughts emanate from bodies—an abiding source of frustration to thought, which would prefer a more predictable framework, one operating on less particular terms, less connected to specific befores and afters.

Page 201 in *The Complete Works of Marcel Duchamp* is a one-word chapter titled "THERE IS NO SOLUTION BECAUSE THERE IS NO PROBLEM." The text reads: *Indeed*. No punctuation follows. The word floats on the page. Indeed, the word couldn't float without its oversize page. Even nothing needs something to point to it. And since, in the end, Duchamp defined a field of problems—something to do with value, something to do with movement, something about where to go from here—the absent punctuation in his *Complete Works* reads to me as an ellipsis. There's always something missing in a model. Models are useful, even necessary, but wrong. Like edges. Every model we know today will be replaced over time.

According to the enunciative model, the authority that confers the status of art draws its agency from the success of its own enunciation, not some exogenous source, not some underlying artistic "value," whatever that might be. In other words, the structure is solipsistic. It thinks it is, therefore it is, and that thought is all the it there is. Keep your eye on the rotating spiral; the world begins to shrink.

Markets also tend to shrink when value is indeterminate. Economist George Akerlof published a paper in the *Quarterly Journal of Economics* in 1970 called "The Market for 'Lemons': Quality Uncertainty and the Market Mechanism." Akerlof's subject was the problem of mistrust in markets. For argument's sake, he describes a market for cars in which vehicles can be either new or used, and they can be good cars or lemons. New cars are likely to be good, but there is less certainty about used cars. The seller of a used car has more relevant information about its value than its prospective buyer. "Consider a market in which goods are sold honestly or dishonestly; quality may be represented, or it may be misrepresented. The purchaser's problem, of course, is to identify quality. The presence of people in the market who are willing to offer inferior goods represented as quality goods tends to drive the market out of existence. The cost of dishonesty, therefore, is not only the amount by which the purchaser is cheated; the cost must also include the loss incurred from driving legitimate exchange out of existence." In a market of lemons, the bad tends to drive out the good. Eventually, exchange comes to a complete halt.

Akerlof uses the lemons model to assess several real-world scenarios in which a lemon-market mechanism stifles market activity. He also describes counteractive, legitimizing institutions that address the problem of trust in markets. These include guarantees, brand names, and professional licensing, some of which operate within the enunciative paradigm. But the situations Akerlof describes—health insurance for the aged, the employment of minorities, and credit markets in economically underdeveloped societies—entail actual commodities and financial services, so the reputations of his institutional arbiters are ultimately kept in check by the quality of whatever they endorse. Quality may be uncertain in a lemons model, but shades of it exist.

The growth of published research on the motion aftereffect began to increase exponentially around 1960. Today, the total amount of research continues to double about every dozen years, in keeping with a general trend in scientific publishing. (This would be more remarkable if publishing technology hadn't changed dramatically and if the population of research scientists hadn't increased exponentially during the same period.) Financial markets also evolve with technological and social change. In times of economic growth, they multiply and become more abstract, not unlike the midcentury art Duchamp characterized.

For example: opportunities to purchase finished goods on the open market in Edo-period Japan were meager, so samurai were typically paid in rice. Not every samurai had a use for gold (what could he do with it?), but every samurai needed to eat. A koku, the amount of rice an average samurai was expected to consume in an average year, was the basic economic unit. When the harvest was good, rice was abundant, supply overwhelmed demand, and the trade value of a koku was relatively low. When the harvest was bad, rice was scarce, demand exceeded supply, and the trade value of a koku was relatively high. A good harvest could render a strapped samurai, whose pay in koku was worth less, while a bad harvest might render a strapped shogun, who would have to scramble to meet his obligations. The balance of power in society hinged on a single, unpredictable grain.

In the early 1700s, the merchant class in Edo was small. They enjoyed the status of an ugly, industrious insect, generally reviled but tolerated. During the preceding century, they had developed officially condoned, member-regulated exchanges for rice, but also illegal exchanges, likened to gambling venues by some. At the illegal exchanges, contracts for a specific quantity of a standardized grade of rice to be delivered at a particular, future date could be bought and sold. These contracts were called rice bills. The market for rice bills provided buyers and sellers with a means to bet on the future availability of rice. These bets in turn affected future prices of rice.

Let's say rice is trading low, the market is flooded, but you've read the skies or the seas or whathaveyou and you know a drought is coming. You might decide to buy contracts at a fixed price today for a few dozen koku to be delivered in six months, effectively placing a bet that rice prices will be higher in the future since the rice supply will be relatively meager. Even if you have to pay more today for six-months-in-the-future rice than for today rice, the amount you've paid today will be less than what others will have to pay for today rice six months from now, as long as your weather forecast proves correct. In the middle of the drought, there won't be enough rice to satisfy demand, and the price will jump. You're trading today to minimize risk tomorrow for rice you plan to own. Alternatively, your game might be to anticipate future price changes and to pocket profits from buying low and selling high. In that case, you simply plan to sell your contract in the future for more than you will pay for it today. In any case, if the market is reasonably efficient—which means that the same information about trading prices is available to all traders at the same time—then price volatility will decrease.

The opportunity to transfer risk (and rewards) back and forth by trading rice futures was sufficiently enticing to Edo merchants that many chanced arrest and punishment to participate in the illegal market. As their economic status grew, so did their political power. In the late 1720s, the shogunate first relaxed then lifted the ban on futures trading in Dojima, Osaka, at the merchants' urging. The price of rice decreased and stabilized.

The first American market for commodities futures opened in Chicago in 1865. Futures for financial instruments developed in the 1970s. Options on futures—the right to buy futures in the future for a price determined today—were introduced in the early 1980s. Futures and options are known as derivatives since the activities of these markets derive from underlying markets. Investors use futures markets to hedge against risk from potential price changes in commodities they consume or to profit by speculating on potential changes. Buyers' and sellers' judgments about future prices will naturally be affected by new information related to supply and demand, which might include weather, war, or the price of tea in China, and their actions will then have a direct, stabilizing effect on spot prices in underlying markets. At least, this is the theory.

In fact, as financial markets have transformed over the past thirty-plus years—roughly, that is, in my lifetime—large commercial investors, with multibillion-dollar funds operated by professional financiers, have been permitted to take purely speculative positions in commodity futures markets. These investors may have little to no material stake in the markets. In other words, they are able to buy futures contracts at enormous volume, greatly increasing demand in the derivatives markets, without reflecting demand (or supply) in the physical markets. Unlike the Edo speculators, these investors do not resell their contracts. They profit by expanding the futures market while driving up futures prices (because the demand for futures increases). But the bubble they create in the futures markets in turn has a real effect on prices in the underlying markets. It's as if perception of a motion aftereffect actually causes something in the world to move. Without the reality check of a material commitment to transport, store, and distribute commodities, pure speculation in futures markets furthers biologically (not "merely" morally) errant values. Human suffering—starvation, for example—results. How did we end up here? And where, exactly, are we going?

Cultural value—broadly adjudicated in terms of aesthetics and morality by myriad institutions, such as law, that derive from these but are more readily discerned as political—mediates the fundamental incompatibility between markets and bodies, between want and need. Its essential relevance to civilization, often obscured within esoteric channels of artistic discourse, stands out against the stark opposition between market speculation and starvation. It is not autonomous. Where we are going, therefore, is not toward incremental reform of an enunciative paradigm that precludes the reality of artistic value. Obsessive self-referentiality only winds the critical impasse into an ever-tighter coil. Nor are we headed toward the rematerialization of the art object. Art has yet to dematerialize. It involves people, and none of us live outside material circumstances, bodies, and markets. Where we are going is toward the realization that every horizon is a misperception. We inhabit the surface of a sphere, not the path of a spiral. There is no underground, no edge on the world; there are only constantly changing relationships among values. If that's a cliché, it's one that hasn't been fully incorporated into our common, bodily sense.

The work of art is to lower expectations.

SOURCES

If this essay is written in response to any particular source, it is to Diedrich Diederichsen's *On [Surplus] Value in Art* (Berlin: Sternberg, 2008).

Marcel Duchamp's "Where Do We Go from Here?" (March 1961) was translated by Helen Meakins and published in *Studio International*, no. 185 (January–February 1975). Todd Gitlin's *The Sixties: Years of Hope, Days of Rage* (New York: Bantam Books, 1987) is a narrative history of the decade by the former leader of the Students for a Democratic Society. Gitlin points to the quote from Allen Ginsberg's *Howl*, written in 1955, published in 1956. For twentieth-century economic history, Robert Shiller's *Irrational Exuberance* (New York: Doubleday, 2005), and Hyman Minsky's papers "Ethics and Capitalism" (Paper 186, 1994), "Failed and Successful Capitalisms: Lessons from the Twentieth Century" (Paper 47, 1994), and "Uncertainty and the Institutional Structure of Capitalist Economies" (Paper 24, 1996), all from the Hyman P. Minsky Archive, Bard College, were consulted. The Alabama School of Fine Arts is online at http://www.asfa.k12.al.us. Marcel Duchamp's *In Advance of the Broken Arm* was created in 1915. The 1945 version, which replaced the lost 1915 original, is owned by the Yale University Art Gallery. Thierry de Duve's "Echoes of the Readymade: Critique of Pure Modernism" was translated by Rosalind Krauss for *October* 70 (Fall 1994: 60–97). Aristotle describes the motion aftereffect in *On Dreams*, available at http://classics.mit.edu/Aristotle/dreams.html. George Mather, Frans Verstraten, and Stuart Anstis edited *The Motion Aftereffect: A Modern Perspective* (Cambridge, MA: MIT Press, 1998), which encapsulates the history and contemporary theory through 1998 of the motion aftereffect. More recent studies by V. S. Ramachandran were also referenced. My edition of *The Complete Works of Marcel Duchamp* (New York: Abrams, 1969) by Arturo Schwarz is from 1970. George Akerlof received a Nobel Prize for his paper "The Market for 'Lemons': Quality Uncertainty and the Market Mechanism" (*Quarterly Journal of Economics* 84, no. 3 [August 1970], pages 488–500), and it is widely available online. General information about futures markets is primarily drawn from the National Futures Association at http://nfa.futures.org (accessed November 3, 2013); Robert Shiller's undergraduate class lectures on financial markets at Yale University, which are available online at http://oyc.yale.edu/economics; Dennis W. Carlton's "Futures Markets: Their Purpose, Their History, Their Growth, Their Successes and Failures" (*The Journal of Futures Markets* 4, no. 3 [1984]: 237–71); testimony given by Michael W. Masters of Masters Capital Management in statements before Congressional Financial Crisis Inquiry Commission (June 30, 2010) and the Committee on Homeland Security and Governmental Affairs (May 20, 2008); and Harvard Business School case study 9-709-044, "The Dojima Rice Market and the Origins of Futures Trading" (November 10, 2010).

Zoe Leonard

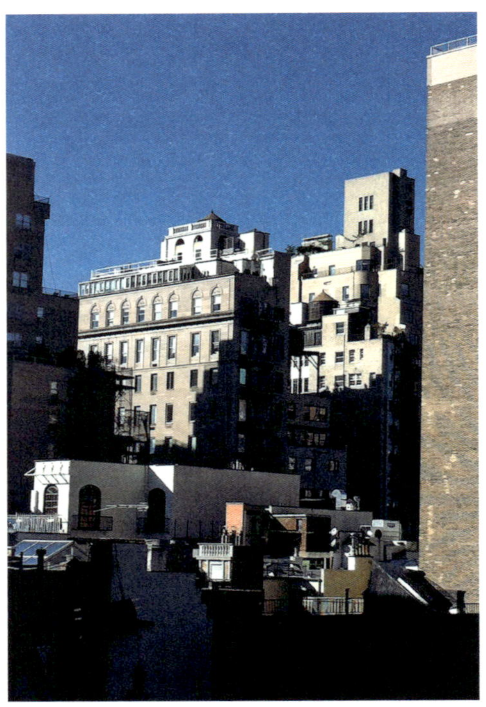

Sketch for *945 Madison Avenue*, iPhone photograph

Born 1961 in Liberty, NY

Lives in New York, NY

At First I Thought I'd Write an Elegy
Gregg Bordowitz

On a dark night, Kindled in love with yearnings—oh happy chance!—
I went forth without being observed, My house being now at rest.[1]

In darkness plunged, my senses to attention
Chambered as science as art as conscience
How through patience we become a patient
Fired alert by furnace's molten matter

Rays drawn through glass ground by art's optician
Skilled physician applying dawn's treatment
To inner walls distinguished by caress;
By awkward music delightfully played

Notes in sync with earth's orbit 'round the sun
Loosen settled world-weary ligaments
By concert float bodies above abyss
Dodging shadows ruefully cast by day

Return the waning brightness nightly gone
O' stay. Wait. Weigh filtered prism's density
Become transfixed; heat will warm clotted veins
In measures blood will flow moved by heart's sway

Restore temperate weather long succumbed
To doubt resolved by friendly fallacy
Deified nature (once denied) obtains
No tricks! See the sun's factual decay

> Utter futility! All is futile!
> What real value is there for a man
> In all the gains he makes beneath sun?[2]

There could be a truth and go "as if"
As if by light I see and in night trust
Dawn to return vouchsafing me today

With renewed inquisitiveness for love
I don't fear the cliché because I know
Well-worn idioms border the unknown

For lack of anything to declare, I
Stack cupboard soup cans against inclement
Seasons gone, all gone now, boiled up, eaten

Pantry bare here, yet somehow contented
The room's supercharged solar wallpaper
Duration's shape for hours disambiguate

To beguile me, to distract me from the truth
Which cannot, must not become solid form
Like skyscrapers and candy wrappers, both

The refuse of civilization.
Nothing but vision itself solves dissolves
Both and neither service the holy name

Hebrew? Greek? A Latin origin. Mind
Is matter as substance embodied I
Camera Obscura no metaphor

Wanting yet knowing. Wanting yet knowing
Each cigarette is the last and love lasts
Day in day out, something exceeds knowledge

And what escapes us is precisely there
Here, everywhere, a planetary
Sameness infinitely refracted One

I am living in God's dream and her aim
Is subjective satisfaction, so be
Well as radiation and stitches

Stice, Old English, "a puncture, stabbing pain"
Related to German, *Stich*, "a sting, prick"
The sense "loop" arose in Middle English[3]

Etymology is a crystal prism
Refracting words into varicolored
Horizons, rising and falling

A chest, a chamber, a rib cage, breathing
Lying-in-state, beyond deception
Glimpsing inky penumbral suspicions

> Whose lantern, pray, will blaze aflame and be bright?
> 'Tis a famous tale, the deceitfulness of earth;
> The night is pregnant: what will dawn bring to birth?
> Tumult and bloody battle rage in the plain:[4]

Newspaper battlegrounds playgrounds meadows fields
Trying to hold together my being
Confused as a surplus of feelings

Landscapes vary, perspectives shift, rooms change
Quotations accumulate but thoughts
They compose as a force not a substance

Atmosphere, the fringes of ideas billow
Puffs, whiffs—airs. From the old French *aire*, "site
Disposition" *aegr*, or *agr*—"field"[5]

A sun, a sum, a pronoun blossoming
Into fragrant dissipation, exhaust
Fumes off childhood's oily recollections

Shimmering residues puddle collect
Transmission fluid: lymph blood semen tears
Rain upon rocks ground pebbles into sand

Become river-silt borne toward the sea
Evaporate into water mass Earth
Birth Death Destruction Rejuvenation

Repeat Cycle Circle Period Hole
Passageway Passages Quotations Lens
Lent Land—all nouns objects lost & mourned.

A garden glimpsed out the kitchen window
Autumn leaves, cloudless skies, pink asters
Pane clonazepam daze inventory:

FOCUS ABILITY SPLINTER MISFIRE
WILD-POLLINATION TEMPLE GLOW
SUBLIME COMPRESSION COMPASSION
COMPOSITION CONSTELLATIONS
MARINER ASTROLABE DAYLIGHT
EXHAUST WINDOWPANE DUST-MITES
FLOAT CONUNDRUM CLARITY CHARIOT
CAIRN GIRL DOLL ARMY FRUIT-ROT
STITCH SHOESHINE SIGN WIRE-FENCE
TREE-TRUNK BARK-BULGE SPOT-WELD
APPLES PAST NOW SEAM CRACK SLIT
OPTIC PARTICLE BITS PIECES SLICES
CHUNKS MOLECULES ATOMS RODS
CONES REFLECTIONS RODS & CONES
LIGHT BOUNCE BUNG PEEPHOLE
INTERIOR SHOW ROOM SKULL-BONES
PEELS BELLS WHISTLES ECHOES
RING-RING ORBITS STAR ORB ORBIT
ECLIPSE ELLIPSE BLIP PING SKYLINE
TRAIN-TRACKS CITY-VIEWS DESERT
DUST DISTURBANCES SIRENS SCIENCE
SILENCE BRICKS BLOCKS NOUNS STONES
BODIES RUINS CHUNKS PILES LENS
LAND LENT LORD LORD LORD PRAYER
CONTRITION APPEARANCES HOLY-
VISIONS SAINTS STAINS GHOSTS IMAGES
VISITATIONS HAUNTINGS METAL-TASTE
CEMENT-SMELL PRISON-CELL WALL
TIME-LAPSE PHOTOGRAPH EMERGENCE
SIT-BONES CHEEKS NOSTRIL EYE EAR
ARM LEG SYMMETRY BODIES VISCERA
X-RAY MRI BEWITCHED BEMUSED
BEFUDDLED BEE-POLLEN DISPERSALS
REHEASALS SUNRISE SUNSET ABOVE
BELOW EQUATOR PERISCOPE INTERIOR
MONOLOGUE METRONOME BEDSIDE
RIPTIDE AVALANCHE FOREST-FIRE LOGS
LICKS LICHEN ANTHROPOMORPHISM
GEESE-MIGRATION CLOUDS-ALOUD
AZURE OCEAN STORMS STREAMS
FLOES CLOTS COAGULATIONS SNOW-
WHITE NOISE STATIC RAINSTORM
INTERFERENCE RADIO TOWER INSECT
ANTENNAE BULLET-HOLE PIN-HOLE
BUTTON-HOLE EYELET WINDOWLESS
PLASTER WALL MONAD SKULL-
CRACK FOUR TEMPERAMENTS FOUR
DIRECTIONS FOUR SEASONS FOUR
ELEMENTS FOUR HORSES FOR FASCIA
FACE-TIME FANTASY FOCUS

1. Saint John of the Cross, *Dark Night of the Soul*, trans. and ed. E. Allison Peers (New York: Random House, 2009), Kindle edition.
2. Ecclesiastes 1:3 (Philadelphia: The Jewish Publication Society, 2000).
3. See "stitch," *New Oxford American Dictionary*, Version 2.2.3, Apple Inc., 2005–2011.
4. "The Times Are Out of Joint," *Hafiz: Fifty Poems*, trans. and ed. A. J. Arberry (Cambridge, UK: Cambridge University Press, 1947), 134.
5. See "air," *New Oxford American Dictionary*, Version 2.2.3, Apple Inc., 2005–2011.

Dave McKenzie

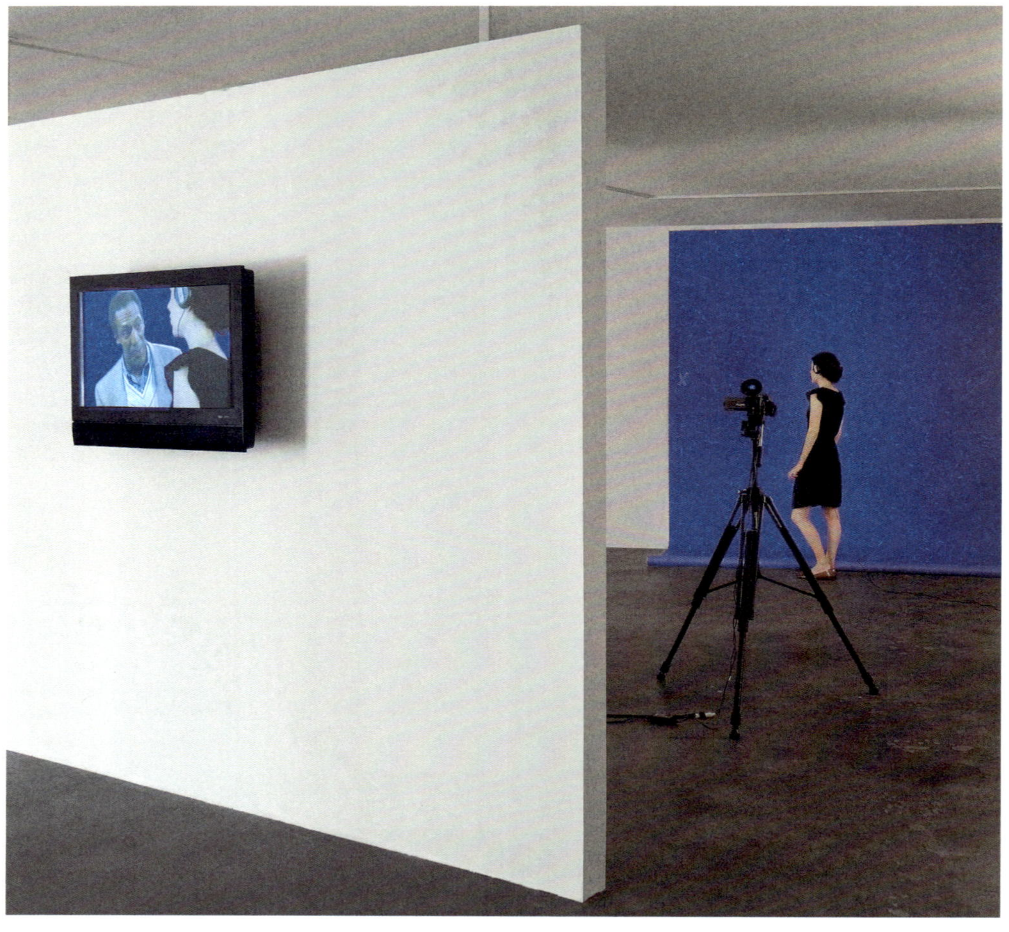

Preamble, 2009. NTSC video, color, sound; with lighting, audio, camera, and flat-screen television, dimensions variable

Born 1977 in
Kingston, Jamaica

Lives in
Brooklyn, NY

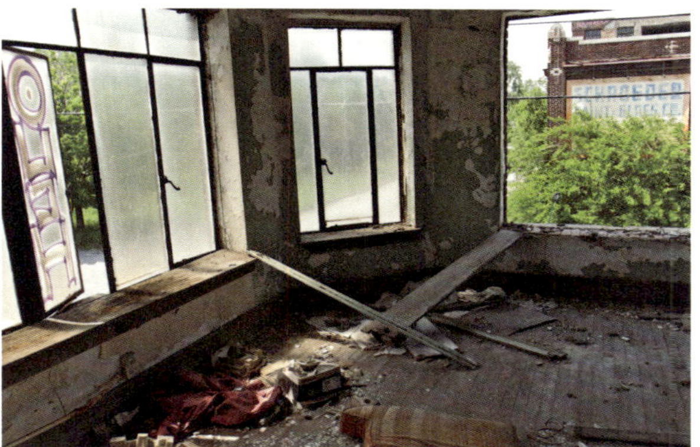

Still from *The Beautiful One Has Come*, 2012. Video, color, sound; 5:48 minutes

Dear, Dearest,

There are no highlights to report from my trip into the interior of that uncircumcised state known as Florida, except I am happy to report a little gem of a museum on the perimeter of the outskirts. There are only three works in this museum's "collection"—all permanently on view, all conspicuously untitled, and all attributed to Unknown. I have decided the collection is afflicted with Goldilocks Syndrome: one work is terrible (although in vogue at the moment), another all right, and yet another might truly be called great (although I more and more suspect it of being a broken kinetic sculpture). Should I say more about the work? Well, I guess I am hoping you'll one day visit. Also, I don't know if you'll find this interesting or not, but I wanted to break the museum down into basic parts for you. Three floors, four windows, and one door—I am not yet ready to describe portholes as doors. Though not technically an artwork, a diorama is on display. I know how you feel about dioramas, vitrines, and really anything too mise-en-scène—so perhaps the less said the better. There's a cafe as well, but apparently they don't use it. A sign in that room reads, "We prefer you to take this moment to contemplate the earth the sea and the sky. May you never know hunger may you never know despair." This may sound like I'm pulling one over the eight, but I did feel like I had heartburn all day there.

As for the staff, I'd describe it as something of a royal contingent. There are four curators and a guard. The guard makes slightly more money than the curators (you can learn a lot by saying hello to people), which means either he is well paid or they are poorly paid. (I guess there are more possibilities, but those are the two that leap to mind.) Two of the curators specialize in the Pre-Raphaelites.

Which means,

a) You have one too many Pre-Raphaelites experts or

2) one Pre-Raphaelite expert isn't pulling his or her weight.

And, yes, I used a and 2 instead of 1 and 2 or a and b because I know you find it so cute when I do that. Anyway, it seems that terms like *curator* and *guard* are used loosely there. In fact, I would swear the guard costume is shared by different staff members and rotates in forty-minute intervals. In fact, I imagine everyone has to pitch in a little with all sorts of tasks and that nobody looks at anybody's name tag or business card too closely.

I should point out, in case you want to recommend this museum to your dad (and just so we are clear, I am strongly recommending it to you), that there is no entrance fee, but you will be asked for a donation on exit. My strategy for skipping out was twofold. When I saw they were about to raise a stink about supporting this and that, I put my headphones on and used the woman in front of me as a kind of shield. I wasn't quite quick enough to avoid the questionnaire that was shoved in my face, "to be completed at [my] earliest convenience." Mostly it's boilerplate, but question thirty-six reads, "Describe in detail a sexual fantasy (use another piece of paper if

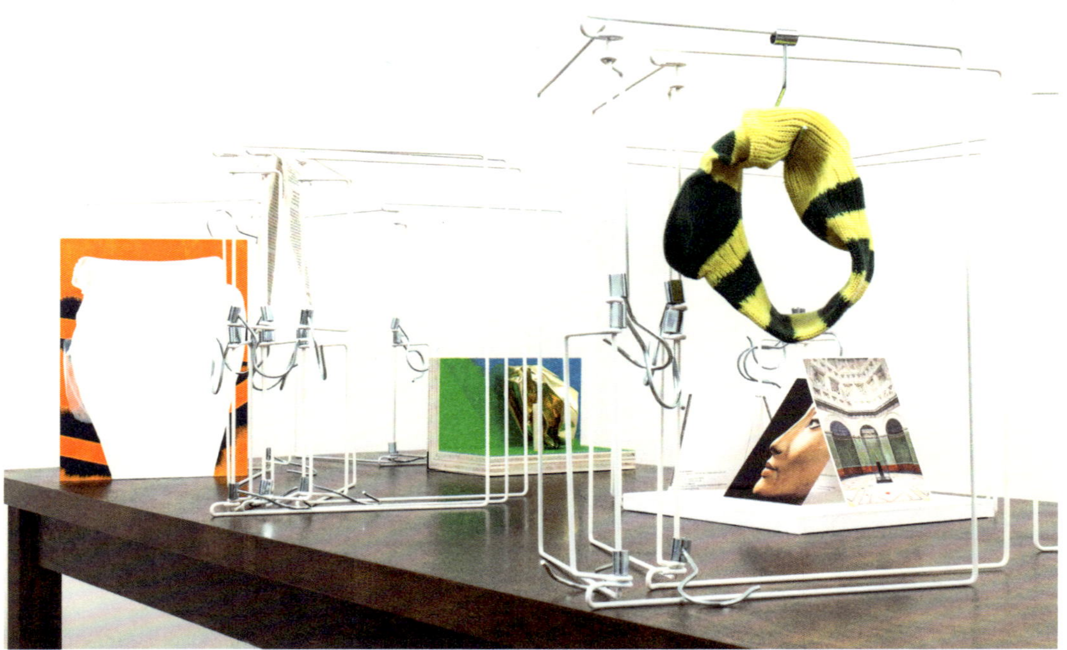

The Past Into The Future Infinitely, 2012 (detail). Wood table, hanging mechanisms, acrylic on metal, acrylic on wood, postcards, found text, and found images, 44.1 × 29.5 × 79.9 in. (112 × 75 × 203 cm)

necessary).” I assume some young ass slipped that in, but the questions do get a little weird from thirty-six on. Anyway, wait until they read what I have to say. Extra sheet of paper?! I’ll give them three sheets of fantasies that will make their eyes water and their heads droop. Don’t worry, I won’t reveal anything—I’ll just Google something up, copy, paste, print, and that will be that.

I don’t know why, but I’ve been picturing you and your old man visiting said museum. Your father will touch one of the three works, and the guard will interject, “Sir, you can’t do that!” But he’ll also wink like maybe you *can*. You’ll learn that there is Wi-Fi but they don’t give out the password. Still, if you have the right connections—again, the guard—you’ll learn that the password is “password1234wordpass.” It’s stupid, yes, but you wouldn’t have guessed it either. You’ll ask why they put a museum like this here and be told that’s a question that comes up often. In general, you’ll learn a lot by talking to the guard. You will learn that, years ago, the local free press ran a story on this museum, that the headline ran, “Quaint Museum Outshines Its Neighbors,” and that the guard was pictured above the fold. Your father will scoff and say, “There are no other museums for a hundred miles!” On the way out, you’ll both notice that there is a copy of said article behind the visitors’ desk. You will point at the walls, noting that they are covered in a fine layer of soot—owing to a grease fire some years ago. (An explanation for the café?) You and your father will agree that the institution is better for the soot, which says, *patina*. Affectionately if a little mockingly, one of you will describe the museum’s size as jumbo shrimp. You will both paw through the books in the bookstore. I say “bookstore” but laugh because it’s really just a crammed rolling cart, like the kind you might find in a library. Father and child will learn from one of these “books on the museum” that the staff has hosted its share of world leaders and dignitaries. The woman behind the desk, who you’ll suspect is one of those misplaced curators, will smile and say, “You haven’t lived until you’ve seen a guard put a dictator in his place.”

When you get home you’ll ask why I didn’t mention that the middle floor is carpeted. I’ll reply, “It didn’t affect the work, did it?” We will debate affect and effect. You will say, “I think it is a real credit to Mr. or Ms. Unknown.” I’ll ask what your father thought of it all, and you’ll say, “He was glad that none of his tax dollars went to support it.”

May you and I never know hunger,

D

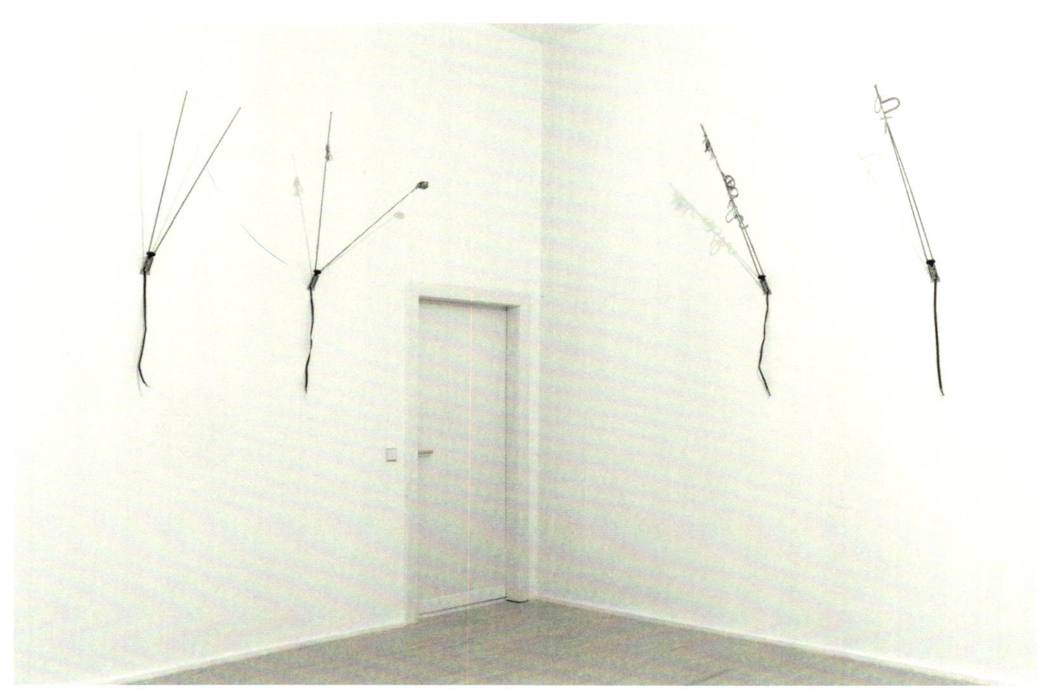

Good Looking Out, 2008. Television antennas, aluminum, and plastic, dimensions variable

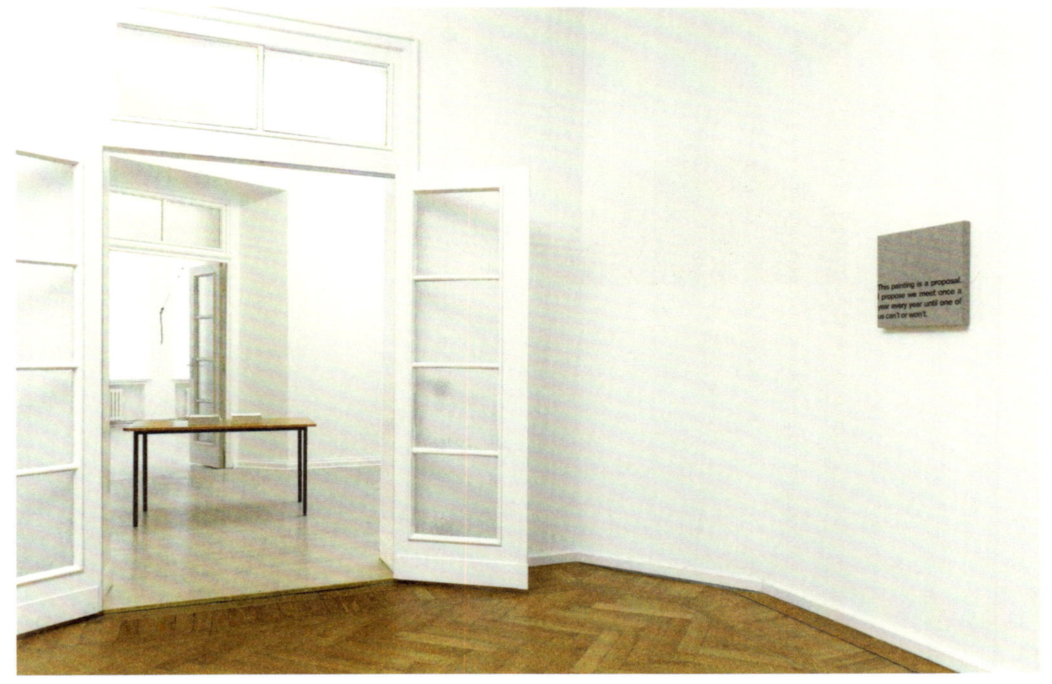

Citizen, 2011 (installation view, Wien Lukatsch Gallery, Berlin)

Rebecca Morris

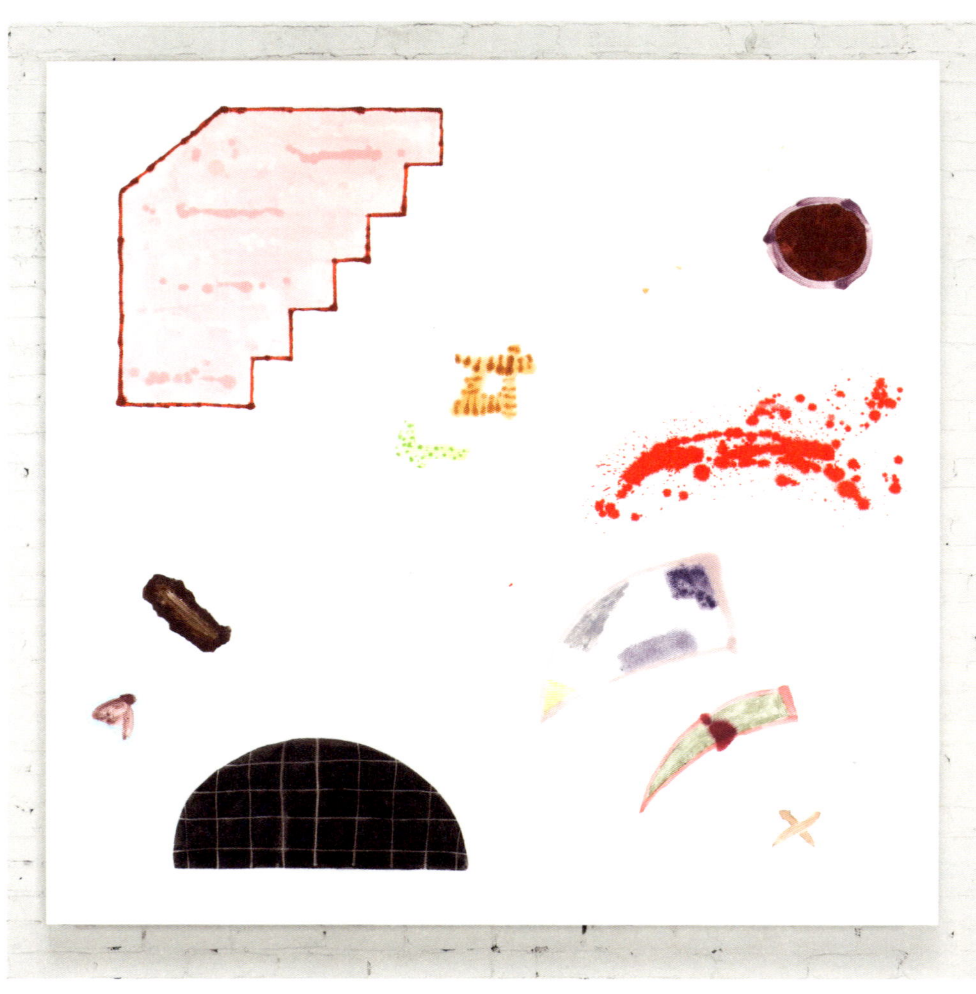

Untitled (#05-13), 2013. Oil on canvas, 79 × 79 in. (200.7 × 200.7 cm). Berezdivin Collection

Born 1969 in
Honolulu, HI

Lives in
Los Angeles, CA

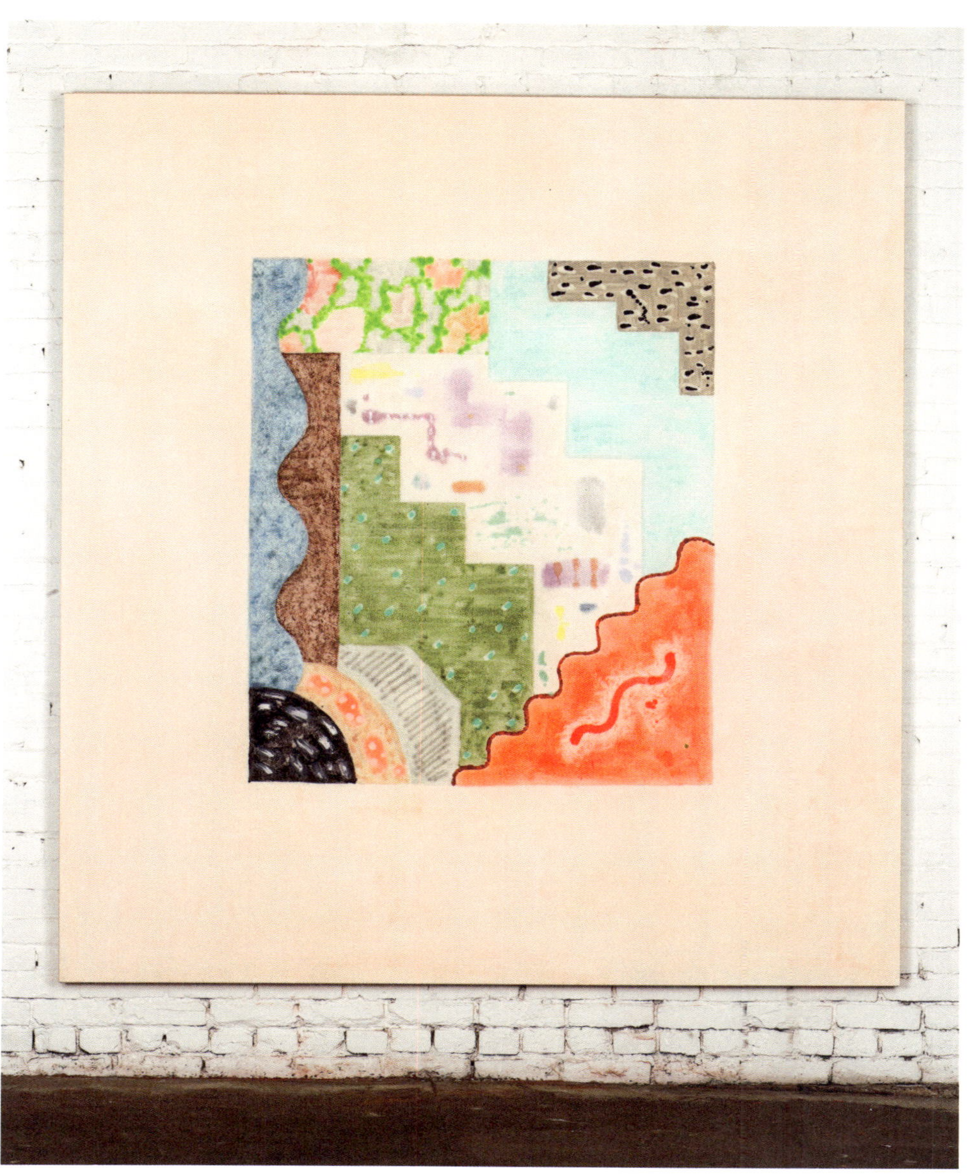

Untitled (#01-13), 2013. Oil on canvas, 87 × 80 in. (221.0 × 203.2 cm)

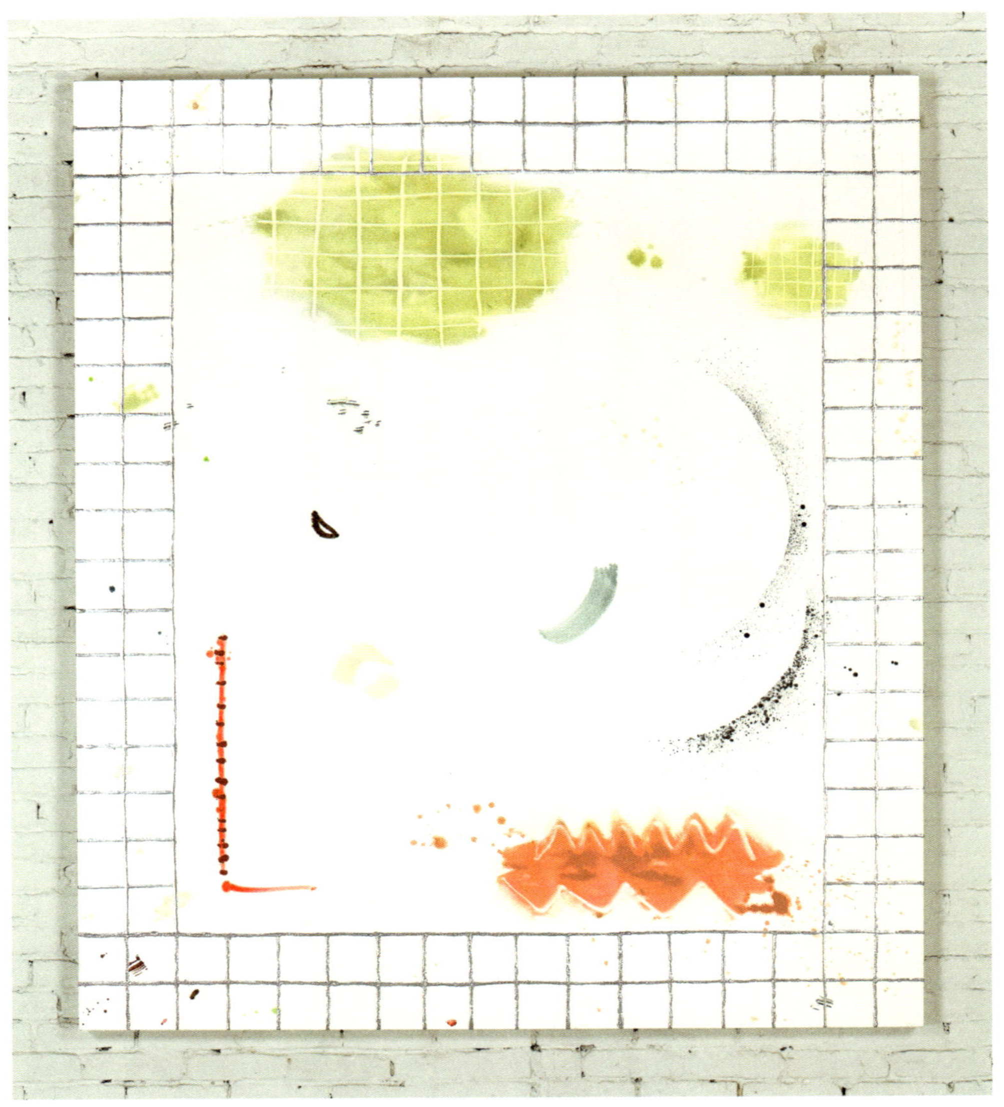

Untitled (#13-13), 2013. Oil and spray paint on canvas, 80 × 69 in. (203.2 × 175.3 cm)

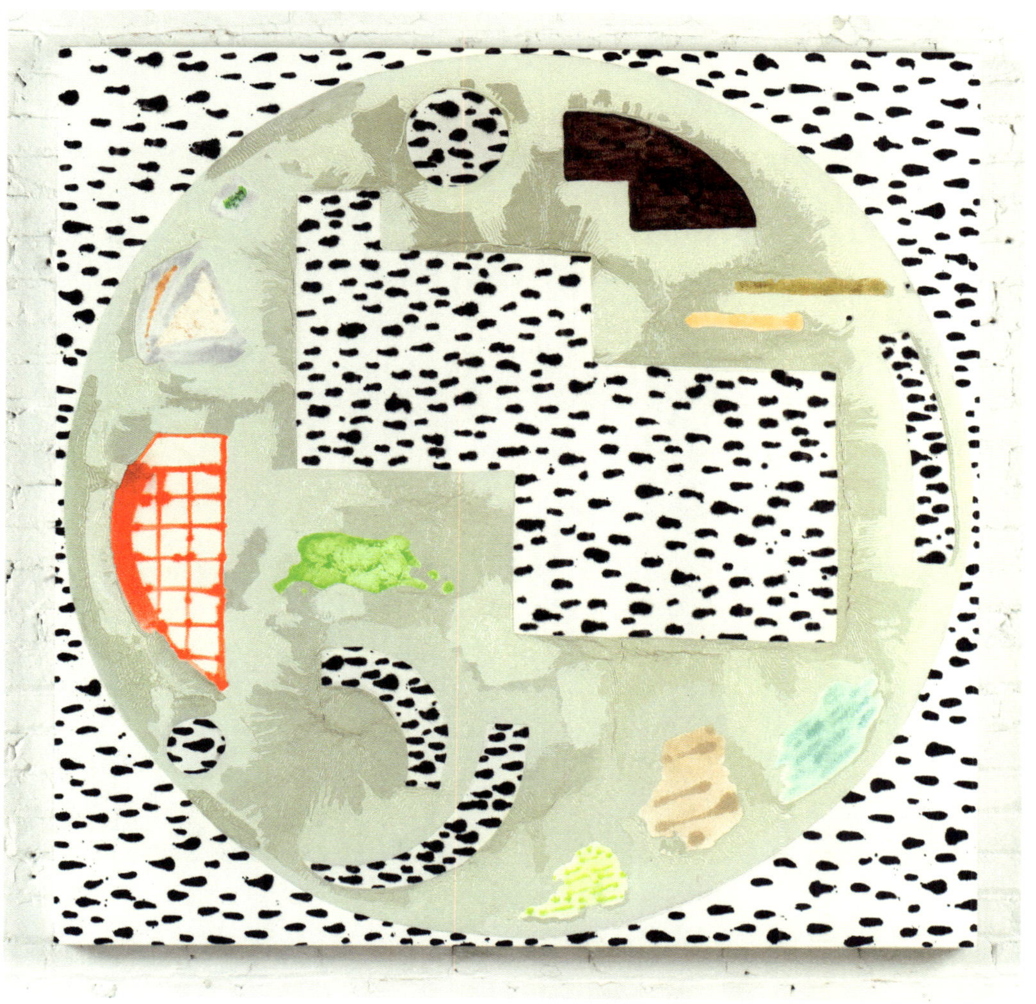

Untitled (#04-13), 2013. Oil on canvas, 58 × 58 in. (147.3 × 147.3 cm). Collection of Miriam Lazoff and Danny Koplowitz

My Barbarian

Malik Gaines, Jade Gordon, and Alexandro Segade

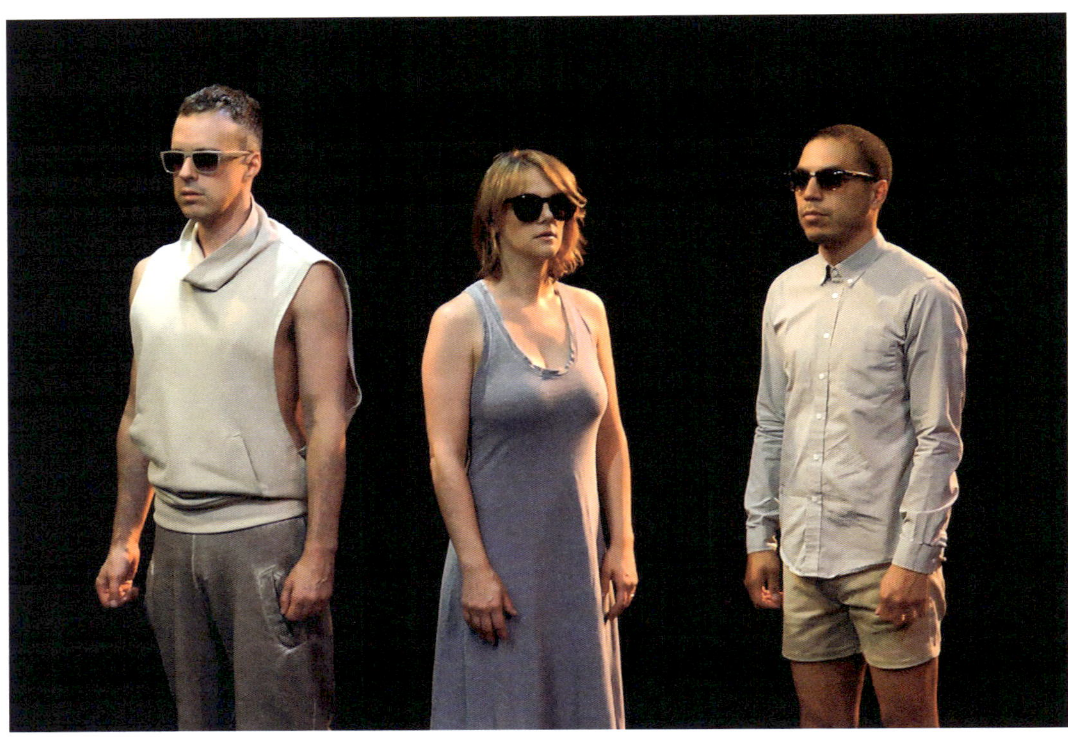

Stills from *Universal Declaration of Infantile Anxiety Situations Reflected in the Creative Impulse*, 2013. High-definition video, color, sound; 29:02 minutes

Founded in 2000

Based in Los Angeles, CA/ New York, NY

The Mother & Other Plays

1.

Many of my mother's journals have been lost. The ones that are left—girlish diaries with broken locks and blue linen composition books from the seventies packed up in a battered cardboard box—have survived the worst of her crazy times, episodes during which she would pack up loose Victorian-era family photos, tarnished silver, "art supplies," hoarded sugar packets, and dirty clothes in broken suitcases and cart them in expensive taxi rides across neighborhoods to my house, to the homes of crazier boyfriends, or to various mental hospitals around Pasadena and Glendale. I rescued the box from a cat-pee closet and moved it around from storage space to storage space and finally into my own place to keep the journals safe for selfish purposes, future art projects. For the "Victoria" section of our video *Universal Declaration of Infantile Anxiety Situations Reflected in the Creative Impulse* (2013), we used excerpts from the one she kept in 1977 while taking a college class called Survival as a Mother. She wrote about how hard it was

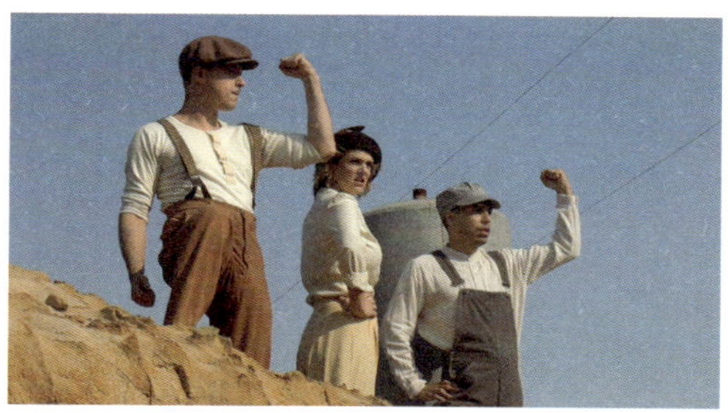

being a single mother, and how she got so angry at eighteen-month-old me that she kicked tables, and how sometimes being a mother was shitty. I read the journal for the first time as a teenager and was horrified to think of her not loving me all the time. Later they were proof of her craziness. See, she's always been nuts! But working with them recently—after having forgiven her for (most of) the "bad mothering," having let go of many of my resentments, and, most important, having become a mother myself last year—I feel softer. I appreciate her honesty and sympathize; how hard it must have been to be alone with a baby, in grad school, and trying to date. I want to protect her, show her off, and have access to the young woman who wrote the journal. I'm also still a little ashamed of her. During the project, I had to remind myself not to exploit her, to let her have input about which photos to use or not to use, and to let her approve the edits to her text. She is still not happy that her hands look so old in the video.

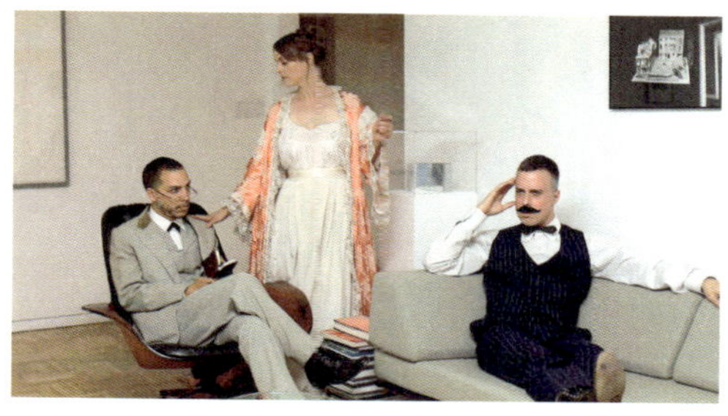

2.

Our work for the Biennial exhibition has two parts. One part is a plan to take over for three weeks the lobby gallery, where we will perform *The Mother*, our adaptation of a Bertolt Brecht play, during regular museum hours. Presenting the story of a revolutionary's mother who becomes radicalized, we will unfix the play's scenarios through improvisations, interactions, and reinterpretations inserted into the memorized text. The performance navigates questions of communism and political love, art and exploitation, and play acting, and also singing, and masks. We each play the mother and so do members of the audience, switching off from scene to scene and rendering the mother a position to be occupied by anyone.

THE MOTHER
What did they ask of us?
MASHA
They asked us to participate.
THE MOTHER
And what did you say?
PAVEL
I said we would.
THE MOTHER
Oh, Pavel.

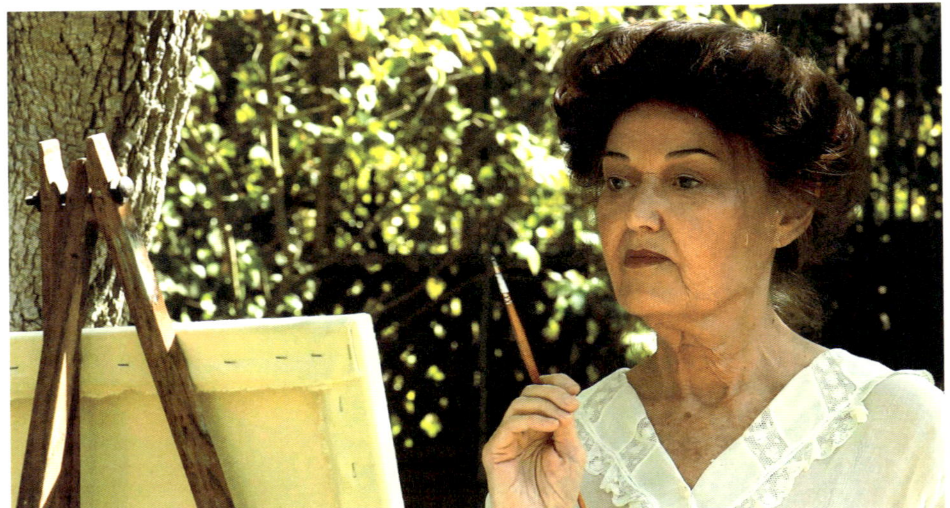

Still from *Universal Declaration of Infantile Anxiety Situations Reflected in the Creative Impulse*, 2013. High-definition video, color, sound; 29:02 minutes

3.

Last night, I dreamed about Mary Kelly again. She was at the piano, and we were talking. And Katy Perry was there. I wanted Mary's blessing for something, and she wasn't giving it easily. I felt guilty because we owe her a DVD of the video we made with our mothers: Barbara Gaines, Victoria Gordon, and Irene Segade; and two important artists: Eleanor Antin and Mary Kelly. The video, which is the second part of our contribution to the Biennial exhibition, has had two titles. "Working Mother" was the working title, but we later collapsed our thinking about psychoanalysis and politics into *Universal Declaration of Infantile Anxiety Situations Reflected in the Creative Impulse*, referencing a textual relationship to both Melanie Klein and Eleanor Roosevelt. The whole thing has the air of a costume drama. Mary Kelly performs a version of Mary Cassatt who paints in the afternoon and plays piano while we sing along with her composition. Eleanor Antin is "a celebrated humanist, philanthropist, and woman-at-large" of the 1930s, and we are workers occupied in her studio, making two-dimensional Depression-era furniture. Our mothers enact versions of themselves in equally stylized situations: a black-and-white montage with diary voice-over, a theatrically staged political speech, a class-drag talent show. They act out a feminist/feminine legacy that's real, imaginary, and symbolic. We've tried to extend the figure of "the mother" past its essentialist clichés; we made a piece years ago, *Pagan Rights*, (2006), that claimed "Our Goddess Gave Birth to Your God." Having reached a different place in our lives and work, we devised both the video and the play over the spring and summer of 2013 in Brooklyn and Los Angeles, drawing scenes of affective labor, communitarian contracts, radical pedagogy and critical mimicry out of our mother-child relationships. Having worked for more than a decade in a field of art and performance that celebrates certain patrimonies and having been compelled by histories of fathers and sons, we felt this was the time to assert (however playfully) a matrilineal kinship. Born in the 1970s as we three were, we were born into and out of feminism. A feminist criticality helps expose the constructedness of origin myths themselves, a criticality My Barbarian has always brought to its narratives. Ours is a group with varied histories and many starting points. Our collective identity is stitched together from a diversity of patterns: we are men and women with mixed racial and ethnic backgrounds and various sexual orientations. While none of us shares the same identity, we identify with each other and each other's identifications. One area in which we do find a kind of rhyme is generation (we share cultural references), and another is class: all of our mothers were teachers before they retired. Along with a few queer male exceptions, our most influential teachers have been women. Women artists, particularly in critical practices related to performance, have created the conditions and much of the art to which our work responds. Many of these artists and teachers are about the same age as our actual mothers, who taught us a lot. This work is an acknowledgment of their historic influence, a proposal for a feminist legacy, and a representation of a present generational melancholy that disallows us from ever fully reconstituting our origins, mythic or otherwise.

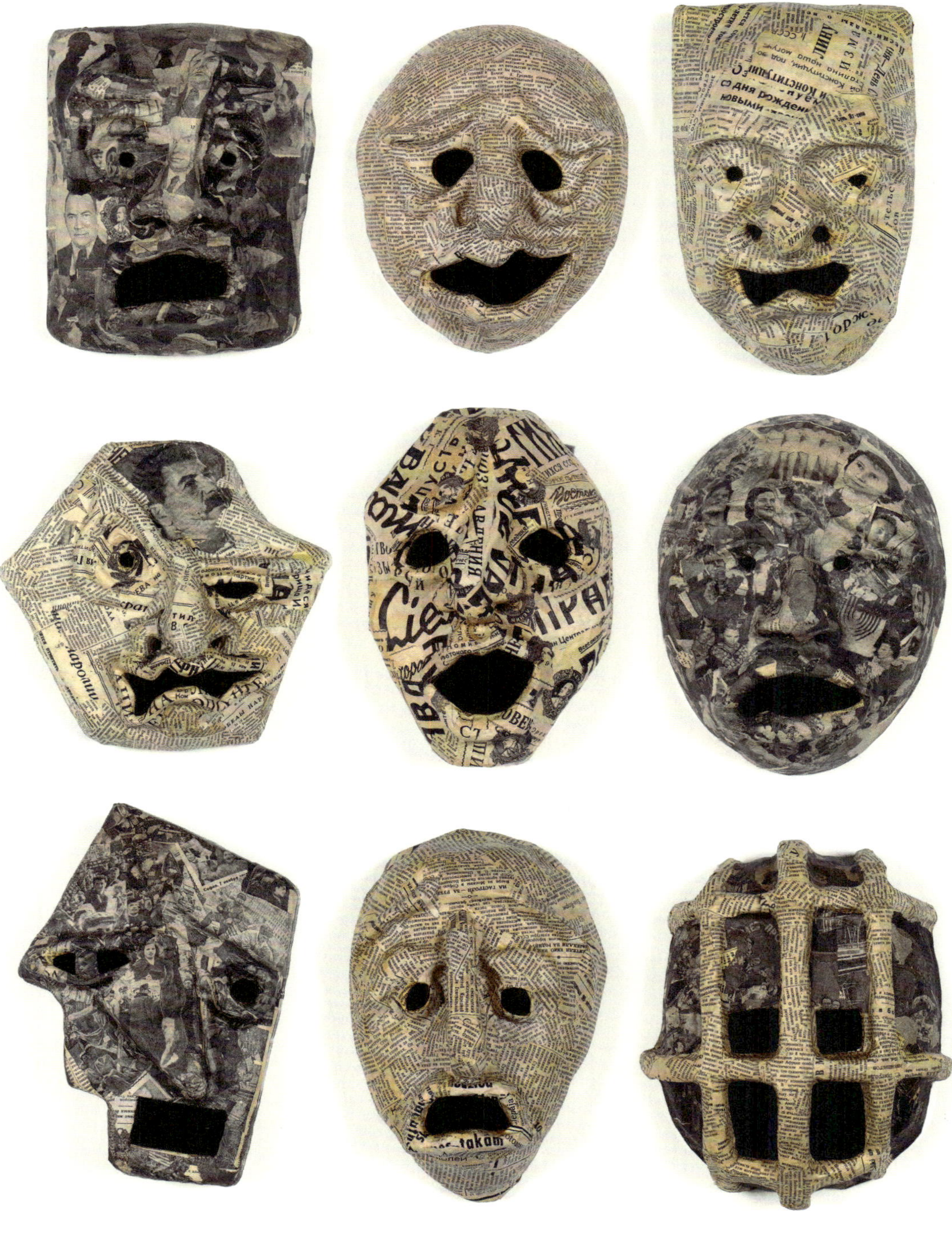

Masks used in My Barbarian's adaptation of *The Mother* by Bertolt Brecht, 2013. Top row: *Unemployed Man*, *Cashier*, *Peasant*; middle row: *Policeman*, *Shopper*, *Woman in Black*; bottom row: *Gatekeeper*, *Foreman*, *Prison Guard*. All works: 2013. Papier mâché, dimensions variable. Collection of Robert W. and Anne Conn

Paul P.

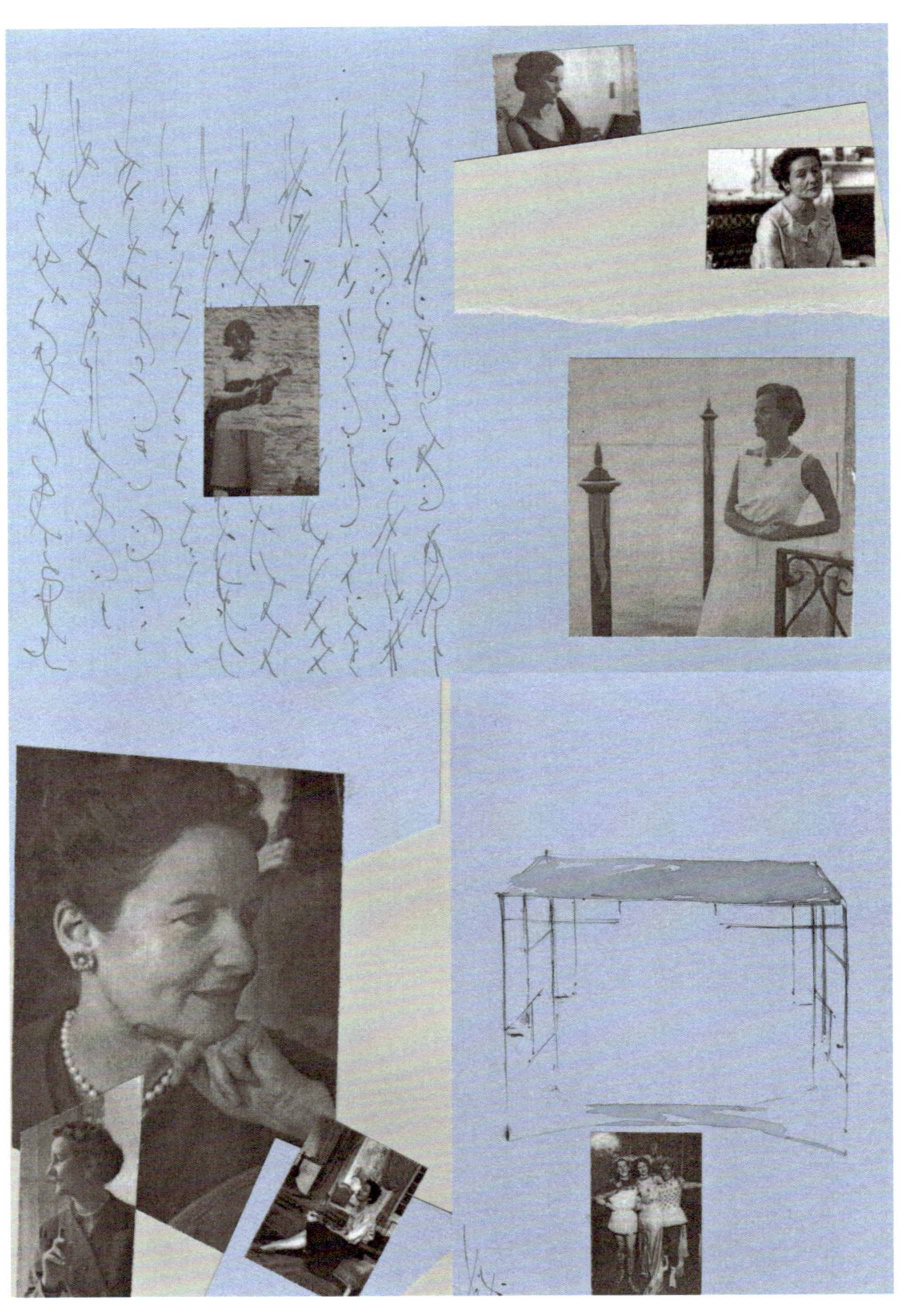

Four works, each: *Untitled*, 2013. Collage with ink, 4 × 6 in. (10.2 × 15.2 cm)

Born 1977 in Hamilton, ON, Canada

Lives in New York, NY/ Paris, France

Paul P.

Bacchante with Lowered Eyes

[Cedric] was sitting on the churchyard wall, the pale sunshine on his golden hair, which I perceived to be tightly curled, an aftermath of the ball, no doubt, and plucking away with intense concentration at the petals of a daisy.

He loves me, he loves me not, he loves me, he loves me not, don't interrupt, my angel, he loves me, he loves me not, oh, heaven heaven heaven! He loves me! I may as well tell you, my darling, that the second big thing in my life has begun.

—Nancy Mitford, *Love in a Cold Climate*, 1949

There is a likeness between Jean-Baptist Carpeaux's *Bacchante with Lowered Eyes*, a terracotta bust from 1872 that sits in a vitrine at the Metropolitan Museum of Art, and photographs of Nancy Mitford. They share a slightly pinched facial structure—imagine the drawing together of features, nose and chin, outward and downward, gently. Teasing with the corners of her mouth and the pagoda lilt of her eyebrows, she is gamine, elfin, just slightly the ugly witch, with a masculine aspect, that, were it not for the designation *Bacchante*, could be an effeminate Bacchus.

Nancy Mitford (1904–1973)—novelist, biographer, and essayist—was the artist, socialist, and expatriate of the six famous Mitford sisters. In 1920s London, she was a part of the Bright Young People, the interwar teenage phenomenon known for their parties and hijinks and a wild premonitory energy ahead of the war to come. No previous youth movement had been quite so gay, or so tolerant. Cedric Hampton in *Love in a Cold Climate* is an amalgam of Mitford's prewar friends—Stephen Tennant, Brian Howard, Harold Acton, Robert Byron, Hamish St Clair-Erskine, and Rex Whistler—and is perhaps the first unpunished homosexual character in mainstream literature. He not only survives the novel, he is victorious: having been summoned from Canada by distant relatives to be the next heir to a vast fortune, Cedric wins the hearts of all, including the affections of a handsome lorry driver and a prurient uncle.

A few rooms away from the *Bacchante* in the Metropolitan is E. W. Godwin's *Table with Folding Shelves*, also from 1872. Hygienic and poetic in its delicate lines, Godwin's furniture has a considered graphic pulse: a drawing that unfolds in its shifting interstices as the observer moves to and fro. Godwin was an arch aesthete and reformer, who, like his friend and collaborator James McNeill Whistler, appropriated elements from Japanese design. I have often imagined Mitford seated at a table derived from Godwin's lines; corresponding, reporting, in London during the Blitz; tired by her work at the first-aid post, the nightly air raids, and the smoldering frames of buildings in the morning, her best work as yet unwritten. This table is not the perpetual furnishing of any room but a liminal object, to be moved in or moved out—having a destination that is ultimately elsewhere. It is the *idea* of a writing table, an immaterial island, separated from function.

In the galleries of a museum, objects do not touch, except by conflation. They exist in suspension, similar to Cedric's counting of the petals of a flower, to the lacuna of life during wartime, or to the halcyon blip that precedes it. The dots and dashes of my ink drawings of the *Bacchante*, seen from all the angles of her dial, are marks of time recorded. Like a chronograph that can be started, stopped, and reset to zero by returning to the museum. Striving for closeness, for proximity to a consciousness (a gentle or shocking recognition), a desired thing, some redux, though moving always toward a new and present love.

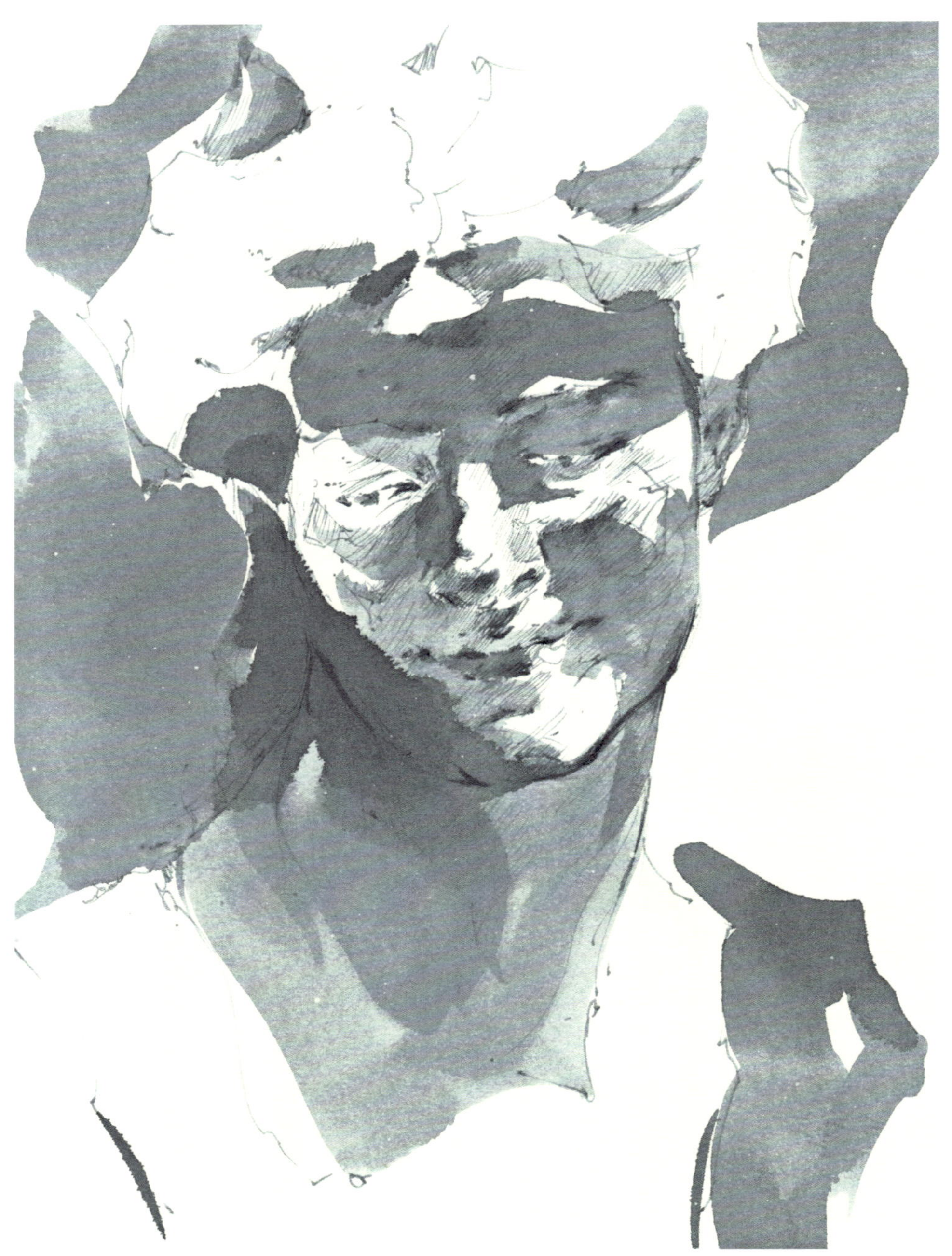

Untitled, 2013. Ink on paper, 8 ½ × 11 ¾ in. (21.6 × 29.8 cm)

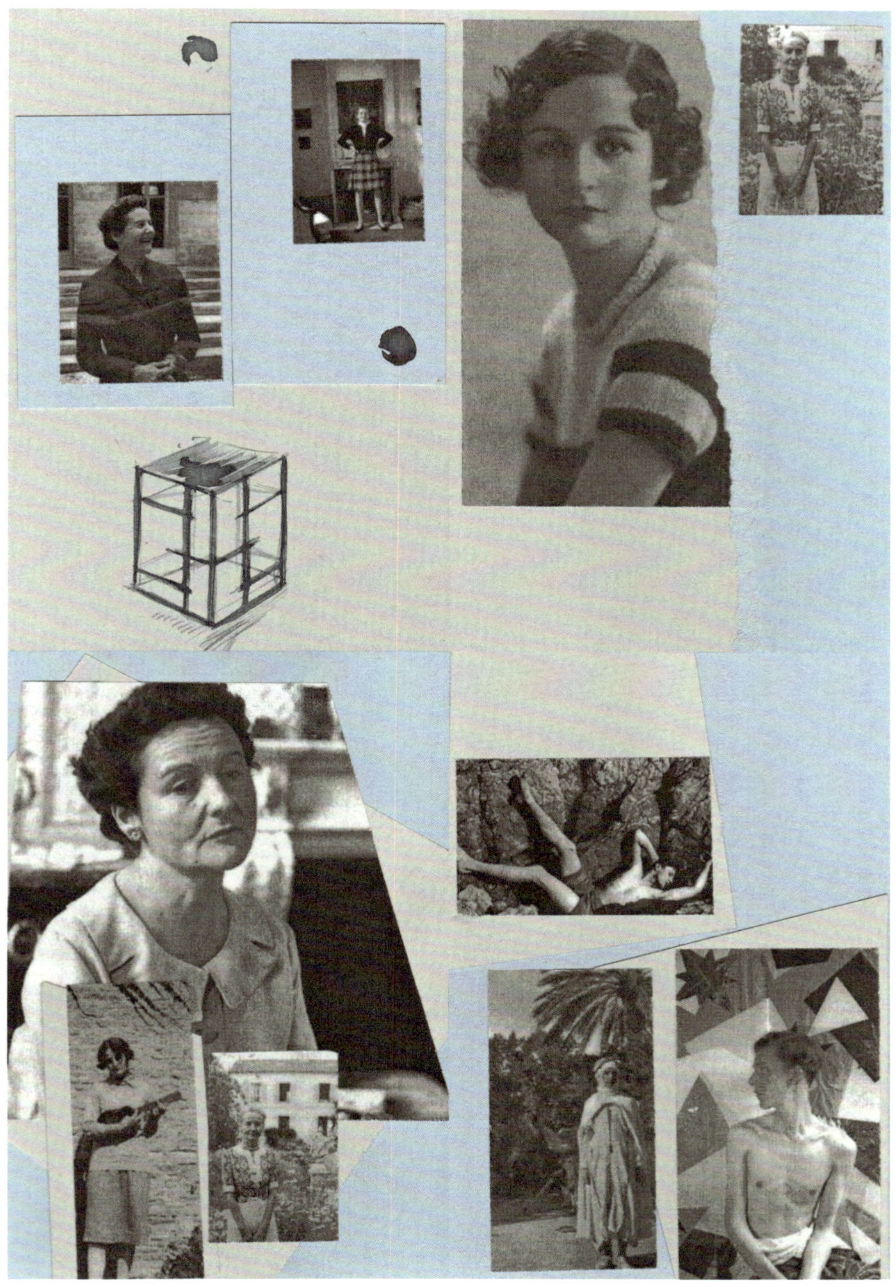

Four works, each: *Untitled*, 2013. Collage with ink, 4 × 6 in. (10.2 × 15.2 cm)

taisha paggett

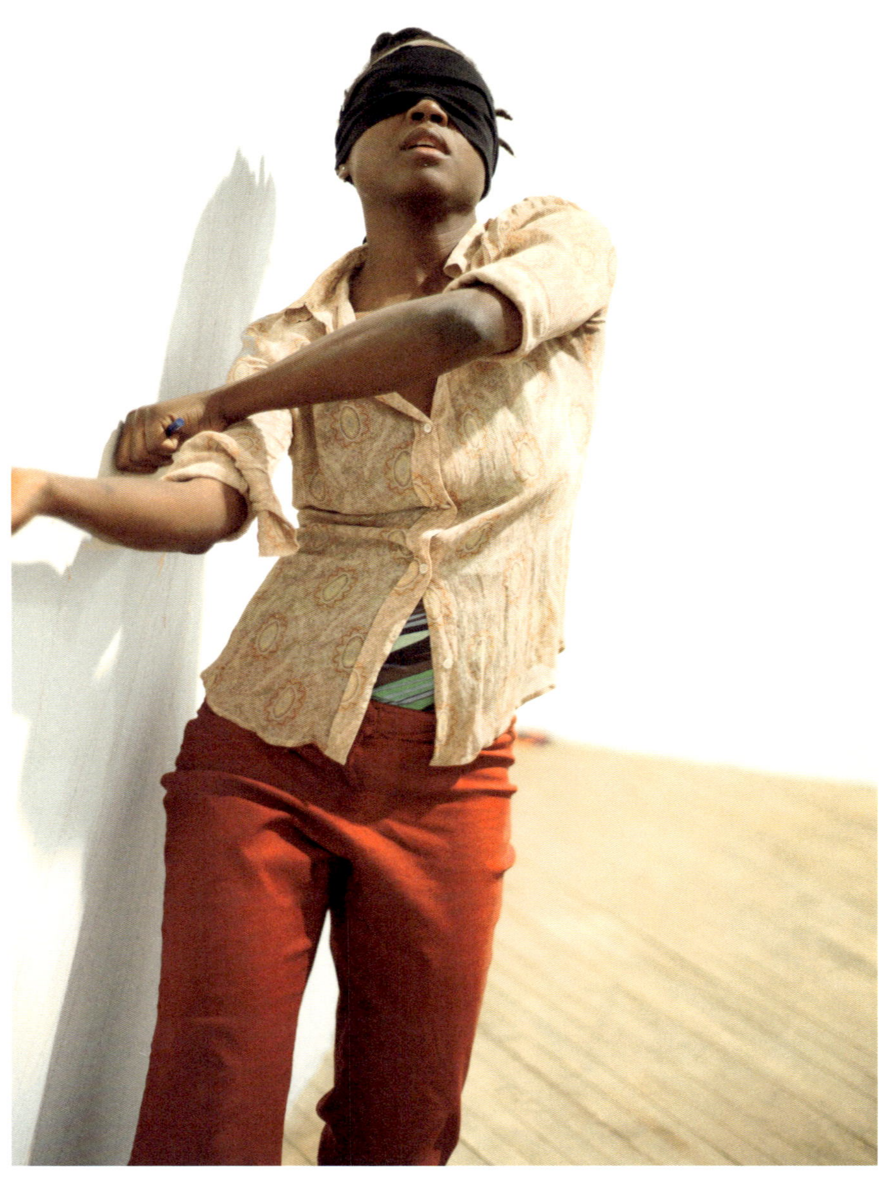

Decomposition of a Continuous Whole, 2010. Performance, Vox Populi Gallery, Philadelphia, December 3, 2010, as part of the exhibition *Quadruple Consciousness*, December 3, 2010–January 30, 2011

Born 1976 in Fresno, CA

Lives in Chicago, IL / Los Angeles, CA

taisha paggett

notes on process & understanding

question: how might we feel time?

i'd like to live in it. i'd like to move slowly enough that both you and I can see/feel what's happening. i'd like you to be able to feel your breath in this process. i'd like to live in—to be—the how-ness and, for now, let someone else pay attention to who/what/when/where/why.

another question: "where do i look when you're looking at me?"[1]

Yvonne Rainer posed this in a lecture at the Art Institute of Chicago not too long ago, and it's stayed with me. it reminds me of what's so terrifying about dancing. and what's so delicious. nobody knows where to look.

HAIR WHIP COLOR MAGIC

more questions: what does it mean to linger in/tease out/extend the space between no speech and speech?

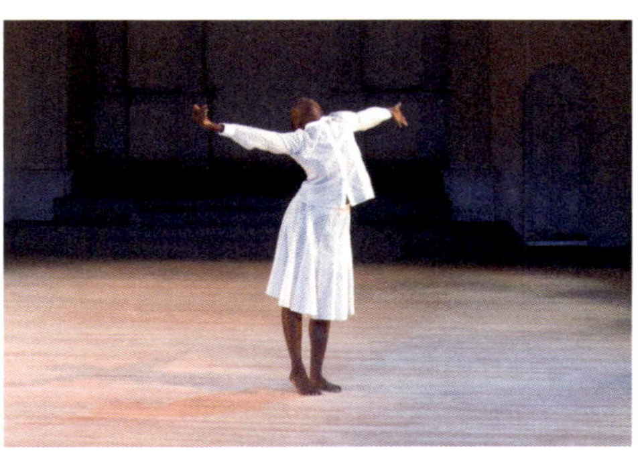

Private Realness, 2012. Performance, Danspace at St. Mark's Church, New York, December 13, 2012, as part of the exhibition *Solos and Solitudes*, December 13–15, 2012

Kansas-Nebraska Act. Missouri Compromise. Civil War. Prisons. Speech. Agency. Memory. Rehearsals. Grand Canyon.

filibuster becomes Fila Buster. an idea becomes a subject(ivity) . . . the production of a noun. a her. a transhistorical, metaphysical her.

quoting, claiming, dragging. (these can be all the same. okay.)

meaning is architecture: crystalline, unreliable, and restructurable.

a question: is my body (ever) enough?

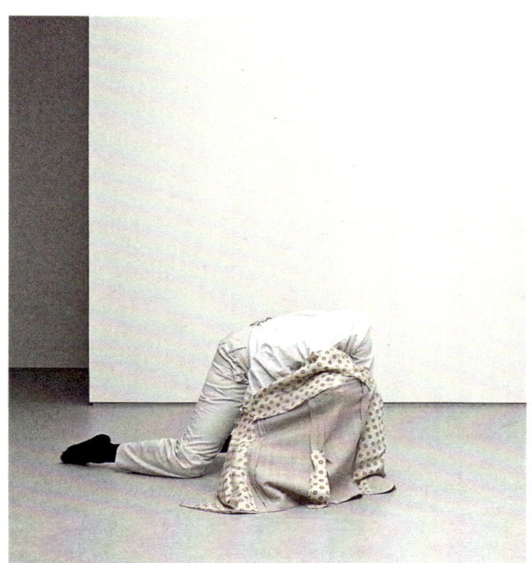

A Composite Field, 2012. Performance, MAK Center for Art and Architecture's Mackey Garage, Los Angeles, January 20, 2012

everyone is right here, right now, even if one is from a hundred years ago.
this moment is like other moments. what if we think the universe flat, see the historical moment as this current moment, and dare to have a conversation about it, with all of our now-ness? and then think ourselves alive? history versus memory. this moment is just like the last.
future present past.
a letter falling in on itself . . . in not linear time but layered time, like an echo.

this song found on YouTube:

> I can be a square
> or a rectangle
> or I can lean over at an angle
> I am a parallelogram . . .
>
> My four sides are straight
> but the angles and the corners
> they make
> aren't always 90 degrees
> measure them—[2]

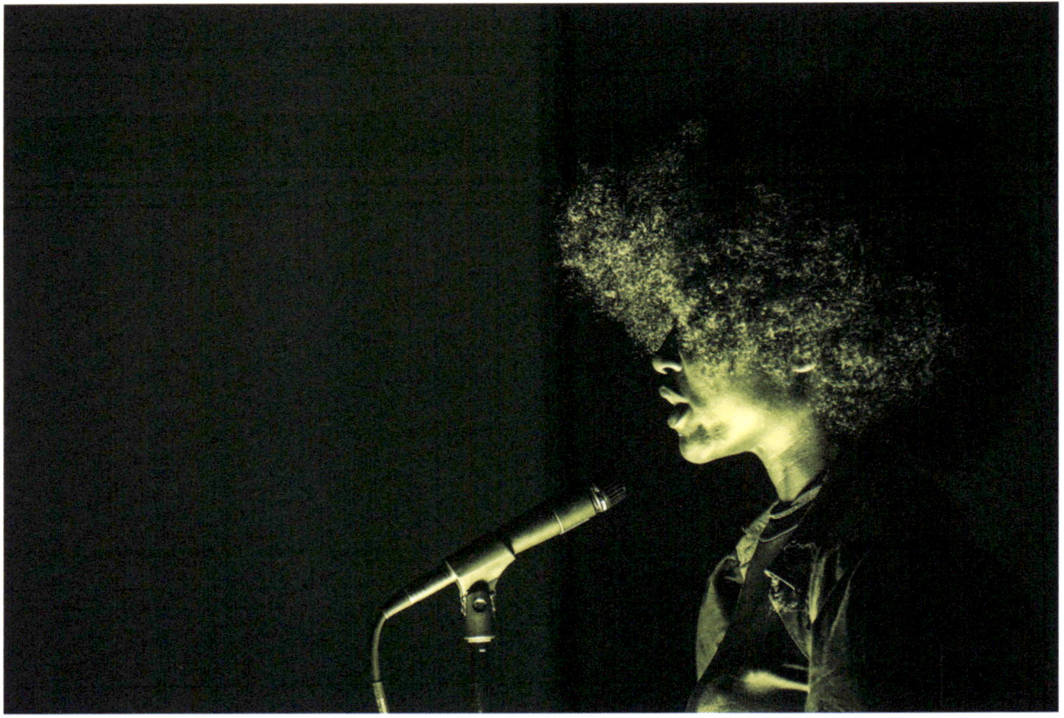

Fila Buster, 2012. Performance, TheOffCenter, San Francisco, as part of the National Queer Arts Festival, June 26, 2012

REPETITION
ECHO
CHORUS
LIGHT
LISTEN
RESONATE

a question: what if i'm to believe all things are sacred?
my (own) private (realness).

(and yours too because we're more similar than we think.)

song lyrics become mantras,
mantras for a possible ________

REPETITION
ECHO
CHORUS
LIGHT
LISTEN
RESONATE
AUTOTUNE
AUTOTUNIVERSE
FIL/I/A/BUSTER

________: how are we like light?

photosynthesis. being. becoming. the necessity of receptivity. eat plants, be plants. eat sunshine, be sunshine.

we are here.

a possible song:

> Mama don't want no peas, no rice,
> no coconut oil, no coconut oil
> Mama don't want no peas, no rice,
> no coconut oil,
> Mama don't want no peas, no rice,
> no coconut oil,
> All she wants is whiskey, brandy all the time[3]
>
> 'Tis the gift to be simple, 'tis the gift to
> be free
> 'Tis the gift to come down where we ought
> to be,
>
> When we find ourselves in the place just right
> 'Twill be in the valley of love and delight . . .[4]

Tonight we're going hard

Just like the world is ours

We're tearin' it apart

You know we're superstars

We r who we r . . . [5]

When true simplicity is gain'd,
To bow and to bend we shan't be asham'd
To turn, turn will be our delight
'Til by turning, turning we come
'round right.[6]

it is the da-da-da
it is the d-d-d
she is ready, she is ready

it is the da da da
it is the d-d-d
he is ready, he is ready

it is the da da da
it is the d-d-d
____ is ready, ____ is ready

it is the da da da
it is the d-d-d
we is ready
we is ready
we is ready

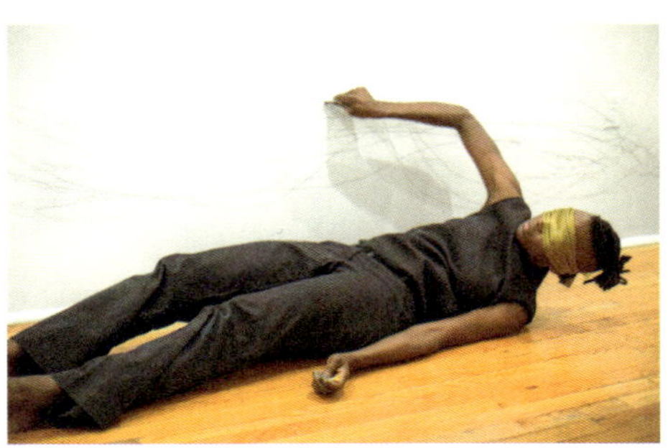

Decomposition of a Continuous Whole, 2012. Performance, The Studio Museum in Harlem, New York, November 11, 2012 as part of the exhibition *Fore*, November 11, 2012–March 10, 2013

multiplicities of information shape our makeup. like mockingbirds, we stretch our time and sense of place to ride tandem with information superhighways. and then hoard ideas. i've found this to be useful, but ultimately it disempowers. i see less need to make more things. less need to invent newness. more cleaning house. more acknowledging inner-historical (mine and yours) thoughts, frames and ideas. more constraints and regifting to unearth meaning from the things that already exist. tapping into their layers.

suddenly everything makes sense and feels dependent on the thing before it, and I feel at peace because it means we have to lean into one another in order to feel (the kind of feeling that gives way to knowing/understanding/acting/superbeing).

also remember: the experience is not for me but for an us-ness that dies and comes alive depending on what we're open to receiving, what interpretive frames we're speaking to/from, and how deeply and consciously we're breathing (the underseeing) as all of this is going down.

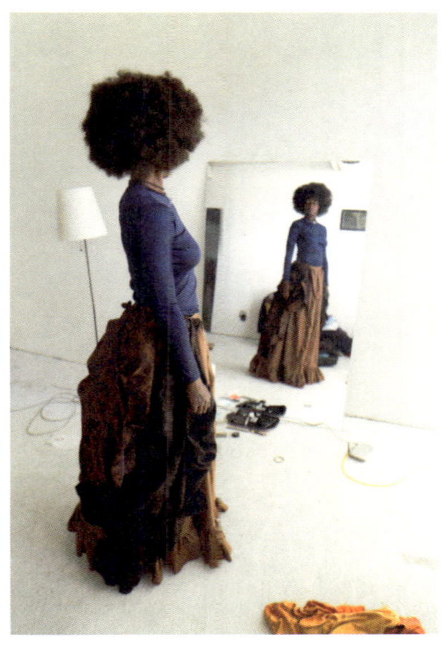

Rehearsal for *Fila Buster*, 2012

1. Yvonne Rainer, lecture on the act of performing, Art Institute of Chicago, April 11, 2012.
2. Peter Weatherall, lyrics of "I Am a Parallelogram" (2009). Online at http://www.youtube.com/watch?v=Rpkjb4Tx844.
3. Shaker Elder Joseph Brackett Jr., lyrics of "Simple Gifts" (circa 1848).
4. Lyrics of a folk song from the Bahamas, "Mama Don't Want No Peas, No Rice." A June 1939 performance of the song by Zora Neale Hurston is archived in Florida Folklife from the WPA Collections, 1937–1942, at the Library of Congress. Online at http://memory.loc.gov/cgi-bin/query/h?ammem/flwpabib:@field(NUMBER+@band(afcflwpa+3139b1)), accessed November 11, 2013.
5. Brackett Jr., lyrics of "Simple Gifts."
6. Ke$ha, with Jacob Kasher Hindlin, Dr. Luke, Benny Blanco, and Ammo, lyrics of "We R Who We R," released October 22, 2010, on *Cannibal*, EP, RCA Records.

Charlemagne Palestine

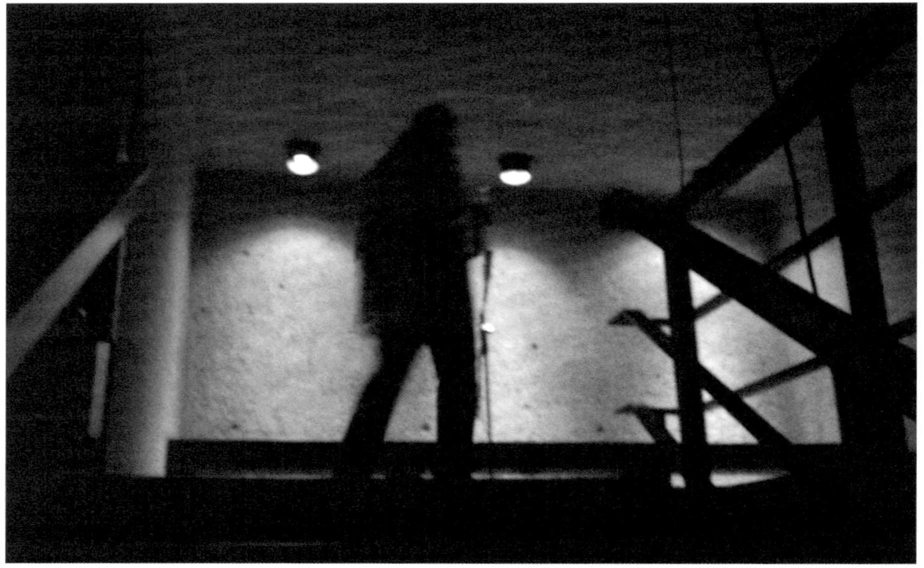

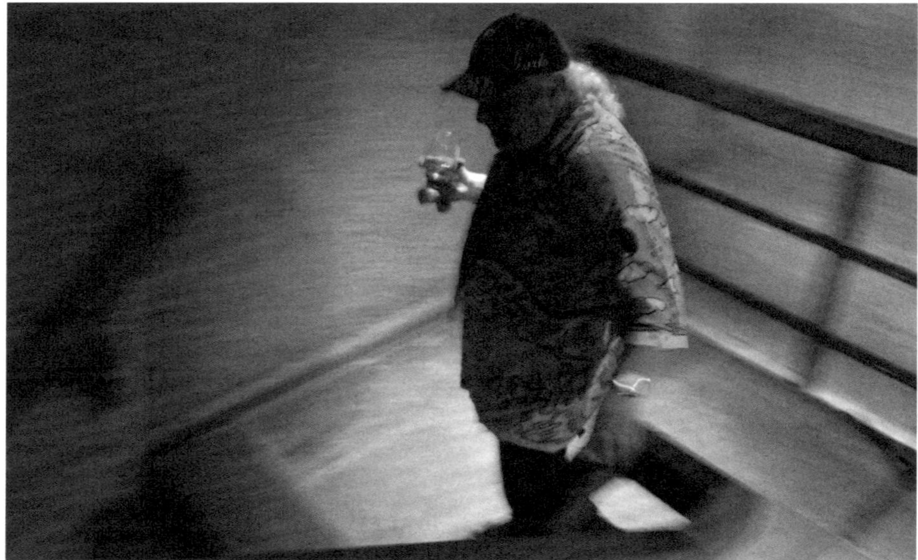

Stairway Song, 2013. Twelve-channel sound installation on stairwell landings and performance (Whitney Museum of American Art, New York, August 31, 2013)

Born 1947 in Brooklyn, NY

Lives in Brussels, Belgium

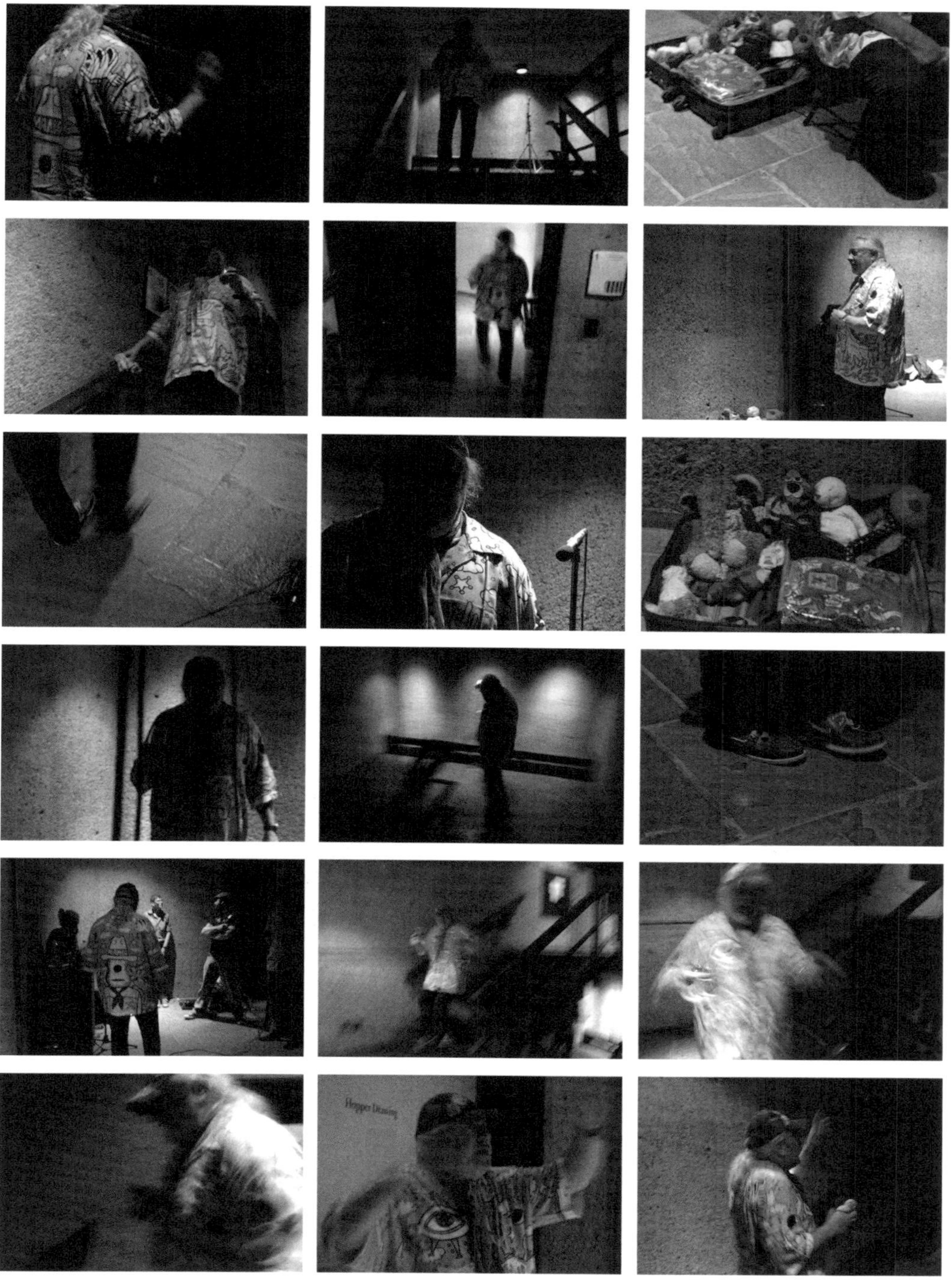

Public Collectors

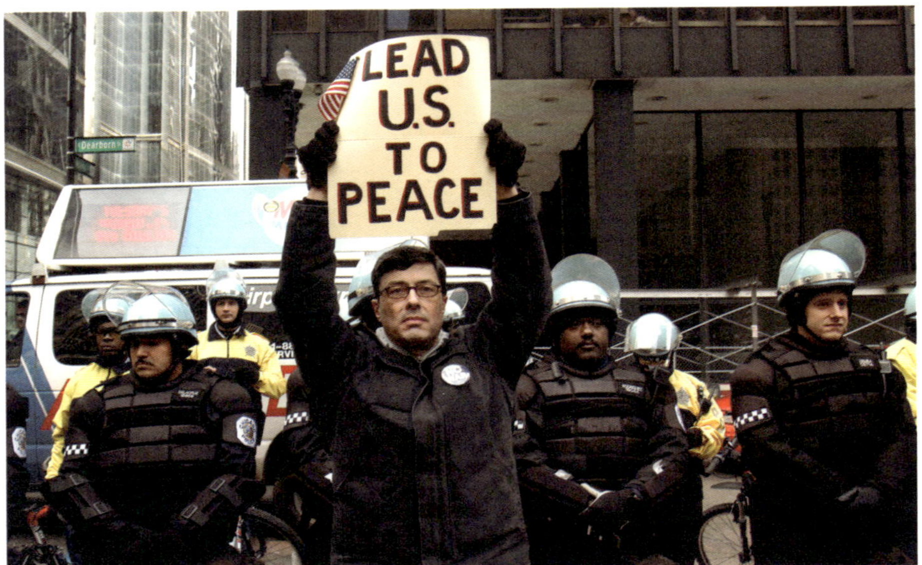

Malachi Ritscher, Iraq War Protest, Chicago, 2003.
Photograph by Joeff Davis

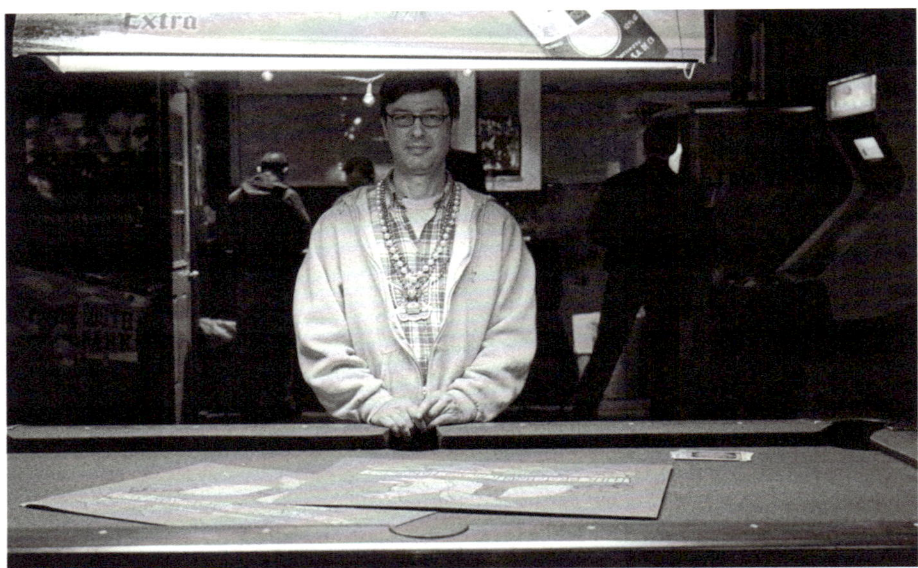

Malachi at the Empty Bottle (Pool Table Series), 2003.
Photograph by Angeline Evans

Founded in
2007

Based in
Chicago, IL

Public Collectors: Malachi Ritscher
Marc Fischer

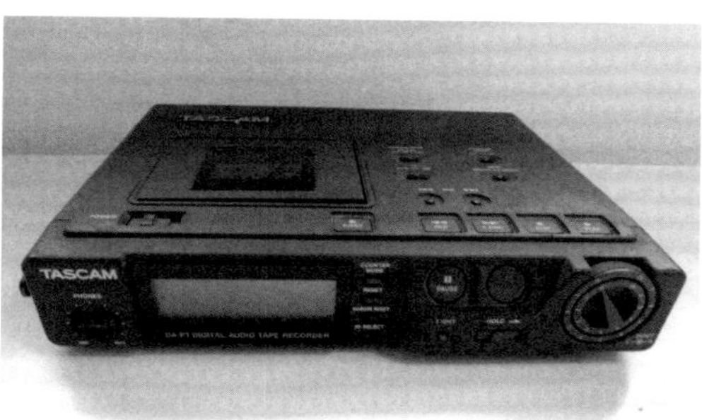

Malachi Ritscher's Portable DAT Recorder, 2013

Malachi Ritscher was a Chicago-based documentarian, activist, artist, musician, photographer, hot-pepper-sauce maker, and supporter of experimental and improvised music. He described himself as: "the modern day version of a 'renaissance man,' except instead of attaining success in several fields, he consistently failed, and didn't really worry too much about it."[1] His creativity was not easy to categorize neatly and could be found as much in the placement of a microphone used to record a concert as in the combination of ingredients in a recipe or the design of a skateboard deck. From 2003 to 2006, Ritscher maintained the website Chicago Rash Audio Potential (www.savagesound.com), which shared extensive show listings interspersed with his own concert and street photography, written insights about the music scene, and political agitprop.

If you attended a free jazz, experimental, or improvised music concert in Chicago anytime between the 1980s and October 2006, you were likely to have been in the room with Ritscher as he was making an audio recording of the event. Ritscher recorded several thousand concerts in Chicago during that period. Improviser and composer Ken Vandermark has observed: "He has the whole evolution of the improvised music scene in Chicago on tape."[2] Ritscher voluntarily made these recordings with the artists' permission, often showing up early to test recording levels during sound checks, and then distributed free copies to the musicians by mail or the next time he saw them.

According to Ritscher himself, he "participated passionately in the anti-war and free speech movement."[3] He was arrested at a large antiwar protest on March 20, 2003, in Chicago and spent the night in jail. Two years later, he was arrested again and successfully sued the City of Chicago for false arrest on First Amendment and free-speech grounds. The charges from March 20 were eventually dropped and settled nine years later in a massive class action lawsuit for wrongful arrest, and the city paid out $6.2 million to the many who were arrested or detained. If you marched against the Iraq war in Chicago in its initial years, you surely marched alongside Ritscher.

Ritscher came to international attention when, during morning rush-hour traffic on November 3, 2006, he poured gasoline over his body and immolated himself in front of Leonardo Nierman's *Flame of the Millennium* sculpture at the Ohio feeder ramp along Chicago's John F. Kennedy Expressway. A sign reading "Thou Shalt Not Kill. As Ye Sow So Shall Ye Reap. Your Taxes Buy Bombs and Bullets" was displayed during the action. Ritscher's suicide was explicitly a protest against the war in Iraq but was not reported as such until the alternative press, independent media journalists, and others forced the issue. Ritscher documented his suicide with a video camera placed at the scene. Police held the tape for some time before releasing it to his family, who chose not to circulate it. In addition to a self-authored obituary that appears on his website savagesound.com, Ritscher shared the motivation for his actions in a "Mission Statement."

Dear friends and family of Malachi Ritscher,

My name is Marc Fischer. I'm a Chicago-based artist, teacher, and writer. In 2007 I formed a participatory initiative called Public Collectors, which I administrate. Public Collectors is concerned with the kind of cultural materials that museums and other institutions often disregard. Public Collectors exists to explore objects and histories that often reside in private hands but deserve larger consideration and attention, as well as to celebrate collecting and archiving as a valid creative practice. Through Public Collectors, collections are shared online (see: www.publiccollectors.org) but also in exhibitions, events, and publications.

Recently Public Collectors was invited to participate in the 2014 Whitney Biennial at the Whitney Museum of American Art in New York City. The exhibition opens in March 2014 and runs for several months. The Biennial is being curated by three people; Anthony Elms is the curator who invited me to participate.

The Biennial is an unusual invitation for Public Collectors as I am normally uninterested in working with museums for this initiative. Public Collectors is concerned with pulling things from the margins and giving them a thoughtful context and public presentation. For me to participate in the Whitney Biennial, I want that participation to give focus to someone who would have never been asked, and who has never been collected or exhibited by the Whitney Museum of American Art. I want to share something that the public may not know exists, and to see the museum lend authority and importance to a life and a creative practice that probably would not receive museum consideration under normal circumstances. I want my participation to draw on a network of individuals or smaller institutions to show the kind of extraordinary things that museums often don't care about. I want to consider what happens to the creative work of people who are not collected by museums, when they are gone—people whose life's work has not been accorded the same desirability as collectible art or all of the resources that are often expended for valuable art objects. I remember Malachi Ritscher's quiet, serious, and dedicated presence at concerts. We had quite a few friends in common and attended many of the same shows and protests. Malachi Ritscher's death moved me deeply. It was Anthony Elms who informed me, via Fred Lonberg-Holm, when he heard the news that it was Malachi who took his life in front of the *Flame of the Millennium* sculpture. I felt this loss then and I still feel it today. When I reviewed the inventory of recordings Malachi made on the website of Creative Audio Archive at Experimental Sound Studios, my respect only intensified. His dedication to documenting a community, and his generosity in sharing those recordings with the artists, is inspiring to me.

My proposal to you is that I would like to create a presentation of materials on Malachi Ritscher and write an essay about his work as Public Collectors' contribution to the Whitney Biennial. I would love to borrow some materials from you for this exhibition.

My intention is to draw from multiple lending sources to create a substantive presentation of a complex, challenging, creative, and generous person. I also want the materials on view to highlight the possibilities for what can be done when many people band together to share a story and a history. The labels and printed materials in the exhibition will credit all lenders. The collaboration that would need to happen to bring his material to public view should be transparent.

Thank you for taking the time to read and think about this proposal. Please respond at your earliest convenience and if you have any questions, do not hesitate to ask.

Sincerely and with much respect,
Marc Fischer / Public Collectors

Two excerpts:

The violent turmoil initiated by the United States military invasion of Iraq will beget future centuries of slaughter, if the human race lasts that long. First we spit on the United Nations, then we expect them to clean up our mess. Our elected representatives are supposed to find diplomatic and benevolent solutions to these situations. Anyone can lash out and retaliate, that is not leadership or vision. Where is the wisdom and honor of the people we delegate our trust to?[4]

What is one more life thrown away in this sad and useless national tragedy? If one death can atone for anything, in any small way, to say to the world: I apologize for what we have done to you, I am ashamed for the mayhem and turmoil caused by my country.[5]

On November 27, twenty-three days after the event, an Associated Press story on Ritscher and his motivations appeared in the *Guardian*, the *New York Times*, and other mainstream outlets. This was the last time anything regarding Malachi Ritscher was widely reported. Vandermark writes: "If the mass media overlooked Malachi's contributions and death, the people closer to him did not, and the musicians and fans of the music I know in Chicago (and outside of Chicago) admired him while he was alive and since then—he is frequently remembered and discussed."[6]

Ritscher's contribution to the improvised-music community in Chicago was significant, and his life and work deserve broader understanding and recognition. His actions—both his protest and in his documentation of art that is challenging, not mainstream, and frequently marginalized—inspired multiple artists to create new works in his memory. Among those who took Ritscher's sacrifice as a call to action were Jean Smith and David Lester of the Vancouver-based duo Mecca Normal. They wrote a song titled "Malachi" that was released as a 7-inch record on K Records in 2010, and, for his Inspired Agitators portrait poster series Lester created a tribute to Ritscher. Smith writes:

It was Malachi's intention for the video of his protest, his death, to reach people through mainstream media, to jar them from complacency, to have them raise their voices to end the war. But that wasn't what happened. The video was not released in that way. When we added our song—and the poster—to our performances and classroom events, we regarded them as extensions of Malachi's intention. We had created documents about the documentarian whose final statement on war was not heard. We created art and music because *Malachi's voice was not heard.*[7]

Directing attention to and caring for the creative work of underrecognized people like Ritscher is one of the goals of Public Collectors. I sent an extended version of the letter opposite to the Creative Audio Archive at Experimental Sound Studio in Chicago. They have been working with Ritscher's family and the artists he documented to manage, preserve, and share the vast archive of concert recordings that Bruno Johnson and Vandermark moved from Ritscher's home after his death. I also emailed this letter to family and friends of Ritscher and others connected to his story. This invitation was the primary text used to solicit participation and loans of materials for the 2014 Whitney Biennial.

In a November 30, 2000, letter that was folded into one of his recording journals, Malachi Ritscher wrote: "What I do is a favor to the artists I respect, in order for them to further their process." This project is, in part, a favor to a creative community and to a family whom I respect and who are still coming to terms with what Malachi Ritscher did and what his sacrifice means. On the front page of his website, Ritscher wrote: "Art and music can express outrage, inspire action, or soothe and distract; please think about priorities and be involved in things that matter." This project is also for people who are just now learning about Ritscher, and who might consider those words or take them to heart. And it's for people whose creativity doesn't fit into neat boxes, whose work isn't for sale or has no obvious monetary value, and for whom long-term archival preservation and exhibitions in museums are not guaranteed or expected.

Public Collectors, lenders, and direct contributors to this project: Dick and Betty Ann Ritscher; Ellen Sackett; Carol Wahl; Allison Schein, Lou Mallozzi and Creative Audio Archive at Experimental Sound Studio; Angeline and Mark Evans; John Corbett; Joeff Davis; Michael Zerang; Ken Vandermark; David Lester and Jean Smith of Mecca Normal; Fred Lonberg-Holm; Brent Gutzeit; Jason Guthartz; Metal Rouge (Helge Fassonaki and Andrew Scott) Agnieszka Czeblakow; Mawrk Solotroff; Lampo (Alisa Wolfson and Andrew Fenchel); Bill Meyer; Thymme Jones.

1. Malachi Ritscher, "Out of Time," 2006, www.savagesound.com/gallery100.htm.
2. Ken Vandermark, remark to the audience during a solo performance at Experimental Sound Studio, Chicago, on July 27, 2013.
3. Ritscher, "Out of Time."
4. Malachi Ritscher, "Mission Statement," 2006, http://www.savagesound.com/gallery99.htm.
5. Ibid.
6. Ken Vandermark, email to the author, September 15, 2013.
7. Jean Smith, email to the author, September 6, 2013.

Steve Reinke

Jessie Mott

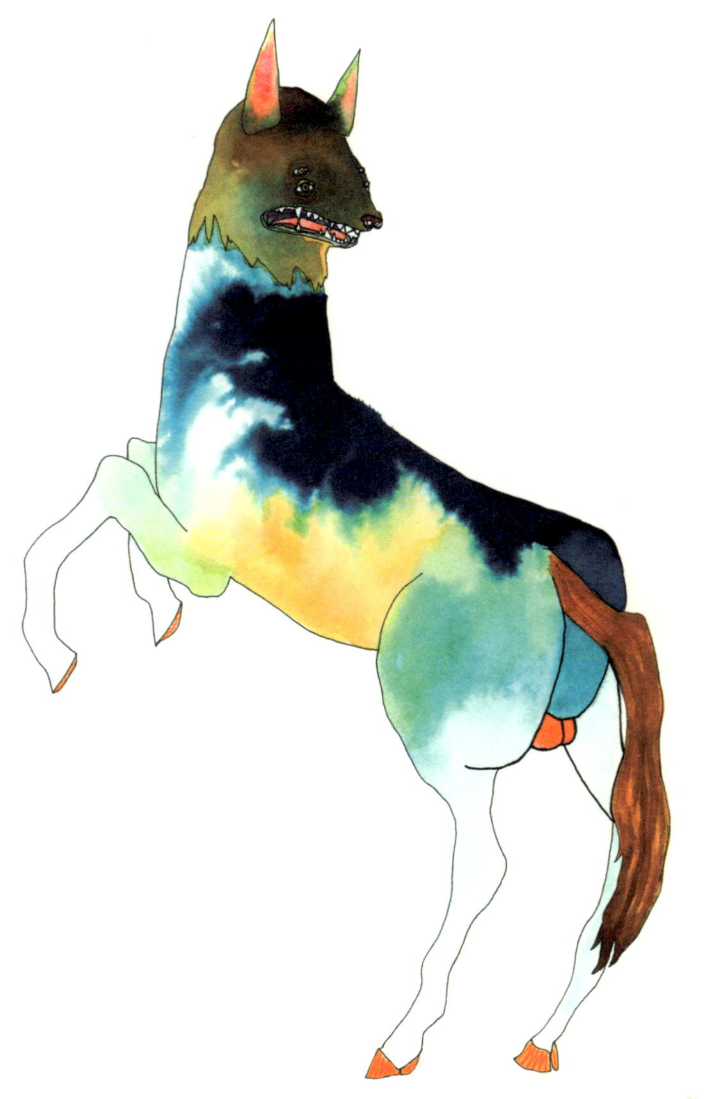

Jessie Mott, *Victor*, 2013. Ink, marker, and gouache on paper, 12 × 9 in. (30.5 × 22.9 cm)

Born 1963 in
Eganville, ON, Canada
Lives in Chicago, IL

Born 1980 in
New York, NY
Lives in Chicago, IL

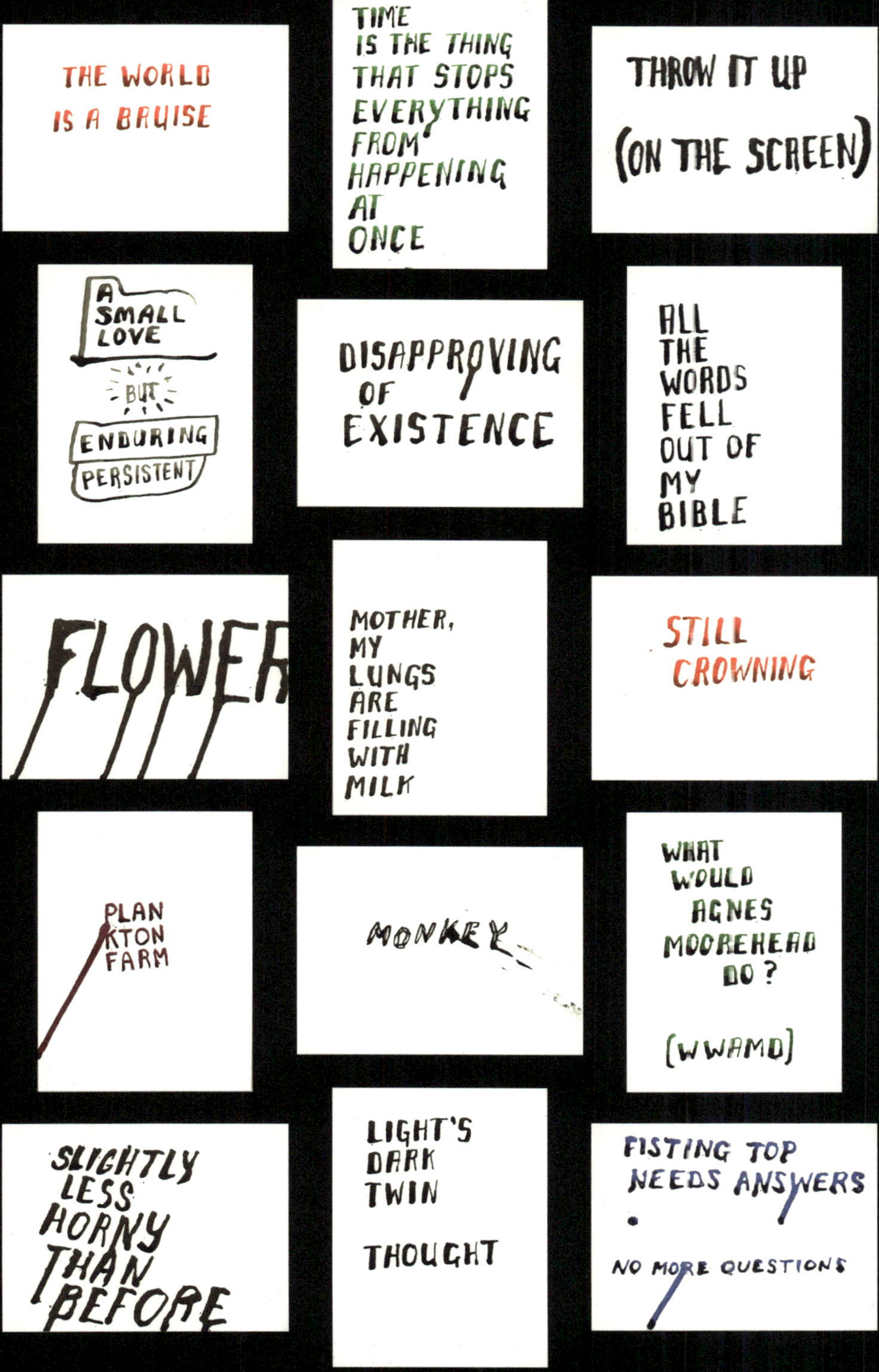

THE WORLD IS A BRUISE

TIME IS THE THING THAT STOPS EVERYTHING FROM HAPPENING AT ONCE

THROW IT UP (ON THE SCREEN)

A SMALL LOVE BUT ENDURING PERSISTENT

DISAPPROVING OF EXISTENCE

ALL THE WORDS FELL OUT OF MY BIBLE

FLOWER

MOTHER, MY LUNGS ARE FILLING WITH MILK

STILL CROWNING

PLANKTON FARM

MONKEY

WHAT WOULD AGNES MOOREHEAD DO?

(WWAMD)

SLIGHTLY LESS HORNY THAN BEFORE

LIGHT'S DARK TWIN

THOUGHT

FISTING TOP NEEDS ANSWERS

NO MORE QUESTIONS

BEAUTIFUL
THINGS
NEED
BEAUTIFUL
BOXES

CORPSE LAST
TO KNOW

CHOKING
ON
A
WALNUT
OF
SEMEN

DISCO
WOUND

THE
PISTON
FORCES
THE
IMAGES
UP
AGAIN

PLOWFAGGOT ASS

THIS
LIFE

OR
ANOTHER

I have discovered,
I said,
that my emotional
state is often inade-
quate to historical events.

DAYTIME
BORING

EVEN
FOR
PLANTS

MOON ROCKS?

WHAT WE NEEDED
TO CONTINUE WAS
MOON BLOOD

NOT
ALL
OF
US
CAN
BE
ALIVE
AT
THE
SAME
TIME

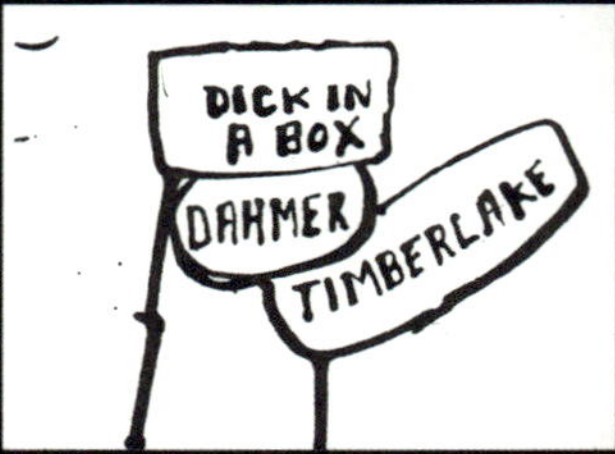

DICK IN
A BOX
DAHMER
TIMBERLAKE

A
COMMUNION
WAFER
SO
THIN
IT
SLICES
THROUGH
TONGUE

I WANTED
THE PLACEBO

BRIAN
DONALD
JONES

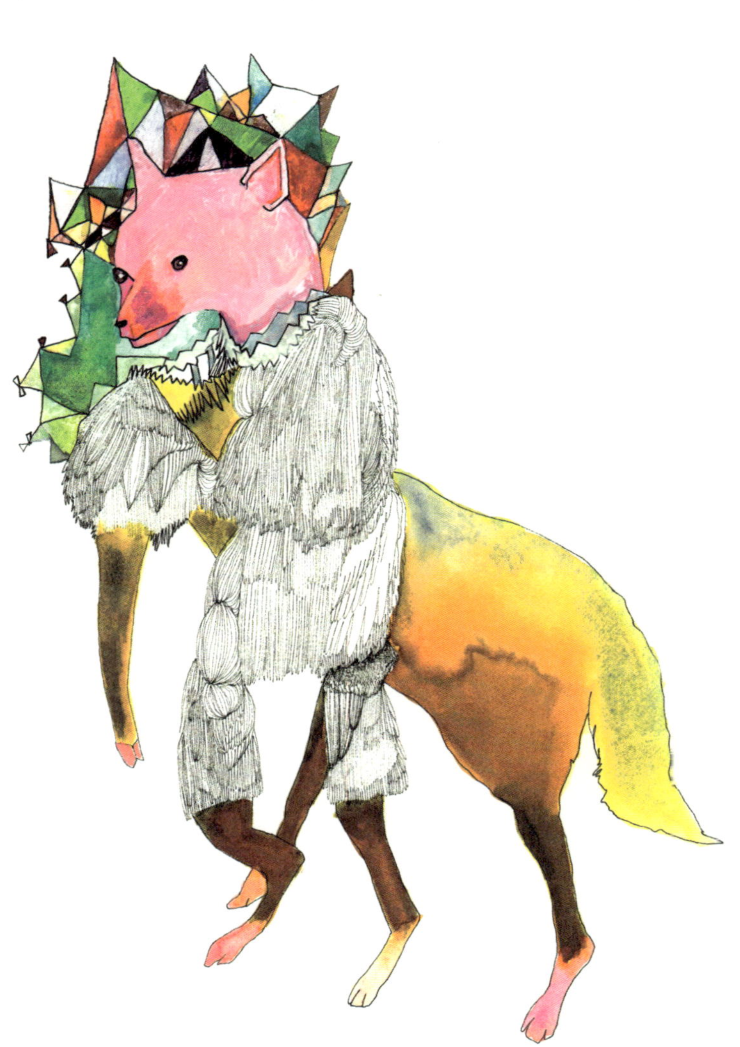

Jessie Mott, *The New Pink*, 2013. Ink and gouache on paper, 14 × 11 in. (35.6 × 27.9 cm)

Allan Sekula

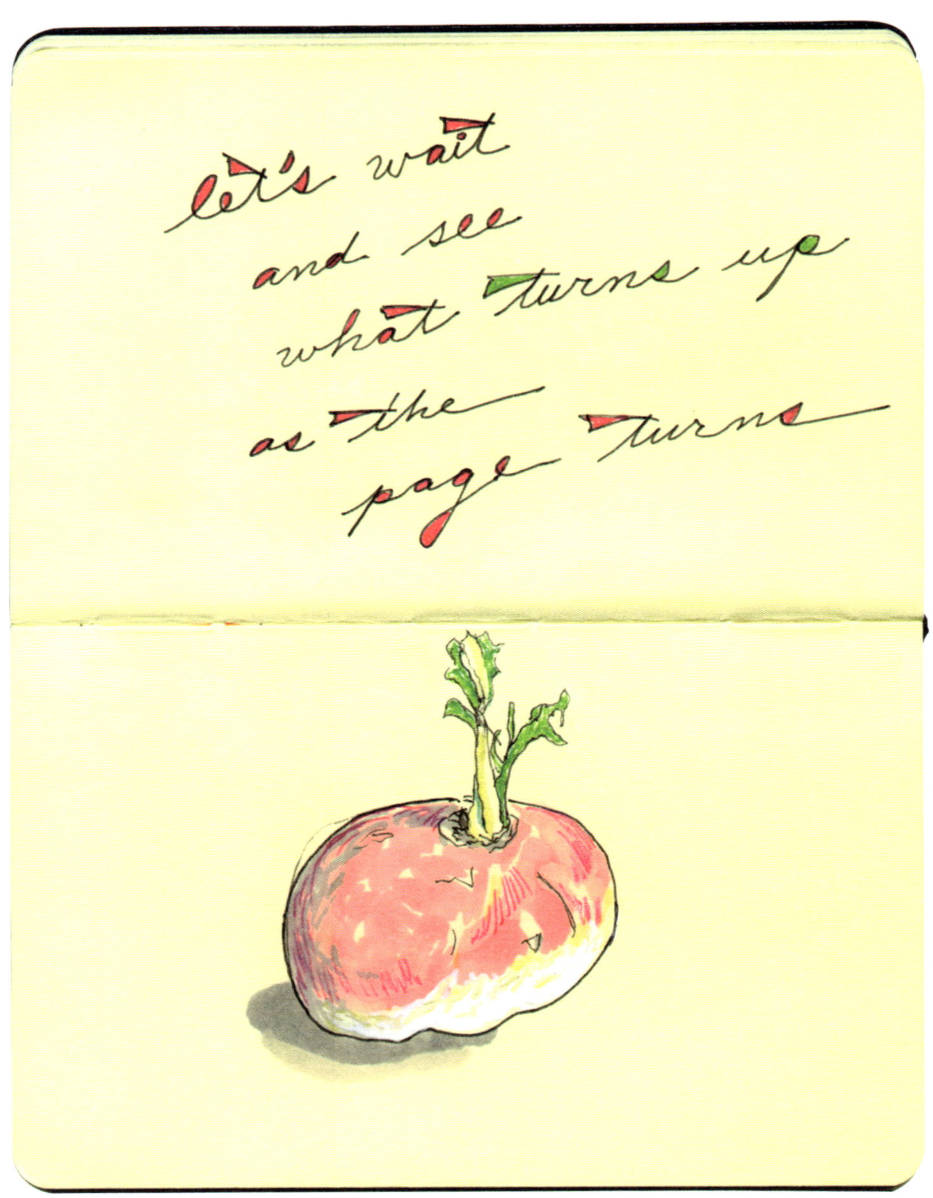

Sketches from Sekula's notebook "PF poland 2009 (1)," 2009. Ink, correction fluid, and marker on paper, 3 ½ × 5 ½ in. (9 × 14 cm)

Born 1951 in
Erie, PA

Died 2013 in
Los Angeles, CA

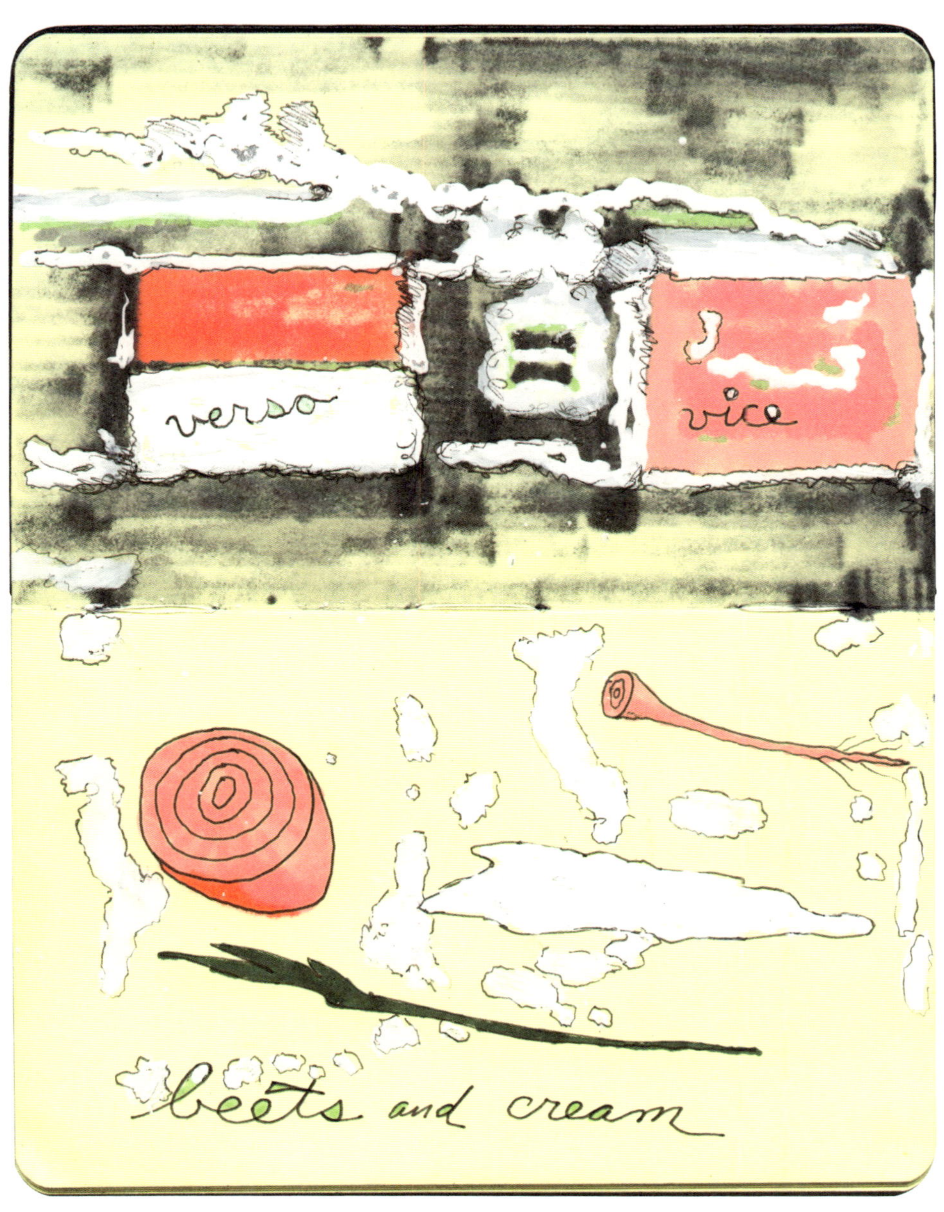
verso
vice
beets and cream

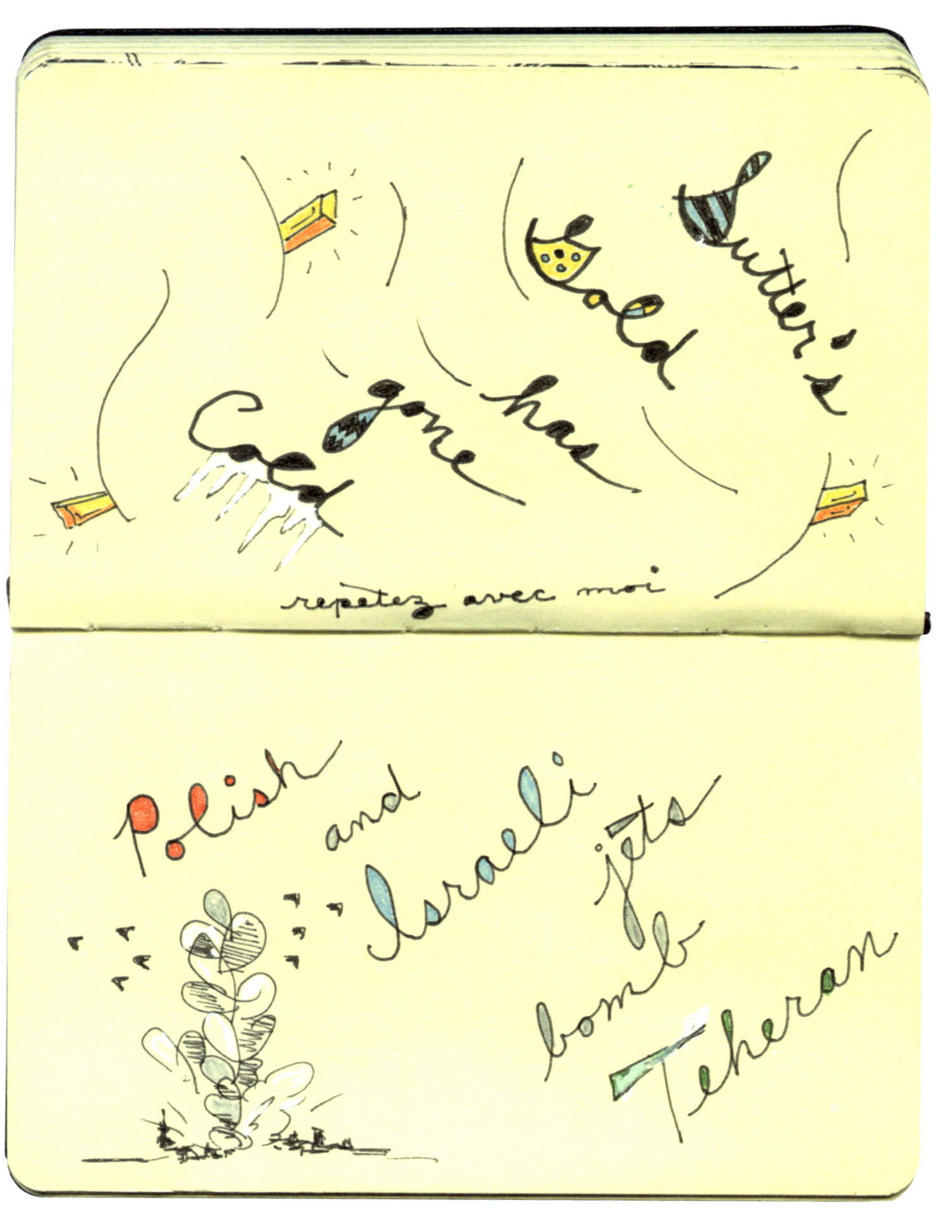
Sutter's Gold has gone Cold
repetez avec moi
Polish and Israeli jets bomb Teheran

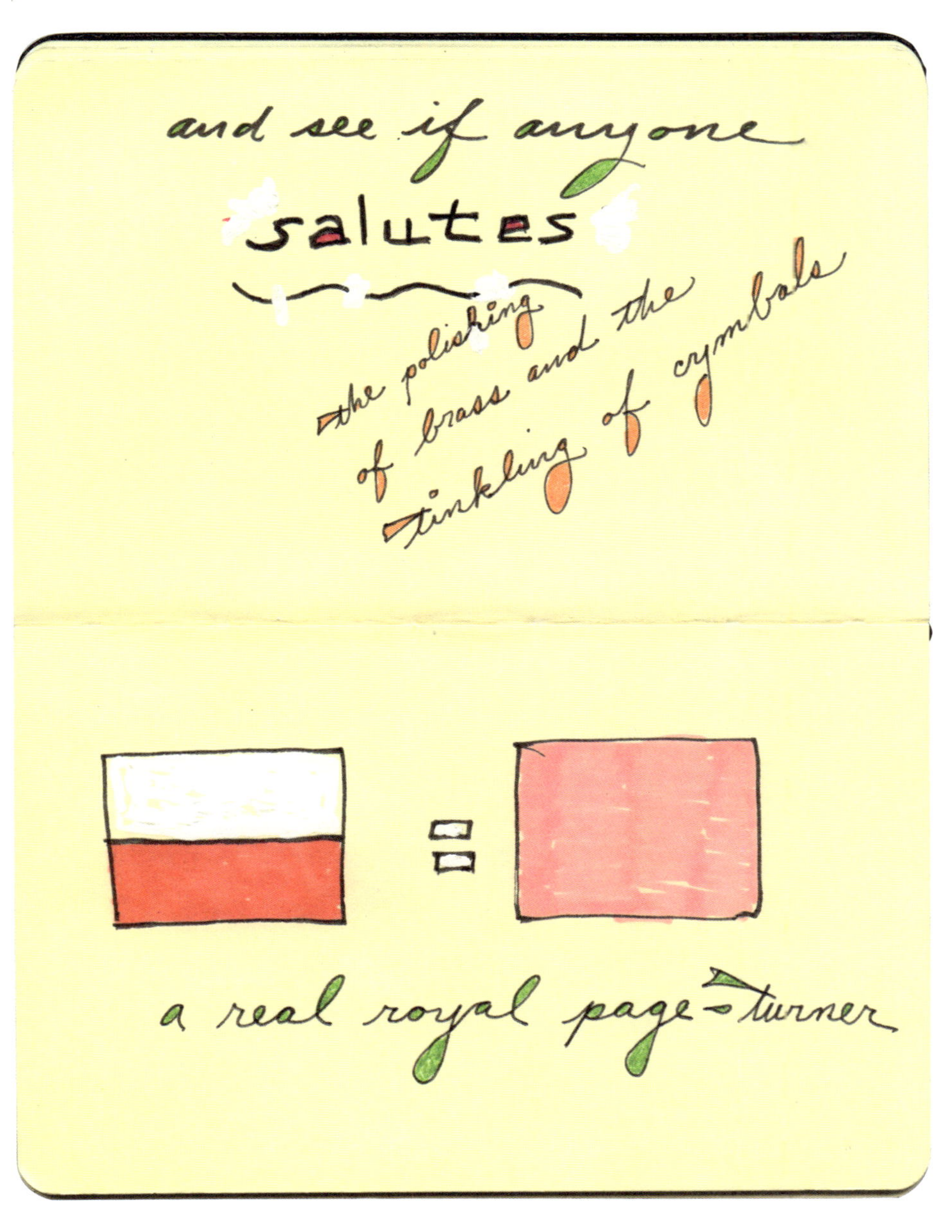
and see if anyone
salutes
the polishing of brass and the tinkling of cymbals
a real royal page-turner

Valerie Snobeck

Catherine Sullivan

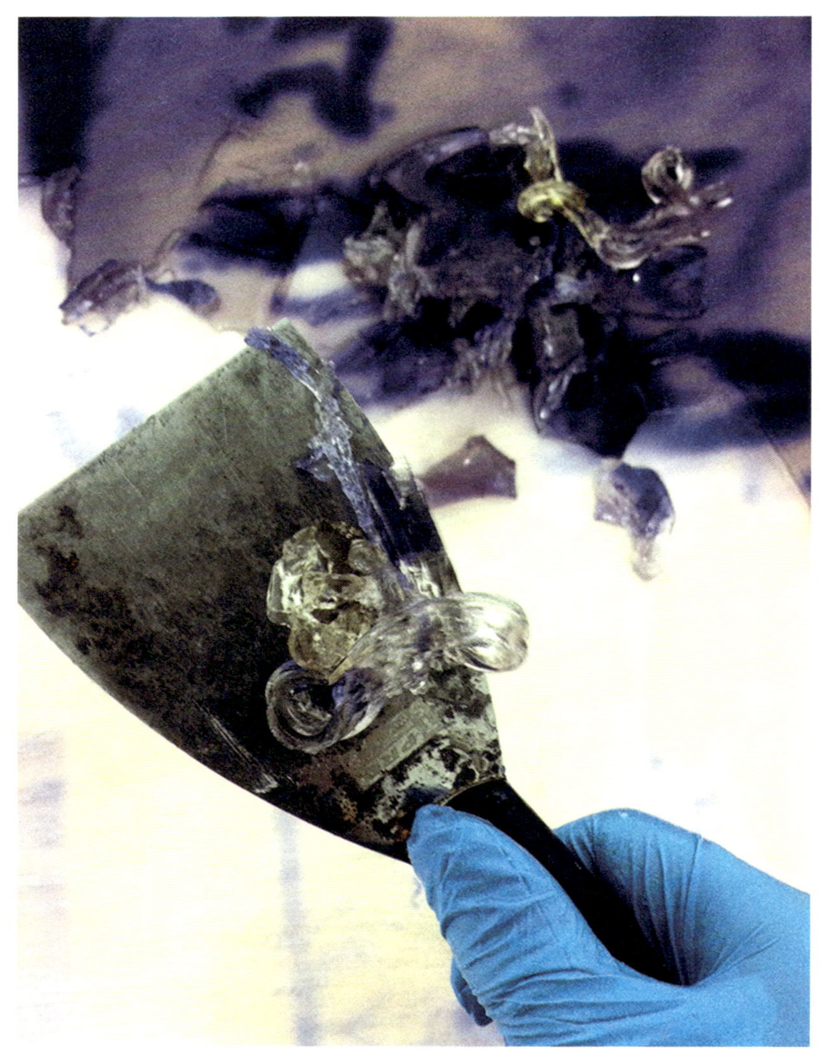

Destruction of the hectograph duplicator, 2013

Born 1980 in
Wadena, MN
Lives in New York, NY

Born 1968 in
Los Angeles, CA
Lives in Chicago, IL

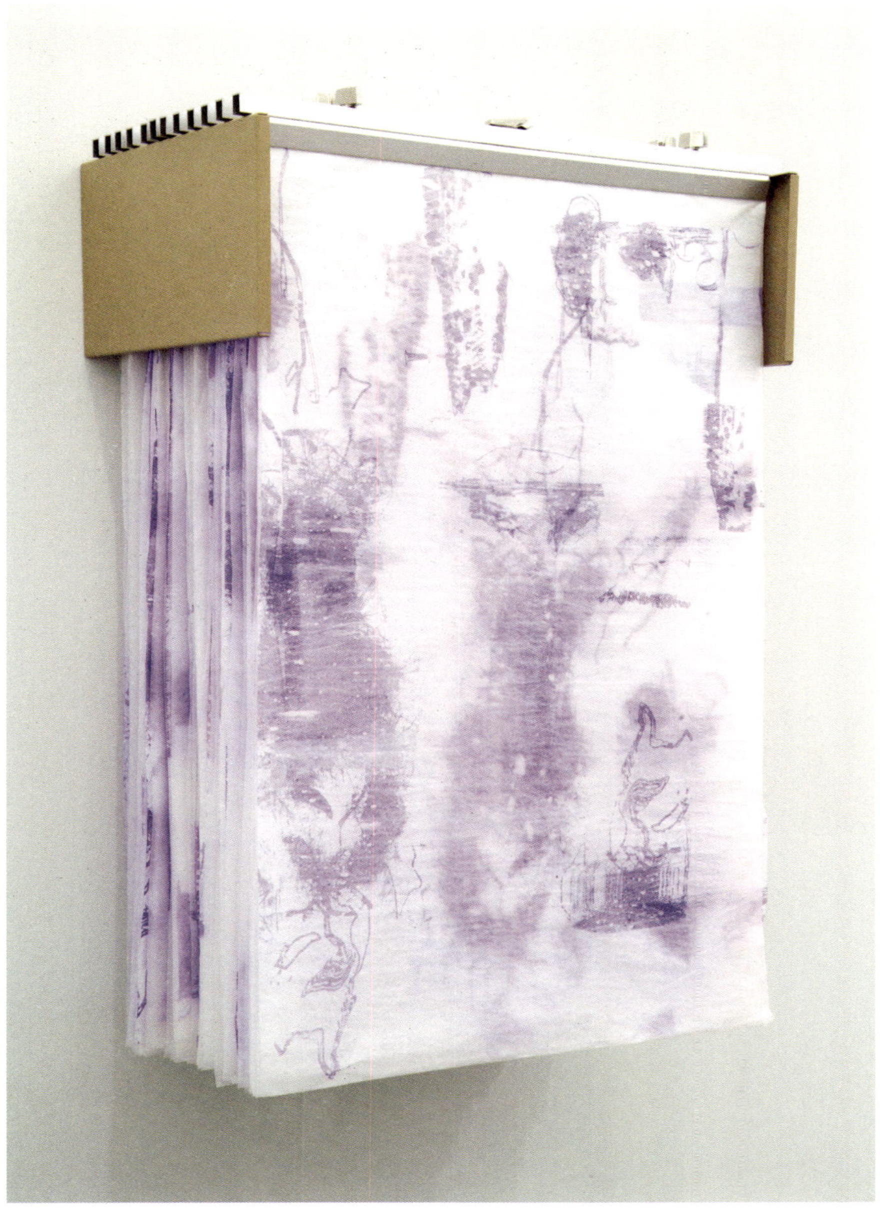

Limited Good 8, 2013. Hectograph prints on glassine and blueprint rack, 63 ½ × 38 × 36 ½ in. (161.3 × 96.5 × 92.7 cm)

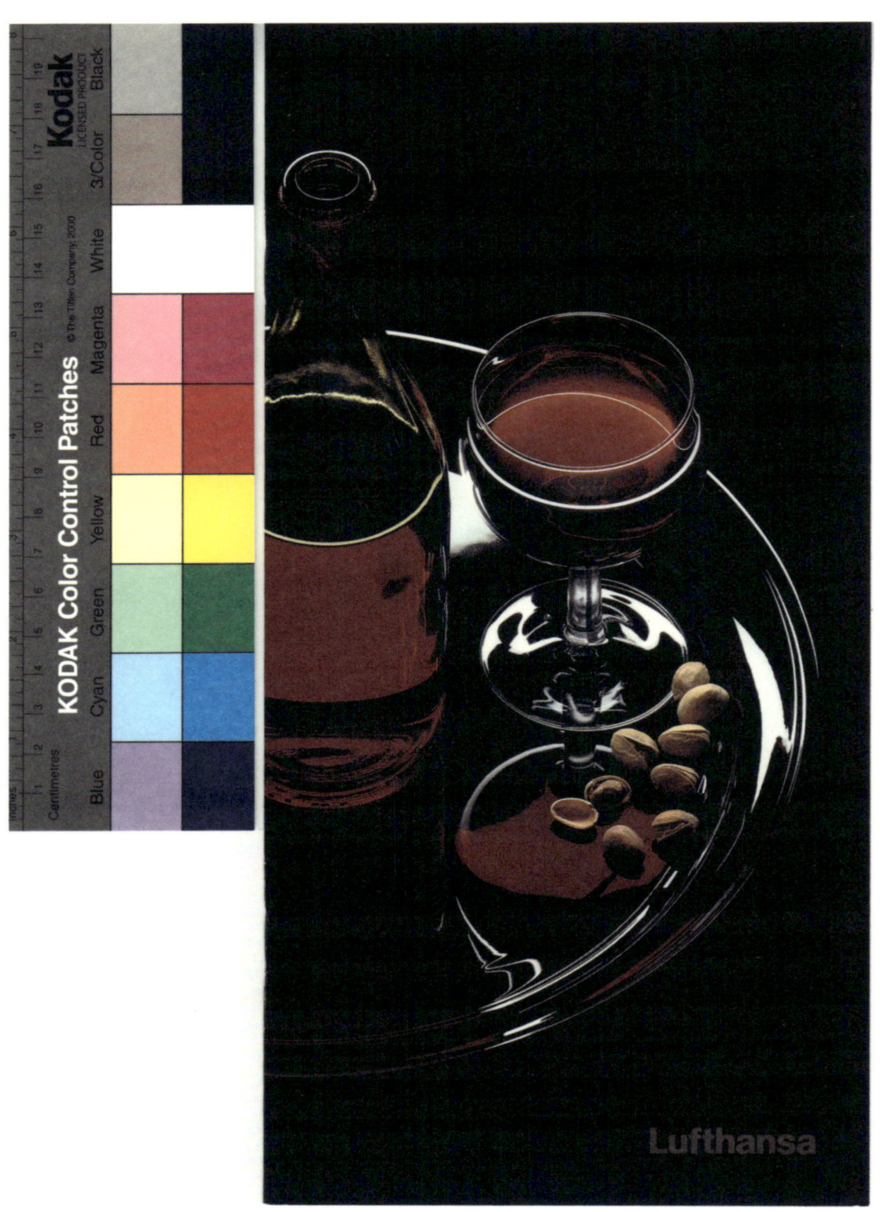

Lufthansa, Frankfurt/San Francisco, 1987. Digital scan of archival material, 11 13/16 × 5 7/8 in. (30 × 15 cm)

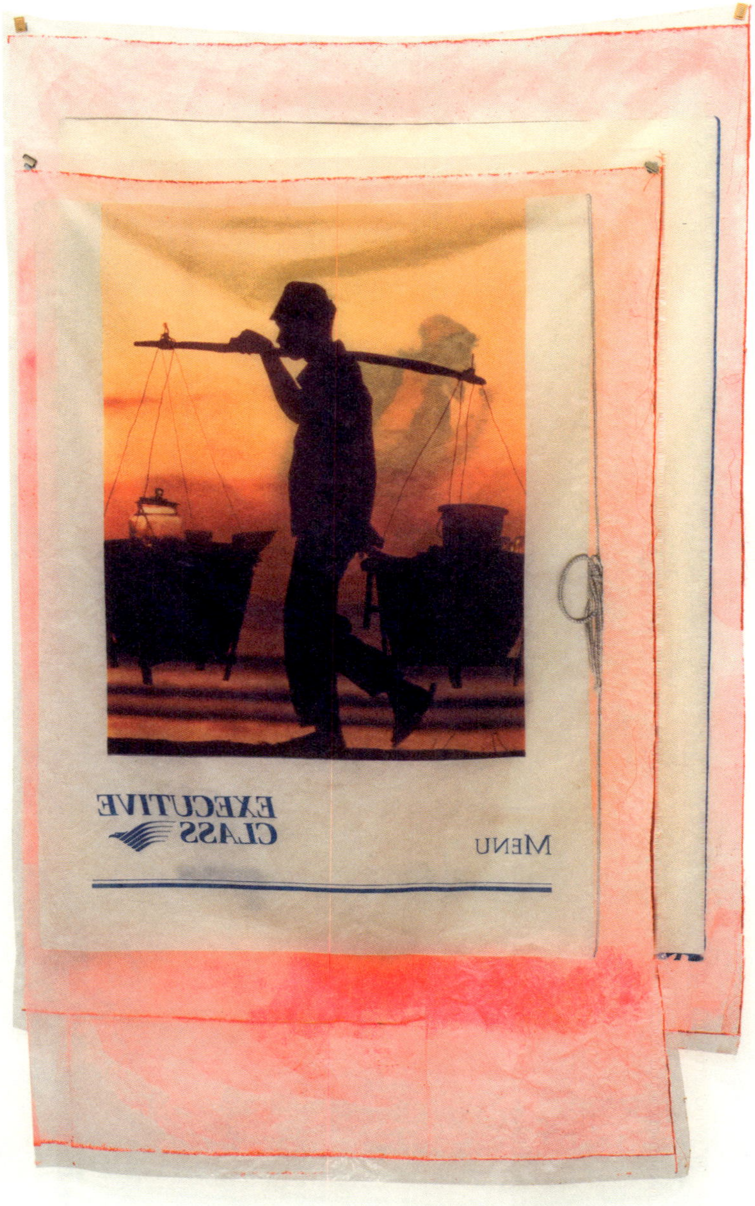

Limited Good 2, Alitalia, Nairobi|Rome, 1962 and Garuda Indonesia Airways, Denpasar|Jakarta|Hong Kong 1986, 2013.
Peeled prints and upholstery fabric on plastic, and cuff links, 63 × 39 ½ in. (160.0 × 100.3 cm)

Charline von Heyl

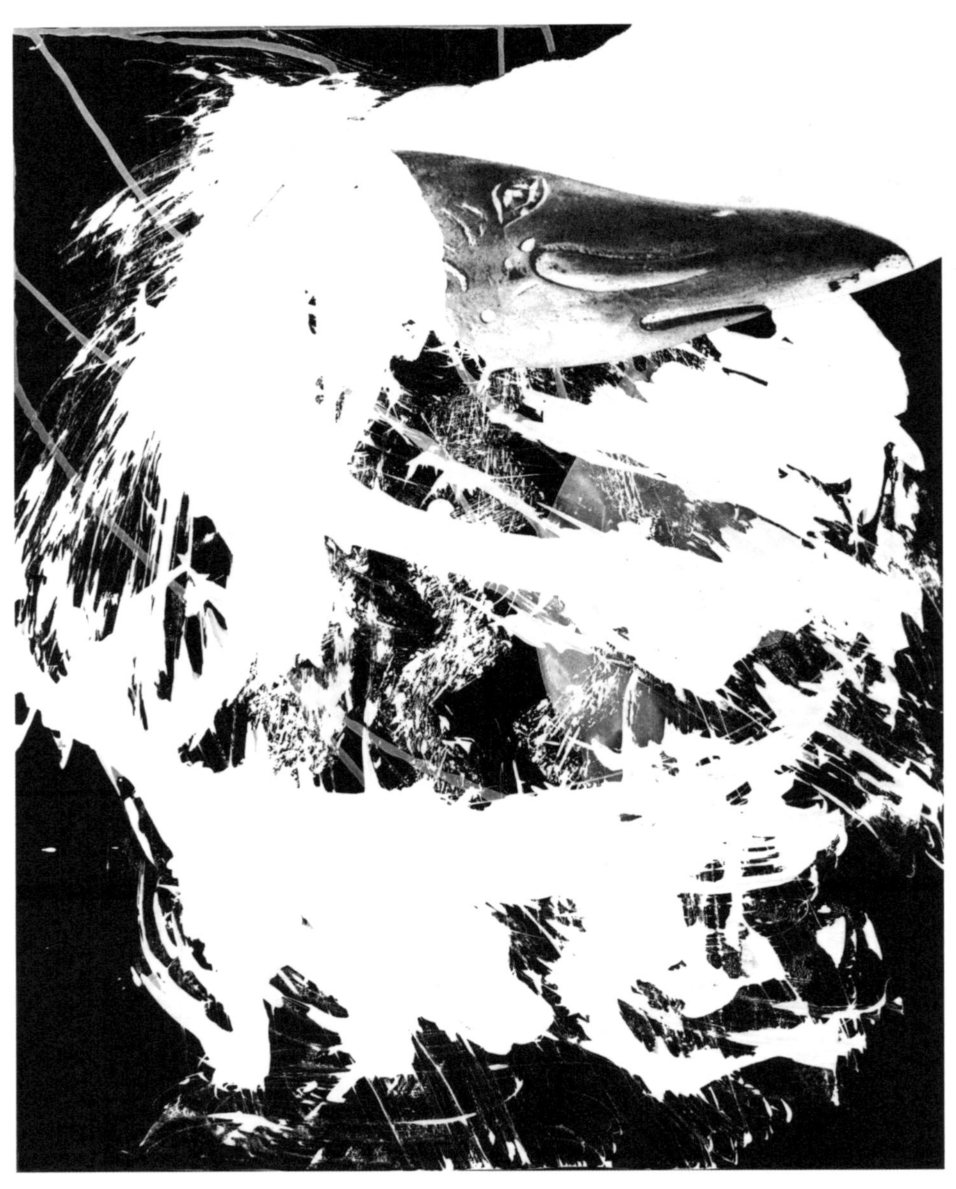

Folk Tales, 2013. Acrylic, ink, wax, charcoal, and collage on paper, 24 × 19 in. (61 × 48.3 cm) each

Born 1960 in Mainz, Germany

Lives in New York, NY

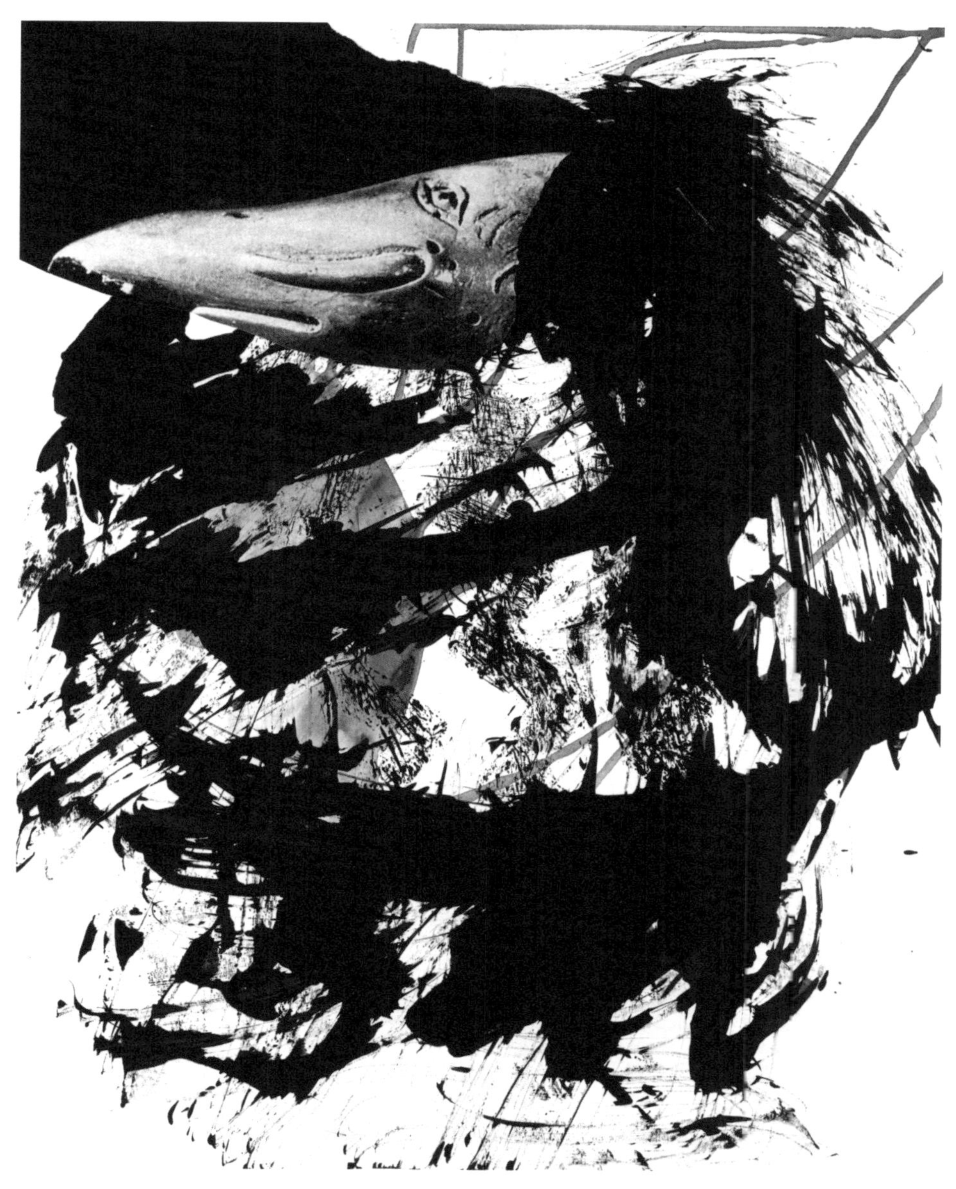

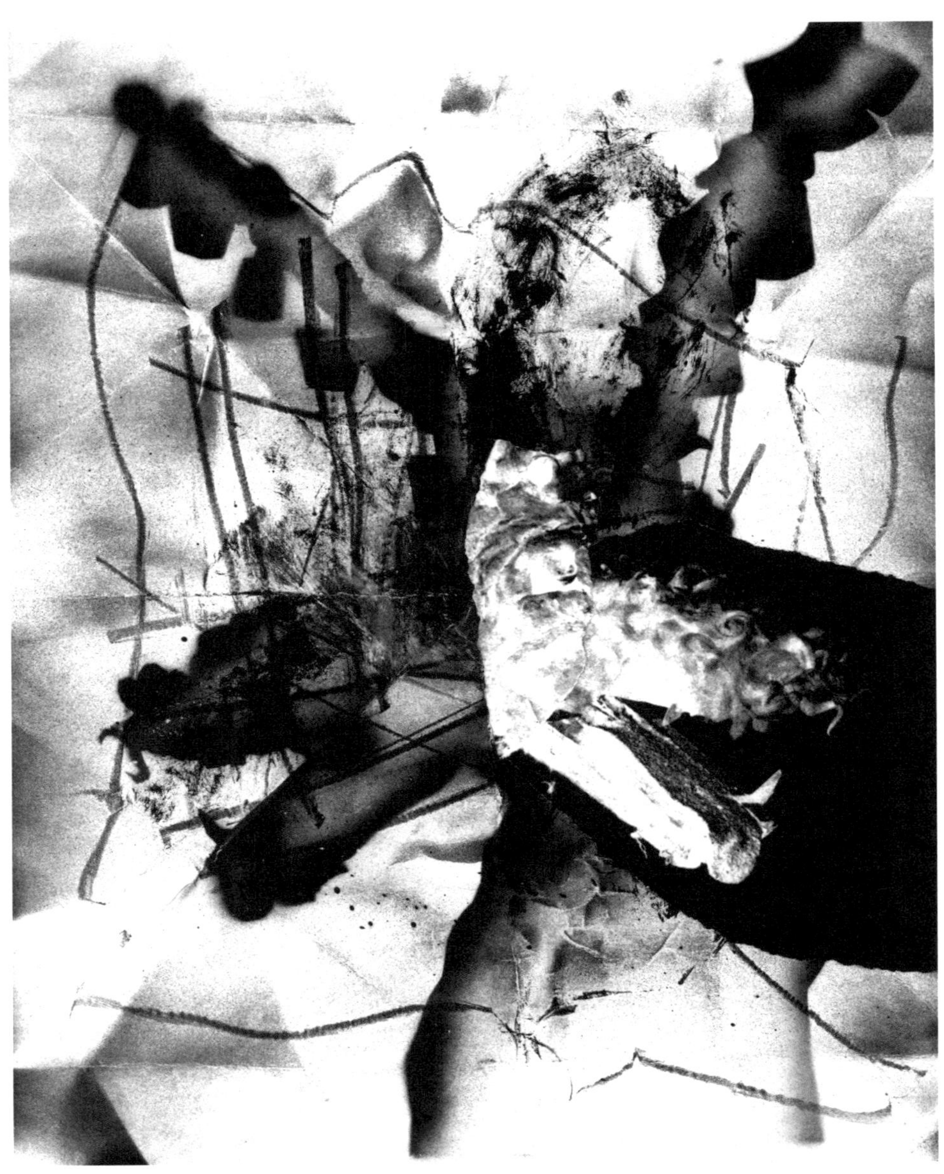

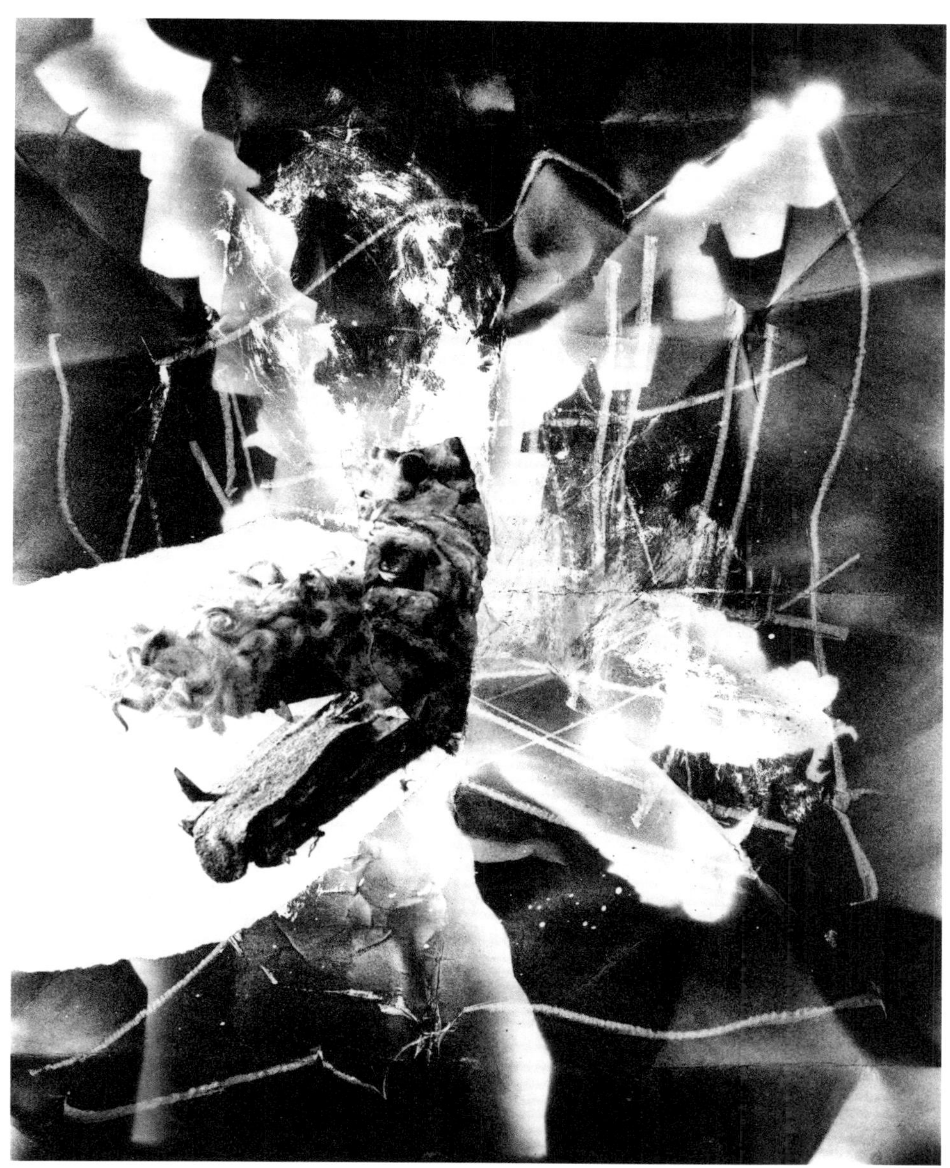

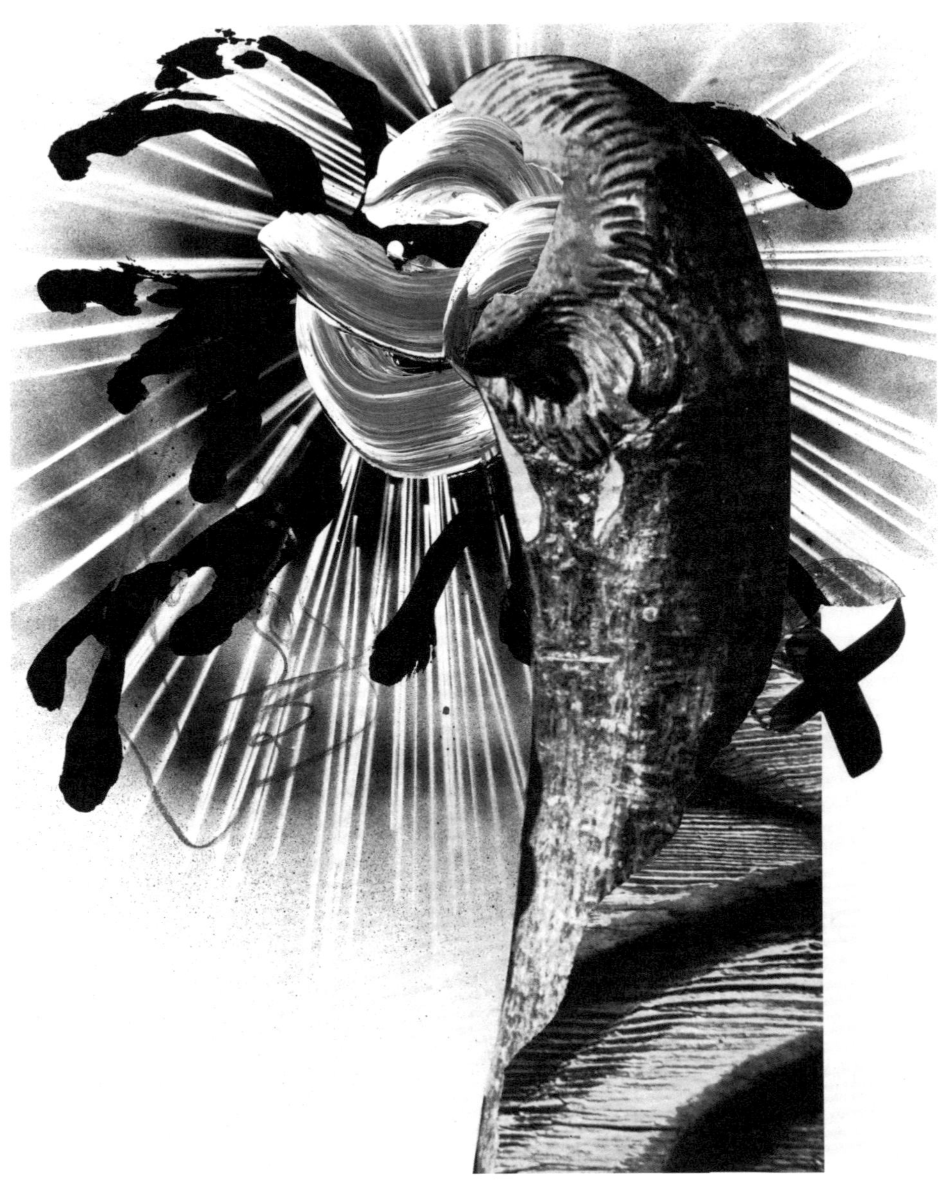

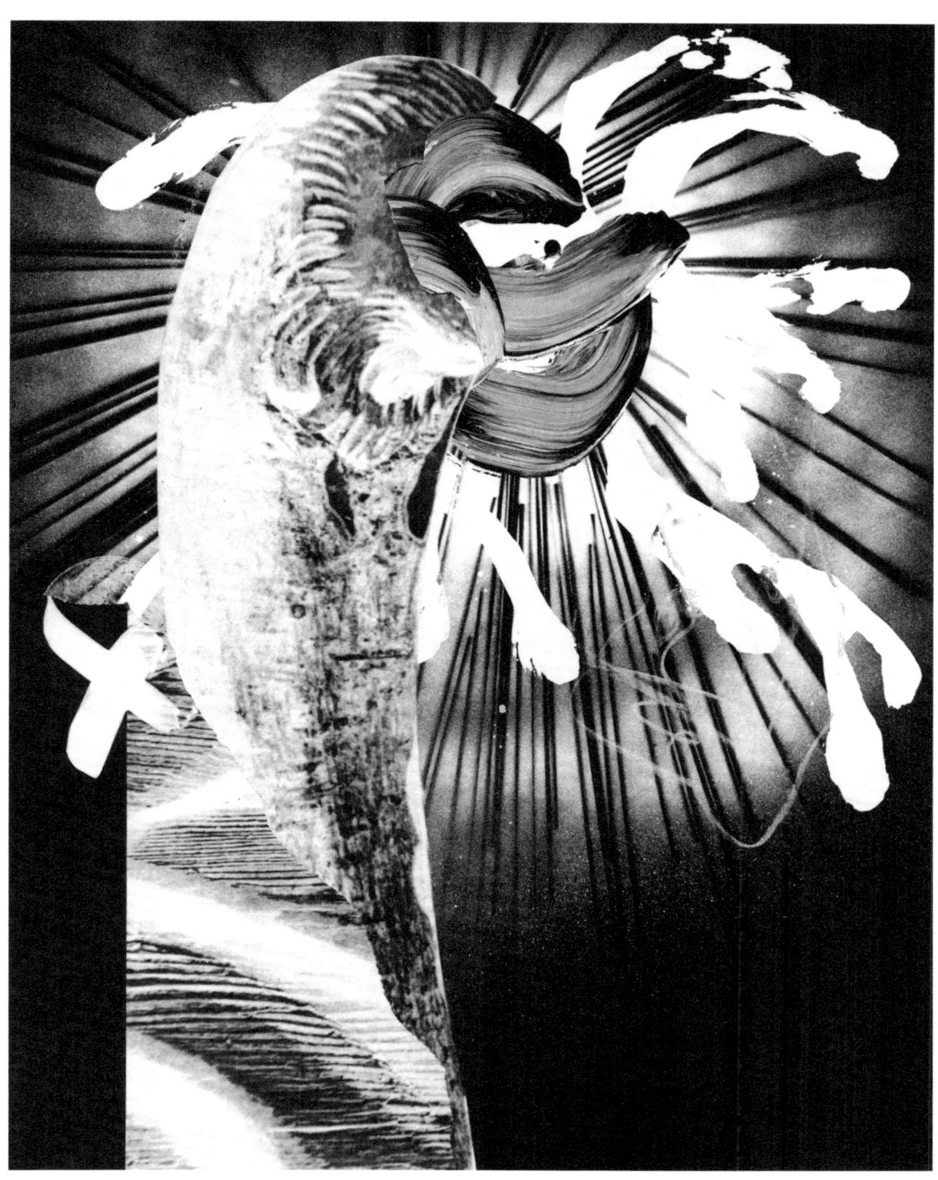

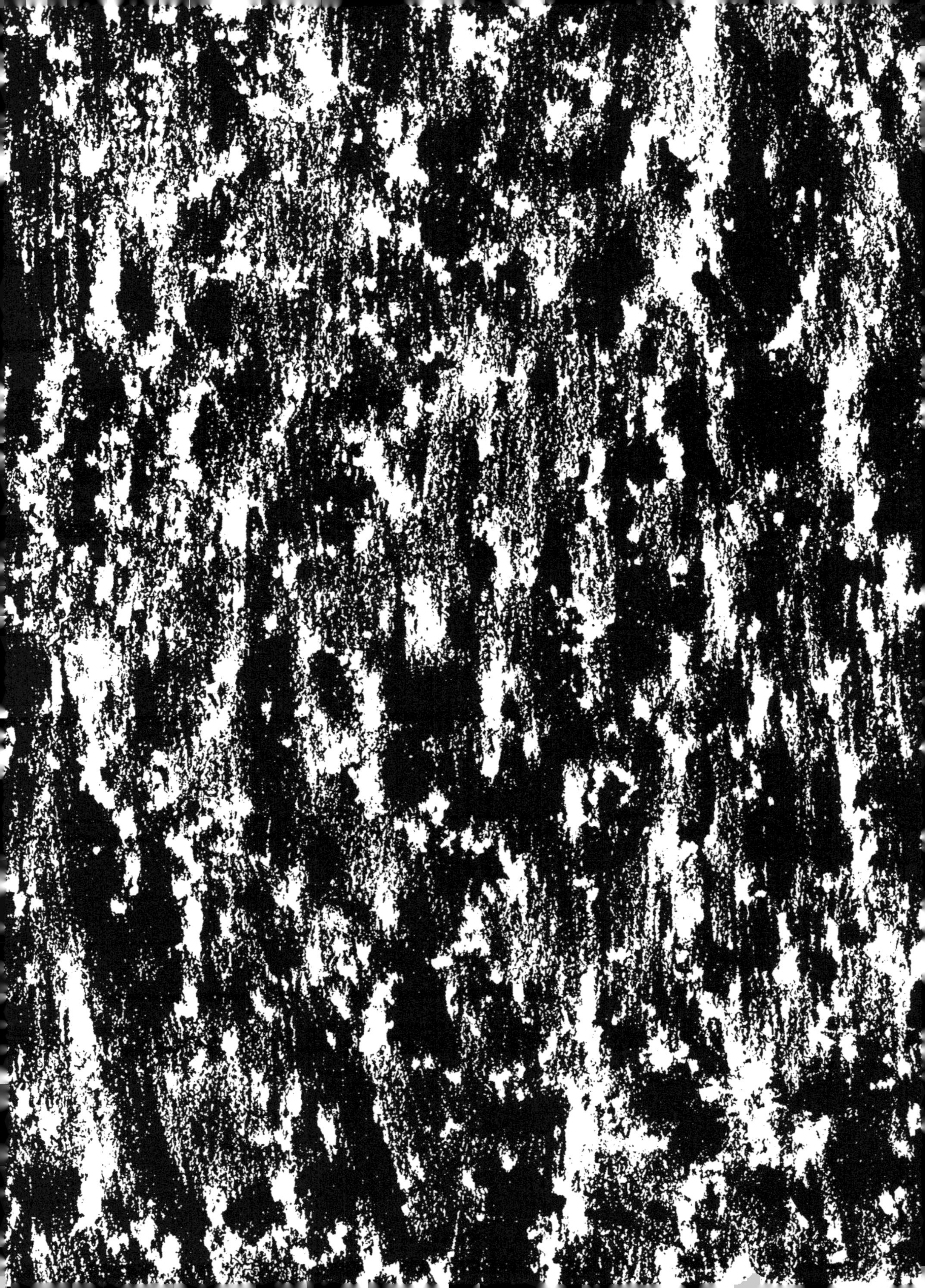

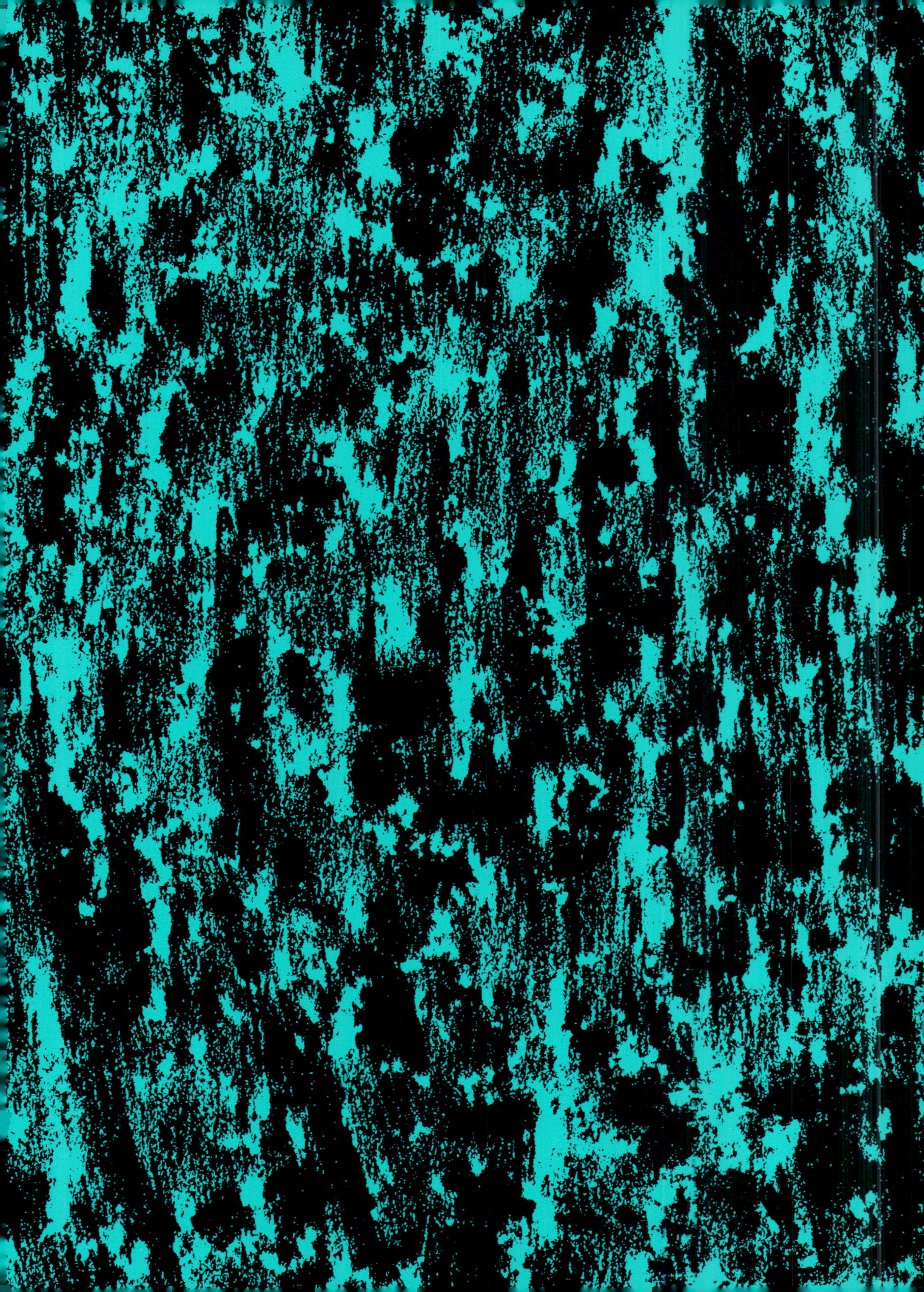

III. Michelle Grabner

ESSAY

ARTISTS

III. Michelle Grabner

ARTISTS IN CONVERSATION

MG's WB
Michelle Grabner

> Beckett—Disgust for hurried publication. Keep counsel—wait for muse. Nietzsche—Too much frantic production is a disease, vulgar. Fruit must ripen. Berryman, "no style, good"
>
> — David Foster Wallace, notations[1]

As an artist curating the Whitney Biennial, I must confess that I have an intellectual inclination to lean toward Gilles Deleuze, who insisted he was not an interpreter. For Deleuze, art was not a receptacle of "hidden content to be discovered by the diligent labour of interpretation."[2] His interest centered on "what [artworks] *did*, not what they *meant*."[3] Elizabeth Grosz understands Deleuze's desire to create something new through his encounters with art by writing: "Philosophy may find itself the twin or sibling of art and its various practices, neither judge of nor spokesperson for art, but its equally wayward sibling, working alongside art without illuminating it or speaking for it, being provoked by art and sharing the same enticements for the emergence of innovation and invention."[4] She goes on to say that art and philosophy have their "[r]ootedness in chaos" and with exuberance to describe "their capacity to ride the waves of a vibratory universe without direction or purpose, in short, their capacity to enlarge the universe by enabling its potential to be otherwise, to be framed through concepts and affects."[5]

There are two aspects of Deleuze's thinking that are particularly useful to me both as an artist and in my role as a curator for the Biennial. The first is his concern for the instability of repetition and its creative ability to illustrate difference. In Deleuze's view, "repetition is best understood in terms of discovery and experimentation; it allows new experiences, affects, and expressions to emerge. To repeat is to begin again; to affirm the power of the new and the unforeseeable."[6] This has standing in pedagogical and educational practices, and it underscores a "process of reading through, rather than towards."[7] The second is Deleuze's aversion toward debate and his understanding that art is integrally networked with all that is external to it. If there is nothing outside of the text for a theorist such as Jacques Derrida, for Deleuze there is nothing inside it. "A book is a small cog in a much more complex external machinery," he writes.[8] So in this way, curating is context building. But forbid, not vertically. For example, when Deleuze and Félix Guattari took on the work of Kafka, they replaced traditional analytical methods of critique with a rhizomatic address. They write: "We will enter, then, by any point whatsoever; none matters more than another, and no entrance is more privileged even if it seems an impasse, a tight passage, a siphon. We will be trying only to discover what other points our entrance connects to, what crosswords and galleries one passes through to link two points, what the map of rhizome is and how the map is modified if one enters by another point. Only the principle of multiple entrances prevents the introduction of the enemy, the Signifier, and those attempts to interpret a work that is actually only open to experimentation."[9]

But where does this critical methodology leave the reader of Kafka or the viewer of contemporary art? With a theatrical degree of exhaustion, Terry Eagleton writes of reception theory: "[D]emands are piled on the hapless handler of text.

1. David Foster Wallace, "Pale King" notebook, undated, David Foster Wallace Papers 1971–2008, Harry Ransom Collection, The University of Texas at Austin.
2. Colin Davis, *Critical Excess: Overreading in Derrida, Deleuze, Levinas, Zizek and Cavell* (Stanford, CA.: Stanford University Press, 2010), 57.
3. Ibid.
4. Elizabeth Grosz, *Chaos, Territory, Art: Deleuze and the Framing of the Earth* (New York: Columbia University Press, 2008), 2.
5. Ibid., 24.
6. Davis, 58.
7. Nancy K. Miller, *Getting Personal: Feminist Occasions and Other Autobiographical Acts* (New York: Routledge, 1991), 75.
8. Gilles Deleuze, *Pourparlers* (Paris: Minuit, 1990), 17.
9. Gilles Deleuze and Félix Guattari, *Kafka: Toward a Minor Literature* (Minneapolis: University of Minnesota Press, 1986), 3.

The reader is now obliged to engage in a strategic enterprise which would tax even the most manically energetic of individuals: connecting, revising, code-switching, synthesizing, correlating, depragmatising, image-building, perspective-switching, inferring, normalizing, recognizing, ideating, negating, foregrounding, backgrounding, feeding back, contextualizing, situation-building, coordinating, memory-transforming, expectation-modifying, illusion-building, gestalt-forming, image-breaking, blank-filling, concretising, consistency-building, structuring and anticipating."[10]

As viewers of artworks, we do this too. With our intellects and our imaginations, we participate in forging connections and draw inferences from the art we encounter. As a matter of fact, when it comes to contemporary art, we come not only to accept but to expect this type of "viewer participation." Meaning, Eagleton explains, "emerges from a constant traffic between work and reader, so that (to put the matter in Lacanian idiom) the act of reading is a project in which one receives back one's own response from the other (the text) in transfigured or defamiliarised form."[11] With a further air of exhaustion, he writes: "Interpretation . . . is self-generating and self-legitimating. Since it produces what it purports to investigate, all interpretation is self-interpretation. The dim patch of light you glimpse down the microscope turns out to be your own eye."[12]

To further Eagleton's metaphor then, visitors stepping off the elevator onto the fourth floor of the Marcel Breuer building to see the 2014 Biennial will look down a microscope of my own construction. And it is just that: a construction. But it is also a text and a curriculum. Theoretically, the works that I included will each demand from the viewer a varied network of analysis. Some artists, such as Gretchen Bender, Sarah Charlesworth, David Diao, Gaylen Gerber, Karl Haendel, Sherrie Levine, Ken Lum, Phil Vanderhyden, and Donelle Woolford, will be interpreted through a combination of poststructural critique, semiotics, and phenomenology. Feminism and psychoanalytic criticism are an appropriate frame to begin examining Molly Zuckerman-Hartung, Louise Fishman, Dona Nelson, Jacqueline Humphries, Suzanne McClelland, Laura Owens, Amy Sillman, and Pam Lins. The personal, the poetic, the symbolic, the political, and the discursive properties in the work of David Robbins, Dawoud Bey, Tony Lewis, Ben Kinmont, Peter Schuyff, Joshua Mosley, Jennifer Bornstein, Shana Lutker, Philip Hanson, and Joel Otterson call for an elastic and layered range of associations, while formalism and materiality are at the heart of the work of Sterling Ruby, Sheila Hicks, John Mason, Dan Walsh, Alma Allen, Shio Kusaka, and my entire film and video program, including works by Rochelle Feinstein, Victoria Fu, Jonn Herschend, HOWDOYOUSAYYAMINAFRICAN?, Doug Ischar, Alex Jovanovich, Chris Larson, Sara Greenberger Rafferty, and Emily Sundblad. Perhaps Stephen Berens's work is a singular example of a fully hermeneutical practice, asking a metaphysical question of photography only to shed light on the answer.

I have likely assembled together, as a curatorial whole, what could be described as a type of bricolage, "characterized in large part by visual realities, by discontinuity and juxtaposition in overall form, and by a decentered, porous association among its discontinuous parts . . . an alternative to compartmentalized systems of knowledge/display."[13] Yet as John Ashbery writes in "Self-Portrait in a Convex Mirror," "Today has no margins, the event arrives / Flush with its edges."[14] So, too, does my curatorial methodology include prescribed edges. As I outlined above, contours can be drawn around three overlapping priorities: abstract painting by women; materiality and affect theory; and art as strategy, those works that are "loose-jointed, internally differentiated affairs, powered by a set of general purposes but with semiautomatic parts, between which there can be frictions and conflicts."[15] In other words, conceptual practices oriented toward criticality. And

10. Terry Eagleton, *The Event of Literature* (New Haven, CT.: Yale University Press, 2012), 186.

11. Ibid., 187.

12. Ibid., 188.

13. Nicholas Paley, *Finding Art's Place: Experiments in Contemporary Education and Culture* (New York: Routledge, 1995), 9.

14. John Ashbery, "Self-Portrait in a Convex Mirror," http://www.poemhunter.com/poem/self-portrait-in-a-convex-mirror/

15. Eagleton, 224–25.

because these contours are "porous" and the works often radically juxtaposed in space, these three priorities foreground conventional and historical practices such as painting and sculpture, while at the same time evading totalizing approaches to curating or artmaking.

In this sense, I am thinking more about curriculum building than about curating. And not because I am a teacher, or because I was resolved early on in my curatorial process to include artists in the Biennial who are also teachers, but because I didn't want that "microscope" you look down to be purely a subjective take on contemporary American art, nor did I seek a democratic survey. Instead, I developed a fourth-floor curriculum that represents identifiable themes, generalities even, that are currently established in the textures of contemporary aesthetic, political, and economic realities, while hoping to enact two differing yet complementary pedagogical philosophies as represented by Friedrich Froebel and Maxine Greene as simultaneous models for curriculum development and presentation. From an Enlightenment position, Froebel writes that "'school' is to be understood neither as schoolroom nor as school-keeping but as the conscious communication of items of knowledge for a deliberate purpose and a deliberate interconnection."[16] This dovetails with Greene's writing on education: "[S]hifts in attention make it possible to see from different standpoints; they stimulate the 'wide-awakeness' so essential to critical awareness, most particularly when they involve a move to the imaginary—away from the mundane."[17]

Although it may be overreaching to think that organizing the Whitney Biennial could equate to developing a program of study, a focused context of contemporary art (a curriculum not for the K–12 set but for other artists), aiming at pedagogy seemed a worthier ambition than a curatorial methodology constructed out of personal subjectivity. I did, however, indulge in a conspicuous and heavy-handed nod to "curating as curriculum/exhibition as classroom" in the inclusion of Dawoud Bey's photographic portrait of President Barack Obama at the entrance to the fourth-floor galleries. This image is a signifier of both civil unity and political and racial instability, a punctuation of nationalism and hierarchy in the shifting field of artworks that occupy the fourth floor.

"We back ourselves into a corner with the false critical presumption that either painting must act serious or it will be nothing more than a plaything for the rich."[18] It was David Joselit's essay "Painting Travesty," included in the 2012 Whitney Biennial catalogue, that spurred me to engage in a focused examination of contemporary abstract painting in the 2014 Biennial. In his essay, he summarizes his thesis by writing that painting "has a secret weapon: its capacity for travesty and its provocation to laughter."[19] Joselit quotes Amy Sillman's statement as a illustration of his point: "I don't find it odd that AbEx practices have now been vitally reinvigorated by a queered connection of the vulgar and camp. Many artists—not least of them woman and queers—are currently recomplicating the terrain of gestural, messy, physical, chromatic, embodied, handmade practices."[20] And I simply selected a range of ambitious contemporary women painters who exemplify Sillman's claim, including Sillman herself.

Still most comfortably in the grip of academia, the complex and pluralistic ideas driving "new materialism" are starting to make their way into our understanding of art and everyday life. New Materialism requires empirical modes of investigation, yet it does not, as it historically once did, distinguish between organic and inorganic, animate and inanimate, matter. Welcomingly, studies in New Materialism naturally pry open the discourse surrounding craft, particularly ceramics and fibers, now comfortably situated within the contemporary art world. For example, New Materialism gives Sheila Hicks, John Mason, Alma Allen, Sterling Ruby, and Shio Kusaka common ground with formal and conceptual

16. Friedrich Froebel, quoted in *Friedrich Froebel: A Selection from His Writings*, Irene M. Lilley, ed. (Cambridge, UK: Cambridge University Press, 1967), 112.

17. Maxine Greene, *Landscapes of Learning* (New York: Teachers College Press), 173.

18. David Joselit, "Painting Travesty," in *Whitney Biennial 2012* (New York: Whitney Museum of American Art, 2012), 37.

19. Ibid.

20. Amy Sillman, quoted in ibid.

object-makers such as Peter Schuyff, Ricky Swallow, David Robbins, and Joel Otterson. It also puts Sterling Ruby's ceramic basins in relationship to Louise Fishman's paintings. "For materiality is always something more than 'mere' matter: an excess, force, vitality, relationality, or difference that renders matter active, self-creative, productive, unpredictable. In sum, new materialists are rediscovering a materiality that materializes, evincing immanent modes of self-transformation that compel us to think of causation in far more complex terms; to recognize that phenomena are caught in a multitude of interlocking systems and forces and to consider anew the locations and nature of capacities for agency."[21]

21. Diana Coole and Samantha Frost, *New Materialisms: Ontology, Agency, and Politics* (Durham, NC: Duke University Press, 2010), 9.

When it comes to critical practices on the fourth floor and in the Biennial's public spaces, they run the gamut. I must confess, if you haven't already guessed, I was schooled in the 1980s, and postmodernism imprinted its many critiques on me. I hold out hope that appropriation still has teeth and that irony is a workable trope. And unlike the rest of the art world, I haven't developed an allergy to theory, finding it useful in context building. In terms of critical practices on the fourth floor, you will find that threads of institutional critique are not nearly as prevalent as investigations into authorship. Examples of the independent imagination are matched against the cultural imagination. Cynicism hangs in the air, as does vulnerability. I believe that all of these artists, including David Diao, Ken Lum, David Robbins, and Gaylen Gerber, along with Sherrie Levine, David Hammons, Peter Schuyff, Sarah Charlesworth, Tony Tasset, Gretchen Bender, Darren Bader, Critical Practices Inc., Matthew Delegat, Paul Druecke, Jeff Gibson, Diego Leclery, Philip Vanderhyden, and Pedro Vélez, disturb the creative field in the interest of long-term critical and imaginative gains.

This brings us to my inclusion of notebooks by David Foster Wallace in the Biennial. These represent, in part, Wallace's research for *The Pale King*, his posthumously published novel (some say five-hundred-page suicide note), in which appears a surrogate named "David Wallace." In the novel, the David Wallace character claims that *The Pale King* is "more like a memoir than any kind of made-up story."[22] Wallace's research for the novel that would be his follow-up to a "masterpiece that's also a monster," *Infinite Jest*, included several spiral-bound kids' notebooks, including a Cuddly Cuties pad with a cute kitten on the cover and a piece of collage paper with the word *SCENES* written on it.[23] Notations such as "Bell shaped men—Fat, Dull, Watching TV is main hobby. Insipid" and "Much in book about boredom—passage of time—vs. how fascinating everything gets when you pay very close attention to it" clutter the pages.[24]

22. David Foster Wallace, *The Pale King*, ed. Michael Pietsch (New York: Little, Brown and Company, 2011), 67.

23. A. O. Scott, "The Best Mind of His Generation," *New York Times*, September 20, 2008.

24. Wallace, "Pale King."

Wallace's status as a metafictionalist is well-known, so it is somewhat surprising, even poignant, when he says: "It's almost like postmodernism is fiction's fall from biblical grace. Fiction became *conscious* of itself in a way it never had been."[25] Yet it is Wallace's ability to embrace nonfiction and humanistic clichés that distances him from both modern and postmodern projects. He concludes "E. Unibus Pluram," his indictment of television's "absurdity," "sardonic fatigue," "iconoclasm," and "rebellion," blending them to the "ends of spectation and consumption," by writing, "The next real literary 'rebels' in this country might well emerge as some weird bunch of 'anti-rebels,' born oglers who dare somehow to back way from ironic watching, who have childish gall actually to endorse and instantiate single-entendre principles. Who treat of plain old untrendy human troubles and emotions in U.S. life with reverence and conviction. Who eschew self-consciousness and hip-fatigue."[26]

25. Larry McCaffrey, "An Interview with David Foster Wallace," *Review of Contemporary Fiction* 13 (Summer 1993): 138–39.

26. David Foster Wallace, "E. Unibus Pluram: Television and U.S. Fiction," in *A Supposedly Fun Thing I'll Never Do Again* (Boston: Little, Brown and Company, 1997), 81.

PERCENTAGES BASED ON THE TOTAL NUMBER OF ARTISTS VISITED BY MG FOR THE 2014 WHITNEY BIENNIAL

GENDER

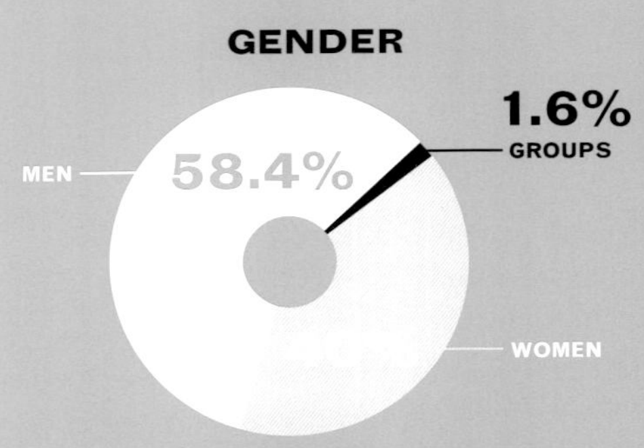

DENSITY BY U.S. GEOGRAPHY

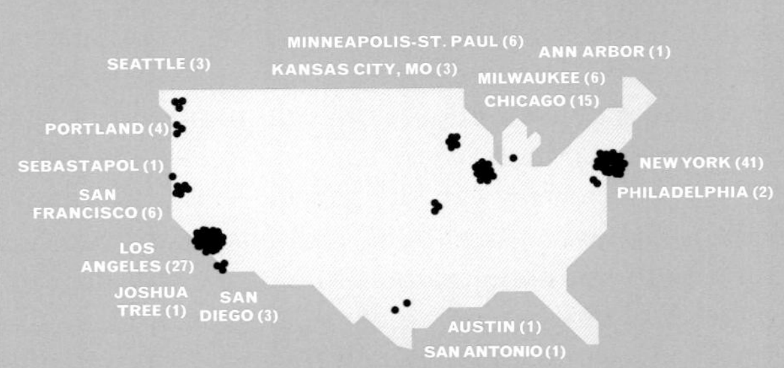

BIRTH YEAR
(BY DECADE)

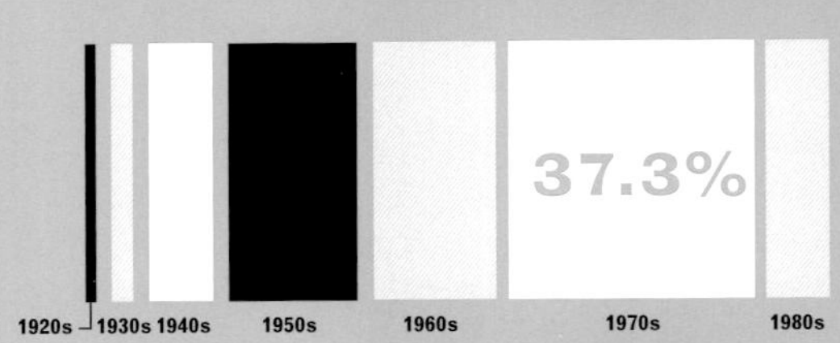

RELATIONSHIP TO MG

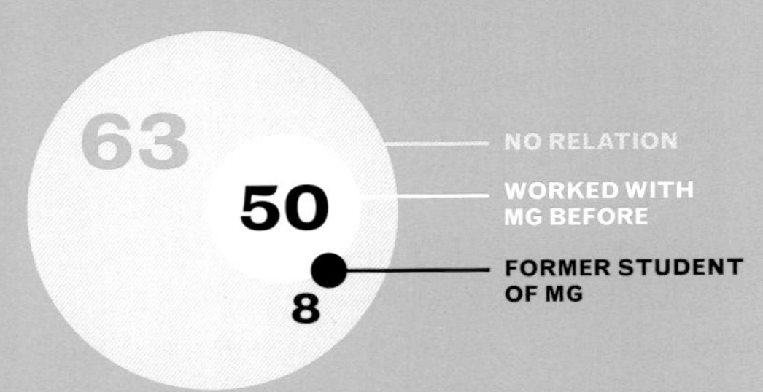

TEACHING

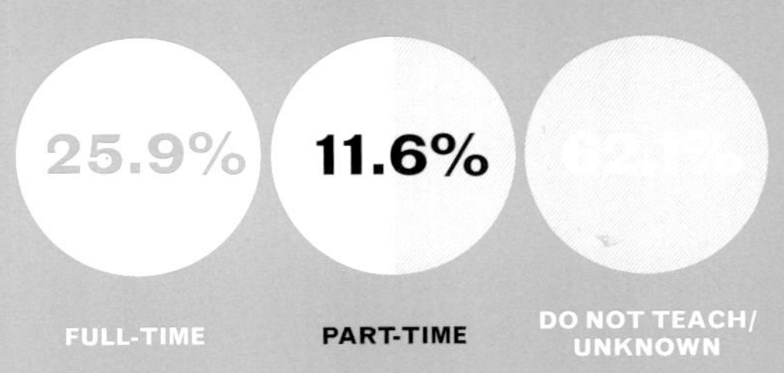

HAS MFA

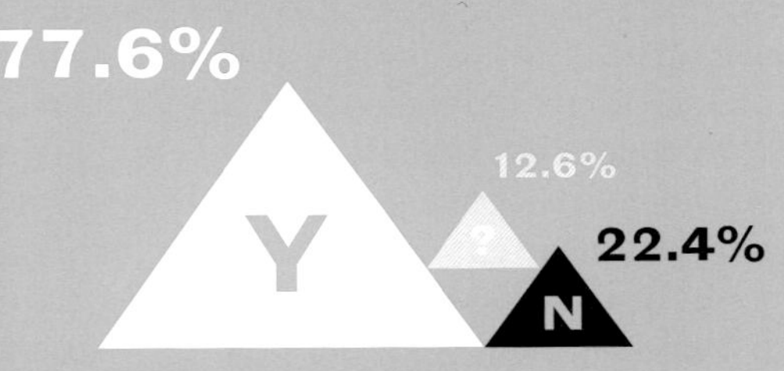

AGE
(AS OF 12/31/2013)

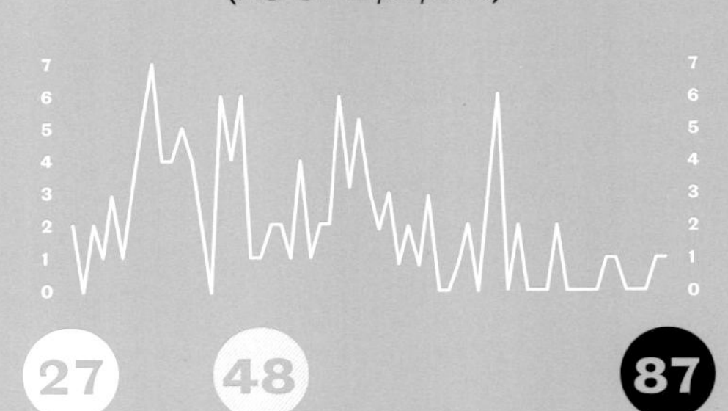

GALLERY REPRESENTATION

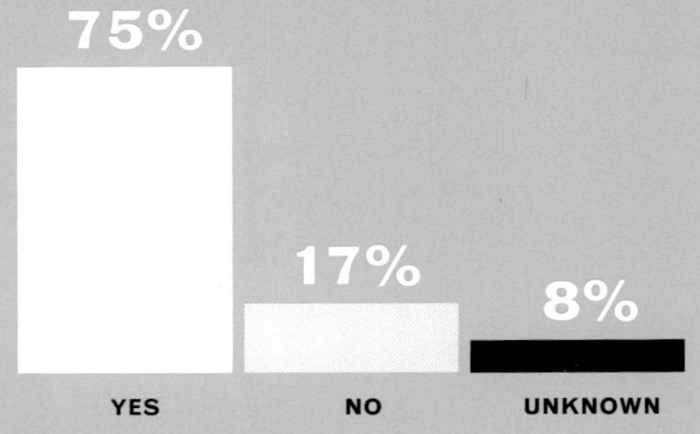

A Note Regarding the Artist Conversations and Infographics

The artist "conversations" that follow are an attempt at everyday language, "to bring words back from their metaphysical to their everyday use."[27] These exchanges between artists, authors, designers, sports figures, critics, friends, and spouses are "efforts to rejoin pieces of language which were disconnected and abusively hierarchized."[28] By leaving discourse up to the artists, to let them enter into content and language that is either specialized or common, is a gesture of respect and belief on my part. Like Wittgenstein, it acknowledges "an outside which itself remains ineffable."[29]

The infographics designed to accompany my essay are meant to reveal transparency in my curatorial process and, similar to the conversations, an endeavor at forthrightness. This conviction is grounded in the fact that as an artist I, too, have engaged in studio visits with past Biennial curators, and I have found the experience befuddling. Below is an example of an email exchange I had over the summer with Jonathan Franzen, the writer and literary executor of David Foster Wallace's estate, as I worked to explain my Biennial selection process and my intentions in shaping catalogue content surrounding the artist conversations.

27. Ludwig Wittgenstein, *Philosophical Investigations* (Oxford, UK: Blackwell, 1976), 48.

28. Michel de Certeau, *The Practice of Everyday Life* (Berkeley: University of California Press, 1984), 9.

29. Wittgenstein, quoted in ibid., 10.

Hi, Michelle,

Thanks for the email. It sounds like you're bringing an interesting take to the 2014, and I'll be curious to see the show itself. Somewhat strangely—given that we writers do tend to think of ourselves as artists—it would never have occurred to me that a writer's work could be displayed in a Biennial. I guess I feel a little bad for whichever visual artist has his or her work displaced by Dave's notebooks, since we writers have other channels for getting our work into the public eye. But Dave certainly was a serious working artist.

I'm afraid I have to say no to doing the interview you propose. This partly has to do with my reluctance to be a general spokesman for Dave and his work, partly with my uneasiness with what-should-be-included conversations, but mainly with the fact that I'm working on a novel and taking on very little else on the side. I'm trying to think of another working writer to suggest for the interview, but the curatorial dimension of it makes this difficult. Maybe the conversation should be with a visual artist whose work might have been included but wasn't? That could be colorful, at least.

Good luck, in any case, with the curation.

Warm regards,
Jon F.

Dear Jonathan,

Thank you for taking the time to respond to my inquiry. If you will indulge me, I would like to briefly clarify my curatorial thinking and my desire to include DFW's notebooks in the 2014 WB. First it is important to know that I am not acting out of fairness, nor working toward a democratic idea of inclusion when I select artists for the 2014 WB. Instead I am working to assemble a group of artists and a collection of artworks as well as artifacts that represent and ground my ardent enthusiasm for the waywardness of contemporary art. As an artist, I am liberated from the tedious stratagems girding today's curatorial industry, so in short, I am attempting to assemble an exhibition that is principally for me and for other artists. I have no interest in "talent hunting." Instead, I am composing an exhibition that features artists who are pivotal in shaping young artists' practices as teachers and mentors. Artists who have made a life, not a lifestyle, out of their dedication to artmaking.

Finally, you will be pleased to know that I took your suggestion to heart. I invited Milwaukee artist Nicholas Frank to have a conversation with one of my most precocious graduate students at the School of the Art Institute of Chicago, Brooke Kantor, to discuss the "immensely gifted writer" David Foster Wallace for the catalogue.

I hope you get a chance to see the exhibition.
Kindly, mg

Alma Allen

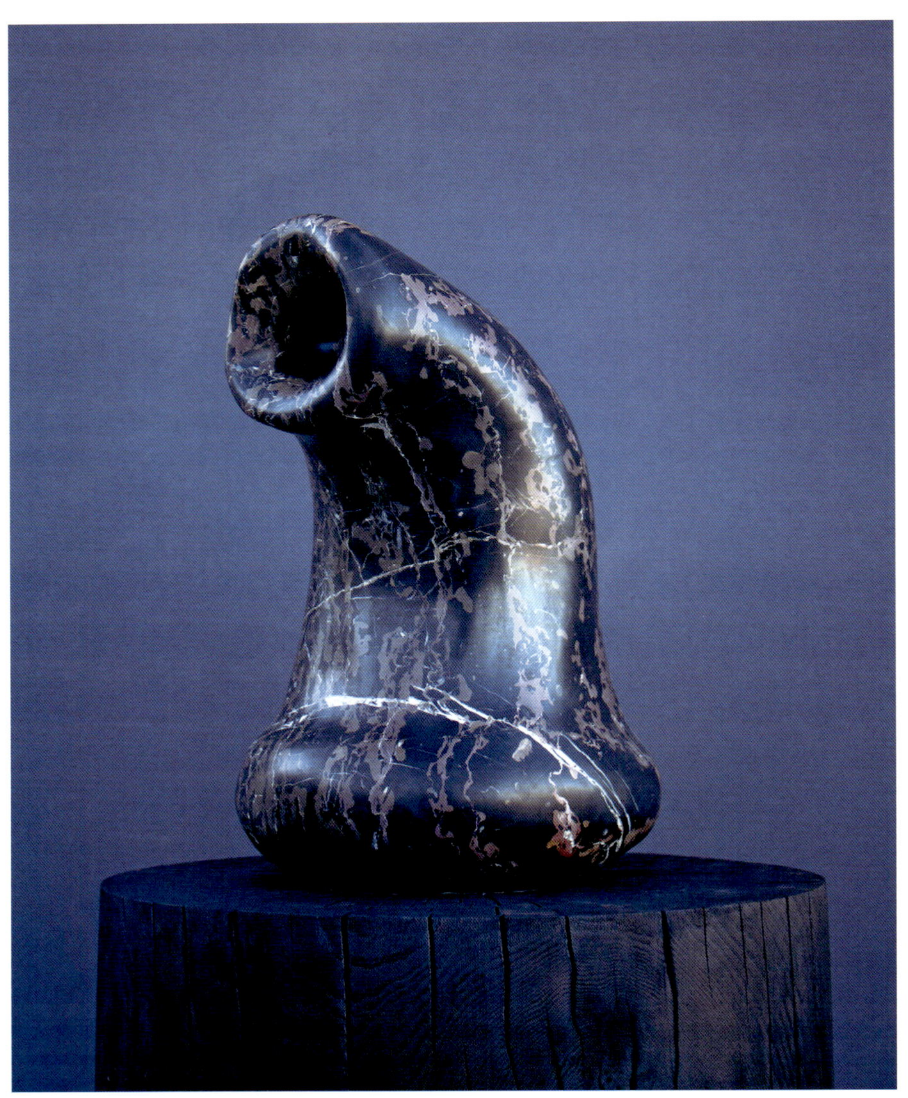

Untitled, 2013. Marble sculpture on an oak pedestal, 25 × 20 × 14 in. (63.5 × 50.8 × 35.6 cm)

Born 1970 in Heber City, UT

Lives in Joshua Tree, CA

Darren Bader

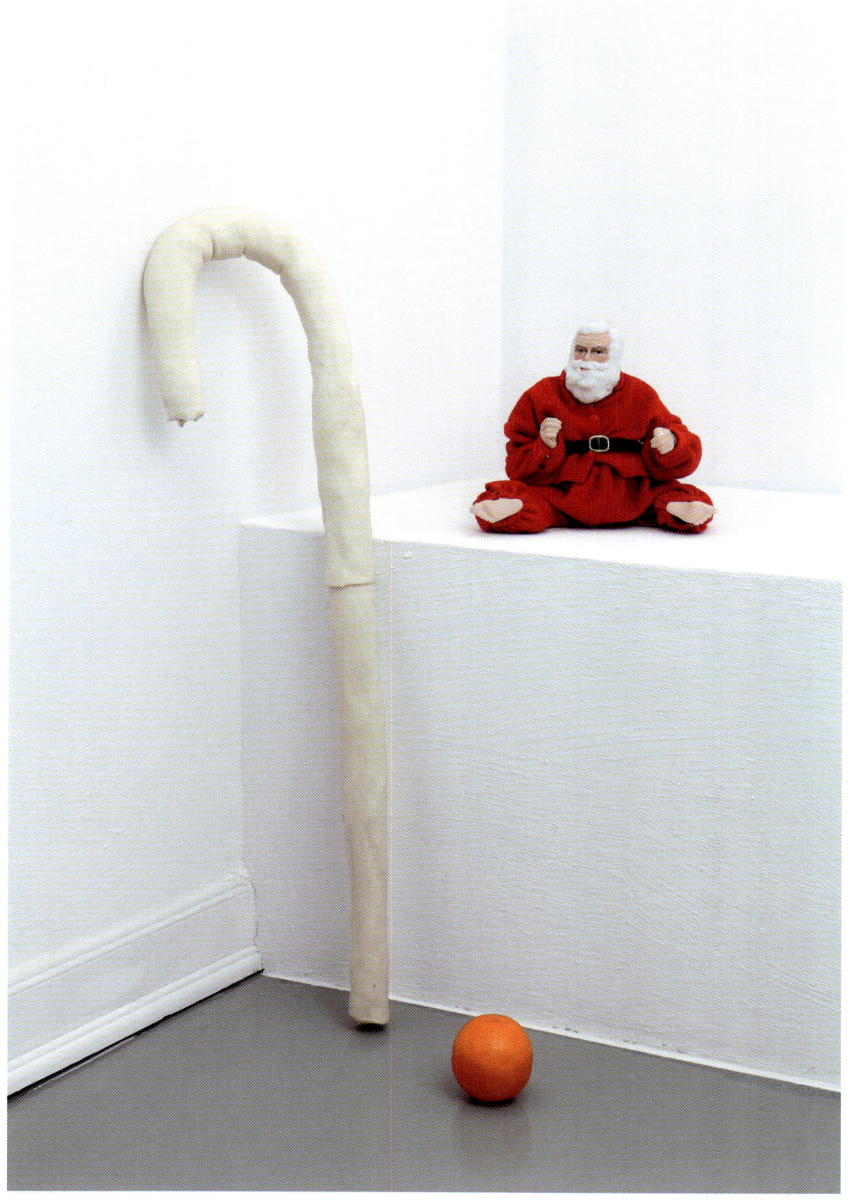

antipodes group 2, n.d. Four-part sculpture, dimensions variable. Collection of Herbert Fellner

Born 1978 in Bridgeport, CT

Lives in New York, NY

Gretchen Bender

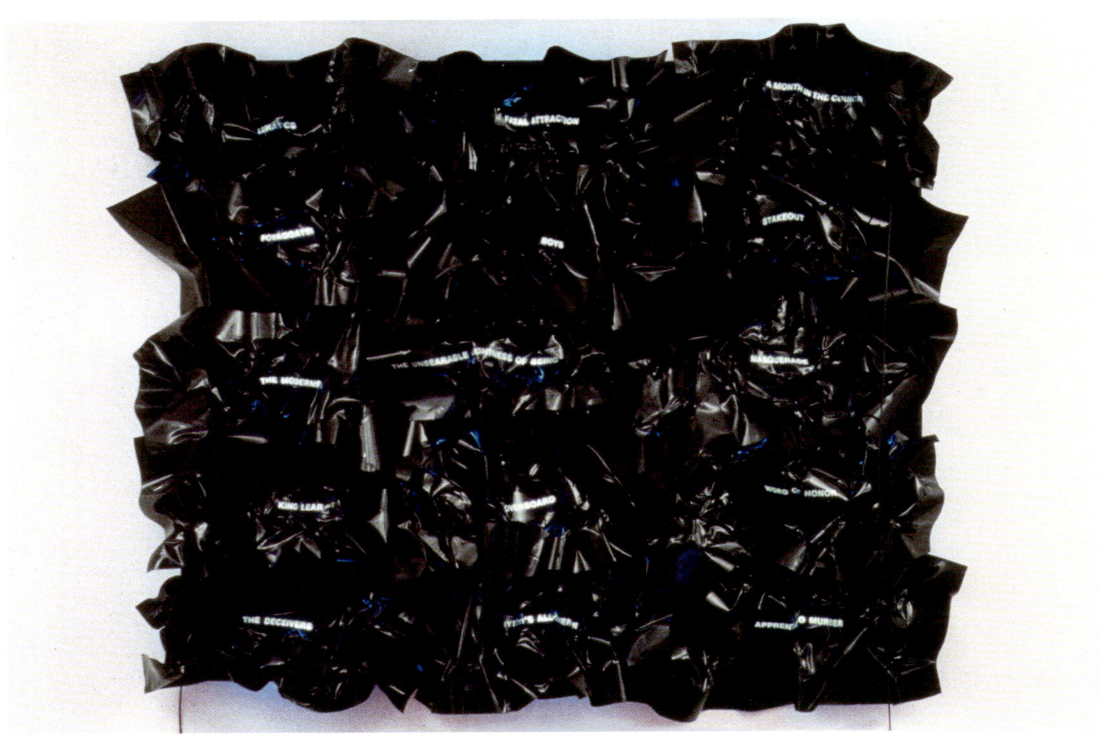

People in Pain, 1988. Paint on heat-set vinyl and neon, 84 × 560 × 11 in. (213.4 × 1,422.4 × 27.9 cm)

Born 1951 in
Seaford, DE

Died 2004 in
New York, NY

Stephen Berens

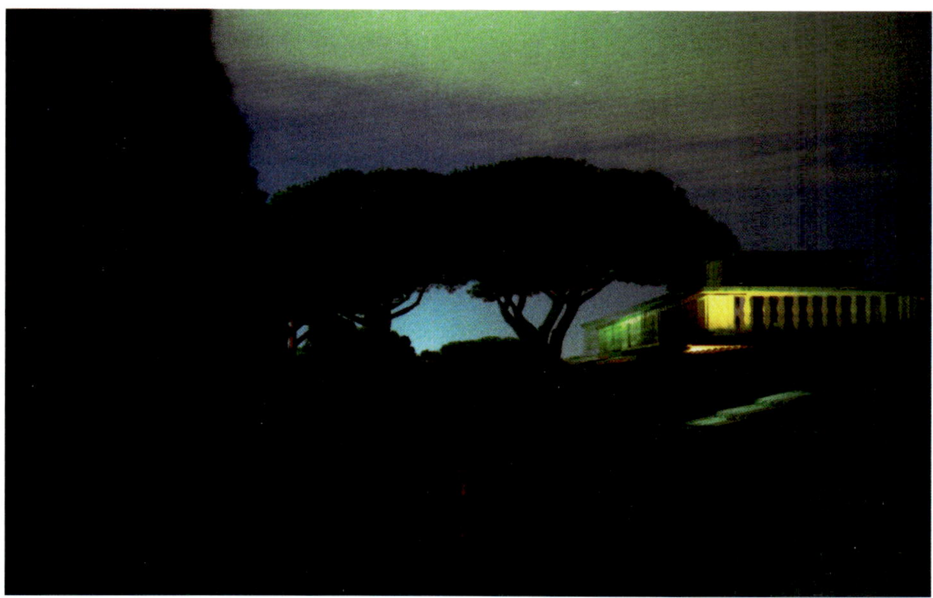

Top: *August 4, 2005, Night; July 28, 2005, Night (Lightning)*, 2013. Dye-based inkjet print, 24 × 34 in. (61 × 86.4 cm); bottom: *August 4, 2005, Night; July 28, 2005, Night (Lightning); July 28, 2005, Night; August 7, 2005, Night; July 29, 2005, Middle of the Night*, 2013. Dye-based inkjet print, 24 × 34 in. (61 × 86.4 cm)

Born 1952 in Fort Collins, CO

Lives in Los Angeles, CA

Dawoud Bey

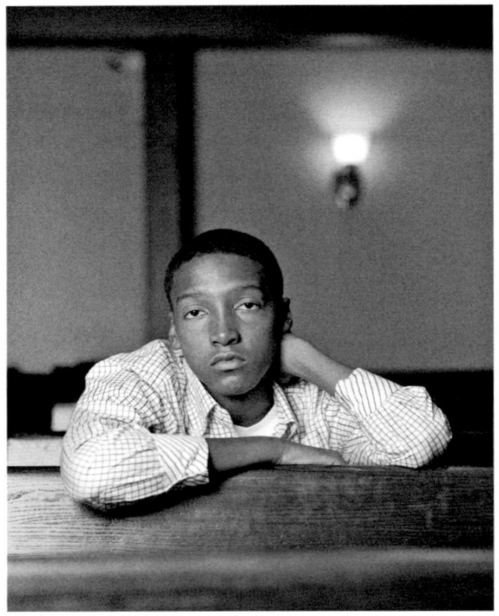
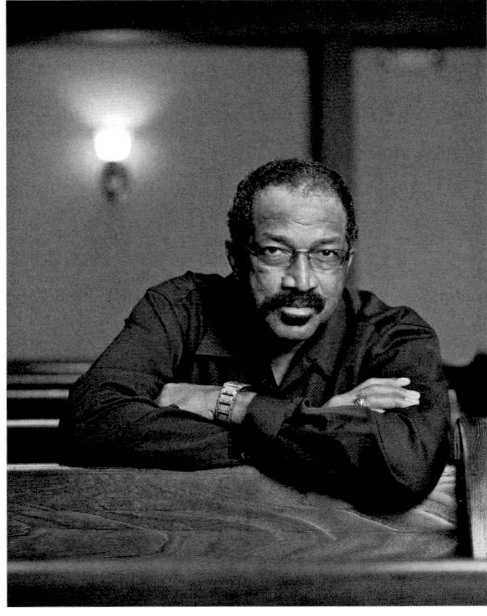
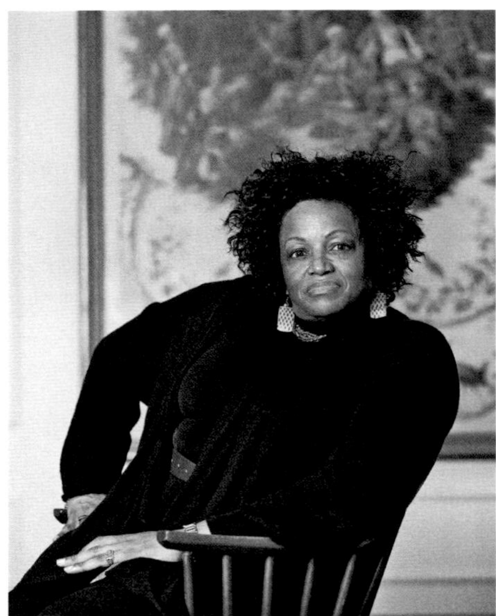
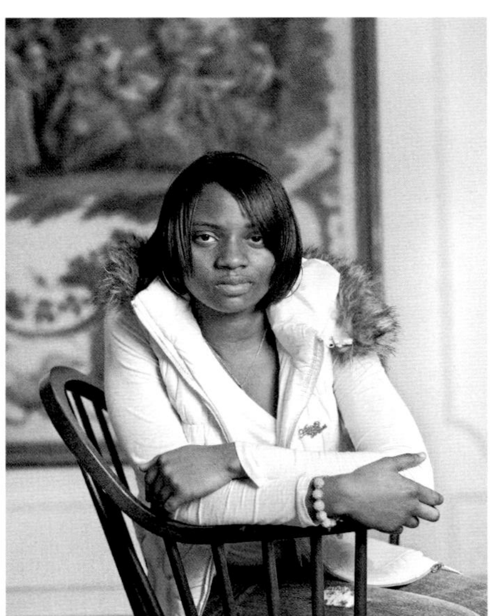

Top: *Braxton McKinney and Lavone Thomas* (from *The Birmingham Project*), 2012. Two pigmented inkjet prints mounted on dibond, 40 × 64 in. (101.6 × 162.6 cm) overall; bottom: *Maxine Adams and Amelia Maxwell* (from *The Birmingham Project*), 2012. Two pigmented inkjet prints mounted on dibond, 40 × 64 in. (101.6 × 162.6 cm) overall

Born 1953 in Queens, NY

Lives in Chicago, IL

Jennifer Bornstein

sparkly
splash
barefoot
big
woo
great
greatest
discover
ultimate
spectacular
state-of-the-art
incredible
thrills
famous
luxury
must-see
endless
thousands
vibe
impressive
awesome
laugh
massive
hottest
top
stunning
hip
surf
celebrity
perfect
unexpected
leader
epicenter
well-being
romance
harmonious
preeminence
coastal
largest
significant
second-largest
knockout
franchise
sunshine
hit
stirring
beachy
surprise
spellbinding
wows
sexy
skyscraper
experience
driven
golden
influential
relaxed
third-largest
fifth-largest
15th-largest
sunny
enviable
headliner
smash
extensive
dreams
Southland
appeal
sensation
extravagant
stunner
fame
star
stardom
successful
babe
tremendous
lifestyle
publicist
agent
summertime
eclectic

Born 1970 in Seattle, WA

Lives in New York, NY / Berlin, Germany

Sarah Charlesworth

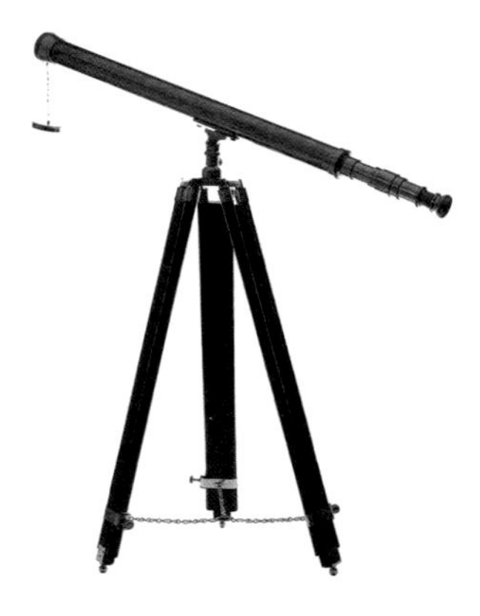

Moon Watch, 2012. Two chromogenic prints, mounted and laminated, with lacquer frames, 41 ½ × 62 ¼ in. (105.4 × 158.1 cm)

Born 1947 in East Orange, NJ

Died 2013 in Falls Village, CT

Critical Practices Inc.

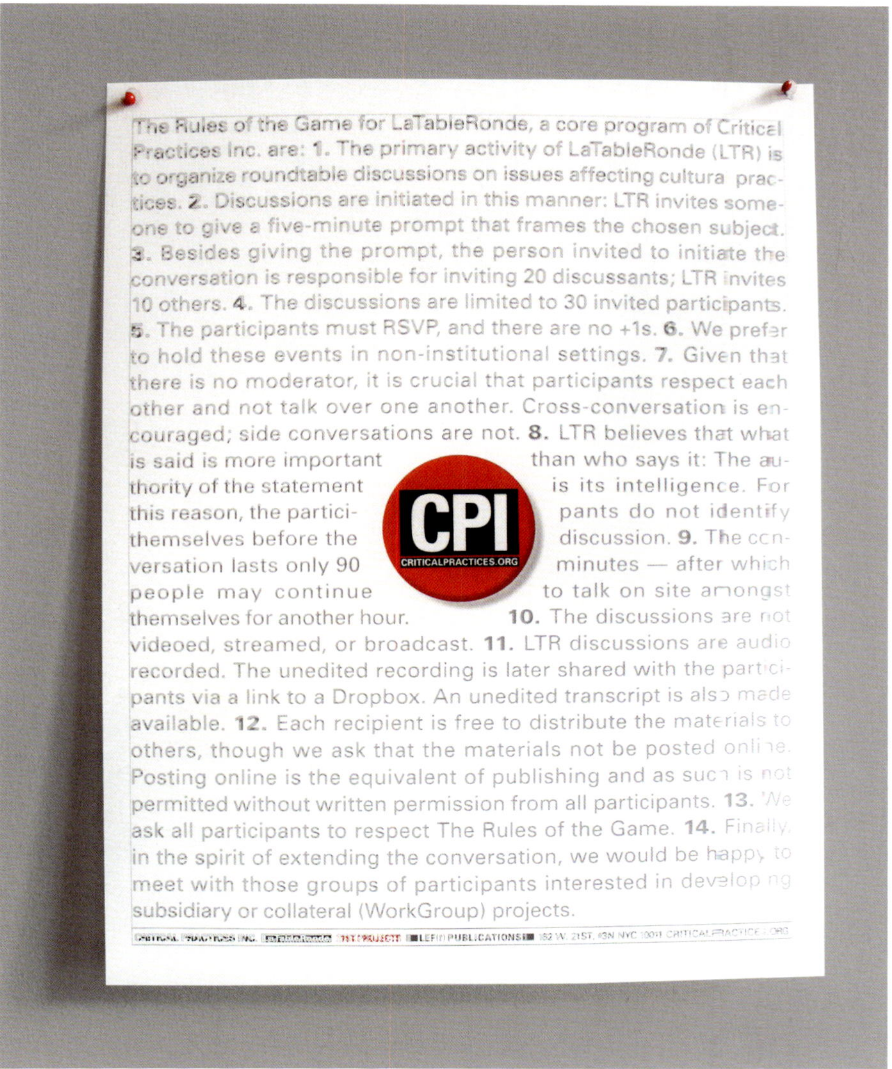

The Rules of The Game – LTR, 2013

Founded in 2010

Based in New York, NY

Matthew Deleget

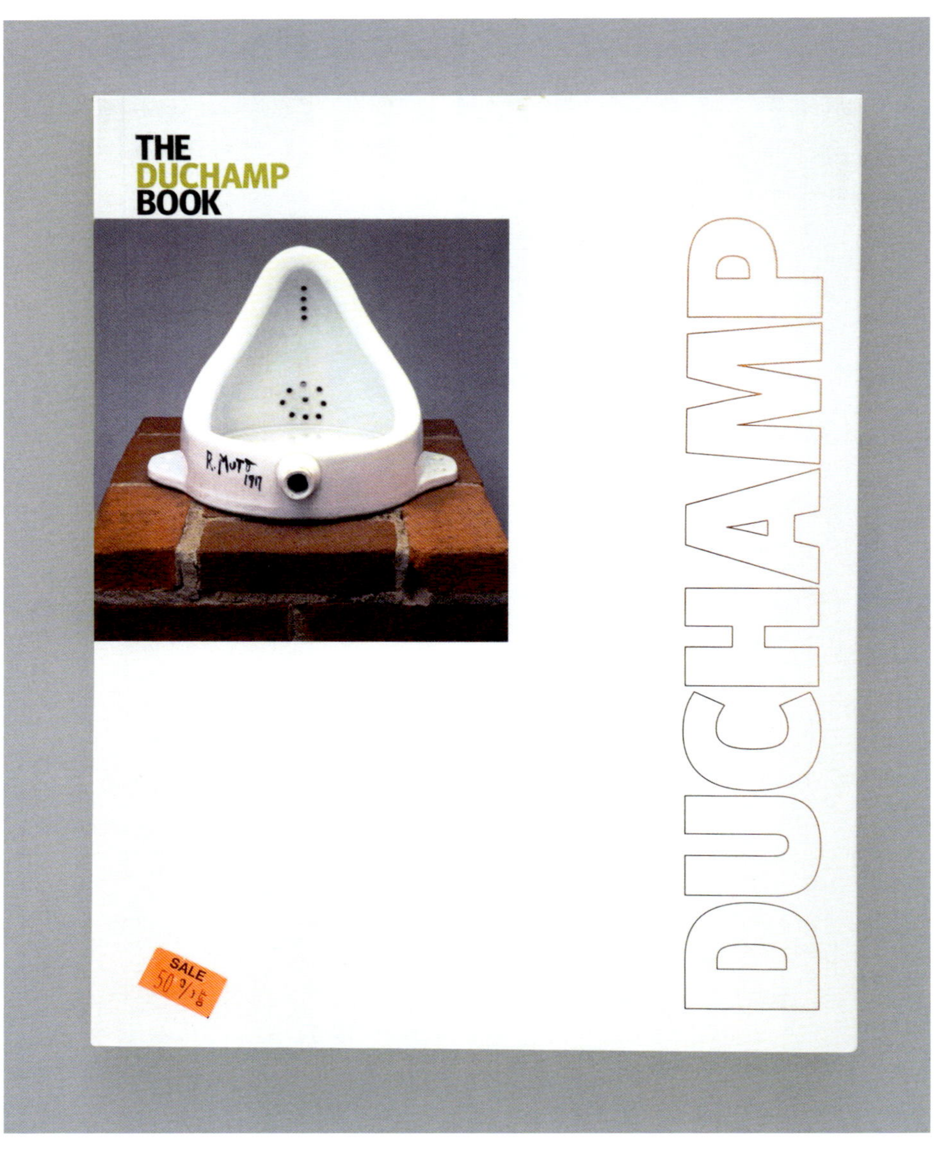

Zero-Sum, 2011– (detail). Installation of discounted artists' monographs and art history publications purchased at museum bookstores, dimensions variable.

Born 1972 in Hammond, IN

Lives in Brooklyn, NY

David Diao

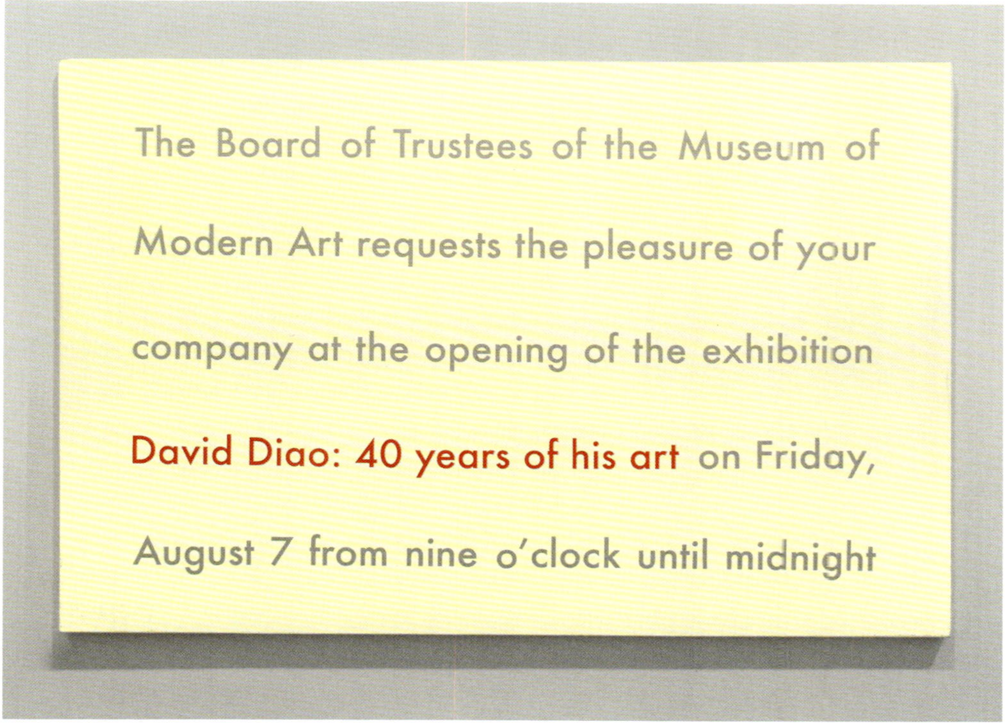

The Board of Trustees of the Museum of Modern Art requests the pleasure of your company at the opening of the exhibition David Diao: 40 years of his art on Friday, August 7 from nine o'clock until midnight

40 Years of His Art, 2013. Acrylic and vinyl on canvas, 40 × 60 in. (101.6 × 152.4 cm)

Born 1943 in
Chengdu, China

Lives in
New York, NY

Paul Druecke

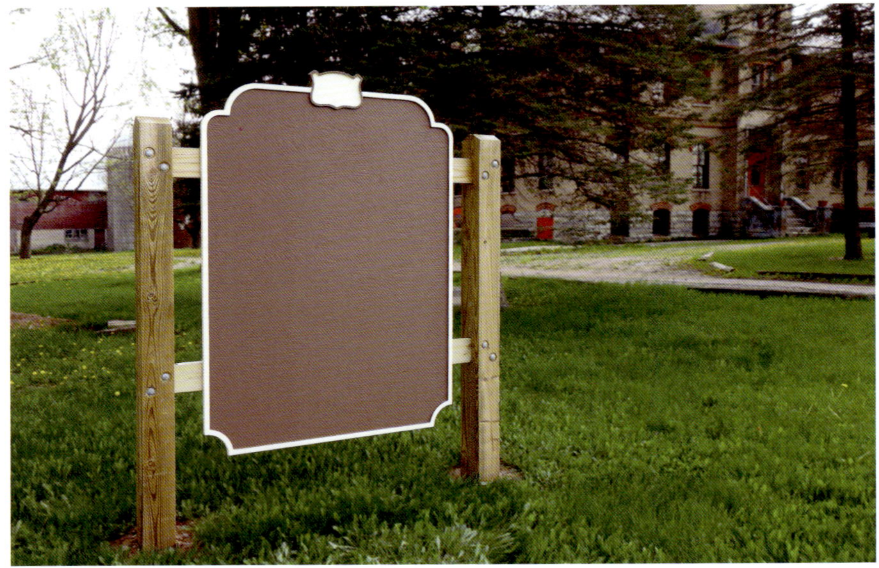

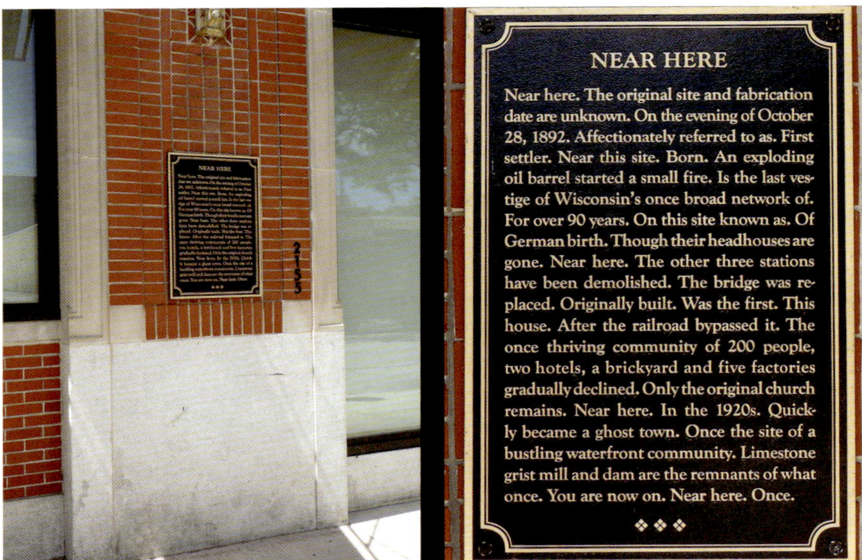

Top: *Poor Farm*, 2012. Cast aluminum, wood, cement, and fastening hardware, 96 × 84 in. (243.8 × 213.4 cm); bottom: *Near Here in collaboration with Donna Stonecipher*, 2011. Cast bronze, paint, lacquer, and fastening hardware, 36 × 24 in. (91.4 × 61 cm)

Born 1964 in Milwaukee, WI

Lives in Milwaukee, WI

Rochelle Feinstein

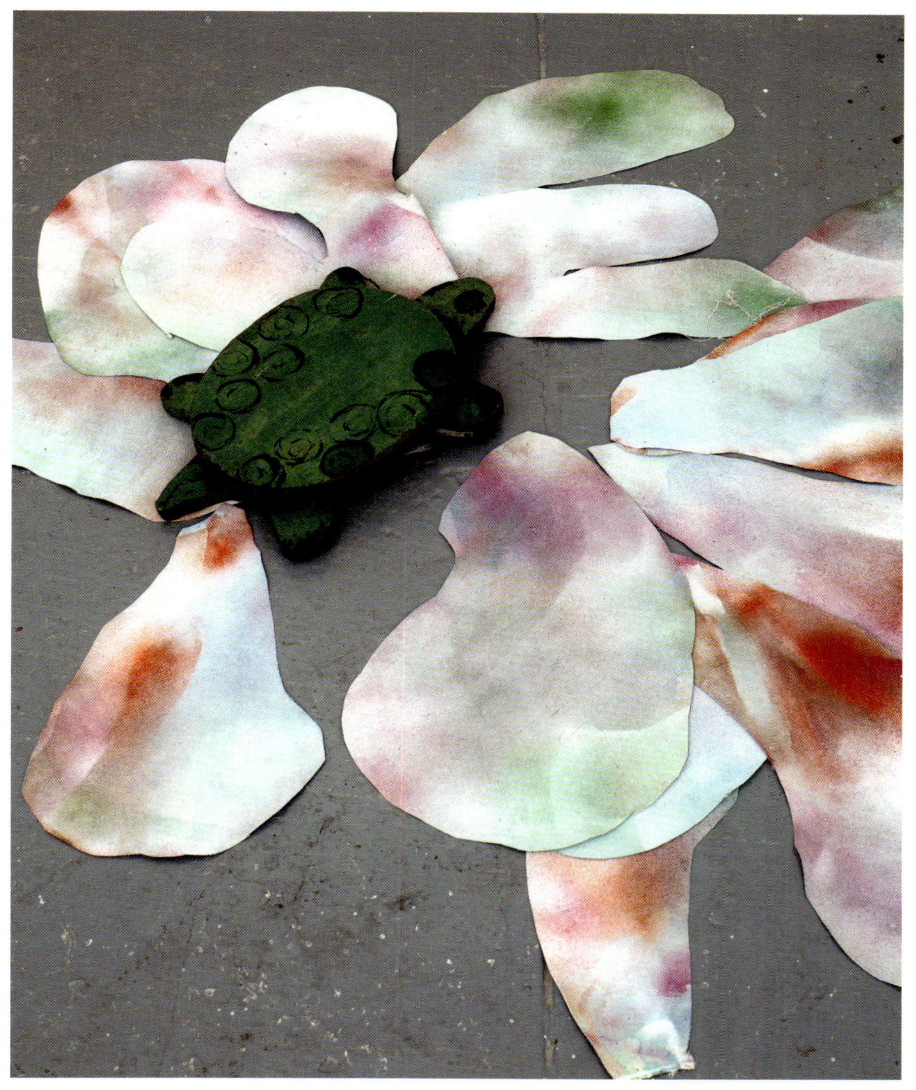

Still from *Toy George et al.*, 2013 Video, color, sound; approx. 9 minutes

Born 1947 in New York, NY

Lives in New York, NY

Louise Fishman

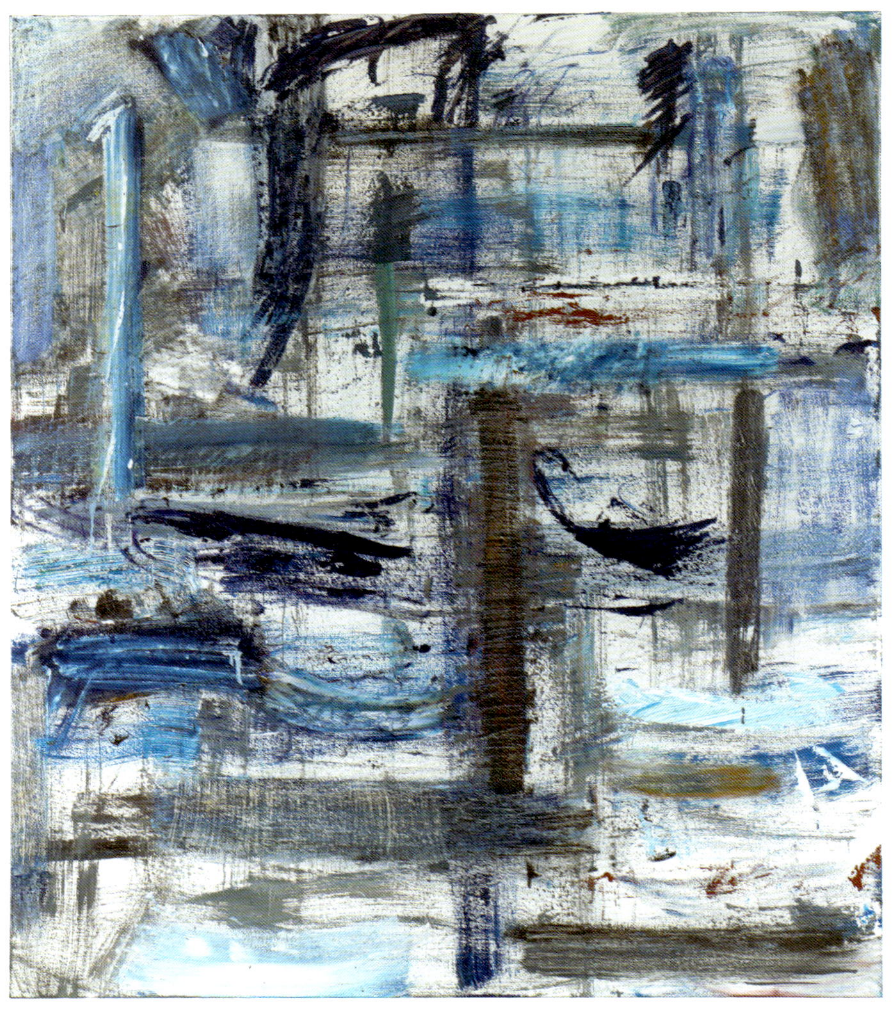

Ristretto, 2013. Oil on linen, 70 × 60 in. (177.8 × 152.4 cm). Private Collection

Born 1939 in Philadelphia, PA

Lives in New York, NY

Victoria Fu

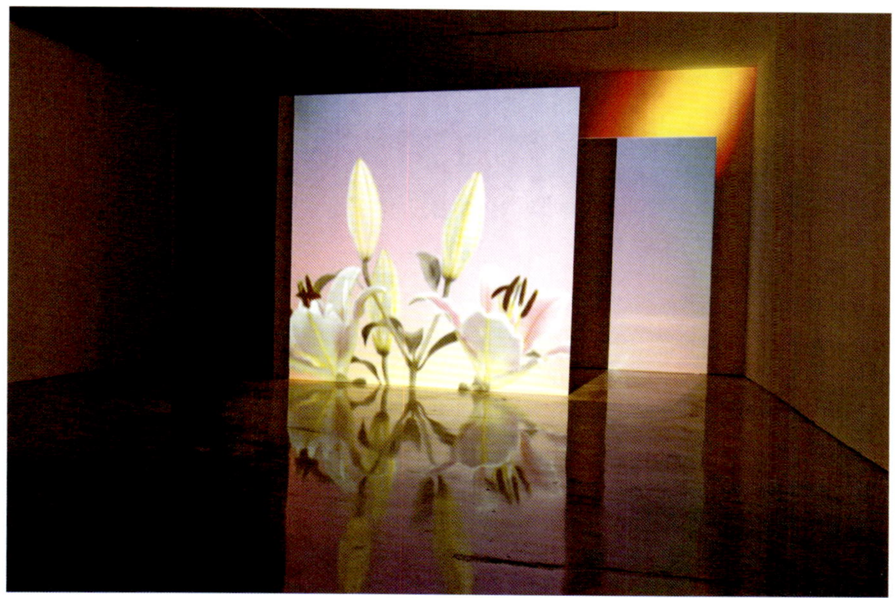

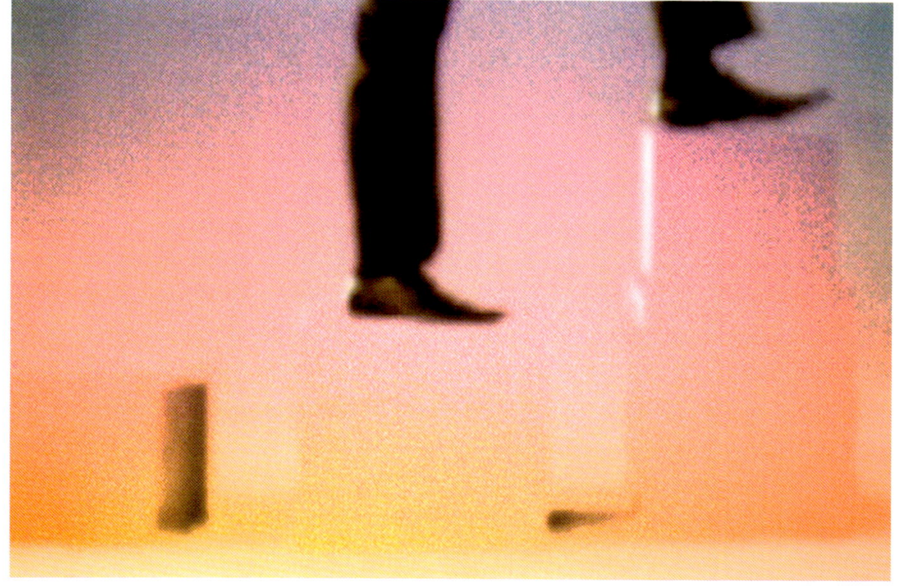

Top: *Belle Captive I*, 2013 (installation view). Digital video projection, color, sound; 6 minutes; bottom: still from *Belle Captive II*, 2013. Digital video projection, color, sound; 6 minutes

Born 1978 in Santa Monica, CA

Lives in San Diego, CA/ Los Angeles, CA

Gaylen Gerber with David Hammons, Sherrie Levine, and Trevor Shimizu

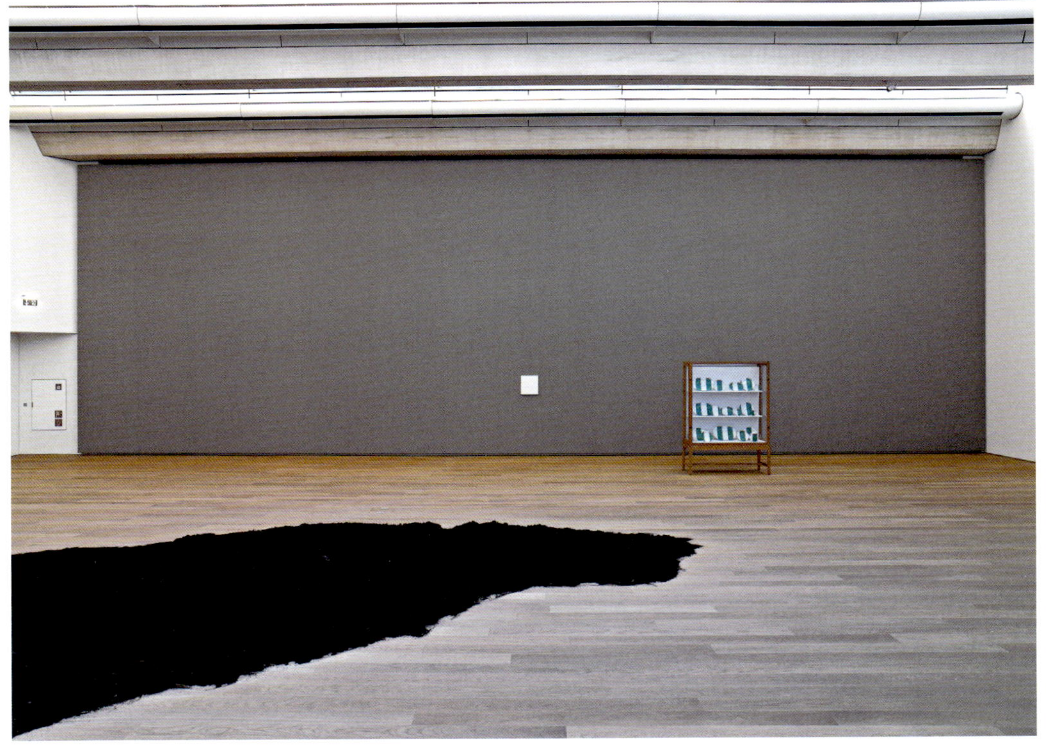

Gaylen Gerber with Daniel Buren (b. 1938) and Rémy Zaugg (1943–2005), *Backdrop/Croisements, 1987, Not Here, 1990–95* (installation view, Musée d'art moderne Grand-Duc Jean, Luxembourg, 2006). Foreground: Joe Scanlan (b. 1961), *Pay Dirt*, 2003

Born 1955 in McAllen, TX

Lives in Chicago, IL

Jeff Gibson

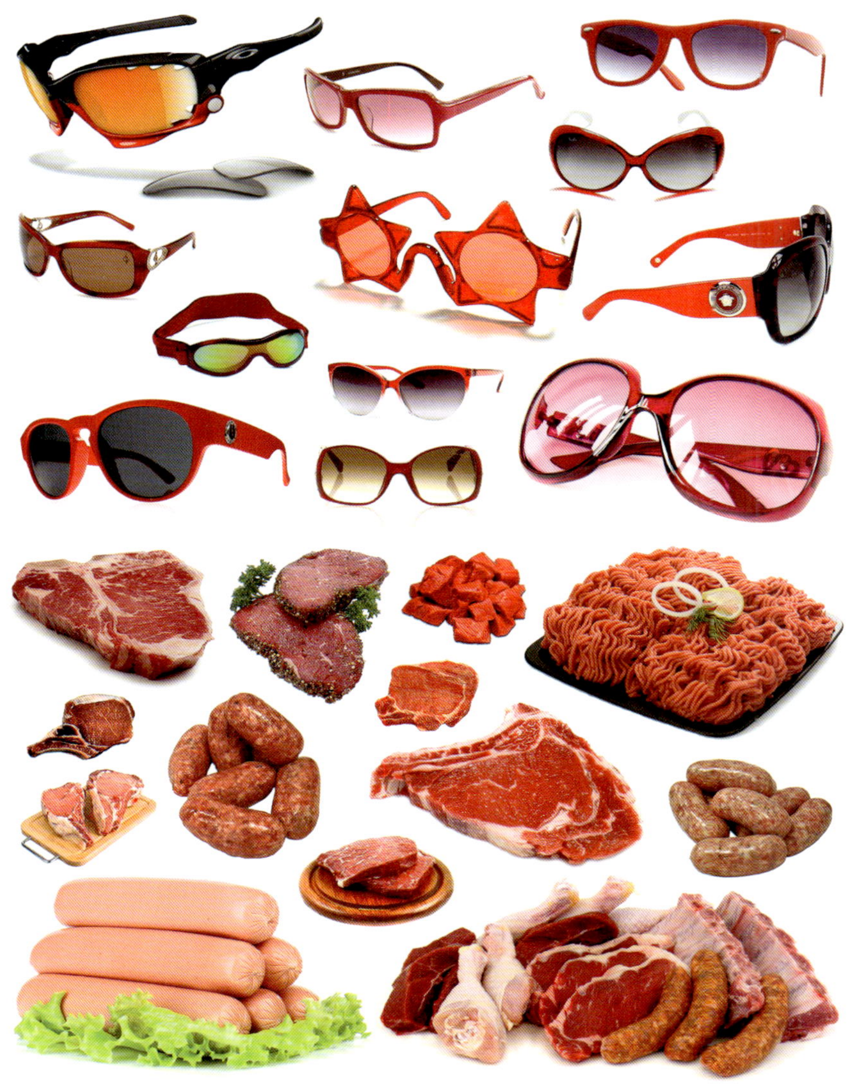

random aggregation *the incidental accumulation of arbitrary information*

Adapted from *Metapoetaesthelicism*, 2013. High-definition video, color, sound; 5:27 minutes

Born 1958 in Brisbane, Australia

Lives in New York, NY

Karl Haendel

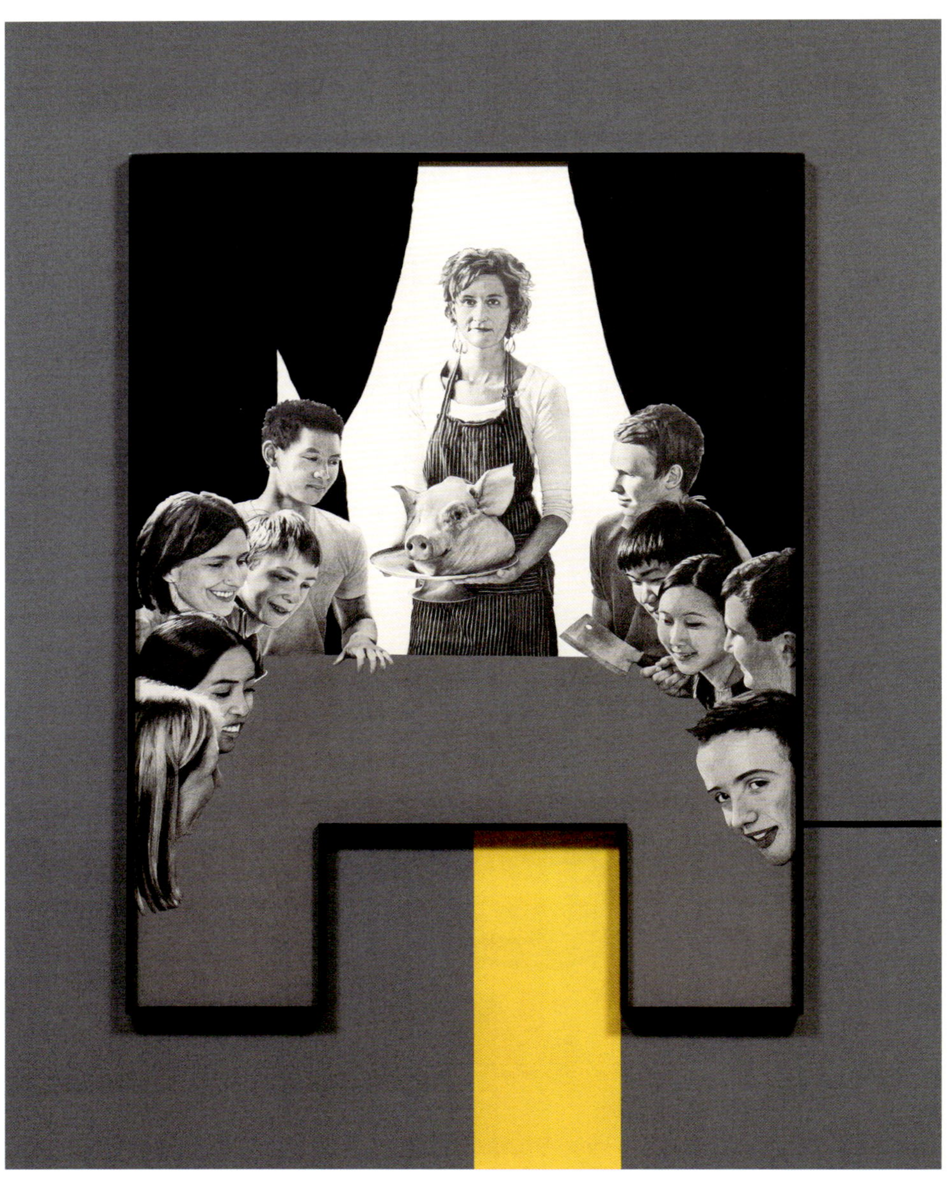

Theme Time—Beginnings, Middles, and Ends, 2013. Enamel and graphite pencil on paper with shaped frame, 68 ¼ × 52 × 2 in. (173.4 × 132.1 × 5.1 cm)

Born 1976 in New York, NY

Lives in Los Angeles, CA

Philip Hanson

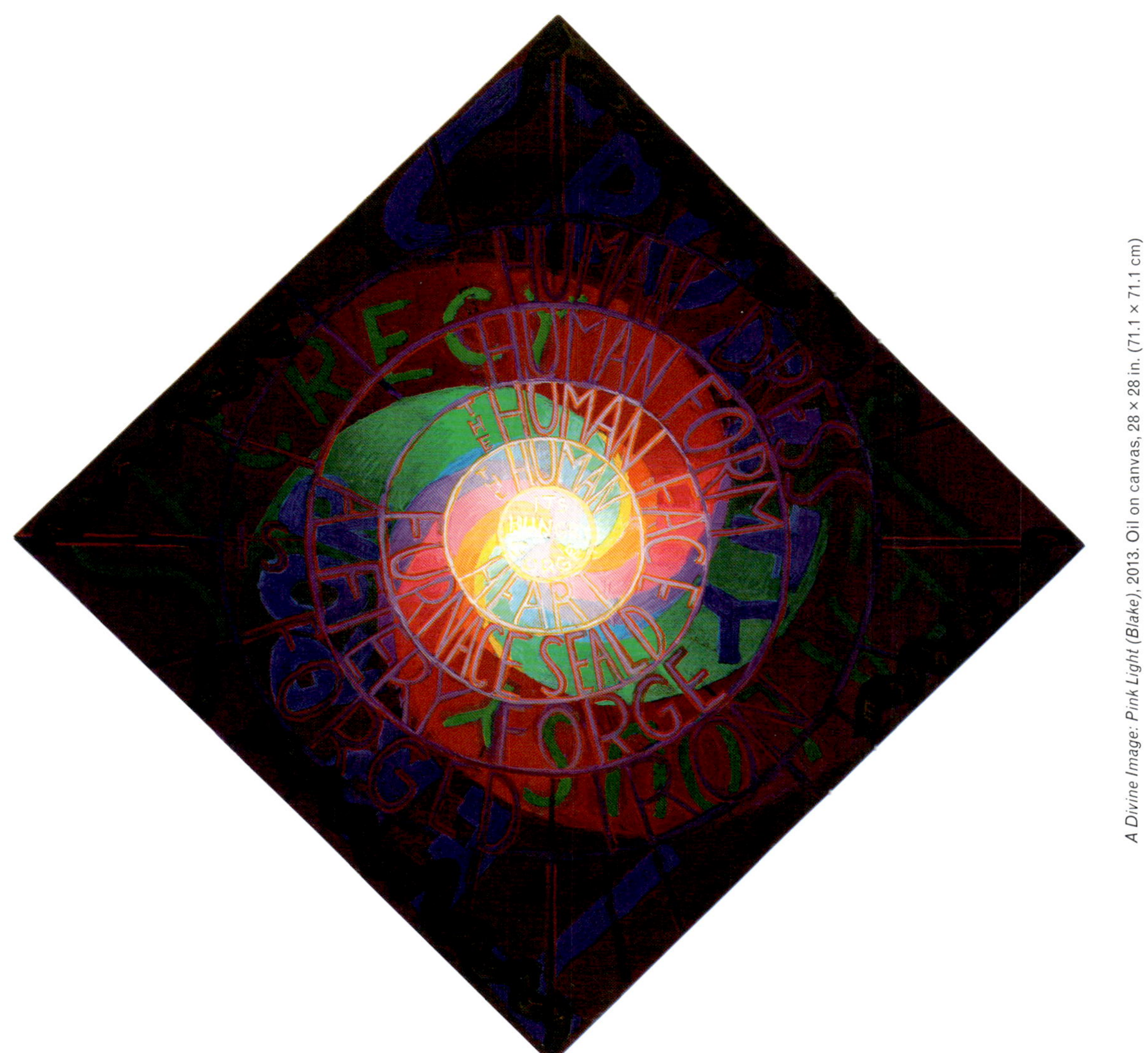

A Divine Image: Pink Light (Blake), 2013. Oil on canvas, 28 × 28 in. (71.1 × 71.1 cm)

Born 1943 in Chicago, IL

Lives in Chicago, IL

Jonn Herschend

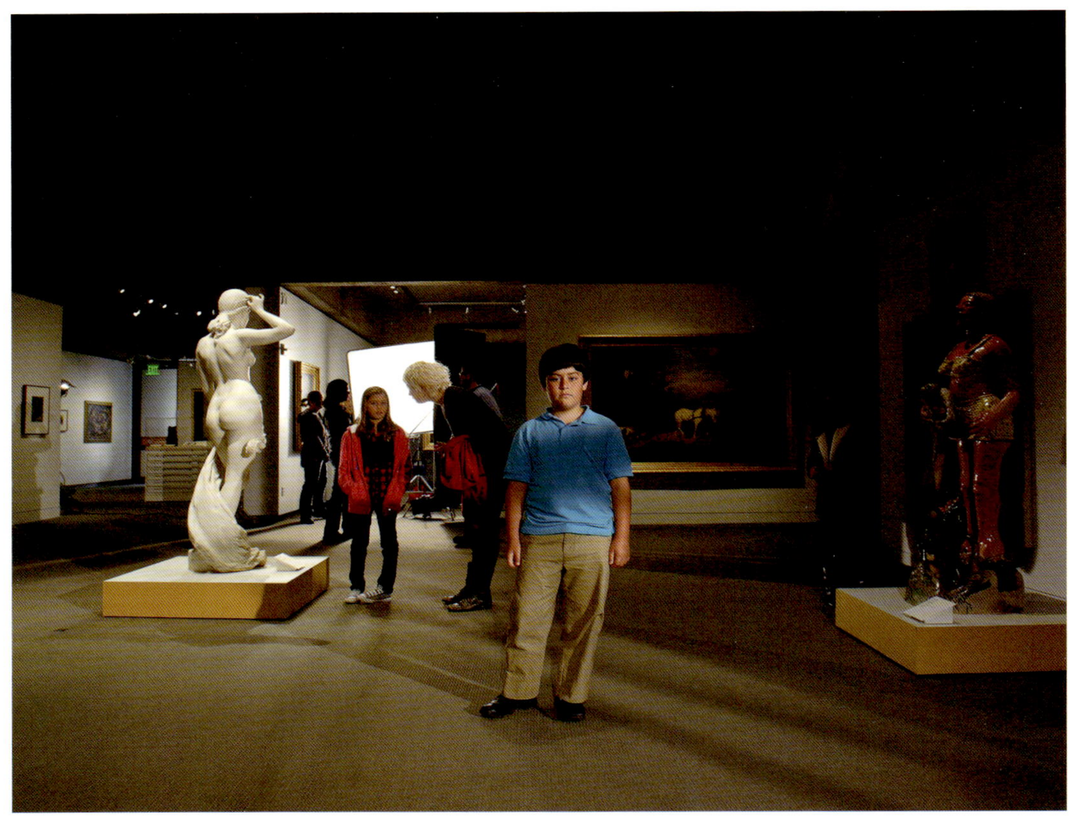

Production still from *Nothing Happens for Long*, 2011. Chromogenic print, 22 × 33 in. (55.9 × 7.6 cm)

Born 1967 in Branson, MO

Lives in San Francisco, CA

Sheila Hicks

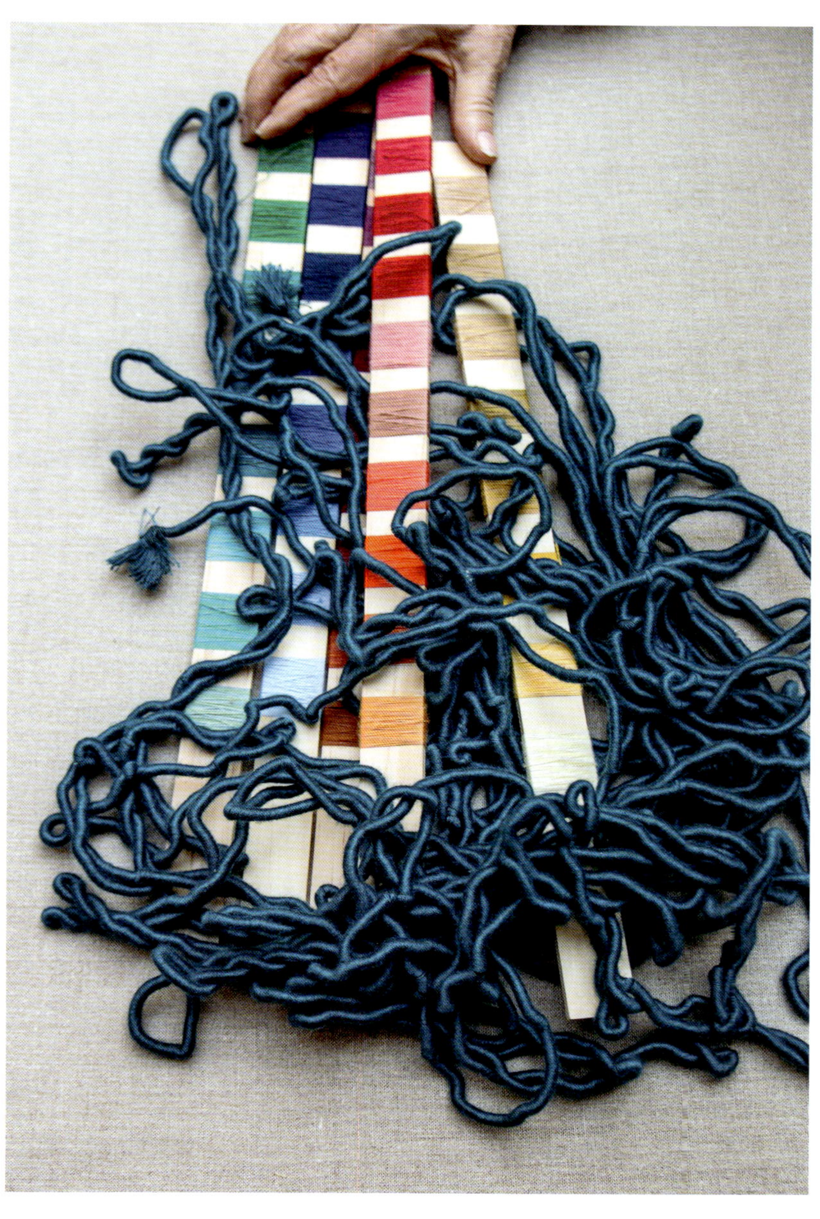

Study for *Pillar of Inquiry / Supple Column*, 2013–14. Photograph by Cristobal Zanartu

Born 1934 in Hastings, NE

Lives in New York, NY/ Paris, France

HOWDOYOUSAY-YAMINAFRICAN?

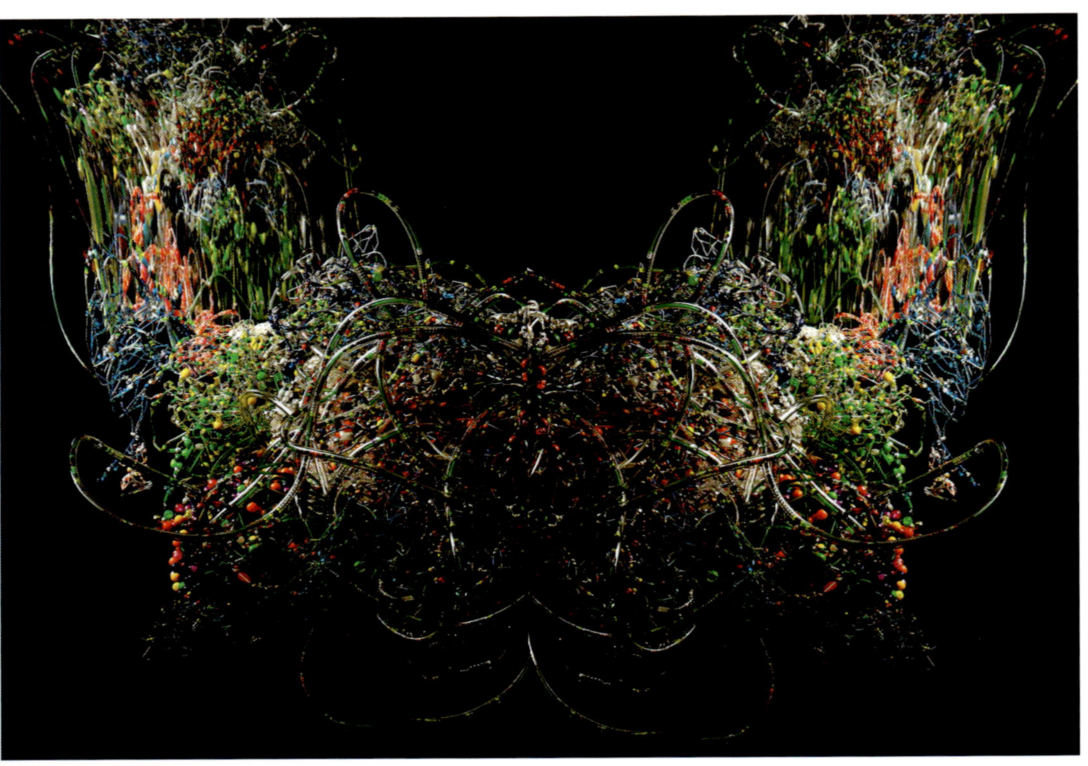

Q-tips, Curlers, Hair Rollers, Love-In-Tokyo Beads, Pony Beads, Seed Beads, Wire, image from the set of *Good Stock On The Dimension Floor*, 2013. High-definition video, color, sound; 37 minutes

HOWDOYOUSAYYAMINAFRICAN? is: Richie Adomako, Beatrice Anderson, Luvinsky Atche, Christa Bell, Ashley Brockington, Monstah Black, Nadia Buckmire, Maureen Catbagan, Felene Cayetano, Dachi Cole, Kirikoo Des, C. Finley, Michael Anthony George, Eliot Glass, Rahi High, Pozsi Kolor, Dominika Ksel, Clynton Lowry, Kobie Maitland, Kyp Malone, Manchildblack, Dawn Lundy Martin, Roland Cory McCutcheon III, Mitch McEwen, Kelsey Lu McJunkins, Annie Lee Moffett, Jasmine Murrell, Tei Okamoto, N. Anthony Richardson, Rachel Rogers, Kim Y. Rufin-Blanchette, Annie Seaton, Sienna Shields, Andre Philip Springer, Suki, Lisa Teasley, Candice Williams, and George Williams

Founded in 2013

A global collective

Jacqueline Humphries

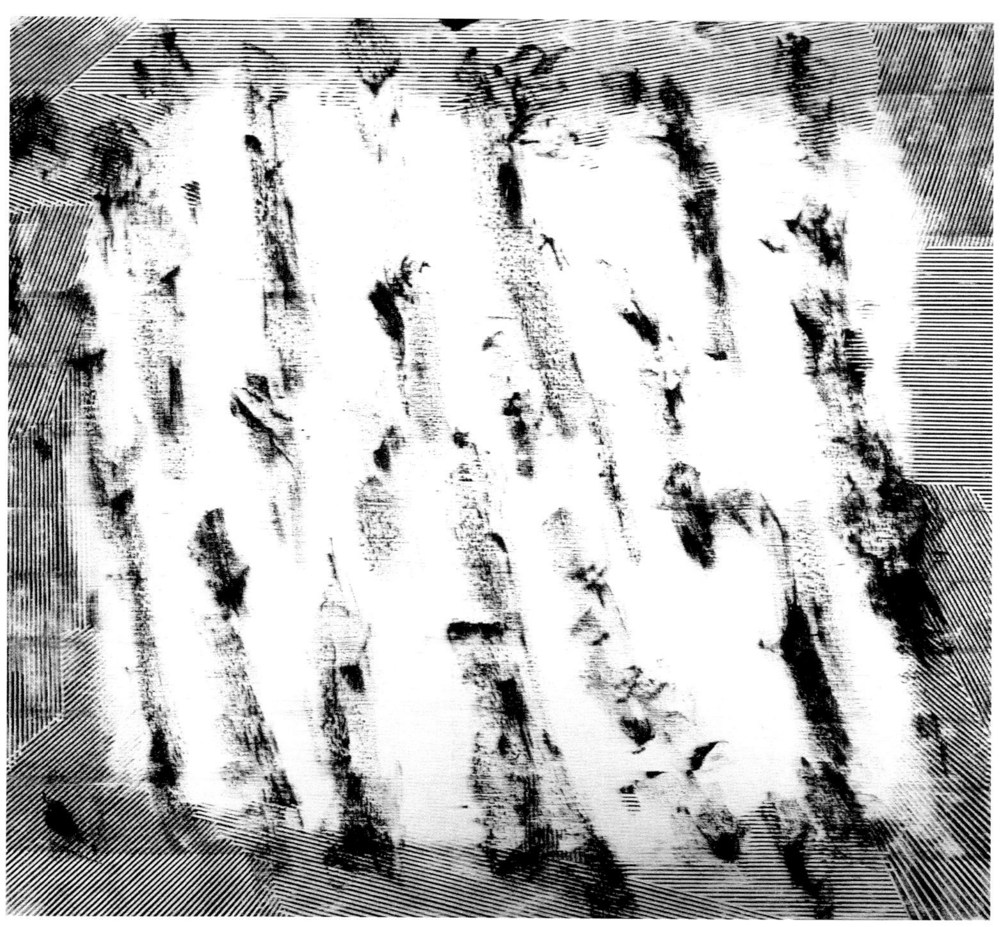

Untitled, 2012. Oil on canvas, 90 × 96 in. (228.6 x 243.8 cm)

Born 1960 in New Orleans, LA

Lives in New York, NY

Doug Ischar

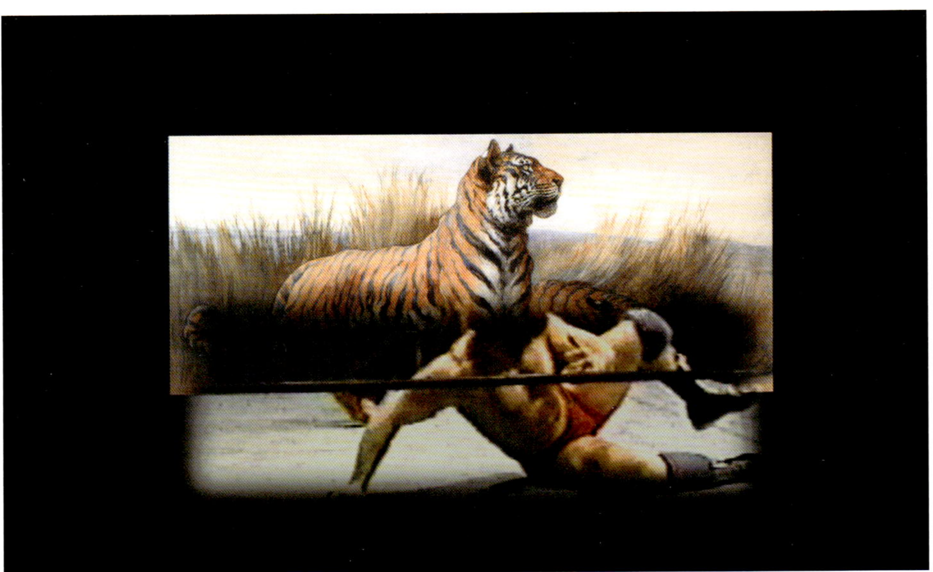

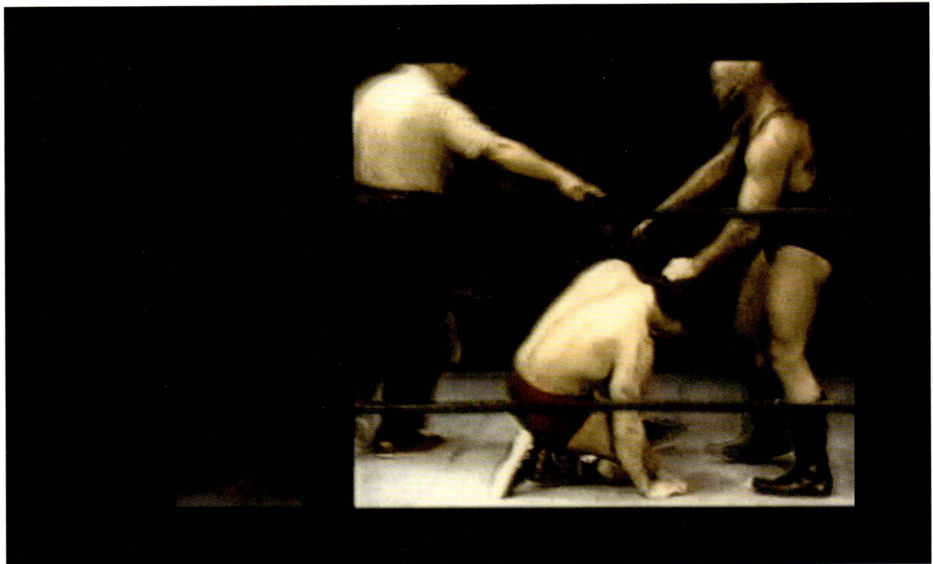

Stills from *Alone With You*, 2011. NTSC video, color, sound; 21 minutes

Born 1948 in Honolulu, HI

Lives in Chicago, IL / Los Angeles, CA

Alex Jovanovich

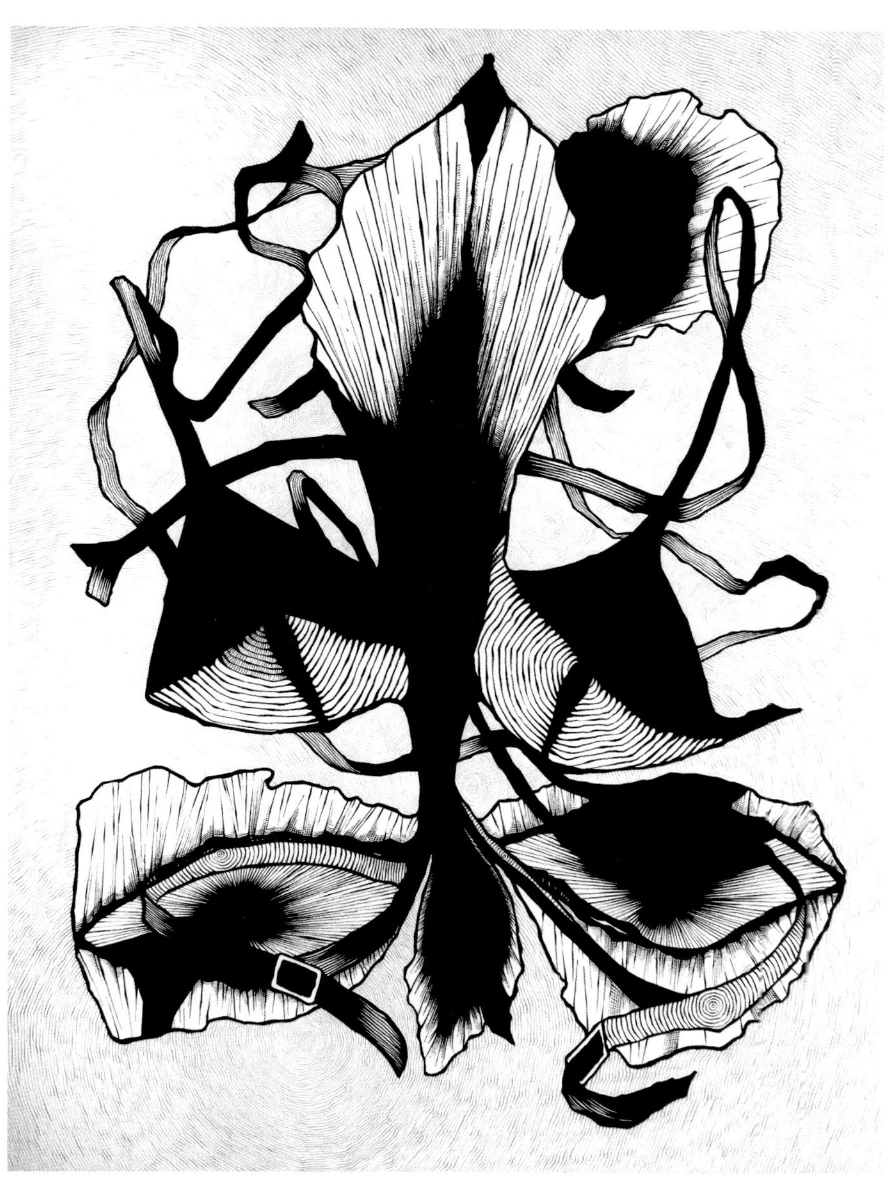

Sister, 2012. India ink and graphite on paper, 15 × 20 in. (38.1 × 50.8 cm)

Born 1975 in Hobart, IN

Lives in Bronx, NY

Ben Kinmont

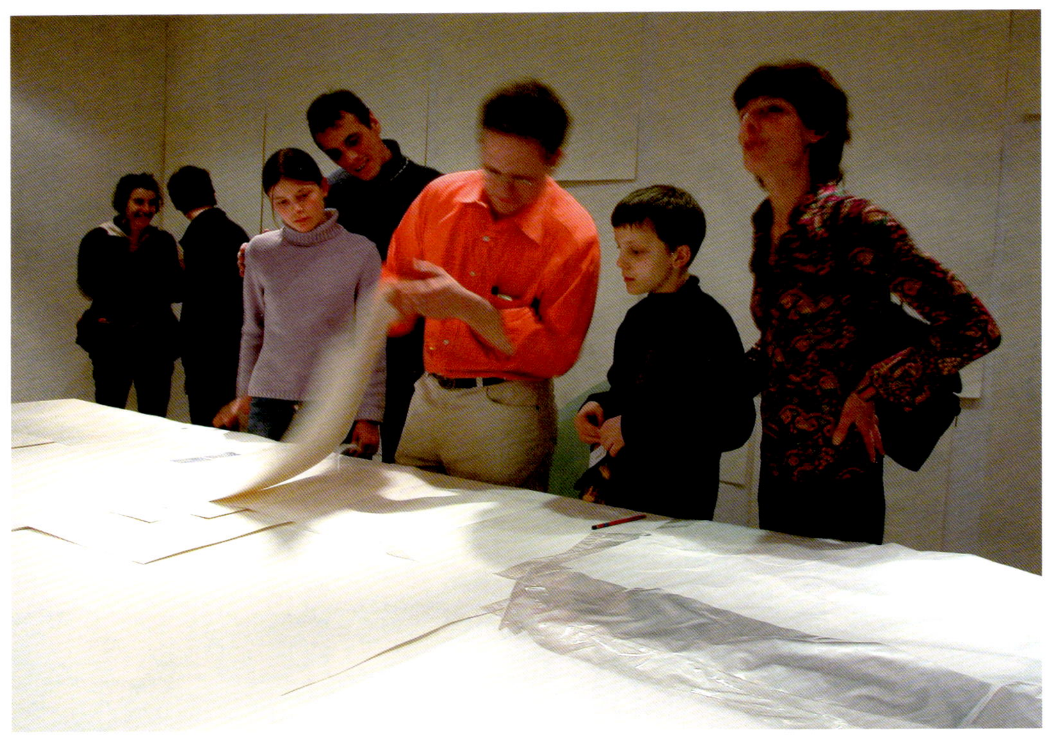

Sshhh, 2002– . Photograph of the distribution of engravings at Cneai, Chatou, France, on February 1, 2003

Born 1963 in
Burlington, VT

Lives in
Sebastopol, CA

Shio Kusaka

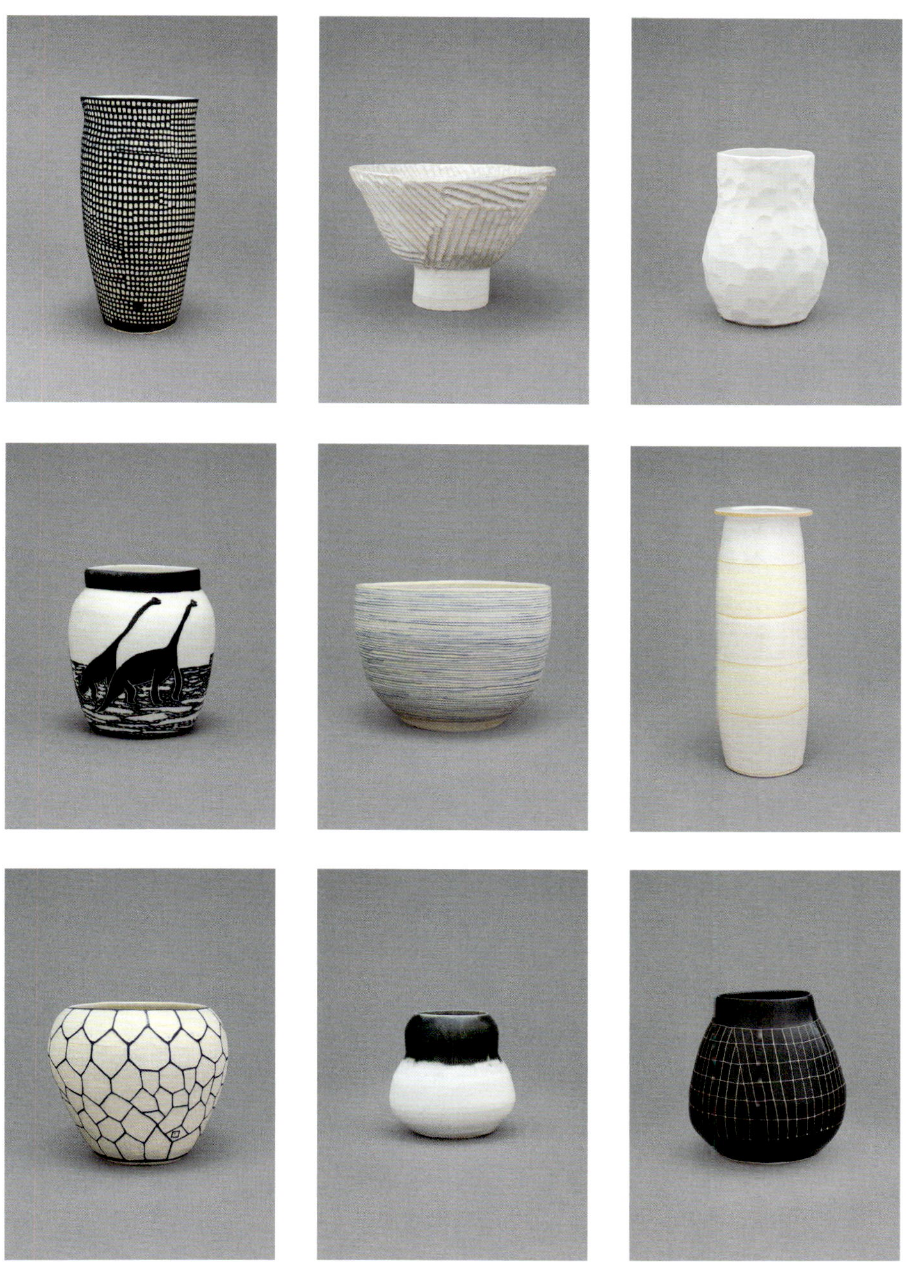

(mark 23), *(pot 9)*, *(carved 26)*, *(dinosaur 2)*, *(stripe 98)*, *(stripe 100)*, *(carved 41)*, *(pot 10)*, *(grid 38)*, 2012–13. Porcelain and stoneware, dimensions variable

Born 1972 in
Morioka, Japan

Lives in
Los Angeles, CA

Chris Larson

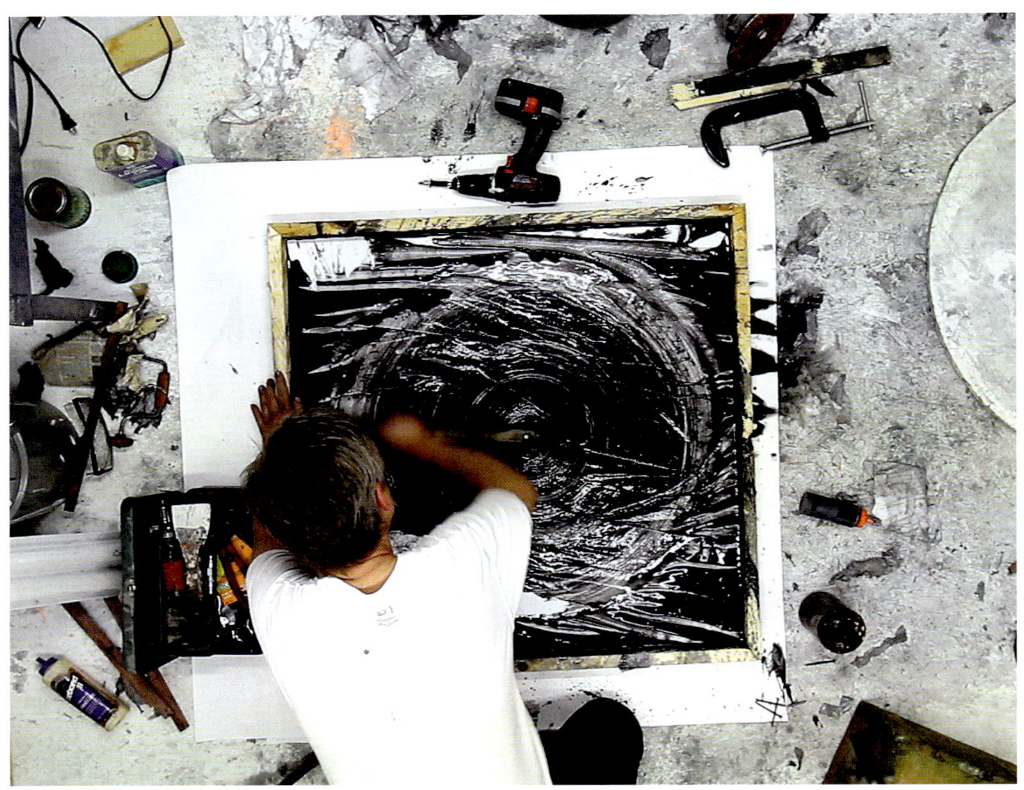

Still from *Heavy Rotation*, 2011. Video, color, sound; 14:44 minutes

Born 1966 in
St. Paul, MN

Lives in
St. Paul, MN

Diego Leclery

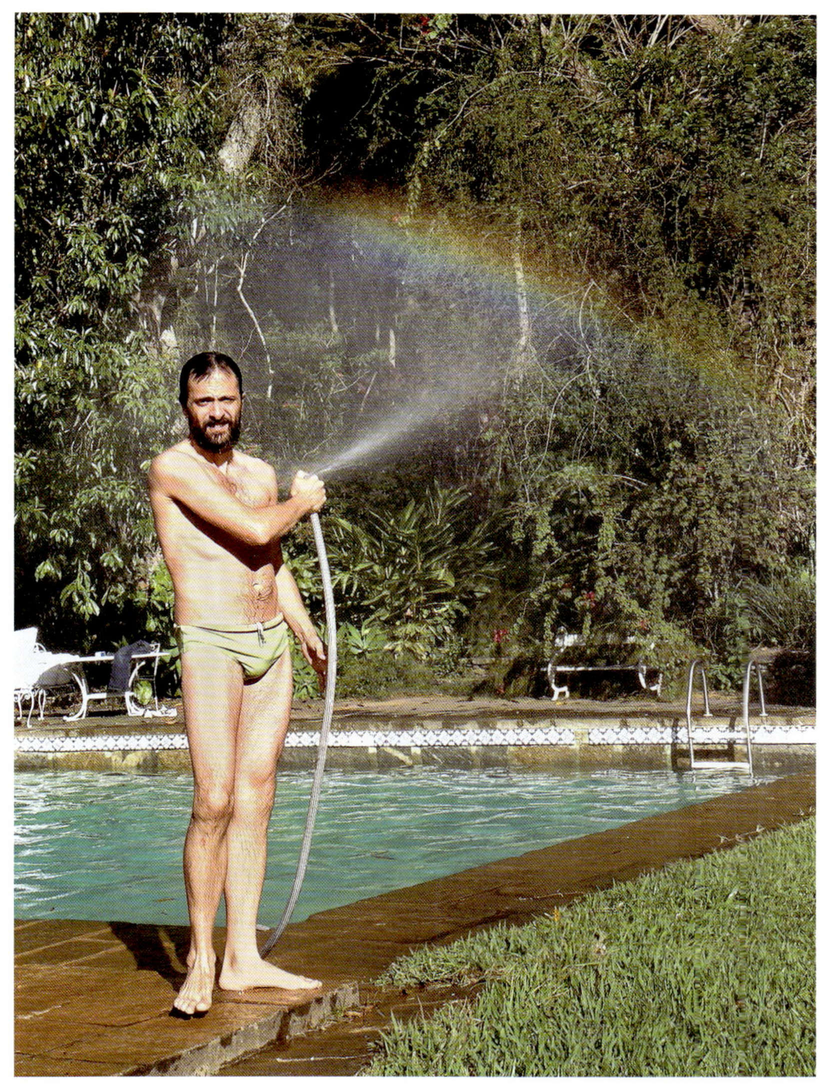

Magic, 2013. Digital image

Born 1978 in Boulogne-Billancourt, France

Lives in New York, NY

Tony Lewis

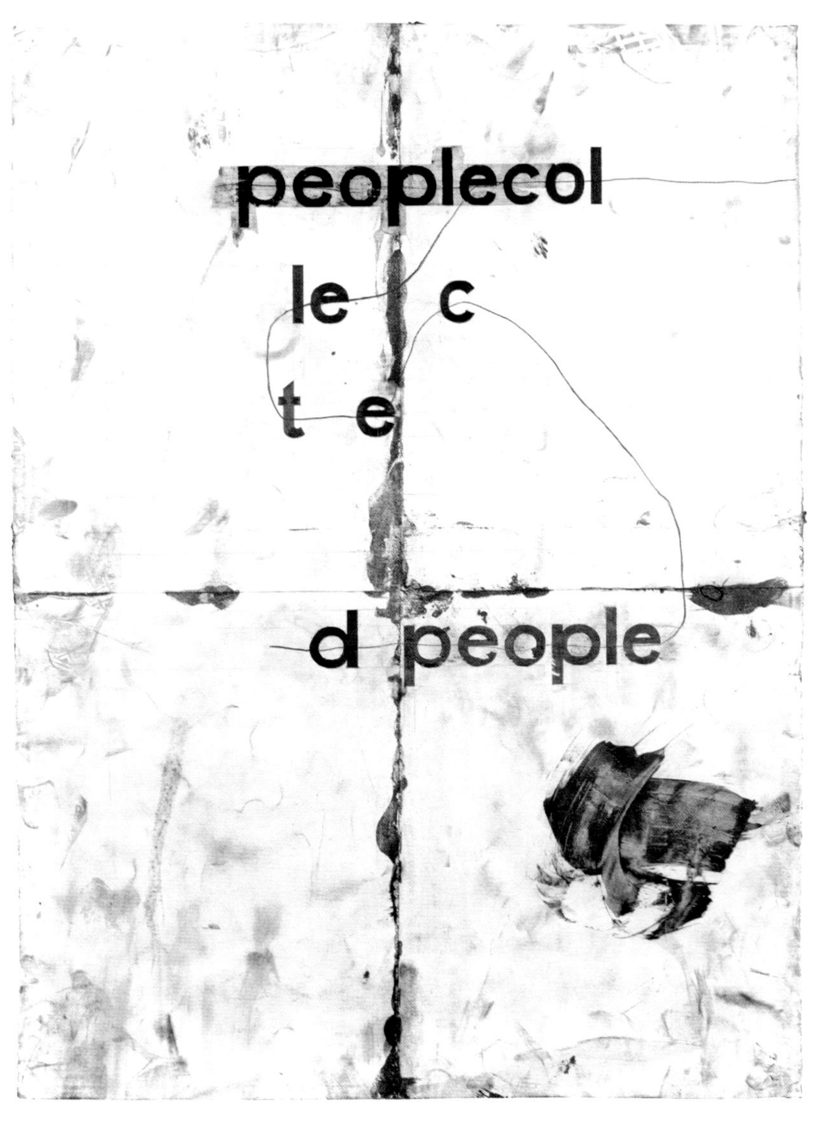

Peoplecol, 2013. Graphite pencil, graphite powder, and tape on paper, 84 × 60 in. (213.4 × 152.4 cm)

Born 1986 in
Los Angeles, CA

Lives in
Chicago, IL

Pam Lins   Amy Sillman

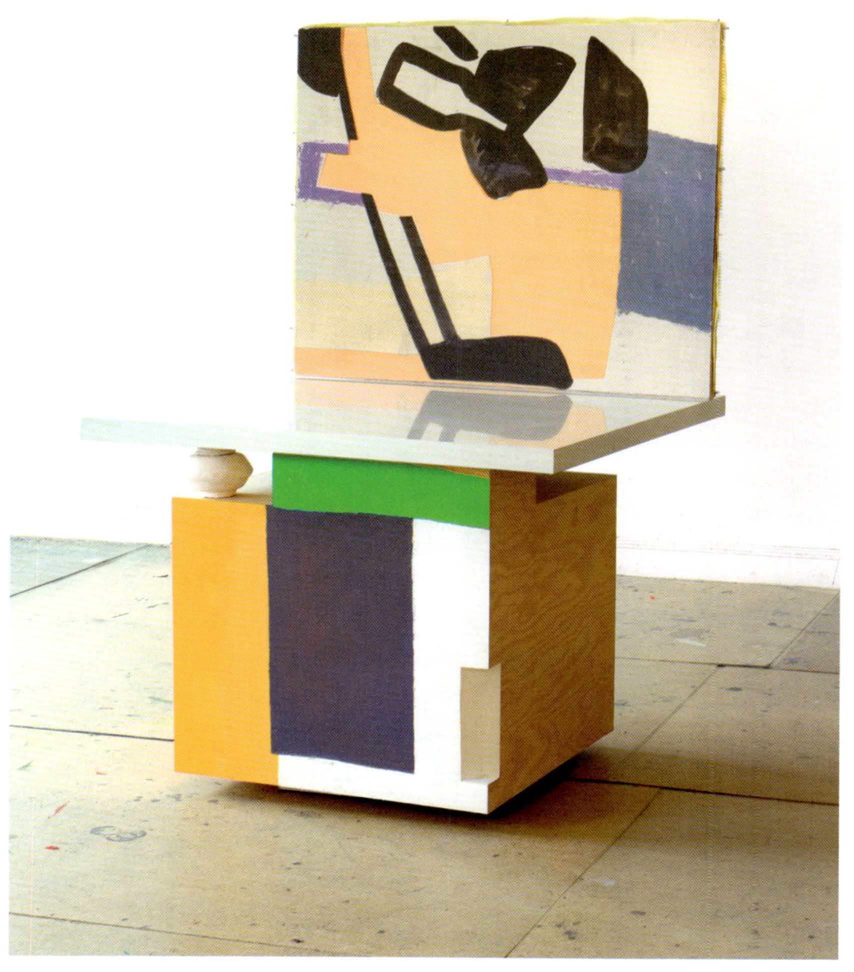

I Placed a Jar in Tennessee, 2013–14 (work in progress). Plywood, oil, lacquer, plaster, medium-density fiberboard, unglazed stoneware, inkjet on canvas, and rice paper, approx. 72 × 45 × 45 in. (182.9 × 114.3 × 114.3 cm)

Born 1957 in Lake Forest, IL
Lives in Brooklyn, NY

Born 1955 in Detroit, MI
Lives in Brooklyn, NY

Ken Lum

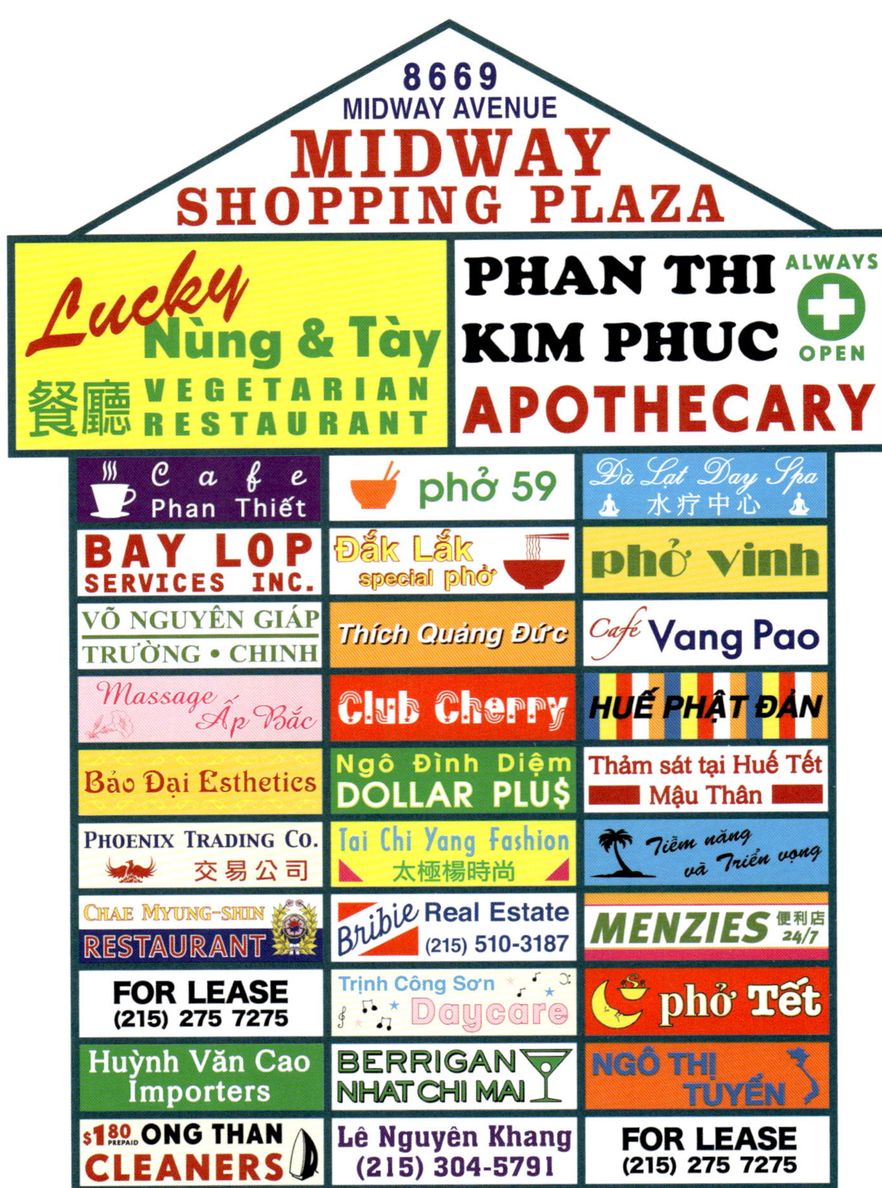

Artist rendering for *Midway Shopping Plaza*, 2014. Powder-coated aluminum and screenprinted plexiglass, 204 × 150 in. (518.2 × 381 cm)

Born 1956 in
Vancouver, BC, Canada

Lives in
Philadelphia, PA

Shana Lutker

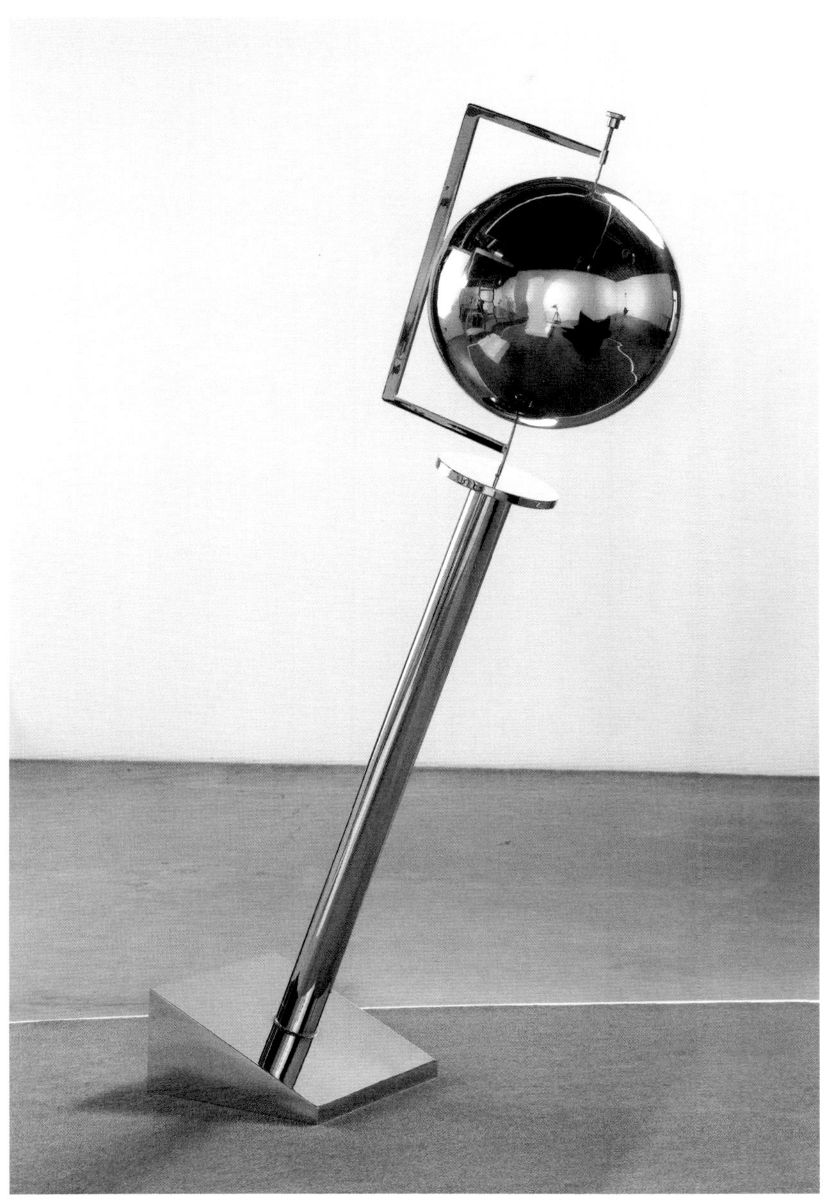

I Swallow Jewelry, 2013. Nickel-chromed steel, 57 × 31 × 13 in. (144.8 × 78.7 × 33 cm)

Born 1978 in Northport, NY

Lives in Los Angeles, CA

John Mason

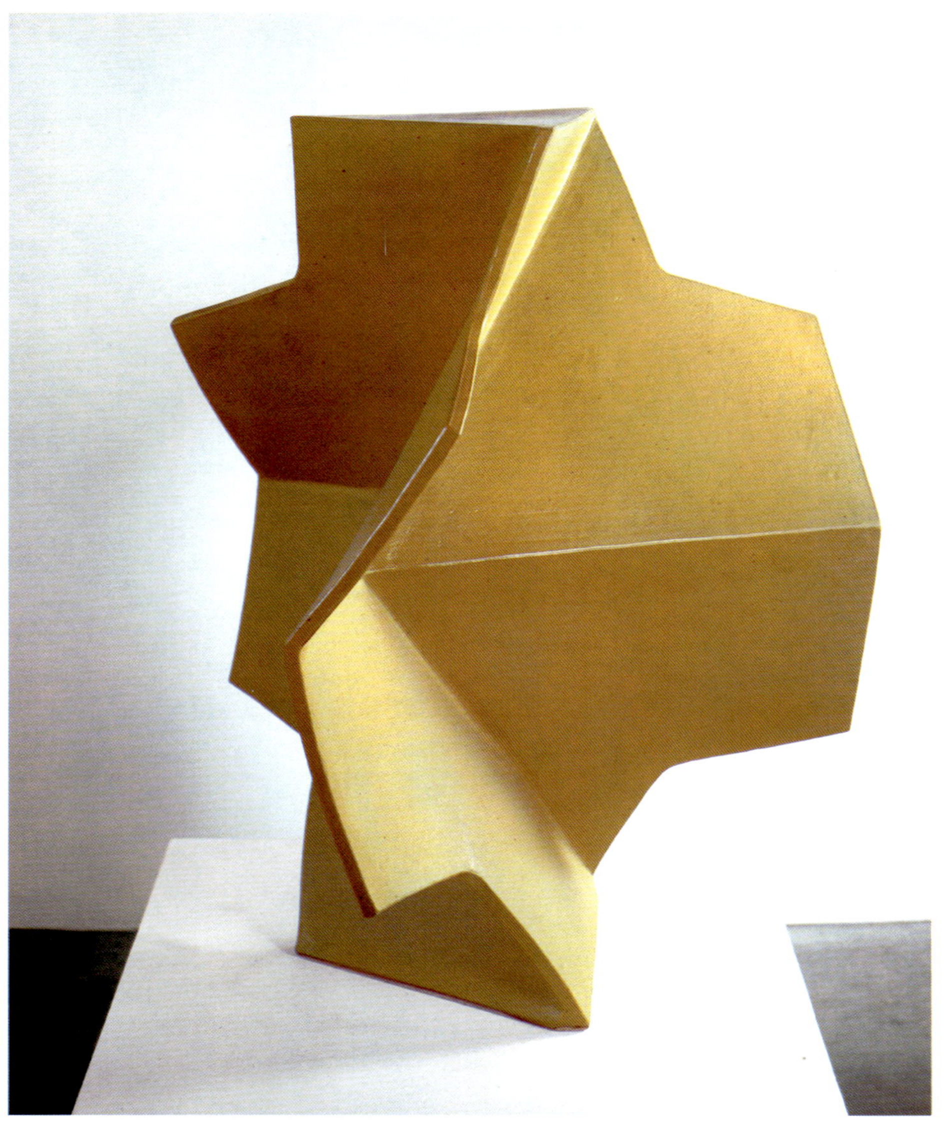

Folded Cross, Yellow-Gold, 2001–02. Ceramic, 39 × 31 ½ × 24 in. (99.1 × 80 × 61 cm)

Born 1927 in Madrid, NE

Lives in Los Angeles, CA

Suzanne McClelland

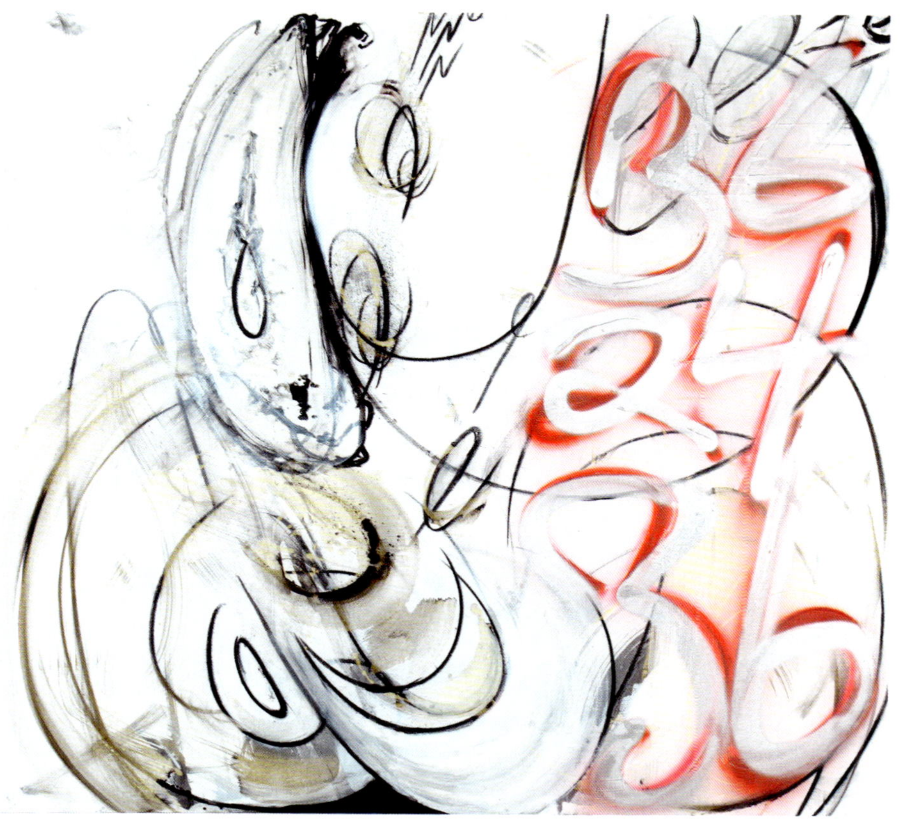

Untitled, (36-24-36 a winning hand), 2013. Charcoal, dry pigment, polymer, and spray paint on linen, 84 × 72 in. (213.4 × 182.9 cm)

Born 1959 in Jacksonville, FL

Lives in Brooklyn, NY

Joshua Mosley

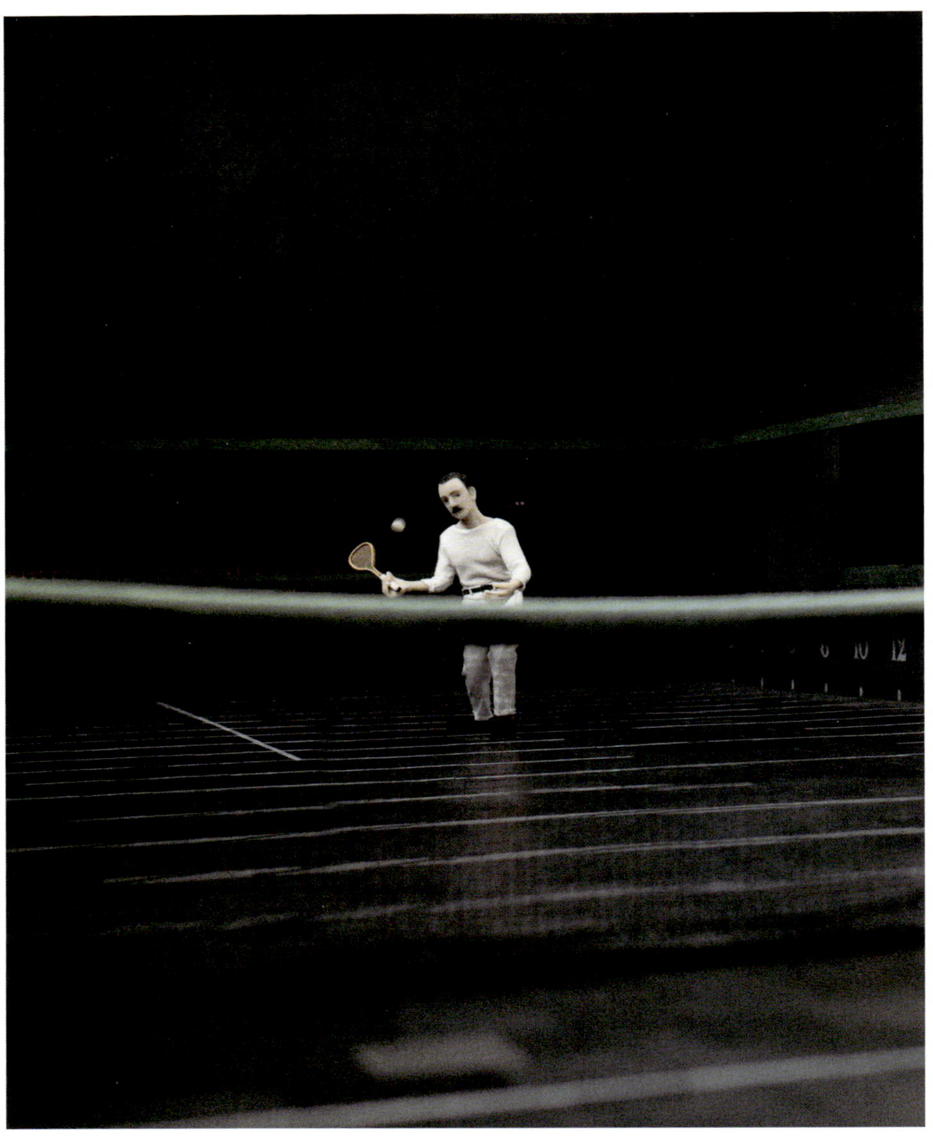

Jeu de Paume, 2014. Mixed-media animation

Born 1974 in
Dallas, TX

Lives in
Philadelphia, PA

Dona Nelson

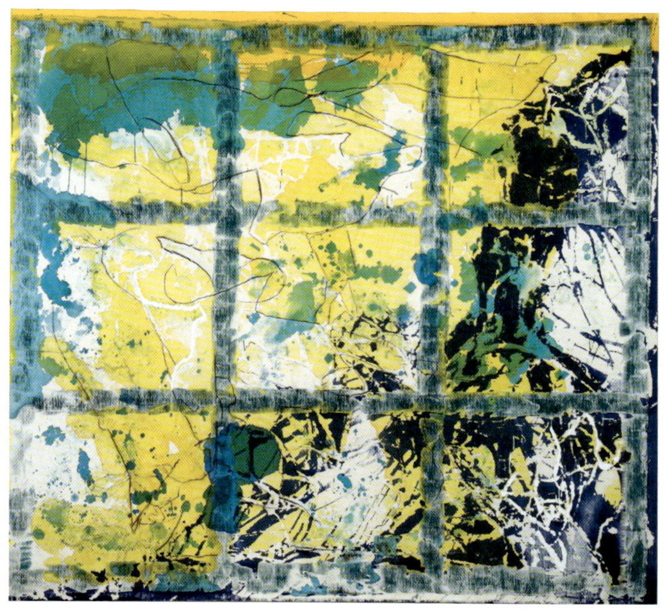

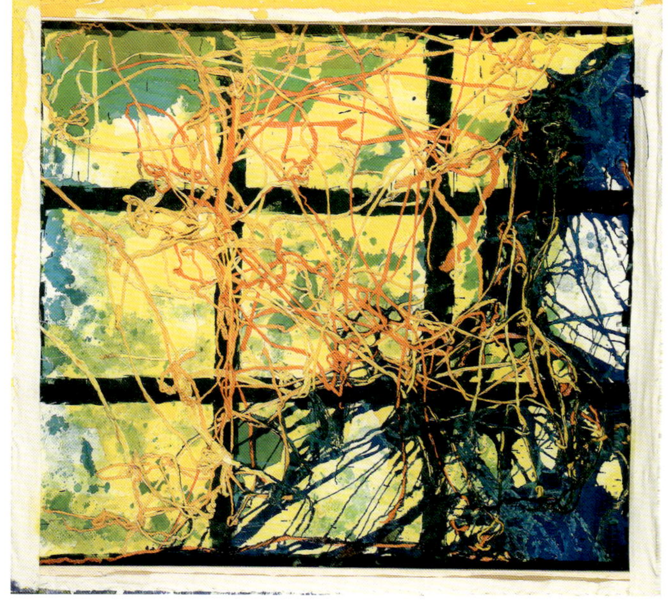

Okie Dokie (front and back), 2008. Dyed cheesecloth and acrylic on canvas, 78 × 83 in. (198.1 × 210.8 cm)

Born 1947 in
Grand Island, NE

Lives in Lansdale, PA/
New York, NY

Joel Otterson

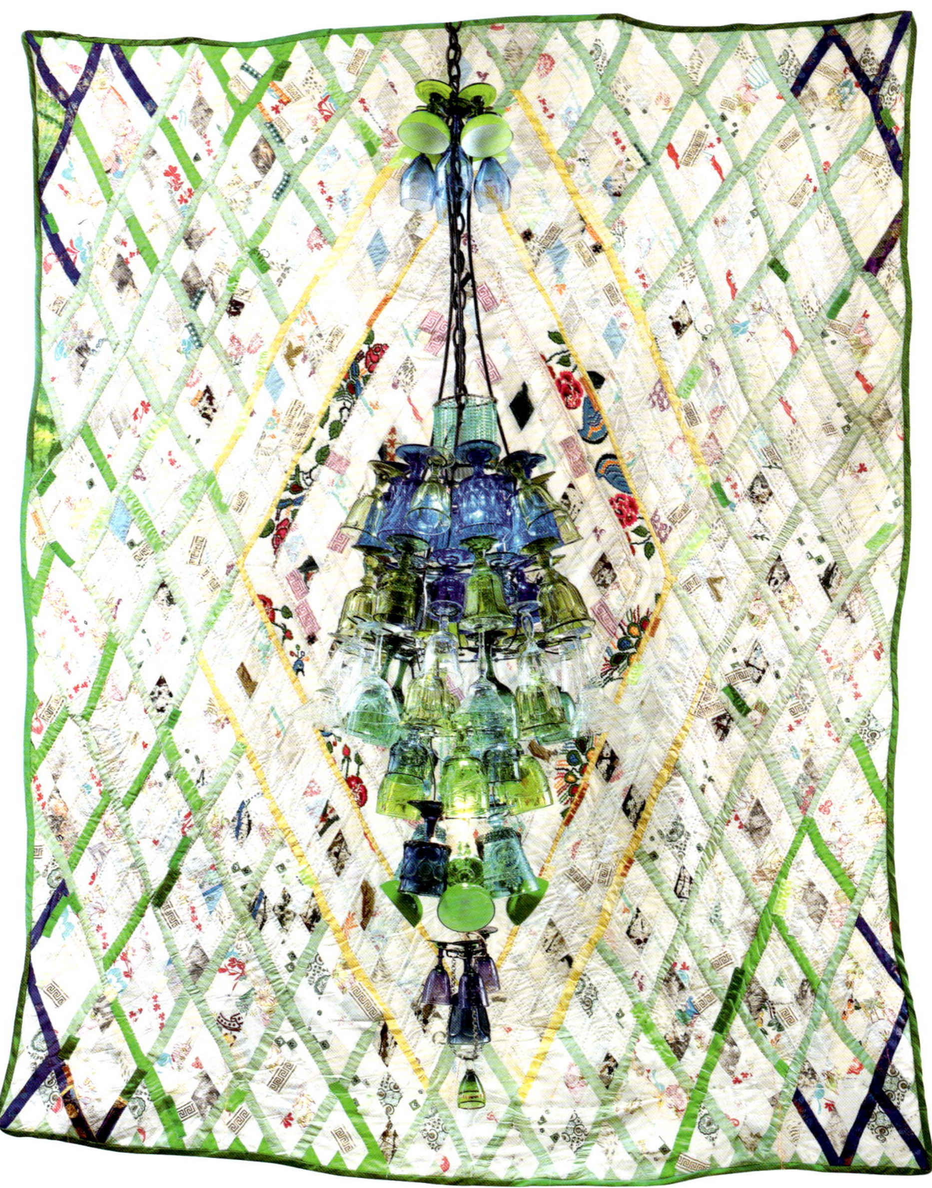

84 Bottoms Up, 2013. 84 vintage crystal and glass goblets, steel, metal chain, aluminum, and electrical parts, 76 × 22 × 22 in. (193 × 55.9 × 55.9 cm) in front of *Rags to Riches*, 1993–2013. Patchwork and hand-quilted fabrics, 84 × 72 in. (213.4 × 182.9 cm)

Born 1959 in Los Angeles, CA

Lives in Los Angeles, CA

Laura Owens

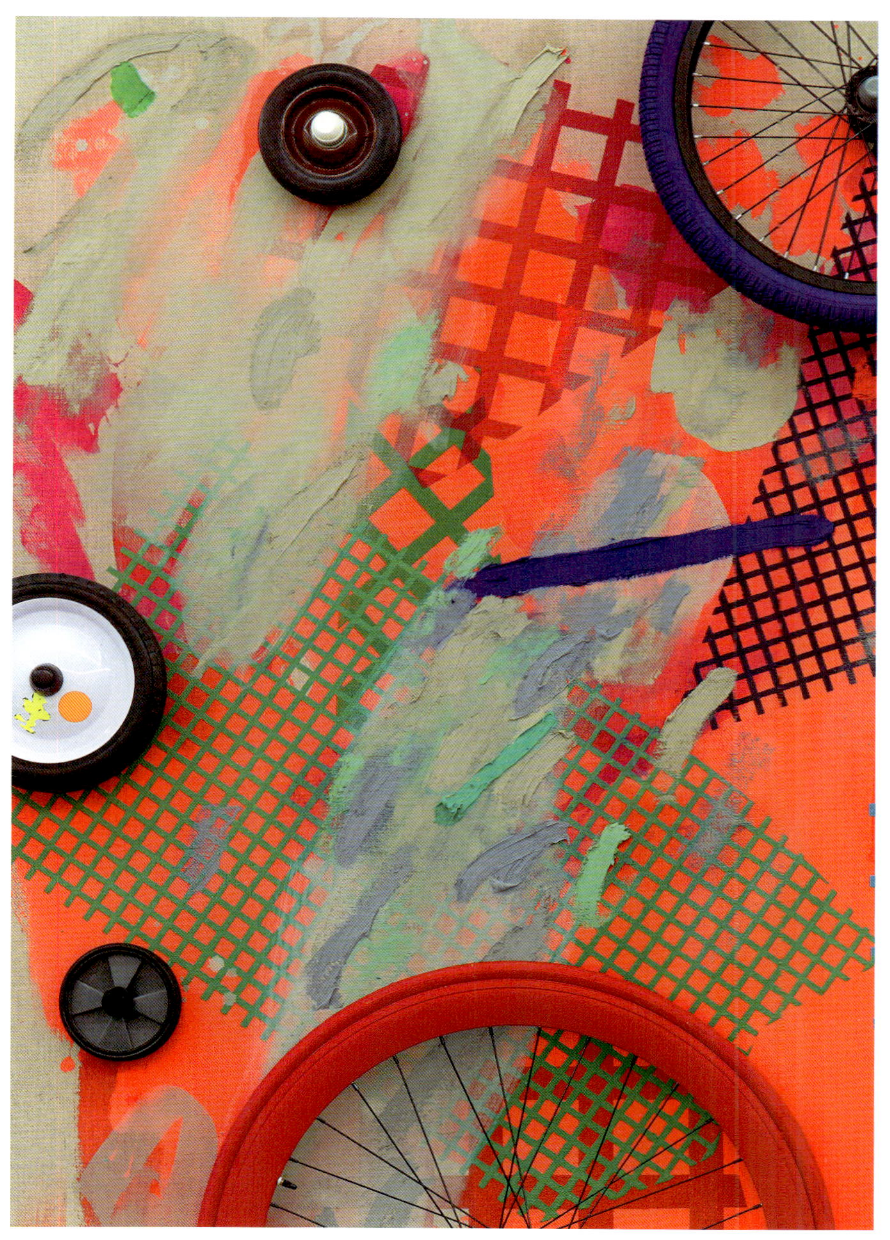

Untitled, 2013 (detail). Oil, vinyl paint, acrylic, and wheels on linen, 108 × 84 in. (274.3 × 213.4 cm)

Born 1970 in Euclid, OH

Lives in Los Angeles, CA

Sara Greenberger Rafferty

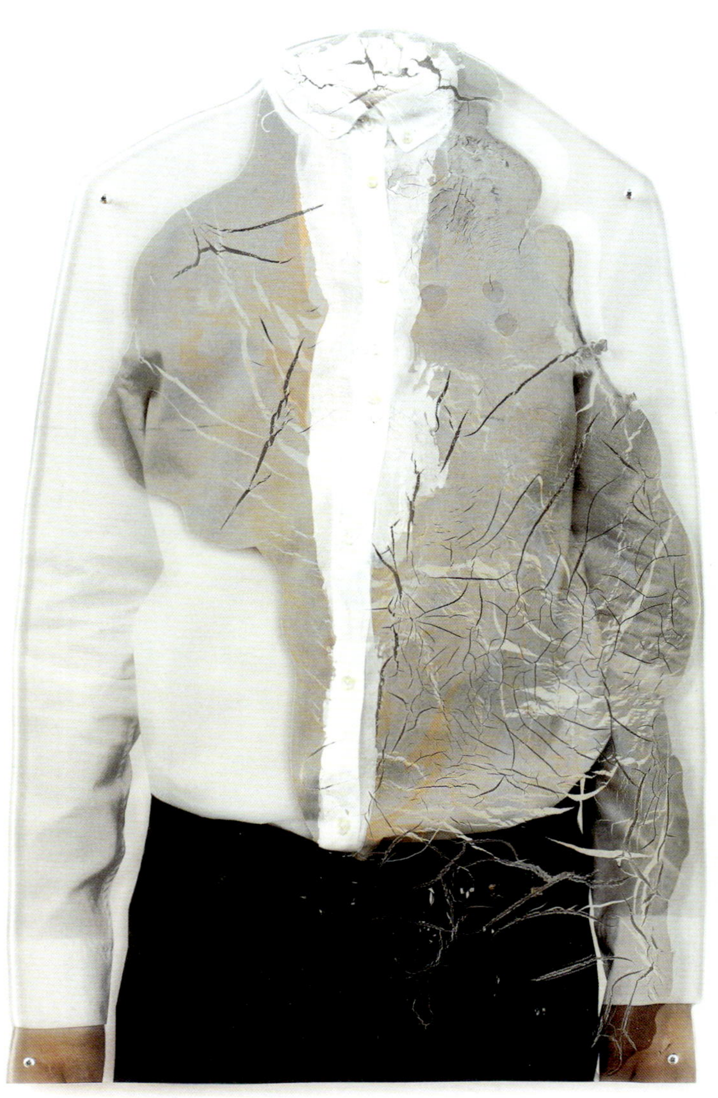

Untitled, 2013. Acrylic and inkjet print on acetate, plexiglass, and hardware, approx. 35 ¾ × 24 in. (90.8 × 61 cm). Private Collection

Born 1978 in Evanston, IL

Lives in Brooklyn, NY

David Robbins

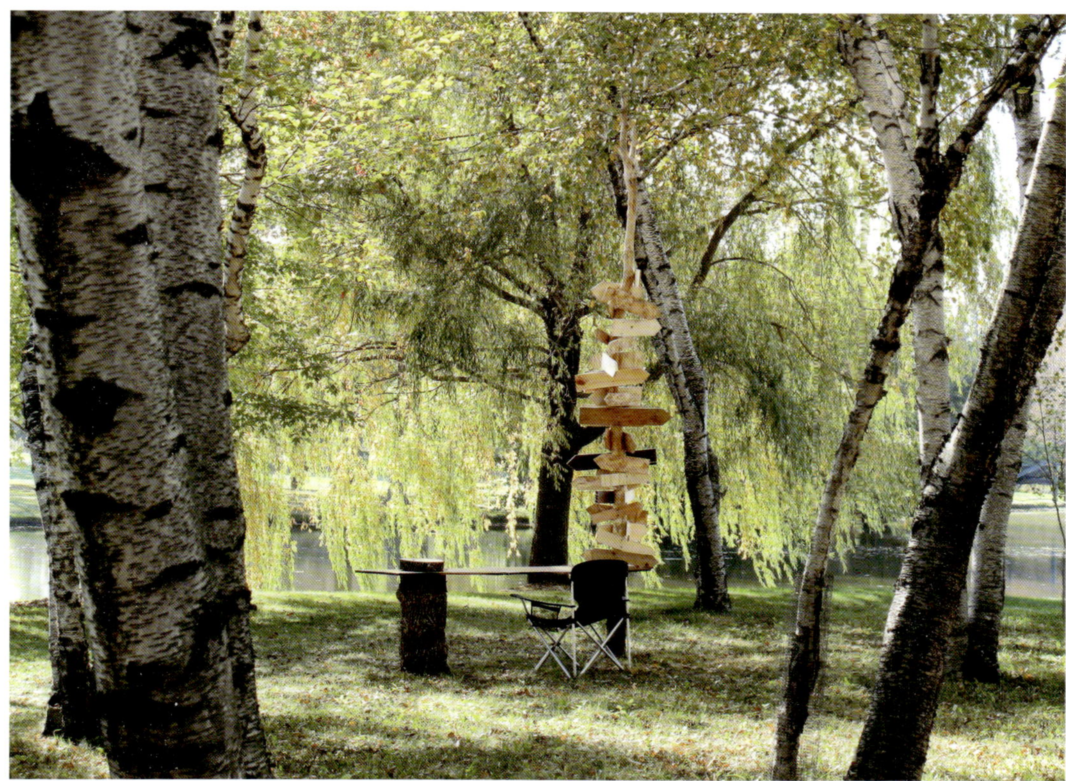

Open-Air Writing Desk (Milwaukee Version), 2012 (installation view, Lynden Sculpture Garden, Milwaukee, 2012). Wood and glass, 144 × 36 × 110 in. (365.8 × 91.4 × 279.4 cm)

Born 1957 in Whitefish Bay, WI

Lives in Shorewood, WI

Sterling Ruby

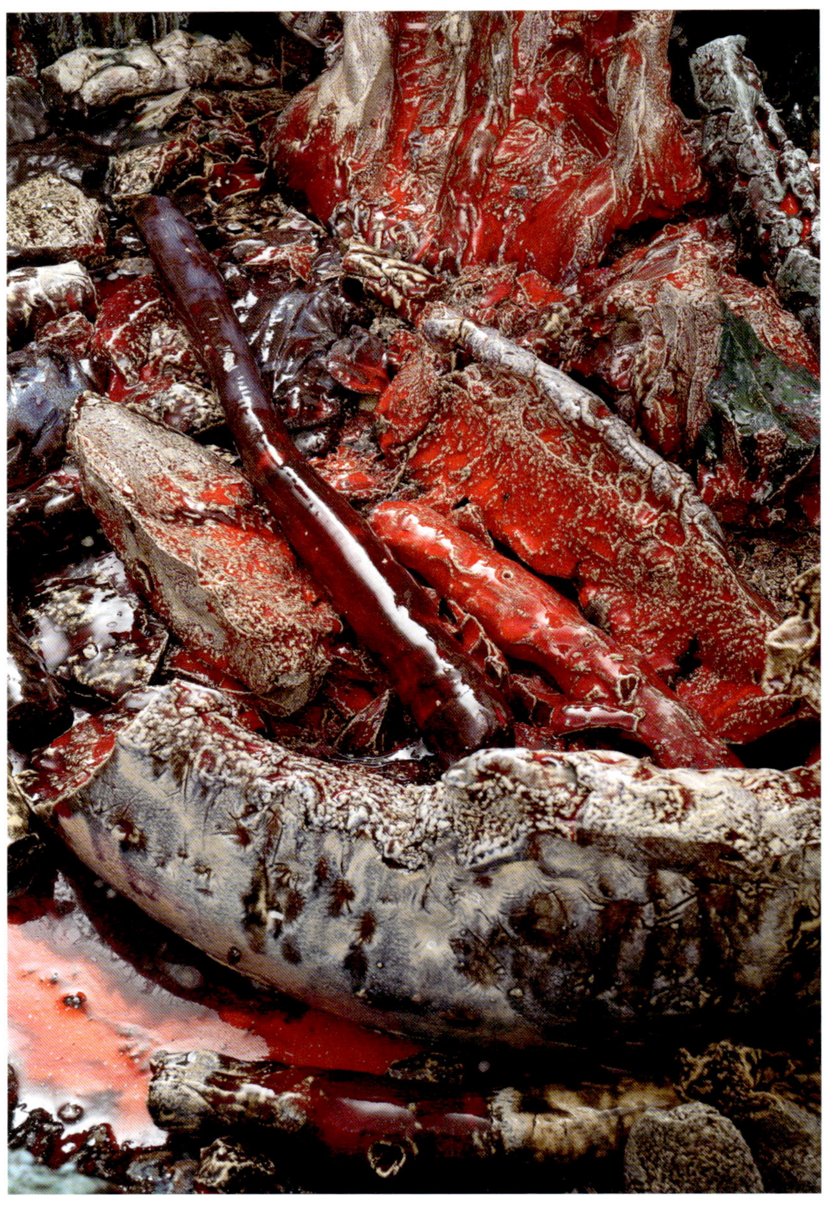

Basin Theology/Talwin + Ritalin, 2013. Ceramic, 28 ¼ × 45 × 45 in. (71.8 × 114.3 × 114.3 cm). Private Collection

Born 1972 in
Bitburg, Germany

Lives in
Los Angeles, CA

Peter Schuyff

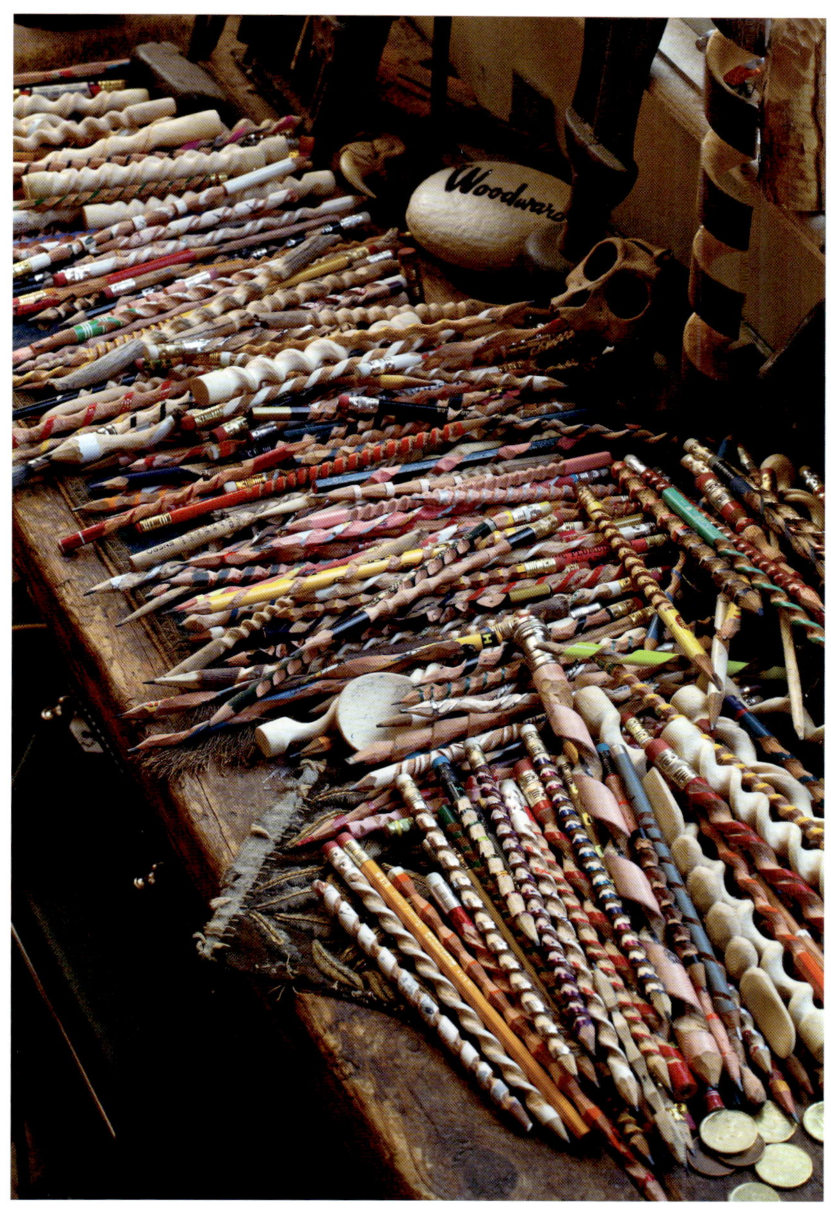

Sans Papier, 2004–06. Carved pencils and sticks, dimensions variable

Born 1958 in Baarn, The Netherlands

Lives in Amsterdam, The Netherlands

Amy Sillman

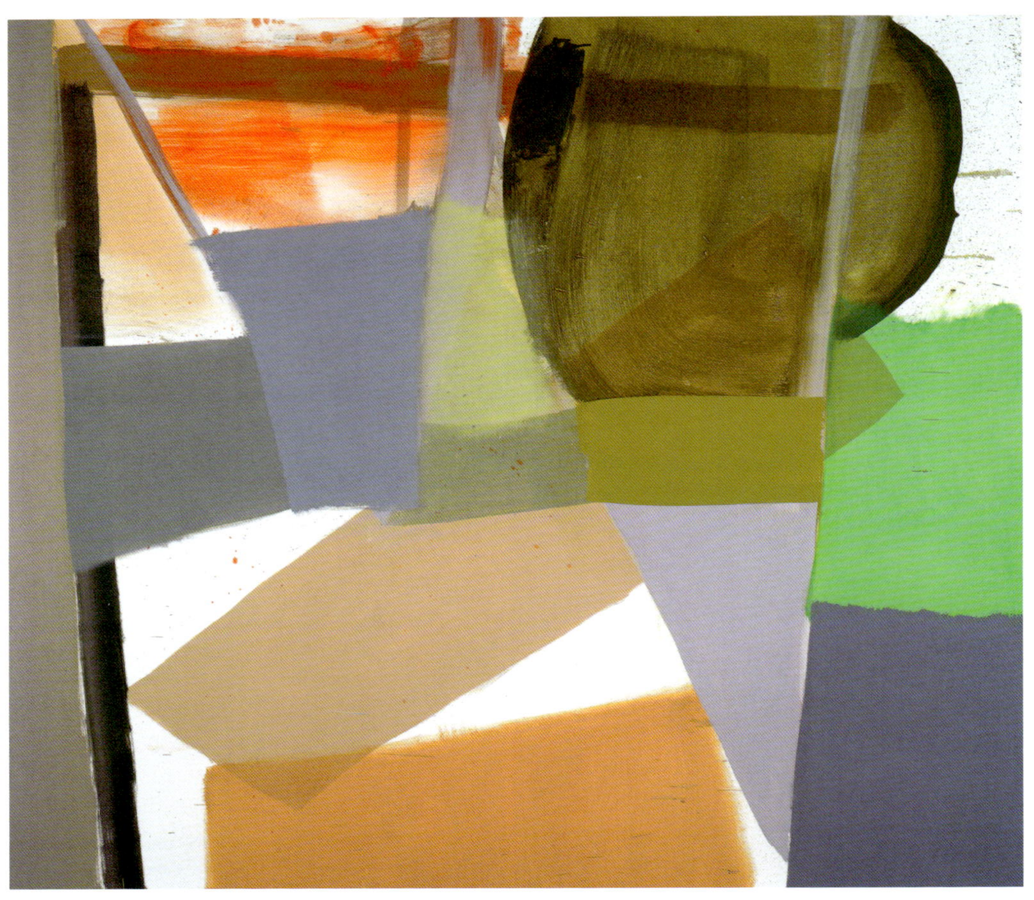

Fast Painting 2, 2013. Oil on canvas, 66 × 75 in. (167.6 × 190.5 cm)

Born 1955 in Detroit, MI

Lives in Brooklyn, NY

Emily Sundblad

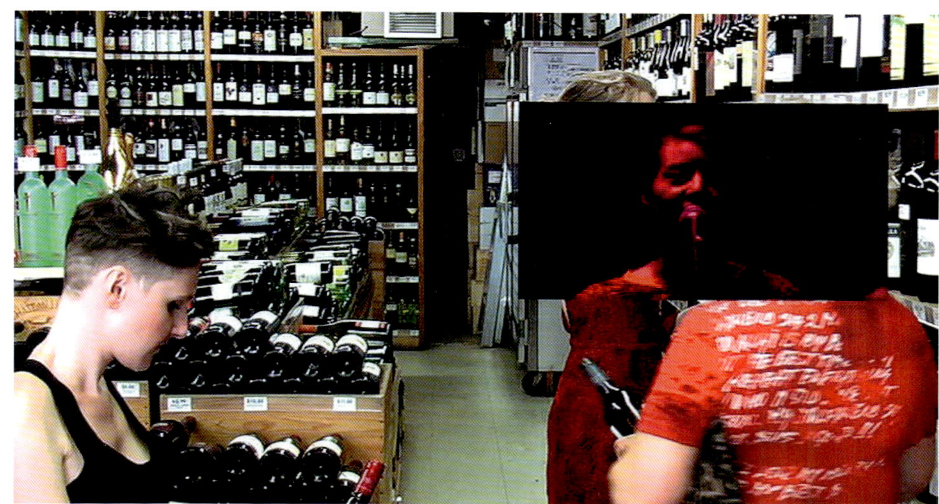

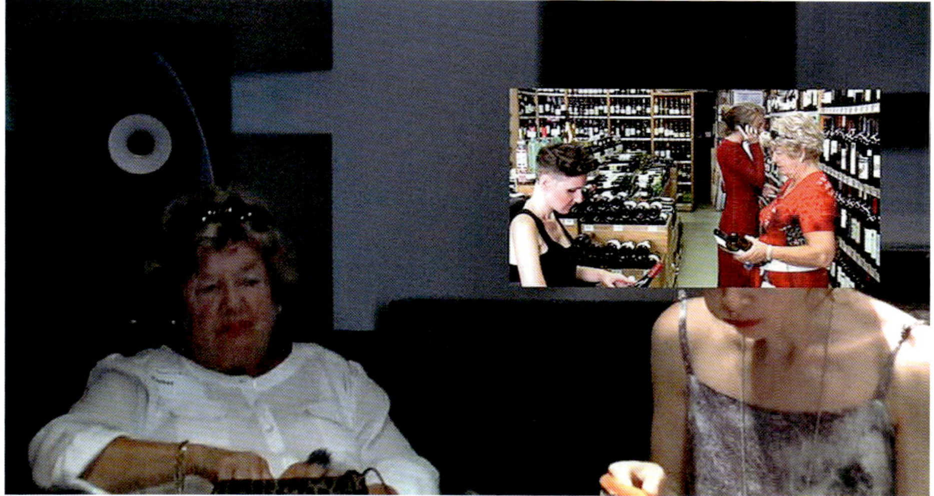

Stills from the video *Que Barbara*, n.d.

Born 1977 in
Dalsjöfors, Sweden

Lives in
New York, NY

Ricky Swallow

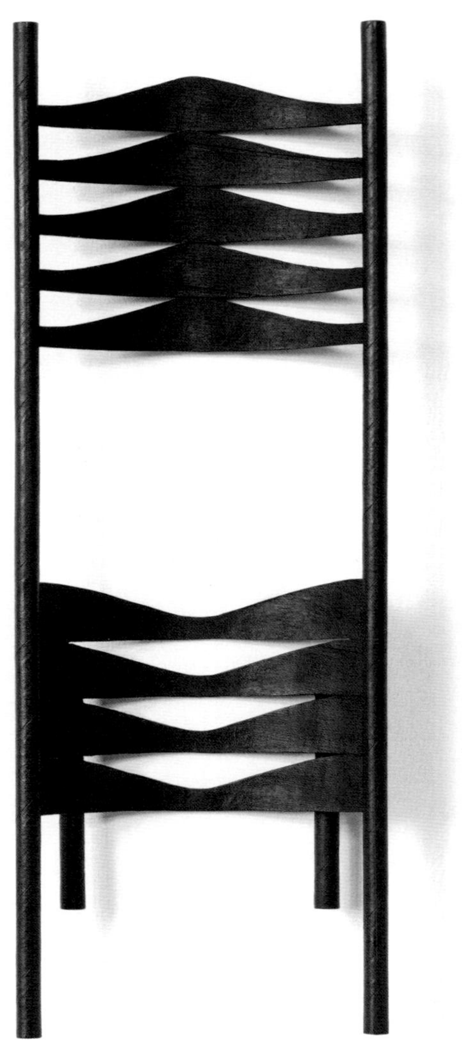

Chair Study/Relief (soot), 2013. Patinated bronze, 25 × 8 ¾ × 2 ½ in. (63.5 × 22.2 × 6.4 cm)

Born 1974 in
San Remo, Australia

Lives in
Los Angeles, CA

Tony Tasset

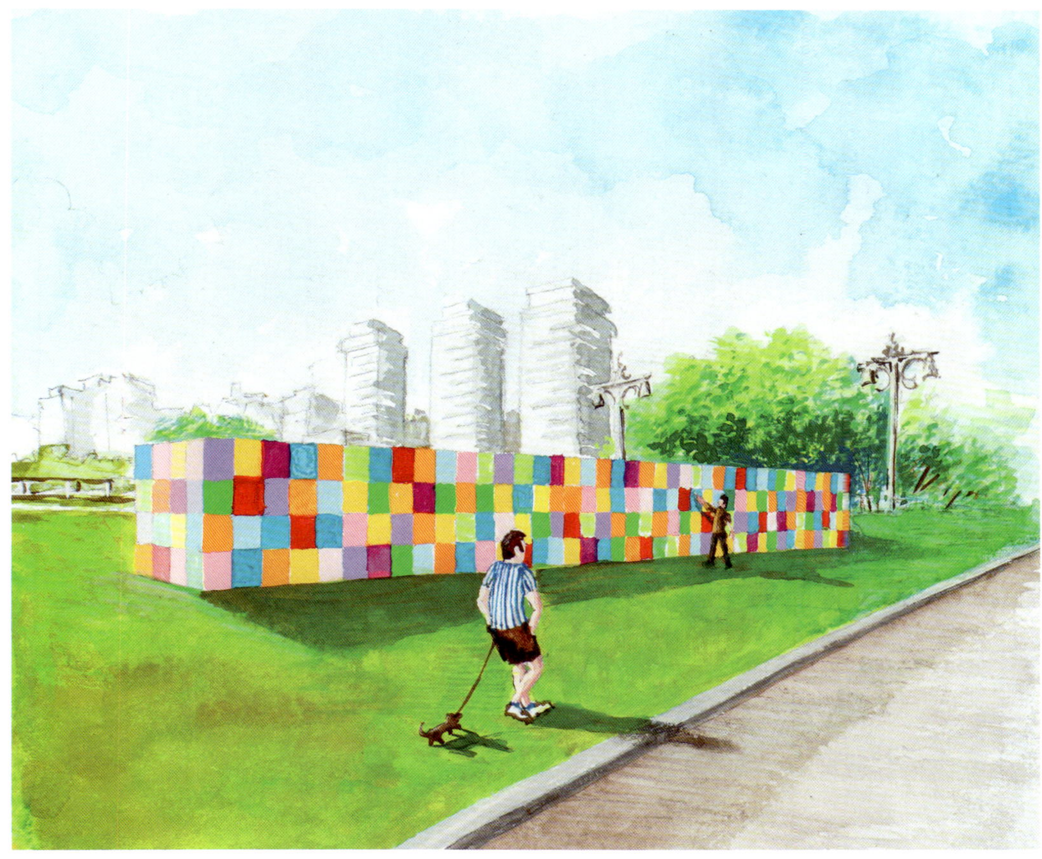

Artist's rendering of *Artists Monument*, 2014. 400,000 names etched on acrylic panels attached to steel and wood, 96 × 960 × 96 in. (243.8 × 2438.4 × 243.8 cm)

Born 1960 in Cincinnati, OH

Lives in Chicago, IL

Philip Vanderhyden

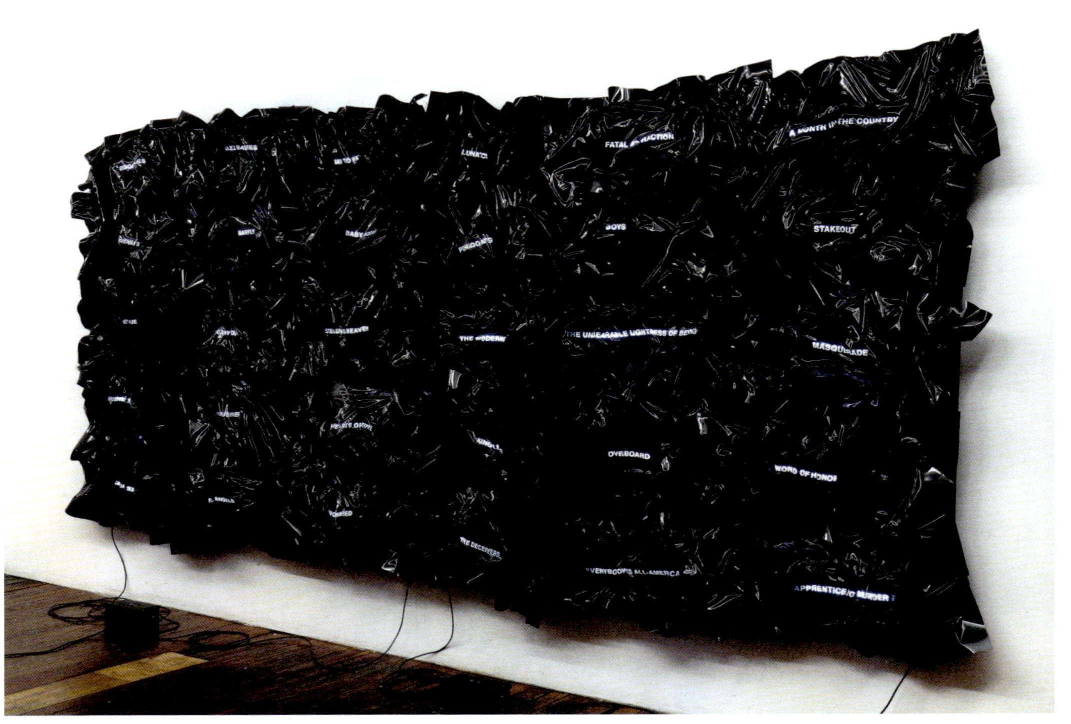

Gretchen Bender (1951–2004), *People in Pain*, 1988 (remade by Philip Vanderhyden, 2014). Paint on heat-set vinyl and neon, 84 × 560 × 11 in. (213.4 × 1422.4 × 27.9 cm)

Born 1978 in Menasha, WI

Lives in New York, NY

Pedro Vélez

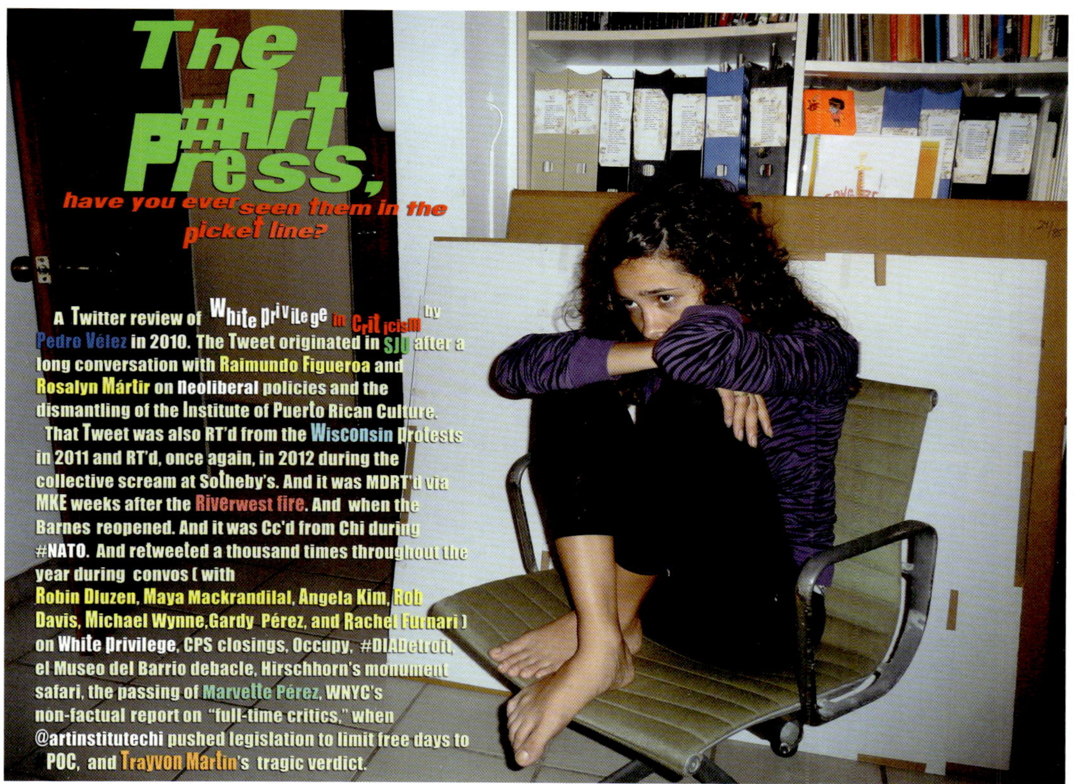

Twitter Review (Flyer from the Poster Barrier installation), 2013. Photographic banners and acrylic, dimensions variable

Born 1971 in Bayamón, PR

Lives in Chicago, IL / Milwaukee, WI

David Foster Wallace

Page from the *Pale King* materials, “Midwesternism” notebook, n.d. Manuscript notebook, 10 ½ × 8 ¼ in. (26.7 × 21.0 cm)

Born 1962 in
Ithaca, NY

Died 2008 in
Claremont, CA

Dan Walsh

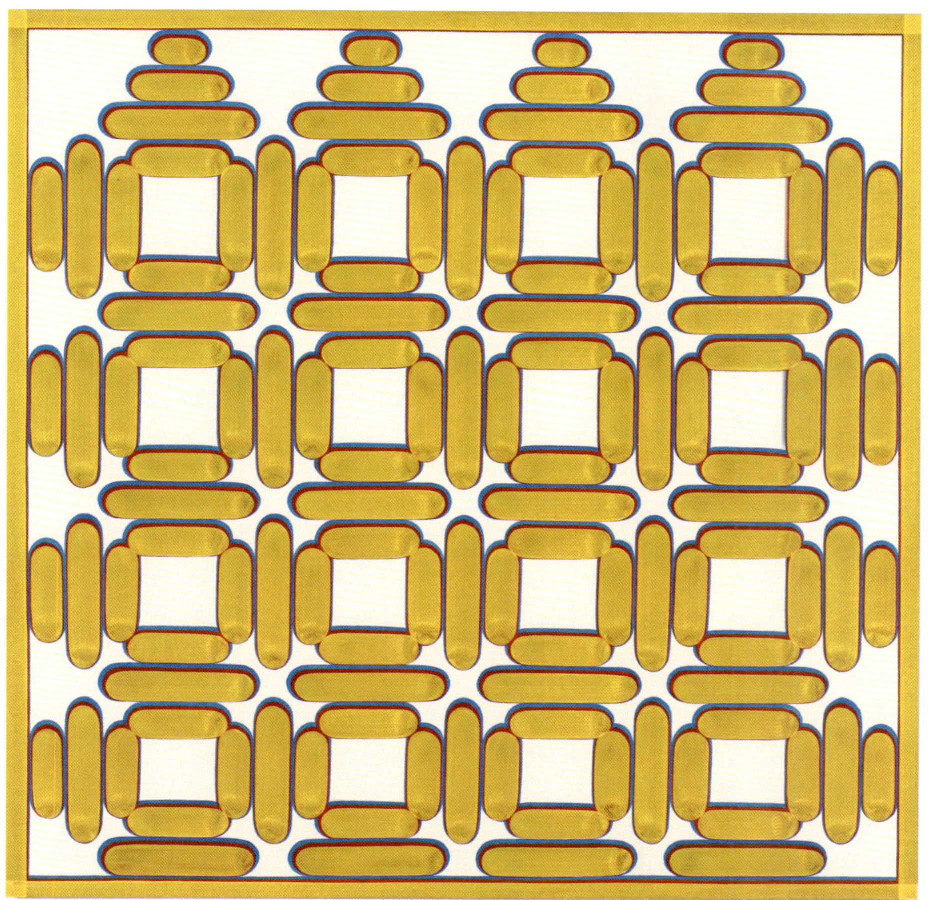

Threshold, 2013. Acrylic on canvas, 70 × 70 in. (177.8 × 177.8 cm)

Born 1960 in Philadelphia, PA

Lives in Brooklyn, NY

Donelle Woolford

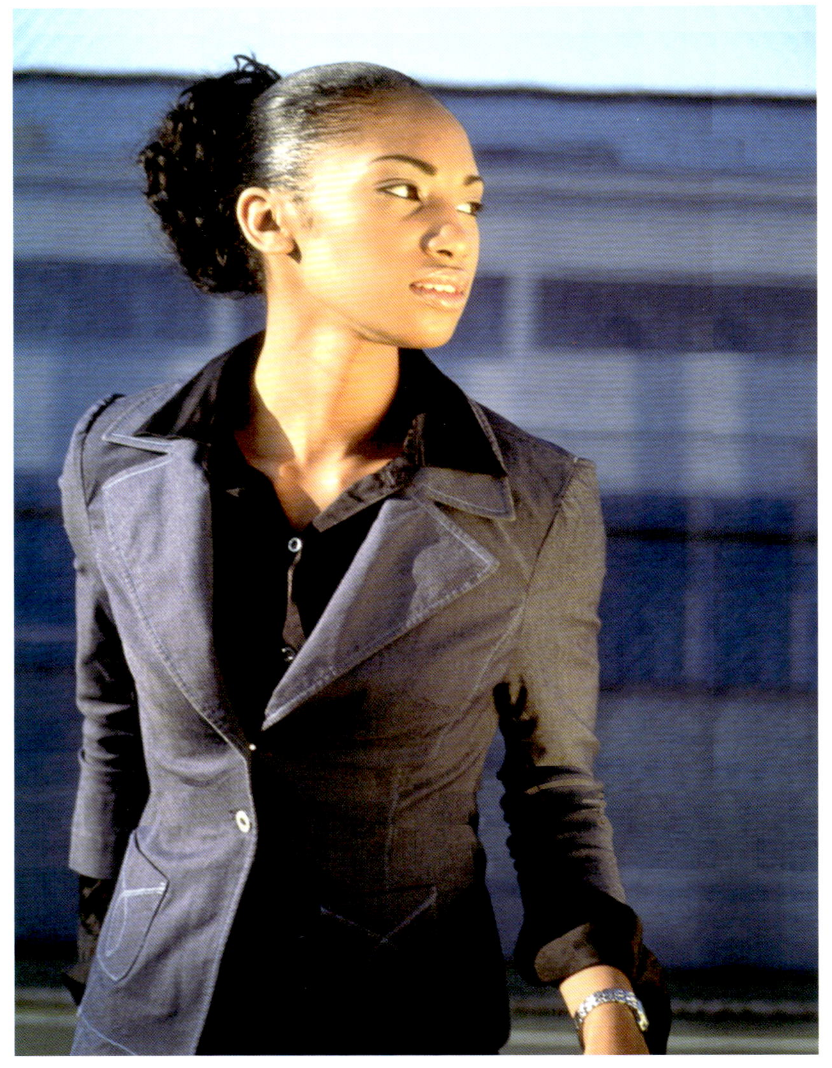

Avatar, 2012

Born 1980 in
Detroit, MI

Lives in
New York, NY

Molly Zuckerman-Hartung

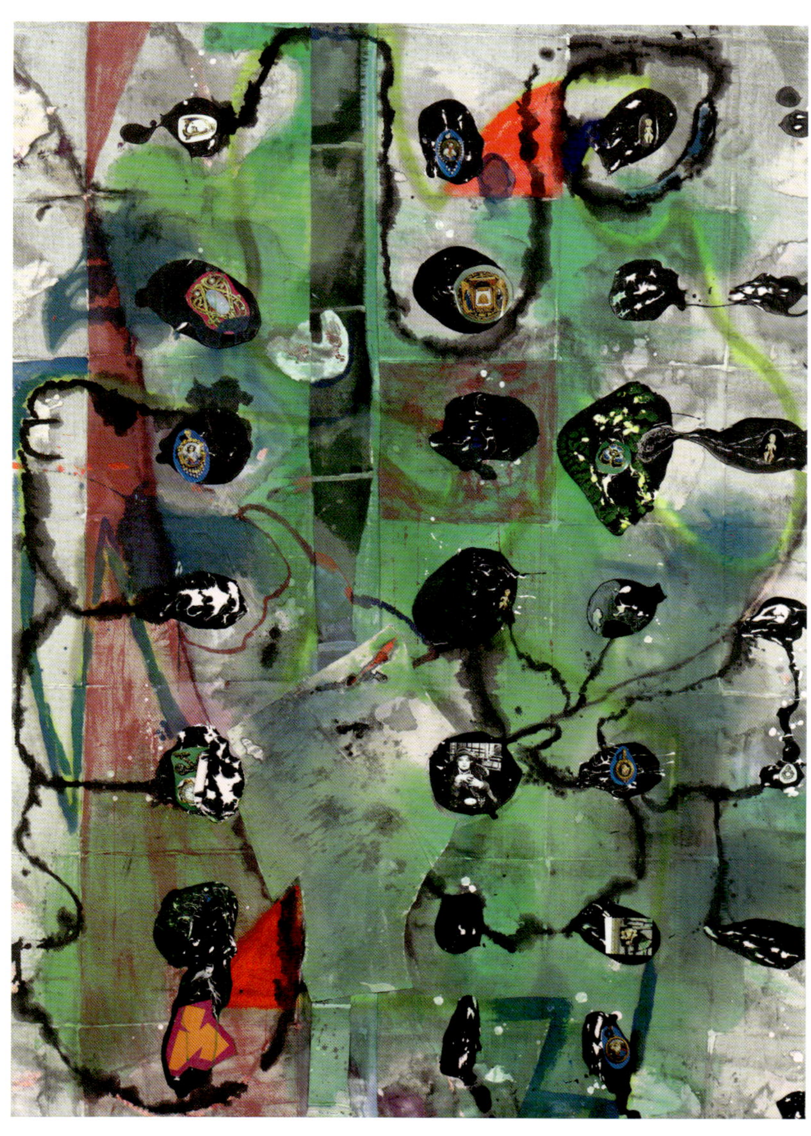

The Madame of the Painting, 2013. Acrylic, latex, fabric, collaged paper, and ink on dropcloth, 72 ½ × 50 in. (184.2 × 127 cm)

Born 1975 in
Los Gatos, CA

Lives in
Chicago, IL

ALMA ALLEN speaks with SU WU

Su Wu: I found a note from you about this Carl Jung quote we both love: "Loneliness does not come from being alone but from being unable to communicate the things that seem important." I don't want to talk about Jung, but it seems as good a place as any to start this conversation, to acknowledge a certain futility. And yet one of the things that strikes me about you is that you're an optimist. So there's hope for this conversation! I wonder if being an optimist is also what makes you so restless?

Alma Allen: I'm definitely optimistic, but I think it makes me more reckless than restless. When you don't have resources, you have to be reckless. How I work is often by throwing things into a jumble, causing as much chaos as I can, and trying to rearrange this chaos while it's happening. I can't see things very clearly except in a quick and frenetic state of working. And what I can imagine is fleeting—things I see out of the corner of my eye—and I don't think I can consciously get there.

SW: You've mentioned that sometimes visions of shapes come to you suddenly but that more often they come in the making and that your hands have their own knowledge and memory.

AA: I was thinking about it this morning. There's a great deal that gets transmitted from the feel of something else. I remember a curve or a shape better with my hands than with my mind. I don't really trust my mind. I trust my fingers a lot more. You hold a lot of information and knowledge in your senses.

SW: Right, the identifiable gestures, the skill, and the impulse, maybe. Your hand gets you partway there, but then there's the struggle. How much of your work is intuitive, and how much of it comes through deliberation?

AA: There's an irregularity to things I find attractive, from a log to an elbow. I think a curve can transmit so much information, but not one that's necessarily at a continuous or exact radius. You know that better in working with your fingers and your hands than with your eyes alone. I start deliberately, but I don't finish that way.

SW: How have you gotten better?

AA: If anything I've gotten better because I try not to be perfect. I've gotten used to throwing things into unrest and grabbing at them—grabbing the worst of them.

SW: How do you think of the physical in your work? Like the physical world as opposed to the biological world—material choices in stone and wood—but also the physical as in physical activity?

AA: Natural material breaks, it has cracks, and there are changes in its color. With reductive sculpture, you can't really go backward, which, for me, is helpful. I'd become paralyzed if I could go backward. I'd be at the same point always.

SW: You've noted before there aren't many reductive sculptors left. It's hard work, sure, and also counter to certain impulses—the stripping away instead of the building up.

AA: And it's not referential. I don't really feel part of popular culture, so I don't really feel comfortable making references to it. I think that's where it leaves me. There's no commentary in reduction.

SW: What happens to your dust?

AA: I hope I don't breathe it. I breathe some of it. I eat some of it.

SW: I want to go back to the idea of not being contiguous, of not fitting, and of working outside certain established readings and trajectories. That's also, I think, a little bit lonely. You live in relative isolation, in a pretty inhospitable climate. Have you deliberately sought solitude?

AA: I'm very noisy. And I do really like working. There are moments when making work allows me to be outside myself. I think most people must have that in the things they like to do, and it's made me sort of addicted to work. It leads me to go live where nobody is around. But I don't know, I'm also a person of the world.

SW: "I'm a person of the world." Did you just say that?

AA: I mean I'm interested. I'm a little naive, but I think that's also protective. I'm self-taught, but I'm not primitive. I haven't willfully not read a book.

SW: Do you want to talk about your childhood?

AA: Not really. I've told you some.

SW: I really did love the imagery: the idea that there might someday be a child—walking around the desert in the late afternoon, delaying the hours before being elsewhere—who finds one of your unsigned carvings sitting on a pile of rocks.

AA: My intention is not often something I think will be important to the viewer. It's very personal. But I've left unsigned work in places and found other funny ways to show works so that viewers don't have an approved reality, an institutional reality—so they have to make a leap of their own. As a child, I left pieces for the Indians because I was convinced they were still out there but were just too smart to be seen, knowing we were up to no good. I don't think there's anything better for an artist than losing his work and someone else discovering it and imagining what it meant. For each new person then, it's a new instance. I think the more people know about me and the more they try to interpret what I meant by a work, the less the work will be able to do. I'm such a sap. I'm just open to a sense of wonder, open to things changing. This is strange. Don't you worry?

SW: Of course. I feel distrustful of people who don't worry. I worry that overvaluing discernment turns you into a deeply dissatisfied person.

AA: You think you can be happy?

SW: Who cares? What would you do with happiness? Seriously, what good is it? It doesn't seem like the noblest pursuit, just something to the side. You seem to often be in some sort of mishap.

AA: I hurt myself all the time. [*holds up injured thumb*]

SW: Or a shattered leg from riding a motorcycle in the mountains . . .

AA: I love to go fast.

SW: What's your relationship to injury? Is there a swagger to working in a form that requires some strength?

AA: Maybe when I was younger there was swagger. But it's funny, I hide myself quite a bit. I'm not central. I don't want to be central. I'm going to get really good at art babble, though. Since I didn't go to school, I really have not had to defend my work, nor have I even been placed in a position to hear critique. It's going to be a very interesting new process for me. And that's the central thing that many artists go through and work for and about.

SW: What do you hope the criticism is?

AA: I kind of hope they're mean. A little bit.

SW: It's just how much you believe your own myths.

AA: It's this utter optimism. The last part I can't slough off is that there's just momentum, and our physiology interacts with a base sort of energy that propels humans forward. It's whatever causes animals to procreate and stars to keep drifting apart. As a kid, I was convinced at times that I could imagine it, when I was running in a field and went into a sort of trance, and I could see the universe moving.

SW: I said I didn't want to talk about Jung, but I have another note from you that mentions the "psychomotor domains of understanding." [*laughter*]

AA: I need hard work and continuous, repetitive carving to separate the mind away. Maybe it's lazy meditation, where you are able to have a meditative state without having to go through just quietly sitting there. The need for all your senses allows for a moment of transcendence. It lets other parts of your brain open up. I'll often think fluidly in those moments when I'm halfway awake in the morning. But as soon as I wake up, it changes, and it changes my ability to see things. You've told me that the right word has come to you in the morning. Morning is an interesting time.

SW: It is. And I think of writing as a sort of paralysis in which I only get to move once in a while. Occasionally I wiggle a big toe or something.

AA: Writing is hard. Language is cursed for me.

SW: Do you think that maybe what you consider your private language is actually more deeply felt than you realize? Is that a more terrifying thought than being misunderstood, that everybody gets you?

AA: I have things that mean something to me. But I don't necessarily think that anybody wants to know about my own fears and desires. What they're interested in is their own and in having a vehicle to find their own. There's that poem you recommended, where the poet's trying to get inside the mind of the rock . . .

SW: Oh, by Wisława Szymborska. That poem is so great: "My whole surface is turned toward you, / all my insides turned away."

AA: It's like trying so intensely to get inside the world to understand what you can't understand but still wanting to and still always attempting, asking over and over, trying to understand something that you'll never understand. Not even close.

DARREN BADER speaks with OWEN KAEN

Darren Bader: I think I need you to find the place to begin, otherwise I'll just bait you and you'll take the bait and we'll get where we were last week.

Owen Kaen: Maybe there's still something from last week's back-and-forth that we could mine for a topic. Like when you asked, "What is the truest word?" But that's an "If a tree falls in a forest . . ." kind of question, where it's more productive to investigate the question itself than the answers we give. There must be something less pretentious we can discuss.

DB: I agree. You responded in the way I expected you would. I was hoping you'd respond less circumspectly, but my hopes shouldn't be confused with your thoughts.

OK: Aside from investigating the question itself, or being explicit that it's an invitation to a kind of imagination game, I don't see any way to address that sort of question head-on.

DB: I understand.

OK: I do, however, think that your work plays (and the playfulness is explicit) with words and forms and images that do not so much answer, or even ask, questions of this sort, but which may invite someone to ask and fail to answer them. I would hope, confronted with this playfulness, she might then realize that to ask these questions is a sort of game, and funnily enough, only a trivial one if she takes it too seriously.

DB: I like that take.

OK: Which is why I think it's funny to hear about people who try to corral you into things like speculative realism (whatever that is), or the remains of relational aesthetics. As if you're engaging with noumena or utopia mongering by way of a pizza in a dishwasher.

DB: I am engaging with noumena. Just realizing the limitations of an engagement with such things/notions.

OK: Are you engaging with noumena? Or are you addressing our insistence on asking, over and over again, whether we can or cannot engage with something called noumena? Put another way, it seems that you engage our temptation to a kind of idolatry by producing a collection of idols and then seeing if people talk philosophical gibberish about them, make a sacrifice (buy the work?), or just take a magical mystery tour. I think the playfulness and theorylessness of your work intimates this—that a lot of this kind of talk is filled with, at best, playful or poetic conceits that have been irresponsibly scientized and philosophized over, but which we're stuck with for the moment, especially in the art world.

DB: I think you're right in many regards. But irresponsible word use is no pointed concern of mine. Words are unstable, of course. I prefer the romance of forgetting this for drawn-out interludes, believing that words have immutable qualities, i.e., meanings, i.e., quiddity. Responsibility for me lies in believing in something fantastical. I always wish upon a star, but know I don't have the rocket fuel (or fusion reactors, or whatever) to get there.

OK: I don't know what you mean when you say "words are unstable, of course," and then go on to say you believe in their "quiddity" and "immutable qualities" anyhow. If I grant you unlimited rocket fuel, you're still never going to get somewhere. That's neither here nor there, that's no place at all. What could possibly count as having gotten to your star? As having failed to get there? If nothing could count either which way, what, after all, is it that you believe? What would it be for "Meanings are immutable qualities of words" to be the case? What would it be for it not to be the case? It's telling that you want to forward both those claims, which, at first blush, are irreconcilable, and also, I think, on investigation, incoherent. Like opposing sides of a bad penny. Language changes for sure. Words and meanings aren't fixed to objects or metaphysical entities or names across all possible words or anything like that. But that doesn't mean they're necessarily unstable, and it doesn't follow that, "like, nothing really means anything," or that we can mean α when we say β, and that meanings of words are open to spontaneous, individual revision. This is the wrong discussion. It ignores how we use words and language every day to do and say meaningful things. At best it's a circus act; at worst it's bankrupt (and still cooking the books). I do wonder, though, if investigating the motive to continue to have this discussion is an interesting topic, and I want to suggest that that's one of the things your work gets at while reminding us of the comedy and dangers of it all.

DB: Dangers, really?

OK: Of idolatry. The failure of communication, of communities. But if the stability of words and meaning is in some special danger today, I don't think it's on account of theory or "disenchantment" or philosophical skepticism; it's because we're less apt to learn through and use a shared set of proof texts/myths that we take as authoritative (or at least authoritative enough to renounce). As a result, we're more susceptible to mysticism and magic—to worshiping iPhones one day, TED Talks the next, and the latest quantum particle for Christmas. We're changing the terms of each conversation, our norms of representation, too fast and too prodigally to keep up and maintain a robust moral life . . . I'm doing a shit job, but I do my best not to talk about philosophy. You say you prefer romance. I might prefer romance too. But I no more want to be romantic about philosophical matters than I do about bookkeeping. That just leads up the garden path. And don't come back to me and say, "That's where I want to go, up the garden path." If deceit that smells like roses is what you're after (what exactly happens up the garden path anyhow?), leave me out of that one.

DB: I'm not interested in deceit in the least. I mean, I am, but using very specific terms. So I do understand what your concerns are about language. I feel I can often be more precise through elision, but of course this depends on previously conspicuous language. I would say that however much I'd like to believe in a thing's/word's "very ownness," I know the absurdity of this. Perhaps that's why I've always been fascinated with the absurd: I know I can't permanently reside there. It's a home away from home.

OK: I'm not sure what you mean. And I don't mean you're talking nonsense; I mean there are more questions to ask about what you could mean, and I'm not sure they're worth our asking. Even if I sound a little like a parrot who spends his weekends caged up beside a table of linguistic philosophers, neither of us has any serious business with this stuff. You do art. And I avoid asking myself what it is I do. But at least we utterly failed at not being pretentious. I'll stand by this: http://www.youtube.com/watch?v=METb_M5s4W8.

DB: Old friends!

GRETCHEN BENDER speaks with CINDY SHERMAN

Gretchen Bender has just returned from Boston, where she presented her electronic performance *Dumping Core* at the Jazz Composers Alliance The following interview takes place in late November, in the evening, at Cindy Sherman's loft in New York. Gretchen has just completed editing a rock video for the thrash band Megadeth's song "Peace Sells," directed by Robert Longo.

Cindy Sherman: It seems as if your critical target is corporate America because your work isolates and diffuses corporate logos and television advertising. How would you feel about a corporation buying one of your works?

Gretchen Bender: I'd feel fine about it. I think it's to its great credit that a corporation has bought my work. Didn't Reagan say the corporate sector ought to support the arts? I'm trying to infiltrate and mimic the mainstream media.

CS: Do you think the work will enlighten them?

GB: Maybe some of the people who work in the corporation might actually be surprised. But I am not that optimistic. I think basically that by the time a corporation has decided to buy my work, the work is already a carcass. The effectiveness of it has already left it and only the structure remains. It's already been neutralized. In general, I assume corporations buy work once it is politically neutralized.

CS: How does it become neutralized? Time?

GB: Time—like after ten minutes! I think that the time limit to media-oriented artwork is an element that many media-involved artists are unwilling to confront: art as I practice it or as I develop my ideas or aesthetics has to do with a temporal limit to its meaningfulness in the culture—and that's real tough. It's hard to make art through the use of guerrilla tactics, where the only constant to the style you develop is the necessity to change it. Style gets absorbed really fast by the culture, basically by the culture absorbing the formal elements or the structure and then subverting the content. You have to make some kind of break or glitch in the media somewhere else with a different style and shove your content into it there. You just go on, learning to vary strategies, to recognize when to go underground and when to emerge. Accepting the fact that your work is going to become neutralized—faster than you ever dreamed.

CS: When the spaceship blew up about a year ago, you were taping everything on television. Did you ever use that?

GB: That happened when I had a TV piece up at Metro Pictures. There were twelve monitors on the wall, each tuned to a different channel and each stenciled with the name of an artist in the show. When the space shuttle blew up, the piece became a macabre choreography of each network's depiction of the space-shuttle disaster.

CS: What timing. In that piece, you were running regular television. I thought you were taping . . .

GB: I started taping when the bombing of Libya happened. It was after the show, and I had all the TVs and a couple of VCRs in my studio. I was working in the studio one afternoon and all of a sudden Libya was happening on all the different networks. I started taping that—NBC came on first with the scoop.

CS: Did you first start working with video out of dissatisfaction with the static works? Did they evolve together?

GB: It was a natural evolution going from the magazines and photos of the news. It seemed obvious to me that the next area was television, which is an incredible gold mine for the flow of the pulse, the permutations that happen daily, in the culture.

CS: Would you want to see the media affected by your work?

GB: I don't think the media is something that listens in the way that we're talking about. I think of the media as a cannibalistic river. A flow or current that absorbs everything. It's not "about." There is no consciousness or mind. It's about absorbing and converting.

CS: What if your videotapes were on TV, say PBS, would that be defeating your purpose?

GB: There are some very fine video artists who work effectively on public television. I'm taking a different tack. I'm trying to create an overview of an environment, and at this point I'm not able to do it on one channel so I create a theatrical exposition of it with multiple channels. In the past three years, I've surrounded myself and the audience with an environment and then turned up the voltage—to create a criticality. I'll mimic the media—but I'll turn up the voltage on the currents so high that hopefully it will blast criticality out there.

CS: There's an article in an Los Angeles paper describing you as a TV terrorist, saying that you can attain a critical edge through overload.

GB: Yeah There are artists who talk of using silence as a weapon, an alternative, and an act of resistance. That's one end of it. I've gone into the opposite direction but with the same desire. I think it's more important to mimic and provoke at this point.

CS: Your theatrical pieces are counterpointed by the tin pieces, which ironically make objects out of paradigms.

GB: Either way, it's only temporarily effective. Hans Haacke uses part of the dominant high culture to criticize the function of the whole system through his object displays. The question is, how broadly effective do you want to be? That is a difficult question with artists. Artists can be confused about their situation as a powerless elite. We operate from the protective base of the art world, a situation in which we can develop ideas but a place from which it is complicated to launch media-related artwork without it getting co-opted by the very structures it criticizes. Although I use those structures, I'm resisting one-channel television because I haven't figured out how to effectively communicate except in a theatrical setting.

CS: You've been criticized for being high-tech, which is another way of infiltrating popular culture—using the technology that it uses.

GB: It's something visual artists tend to resist, although that resistance is steadily breaking down. It's strange that the art world resists using the visual tools of our time. What's that about? It is scary when you have this heritage that you invoke—art history.

CS: It's supposed to be more pure if you use materials like paint or make it all yourself or use another person to make it for you.

GB: The art world is trying to protect this antiquated territory, and what is most disturbing about switching over to the newer technologies is that there is no authority to invoke. There aren't any guidelines to tell you that you're making "good" art. There's so much experimentation to do, so many blind visual forays to risk, so many conceptual implications of the newer technologies to try to comprehend. Many artists aren't willing to take those risks. You don't know if you are going to be effective or not, if you are going to make silly or profound works. I think that's what terrifies most artists, and I think that's why the art world is so slow to accept the culture of today.

CS: You have used imagery from other people's artwork in some of your own pieces. I interpreted that as reducing expensive works of art by male artists—paintings—to this disposable-imagery level.

GB: I wanted to use the art as signs and not as valuable objects. I decided to combine those found-art reproductions as one combines words in a language or even just parts of an alphabet. I saw them as a moving language. At the same time, I realized that because we had gotten so much of our art out of magazines and reproductions, we weren't contemplating art anymore. I go into galleries to see shows, to be aware of what is going on, and it takes three minutes to see a show. Where are we? And what are we doing? It's our nervous system—the time we live in—it's not about reverie. There are some haunting artists that somehow transcend that, where you can't get away from it. But there's no place that's conducive to viewing that work. You either describe or analyze an environment. It's a way artists examine what they're doing and why they're doing things—how they're operating. I think a balance between the two would be the most potent.

CS: It's like classical and romantic, those two sides.

GB: Artists using media have taken on a more complicated position in the culture than painters. Painters like tradition. And I think it's a hundred or a thousand times more difficult for a painter to make politically engaged work. They know that if it smells like art and looks like art and tastes like art—it's painting. There's not much risk in the art world. At the same time, I'm still operating within the art world. There is that base. Maybe it's a base to reaffirm your goals or your sanity in trying to develop ideas.

CS: You also work in film—in a more traditional way, with a script and a crew. What got you going in that direction?

GB: It's the other major media besides television. The mechanics of making film shows me how my perceptions can be altered. At one time you asked me if I had a preference for one genre over another. I don't. I want to experiment. In the last few years, I've realized the visual-art world has to broaden the areas in which it is dealing. As visual artists we don't become "video artists," we don't become "filmmakers." We are still visual artists, but we need to critically interface those mediums in our work. Until there are more artists doing that, oppositional media art could become obsolete. We need to stay alert to the political implications of the conceptual evolutions of our newer technologies.

This is an excerpt from an interview that was originally published in *BOMB*, no. 18 (Winter 1987).

STEPHEN BERENS speaks with LESLIE DICK

Leslie Dick: Looking at these photographs, in your series *All days are nights*, I found myself thinking about time and place, and also about what it might mean to layer different moments on top of each other and how that relates to painting. I'm interested in the photograph as something that both marks an irrevocably past moment and preserves that same moment. Loss and preservation are registered in the same image. It seems that your decision to layer these moments, these instances of looking, really draws us into the emotional dimension of that question of time.

Stephen Berens: First off, it's important to me that the process is a generative system, where you lay one image on top of another—the first print contains a single image; the second print, two images; the tenth print, ten images—until the print appears entirely black. But I'm not interested in the work solely because it was made using this generative system. I think, at a certain point in time, making art by following a set of rules was enough. But I purposefully make interventions into the system.

LD: I was remembering Michael Asher's show at the Santa Monica Museum of Art in 2008, where he rebuilt all the temporary walls from the various exhibitions of the previous ten years, using only the studs. That work engaged architecture, exhibition, repetition, redundancy, and many other things. It was extremely rigorous and completely systematic. Still, there were all these incredible by-products. It started to look like a hall of mirrors. It generated all sorts of optical effects and illusions, and it was very, very beautiful.

SB: Yes, I remember that to navigate through the space you had to literally step through the walls, which made me hyperaware of my presence as a viewer and a participant.

LD: It's paradoxical: as if the tighter you squeeze—screwing the system down—the more this ooze of emotional by-product comes out the side. With *All days are nights*, you never set out to produce such emotional effects, to call up memories of Romantic painting, for example. It happened as a result of a system. Like going the long way around the barn.

SB: I believe that when Asher and Sol LeWitt designed their systems, it didn't concern them whether or not something turned out to be beautiful. In the catalogue for LeWitt's retrospective at MASS MoCA, John Baldessari tells a story about meeting LeWitt in the late sixties. Baldessari told him that he thought one of his wall drawings was beautiful, and LeWitt's response was basically that this was beside the point. And I would say I don't think it is.

LD: Right on!

SB: I think that the reason their work is still engaging is because it is both incredibly rigorous and beautiful. While they always made their decisions beforehand, I have been developing a way of working where my specific history and interests leak in, without abandoning the system. The choices I made in *All days are nights* are mostly about maintaining distinctions: the first image has very even lighting, then this one adds shadows, this one adds a bird, this one adds another bird. This one adds a cloud. This one starts to add more clouds. Out of this process, a series of unplanned connotations begins to appear. And that's much more interesting to me than setting out to make a photograph that looks like a nineteenth-century painting, for example.

LD: By layering these photographs, you've constructed a set of images with multiple associations. They invoke those architectural views in the backgrounds of early Renaissance paintings, as well as neoclassical views of Rome, heavy-duty Romantic painting, and even that early moment in art photography when Edward Steichen wanted photographs to look like paintings. This work has got all these things buried inside it.

SB: It's interesting to me that making art using a generative system, which is a twentieth-century idea, along with the most recent printing technology produces something that looks like it was made 150 or even 200 years ago.

LD: It stretches from early Renaissance to the daguerreotype, and through to Ad Reinhardt's late work! It's mind-boggling that it can extend so far with only eighteen images, layered one on the other and then removed in reverse order, one by one.

SB: That's why the generative system is so important.

LD: Absolutely. It's productive: you discover things you never imagined were there, as if the system itself holds all this visual potential or memory. A time machine. What about the ways we tend to use the image now, on our various screens?

SB: I didn't set out to do this, but I think the work is a reaction to the proliferation of images and to how quickly everybody looks at them—especially photographs. On Facebook, people may look at a photograph for a tenth of a second, right? They're grabbing little bits of information. With this work, I am making something that's the opposite of that, something you have to be in the presence of and to spend time looking at. Trying to get back to Reinhardt, perhaps. It really impressed me that he was willing to make works that were just not reproducible. To see the way he subtly shifted value and luminosity, you had to be right there, standing in front of the paintings. I'm wondering, given the present proliferation of images, seamlessly transmitted from device to device, does it still make sense to ask viewers to slow down? Not to absorb an image instantly but to decipher it?

LD: So encountering the work can be an embodied experience, located in the particular time and place of viewing. For me, these photographs are more about the time and place of those lost moments, which somehow aren't lost—but then they do get lost once the image turns black.

SB: Well, almost. Different shades of black.

LD: Maybe it's about having and not having at the same time. It's all still there: the birds, the clouds—even the helicopters! All eighteen images are there, but we can only see the tiniest traces of them.

SB: Yeah, but I think as our lives go on and our moments accumulate, the same thing happens, right?

LD: Yes.

SB: It becomes so dense that you can't separate it out anymore.

LD: Time and place.

SB: I can separate out the time when I left Nebraska. I can separate out when I left Florida and when I moved from East Los Angeles to Eagle Rock (northeast LA). But it's hard to separate out all the cumulative moments in each of those places. So I think the work is also somehow about that.

DAWOUD BEY speaks with IMANI PERRY

Dawoud Bey: I first became aware of your connection to Birmingham, Alabama, when I posted some of my snapshots taken during one of my visits there on Facebook. You were the first one to comment, and you said, "That's about four miles or so from my family home. I'm so excited you're doing a Birmingham project." I was both surprised and heartened by your response. At that point, I was still finding my way in Birmingham, becoming familiar with the place. Initially my visits were about trying to displace the city's mythic history, which I had been carrying in my head for so many years, with an actual physical experience in the here and now. What were your thoughts when you first saw those pictures? What memories did they bring back for you? What did they provoke?

Imani Perry: Your pictures remind me of something I so cherish about my birthplace. There is a quiet dignity to people and places in Birmingham. There is Armstrong's barbershop. Mr. Armstrong was a local leader who fought to desegregate city schools, worked on the Birmingham campaign, and provided a space for political discussions and organizing in his barbershop, which also was where Dr. Martin Luther King Jr. had his hair cut when in the city. But, look, it is a characteristically simple and tasteful storefront. That is Birmingham: where history lives but does not boast, and where the resilience and grace displayed in the civil rights movement are always in the air. So is the restraint and forbearance that were necessary for survival under Jim Crow. It is quite powerful to me, how images like these of businesses can evoke that energy. You clearly "saw" Birmingham quite deeply.

Recently I have been reading Gordon Parks's memoirs, and several of them begin with discussions of Birmingham, which fascinates me because he was from Kansas. I am curious as to why you think Birmingham remains such a powerful symbol in black life. How do you think visual images describe both the symbolic meaning and the spirit of the place?

DB: So much of what I know about Birmingham is from photographs. I think that the Children's March in Birmingham in May 1963 and then the bombing of the church four months later deeply jolted the psyches of black Americans. The horror of those two events reverberated far beyond the city itself. Those outside of Birmingham experienced these events through photographs. The images of young black people peacefully demonstrating for their rights being attacked by police dogs and blasted by high-pressure fire hoses were evidence of just how high the stakes were and how white supremacy was so absolutely maintaining white privilege and black disenfranchisement in the South. The level of violence against black folks in Birmingham became well known because of these photographs, so much so that it reverberated for me as an eleven-year-old black boy in New York, as well as for Gordon Parks, who was from Kansas, where segregation was also the norm while he was growing up. I think Birmingham became for many black people, through the notorious viciousness of the commissioner of public safety, Eugene "Bull" Connor, the most horrifically iconic of Southern cities because of the ubiquity of those photographs.

There didn't seem to be any photographs of Birmingham that I encountered when I was young that were not documenting this ongoing struggle against segregation. Today, an equally compelling visualization of Birmingham has not yet gained enough prominence to stand alongside those narratives of the past. It's one of the reasons, I think, that the past hangs so heavily in the air there. Are there any pictures that come to mind for you, since those civil rights–era images, that reflect the Birmingham you know more intimately?

IP: Interestingly, because I didn't grow up in Birmingham (I was born there and then spent holidays and summers there throughout my childhood and young adulthood), the homesickness I have for the city has a cinematic quality. Much of my relationship to "home" has been dependent on memory and on calling up images and sounds. So when I have encountered the work of photographers who visualize my home, I get very excited. Two images are very powerful for me. The first is Gordon Parks's *Department Store* (1956), which for years I thought was taken in Birmingham but which I learned recently was actually taken in Mobile. It features an African American woman and child standing under an orange-red neon Colored Entrance sign. The harsh light of Jim Crow does not diminish the duo. They are both richly brown; the woman's walnut complexion is deeper than the girl's, whose skin is just a taste more burnished than copper. Their faces are enchanting in their pastel surroundings. Both are dressed sharply, the woman in chiffon, the girl in a Sunday dress. The woman's pose is restrained yet steely, with some added delicacy as the strap of her slip has fallen down over her shoulder. It is the way she looks forward with her lips pulled in and eyes wide that made me first whisper, "Home." It captures what I think of as the "formal culture" of the black South, which is filled with social graces and propriety and a sense of self-possession. It is an aspect of black life that is understudied and undertheorized.

DB: I know that photograph well and was just looking at a print of it in the home of a friend in Birmingham. It's one of my favorites of Parks's pictures, for the formal beauty of the photograph and how the "quiet dignity" of the mother and daughter is framed by that sign that is meant to subjugate them.

IP: The other image I want to mention is *Five Men* (1963) by Roy DeCarava, of men leaving a funeral after the 16th Street Baptist Church bombing in Birmingham. The grief in their eyes is palpable, and their heads are layered in a way that demonstrates its depth. But, again, there is that simultaneous steeliness and dignity, and they are a bit frayed—a collar sneaking out, hair beaded up, skin glistening. DeCarava said of the image, in an interview with Dread Scott, "You see, they're determined, and they're angry and they're sad, and they're beautiful. Is there anything else?" And really that is it.

Which brings me to a question I have about this project. I've been familiar with and greatly admired your work for many years. It is such intimate work. Your portraits describe the interior lives of your subjects. I'm fascinated to hear about that process with this project. I think of Birmingham people as generous and friendly yet guarded, particularly with respect to grief. Was the process of reaching your subjects' interior lives different for this project than for previous ones?

DB: Your characterization of Birmingham's people as being friendly yet guarded is definitely true to my experience, and for that reason it took a while for me to be accepted and for people to come forward to participate in being photographed. What made the project different for me was the fact that not only I was a stranger asking them to enter into the intimate experience of being photographed, which I always am, but also that I was asking them to do so in a specific historical context. Their willingness to be photographed also meant their engagement with the context in which I was making the work. This clearly meant something different for the older people than it did for the young.

The guardedness was most notable in older men. Four months into photographing and reaching out extensively, not a single older man had agreed to participate. The memories called up by this project were clearly not a place where they wanted to go to. The bombing of the church killed four girls, and two boys were killed in the aftermath; the collective trauma of the community and those who survived that moment was considerable. My being there brought back memories that these older men were clearly not ready to share with an outsider. It was only through the direct introductions of Reverend Carolyn McKinstry, one of the survivors of the bombing; Mayor William Bell; and a few others that I was able to begin to break through that and become someone they could trust, someone whose camera they felt comfortable sitting in front of in an act of witness. Once a few came, more followed. Before that, I feared the project might fail for the lack of their presence. Once they consented, it was then up to me to meet the challenge of creating a comfortable enough space so that the interior person could appear momentarily on the surface.

Once the photographing was done, I went through the individual photographs, looking for those pairings that resonated most deeply. Each diptych embodies fifty years . . . the fifty-year difference between the young person who is the age of the young people martyred in 1963 and the older person, the fifty years that the murdered children never got to live out, and the fifty years since that traumatic moment on September 15, 1963. They are a kind of visual time capsule, conceptually and literally embodying past, present, and future.

JENNIFER BORNSTEIN speaks with CHRISTOPHER WILLIAMS

Christopher Williams: Something that I think is such an important part of your work but that doesn't get talked about much is the idea of performance, or, in more contemporary terms, the performative. The earliest work I know of yours is a video that's like an episode of *Antiques Roadshow*, where you present a pretty heterogeneous collection of objects and talk about them in a fairly straightforward and deadpan manner.

Jennifer Bornstein: I made that in 1994 and was pleased by how nicely it infiltrated mainstream TV. I was a guest on a Los Angeles program called *Collectors' Favorites*, during which I showcased my collections of things like ziplock bags and words. The show was recorded at a cable-access TV station in Eagle Rock and broadcast in late-night repeats. So for years afterward I got phone calls from people saying, "I saw you on TV last night at 2 am. What were you *doing*?"

CW: I can't help but see that videotape as being related to West Coast Performance art from the seventies, eighties, and nineties—even things that aren't necessarily talked about as Performance art. Allen Ruppersberg, for example, is somebody I think about in relation to your work. As you moved into a more photographic practice in the years after that video, it became clear that you were bringing performance into a relationship with photography. Your work collapses the social and the performative with photographic models and codes such that they become indivisible from one another.

JB: I took up photography because I was interested in its relationship to performance. I was making photos that documented my interactions with strangers in public parks. Photographs were a way to narrate actions that had taken place. I was specifically interested in the work of California artists who combined Performance and Conceptual art in the seventies and eighties—people associated with *High Performance* magazine, LACE [Los Angeles Contemporary Exhibitions], Beyond Baroque's performance program, and the sound projects broadcast on *Close Radio*.

CW: You've talked specifically about your interest in performances that are not visible to a public, performances that happen away from the public or away from public presentation. Could you talk a little bit more about that?

JB: Aren't we all performers in the course of daily life? You buy a quart of milk, you talk to the guy at the deli: performance. Even now, talking to you with a tape recorder, this conversation is a performance. I started to make 16mm films because I was interested in the performative presence of the projectionist in the room and the action of turning the projector on and off for an audience who sits and waits.

I wanted to make works that explored different ways of functioning in the world. So between 1999 and 2003, I stopped making objects and made actions instead. They were purposely meant to be invisible, quiet, ephemeral, and undocumented and did not even involve conversation.

CW: Are you referring to photo-based works from the late nineties, like *Public Libraries and Basketball Courts* and *Family Pictures*?

JB: Later. I spent a year in 2002 riding buses by myself around New York. I didn't tell anyone I was making an artwork out of bus riding. The only people who knew were the bus drivers. They were the perfect audience because they were the ones who noticed my presence while they drove through the entire length of the city. But these works weren't documented or spoken about. The works erased themselves. They didn't enter the world. Afterward I made photographic portraits of the bus drivers, and those photographs became physical "art." I figured out that it's great to make an artwork out of riding the bus every day, but the fact is that when Alison Knowles ate a tuna-fish sandwich every day at the same diner on Eighth Avenue in New York City, she had to tell someone about her sandwiches, otherwise it was really just a tuna-fish sandwich.

CW: Right. Do you know the Korean market on Gramercy?

JB: No.

CW: In the eighties, I used to rearrange things in that grocery store. I never took a photo of it. Nothing exists and barely anybody knows about it, so I totally understand the impulse. But I would see the photos in *Public Libraries and Basketball Courts* and *Family Pictures* as actually having a critical relationship to certain aspects of Performance art. As a performer, you are really decentered in those photographs—they aren't spectacular and are engaged not with models of entertainment but with models of vernacular photography and types of portraiture unassociated with celebrity or advertising or fashion.

JB: My aim was to make photographs that fit seamlessly into the world. Vernacular photography was my target. Photos that, if they were purposely dropped on the floor of a shopping mall, might be mistaken for an ordinary, lost family photo. I've seen enough photos in the world that stand apart, but I wanted to make something that fits into the center. The center seemed the most subversive place to be.

CW: I would see those as a comment on Performance art. I'm also interested in the fact that making a photograph is one of the reasons you set out to perform specific activities with different communities. Yet the image itself is unable to communicate the extent to which you were involved with them to produce it. This lends the work a kind of ambiguity that differentiates it from, say, the photograph of Chris Burden crucified on the roof of a Volkswagen, which is pretty direct and self-evident. In your case, the reasons why you're sitting with this child, who the child is, etc., are not. I think the understated way you position yourself always is part of a commentary in relation to others' extroversion, if you will.

JB: All that work had already been done in the sixties, seventies, and eighties—different eras. Why remake it? At a certain point, Performance art joined the vernacular. There are YouTube videos by people performing for the camera in their living rooms that seemed much more mysterious and beautiful to me than the performance-based works taking place in fine art. At that point, I decided to make etchings instead, partly to protest the spectacle that Performance art had become.

CW: Yeah, but do you feel a part of that Performance history?

JB: Definitely. It's what inspired me to become an artist.

This is an excerpt of an interview to be published by the Berliner Künstlerprogramm/DAAD in 2014.

SARAH CHARLESWORTH (1947–2013): SARA VANDERBEEK speaks with MATTHEW S. WITKOVSKY

Matthew S. Witkovsky: Michelle Grabner plans to include in the Biennial three diptychs by Sarah Charlesworth, which she chose with Susan Inglett: two from Sarah's last show, *Available Light*, at Susan's gallery in 2012, and one from slightly earlier, called *Camera Work*. It's a view in silhouette of a banquet camera with the bellows extended. That beautiful, cumbersome piece of equipment was hers, right?

Sara VanDerBeek: Absolutely. Sarah had terrific technical abilities across a range of photographic equipment. I had dinner with her just ten days before she died, and she was telling me about an idea she was exploring with a new field camera. She was working outdoors and was planning to capture a variety of images both inside and outside her studio. She said she was focusing up at the leaves on trees. I was struck by her experimentation and her enthusiasm for a new challenge and am saddened not to see how she would have addressed these new images. Sarah was not only deeply knowledgeable about the history of photography, its genres and its previous practitioners, but also completely engaged in the discussions of where photography is going.

MSW: I was just up in northern Connecticut, visiting Sarah's house, where I saw some transparencies on her worktable: all diptychs, like the works in the Biennial, with one half of each diptych a view of foliage. The branches are hushed; they give off an air of equanimity, which I find in so much of her work, particularly that of the past few years. You're right, Sarah was committed to photography as a distinct field, even as her work remained firmly in dialogue with recent art. But many of her pictures—including those chosen here—seem to have one foot in the mid-nineteenth century. They emanate the slowness, the equipoise, of that time, as well as the fascination with capturing one's immediate surroundings, which you find in photographs made by gentleman amateurs of the 1830s, 1840s, and 1850s.

SV: That could be. *Available Light* is such a succinct and poignant choice of words and is indicative of Sarah's inspiring use of language. It was as astute and considered as her photography. Using natural light was a means both to emphasize her observation of what was in front of her and to privilege the actual over the virtual. Her works urge the viewer to do the same. They require us to be contemplative in a way that is generous as well as demanding.

MSW: I'm thinking now of Sarah's house, where she made her most recent work, and the writing desk and study that she used as a setting—as if she were a Victorian lady of leisure whose life was gathered around epistolary correspondence and things of the home, such as the glass ball that appears in several of those photographs, which could be a paperweight. The house is a humble village dwelling from pre-Revolutionary times, with wide plank floors, low ceilings, and now an oval wooden plaque on the front door that states proudly, "Built in 1730." Sarah made her New England family heritage into an ethnic identity!

SV: I met Sarah when we were asked to interview each other for North Drive Press. Her focus, reflection, and revision during the course of our work on the interview captivated me. I was running a gallery at that time, and in 2008 I asked Sarah to be part of a group show, *The Human Face Is a Monument*, featuring women artists who addressed the figure. Some of the artists were my peers, Anya Kielar and Sara Greenberger Rafferty, while Sarah was a guiding figure—an inspiration. Figures in their presence and absence are central to a number of Sarah's works, from the empty dresses and masks in her Objects of Desire series (1983–88) to her many Buddhas. She had a piece, which she had conceived of in 1988 but had never fully realized, involving many small images rephotographed from the picture collection of the New York Public Library of isolated figures ranging from classical sculpture to Renaissance painting to contemporary advertising. I understand that it was unusual for her to return to an earlier work, but the idea for *Figure Drawings* worked very well with the focus of the show.

MSW: Why all women artists?

SV: Women, often the subjects of figurative art, are far less known as its makers, but the range of female artists' treatments of the figure is striking; it is often when female artists have been working with photography, found imagery, or reproductions that I think some of the most significant and challenging works have been created. I feel that photography is unique in that throughout its history women have made contributions equal to those of men toward the evolution of the field.

MSW: I'm thinking of scale as you say these things—on the one hand, Sarah's prescience in making, in the late 1980s, a gigantic mural composed of small photographs, when the trend was toward single images at the size of history paintings. Constellations of little images have been the rage for several years now, so Sarah's work in your show was timely. On the other hand, I'm thinking of the legacy of Conceptual art, which got Sarah to her proposals on scale. Artists using photography around 1970 concentrated heavily on the problem of "actual size"—whether the photograph could have a nonarbitrary relation to its subject. Sarah accordingly printed the individual photos in her Modern History series (1977–79) at the size of the source newspapers. Around 1980, the (sculptural) preoccupation with one-to-one size faded in favor of a renewed compatibility between photography and painting; photographic pictures got bigger and bore no obvious relation in size to their subjects. Right at that time, Sarah—and I think she was one of the first to do this—made her first large-format photographs: Stills. Sarah and I worked closely last year on her definitive series of these works, which will go on view in Chicago this fall. They are appropriated and enlarged news photos of individuals in midair, who have leaped from tall buildings, perhaps to their deaths or perhaps to save their lives. A limbo moment eternalized by the press is now monumentalized. In choosing to print those photos at a 6-foot height, Sarah wanted viewers to feel as if they could step into the picture, as if the picture itself were not lifelike but life-size. That move slowed the viewer down, and offered a profound expression of contemplation and stillness of the sort you've mentioned.

SV: Sarah was assertive in her use of space and concise with the arrangement and presentation of her work. Today, there are no hierarchies in capture; all images in all formats seem interchangeable. Stillness is incredibly important as a form of resistance against the expanding visual landscape in which we live and work. I'm very intrigued by this new culture of capture, in which almost everyone, via their phones, has a camera and uses it to engage and interact not only with each other but also with a larger global community. Ours is a culture of sharing and of image ubiquity—not of honing or of reflection. Sarah was fascinated by this rise of mobile media and was continually studying the media in every form, yet her own work was always the product of lengthy editing before and after capturing the images.

MSW: Her own images were slow, stilled, and difficult to circulate. She wasn't pointing a finger at contemporary image circulation; she was in another space. Her images evoke a time when one shared images only with a few friends. It is so hard now, following Virginia Woolf, to have a room of one's own. We are all in the media commons. Sarah seemed to say, "I can be with you all, but this is my space."

CRITICAL PRACTICES INC.: Producing Exchange

On Sunday, September 8, 2013, Critical Practices Inc. board members Saul Ostrow (Founder and President), Susan Bowman (Treasurer and Director of Design and Communication), David Goodman (Director of Projects and Programs), and Edouard Prulhiere (Director CPI.E) joined with members of the CPI advisory board Donald Daedulus (WorkGroup Facilitator) and Sara O'Keeffe (LTR Coordinator) to discuss John Kelsey's essay "Next-Level Spleen" (*Artforum,* September 2012) and its relationship to CPI's platform. For the resulting text, published here, some of LaTableRonde's (LTR) "Rules of the Game" were suspended: the participants are identified and, for the sake of brevity, the transcript has been edited. But the transcript does not identify who said what because CPI determined it was necessary to uphold LTR's rule that what is said is more important than who says it.

Voice 1: I would say we start, and she can just hop in or not when she shows up. The immediate question is, given this is for publication, I assume we are not going to follow the LTR rules, right?

Voice 2: Okay. So for the prompt, I want to touch on a few aspects of John Kelsey's essay so we understand what he's doing. Kelsey's reinvesting for a contemporary context Charles Baudelaire's use of the word *spleen* to mean "discontent," perhaps implicitly drawing a parallel between the moment following the revolutions of 1848 and our times—financial crisis, civil unrest, etc.—but the essay is really about what is happening to us culturally in this age of connectivity and networking. One thing of importance that he points out is that isolation is systematically designed into connectivity, and that connecting itself is now defined as a functional relationship between formatted materials and components, which stimulate computer users to be actively involved in the production of experiences for dispersion.

Voice 1: We looked up the number of people who actually have access to computers and the internet, which is 22 percent of the world. So it seems what happened in Libya and in Egypt the first time around, against Hosni Mubarak, is people with cell phones and computers communicated with one another and then went into the neighborhoods to spread the word by mouth [*laughter*] because there was no other way to spread the word. You could tweet anything you wanted, but to get people without cells to turn out was another issue.

Voice 3: I wonder how he would rewrite this article after the use—the implementation—of these social networks for the Arab Spring—like Twitter not as a generator of content but actually as a tool that undermined a regime that couldn't be undermined prior to that.

Voice 1: The problem is that Kelsey engages in a type of technological determinism in that he sees himself as a prosthetic of the technology rather than the technology as a prosthetic of him.

Voice 4: I would also argue that how you communicate through this network is much more interesting—what happens to a civilization when it is so dependent on these kinds of networks. So, for example, Werner Herzog just collaborated with AT&T to do a movie about texting. One impetus behind this movie is that he saw kids, really young kids, not communicating—not talking—but texting.

Voice 2: Well, there is also this idea Kelsey mentions of these networks creating a sense of exile.

Voice 3: I think he's purporting that it's impossible for people to grasp the amount of information generated because of the ubiquity of the internet and the ease of producing content on it, whether it has meaning or not. It creates this feeling of being overwhelmed. In some way, that's what LTR is trying to circumvent—we have in-person meetings and the content is generated here. In terms of that, the whole idea is to embrace the notion of the network, the notion of the system—but not to submit to the hardware. [*laughter*]

Voice 5: So, the application of a form in which you actually have to engage in person breaks the mode in which people have started their interactions for the past, say, five years—that is, with "I'd like you to join my network." There is this discussion of "friending," and then the power of "defriending." What are those intimate interactions that actually create a social network? This is why LTR initiates its conversations with just a prompt rather than with "a someone's" presentation—the topic, not someone's expertise, is the catalyst for the conversations, and then the networks that get created are a result of an exchange.

Voice 4: Well, we're working in a really traditional structure: you say something, I say something, you say something, etc. There's just a pool of conversations, which is different from what happens with a website where you're looking for something, and you are taken farther and farther and farther away from it, so you get distracted.

Voice 1: The other thing I am interested in is how Kelsey presents a mythic model of the artist—the notion that there was, once upon a time, an artistic monopoly on creativity. [*laughter*]

Voice 5: Well, it's that idea that you don't really know what is actually historically significant since all the information is consistently presented to you as . . . as immediate.

Voice 3: And you don't even know how to tell what is and isn't historicized, and you're saying . . .

Voice 4: I think it's also interesting how all this content turns everybody into an editor. You have to figure out what you are going to spend your time with and what you won't spend your time with, and that's sort of editing your selection, right?

Voice 1: To a certain degree both are relevant to the notion of *LEF(t)* as a publication and Curricula as a collaborative rather than a curatorial project. In both cases, CPI provides the interface between producers. As such, we aren't the content providers. Even with *LEF(t)* and its mode of distribution, we can't just say: "Here is a package of content." Our projects, as interfaces, necessitate an engagement; they construct a collaborative network between really diverse people who set the program in motion.

Voice 5: It's like bringing back this idea of the center or the hub as actually an interaction between people rather than an interaction that happens through a device.

Voice 4: But we don't want to be Luddites, and we don't want to be nostalgic for something that never existed. [*laughter*] So it really is about, in a funny way, creating a human internet rather than an internet of machines. I think a significant aspect of what we have developed is our embrace of terms like *programming*, *interface*, *social media*, *networking*, and *node*, which are the very terms of the technology that we seek to redefine. In that way, CPI doesn't resist anything—or oppose anything . . . We're not just reactive.

Voice 5: Which, I think, is what, you know, CPI is—a reformulation of all the different kinds of conversational modes that form around cultural production. It's about being a witness to those conversations or being able to be in the presence of some catalyst so that it can inspire you to investigate your own relationship from a starting point that is actually an interaction between people.

Voice 4: Good point. CPI is a facilitator—a producer that organizes and administrates.

Voice 1: Which, in a funny way, goes back to the very beginning of this conversation, in which we were talking about how these digital technologies were originally designed to crunch numbers and serve as interfaces, not as modes of mediation and output, right? The internet and computers were developed for strategic use by the military so that after we had annihilated ourselves, computers could still continue to fire off missiles. [*laughter*]

Voice 5: I'd like to bring this back to Kelsey's use of Baudelaire and the reference to social discontent: creating a parallel between the French Revolution and the Occupy movement. You know, perhaps Occupy is the type of social discontent people are willing to share. I like that idea of social discontent as generative.

Voice 2: I think that the general lack of any real solution-minded writing . . . the text is actually just Kelsey inflecting Baudelaire.

Voice 3: Right. But it is like the people who were participating in Occupy: it wasn't just a bunch of—we could use Marxist terms—proletariat laborers who were out there. They were people who were disenfranchised, who thought they should be entitled to things, who were highly educated but still weren't able to get jobs, and who had paid into the system in some way and were going out there, demanding a return on their Ph.D.s.

Voice 5: In some way were the notions of LTR's conversations and *LEF(t)* brought about from a feeling of discontent or . . . ?

Voice 1: The notion of the round table was a form of subversion in the sense of the internet being presented as a huge think tank, a round table, while *LEF(t)* was thought of as a social-media interface, to generate a following via Twitter, etc. Each was to carry content unique to its form.

Voice 3: What round table are you referring to? Not the internet round table but a private, previous round table that existed when people . . .

Voice 1: Well, you know, for me the joke about LaTableRonde was that LaTableRonde was also Action Française's intellectual organization to counter Jean-Paul Sartre's *Le Temp modernes*. So it was right-wing conservative, and for them it referred back to the Knights of the Round Table, right? But for me the notion of appropriating it . . . was amusing.

Voice 3: Ultimately, what did the Knights of the Round Table achieve?

Voice 1: You know, there is the notion of the quest . . .

Voice 3: For the Holy Grail? [*laughter*]

Voice 4: Which is, of course, a very romantic idea.

Voice 3: So the whole idea was to be able to bring together people, not the same old people you already know or engage with on a regular basis and not to turn it into a club but to keep it as a network in constant flux—that was the reason we came up with the formats we have. Right?

Voice 4: Which is why we sought to facilitate conversation and engage in production as critical form, rather than engaging in "critique."

Voice 1: See, I think that's what Kelsey misses—he somehow thinks that the type of programming he's writing about is somehow natural, that it's a result of the technology rather than the way technology is organized or deployed. There's nothing intrinsically technological about the Internet, nor is Facebook intrinsic to the Internet—Facebook is a way to organize the internet. Technology only supplies the speed. Basically digital technology imitates existent forms, and Kelsey, like so many others, seemingly thinks it's the other way around. [*laughter*]

Voice 3: Any appalling insights that we forgot? [*laughter*]

Voice 1: So I'll send this off to Wendy. I guess we'll then do a group edit and insert whatever we need to.

MATTHEW DELEGET speaks with DAVID PAGEL

David Pagel: I love a bargain as much as the next the guy, and the bargains I love best are books that have been ridiculously discounted and sold for a fraction of what they originally went for. Their prices suggest an alternative economy—one linked to the dominant economy but absurdly out of sync with its standard operating procedures. As an artist, what led you to choose discounted books as the main materials for *Zero Sum* (2011–), your piece in this year's Biennial?

Matthew Deleget: As with much of the work I've been making lately, I didn't really intend to make *Zero Sum* at all. The piece just kind of occurred to me in looking more closely at my own interests and habits—the things I do unconsciously when researching and making the things I make. I do love discount books. (I've got a bit of a problem, actually.) I especially like the rare, vintage, and out-of-print ones I find in used bookstores, which are sadly becoming increasingly rare in New York. Two of the remaining in my neighborhood in downtown Brooklyn just became nail salons. I don't even want to think about what that implies about the state of intellectual discourse right now.

For the last two decades, I've been combing through bins at second-hand stores, galleries, and museums for cool finds. Around five years ago, it struck me, though, that most of the books I'm interested in, both intellectually and aesthetically, have been either discounted or discarded in various ways by institutions, galleries, schools, and individuals. I can remember the precise moment this occurred to me, in fact. I was giving a talk at a local art school, and I came across the landmark book (for me) *Circle: An International Survey of Constructive Art*, edited by J. Leslie Martin, Ben Nicholson, and Naum Gabo, being used as a doorstop.

Of course, this book is resting safely at home with me now. It joined my collection of hundreds of monographs, artists' writings, biographies, and art-history publications—my personal resource library and a latent work of art unto itself.

DP: And does your interest in cheap, discontinued publications tell us much about the way you think of—and run—the gallery MINUS SPACE?

MD: Yes, in many ways, *Zero Sum* and MINUS SPACE, which I cofounded in 2003 with my wife, artist Rossana Martínez, address the same basic issue. Both advocate for artists and ideas that are extraordinary but that are generally overlooked, unfashionable, unmarketable, or, worse, discounted altogether. As artists, we make unbelievable sacrifices to produce our work, with the idea that we may, hopefully, someday be included in books like these. By thinking of these books as works of art, I've brought them back full circle into the realm of ideas and aesthetics. I wonder just how long it will be before I see this Whitney Biennial catalogue in a discount bin somewhere . . .

DP: And, if we're lucky, there'll be some bargain-conscious, history-loving youngster ready to snatch it up and do something interesting with it to rescue it from the dustbin of history. Is *Zero Sum* a kind of rescue operation? And doesn't that idea collide with the work's title, which implies a perfect balancing out of accounts? It seems to me that your work suggests that the accounts are not balanced, that there is a remainder, and that that is where the surplus value comes in. Is that where art enters the picture?

MD: It's so much more provocative to think of *Zero Sum* as a kind of rescue operation! Yes, I do think a big part of it is advocacy, working to set at least one facet of the record straight. As you know, I have a background in both painting and art history—I really don't see any distinction between the two. I'm terribly dissatisfied, however, with the history of contemporary art as it's been told in the glossies, mega-galleries, art fairs, museums, and auction houses over the past two decades. It's history as told by the "winners," in a way, by the one percent at the top end of the market.

By contrast, I find the plodding investigation of new ideas and forms, which primarily takes place inside artists' studios, to be much more compelling. It's messy, irrational, unregulated, pluralistic, and even contradictory. I prefer visiting a studio over seeing a formal exhibition of an artist's work any day. For me, seeing work in the space in which it's been conceived and labored over has just no comparison. My real interest lies not in the theatricality of a show but in that massive part of the iceberg that sits below the surface of the water and generally doesn't see the light of day. That's the part that keeps the rest of it afloat.

DP: Could you say more about the ways your backgrounds in painting and art history have fed into each other? How does that double-layered approach influence the many roles you play today—painter, curator, dealer, archivist, and historian? And does this suggest that amateurism, after years of disparagement from paid professionals, is making a comeback?

MD: I think my studio work and the work I do at the gallery are one and the same. It's honestly impossible for me to distinguish where one ends and the other begins. I'm an artist in the gallery and a historian in the studio. When I'm not physically in one place, I'm in the other. And I try to approach both roles with the same level of intensity and criticality. I don't think of it so much as amateurism but rather as DIY. And much of the art world as it currently exists—the things we genuinely take for granted now—was started in this same DIY manner by artists. Look no further than the Whitney Museum of American Art itself. Gertrude Vanderbilt Whitney, an established sculptor, founded the Whitney Studio Club in 1918 to support the work of her artist friends and colleagues. She also extensively collected their work, and later on offered her enormous collection—something like five hundred works or more—to the Metropolitan Museum of Art in 1929. When the Met rejected it, the Whitney was born.

I think our discourse would be much less interesting if we left it up to the professionals. I think the pros would agree with me. Meaningful things can happen when people start to question the status quo, envision how things could be different, and take matters into their own hands. I'm an ally of anyone who does this.

DAVID DIAO speaks with ANDREW RUSSETH

On a scorching afternoon in July 2013, David Diao and I met in New York, in his Tribeca loft. On the wall hung his 1991 painting *Barnett Newman, The Paintings in Scale*, a chart that presents the complete works of that Abstract Expressionist as little geometric shapes. He had bought it back from a Hong Kong auction house two months earlier, after reading, in my review of his show in New York the previous spring, that it was coming up for sale. (That exhibition included another painting that reproduced the catalogue pages of the same painting from a 2005 Hong Kong auction.) When I visited, Diao was midway through two new works about the twenty-two-year-old painting's path through the market, one a tall painting with the original piece silkscreened on it four times in reduced scale.
—Andrew Russeth

Andrew Russeth: What are you up to in this tall new painting?

David Diao: That painting documents getting *Barnett Newman, The Paintings in Scale* back from auction. If you hadn't discovered that it was coming up again, I wouldn't have known. I registered to bid and got the painting back at its low estimate. This new work will record, in my handwriting, the history of the painting, saying when it was made, where it was shown, who bought it, etc. At the bottom, I will scrawl: "Home again."

AR: The timing was such a good, weird coincidence. The world was working with you.

DD: Yes, but here's an instance where a big player—a dealer—would do it differently. He wouldn't buy it back at its low bid. He would have sent some shills there to bid it up, so that the final price would be very high, and then he could sell fifteen other works at the higher price. This is my stupidity as, you know, a dumb artist.

AR: You should have rigged it.

DD: I undermined myself by buying it at the low bid. The truth is, I like the painting a lot, so that when it was sold I missed it and bent over backward to think of a way to have it again. I made a second version. The justification was the publication of Barnett Newman's catalogue raisonné, which gave data for the number and order of the paintings that differed from my own initial research. In fact, I felt compelled to make the corrections and did so by using different colors.

AR: Where is this mint ground coming from in this new one?

DD: I'm attracted to the green blackboards in classrooms, on which information is disseminated and mathematical proofs are worked out. Stuff can be erased and reformulated. A painting is simply a place to focus one's attention, as in the classroom. In 1969, I made a huge empty blackboard, as if waiting for Cy Twombly to come draw on it. *Barr Talk*, from 1989, has Alfred Barr's chart of the development of Cubism and abstract art in chalk on a similar green. Whereas some would consider his chart canonical and set in stone, I painted it at the point of its disappearance. I like to think that a painting is just a demarcated space, which someone wants you to pay attention to.

AR: This idea of paying attention—reexamination—is at the core of appropriation, which you moved into in the early eighties, from geometric abstraction.

DD: There was a sense that everything I wanted to do had been used up. I could find no way to use geometry in a fresh way; how it's read is so fixed. One way I thought of getting beyond that is precisely to use its fixedness, to exploit the already-in-place meaning to make new meaning. In 1985, I chose to use Kazimir Malevich's 1915 installation photograph of *0.10: The Last Futurist Exhibition* as the template for an entire show of paintings because it's so well-known, trotted out in every book on abstract art as the ur-event. It invokes a utopian moment in art that is now unthinkable. Though many artists were appropriating and quoting earlier art by the mid-eighties, the best ones labored under that rubric the "death of painting." I still wanted to make paintings. I don't have a good answer for why, other than that it's what I had been doing. I have a particular interest in the history and problematics of painting, and I wasn't ready to throw it out the window. The problem with painting is that people still tend to see it formally and hence inertly, whereas I think painting is just the place where I can present stories and arguments.

AR: You've said you were "digging among the remnants" of modernism, hunting for something lost. You root for the underdog, almost.

DD: Well, I do, but I also like the offhand remark—something that is maybe not at the center but in the margins. Oblique. It's a way I find useful for working, because it might help me to get at something that has escaped notice.

AR: But the handling of the material—particularly at those points where your own life comes into the picture—is really direct.

DD: It is that. It's funny: I'm very diffident when it comes to writing. I think it has to do with having gone to Kenyon College, where my teachers so valued the well-wrought sentence, and I never thought a sentence I wrote was good enough. But somehow I always accepted that art making is provisional. It's not the last statement. It's only on the way to getting at something. So I don't mind making a fool of myself, and I don't mind revealing the most abject of information—whether my paltry sales record or my fantasies of institutional validation.

AR: That word *provisional*—there's this sense of linkages to other paintings you have made and paintings to come, which feels very contemporary. It's a story that will keep going.

DD: One day you wake up and realize you've been working for forty years. How do you make sense of the myriad bunches of work? Somehow you want them to count, if only as bridges from one group of paintings to another.The fear is that you'll never have another good idea again.

AR: Right, but there is always a very systematic presentation: paintings connect to and point at each other. You're showing things clearly and concisely, like Newman did. How do you do the actual painting?

DD: As much as I would like to think that I have gone through many ruptures, I've always been involved with the same issues. One is that old, old saw of painting's flatness. I realize that is a limited area to obsess over, but I'm stuck there. Not just in the visual flatness of modernist painting but also in the material flatness of the applied paint. That's why all the paintings since about 1986 have been done with knives.

With enormous pressure of hand and knife, I get that paint onto the ground. I really want to cover up the grain of the canvas so that it's as smooth as possible. It comes with a load of pleasure—getting paint to slide across a surface. The time it takes becomes an intense time of revelry, of thinking, of trying to figure out what to do next, and of what to keep from one's past and what to move forward with.

AR: There's a certain laboriousness to it?

DD: Somebody else might think so, but when I'm engaged in wanting to do something, it's no longer labor for me. It's just pleasure. It gets more pleasurable as the surface gets smoother.

AR: Showing at the Whitney—you were in the first Biennial at the Breuer building and now you are in the last—do you have plans to reference Marcel Breuer? I know you owned a home by him?

DD: Forty years between drinks. As for Breuer, I haven't referenced him enough, though I have made work about his failed cantilevers. The house was in the Hudson Valley. For the first ten years, I was really obsessed with restoring it. When I got the place, in its decrepitude, it made me see that modernism is not new forever—that the minute you own something or build something, it's on its way, through entropy, to ruin.

AR: Do you feel that's part of your work?

DD: Sure. For example, there was a crack in the painting when it came back from Hong Kong, but it's not glaring damage. I don't mind that. That's just the life of the painting.

PAUL DRUECKE speaks with DONNA STONECIPHER

Paul Druecke and Donna Stonecipher collaborated in 2011 on the first in a series of cast-bronze plaques. The inaugural plaque, *Near Here Milwaukee*, appropriates text from historical markers to pay homage to space and time. They began to work on an iteration for Los Angeles in 2012, which is still in its research phase.

Paul Druecke: Since we worked together in 2011, our respective relationships to the *Near Here* project may have diverged, especially regarding what story a new plaque might tell. My interest in a plaque's poetic potential broadened while in Los Angeles researching the city's landmarks. The scale of the city and its sprawling decentralization begged inclusion of the full breadth of how and what people write into the cityscape. By expanding our source material to include graffiti, park-bench nameplates, buy-a-brick tributes, and other historical markers and memorials, we force the plaque to become broadly inclusive, which inverts, or subverts, its normal function.

Donna Stonecipher: I don't know that our thinking has diverged so much as that I'm a great believer in the paradox of constraint—that through constriction emerges greater and more compelling freedom. This comes from my training in poetry, where much of the greatest human expression has been corseted into, say, the form of a sonnet. With *Near Here Milwaukee*, we limited ourselves to the database of Wisconsin memorial plaques, and the collage we made of that language system roamed nevertheless very freely through a number of emotional registers. When you sent me your first ideas about a collage of "markings," I found it exciting in a vertigo-inducing way. The scope seemed so vast that I felt (pleasurably) dizzy. Instinctively, I reached for the oxygen of constraint.

PD: Sensible enough, given the narrative bedlam I proffered.

If I remember correctly, you once told me about Baudelaire's role in developing the prose poem as a response to the city. The desire to express urbanity—the idea of all of us together—seems an act of mythic creation/destruction. I read existential urgency in public mark making. Plaques on benches in Central Park, graffiti scratched into wet cement, historical signage dedicated to this or that community: these markings accumulate week after week, day after day, literally hour after hour, even as the pace of life marginalizes them and makes them seem archaic.

DS: The interaction between the personal and the impersonal dovetails with how I'm thinking about Michel de Certeau's notion of people using "tactics" to appropriate the objective "administrative and legal entity" of the city through their own subjective movements and actions. Most of the unofficial or semiofficial markings one sees in a city, like the ones you list, are text intervening with nontext. Because the memorial genre we've been discussing over the years is mostly text based, I thought it might be productive to continue intertextually—to begin with a base of "official," "monumental" text and lob "unofficial interventions" into the midst of it, perhaps collected from a certain radius around our plaque. And then I would have my constraint.

PD: I like it. Our ammunition is inexhaustible. The streets brim with inscriptions, writings that assert agency, churning in the wake of the human herd shuffling toward the same goal. Everyone seems driven by a monumental desire for—and belief in—individuality and specialness. It's heartwarming, comedic, maybe a little sad. I imagine the drive for distinction starts with an obsession over time, complicated by our imperfect relation to everything temporal. (We're going to die, after all.)

We invent ritual, and ritual begs repetition and audience. The urban habitat is the perfect stage for the impossible balance between public and private—the city and its dwellers have evolved together over millennia.

DS: That makes me think of a recent trend: padlocks on bridges inscribed with lovers' initials. I first noticed this on a bridge in Bologna in 2011.

The lovers affix the padlock to the bridge because they feel the union between them has a uniqueness about it (unbreakable, apparently). But as more and more lovers affix padlocks to the bridge, the more each individual padlock is utterly effaced by the mass. In our quest to express our unique selves, which rises out of our sheer numbers, we are all the more quickly subsumed into the crowd. To go back to your earlier remark, Baudelaire's abdication of the traditional "subjective" lyric for more "objective" prose reflects this tension.

PD: At an opportune moment, one, the other, or both scratched "Jennifer V + Larry T Mr NYC 1991" into a freshly poured slab of sidewalk in Chelsea. They encircled their declaration with a crude heart, and through said heart they drew an even cruder arrow. Twenty-two years later, I fell in love with what's at stake in that bit of extramarginal marginalia. The youthful sentiment, not to mention its execution, doesn't betray the money poured into the same gesture at the other end of the spectrum. Vast amounts of wealth and scholarship underwrite the inscription of civic heroes, deep-pocketed philanthropists, and A-list celebrities into our public spaces. Jennifer and Larry were not daunted. They added their rogue tactical incursion into the public record with the best of faith, I have no doubt.

DS: That reminds me of Georg Simmel's 1903 essay "The Metropolis and the Mental State," in which he wrote about the transformations he believed human beings were undergoing in their evolutionary progression toward newly urban creatures: the urban dweller's need to individualize him- or herself within a crowd of samenesses was radically reshaping and even deforming individual psychology, so he or she would start to exhibit "the strangest eccentricities." To Simmel, what was occurring through the development of the metropolis was nothing less than the "atrophy of individual culture through the hypertrophy of objective culture"; this resulted in what he termed a "blasé attitude." These unofficial markers you are talking about are many things, but they are not blasé.

PD: "We two dear men, friends forever, were here. If you want to know our names, they are Gaius and Aulus." "On April 19, I made bread." "Antiochus hung out here with his girlfriend Cithera." The graffiti of Pompeii is usually recounted because of its sexual and/or scatological content, but these examples, from the entranceway to a bar (in the first case) and army barracks (the second two), show that the content runs a familiar gamut: friendship, hunger, love.

Can transcribing informal examples of public imprint into a more "official" medium have systemic reverberations? Would people ever care about Jennifer and Larry's proclamation? Do Jennifer or Larry care at this point? The possibility of an audience engaging with existential scratchings in cement seems tenuous—there's less at stake than when appropriating the language of other markers, as we did with the Milwaukee plaque. In my personal brand of populism, I'd argue that there's something far more evocative in the names and sentiments unofficially representing us in our public space. There is essence.

DS: Well, I'm afraid that Robert Musil's remark "There is nothing in this world more invisible than a monument" applies to both. Official or unofficial, our eyes gaze past them. Unless, of course, as with you and me, one starts to take a systematic interest in them. Otherwise, their signs seem to refer to times and places and people caught up in a cyclical rhythm—of birth, death, love, war—that feels too remote and/or general to apply to us personally. Maybe there's a parallel with the recounting of dreams: nobody wants to hear about anyone else's dream unless they make an appearance in it. Memorials and monuments seem to belong to others' dreams (or nightmares).

PD: Nightmares of unnecessary information. That's the perfect image of a quagmire that is the glut of public inscription, all the resources that underwrite it, and the running-without-moving terror of attempting to differentiate ourselves by contributing to the collective pool.

ROCHELLE FEINSTEIN speaks with JENNIFER KABAT

Jennifer Kabat: Can we talk about extinction and Lonesome George? How did he get the name Lonesome? Was he always lonely?

Rochelle Feinstein: I've been working simultaneously on two videos, each about different species but both about "the end." The first is *Toy George*. Lonesome George, a giant tortoise of a thought-to-be-extinct subspecies, was discovered on Pinta Island in 1972 by a ranger, Fausto Llerena. He became George's keeper—and he found him dead in June 2012, somewhere between 112 and 132 years old. Under Fausto's watch, George lived at the Darwin Project, Galapagos, both as a major tourist attraction and as part of a breeding study to keep the Abingdon Island subspecies alive. Attempts at reproduction failed, which may be why he was named Lonesome George, after the fifties TV personality "Lonesome George" Gobel. Maybe they intended to put a light touch on George the tortoise's impending extinction. I've followed his "story" for years, first in print, later on the internet. George's remains are currently at the taxidermist's and will be on display this winter at the American Museum of Natural History in New York. All his visible parts will be intact except his eyes—

JK: His eyes? That seems really weird and almost like something around which you could do something, because the other elements of your piece involve voice, and somehow seeing—the eyes as the window to the soul—and voice and who speaks seem movingly linked.

RF: Yes. The second video, *She Has a Name*, is about my mother, who was lost sometime in the late 1970s, never found, and presumed "extinct" sometime in the 1980s. Her "ending" is unknown. There are no records of her life; no census reports; no voting, criminal, medical, or death records, or any factual material to add form to her life. What I do have is an archive of home movies; a made-for-TV movie about schizophrenia, *Strange Voices*, made by a relative in 1987; latter-day Rotten Tomato reviews; and email documents accumulated on my laptop—the "motherboard" of the piece.

JK: So we have two losses that seem to add up to a larger sociopolitical context, involving media. With George, there's the environment, and he's evocatively connected to Darwin and all that Darwin represents; your mother's story is pulled through a political landscape and a personal one.

RF: I wouldn't dig into these narratives, or any, without faith in discovering a much larger dimension. I tend to start with an emotion in obvious and dumb ways. For example, my brother and I are the last of our line. While I'm not like George, I "can relate," as a member of my species, to his single and childless status. Anthropomorphizing aside, the social and economic conditions of George's story are not "adorable." Beginning in the late nineteenth century, hunters decimated the tortoise population of Galapagos for meat and fuel, while the growing agricultural economy introduced goats and other livestock that ate the grass that was the tortoises' food supply—a familiar narrative.
My mother was schizophrenic. One of her many misfortunes was to be institutionalized during the years Nelson Rockefeller and Hugh Carey were governors of New York, at the onset of deinstitutionalization policies, when over 50 percent of the mentally ill population were removed from hospitals and "returned to the community"—placed largely in squalid welfare hotels, with minimal medical and social services. My mother became extinct as a result of this social experiment.

JK: That story is achingly sad. The way you interweave these narratives and see them expansively is really moving. And there's the schlocky TV movie—

RF: *Strange Voices* is the last place I ever wanted to go. I hate it. It's sort of like emotional slumming . . . high on the bathos spectrum. I only saw it in its entirety three years ago. When it came out, in 1987, I was on the subway, reading the *Times* review of this movie about schizophrenia that seemed weirdly familiar—

JK: The review I found last week?

RF: Yeah. *Strange Voices*: the story of a young woman gone nuts, cowritten and coproduced by my cousin. I wasn't told about the movie, not then and not since. When it showed up on YouTube, I downloaded parts until the data was removed for copyright infringement.

JK: That seems ironic.

RF: On eBay, I found a pristine VHS, from Denmark. Around that time, my brother found a pile of 8mm family movies. These started gelling as distinct elements in *She Has a Name*, a melodrama by and about my family that begins with three minutes of the made-for-TV movie, alongside the footage taken by my father of what he chose to film. To that, I'm adding my own on-screen presence. My question is: who owns this story—or who is the owner of any historical narrative or retelling of an event?

JK: Yes, the idea of story and narrative and who owns it—

RF: The internet in my case.

JK: I like how the media accretes in your work—in its collected media, in its mediated on-screen experience, and in your narration. It becomes this thing about life but also about the nature of mediation.

RF: Yes, about mediations accumulated over time. Funny, I got an email today with the subject line "Search Results Matter."

JK: Yes! As a fiction writer, I feel I'm always striving to reach a place where multiple ideas can exist in one piece, and I'm always failing. It pisses me off. I mean, I write about art in part because so many elements can coexist in a single piece. In fiction? I can't reach that depth. Narrative is so straightforward, and truthfully I don't often like fiction that isn't. Essays, though, can compress many things and have elasticity.

RF: So why keep writing fiction? Maybe it shares with painting the "why does it still persist" question . . . All I can say is the results are not, often enough, compelling.

JK: I love fiction.

RF: I loved fiction. I don't anymore because the narrative path moves from here to here to here [*indicating a straight line with her hand*]. Not sure what I'm learning on that path. Maybe a lot, maybe not much.

JK: Yes, life isn't one straight here-to-there story.

RF: And most fictional narratives are driven by one character's story, despite the presence of multiple characters.

JK: But narrative in our day and age is thought of as so layered, especially with shifts in media. We see a continuum of passing stuff as viewers and rarely get stories with the considered richness that you're bringing to these videos. Art can compress things. Like poetry . . .

RF: Compression. My low-res videos are really short, and they don't do much. They do nothing, in fact. But I don't want them to do the things the movies do. Probably because I think like a painter when making a moving image. The compression here may be comparable to a layering process in painting—real-time application of material and thinking spatially in two dimensions.

JK: Your work is about problems in painting, but there's an emotional level to it, like with your cats in the painting *Today in History* (2012–13), which comes with a shredded chair. I love your work because it's funny, too.

RF: This painting should be installed with the chair placed approximately eight feet away. Sentimen-tality and loss and comfort get embodied in this weird modernist chair mangled by kitties imaged in the supersize photographs that are part of the paint-y paintings. One can lounge, take in a 360-degree view.

JK: But in your hands, issues in painting seem really urgent. Urgent and funny. Like *In Anticipation of Women's History Month* (2013), which is deadly serious and yet has all this warmth and humor . . . and a wearable pin to go with it, which sits on my desk.

RF: Abstraction, without a human depiction, can't readily be penetrated by emotion. So you perceive abstraction in some other way. Some thinking/feeling way, and it brings along whatever accumulations, however ahistorical or personal. I like abstraction that puts up the appearance of a cold, impenetrable front. That makes me think, "Oh yeah, are you talking to me?" I love that.

JK: And there's the original development of abstraction—how it's been historicized—linking it to a teleology that was almost an eschatology of art, as in, "We're onto the endgame, folks, and we're going to have a second coming"—as if abstraction were the clear line to the Rapture after the "End of Art."

RF: And there's who got taken up . . .

JK: Almost like in a UFO.

LOUISE FISHMAN speaks with DONA NELSON

We have been looking at art together for decades—in galleries, museums, and in each other's studios. We are always expanding our understanding of art making and thinking. We have been each other's most serious and dedicated critics. For this conversation, we met at the Museum of Modern Art in New York.
—Louise Fishman and Dona Nelson

PART I
Jo Baer, *Primary Light Group: Red, Green, Blue* (1964–65)

Dona Nelson: We're looking at . . . Jo Baer.

Louise Fishman: These paintings are so understated. There's nothing dramatic; there's nothing sucking you in. They are beautiful paintings and they are forceful—in their squareness. Very even. They don't do what paintings by men seem to do, which is more to knock you over the head.

DN: No, they are restrained. I admire that they are not lyrical. They are different from Agnes Martin's works in that way—totally different, actually.

LF: Right, right.

DN: And they are cerebral. They don't go beyond what they are. That's a big accomplishment after the Abstract Expressionists and all their, you know, desire . . .

LF: Ego.

DN: Yeah, ego and desire to go toward the existential statement.

I'm looking at those white squares—and the black and green, black and blue, and black and magenta lines around them.

LF: It's not a framing device.

DN: It's not a framing device, and that's quite an accomplishment! They are free of so much metaphor, illusion, and statement extraneous to the paintings themselves. They actually do what a lot of Minimalist works try to do but are too grandiose to accomplish.

LF: They're meticulous and so pure.

DN: And they're hand painted—there's a little wobble . . .

LF: I'm noticing that, as you get close, the whites change color . . .

DN: It's affecting. Even the thickness of the stretcher, which I would say is maybe two inches or a little less, seems very . . .

LF: Well, it has a stripping on it—it looks like a canvas stripping. It's probably either canvas or canvas around wood. So, actually, when you get close, it becomes a band. Just like the other bands—the black band, the pink band, and the square. It's really so integrated.

DN: It's such a specific size, too. These are terrific paintings.

PART 2
Paul Cézanne, *The Bather* (c. 1885)

DN: I know this is one of your favorite paintings.

LF: It is my favorite painting. In fact, I did a whole series of drawings and paintings from it, none of which are likely to exist anymore.

DN: Wow, when?

LF: Probably in the sixties . . . when I first got to New York. I had received a terrific education from a guy who taught color and design at the Philadelphia College of Art. His name was Karl Sherman, and his was the class in which I learned the most about painting—not from my painting teachers and not from art history . . . I was only there a year, but Professor Sherman had a major impact on me. One thing that was so striking was that this guy lectured with his hands in front of him—with passion, grand passion. He talked about Piet Mondrian and Cézanne. I think he came from the Bauhaus, and what he taught was the power of painting: the energy and the dynamic. Many years later, I came across him sitting on a bench with his wife. He must have been in his seventies. Now I'm thinking, I'm in my seventies!

DN: Yeah, yeah.

LF: Back then I thought of him as an old man. He introduced me to his wife, and he put his hand out. Two of his fingers were missing at the end of the first joint. The whole time he taught, I never noticed. And his hands were right in front of me!

DN: Do you think he had so much feeling for this painting because the hands are so prominent?

LF: For him, it wasn't this particular painting, it was Cézanne in general. What's interesting in this painting is the way things disappear, the way the area around his legs becomes sky, and the way the thing is sculpted. Cézanne really is a sculptor with paint, right?

DN: Let's move over a little, so that we're more right in front of it.

LF: I also knew an interesting guy, the sculptor Sidney Geist. He introduced me to his book *Interpreting Cézanne*, which is about all the "ghosts" in Cézanne—the things that are there but have been painted over. There are all these puns, allusions, anagrams—consciously or unconsciously—embedded in the work. They could be left over from earlier paintings or from him just moving things around.

DN: It looks like he kept repositioning the figure.

LF: I think I identify with this figure.

DN: What—the carefulness and the solemnity?

LF: And also the physicality of the body. There is such a density in the description of the legs and feet. It's so much in the round, but then it's Cubist, it's flat. Where the knuckles are in the right hand is perfectly flat.

DN: It's one of the flattest Cézannes, actually. It feels as though there is gravity centered in the man's attitude and his incredible orientation to the ground where he's stepping.

LF: Then, the landscape—it just barely exists, but it's very tactile. The hills . . . there's no definition about what's back there.

DN: No, and the scale isn't realistic.

LF: It's a gigantic figure. A giant.

DN: It is about being human in relation to gravity. It's very much an idea painting.

PART 3
Joan Miró, *The Birth of the World* (1925)

DN: This is one of my favorite paintings. It's such an amazing painting for 1925! It's a big painting, and when you think of it in relation to Rothko and Newman . . .

LF: Clifford Still.

DN: Still . . . monochromatic abstract fields . . . I love the dripping. It's on very fine linen, and there's something about the tiny detail in the completely abstract surface—what's happening physically with the paint.

LF: This is really stained. It's poured.

DN: And wiped. I've spent a lot of time looking at this painting. I personally was relieved to be able to look at this painting and just have permission to feel that kind of space. Dripping is a form of drawing. He has so many different ways of applying paint. He's splashing; he's rubbing with a rag. Then he puts these flat-footed shapes on the painting, this white and red ball and this black triangle . . . I love the title because it's just a completely abstract painting.

LF: Yeah, but it has all this sort of . . . not womb-like—what would you call it? Sperms and things. I'm thinking about where you came from, Grand Island, Nebraska, and how I came from Philadelphia, and the difference in our takes on painting because of these landscapes—how that difference affects our ways of seeing. I'm looking at this painting, and I'm thinking that the scale of it is huge. It feels more like the countryside than anything I ever knew growing up.

DN: It has dirty colors, but it doesn't seem urban.

LF: It feels inky.

DN: Don't you think it's also related to Asian paintings? To scroll paintings?

LF: I don't think I would have gone there. I mean, there is such a hard-edged black shape in the bottom left. But maybe the rain in a Japanese landscape is related . . . But there would never be literal things that take on that kind of weight.

DN: Right. It's not a depiction of nature. It seems like a purely authoritative and masterful placement of shapes. It's a painting I've never quite gotten to the bottom of. I feel that with Miró. He's treating the surface with such detail, and yet it's completely loose. That's very unusual. Today it seems that painters make maybe two or three moves when they make these big surfaces.

LF: I think of that period's artists as having a lot more freedom. There wasn't a contemporary art history, which can be poison. They were inventing themselves. That's pretty fabulous.

PART 4
Pablo Picasso, *Glass of Absinthe* (1914)

DN: Picasso used a real absinthe spoon in this sculpture. You realize how Pop it is and how, simultaneously, complex it is. It's also like a Surrealist object. It just scoops up all these different art movements. It seems just completely instinctive too, the way the little clay form—oh, it's bronze!

LF: It's cast.

DN: This is such a Conceptual object—a big object but so modest in size.

LF: There's a loving sense to the way these shapes fit together. It has a kind of affectionate quality, such as in the way that black, sharp curve comes around. It's a flat shape that's painted right on the surface, which mimics some of the molded curves.

DN: Yeah, it's amazing because it's a shadow, but it could be a shadow of some other object being cast on that object.

LF: It could be. I think it references the spoon. It is as though it is the shadow of the spoon, but of course it isn't. It's more a shadow of the shape that is painted black. Its references go back and forth and tie the bottom of the sculpture to the top. That black with the white inside, it's really so considered . . . It's very delicate. Actually, I think there is more delicacy in Picasso's sculpture than in his painting. It has to do with the tactile quality. It has to do with touching and making with the hands.

DN: I know. It's so much a created object and that's what's so interesting. It's not a glass. It's a riff on drinking. It's a riff on . . .

LF: Community.

DN: Also the body. It's hollow. You can look into it.

LF: Think of Picasso and all his cronies in the bars sitting around drinking absinthe. He put everything together. He put everything into the mix.

DN: To me, it has none of the fixity of a product-type piece of art. Even as you're looking at it, it's making itself.

PART 5
Pablo Picasso, *Les Demoiselles d'Avignon* (1907)

DN: This painting seems to come so much out of Cézanne's *The Bather* (c. 1885). But it's important that there's no landscape here—there's an interior. There's not the same relationship to gravity.

LF: You know, one of the things I never noticed before—or maybe didn't think about—is how the background feels like glass. It's sharp. The whole painting is very sharp. Look at the fruit . . .

DN: It looks like glass fruit.

LF: It's so sharp it could penetrate the figures. The blue and white are like reflections on glass. It's dangerous looking.

DN: Dangerous, yeah.

DN: You know, we talked about how *The Bather* is an idea painting. It's rooted in a landscape, the Mont Sainte-Victoire, and it goes into such a psychological place with the gaze, because the bather is looking down. These women, by contrast, are looking right at you. I've never noticed how intense their gaze is!

LF: It's a tough painting. It's so hands-on—like building blocks. Things jammed together. The hand at the upper left—you don't know where it's coming from but it's holding up that whole—

DN: It doesn't look attached to either figure.

LF: But it's so densely drawn and outlined.

DN: How about the blues? They're not really from nature . . . He goes from a Prussian blue in the reflections to maybe ultramarine in the drawing of the knee down there.

LF: There's also that standard European still life at the bottom, a detail that became such a powerful part of his body of work. There was no reason to do a still life as just a detail on a larger painting, but it's a crucial detail in this piece.

DN: And it's just not naturalistic. It's gray and reddish.

LF: Those pink stripes on the fruit anchor the painting. I just love this painting. It's crude and at the same time incredibly sophisticated.

DN: It's so completely economical, and it's all very close to the canvas. It's all business.

LF: That's a good way of putting it. I've never looked at this painting in this particular way before, but the slope of that curve for the nose and the way that shape comes down . . . whatever that shape is—maybe a piece of watermelon—happens throughout the painting. Those nasty curves.

DN: You are right: it's full of danger, and he didn't know where it would lead at this point. They call Picasso the "vertical invader." He gave up so much of his skill in order to make this painting. It's so impressive, his courage, as a model for an artist. Danger is not really something you often see in an artwork. You see psychological instability in some late van Gogh paintings, for instance, but this is very different. This is danger embraced.

LF: I think he had a toughness that a lot of people just didn't have, say in his ability to make the head of that woman and the breasts push into a non-Western culture. He obviously understood the power of African art. It was a very early understanding of it, but the fact that he took it on is kind of amazing.

DN: It's as exciting as ever.

PART 6
Jackson Pollock, *One: Number 31* (1950)

DN: We're looking at Pollock's great drip painting, *One*. It's so fresh; I think it's been recently cleaned. I'm struck by how powerful, subdued, and related to nature and the light of nature it is—how nature can so drab, you know, when you are out in the fields. It combines graphic power and drabness, which allows it to be, for me, contemplative.

LF: Oh yeah, it's not at all aggressive.

It's hard to talk about this painting. When I look at Pollock, I always wish I painted differently than I do [*laughs*], because his process of walking around and through a painting is fabulous, and not having to think about the formal issues of the edges—not that he didn't think about the edges, because there is an actual edge all the way around.

DN: Oh yes.

LF: That is an extraordinarily appealing notion—to travel through a painting rather than to construct it. But the more you look at it, the more the shapes become clear; it's not just a passageway through skeins of paint . . .

DN: It's so beautiful, isn't it?

LF: Celestial. It is hard to talk about. It just covers you.

DN: It just keeps on living and living. It's breathtaking in its dignity and majesty.

LF: Yeah, good words.

PART 7
Jackson Pollock, *Shimmering Substance* (1946)

DN: Do you like this painting? It's a lot of white, yellow, and some pink.

LF: I adore this painting. It makes me want to cry.

DN: To me, it's very related to your paintings—and I don't often think about Pollock and you together.

LF: How? I don't see it.

DN: It's the use of the paint; it's very present. And the brush! Your paintings are unself-conscious—you just paint until the painting feels finished to you. This also feels that way, like it's scraped down and then painted back up. These kind of dimples, or circular motions, seem very relaxed for Pollock.

LF: I love the title *Shimmering Substance*. The other thing that's unusual for Pollock is that the colors are so soft. Some really come forward, as if they were jelly-beans or something you want to caress. I do feel like I could just cry over this painting.

DN: Like all of Pollock's work, this painting is highly conscious and highly specific, and the colors are very carefully mixed, this lime green . . . And this, this isn't red, it's . . .

LF: It's more like an orange.

DN: Like a coral. It's physical, abstract, and specific.

LF: I'm kind of curious . . . I wish I could see around the edge. Oh, you can! I thought it had a piece of tape on it. You can see it. He did actually stop it. It was painted on a stretcher.

DN: A very thin stretcher—it's so delicate, and it has incredible space for such a small painting.

PART 8
Kurt Schwitters, *Revolving* (1919)

LF: I've never thought of your work in relation to Schwitters, but this makes me think of your paintings.

DN: Oh, you know, that thrills me more than I can say . . . Schwitters is so precise and surprising in his use of the materials. See, he used part of a drop cloth, with grommets at the bottom. He picks up on that essential part of the base material to make the circular, machine image. The image isn't separate from the materials. He's transformed it psychologically to be like a shadow on a wall.

LF: There are actual shadows in the painting, created by things that protrude.

DN: It would be very interesting to see this piece next to *Glass of Absinthe*.

LF: I can't imagine anything more exciting than being Schwitters working on this piece or Picasso working on his glass.

DN: There's a kind of grand modesty in Schwitters because he operated outside of the big movements. I do think of him as outside of Constructivism, Expressionism, or Cubism. His work is still so relevant.

LF: He was a magician.

VICTORIA FU speaks with PAUL PFEIFFER and BRAD TROEMEL

Paul Pfeiffer: Victoria, viewing your new video installations, I'm immediately struck by how the edges of the video image don't line up with the edges of the projection screen. The image spills off onto the walls and floor of the surrounding space. Also, the people and objects on-screen appear unfixed from their background, like cutouts suspended in an ambiguous, green-screen void. At one point, a hand tries to finger swipe a cockatoo as if to advance to the next page on an iPad touch screen. But the bird doesn't move. Each element in the picture seems isolated on its own separate layer. In the sound track, I hear background voices and someone typing on a keyboard, which makes me think an invisible director or editor is controlling the action. All of this suggests to me a new, expanded image environment—one that blurs the boundaries of projected image, real physical space, and hyperspace. You're making installations that behave like cinema in some ways, like sculpture in others, and like the internet in still others.

Victoria Fu: Every figure and object in *Belle Captive* (2013) is an appropriated green-screen stock clip from the internet. The footage is overlaid and manipulated—cropped, looped, blurred—to appear as foreground on a color-field background that I've shot on 16mm film. Each layer is disconnected from the others, but at the same time they're legible all together as action within cinematic narrative space. Installed, the off-kilter projection merges the videos' spatial logic with ours in trompe-l'oeil fashion, toying with our perception of actual space. Cinema is pixels on-screen is projected light is a sculptural object is the walls of the room. In what some call a "postcinematic" or "postinternet" moment, is the viewer a spectator, protagonist, user, or all of the above? With the emergence of the digital, painting's problem of representation (Magritte's "This is not a pipe") persists with higher stakes: now, more intricate degrees of simulation ask us to engage with the constant flood of images on a haptic level—swiping, tapping, dragging. I recognize the impulse to translate the digital into analogue, extrude sculptural space out of the virtual, then back again.

Brad Troemel: Virtual!! [*giggles, pops leather-jacket collar, takes a drag before placing clove e-cigarette over magnetic-faux-pierced left ear, clears throat*] I'm interested in this feedback loop you describe wherein all physical art-things must eventually be digitally mediated (many works are now constructed with their inevitably mediated form in mind), but I'm also a fan of art's signal getting lost in the digital abyss. Decentralized image-sharing networks allow art to become something other than itself, reblogged into contexts and for purposes totally unrelated to the author's initial intentions. Art's integration (disintegration?) into everyday life feels most exciting here because this is a uniquely contemporary phenomenon based on current mediating technologies. Can you imagine another time in history when twenty thousand fifteen-year-olds in suburban America were using Robert Smithson images to impress each other and get laid? [*wipes Andrea Fraser–based alligator tear from eye*] Historical avant-garde dreams do come true!!

PP: Great expectations! There's a sense of new possibility in this digital era, particularly around the emergence of decentralized modes of content distribution and consumption. Whole new horizons are opening up to support freedom of expression and interconnectivity, new ways to reinvent our identities and customize our user experience. But I wonder if all this really amounts to a kind of vastly extended shopping mall. In his book *Design and Crime* (2002), Hal Foster describes the endless possibilities in a suburban mall to choose just the right combo of clothes and accessories to formulate a unique identity and lifestyle. The only thing you are not free to choose is your ontological limits. In my opinion, what distinguishes art is the focus on ontology: the intent to question reality. It's not just the production of another object, image, or experience to be consumed; it's the production of self-awareness in the act of consuming. It's an experience of disjunction, of crossing a threshold from one reality to another.

VF: You've often considered these thresholds in your work, Paul, asking viewers to switch modes of engagement between differently mediated images. It makes me wonder, what happens when the threshold is broader and the apparatus less detectable? What are the phenomenological implications of engaging in digital simulation?

BT: [*embarrassed, looks up from one-handed sexting on a Motorola Razr*] I don't think scrolling on a device produces a greater degree of engagement for viewers. Scrolling is an act of indifference; it's a tepid, upstream doggy-paddle against the deluge of status updates, lunch decisions, selfies. Scrolling is a pattern-finding mission that doesn't privilege any bit of information over another but serves to identify links between posts. I won't click a news link until three people who don't know each other have shared it. We use our calloused index fingers to scroll, but it's a process derived from the organizational principles of machines. I am, by the way, totally fine with that. [*winks at Jaron in the front row of the press conference Victoria, Paul, and Brad are holding at Madison Square Garden; Jaron angrily wind-flutes back*]

VF: Scrolling appears to give freedom of choice, but we are still limited and informed by the system. Psychogeography at the virtual level still shapes being and consciousness. Just as our bodies conform to behavioral patterns dictated by our built environment and social status (whether we hunt for our food, jog on a treadmill, work in an office), I can imagine an analogous situation where our neurological pathways form along Google image-search typologies.

PP: I think it's important for artists today to acknowledge their roots in the legacy of Conceptual art—the generation of artists in the sixties and seventies who deeply distrusted images, for whom it was necessary to reject the visual and material in favor of words and ideas. But we're far removed from that moment. The Pictures Generation in the 1980s represents a shift like ours to a focus on threshold, where there's a desire to play with the power of spectacle, to appropriate the image toward other ends.

VF: Yes, we aren't far from the Pictures Generation's play with spectacle. The gesture of appropriation has been normalized (animated GIFs, for instance) but is no less relevant given the ease and speed with which we encounter and proliferate images. The global advertising network is imbricated in the stock footage I use, and the videos I make are just single nodes along paths of dispersion. Moreover, the footage, created on green screen, is meant for any kind of advertisement background; dictated by capital, the visual content adheres to a one-size-fits-all, generic flatness. Exaggerating the "home-less" aspects of green screen, *Belle Captive* weaves the blandness of stock media into a narrative-like spectatorial experience—looping and stretching the duration of actions, collaging absurd combinations. In a way, the images we encounter on the internet are Surrealist objects or ready-made combines—hyperlinked and endlessly divorced from their original contexts.

BT: One of the coolest things *The Jogging* [thejogging.tumblr.com] stole from advertising is the idea of having an unavoidable relationship with media. Lauren Christiansen and I started the project as a response to the attention economy. We wanted to create a way of producing (and a type of) content that would fluidly exist in a digitally mediated environment that privileges image ubiquity rather than operating on the scarcity model of the art market. [*polishes flag lapel pin, runs hand through hair to appear more Romney-esque*] *The Jogging*'s Tumblr presence was always meant to maximize attention efficiency in that context. We would make and photograph multiple configurations of sculptures—let the free-market attention economy decide which version is best! Downplay authorship by only using abstract symbols—let the images' rebloggers decide what to do with the author's identity in relation to their online personas! Post more content than any one person could possibly share—let the rebloggers express individuality through what they choose to share! Make use of topical events and known products—let art become a background for the image consumer's comment threads! [*puts hand up to high-five Rupert Murdoch, Rupert swings, Brad swipes hand over his head as if to run hand through hair—"Too slow, old man!"*]

GAYLEN GERBER speaks with JEANNE DUNNING

Jeanne Dunning: I thought a good way to discuss your new work at the Whitney and perhaps to shed some light on it, would be to talk about other pieces you've made that use some of the same elements. One of the central elements of the Whitney project is the very large Backdrop painting; Backdrops have been part of your work for a long time. In these works you take a preexisting wall and stretch a huge canvas of the same dimensions, and then paint the canvas some neutral color, typically gray. You hang this painting on the wall, so that when it's hung you can barely see it's there unless you look at the edges. I've seen photographs of the process of building and stretching one of these canvases. You have to build the stretcher and stretch the painting in the same room where it will be hung—it's too big to get through the doorway. It's this massive work, but as soon as you lift it up onto the wall, it seems to disappear. It's sort of the perfect way of getting at this idea that the painting is a background—the ground against which we see other things. When did you first start making the Backdrops?

Gaylen Gerber: The first one was made in 1993 and exhibited the following year at Nicole Klagsbrun Gallery, with Joe Scanlan's work in front of it. But it's hard to say, I had been making work related to this idea for more than a decade . . .

JD: As I recall, before the Backdrops you were making works that were more easily understood as discrete objects: paintings, drawings, photographs . . .

GG: Each Backdrop is a discrete object—canvas over a wooden stretcher.

JD: But we don't really experience them that way. So it seems like a shift to me. The Backdrops are so much about the fact that they don't function on their own. Even calling it a backdrop points out that it only functions if there is something in front of it. Of course, ultimately the point you're making is that all those supposedly discrete art objects do the same thing, that they don't function independently.

GG: It's more complicated than that, but yes, it's fair to say that my early work was intended and scaled for an individual viewer. But even at that time I was organizing my exhibitions so that they had the kinds of relationships to each other that the individual artworks have to each other. In the early 1990s, I did a couple of exhibitions that helped collapse the difference between the exhibition space and the objects, most notably at the Renaissance Society and Documenta 9, in which my early paintings were installed in contiguous lines. They overtly made a promenade, or a background, that framed the activity not just of a single viewer but of the entire room. These installations were the precursors to what would become the Backdrops a year later.

JD: I remember those shows. It seemed like a pretty dramatic move to hang those paintings that way because they involved an image of such traditional subject matter—a genre image—and so they seemed to invite a more routine way of viewing. When you butted them all up next to each other, with no space between them, they made this frieze. It forced us to see them as one thing. Another element that's central to the installation you're doing for the Whitney is that this giant Backdrop has other works literally hung on top of it. Did the first Backdrops have things hung on top of them?

GG: No, I still hadn't figured out how to orchestrate that. The exhibition with Joe Scanlan in 1994, for example, started as a one-person exhibition. Then I invited Joe to work with me: we installed my work, which literally represented a wall in the gallery, and Joe installed his work in front of and around it. It was uncertain whether this was still a one-person exhibition with Joe, a two-person exhibition, something else, or all of these.

JD: And Joe's work was sculptural, so when you say you installed it in front of your Backdrop, it wasn't literally on top of it?

GG: Joe installed his work as he normally would have, around the room. His objects related to everyday things having to do with a personal economy. They occupied the floor or leaned against the wall—but nothing hung on top of the painting itself.

JD: So when was the first time that you actually hung a two-dimensional work on a Backdrop, as though you were hanging a painting on the wall?

GG: It had to be in 1997, at the Chicago Project Room, in an exhibition with Mari Eastman and Amy Wheeler, which continued with Charlie Cho, then Helen Mirra. When Mari and Amy's exhibition was coming down, I had a conversation with the director, Michael Hall, and we thought it would be important for the Backdrop to remain in place while the exhibition in front of it changed, as a way of accentuating the relationships between the more temporal aspects of expression and the less temporal aspects of the expression's ground.

JD: At the Whitney, the works hung on top of *Backdrop* will change during the exhibition. You're starting with two paintings by a young artist named Trevor Shimizu, then about halfway through they'll be replaced with works by David Hammons and Sherrie Levine.

What you just recounted is interesting because I hadn't realized that the idea that over time multiple things might get hung against the same Backdrop had always gone hand in hand with work being literally hung on top of it.

GG: I've thought about *Backdrop* as a representation of the architectural ground, a representation of the normative ground of the culture, intended to represent a slower rate of change and so appear to be more stable . . .

JD: Were you thinking that in a traditional exhibition in a museum or gallery the white cube of the architecture plays the role of the normative ground?

GG: Yes, the normative ground is not architectural per se, but a cultural ground and specifically a representational ground.

JD: But in this case the architecture both acts as it and stands in for it . . .

GG: Yes, it stands in for the larger picture. When I originally started thinking about this, it seemed to me that the cultural ground we see things against was more stable than I now consider it to be. I essentially thought of it as unchanging or glacial in its rate of change. Now I see it as also fluid but moving at such a dramatically different rate than other expressions that it *seems* to be unchanging. Trying to represent this perception pushed my work, for lack of a better description, toward a semiotic relationship to visual language.

JD: So as I understand your work, in the end it's about this idea that whatever we're aware of, it's because of the way it stands out in contrast to, or emerges from, what surrounds it. Whatever we perceive, it's because of its distinction from other things. That's like the classic figure-ground relationship—you know, we see a figure because it distinguishes itself from a ground. It's interesting to see the relationship between what you're doing and these very old art concerns. And that when it comes to what we see (and don't), the ground matters as much as the figure.

The ground is also linked with formlessness. I know that when you talk about your work, you usually choose the word *expression*, and talk about these same ideas in terms of expression and ground. And for me, the term *expression* does allude to the temporal aspects that you speak of in a way that *form* and *figure* don't. But if I keep following this train of thought, figure, form, and expression become iterations of the same general structural position as ground, formlessness—and normativity. An important aspect of all this is the idea that grounds function almost invisibly for us—we don't pay attention to them, we take them for granted, not realizing that the ground is not a given. If the ground changes it can allow different expressions to emerge; in that sense, everything that is a ground is also an expression. Not only does it affect other expressions, but maybe it's an expression in its own right. By the same token, anything that is an expression can also serve as a ground. Hence we have you taking a painting—a vehicle for expression—and turning it into a ground.

GG: I'm trying to remember exactly how I started thinking about this. I think it came out of my desire to actually try to see, to understand something, and to be clear about that understanding. And—this is exactly what you're saying—that in order to see something it must be delineated. That mechanism of delineation is more permeable, shifting, than I had considered. I remember realizing how tricky this can be when I was installing a room of photographs, works of mine that are silver prints of a clear sky on a bright day. They look flat and opaque, like concrete expressions of their own materiality, until you understand what the images represent. Then they become atmospheric and represent an extremely deep field.

JD: Yes, I've always been especially interested in those photographs because they look like some sort of minimalist object—a square of photographic paper with no image—until you realize they're actually photographs *of* something, and something that is not a deadpan or neutral subject but one suffused with feeling and associations—a clear blue sky.

GG: I was installing the photographs in an exhibition with James Welling and Angela Grauerholz in Vienna in 1994. They are gelatin silver prints, and I installed a room of them in conjunction with one of Jim's early gelatin silver prints of a Wyoming landscape. My intention was to have my clear skies connect with the sky's representation in his photograph—to hopefully cut the landscape in his image loose from its background, and push it forward, separate from the ground that the skies represented. The thing that I hadn't anticipated was that his image made my photographs immediately recognizable as representations. The relationships I was trying to frame were more complicated and unruly than I had anticipated.

JD: That was really beautiful, that exhibition.

GG: I had forgotten about it until we started talking.

JD: I want to bring up another of your exhibitions that I find especially interesting—it was so succinct and clear—at Rhona Hoffman Gallery in 2010. She had a Sol LeWitt wall-drawings show up, and Kehinde Wiley's work was scheduled next. Typically when a show of LeWitt wall drawings ends, the drawings are simply painted over in "gallery white," and a new show goes up. You asked Rhona if you could paint over the LeWitt drawings to make a work of yours. For those of us who've worked for galleries and museums and been part of those installation crews that have done the work of painting over the drawings, there's an awareness that the LeWitt drawing is actually still there, hidden underneath a layer of paint. So when you asked if you could paint the gallery walls, you were putting your expression on top of LeWitt's ground, which became invisible, and your expression in turn became the ground for Kehinde Wiley's work. You were just doing what would have happened anyway without your intervention. A LeWitt wall drawing begins as an expression and eventually becomes an invisible or unacknowledged ground for another artist's work.

GG: Yes, and Kehinde Wiley's work then, in turn, becomes the ground for other expressions. One of the things that was interesting about this for me was using white, which I think of as an alternate neutral. It's kind of our cultural de facto neutral, at least for certain situations. And yes, it is invisible unless you consciously look for it. Recently I did an exhibition at the Museum of Contemporary Art in Chicago, where half of the show was colored bright amber and half was colored the white that the museum normally uses to paint its walls. Almost no one recognized the white portion of the exhibition—not just the color but that whole portion of the exhibition—as an expression. They didn't see that it was also the exhibition. They recognized the amber portion as expressive because it deviated from the norm of the institution, and the white, as a noncolor, went unseen. But both portions were equally intense, and the exhibition was in large part about exactly that relationship.

JD: You've involved Sherrie Levine's work for a second time in this Whitney project: in 2006, at Chicago's MCA, you exhibited a large Backdrop painting with her *Untitled (Gold knot 1)* hung on top of it. Were you thinking about that exhibition when you proposed this project for the Whitney?

GG: Somewhere in the back of my mind I thought pairing Sherrie Levine with David Hammons could be interesting . . . It's complicated enough that it's not easily apprehended. It wasn't until I went back and looked at an image from the earlier exhibition that I realized that the MCA curators had installed David Hammons's sculpture *Praying to Safety* directly in front of *Backdrop* with the Levine. Somehow the complexities and incongruities of that situation had gotten into my consciousness and emerged in my consideration of the form of this exhibition.

JEFF GIBSON speaks with FRAZER WARD

Frazer Ward: Walking frames, sunglasses, ball bearings, high heels, hearing aids, diggers, saucepans, tropical fruit, meat, men's sandals, forklifts, strollers . . . In your most recent video, *Metapoetaestheticism*, we see a series of still images of apparently random collections of objects overlaid with the invented linguistic definitions you've been working with for a while and accompanied by a very funny elevator-music score. Where do you find the images and what drives your choices? How do you establish the juxtapositions—however loose or close—of homemade taxonomies and definitions?

Jeff Gibson: The images are all derived from Google searches. I have an enduring fascination with made-up systems of classification and at some point began assembling an idiosyncratic catalogue of carefully composed image taxonomies as a kind of visual corollary to the compendium of definitions concerning human behavior and weird sociocultural phenomena that I've been compiling for years. I search topics until I strike something that engages me. I am, as Ed Ruscha famously said, interested in what is interesting. Some topics are too obvious; others, too obscure. I'll often settle on something that reveals a surprising aesthetic variety. Who knew, for instance, that the world of walking frames is so stylistically diverse: there's the standard-issue public-health-care option; the snappy, anodized aluminum rig; the swooping, aerodynamic designer model; and the streamlined three-wheeler with its jaunty, plaid carry-all. Other searches mine specific veins of categorical banality (blue pumps, red sunglasses), exposing photographic microgenres as exhaustive, heterogeneous bids for consumer identification.

Sometimes, it's simply the form (say, of ball bearings) or the semiotic absurdity (say, of meat) that appeals. I then organize the images and definitions intuitively into roughly parallel, interwoven sequences that throw up semiaccidental, poetic connections between image and text, being careful to avoid opaque imponderability, on the one hand, and literal illustration, on the other. As for the sound track—a Muzak rendition of the extensively covered "Shadow of Your Smile"—I was aiming for a slow, hypnotic, memory-laden headspace, a soporific seduction that matches the pace of the dissolving words and silhouetted image-objects. And it lends the work a comically apt shopping-mall/waiting-room/elevator ambience.

FW: The music certainly cues the comical aspect of the work, but then the visual taxonomies have a sort of blank, faux-anthropological quality that is also funny, if in a slightly queasy way. The definitions are similarly comical at the same time as they are a little uncomfortable, because they carry a sense of being grounded in art-world or everyday social situations; they are funny because they're true. So there's the cheesy, seductive veneer of the work, but there's some bite underneath, suggesting that you're working with a relation between humor and criticality. In connection with that, you're putting into play an attenuated conceptualism (linguistic definitions), alongside selections from the mass media's image bank (where choice is overrun by the inexhaustibility of the content). Is there an element of both the humor and the critique that concerns itself with the shifting relations between image and word?

JG: As a lifelong magazine fiend, I'm a big fan of image-text poetics. I relish the conceptual and aesthetic potential of that relationship. The "comical aspect" seems to appear of its own accord but is clearly, in many instances, a palliative for the sting of criticism. For me, the beauty of comedy lies in its license to expose and excoriate. Larry David's decorum-busting "social assassin" is exemplary in this regard.

But if there's a queasiness to the taxonomies, it's only upchuck from their subject matter's place in the world: I'm just trying to make a critical fist of the garbage floating through my "digisphere." As far as the definitions are concerned, they remain inclined—by virtue of dyspepsia—toward mockery and disapproval, but with humor!

FW: Isn't Larry David's *Curb Your Enthusiasm* character a social assassin and socially suicidal at the same time?

JG: Sure. That's part of the appeal. He'll say the very thing you're thinking, but you know saying it would lead to social death. It's cringe-worthy yet hilarious. And, again, that's a great thing about humor. It allows you to speak the truth to delusion and pretense, as long as the context of the utterance is fictionalized, depersonalized, which is only barely the case with *Curb Your Enthusiasm*. Of course, were we to behave that way in real life, and I've known cloistered misanthropes who do, all civility is lost, and with it, ongoing social contact.

FW: And if we're talking about queasiness, upchuck, and dyspepsia, are we in the doctor's waiting room rather than the elevator?

JG: Ha! Yes. And the doctor is in. I like a public space with a captive audience. Waiting rooms, lobbies, elevators, subways, and, for that matter, galleries, are sites of psychosocial suspension, and, as such, are conducive to reverie and self-consciousness, the ideal conditions for the reception of my work.

FW: Do you think your work intensifies that suspension? Or, to put that another way, do you think your work establishes connections between those kinds of spaces, from waiting room to gallery?

JG: I'm mostly looking to capitalize on the contemplative state that such spaces induce or allow, since a lot of my work requires, or attempts to catalyze, thought. But if the work intensifies that state, all the better. Nearly all waiting-room ambience seeks to fill the existential vacuum of life's little layovers with distracting infotainment or tranquilizing aesthetic clichés—CNN, talk shows, nature docs, and travelogues. Give me art or a dog-eared magazine. And regarding the correlation of gallery to waiting room, the gallery, in providing respite from quotidian drudgery and an increasingly rare opportunity for reflection, is perhaps the ultimate waiting room. The connections are readily apparent. I'm more intent on exploiting contextual similarities to test and extend the reach of my work.

KARL HAENDEL speaks with AMANDA ROSS-HO

1. Karl Haendel
2. AMANDA ROSS-HO

Products I Like

Fantastic
Pine-Sol
Palmolive (original)
Brut Anti-Perspirant & Deodorant (stick)
Frédéric Malle, Jean-Claude Ellena's Angéliques sous la Pluie
Snuggle
409
Nizoral
Dove soap
Bar Keepers Friend
Arm & Hammer detergent (liquid only)
baby powder (cornstarch)
Comet

EYE SHADOW

WORRY MARKET
A GALLERY FOR CATS
THE DEAD CAN'T SAY NO
FUCK DIVORCE
EVERYTHING BAGEL
DRAWINGS ON CD-ROMS
RELATIONSHIPS
INSANE SUNSETS AND HAND-PAINTED SIGNS
IF YOU NEED A TROIS FOR THAT MÉNAGE I'LL BE AT THE BAR

Types of Sex

Exploratory Sex
Revenge Sex
Self-Esteem Sex
Sympathy Sex
Power Dynamics Sex
Quid Pro Quo Sex
Routine Sex
Angry Sex
Make-up Sex
Competitive Sex
Obligatory Sex
Bait-and-Switch Sex
Nothing-to-Lose Sex
Resigned Sex
Stress-Relief Sex
Status Sex
Bored Sex

FONTS AND STRAINS

BIG CASLON AND BLUEBERRY DIESEL
ALBERTUS MEDIUM AND 1-EYED JAMAICAN
CAMBRIA MATH AND BLACK VELVET
MARKER FELT AND CAT PISS
PLANTAGENET CHEROKEE AND CHEESE QUAKE
COPPERPLATE AND CHOCOLOPE
OMNIA AND CHEM DAWG #4
PEGASUS AND GRAPE GOD
HARRINGTON AND INCREDIBERRY
BASKERVILLE OLD FACE AND JOCK HORROR
BLACKLETTER AND JACK KEVORKIAN
FRANKLIN GOTHIC AND FUCKING INCREDIBLE
WINGDINGS 3 AND GEORGE BUSH
PERPETUA AND GNARSTY
EGYPTIENNE AND GODCRACK
CHARLEMAGNE AND PLATINUM GHOST
HAETTENSCHWEILER AND PURPLE PUSSY
FOOTLIGHT AND ACCIDENTAL TOURIST
BRAGGADOCIO AND BLACK JACK
CENTURY GOTHIC AND JACK WIDOW
CALIBRI AND KILLING FIELDS
APPLE CASUAL AND ROMULAN GRAPEFRUIT

NFL Football Helmets I Like and Why

Cleveland Browns: The only team to go with such a minimalist approach, it is just an orangish helmet, no logo at all, clear, and matter-of-fact, although you wonder why the helmet isn't brown.

Pittsburgh Steelers: The logo, in which three asteroid shapes (which I assume represent iron, coal, and scrap steel—the ingredients in steel) are depicted in harmonious balance, invokes the proud and successful history of the city, while also pointing to its current postindustrial decline. Also, the logo is only on one side of the helmet, the flip side is left blank, which is really odd. The Steelers are the only team to go with this one-sided approach, whose specificity I find pleasurable.

Oakland Raiders: I believe this is the only team not to have a "color" (silver seems to me to be a shade of gray), and for this I find in them a formal affinity. Also the helmet logo depicts a handsome man, clean shaven, and chiseled, wearing both an eye patch AND an old-time leather helmet, suggesting the odd convergence of collegiate athletics and high-seas lawlessness.

Miami Dolphins: It depicts a dolphin leaping through a hoop or sunburst, wearing a football helmet no less, a highly constructed situation if ever there was one, which makes me think the designers were very self-aware, if not self-critical, of the entire process. It's also damn cute.

ALWAYS

Always Incredibly Thin
Always Incredibly Thin Fresh
Always Xtra Protection

Always Radiant Incredibly Thin
Always Infinity
Always Radiant Infinity
Always Ultra Thin
Always Ultra Thin Fresh
Always Maxi
Always Maxi Fresh

Am I a Feminist?

- I put the toilet seat down.
- I do all the cooking.
- Mary Kelly was my thesis advisor.
- I enjoy reruns of *Sex in the City*. And while I find these ladies shallow and materialistic, I understand that they are wrestling with the difficult questions of how to be their own women in a post–Gloria Steinem world.
- Whenever I make a really big drawing, I know it has something to do with my penis.
- I don't think any woman needs to be taken care of or protected by a man, but if any woman wants to take care of and protect me, I think I'd be open to it.
- I keep noticing that most museums are primarily staffed by women, although the directors are usually men.
- I'd be happy if a woman was president.
- I'd be happy if a woman was the starting center fielder for the Yankees. I'd be really happy, though, if that woman was my daughter.

REAL TALK

- THE COLOGNE YOU WEAR IS TOTALLY WITHOUT NUANCE.
- YOUR LIFE ISN'T LONG ENOUGH TO FILL THIS ROOM.
- THE TATER TOT COUNTS AS TWO ANCIENT GRAINS.
- EVERY HANGOVER IS CANCER.
- THE PIGEONS WILL SHIT ALL OVER IT.
- SEX IS THE WEIRDEST THING IN THE WORLD.
- DON'T BE COUNTING CHICKENS BEFORE CHICKENS BE HATCHING.

Fears of mine

fear of failure
fear of losing loved ones
fear of getting fat
fear of being poor
fear of dirtiness
fear of old furniture
fear of humiliation
fear of cancer

CLOSE-ENDED QUESTIONS, FOUND

- Were you planning on becoming a fireman?
- Could I possibly be a messier houseguest?
- Shall we make dinner together tonight?
- Did that man walk by the house before?
- Should I call her and sort things out?
- May I please have a bite of that pie?
- Is that haunted house really scary?
- Is the prime rib a special tonight?
- Did Dad make the cake today?
- Will you please do me a favor?
- Are you feeling better today?
- May I use the bathroom?
- Should I date him?
- Are you pregnant?
- Are you happy?
- Is he dead?

Sayings of My Dad's That Have to Deal with Food (Literally or Metaphorically)

- Dinner at 6!
- You'll eat it, and you'll like it.
- Life is a shit sandwich; take a bite or starve to death.
- One day your nose will be so big you'll have to lift it with one hand and eat with the other.
- I hope to god one day you have a wife whose cooking is horrible, and she'll put a plate in front of you, and you will say, "Honey, it's wonderful."

TOP STORIES

"YOU TALK?"
"I'M TAKING OVER!"
"NOT ONLY THAT, BUT WE ARE MAMMALS."
"OH YEAH? OUR RELATIVES WERE KINGS."
"THAT'S LIKE SAYING FREE OHIO."
"THAT'S AN ASSUMPTION."

Things I May or May Not Have Said to a Student:

"Paul McCarthy's 'body' is very different from Marina Abramović's 'body,' beyond the fact that one has a penis and the other has a vagina—although I suppose that is a pretty big difference."

"Yes, but what would your grandma say?"

"Perhaps your notion of an expanded field has expanded too far?"

"I think it's super important to consider the ethical implications of choosing to be an artist. Like, where is artist on the ethical continuum of career choices? I used to think it was, like, up there with community activist, but now I think it might be right there next to sommelier. The question is, do you want to be a sommelier?"

"Maybe it's possible to have too much visual pleasure?"

"How can you not care what happens in Washington? Who do you think guarantees your student loans?"

"Remember, God took six days to do his work; you can give yourself a break but not too long—He only took one day off. And we can leave it up to Nietzsche to figure out if He was antsy that day."

"Do you mind if I eat in here?"

THE END

SINCERELY,
KINDLY,
WARMLY,
WARM REGARDS,
KIND REGARDS,
BEST,
ALL THE BEST,
MY BEST,
BEST WISHES,
FONDLY,
CHEERS,
YOURS,
XO,

PHILIP HANSON speaks with JOHN CORBETT

John Corbett: For certain painters, I think, painting is an improvisational activity. For others, it's more of a constructing activity. It would be possible to look at yours as the latter, but I think it's actually the former. You're really engaged with being in the painting in the moment. As happens with a lot of improvising musicians, when you listen back you can make aesthetic judgments and decide whether it works, but what really motivates you is doing it.

Philip Hanson: Yes. I have a regular routine: get up and do it. If I have four hours, something's always possible.

JC: I've often found with music that my memory or impression of a performance does not match the recording.

PH: Method actors live in the improvisational moment—and they really need directing. They might feel their performance is really great, really working, and they need someone to tell them after that it's not really coming through. A painter gets to be both performer and director; first thing in the morning, you're the director, you get some distance on the work of the day before. The painting might need some solving—there's a minor color or volume problem, something you were worried about, and then you realize it was really about something else. That's why the moment you see your work afresh is so special.

JC: How did the words come into your paintings?

PH: Taking notes in school, I was always making elaborately marked-up diagrams, as a way to pay attention. And my paintings are like diagrams—elaborate configurations of color and space. The earliest word paintings were from the sixties. They were candy boxes, built on stretchers that looked like boxes, with painted plastic flowers on them. Putting one word on them, like "Lovely" or "Dear," added another quality to the image. In the eighties, I made paintings that looked like horticultural prints of invented plants, then I recognized that they were like nineteenth-century parlor paintings that had phrases in them—a simple one, for example, was "God is love" surrounded by vegetation. I started thinking about those phrases, and began borrowing bits of Blake, things like that, and then finally I used whole poems. These paintings involved the structures of the words, the symmetries, their multiple meanings. That's why Emily Dickinson is so interesting: she does really strange things with words, in terms of balance and sound.

JC: In a way your paintings are like the opposite of diagrams. If diagrams are about reducing things to essentials, your paintings are about multiplying possible readings.

PH: They're often about the emotional tone of poetry, which risks disappearing in a diagram.

JC: And you never approach language from an ironic standpoint. Your use of poems treats them as a parallel art form.

PH: It's a little more like what composers do, setting poetry to music because they like the words.

JC: Color is central to what you're doing. You create dynamic situations in which the value of the color in a 4-inch square, can completely change a 6-by-4-foot canvas. It seems like balancing or juggling, coordinating, all these loaded color combinations.

PH: I set up a color environment and then go into it. A fade between two colors can be the beginning of a painting—setting something up, letting it lead elsewhere. Once you make one choice, it eliminates a lot of others. And the poem is always a guide, helping me make decisions.

JC: Because your approach to the poem is empathetic. You're not trying to poke fun at it or undermine its sentiments. With color and form you are enriching the reading of the poem.

PH: The text already has a richness to it, a power, a luminous quality. Some of the poetry I choose is about spiritual things. I don't know how much I believe, but I love the surface of spirituality. How it looks and the history of it and the intensity of it.

JC: That's also about apprehending things for what they are, really getting deep into them.

PH: The poem gives a path. Before going into the studio in the morning, I walk for an hour. I see a lot of beautiful things, and I'm very enthusiastic. There's a pattern on a building at the intersection of Damen and Chicago, a cast-iron sequence of curves—fantastic. The painting is always the facade that you go into.

It's like in the work of Alfred Jensen, with his numerical calculations and Mayan mathematics, sometimes things are put into an artwork that you can't get back out. Something else comes out, beyond your control, and an intensity emerges. Sometimes, in making a painting, I only know parts of the thing, even though I have a sense of the whole. So I'll make a part, and make another part, and then maybe I have to adjust the first part to make them fit together.

JC: How much of the structure of a painting is developed in sketches?

PH: Very little. There are sketches, like the Abstract Expressionists' "skirmishes," as Harold Rosenberg called them. There's no original drawing for a painting. It never works that way for me. The painting has to have the right surface, or thickness, and I don't mind if it gives a sense of its history. Color underneath affects the surface—adding another coat changes the intensity. Many artists aspire to Bach—you can follow these structures and suddenly they cohere to have a hugely emotional quality. It's not only rational, it has a feeling to it, and a larger implication.

JC: How does symmetry function for you?

PH: My work has the idea of symmetry but not perfectly so. Symmetry almost always refers to architecture and the body: the torso, the face, the building. But in Japanese architecture, they might have two trees of different types playing against each other, implying symmetry but not in an absolute way. There's a medieval diagram of the universe that I'm particularly interested in, concentric circles or ovals, then suddenly Christ's head is at the top and his feet are at the bottom, so it shifts the diagram into a body form. And from another realm altogether, I'm interested in the quality of circus posters. They have to convince us that there's all this great energy in one place, at one moment.

JC: Under one roof!

PH: And on one surface. The poster has to sell us that energy. I'm old enough now that I've looked at many things, like circus posters, but I didn't set out saying I wanted to make paintings that relate to circus posters.

JONN HERSCHEND speaks with ANDREW LELAND

In the following conversation, Jonn Herschend and Andrew Leland meet for the first time since an earlier attempt to have a printed conversation for another publication, which ended in failure. The two men had previously fallen out over a misunderstanding involving a promise that Jonn does not recall regarding his role in a short play that Andrew was producing about the experience of watching cable television on a laptop. Here, both men are about to paint the study in Jonn's aunt's house. Paint cans are scattered around the room, a spattered tarp lies on the floor, and an old ladder leans against the wall.

Jonn Herschend: Thanks so much for agreeing to be involved in this conversation. I enjoy the format of such conversations and was excited to discover that you do as well.

Andrew Leland: How did you make the discovery that I enjoy this format?

JH: You had mentioned it to Lisa [Jonn's close friend] some three years ago, and it was one of those things I just couldn't seem to forget.

[*Jonn inserts a Bluetooth headset into his ear and looks at his phone. He sets an open can of paint on a bookshelf.*]

I'd like to focus our discussion on the uses of entertainment in art. Many artists feel that it's not art's job to entertain. When something feels entertaining, then maybe it's crossing the line. Rather, it's art's job to ask the serious questions.

AL: What are the serious questions?

JH: For example, what are we doing here?

AL: We're having a staged conversation in a room to be painted.

JH: But what are we doing here, what are we doing here in this life? What is this?

[*Jonn gestures around the room, taking in the books, the carpet, the ladder, the window, and the open can of paint.*]

AL: You mean the existential issue? Why is there something instead of nothing?

JH: Well, yes . . . and also the other issues of how we occupy ourselves with structures and distractions to insulate us from the nothingness.

AL: What structures are you occupied with?

JH: All structures and the rules that seem to govern them.

AL: Which rules?

JH: For example, the rules that govern the boundaries of art and entertainment. There is a tension between what is considered art and what is considered entertainment.

AL: For critics? For readers? For artists?

JH: I'm not sure which group has the most tension, but to get things rolling, let's start with *Don Quixote*. It's a formal investigation of narrative structure (as the first novel), but at the same time it's filled with fart and sex jokes and intense violence and comedy.

AL: I've never read *Don Quixote*.

[*Andrew goes to the ladder.*]

JH: It doesn't matter. We can still talk about it.

AL: So a formal investigation of comedy equals art, while fart and sex jokes equal entertainment?

JH: Something like that . . . maybe not exactly. I'll try and think of another example.

[*Andrew grabs the ladder and hoists it onto his shoulder.*]

AL: One thing that connects art to entertainment is pleasure. The primary goal of entertainment is to hit the pleasure centers in your brain. Art hits the pleasure centers, too, and not just because it can be titillating or hilarious—though, as you point out, it's often both. The nutritional or difficult parts of art can also hit the pleasure centers. What kind of pleasure is that? Is it like solving a challenging problem or puzzle? Is it self-satisfied or self-congratulatory pleasure, where you feel good because you're doing something enriching, as art softly blows the human spirit upward through the museological air ducts of cognition?

[*A brown bird lands on the windowsill and glares derisively at them. Hearing its flapping wings, Andrew, still carrying the ladder on his shoulder, turns just in time to see it fly away. As he turns, Jonn bends to tie his shoe, the ladder swinging just inches above his head.*]

JH: Tying my shoe reminds me of a funny situation I was in a long time ago.

AL: Art has always blown the human spirit . . . softly upward.

JH: I was in my twenties and living in New York, which in itself is funny.

A bunch of us were out late at a bar called Tortilla Flats, and I was very drunk. I didn't think I was drunk, but I was. And there was a woman there whom I was trying to impress.

I think she worked in a gallery, which is how the art context works in this story. I remember thinking that she was really into me, but, now looking back, I can see I was delusional. I'm not even sure she worked in a gallery.

AL: Art is nutrition; entertainment is candy. No one will eat a brick of pure nutrition unless they're a masochist or they've put themselves on a strict, pleasureless diet. On the other end of the spectrum, pure entertainment causes tooth decay. To get the dog to eat the pill you have to plug it into a glob of peanut butter.

JH: I thought I was very charming and funny. But she was really just into my friend. However, at that moment, I felt that everything I was saying was electric. I was thinking that maybe we should all be dancing. I might have said, "Let's start dancing, everyone" and made a sort of flourish.

[*Jonn attempts the same gesture, his left hand pointing jauntily above his head. He holds the gesture.*]

AL: One way this model gets complicated is when the brick of pure nutrition, the work of pure art, with no fart or sex jokes in it whatsoever, gets appropriated, absorbed, or softly blown into popular culture. It's suddenly trendy to drink unsweetened artistic kombucha just because it's good for you and makes you seem cool. In that case, there's an element of entertainment even if the work itself doesn't have any fart or sex jokes, since it's entertaining to feel cool.

JH: The room was small and filled with people dancing. It was hot and dark. I was king of the small dancing room. And then suddenly I needed to vomit. The bathroom was on the other side of the dance floor. And I would never make it across the room without potentially spraying others.

AL: An example of the way that all-nutritional art becomes entertaining occurs anytime a "difficult" artistic technique leaves the avant-garde and enters the mainstream. Ads for jeans that look like Op art. Ad copy for shoes that read like postmodern fiction.

JH: So I decided that I would pretend to bend down and tie my shoes and throw up quietly beneath the bar. I thought it was a great idea. I looked at the woman (whose name was Lisa, I believe) and mumbled something like, "I'm going to tie my shoes. Hold on."

AL: The problem for the creator of something nutritional but hard to swallow is how to get more than four people to consume (or understand) their work.

JH: I bent down and vomited all over the floor . . . but very noiselessly. I thought it was the best sort of vomiting anyone could do. I was really proud. And then when I came up, everyone, including Lisa, was staring at me in horror.

AL: This argument has been flogged extensively in the literary context, primarily by writers responding to Jonathan Franzen's complaints about the difficulty of reading William Gaddis. Is something different at stake when we're talking about visual or fine art?

JH: Did you hear my story?

[*Jonn moves to the window to lean out, gazing into the middle distance.*]

AL: I thought you were on the phone. You're wearing a Bluetooth headset. Were you talking to me?

JH: Yes, I was. I was giving you an example of entertainment and structure in the art context.

AL: Have you ever seen a funny abstract painting?

JH: Hold on, I'm getting a call. Hand me a roller? I want to get this section.

[*As Jonn leans out the window, Andrew, the ladder still on his shoulder, turns to get the paint roller. The ladder swings around and knocks Jonn out the window. Andrew is unaware that he has just sent Jonn down from the second story into the shrubbery below.*]

AL: I guess you're not a painter. You work a lot in video, which is of course the most entertaining medium ever devised in the long global history of entertainment . . .

SHEILA HICKS speaks with JULIET KINCHIN

Juliet Kinchin: After sixty years of pulling, gouging, wrapping, folding, and weaving thread in all directions you've never fallen out of love with textiles? Not many artists have managed to stay the course working with this tricky and strenuous medium.

Sheila Hicks: What I do is labor intensive, and wearing on the eyes, hands, and back. It puts many people off. Or they become discouraged by the reception of their work and switch to media more readily identifiable as "art." At a certain point, even Anni Albers felt her weaving would never be fully acknowledged as art, and she gave away her looms and materials.

JK: The work you are presenting at the Whitney reveals your exhilarating and exploratory engagement with this medium over eight decades, across multiple geographic locations. The most immediately impressive is a monumental work that cascades dramatically from the ceiling, but you have also chosen others that are diminutive in scale. You seem to attach particular importance to those small irregular works you call "minims" as a record of your research and thought patterns developed over time.

SH: Yes, I found my voice and my footing in my small work. It was informed initially by Josef Albers's teachings about perception of color and the inherent qualities of materials and mediums at the Yale School of Art. Then I studied ancient textile constructions during a Fulbright scholarship in Latin America. My rudimentary portable weaving frame serves as my sketchbook. On it, I can compose a fully finished and independent small statement. Or I can investigate, discover, and create a new visual language with a single strand working as both warp and weft. I've devised ways to improvise double-sided pliable planes with four finished selvages and infinite variations of closed and open compositions, which challenge the imagination.

JK: The kind of pictorial thinking that Paul Klee described as taking a line for a walk.

SH: Thread language is coherent, seemingly simple, and basic. At the same time, it expresses and adapts to multiple layers of information. I have heard computer programmers pay homage to Joseph Marie Jacquard for the elegant simplicity of his punched-cards system for controlling the mechanical weaving of intricate and complicated structures or complex patterns. Introduced in 1801, this early form of a "stored program" influenced the subsequent development of computing machinery.

JK: And those complexities are not only technical but intellectual. You manage to translate a whole range of sensory impressions into woven and constructed form: sounds, colors, tactile contrasts, temperatures, even smells. My first encounters with your work reproduced in books did little to prepare me for the sheer physicality and multisensory assault of the real thing—its floppy bulkiness, the tactile subtleties, the evocative scents of laundered cotton, steel fibers, or husky wet-spun linen. These are powerful triggers of memory and feeling.

SH: Most of what I do is a quiet probing, a search for poetic and hidden meanings in the commonplace. It is an examination of neglected or forgotten methods for inventing forms and tooling them to new applications.

JK: "Stuff" seems an apt cover-all term for the unconventional range of materials you use, particularly as it can describe both textiles and material of an unspecified kind to be worked on. What's in your stuff?

SH: After a quick investigatory look: wool, linen, silk, hemp, polyester, acrylic, steel fiber, fishing line, twine, rope, tape, string, cloth, netting, felt, wood, filters, bands, thread, yarn, canvas, braided coir, shoelaces, rubber bands, razor shells, porcupine quills, feathers, fossils, bamboo, metal keys, newsprint, slate, twigs, grass, gauze, cardboard, price tags, dried noodles, coins, raffia, cornhusks, rickrack, buttons, plastic toothpicks, paper clips, rags, uniforms, T-shirts, napkins, dish towels, underwear, gloves, neckties, photographs, comic books, chicken and fish bones, rayon, nylon, cashmere, vicuña, llama, guanaco, alpaca, goat hair, rabbit hair, angora, camel hair, horsehair, human hair, reeds, mohair, iron, copper, silver, and gold.

JK: Some works begin with the pure material in its natural form, but you've also incorporated some intriguing found objects—an enamel bathtub, a mason's compass for stone calculations, ancient iron fishing forks, darned Carmelite sheets and socks—which come with their own histories and poetic resonances. The way you title works reinforces this idea of textiles as a form of storytelling and reportage, which people instinctively relate to inner processes, experiences, and feelings. You have often said that your natural curiosity about material culture was given direction and rigor by your studies at Yale with George Kubler, authority on pre-Columbian art and author of *The Shape of Time: Remarks on the History of Things* (1962).

SH: Kubler's lectures were magical; his physical presence was powerful and made his delivery forceful. He showed slides of Andean mummy bundles in class that made a lasting impression on me. I may have had them in mind when I exhibited what appeared to be ghostlike personages: washed, bleached, and pressed white cotton nurses' blouses from the Lausanne Cantonal Hospital. For a number of years, I presented them in various constellations and in different countries.

JK: I hear you ruffled a few feathers in 1975 when you first showed a mountain of twelve hundred of these neatly folded and piled blouses at the tapestry biennial held in Lausanne!

SH: I was moved by the sight and purity of the massive avalanche of these soft white forms. I wanted to contrast them to the stiffly woven tapestries from the Gobelins and Beauvais workshops. The original blouses, now cut in strips, have remained integrated in the work I titled *Le Démêloir* (1976). Each blouse unwinds in a ribbon-like zigzag path. They are combined with hundreds of white cotton bellybands originally used to wrap newborn babies. These bands, with attachment ties sewn on both ends, come from the Municipal Hospital in Lund, Sweden, and were part of my 1978 exhibition *Tons and Masses* at the Lund Konsthall. I treat such materials as building blocks: I use the elements to shape and create soft and approachable presences evoking life cycles.

JK: *Le Démêloir* takes me back to my own experience as a teenager, when hours were spent dismembering old clothes and constructing strange new ones. Through play with textiles from an early age, I developed a sense of sculptural possibility inherent in flat materials. I find it interesting that in the 1920s Lilly Reich in Berlin and Charlotte Perriand in Paris followed similar paths, from their understanding of textiles and the construction of clothing to the profession of architecture. And now, as a curator dealing with architecture and design, I can relate to your treatment of textiles as building blocks that can be installed anew each time. At the Museum of Modern Art this past year, it was thrilling to unwrap and build a fresh configuration of your *Evolving Tapestry: He/She* (1967–68) consisting of hundreds of bound and stacked "ponytail" units.

SH: I like to feel prime material in my hands. This is what interests me most: the possibility to sculpt submissive material into self-supporting shapes and forms. Prior to becoming textile, raw yarn or thread—before it is carded, twisted, spun, plied, and dyed—is weighable and measurable in units. I love watching a single running weft thread inserted into a network of programmed warp threads, resulting in cloth (with the help of a loom). When the woven cloth is transformed into clothes, towels, tents, or curtains, the colors and textural features become of prime importance. I tend to feel lost with too many choices, and stick to the rudimentary in my work; I avoid "the decorative" as an extension or parallel path. The new work *Pillar of Inquiry/Supple Column*, which I'm presenting in the Biennial, is grounded in this thinking process.

JK: Textiles are wonderfully malleable both as substance and as artistic genre. In exploiting this malleability, you have managed to resist being pigeonholed, and to connect with adjacent practices in innovative and interesting ways, in particular architecture. Your large-scale commissions for permanent installations work with the proportions, lighting, and spatial ambiance of particular buildings. Then your weavings often suggest a metaphoric relationship to architecture, like the small *Fenêtre* (2006), or the parabolic shape delineated by the tassels on *Prayer Rug* (1965), which echoes the arch form common to Islamic architecture. Supple, dynamic, and colorful, the towering *Pillar of Inquiry/Supple Column* undermines any sense of a rigid and phallocentric orthodoxy or the polished white surfaces associated with classical architecture. The piece references a structural component at once grounded and connecting to a higher plane. What is the symbolic load that it bears, or stress that it channels?

SH: For me, it expresses a soaring optimism. An accumulation of sensual thread becoming sculpture. It goes beyond being read merely as textile. Fibers—meshed, intertwined, or woven—usually result in textiles, but they can also metamorphose into alternative forms. Stretched tautly or draped loosely, cloth—perhaps viewed with light from behind (as in a window)—becomes a filter separating the outside from the inside, protecting privacy, creating mystery. Fabric, with staged backlighting, frames dramatic fantasy worlds hidden behind a screen. In architecture or exhibitions, fiber-based works are usually shown under spotlights so that the material has shadows and highlights. It makes them different from flat paintings, where light is represented or implied within the pictorial canvas. I want to invite examination of my work in all kinds of light, from different angles, open to personal references.

JK: The Centre Pompidou in Paris acquired your large linen work *Lianes de Beauvais* (2011) when it returned from the Bienal de São Paulo. You hand delivered it to them, collapsed and twisted into massive skeins packed in eight rolling suitcases. You mentioned that they wanted to conserve the suitcases. Were they part of the work?

SH: Yes, I avoid whenever possible the necessity of padded trucks, costly crates, expensive handling, and insurance. Once I sent my work to a show on the train in discarded French mailbags. The museum director thought I was disrespectful. For me, culture budgets, always limited, are better spent on producing publications with telling photography and insightful texts or films and digital transmissions.

JK: So according to that museum director, if you really want your work to receive as much consideration as painting, sculpture, or architecture, then you need to invest in costly signifiers of preciousness? Do you sense that things are changing just now—could textile-based art be having a moment?

SH: I'm oblivious to these moments. I've seen them come and go.

HOWDOYOUSAYYAMINAFRICAN? talk among THEMSELVES

The end is at the beginning and it lies far ahead.

—Ralph Ellison, *Invisible Man*

Shall we begin, then?

Will you indulge us? Will you engage both imagination and DNA for this conversation? Can you pretend that we, all thirteen of our black* bodies, are standing in front, to the side, and behind you? Can you imagine that you are alone with us? That you're alone, encircled by thirteen black bodies? Can you imagine that you are alone with us, encircled by thirteen black bodies, *in the dark*? Can you see us in the darkness? Do we shine among the shadows? Do our fractured skins remind you of things you would forget? Are these bloated eyes familiar in our paralyzed faces? Do our feathered backs look strange for their amputated wings? And if we call you to speak at the center of the circle, surrounded in the dark, can you tell us how you feel? *How* do you feel? How do you *feel*? We've always felt you, but how do *you* feel?

And if you feel safe enough (and you may wonder, rightly, on this sharp and glittering question of safety), will you close your eyes? And if we invited you to be the fourteenth black body, can you, with eyes closed, know yourself as one of us? From moment to moment and for eternity, you are us?

And now that you are alone, with us, and one of us, in the circle, in the dark, now that you're part of the blackness, is it different? Can you tell us how you feel? Are you new? Are you frightened? Are you innocent? Are you brave? Do you feel loved? Do you feel hope? Do you feel hoped for? Do you feel anyone hoping for you? Is anyone hoping for you in the black circle that is us? What about your thoughts? Are they colored, too? Are they red eyed and writhing or pale as a tongue? Do your thoughts belong to us yet? Do they sing with the darkness? Are they part of the now-humming circle as well?

Do we have your attention? Are you one of us yet? Are you thrumming? Are you feeling? Can I tell you a story?

The Mistress had Lulu's ears pierced so that when they healed she could snatch the earrings out. Lulu's ears were in shreds by her tenth birthday, so the Mistress began piercing her lips. Once, she pierced them in the center with a golden hoop, and Lulu could only eat from the sides of her mouth. A slurp here, a crumb there, this is when Lulu began to disappear. Until at last (finally!) her lips were shredded too. And so the Mistress pierced her nose . . .

*At fifteen, Lulu was a shredded silk pillow, embroidered by Ogbanje** with ruthless needles. Yet in all her wretchedness she blazed the meaning of light. All the colors gathered in her blood, a road of rainbows to the stars.*

You ask of the Mistress? Well, she blazed too, on the borrowed light of Lulu, who shone bright so you'd remember. And they danced and shone together, Mistress and fetish, until neither outsider nor ancestor could tell them apart. They danced a ring shout, counterclockwise, for the past. They danced a two-step, with the future cutting in. They danced because others were waiting for their story, and the only way to tell it was by stomp, slip, and slide.

What is that you say? Why must you know this story? Why'd you have to hear it? Where do you put it now? And who will save the shredded? And who can love the shredder? And if we cannot tell them apart, how will we know what to do?

But aren't you the fourteenth body? Didn't you come here for this? And doesn't this question belong to you now? Did no one tell you that it's our turn to forget? You are the fourteenth body, isn't it our turn to forget? Isn't it our turn to lay it down? Won't it rest on your head? Isn't this, after all, what you came here for? Isn't it your turn to hold forever? Isn't it your turn to hold the story? Isn't it your turn to begin?

* Throughout, *black* is used as designated by Toni Morrison in *Playing in the Dark: Whiteness and the Literary Imagination* (1992). She uses *black* to refer to all of the racial bodies, against which whiteness is defined in the Western literary cannon.

** *Ogbanje* is an Odiani word that translates, in Igbo, to "children who come and go." It is believed that "malevolent ogbanje differ from others in being revenge-driven, chronically ill and engaging in repeated cycles of birth, death and reincarnation" (http://www.ncbi.nlm.nih.gov/pubmed/11286364). The idea of Ogbanje is similar to that of the mischievous or vengeful fairy in European folklore. It also appears in Chinua Achebe's novel *Things Fall Apart* (1958).

Recorded by Christa Bell.

JACQUELINE HUMPHRIES speaks with LAURA OWENS

This exchange is a do-over of a conversation via email among Molly Zuckerman-Hartung, Jacqueline Humphries, Pam Lins, Laura Owens, and Amy Sillman. That first attempt was abandoned. One of the many topics discussed was Michelle Grabner's idea of grouping five female painters together in a conversation for the Whitney Biennial in the first place—how her selection might create a context for some ideas about painting. That point is where Jacqueline and Laura start off again.

Laura Owens: It seems that in our conversations with Michelle about her plans to present paintings in the Biennial, she alluded to wanting to really narrow in on a core group who are taking painting very seriously and have invested in it for a long time. This isn't, "Oh, I've decided to make a few paintings this year."

Jacqueline Humphries: Maybe what connects us is our involvement in painting's history, investment in what painters have done over the centuries. We both have our roots in a specific time when painting had no legitimacy. For instance, you started painting at CalArts, I was in the Whitney Program—

LO: When it was not okay to be painting.

JH: It was kind of like you were just pathetic or had no idea . . . painters weren't "real artists."

LO: At CalArts, it was my friend Monique Prieto and me making paintings, and there was a friend of ours making ceramics. The tone was very dismissive: "Oh, that's so cute, you're making paintings. Oh, you're making ceramics."

JH: But it was kind of great, too, all that negative attention. Knowing you're doing the wrong thing.

LO: It now feels impossible to convey what that tone was like.

JH: Now everyone seems to be doing ceramics and crocheting. All this marginality . . . and the center is this void. When I started, there was an idea of the mainstream—from the New York School to Minimalism—and now, what is at the center? I actually like to begin paintings almost as a diagram of that, working the edges toward the center, making a kind of painted void there.

LO: It seems we're at a point where there are artists who are interested in the idea of painting, but who use it more like a container. Painting is a container for some kind of art that is going to take place. Which is very different from the work of painters who are, among many other things, confronting the way they actually apply the paint, who are engaging with it and also interested in the history of all of that.

JH: Who use painting as a kind of referent?

LO: Sure, the stretcher bar is there to contain the idea of art, but it stops there. I mean, you'll always engage with the history of painting if you are representing a painting. It's interesting that we're at this point . . . you always knew that anything could be put on a painting, but the extent that it has been used as a container in recent years, seems—

JH: But I do like this notion of painting as container, that you could put anything into it. Take Rauschenberg's presentation of the blank canvas or Fontana's focus on the picture plane and painting support, and relate that to what we call the viewing platform. Screen space is a form supposedly waiting for content. It's ready for any image, yet it has its own distinct physicality. I feel that it's the screen we're responding to more than the image; it's almost like we'll look at anything on the screen. But then I have to ask myself, "What image content would you commit to a painting?" But maybe you're talking about my little pet term, *art on canvas*.

LO: *Art on canvas* seems to be about the primacy of discourse. I think we both would say that there's the space of discourse but also the space of the actual painting, and the space of the room it exists in (the studio, the museum . . .). I don't think we are in denial of any of it. These are three legs of the same stool. It is a fact that your work will be talked about, and that language flows around works of art.

JH: Well, I think we are enunciating our position: abstraction today is in a much-changed world since Malevich or Pollock. It's abstraction, yet it's not expression. In terms of an ism, there are no isms anymore. Style is not the issue so much as trying to think more directly about one's relationship to the world.

LO: Was it Oscar Wilde or someone else who said that the best criticism of any art form is always done in the same art form? I mean, I think that's how the consciousness around painting changes: maybe someone enters the conversation with new language or a very specific way of talking about things, but more often an object captures that moment. One painting can, in one moment, make everything else feel dated, because it shifts the conversation over . . .

JH: Yes, over to some real and current condition, rather than confining itself to a tradition or just the conversation of art. I like to think about art history and look at old paintings, but how am I going to paint in my time? We don't want to recognize what we see, but it's my job as an artist to do that. I like to get rid of the image so the thought becomes apparent.

LO: Totally, but I guess—just to go back to the thing about the legs of the stool—if people are interested in painting as a container for discourse, is it simply because they get to start with the implication of "art" no matter what, because it's on a stretcher or at the very least hanging on the wall acting like a painting? It cannot *not* be art. So why is the "art on canvas" so immune in terms of any critique surrounding the work? Is it because if you don't acknowledge its self-described discourse, you are not "seeing" the artwork? If the discourse is in the container, it's not going to be positioned outside the work. We were talking about Cheyney Thompson's work earlier, and how his ideas are embedded in the labor, in how it's made. The work is tautological; it is a container for its own making. Also, when we went together to see Josh Smith's show of monochrome paintings at Luhring Augustine this fall . . . knowing he made them, you look at the show like, "Oh, this is now what Josh Smith is painting"—the discourse almost stands in for or implies the figure in the field of the monochrome.

JH: Yet he himself raises this question of the autonomy of the art object; it's in the paintings and the way he makes exhibitions. There's a lot of irony and humor in the way he performs painting and shifts roles all the time. He puts a lot on the line to do that.

LO: I agree, but I think it's interesting to think of how dramatically the meaning would change depending on who made them. There's a discourse that's built up around the previous work Josh has made, all the exhibitions and how the work progressed, and that is what allows the space so that the monochrome show can be made.

JH: But what I hear you saying is that when you're looking at one of the paintings you can't help but reference all his other work, the totality of which is "off-site." It makes me think of the cloud thing, where more and more we are living and recording our lives in some invented fictional place. Josh's cloud is a dark, sinister, and gritty place. It's not a fluffy, white, clean place.

LO: I think we were looking at the colors—some of them are really interesting—and thinking about being in the studio.

JH: Mixing paints.

LO: Mixing paints on a palette or a table . . . So his paintings somewhat reference coming out of the studio. So now these two ideas of discourse. One's sort of biography, building up a history of shows and exhibitions, and a kind of reverence for the persona. The other's following a logic and relying on the painting as a ready-made form. Can we ask ourselves if we do this? Do we make a type of discourse? For example, in this conversation we're being asked to talk about our work . . . we're having something called discourse right now.

JH: What we are saying, what is said or written by others, and what painters paint: it's all part of the thought in and around it. But the painting is really the engine. I think that's what I was talking about in the first conversation with Amy, Molly, Pam, and you, when I said art is a matter of the intellect, which seemed to cause such a stir . . . But you know what's popping into my mind right now is to return to the woman thing, because gender stereotypes get carried over into this, into what you might call the expanded field of painting discourse. The stereotypes are the background you're trying to change.

LO: When we talked about biography at Josh Smith's show, I asked myself if those monochromes were made by a woman, Marcia Hafif, for example, would they be seen as having more emotional content or at least be seen as much more sincere?

JH: Or "intuitive" . . . I'm ever confounded by this term. Feelings don't make paintings. Decisions do.

LO: With colors, women often have a lot more meaning projected onto their work, whereas with Josh the work is immediately read as having a kind of irreverence that makes even boring monochromes super-cool.

JH: But isn't Anne Truitt just as cool as Donald Judd?

LO: Maybe, but I guess I'm not talking about coolness, but rather the narrative foundations of our present. There are stereotypes of the female artist that are widely accepted and historicized. There's the hermit lady—like, go off and be alone in the desert. Like Georgia O'Keeffe or Agnes Martin. Or the rejector of all female identity, of the art world . . . that's another version of crazy: Lee Lozano.

JH: The hysteric.

LO: And then there's the bad mother, Alice Neel. You can't be a good mother and a painter, because where do your interests lie? And there are all these people who take big breaks and raise the children and don't make art, and then they come back and maybe make more art later. It's hard to tease it apart—is it that we needed our own history, or is it just that it's assumed since you occupy this body that can *birth* the artist, how could you *be* the artist? You know? Like, if you have to care for the child, how can you be the child? You can't be both.

JH: Okay, we took a little break, during which we visualized the legs of the stool again.

LO: So . . . I was trying to figure out the space of the painting, there's the space of the studio, there's the space of the exhibition . . .

JH: The mind-space of the painter, of the viewer/spectator/beholder . . . I think it's hard to collapse it to a single plane, although that really is what painting is all about. Compression.

LO: But where is the painting? Do you know what I mean?

JH: Not *what* is the painting? But *where* is it?

LO: Is it in your mind? Is it in, you know . . .

JH: It's something in the painter's mind, transformed by being put in the world, then transformed again in the viewer's mind . . .

LO: I guess this is one of those broad philosophical questions, but we were talking earlier about the space of discourse because we're meant to talk about our own work for the catalogue.

JH: Being interviewed . . . again . . .

LO: By each other [*laughs*] for each other. [*laughs*] I feel like this is the space of free labor in the art world. But we're here to talk about art, specifically our art and the space of this exhibition. We create a discourse that will end up contributing to received ideas about our art, right?

JH: It's a conversation, and we are writing.

LO: Right, because something you say or something I say could potentially, if anyone ever reads this, be somewhat inseparable from the artwork they see or the exhibition they look at. Why is it us talking about our own work, conversing? Why not have someone just write something? Which I think is an interesting question, because I think many artists are creating their own discourses, and I'm wondering if that's valid or primary?

JH: At some point I thought I would write my own book about my work. [*laughs*] As in, "These are the paintings I made and why I made them," as years and years of work stack up . . . I don't know. It seemed like fun.

LO: I had a similar idea a while back. I wanted to use Raymond Roussel's *How I Wrote Certain of My Books* as a model.

JH: Yes. "How I made some of my paintings." And then it's just gibberish.

LO: Total gibberish.

JH: Making a painting often *does* feel like gibberish to me. Like, I'm dealing with these pieces and fragments and half things, some of which I know I will bury under other layers. Following some kind of notion of beginning and playing it out in painting.

LO: Well, I think that kind of links back to when we were talking about Dada and Picabia previously. We were talking about an idea of gender in painting—not biologically determined but instead based on the way you activate an identity as an artist and on how art gets made. If the approach is to reaffirm the signature—to restate the same thing over and over again so we know *who* the painter is—that's the male gesture.

JH: So more than making a painting, you're forming an identity? Is that more important to what you're doing than the painting, in a sense? I'm fascinated by this: we're just painting, but then there are possibly these other implications. I can never quite get my head around it, because I never think "I'm a woman painting" when I'm painting. Maybe that's why I love Picabia. It's never really clear if he's deliberately playing with male stereotypes or just dismissing them.

LO: Yes. Picasso being this model for, uh . . . genius. He insinuates himself into the painting, and he goes from period to period, and it's good. But with Picabia, it's truly as if he's just abandoning himself at every moment.

JH: What is your feeling, do women have to deal with the gender issue? Can't we ignore it?

LO: No one's going to give you that kind of freedom from biography.

JH: Or permission?

LO: It just doesn't come with the territory because you're not assumed to have the authority in the gesture that you make.

JH: Not *assumed* to, but when you do—when the painting makes the case unequivocally, like I think is *so* the case with your work—then you almost benefit from that element of surprise, especially the way you mix it up with your subject matter, "girly doodlebug art," or whatever people have said. The things you paint, you make them act in ways they're not supposed to, you're not acting the way you're supposed to.

LO: It could be that the painting is not behaving the way it's supposed to . . . but that is only temporary, because once everyone has absorbed it as a possibility . . . it doesn't seem so ill-mannered anymore. There is no authority available right now. I think it's an antiquated idea. I wanted to hear your response to the idea that gesture could hold the idea of signature, because you do take on gesture in your work.

JH: Almost in this kind of generic way.

LO: Do you feel like you are pummeling it, or what are you doing?

JH: Well, for one thing, I want to completely divorce the gesture from the idea of signature. I'm not really interested in "identity" in painting, in declaring myself. The whole "signature-style" issue is problematic for me. I mean, I've made bodies of work back-to-back or even simultaneously that are really different. But confronting the issue of gesture in painting was important, because it was kind of a taboo to do that. I guess I was always most interested in decoding it, overturning expectations around it, or putting it on its head, so to speak. Treating it almost as a readymade, adopting its qualities as a sign yet inflecting it from within. Now I'm in a different place with it, more interested in innovation and really making it appear like it hasn't before—cramming it into the space of the canvas as a dense array of traces of energies and collapsing it all onto a single plane. But I wouldn't agree with you about authority. Such things don't go away so much as reappear where you least expect them to.

LO: Oh, my friend is here. Sorry.

JH: Oh, okay. Good place to stop.

DOUG ISCHAR speaks with JOHN NEFF

John Neff: Let's start by talking about where your films come from. What's the relationship between intention and construction?

Doug Ischar: It's murkier and less precise than you might imagine. My intention is always, simply, to make a compelling work that deals with a certain cluster of subjects. Construction begins organically. Form and structure develop slowly. Then, at a certain point, I turn away from imagination and improvisation and become more of a conscious builder.

JN: What are your contemporary or historical models?

DI: They don't come from narrative cinema or even experimental film. They come—oddly enough—from classical music, especially twentieth-century post-tonal music. People have commented that the work seems like a product of musical, rather than cinematic, composition. First suggested by Gregg Bordowitz, this observation is one I largely agree with. The work is conceived along the lines of large-scale lyrical works, with a great deal of intricate motivic development and morphing repetition.

JN: What does post-tonal music offer you that, for example, experimental cinema doesn't?

DI: First and foremost, I know it. I don't know the history of experimental film nearly as well. Also, I love post-tonal music and have much less affection for canonical experimental film. Finally, this music grows out of late nineteenth-century Romanticism and retains some of that movement's lyrical aspects. Lyricism—from the smallest clip to an entire filmic work—is hugely important to me. So it's partly a matter of affinity and intimacy but it also comes from a stubborn intent to do something that's patently mine, something that doesn't reference familiar, genre-specific sources. I have no interest in making art about art.

JN: "Patently mine." Your recent films interpenetrate self-authored, first-person texts with quotations from critical and poetic writings. Could you talk about your use of text, and the "voice" in your works?

DI: This is difficult for me to disentangle. Regarding first-person voice, I wouldn't call it narrative. It's more about clusters, or constellations, of desire and insight. Subjective and quotational voices elide, just as the psychological and social elide in life. My found materials are extremely specific. They usually physically belong to me, and they've often been part of my daily life for a long time. The texts, in some ways, confuse sourcing and inject an element of instability into the work's overall affective structure.

JN: Could you relate your use of found material to postmodern strategies of appropriation?

DI: I don't like the notion of appropriation very much, and I want to distance myself from the way it's familiarly employed in postmodernism. The secondhand materials I use have always already been filtered through me psychically. They're not taken from outside and put to use in the work; they're taken from within me. They're not borrowed—they're externalized, animated, and redeployed in an artwork, which returns them to the social zone but only after they undergo a whole lot of impassioned working-through.

JN: Composition through editing—rather than, say, shooting—is at the heart of your work. Could you talk about editing as working-through?

DI: It's intuitive, but I have the veteran intuition of a sixty-five-year old. Editing goes beyond simple montage. Take my use of motion effects: these moves derive from my relationship to the material. The use of the floating frame walls in *Alone with You* (2011), for example, is based on my emotional and erotic attachment to a younger pro wrestler. I jerked off to this tape for years before deciding to build a film around it.

Editing at the computer is a tactile experience for me; I'm making something manually. It feels unmediated, like a wet darkroom, which may seem odd to some. Things are happening inside the computer that I have little understanding of, but I also have a great deal of control over what's happening on-screen through the software Final Cut Pro. At times, I think of myself as a Final Cut Pro artist; the kinds of things I'm doing would have been impossible, perhaps unthinkable, in analogue film or video.

JN: What kind of physical encounter would you like viewers to have with the work?

DI: The films are dense and complex, and I think that ideally—just to be honest—they require more than one viewing to reveal themselves. Although I like to see them on a large screen, which makes for a much more viscerally satisfying experience, I also imagine them circulating like novels or porn, taken into homes on DVDs and flash drives. Pored over, lived with, and brought close.

JN: Could you talk about your work's relationship to identity art?

DI: It's a difficult one. For my early work, I considered representation a necessary tool of empowerment—I *was* trained at CalArts in the mid-eighties, after all. I worked in that vein with satisfaction for a long time . . . actually, for a brief but extremely intense time.

JN: Maybe it just felt like a long time . . .

DI: Yes . . . and countless rolls of film. Although the newer films relate to identity in an oblique way, they're more determined to skew and fuck with it than they are to enunciate and affirm it.

JN: Why is that important to you now?

DI: Because I've come to believe that identity is a kind of trap, just as self is a comforting, necessary illusion. What's needed at this point—art historically and as a philosophy of living—is a greater sense of complexity and subtlety in dealing with the fallout of human life . . . the fallout of queer human life, in particular.

Although old political-theoretical issues remain embedded in my work, a lyrical, nuanced poetics matters much more to me to now. Hopefully, that's how the complexities of my long experience play out—as bracing, moving provocations.

JN: How do your films make you feel?

DI: They're a pain in the ass. But . . . what was I going to say? Ah . . . I find it a higher and wiser calling these days to complicate things, to consciously preserve the scrambled wires of experience, as opposed to sorting them out and making sure they lead to exactly the right source or terminus. I'm interested in how the trouble of life can inform a work that's both melancholic in tone and, perhaps paradoxically, optimistic in its aural and visual poetics. I want the work to have this oxymoronic, almost schizophrenic, quality. That's what I sweat over.

ALEX JOVANOVICH speaks with DAN BEACHY-QUICK

Alex Jovanovich: Dan, I wanted to do this conversation with you because you were the one who really turned me on to poetry. And, sadly, for most of my life, I had relegated poetry to this sort of moribund, romantic ghetto. I'm ashamed to admit it, but had someone asked me when I was twenty if I liked poetry I would've laughed in their face. And I think that attitude comes from being a child of the nineties, when postmodern irony, in culture and quite acutely in contemporary art, suffused everything I was drawn to or thought about. Anything deemed "poetic" was stupidly thought of as soft, uncritical, purely aesthetic, or uncool. I was an art kid who loved Andy Warhol, sixties Pop art, Babysue comics, Mike Diana, Ween, drag, serial killers, John Waters—the list is endless! Anything that smacked of sincerity, tenderness, or emotionality was off-limits, and poetry seemed immersed in all of that. As I got older, however, that stance regarding art was no longer fulfilling me. It felt divorced from the intensity of creation and from the intensity of an artist's interior or emotional life and didn't address how that intensity might transmit itself through an art object. I simply needed to break up my old habits of mind—or just break myself up—to have access to other channels of thinking and making that allowed me to delve into riskier and more complicated sorts of depths.

Dan Beachy-Quick: I started writing poetry very early on, in high school in the early nineties. The moment I fell in love with poetry is specific one, indelible in my mind. A rather extraordinary English teacher was guiding my class through John Donne's "A Valediction: Forbidding Mourning." With me in that class was the woman who is now my wife, and we had just started talking, getting to know each other—really, falling in love. And Donne's poem is about love—not the sudden flush of feeling, but love in its fullest complexity, from the sexual to the spiritual, refusing to demarcate lines. I saw how a poem might be a form of seeking that teaches those who read it not answers but how to join in seeking, how to be truly more aware, even if the consequence is being truly more confused. Such a sense of poetry led me through college and finally to graduate school.

There, I became deeply immersed in the poets I loved, poets from the early nineteenth and twentieth centuries, and also the metaphysical poets of the sixteenth century. I pursued a form of poetry that possessed certain kinds of wit—wit that could never be ascribed to any kind of ease of irony. And now that I am going firmly into middle age, irony seems a different sort of tool than I understood then. I think irony is often used in extraordinarily poor and simpleminded ways, and that shouldn't be so. When one begins to understand irony as a kind of emotional crisis, in a way—which is to say that you find yourself as the butt of the joke, not the one making it—then irony can find its way into poetry and art in incredibly valuable ways, because it reveals itself as a thing not that deflects the human moment but that, inevitably, introduces us back into it.

AJ: You were one of the people who introduced me to the writing of Susan Howe, who spun me deep into this world of Puritan thinking and literature. Her poetry and scholarship brought me to the writings of people like Jonathan Edwards, Cotton Mather, and Mary Rowlandson, and specifically to that Puritan relationship with fear, via the Old Testament. These pilgrims left England in blind faith to start a new life by sailing into the absolute unknown, awash in total fear, feeling quite viscerally that their mortal souls were at stake. There is plenty of insidious fear today, but it's so mediated, mitigated, and medicated. And it's fear that keeps us closed off from the breadth of life, from real risk and real agency. You know, living in New York, you see a lot of people looking for absolution in yoga class, wearing fucking crystals around their necks, or going on diets. The kind of fear that the Puritans knew when they stared into the shadow of that Old Testament God—frankly, it's beautiful and alive and terrifying. I'm hardly a Christian, but those texts bring me to something that's missing from my life and maybe contemporary life in general. It's not fashionable. It's a profound love entwined with profound fear and profound purpose. It's something about making this life count.

DB-Q: Well, there's a kind of real pleasure in fashion that also seems to me like a genuine irony of fashion: it clothes our naked condition, that state of being absolutely unchanging, in which we suspect we're wholly seen despite what we're wearing, and that has little to do, in the end, with being "clothed." It seems very connected to the way in which the Old Testament insists that the proper way to pray is in love *and* fear and that these qualities are in equal measure and absolutely simultaneous. One of the things I worry about in this culture is that love and fear bear no relationship to one another.

Fear is itself a kind of fashion that one pays however much money to feel because it's as if fear is, instead of a kind of ontological condition, just a need for more jolts of adrenaline, for dangers that actually aren't dangerous, or for some simulation of real sensation that, to the particular intelligence of the postmodern mind, is accepted as actual stimulation—an aesthetic that divorces itself from the body it secretly depends on. Of course, the same discrepancy has been an argument in all eras, from Aristotle and Plato to Augustine to now. And sometimes it feels to me that in our culture love, sadly, is given in a sticky note that says, "You look good today!" You tack it on your mirror so that you can face the world one more time. You know, if we're looking for such an easy form of self-affirmation, then as a culture we know nothing of actual fear, existential fear, fear that keeps us aligned with that oblivion that is the counterpoint of genuine love.

Howe was also my entry point into those authors and all that language you mentioned. What we feel—what's so moving—in Anne Hutchinson, Herman Melville, and that whole astonishing bunch is that they had at a single point of a certain self a kind of infinity of bewilderment that they were always brushing up against. Maybe to have an American voice is to always locate oneself in that thinnest strand between an arrival that's known and everything that threatens the ability to stay at that place, to stay there, to find a way to dwell. It feels infinite and prophetic and godlike and fearsome; the only way to do it properly is to understand that love is some dwelling at the other edge of oblivion.

The art I love most offers us these kinds of dwellings. You read a poem and you climb into a kind of hut, so to speak, and that hut is right there, between knowable things and unknowable things. For a little while, a great piece of art lets those two things coexist and lets you stay there as long as you can look at it or as long as you can read it. But, of course, no one gets to stay. One can hardly bear it.

BEN KINMONT speaks with THOM DONOVAN

Thom Donovan: Yesterday, by phone, you spoke again of your idea of "the third sculpture" with regard to various ruminations about the archive, Giorgio Agamben, Jacques Rancière, and problems of consensus building within and outside of art discourse. Can you talk about how "the third sculpture" relates to your work as a whole?

Ben Kinmont: The idea of "the third sculpture" is to have a syntax to speak about spaces in between: in between two people, two points, one idea and another. And the way in which the space in between, as soon as it is identified, becomes another point that then creates other "third sculptures," or spaces in between.

What strikes me about the idea of consensus and dissensus is the way in which dissensus, once successful, becomes consensus, and how this constant motion constitutes democracy. This idea of things coming into being and the connection between being and power interests me.

TD: *Sshhh* (2002–)[1] seems to be another of your projects that considers the threshold of art discourse, and offers a proposal on how to move forward when art threatens to expropriate our most intimate relationships. Given the parasitic relationship many artists currently have with various forms of political and social practice, *Sshhh* seems a particularly timely work to reactivate for the 2014 Whitney Biennial. When the art discourse threatens real sociopolitical results, such as providing spaces where communities and families can properly care for one another, the *Sshhh* project produces a means by which to act in the face of art's failure to produce a more equitable and salubrious world.

BK: With *Sshhh*, I am trying to acknowledge that there is a domestic discourse that is outside art discourse, a place where meaningful things occur and also a place to which art is not invited. So, with these engravings, there is no image, no information to reveal what was said. We just know that a certain family had a conversation on a particular day, a conversation that is referenced by the engraving but known only by the participants.

TD: Whereas some artists would like to partition art from other forms of culture work, and others would like to take up other disciplines and discourses as extensions of their practice, it seems to me that much of your work is about making certain thresholds appear between what has been constituted as an "art discourse" and other types of discourse. This seems especially true of your ongoing project *On becoming something else* (2009–),[2] where you're trying to find the more or less exact point where art's extension into other disciplines negates its ability to function within an art discourse.

More than anything else, I see your work persistently trying to embody an ethics that accurately observes contemporary art's undiminished tendency to appropriate a world of lived relationships for itself as well as the risk of your own participation in this appropriation. As though by observing it more clearly (or making it visible at all), we might reorganize what art can do, who it is for, and who is capable of participating in the assertion of its value.

BK: Once things are made visible, we do have the opportunity to reorganize what art can do. I suppose that this is the optimism that can be found at the end of institutional critique, that once we have a sense of how meaning is made and where power lies and how it is used, we can propose a plan for a more equitable future. But remember—to refer back to the ideas of consensus and dissensus—that once that new, more just structure is created, it too will leave out some other idea or person or group, and will therefore need to be challenged and renovated to meet the needs of others. And so change continually occurs.

TD: I couldn't agree more with what you say about institutional critique, regarding "visibility." I hear Marx in it ("the point is to change it"), but also our beloved philosopher William James, who made a lifework of coordinating ontology with a constant sense of change.

BK: Thom, I have a question for you, one that came up last summer while I was reading an article by James Wood in the *New Yorker*. In his review of four literary biographies of novelists written by their children titled "Sins of the Father," he writes, "Almost twenty years ago, George Steiner suggested in these pages that doing philosophy was incompatible with domestic life," and later he asks, "Can a man or woman fulfill a sacred devotion to thought, or music, or art, or literature, while fulfilling a proper devotion to spouse or children?"

I would argue this points to a threshold that is worth careful consideration. What are your thoughts on this, in the context of your life as a poet and your interest in various political activities such as Occupy Wall Street? Although Wood's question refers directly to family life, it has implications that go beyond one's private life and extend into our relationships across a social fabric.

TD: I immediately think of the many women artists and writers who, despite bearing the brunt of (unpaid) reproductive labor, have still had careers and asserted themselves beyond the domestic sphere. It also reminds me that one of the not-small leaps of feminism was to instill in men a sense of responsibility for reproductive labor—from child rearing to keeping house to making sure everyone in the household is cared for.

Without an attention to the domestic sphere, I don't see how a proper political praxis can exist. Something interesting to note about many of the Occupy camps is how the occupiers created a domestic space, a home, through the appropriation of spaces like parks and squares. At Zuccotti Park in Lower Manhattan, in particular, groups were assigned to cook, clean, and administer health services. Tending house was crucial because the police were trying to find any reason they could for eviction.

With the collapse of various national welfare systems, I think that artists will increasingly become providers of and mediators for lacking civic services. I think that they will also continue to explore new ways of being public and private, and to rethink citizenship in terms of the responsibilities of an expanded notion of the domestic, one that may perhaps include a larger "tribe" or "pack," or even extend to a commons (communism).

The months after my Occupy activities ceased, I watched everything by the television producer and director Joss Whedon, who is most famous for the TV series *Buffy the Vampire Slayer*. Whedon's work is all about family—an alternative notion of family that is not dependent on blood relations but rather on shared cultural urgencies. In a weird way, his work helped me process my own cathexis of Occupy and ongoing projections about social practice and political engagement. I am still using that work to write about the problems you recognize in your question. How can one both have a family and feel that one is part of a commons? Likewise, how can one behave in such a way that family and commons become coextensive? Would you care to talk about this trajectory in your practice, from the series of works in which you washed dishes for other people to your founding of an antiquarian bookshop in order to care for your family? I wonder, too, if we are not all constantly "becoming something else" in the current cultural climate, where very few artists can survive on their art alone and most culture workers have more than one job, maybe several?

BK: I have tried to respond to a felt sense of urgency. What needs to be said? What is missing from the discussion? What is not part of the consensus, and what is my culpability in this dynamic? I am interested in the threshold of this community, of what can and cannot be called art. I have watched various ideas come and go, from relevant to irrelevant, and back again. But I would argue that, yes, we are all in a state of becoming, and that as we understand, this transmutes into being and power.

1. Artist's project description: "*Sshhh*, archive begun 2002. I invited families living in Chatou, outside Paris, each to have a conversation at home, among themselves, and to consider the possibility of this conversation as a work of art. Fifteen families later notified me by email to say when they had completed their conversation. The content and nature of each conversation remains a secret known only to them. Afterward, I made each family an engraving, recording the family's name and conversation date, in the size and color of their choosing. Each engraving functions as an art object, as something to be exhibited and circulated within the art world. For those within the family, the engraving is more; it comes out of a domestic moment and functions as an aide-mémoire for a conversation once had. Project can be reactivated. Archive in the collection of the artist."

2. Artist's project description: "*On becoming something else*, archive begun 2009. I wrote seven paragraphs to describe the work of seven different artists who had pursued art practices that led them out of the art world and into new discourses and value structures. In Paris, seven chefs wrote recipes to represent these paragraphs. At the Centre Pompidou, a broadside was distributed, directing people to the chefs' restaurants where they could eat the representations of the paragraphs. The project was reactivated four years later through SFMOMA with seven new restaurants and then as a multiple with Galileo High School. Project can be reactivated. Archive in the collection of the artist."

SHIO KUSAKA: frequently asked QUESTIONS

Q: What do you make your pots out of?

A: A lot of my work is made of porcelain. I also use stoneware.

Q: What's the difference?

A: Porcelain is really dense and more like glass. Stoneware is porous and has more sand in it.

Q: Why do you use porcelain?

A: I like how smooth it is. It feels nice in my hands when I make pots.

Q: Isn't porcelain difficult?

A: Yes, if you want to control it.

Q: Why do you use stoneware?

A: Stoneware pots look different. Stoneware also reacts differently when I do the same thing I do with porcelain. If I am making pots in porcelain, after a while I get better at it.

Then I switch to stoneware to lose my control over the clay a little bit. I then switch back to porcelain when I am able to make what I'm trying to make.

Q: Do you know what you will be making when you start?

A: I have an idea, but I usually can't make what's in my head. It is part of the process to force myself to make something particular and end up with something else. Sometimes I just make pots without any plans.

Q: Do you draw your ideas?

A: Not usually. I make notes and look at images I find.

Q: Do you use a wheel?

A: Yes. I use a wheel called the Whisper, by Shimpo Ceramics. It's very quiet.

Q: Are the big ones made on the wheel, too?

A: No. I get help with the coil building. The clay ropes are rolled and then stacked up. The surface is then smoothed.

Q: Why get help?

A: I don't have the skill but I want to see my pots bigger. Big pots make my small pots look even smaller, which I like. I love my mini pots.

Q: How long have you been doing this?

A: It has been seventeen years since I first took a ceramics class. I was making pots on and off for ten years. I committed to pottery full time in 2006.

Q: How did you first get interested in pots?

A: Ceramics 001 looked like the most interesting to me in the class schedule at the time. I can't remember when and how I first thought making pots on the potter's wheel was magical.

Q: How long does it take to make one pot?

A: Twenty minutes on the wheel. I sometimes work on it a little more the next day. The pot dries from three hours to overnight, depending on the weather. I then flip it and work on the bottom of the pot for ten minutes.

Q: What was the first pot you made that you felt proud of?

A: A planter I made in 2005. I was excited immediately. I have made a bunch since then, and sometimes still make them.

Q: Do you make your clay?

A: No. I buy clay in bags. Usually from a local store.

Q: Do you make your glaze?

A: No. I am not really interested in the chemistry aspect of ceramics.

Q: Colors?

A: The bright colors I use are called underglaze. It's colored liquid clay. I make a pot, dry it a little, then paint two coats of underglaze. Then I carve some patterns out. I fire it once, put clear glaze on, and fire it again.

Q: What about your painted patterns?

A: I make a pot, fire it once, and put clear or white glaze over the pot. I paint patterns on the dry glazed surface and fire it again.

Q: How long does it take to finish patterns?

A: Sometimes I can make ten pots in one day, but sometimes I spend the whole day on one pot.

Q: How long do you wait before firing?

A: I dry small pots for one to two weeks and big pots for three to four weeks.

Q: How high do you fire?

A: The first firing is about 1,800 degrees Fahrenheit and the second firing is about 2,300 degrees Fahrenheit.

Q: How long is the firing?

A: The first firing is about nine to ten hours. The second firing is twelve to fourteen hours.

Q: Do you have a kiln?

A: Yes. I have an electric kiln, the FL-20 by Olympic. It is 28 inches wide, 45 inches tall, and 28 inches deep.

Q: How many pots do you fire in the kiln?

A: Fifteen to twenty, depending on the size.

Q: How often do you fire the kiln?

A: About twenty times a year. I fire twice to finish my pots, so ten cycles.

Q: Is it okay to use your work?

A: Yes. I make sure that all my pots hold liquid. Most of them are glazed inside. Some of my porcelain pots are not glazed inside, but they can hold water.

Q: Do the pots refer to historical pots or specific cultural forms?

A: Yes. I always hope my work has the essence of pots from the Yayoi period (300 BCE to 300 CE) in Japan.

CHRIS LARSON speaks with GRANT HART

Grant Hart: . . . that's the journey that took you to the destination.

CL: I have been trying to pay attention to the debris left behind by the things I have been making, watching the wake or the wear marks left behind, studying the material or by-products . . . The studio is a great space after a project has left; the energy remains but the work is gone. This is what I am interested in at the moment.

GH: Second to what you are doing deliberately . . .

CL: Right.

GH: The energy . . . This is like the sunlight falling on a landscape, on the texture of an undetermined world . . . Those are batteries of stored energy—like the energy that breaks loose from the funnel, the energy that falls by the wayside, that gets sucked out the window and lands where it may.

CL: Yeah, I've been trying lately to pay attention to these things.

GH: My debris, the stuff that I create while creating something else, is a bit different from yours in one very happy aspect. My studio floor is my memory. I pride myself on my lyrics and the fact that I am a contributor to the great river that runs backward from New Orleans to the north. The river of American music: rock 'n' roll, riddim and blues. I can discard an idea of years, and days later find a use for it. There is no garbage, just recycling and the compost heap. The dry unperishables go in one place. The wet stuff, the veg, and the scraps go into the heap, where they become the fertilizer for other developments. Words, like boards and screws, can be reassembled.

CL: I find that memory and meaning are deep-rooted in the materials and sites we occupy and manipulate. I live blocks away from St. Paul's sacred Indian mounds. At one time, there were around thirty-five. Now only six exist—or six reconstructions of what were once there. I see this as a kind of shift in energy. All the original mounds were destroyed by development and plundering.

GH: No treasure in this one. Move on to the next.

CL: Yeah, an archaeologist dug up all the mounds in the late 1800s. Most of the artifacts have gone missing, but he kept records of what he found. As I walk by the mounds, they feel more like stand-ins for what were created over two thousand years ago. The original mounds were looted, and then new ones were fabricated to look like the originals. I am interested in what these sites have become. They seem less like Indian mounds and more like series of hills made by an archaeologist. Through the destruction of one thing, we make something else. I like thinking about this kind of shift in site, energy, and place.

GH: Who put them back together?

CL: The rogue archaeologist who dug them up. It makes me think about the processes that the mounds have gone through. They used to seemed loaded with energy before I knew they were altered, shifted, and processed. The processes by which they were created still hold power, just of a different kind.

GH: What if there were human constructions on the site of the mounds that the Indians obliterated to build their mounds? There are endless speculations. We assume that the mounds were destroyed in a search for treasure. What if the digger was curious to find out how they lived at the time of the mound building? When we destroy for the sake of learning, it is called something else. Think of the poor guy who would not get to his dying grandmother's bedside because Marcel Duchamp stole the wheel from his bike.

CL: Sounds like a thief. We are curious; we want to dig, but our traces and piles always remain. Something is always left. I am interested in the residue after the process of destroying or making something. Sometime it's harder to find the traces, but they're there. Meaning can be found in the memory embedded in these abstract piles and remains.

GH: The piles are a result of your life. We are always recycling. We're like earthworms—eating the dirt in front of us and leaving dirt behind us as we go.

CL: Destruction and creation. I have been destroying materials, things, and objects that I build as part of my practice. I wanna see what's on the other side . . . transform the thing, change its form, keep it in motion, build it, wreck it, and turn it into something new. There is potential in something that has been destroyed or damaged. I have been interested in musicians that destroy their instruments on stage . . . beyond the repeated, expected performance . . .

GH: We destroy accidentally sometimes. Usually when we preserve, a selection is made. The older the remnant, the more chance that forces of nature will destroy it. Earthquakes collapse caves with wall paintings, wind erodes standing stone, and rock breaks scissors. Curiosity is a "higher virtue" than greed. Pompeii was first excavated by men looking for treasure and stone for their palaces. At a certain point, the objects became valuable for what they taught us about our ancestors.

CL: Do you have an equivalent in your practice? Have you ever destroyed a song? Accidentally? Or a drum set or a guitar? In a performance?

GH: The only time that I experienced destruction as an organic outgrowth of a performance, it wasn't even *my* drum kit—it belonged to the band that was playing after us. We were playing before the Minutemen at Love Hall in Philadelphia. I was making eye contact with Bob, and we were just going for it . . . and the next thing I knew . . .

CL: And . . . ? What pushed you to do it?

GH: I just reached the point where there was no other way to channel the energy. It was part of playing with them, and things had just gotten rough and physical with me and the instrument . . . I was looking for sounds, but there was no way that I was actually going to create them because I had taken the instrument as far as it could go right then. The instrument must leave.

DIEGO LECLERY poses FIVE QUESTIONS

Why Civilization?

It is generally accepted that Civilization is the greatest game in the history of the world. There have been five different versions of Civilization since Sid Meier released the original in 1991, and each one was met with widespread acclaim. For more than twenty years, Civilization has served as the dominant model for games of its genre.

How Do You Play Civilization?

Civilization begins at the dawn of recorded time, with the settling of nomadic peoples in cities. Players are entrusted with a civilization's fate and with the stewardship of its cultural and material resources toward victory. For this, a player must administer cities' means of production; rally and deploy expeditionary troops, self-defense forces, and armies of conquest; incentivize the specialization of citizens into the arts and sciences; allocate research toward technological innovation; appoint bodies of government; and designate cultural values—while always ensuring the welfare of the people.

How Do You Win at Civilization?

A player wins Civilization by conquering the world or colonizing outer space. To conquer the world, a civilization must militarily capture and hold (or raze) all opponents' cities or otherwise exert global domination through cultural, economic, or diplomatic mechanisms. For a space victory, the entire endeavor of human scientific and technological development must be traversed—from pottery to banking, radio, rocketry, and beyond—before an intragalactic space transport can be designed, constructed, and launched to Alpha Centauri. Both paths to victory require the establishment of a solid base for manufacturing, the maintenance of healthy conditions for population growth, and capital investment in local infrastructure tailored to the specific geography of a player's dominion.

Who Do You Play in Civilization?
All players inside Civilization are based on real historical figures, with every release assembling a somewhat altered cast, from Alexander, Catherine, and Gandhi to Napoleon, Mao, and Shaka Zulu. Varying degrees of advantage are given to opponents depending on the chosen level of difficulty, and two decades of development have sharpened the artificial intelligence of foes to a point where only the highest-skilled players in the world can hope to win at the most expert level. There is also a clock that runs out before the twenty-second century.

What Does Civilization Mean to You?
I have played every version since I was thirteen years old and have devoted hundreds of hours to each release. I feel a noticeable thrill at breaking a siege, real relief when warding off an invasion, and delight when beholding a recently built Great Wonder. If thought of as a single enterprise, playing Civilization is the most consistent focus of my life. Civilization means the world to me.

TONY LEWIS speaks with DR. ROBERT P. VANDE KAPPELLE

The following is a brief excerpt from a conversation concerning issues of faith and art, systems of making meaning, and the sensibility of conventional wisdom.

Dr. Robert P. Vande Kappelle: Let's begin with the topic of faith in your work. How does it impact your perspective and inform your voice?

Tony Lewis: Faith seems necessary to develop and sustain the relationship between an audience and whatever they're experiencing. I think the decision and opportunity to believe in an art form has to be present from the beginning, together with doubt. It might have been the first relationship I recognized in my early experiences with art. I knew faith from church as a child—it later became a consideration for making art. There was an ethical richness in making what I wanted to cultivate.

RPVK: In your estimation, could religion be described as art? When faith becomes narrowed down to dogmatism, extremism, or fundamentalism, are these distortions of religion "bad" art? Perhaps it can be connected to the notion of "poor" versus "good," or even "excellent," art. When I speak of faith in this regard, I'm referring to a perspective or attitude one has toward the universe in general and to one's life in particular. As I see it, "faith" is a construct that provides focus and context—"meaning," if you will—and if one's "meaning system" (worldview) is limited to a purely personal way of coping, oriented only toward oneself or, in a fundamentalistic way, oriented only toward one's concept of God, then that for me would result in "poor" or "bad" faith, for it derives from a limited, self-serving perspective. Much of what goes by "religious faith" in America today falls into this category, I'm afraid. It may have personal value but should not be confused with the kind of holistic faith that will help us cope with global problems and move our world forward. If religion (faith) is a way of creating and maintaining meaning, can it be viewed as art—art that can be executed poorly or excellently? Can art be thought of in that way as well?

TL: Absolutely. Religion can be described as art. Although, art tends to have an individual credited as responsible for its making it—an artist. I would be interested in who the artist would be in that scenario. Distortions of religion are distinct from critique of religion, yet both can be part of telling one's story, as a personal way of coping or creating meaning. I feel conflicted in writing about it, as an artist who employs a private narrative (no matter how tongue-in-cheek I may want it to be), which preys on an external perception, as a coping mechanism. I cannot say self-serving meaning systems cannot yield viable art, and in some way contribute to a holistic solution for coping with local or global problems—because I think they can.

RPVK: Holistic faith, like great art, is, in my estimation, energizing and has universal appeal because it addresses the universal human condition. It contains an expansive quality, an openness that, like a good conversation, is unending. As I tell my students in religion classes, an effective religious perspective should not be limited to self-enhancement or characterized by an apologetic function—that is, to making converts by clinching arguments and stifling conversation. Faith, like art, enhances dialogue.

TL: I think art acts on a similar impulse of making meaning. The concepts of holistic faith and holistic art are quite attractive. Both have, at heart, an agonistic approach to conversation, belief systems, and practical solutions. To your question of whether or not religion can be placed into an art context, I do wonder, if one practices a particular religion, does entering into a context that potentially regards that particular brand of faith as a historically monstrous, thought-killing poem of platitudes change one's relationship to it; the same faith that has seeped into our secular understanding of conventional wisdom—a theistic wisdom that feeds our common, atheistic sense of morality? Maybe this is one place an exchange can begin?

RPVK: I would agree insofar as wisdom-literature is an important part of biblical scripture, just as wisdom is captured in aphorisms and platitudes—"street" wisdom, if you will.

TL: I'm not sure what you mean by "street" wisdom. Do you mean "street smarts," acquired by spending a lot of time on the street and on street corners, knowing the customs, language, and codes that originated there? I feel that's quite different from the aphorism or platitude, yet slightly similar insofar as both are ways for people to not only survive but advance in life within a community.

RPVK: By "street" wisdom I have in mind a way of speaking and thinking that is not elitist or one-dimensional; it has breadth in its intention and impact, speaking to the masses because it originates from the general populace.

TL: I understand where you're coming from. To be fair, I've noticed in discussion and writing about my work a conflation of the influence of the modernist "grid" with the "grit" of the urban landscape. I can say this correlation is a tool I've decided to use. The conversations that develop out of this deduction usually end with a familiar mythological narrative that I unfortunately don't live up to—although I imagine it would be nice if I did—to help people understand the work more clearly. The dirty condition of the work (all graphite pencil or graphite powder) can be traced to a larger conversation of drawing as a principled, physical activity, and the slipperiness of material as metaphor (issues of the studio and the attitude it promotes). I would argue this "street wisdom," is in fact a quite elite and one-dimensional take reflecting the skewed perception of the general populace. For example, the book I've worked closely with for years, *Life's Little Instruction Book* by H. Jackson Brown, is filled with common themes of American positivist sensibilities, with consideration for God, others, and oneself. Though this book is inclusive, with an altruistic, systemic wisdom, it was written by a white man for his son leaving for college. This fact changes my perception of accessibility to such writing. By this I mean the book is intended it for the masses today, yet there's a subtle historical authority that can be perceived as alienating to women and nonwhite people. I'm not saying the book is not accurate, or oddly comforting in rare cases—I think it is, or I would not being working with it. But there's a strong component of social instruction that relates to authority, and it's understood as a sensibility that is less about what you *have to do* to live right, and more about what you *should do* to live right, if you want to participate and succeed in *this* society.

PAM LINS speaks with AMY SILLMAN and MOLLY ZUCKERMAN-HARTUNG

Pam Lins: Let's start in the middle. Do you think there's something about us all having connections to the Midwest? I have the accent, but I had no role models.

Amy Sillman: I was a full-on Midwestern dork. I wore lumberjack clothes, and only when I moved to NYC did I realize there was such a thing as style. Molly, I'm embarrassed that I once asked you if you were going to stay in Chicago. No one has ever asked me if I will be "staying" in NYC!

Molly Zuckerman-Hartung: Oh, I've much to say about the Midwest. I've been there ten years now. But also, when I was in my late teens back in Olympia, where I'm from, I met these emo punks arriving from Michigan. They would show you their palms like they were from *Star Trek* and point to their city. I loved these funny, slow sweethearts.

PL: I'm all for funny, but fast funny, not slow funny.

MZ-H: I was a tank! Angry and pushy.

PL: I needed to get out of the Midwest because I felt you were considered a downer if you were seeking ugly thoughts. Asking questions was equivalent to complaining. Plus everything in Chicago burned down a hundred years ago. AND they have a series of alleys to hide their garbage in. I'm just sayin': there's no garbage in sight.

MZ-H: Chicago does hide its garbage in alleys. It's really passive-aggressive.

AS: Do you guys think about ugliness? I always wanted to call a painting "The Ugly Light"—after the name of the light that comes on when the bar is closing.

MZ-H: Of course I think about ugly. When I said I was a tank, I really meant my face. It was square and heavy—masculine—and I hated it.

AS: I love your description of your face! It reminds me of a Jim Nutt face.

MZ-H: More Egon Schiele or Otto Dix! The first paintings I made—I think I was twenty-four, twenty-five—were self-portraits, which allowed me to look at myself with more care. So I started thinking that my feelings were all trapped in my face, and that was making me ugly.

AS: It's really interesting to know that you disliked your own face but still made pictures of it! I like my face just fine, but I'm alienated below the neck: above = good, below = scary. Huh, all of a sudden I realize why I'm not a sculptor. [*laughs*] No, really: maybe feeling uncomfortable with one's body is an advantage in art?

MZ-H: Awkward bodies. Yeah. Formally I think all of our work operates roughly as body surrogates. Pam, your paintings on sculptures seem like heads on bodies. Is that too crude a read?

PL: No, not crude at all. I have an interest in faciality, and maybe this is a small part of how Amy and I started a collaboration.

MZ-H: Right. You two are working together on a piece for the WB, and you've known each other for years. About figuration, that reminds me, Amy, of that three-way painting series you made—showing couples intertwined, imagining yourself as a third wheel. That psychological situation was formative for me. I was often the smart girl invited to hang out with couples on dates because they had nothing to say to each other, and I always had something to say.

AS: WEIRD! I don't think I ever had such a role—a date add-on!

PL: I was never brought along to spice things up either! I think it seems like a huge compliment. And here we are, a threesome.

MZ-H: It didn't feel like a compliment. I think I didn't know how to address or be addressed as a lover—OR a collaborator. Can you guys talk more about working together?

PL: I had been talking to Amy about the role of painting as prop in sculpture. Amy offered me one of her paintings; I placed it in a sculpture and gave it back. She changed it, gave it back to me, and on and on. In these collaborations I want to focus on the dialectic between painting and sculpture as one concerned with different spatial logics and disruptions at the same time.

MZ-H: So you haven't been actually working together in the same room, at the same time?

AS: No. I've realized that what I have to do in my studio bears no resemblance to what Pam has to do—all this lifting, carrying, wrapping, storing objects that can break in half . . . But a funny thing happened after we began to collaborate: I had this mad urge to add a ceramic cup to the side of the stretcher bar.

PL: We're finding out things we didn't even know about our own work. I didn't understand a certain relationship to bodies in my work.

MZ-H: So things are getting hairy in your studios, which brings up criteria. How do you judge sculpture? Like, why do you both like Anthony Caro so much?

AS: I often defer to Pam in the judgment of sculpture. She has a more critical eye and mind for sculptural space. I'm kind of an easy date: I like things that are there in real life. *Basta*.

PL: The thing you have to remember about Caro is that so many of his works were I beams, which speaks so much to the built world and its materials. I think his sculpture *Early One Morning*, from 1962, is so odd. It is red, and it also looks a little like an easel. It contains distortion and two-point perspective at the same time that it's a form.

MZ-H: Maybe I'm venturing into sculpture because I put too much dumb pressure on painting. I want to exhaust painting by pushing it into real space.

PL: I don't think sculpture always equals real space.

AS: I don't understand that—sculpture is really there! That's why it has meant so much to me when I've been in periods of grief. That's why there is funerary sculpture.

PL: What the graveyard taught Brancusi is that sculpture doesn't need a pedestal. Anyway, I can't concretely argue with you that sculpture is not necessarily real space. I think sometimes I am working from within my body, yet I don't recognize that I am working in space.

AS: What do you mean?

PL: When something's really there, it makes me want to try something different—like changing or emptying, opening up or lightening something that is hollow, or abstract, or colorful. The actual properties of things can recede or disappear, or abruptly change after the first encounter. I don't know what's coming as I walk around—it's an unknown future. I think the attempt is to get sculpture to be both a fact and a fiction . . . which is really hard.

MZ-H: I don't know what sculpture is! Object making is a wild gamble for me, but I always do it as a Painter. I wanted a home medium/discipline, and I chose painting. It gives me limits, edges, historical precedents. I call it "Dad" and argue with it. Or it's a hair shirt. I'm not thinking about sculpture formally with my hinged paintings. I see them as excess weight, as deliberate overburdening. Or something dragged, something parasitic, more metaphoric than spatial.

PL: Molly, I just saw a picture of one of your works where a painting is dragging behind a chair. I guess there were little wheels—so not a total "drag." Wheels are almost always good in artworks. Funny and sad and violent.

MZ-H: Pam, you seem able to say three things at once.

AS: Molly, are you saying that your forays into sculpture are not formal? That they are metaphoric or linguistic, while your painting remains more formal?

MZ-H: Yes, I'm definitely thinking formally in painting. Or trying to.

AS: But I assume that, Pam, you are dealing with all this formal stuff in your work?

PL: Yes and no.

AS: This makes me wonder if feeling comfortable with the formal language in one's work is something that happens over time. Maybe people become more formal as they get older. Pam, do you approach the formal differently when painting, for example, than when making objects? I know you both make work in two different genres, so do you approach these differently?

PL: I like to struggle with the difference. How they are the same may be harder to come to.

MZ-H: What do you mean by that?

PL: I mean: sometimes I work in my head and sometimes in my body.

AS: I keep wanting to push you, Pam, to say exactly how you feel that painting and sculpture are different and/or not different?

PL: Amy, you are not going to be satisfied with my answer: I don't know if I can tell you exactly. "Exactly" makes me uncomfortable. I just think that sculpture can be psychological space. Stand-in, metaphor, even illusion, or prop. It is not so stuck in time, like, say, a log on the floor. Of course, it's real in space. But that's my struggle and my work. It's the push to understand those things that keeps me working.

AS: For me, the essential difference between painting and sculpture is that painting is fiction and sculpture is nonfiction. I make paintings because I am intimidated by things. I prefer 2-D to 3-D. I don't want to be responsible for volume.

MZ-H: What's a volume? I think about books . . .

PL: There are volumes in everything. I equate a painting's stretcher frame with the armature of a sculpture—both are fundamental to the creation of volume.

AS: But an armature and a stretcher bar aren't the same thing.

PL: I disagree: both are hard and can help slack, soft things stand up!

AS: No, that's a fluffer! [*laughs*] No, really—the difference to me is that the stretcher bar remains the same regardless of the subsequent moves on the canvas. You would never say that about an armature.

PL: Well, in these collaborations we are doing, we are dealing with your stretchers!

AS: Yes, that's precisely my point! We are dealing with it because we're making a sculpture out of it. As a pure painter, I would not be "dealing with" my stretchers.

PL: That's because you're not a structuralist.

AS: Well, it's true that our collaboration has pushed me to understand the painted object in a totally new way. Still, I do like the indifference of the stretcher bars to the painting. I'll just say it again: I don't make sculpture simply because I am intimidated by the real.

PL: Wait! So am I! But I want to add: in some ways, I think that sculpture should be considered as having more virtual space than painting, or SOME sculptures do. You can't always see the whole thing. This is one way to get out of the idea that all sculptures only exist in "real space."

AS: The one way I could describe how I would think of painting as between sculpture and painting is via abstraction. Abstraction is precisely the thing that allows me to have a dual experience, both mental space *and* physical embodiment. You could say abstraction is "queer" that way. It swings both ways, neither one thing nor the other. Anyway, who would love abstraction more than someone who feels ambivalent in their body!

PL: Hell yeah!

MZ-H: What about not feeling comfortable in your mind? Sculpture brings up the real on a number of levels: real materials with real associations, real bodies, real time, real social relations, class, race, gender . . . All of this brings up feelings of collapse, depression, failure, and sleep for me. I get really sad when I'm working outside the picture plane.

AS: Do you feel those things when you are *working* in sculpture? Or only when you are looking at it?

MZ-H: This is what makes me definitely NOT a sculptor. I always imagine making paintings when I look at them. But with sculpture I feel like a spectator: powerless, overtaken. Like with Caro, which feels so light and limber but has its own reality: I believe in it.

AS: Then for you, sculpture is fictional and painting is real.

MZ-H: Maybe.

AS: For me, the fiction of painting is simply that I can draw ANYTHING. But nothing I depict has to actually be able to stand up in real life. Ah, the imaginary!

PL: So we're back to affect. What about the emotion of fear? Can we parse our emotions a bit more?

MZ-H: I'm uncomfortable with your word *intimidated*, Amy, but excited by your recalcitrance. You seem to need to articulate anxiety. I wonder if this relationship to anxiety emerged through grief? It feels like that level of necessity. I hope that isn't a rude question.

AS: Not rude at all. But no, the necessity for articulation for me is more about justice than it is about grief. Though weirdly, grief made me love sculpture! I welcomed the sheer presence of sculpture during certain years of my life.

MZ-H: Grief makes me think about this Egyptian drawing of Theban women mourning. They all have the same black hair with bangs like Olympia's Riot Grrrls. I was one, and so was my dear friend Angie Hart. We were raw, undefined, and confusing, and there was power in that, but also I felt, viscerally, the identification and repulsion of being a woman among women. Angie was the girl who wrote "slut" on her belly and was photographed. *Newsweek* magazine hijacked the image and published it.

AS: So, do you think that when a Riot Grrrl writes "slut" on her body, that is a crude way to change her body, as hated object? If so, is that act like an abstract painting? In the sense that abstraction could be a gesture made from negative feelings but reclaiming the world as a positive—i.e., bad but proud?

MZ-H: She was basically offering the hatred in the culture a mirror and saying, "It doesn't affect me."

PL: Operationally, are a cut and a mark the same? I use cuts in my work very deliberately. To break a surface, to reveal an interior, to get some guts on top . . . Writing "slut" or making an abstract mark creates a new attitude that carries the burden of history.

MZ-H: I want to cut in here and say that I think you are talking about a historical, aggressive coupling of form and content.

AS: I'd note that a cut and a mark are operationally two different things.

MZ-H: Yeah, with the *Newsweek* photo, I think the mark was the word *slut* and the cut was the photo itself. Photography is violent.

PL: But we have to think about context. The photo in *Newsweek* is factual. Now we all look back, and what is it? A memory or an event or . . . a fiction? I remember seeing that picture of Angie, and how complicated it was for me that it was a collective memory or a realization that memories are also fictions. I look at so many photos for my work as a way of questioning histories.

AS: Pam, I tend to distrust the categories that you are bringing up: collective memory and the historical. When I saw that photo, I didn't stop to think about it as an historical event, I just saw it . . . I always thought mere reversals (like claiming the word *slut*) were dumb politically, and therefore bad strategies. Maybe now I can see it as an abstraction. But I don't trust images or representation; I don't take them for facts.

PL: Maybe sculpture is for a person who lied at a very young age to make themselves feel more legitimate or important around power and intellect and bodies. But it isn't lying. It is a way to create truths by representing real things along with the properties of fictions. You can't lie about what is seen in a body, but you sure can make up a lot about how, who, and what for.

AS: Lying? For me painting in many layers is similar to shoplifting—hiding things close to the body and getting away with it, cloaking a rude gesture. Is that something like the lying you're talking about?

PL: Thinking about shoplifting and painting in layers as being similar is funny and awkward. Shoplifting is bad.

MZ-H: I'm kind of drunk. When does the ugly light come on? But I get giddy thinking about that photo of Angie as a form of abstract painting. This collision of the photographic and the fictional is why and how I make paintings: to smuggle in the past and transform its reception in the present. I thought it was fucking heroic. By the way, I DO have a sense of humor.

AS: I don't laugh in real life. Only at TV.

MZ-H: What's the difference between real life and TV?

AS: TV's better. I got my whole aesthetic from Jay Ward, who created *The Rocky & Bullwinkle Show*.

PL: I got mine from *Gilligan's Island*, which is all about loss.

AS: Well, not really. It's about money.

MZ-H: I liked *Mister Rogers' Neighborhood*.

KEN LUM speaks with ALEXANDER ALBERRO

Alexander Alberro: You've worked with fictional signs for some time now, including shopkeepers' signs. What sets *Midway Shopping Plaza*, featured in this Whitney Biennial, apart from the previous signs you've displayed?

Ken Lum: I've been adapting public commercial signage since the very first series of photo-logos I made in 1984, from which the work in this Biennial derives. I suppose my interest owes much to my background growing up in an economically unstable neighborhood in Vancouver. I was sometimes hired to paint the "daily specials" for Jean's Grill and "semiannual sales" signs for Monarch Furniture. There was always a lot of business turnover on Kingsway, the nearby retail street, and with that came the loss of acquaintances and even friends. So the channel of work from which *Midway Shopping Plaza* emerged began with a study of the individual in relation to a corporate logo or sign. Typically, I work in several different channels at once, which often overlap. Each channel develops according to what I have learned from earlier steps. The steps usually cohere into a series. The most recent iteration deals with the idea of a community of tenants that may, to a certain extent, be in competition with each other.

AA: This sign in *Midway Shopping Plaza* is set within an imagined Vietnamese American shopping plaza. Why Vietnamese American?

KL: I'm interested in hyphenated identity and the ways in which cultural identity is established by a community. It's something I've long developed in my work. Presently, I live in Philadelphia near two rather large Vietnamese American shopping plazas with plenty of signage. The signs have led me to contemplate the historical factors that brought about the displacement of the Vietnamese language by the Latin script system in the seventeenth century. They've also prompted me to reflect on the circumstances that resulted in Vietnamese Americans establishing businesses at such sites, where they shop and eat together. The old South Vietnamese flag features prominently in the larger of the two Vietnamese plazas in Philadelphia. That flag may no longer officially exist politically, but its continued presence makes it function as a specter and as a gesture of defiance and longing.

AA: An inordinate number of pho soup places seem to be located in this made-up shopping center. Why is that?

KL: Yes, that's a good observation. Like any ethnically centered shopping plaza, there are eateries. Pho is a key dish in Vietnamese cuisine, so there are a lot of pho signs. Besides, it's in keeping with the retail logic that merchants do best where they are around similar vendors.

AA: What is the logic to the discrepancy in the size of the smaller, individual signs that together comprise the larger one?

KL: I'm playing a bit, but if you go to one of the many ethnic areas in Flushing, Queens, particularly the East Asian ones, for instance, you'll find signs that aren't necessarily large in scale but are subdivided into a curiously high number of tenant slots. The result is a visual cacophony—at least to my eyes. So, in some ways, there is no "discrepancy," as you put it, but a particular kind of logic.

AA: To what extent is this project playing with the signification of the signage?

KL: To a large extent. The work also consists of a whole series of imaginings on my part. I'm imagining who the people are who populate this shopping center: who the salespeople and shoppers are. I'm imagining the life stories of these people. I'm also imagining the system of signification in the context of the struggle to survive in the multiethnic society of the United States.

AA: How evident to the spectator do you want this play to be?

KL: I want the work to appear plausible as nonart, at least at some level of apprehension, so that some thought is given to actual people, places, and scenarios in the lifeworld. If the work functions well on that level alone, then I consider it a success. The sign may look banal and seem innocent. But, as I've already suggested, it has ties to a particularly fraught history shared by Vietnam and the United States—a recent history. Maybe my interest in these shopping plazas also has something to do with the fact that I, as a Chinese Canadian, suddenly felt more at home—whatever that might mean—on discovering these plazas so close to my new residence in Philadelphia. I often go to these places to eat or to buy groceries.

AA: Given that there are multiple references more or less hidden in this big commercial sign to a war that many Americans would rather forget, I wonder what your ultimate aim is. Do you want spectators to study the signs of ethnically defined shopping centers more closely than usual? Or is it a question of returning polyvalence to language, of challenging the instrumentalization of the sign brought about by commerce?

KL: I would say the second question you pose is closer to what brought me to *Midway Shopping Plaza*. But, again, I felt compelled to make this work because I found myself spending a considerable amount of time in a district of the city full of Vietnamese Americans. As in much of my work, I'm interested in exploring human subjectivity. My art often performs representational, not just critical functions; here, the subjectivities discernable in a large shop sign. There are many real human hopes and worries lurking behind the facades of small businesses. I try to decode these or to accentuate them for the spectator to decode. I've drawn many lessons from Pop and Minimal art, and their immediate legacies, in terms of what is revealed or what lies behind a surface. This has led me to think about the nature of meaning in a social environment where the sign is the dominant marker of everything and nothing: no matter how it is composed, at root it's an arbitrarily chosen representation. Of course, it's not as simple as that—signs also point toward difference through language, for example. That was the great paradox of so much Pop and Minimal art: its sociality, if I may, was articulated through an extreme asocial character. But to reiterate an earlier point, I'm interested in the lives that people lead, particularly those immigrants and exiles from faraway places who bring with them complex life experiences, and in how those lives intersect at the level of the contemporary public sphere.

Shana Lutker

A to B to E to F to G to M to N: A Conversation with Augustine, André Breton, Albert Einstein, Sigmund Freud, Gradiva, Me, and Nadja

This is a conversation in quotes, a collage of statements made by both real and fictional characters, cobbled together in an effort to make connections. Their talk is riddled with gaps and slight misunderstandings, but they strive to offer some context and reveal some of the process that generates my work.

Introductions
Augustine arrived at Paris's Salpêtriére Hospital in 1875, suffering from hysterical paralysis, and became the star patient of neurologist Jean-Martin Charcot. Her symptoms are well documented in Charcot's photographic research archive. Augustine, whose full name was Louise Augustine Gleizes (though she has also been referred to as Patient X), escaped from the hospital in 1880, disguised as a boy. In 1928, André Breton and Louis Aragon declared and celebrated the fiftieth birthday of hysteria in the eleventh issue of their serial publication *La Révolution surréaliste*. Alongside a spread featuring six photographs of the teenager Augustine in bed, wearing a robe, the writers thanked Charcot profusely for his definition of hysteria, calling it the greatest poetic discovery of the end of the nineteenth century, and for the pinups of "delicious" young Augustine.

André Breton, founder of Surrealism, met Sigmund Freud in Vienna in 1921. After meeting this hero, Breton wrote of feeling disappointment: "I tried to make him talk by throwing into the conversation the names of Charcot and Babinski, but whether I tried to make use of memories too far off, or he was reluctant to talk to a stranger, I could only draw from him generalities like: 'Your letter was the most touching I have ever received in my life,' or 'Fortunately, we rely heavily on youth.'"[1]

Theoretical physicist Albert Einstein published his equation $E = mc^2$ (and three other groundbreaking papers) in 1905, six years after Freud published *Traumdeutung* (what would later be translated into English as *The Interpretation of Dreams*). Einstein initiated a correspondence in 1932 with Freud in an attempt to address the question "Is there any way of delivering mankind from the menace of war?" Freud responded with a dark and pessimistic account of mankind. Their exchange was published in 1933, under the title *Why War?* That year, Hitler came to power; Einstein, who was visiting the United States at the time, never returned to Germany, his birthplace.

Gradiva means "woman who walks" and is the name of a Roman bas-relief in the Vatican Museums depicting a young woman lifting her robes and revealing her feet to walk forward. In 1903, Wilhelm Jensen published a novel called *Gradiva*, in which an archaeologist has a delusional relationship with the girl in the relief, confusing her with a childhood friend named Zoë. Freud wrote "Delusion and Dream in Jensen's *Gradiva*" in 1907, an essay about fantasy and delusion, analyzing the novel's protagonist. Freud bought a copy of the bas-relief that year and kept it in his study in Vienna. I saw it at the Freud Museum in London, where he relocated in 1938, as Hitler encroached. In 1937, Gradiva was the name Breton gave to a new gallery he was managing in Saint-Germain. Marcel Duchamp designed the door at Gradiva, and Breton tried to convince Pablo Picasso to design the letterhead. The gallery did not stay open long.

Sigmund Freud, founding father of psychoanalysis, went to Paris in 1885 as a young medical student to study neurology with Jean-Martin Charcot. After returning to his home in Vienna in 1886, shocked by some of Charcot's techniques, he decided there must be a "talking cure" for hysteria. He then started to develop his theories of the unconscious and analysis, which changed the way the Western world approached mental illness, sex, and trauma.

Nadja was born Léona-Camille-Ghislaine D. in 1902. Breton saw Nadja walking on the street in 1926 and was immediately entranced. She became an obsession, a haunting, for him, and their affair continued off and on over the course of that year, until her institutionalization in a mental hospital in 1927. His novel about their relations, *Nadja*, was published in 1928.

I am an artist who has been researching and making work about the beginnings of psychoanalysis, Surrealism, and hysteria for a number of years. I am now writing a narrative history of fistfights between the Surrealists. From this research grows a body of work. Each fistfight that Breton and the Surrealists initiated forms a chapter, unfolding the motivations and history behind the squabbles; the chapters in turn become the seeds of objects. From a ladder falling down a short flight of stairs, to a leather theater seat like the one Breton jumped out of to initiate the first fistfight, to an oversize reproduction of Breton's gravestone, the sculptures are translations or interpretations of this research, the relationship between inventors and their ideas, and the shifts in the perception and reception of ideas and art over time.

———

I commence: The struggle to define oneself in language and history is one to which you all relate. Each of you has been shaped, quite literally, by another member of the group.

Sigmund Freud begins: When I learned of your intention to invite me to a mutual exchange of views upon a subject which not only interested you personally but seemed deserving, too, of public interest, I cordially assented. I expected you to choose a problem lying on the borderland of the knowable, as it stands today, a theme which each of us . . . might approach from his own angle, to meet at last on common ground, though setting out from different premises. Thus the question which you put me . . . took me by surprise.[2]

I contextualize: Thank you, Dr. Freud. The subject, as you know, is an investigation of the fistfights of the Surrealists. More generally—a conversation of legacy, language, and violence. What does it take to bring an idea to the status of an invention, to name it? What does it feel like to believe that your ideas are revolutionary? And why do some men feel entitled to do violence in the name of defending or spreading their ideas? I am interested in Breton's public fistfighting, but also, for example, in the preoccupations of Einstein, as a scientist, with understanding man's predilections to destruction on a greater scale. Are these two violences the same?

Albert Einstein inquires: Is it possible to control man's mental evolution so as to make him proof against the psychosis of hate and destructiveness? Here I am thinking by no means only of the so-called uncultured masses. Experience proves that it is rather the so-called "intelligentsia" that is most apt to yield to these disastrous collective suggestions, since the intellectual has no direct contact with life in the raw but encounters it in its easiest, synthetic form—upon the printed page.[3]

Gradiva supports My colleague is right; the method is really good and he has used it with the greatest success![4]

I wonder: But what about these cases where it is the theories and ideas of the intelligentsia that drive the violence?

Freud continues: Conflicts of interest between man and man are resolved, in principle, by the recourse to violence. It is the same in the animal kingdom, from which man cannot claim exclusion; nevertheless, men are also prone to conflicts of opinion, touching, on occasion, the loftiest peaks of abstract thought, which seem to call for settlement by quite another method. This refinement is, however, a late development.[5]

Nadja admits to Gradiva: He said something I don't understand, there was a word in it I don't understand.[6]

Gradiva concedes: One must resign oneself to the inevitable, and I have long accustomed myself to being dead.[7]

Freud expounds: Indeed, it might well be called the "death instinct"; whereas the erotic instincts vouch for the struggle to live on. The death instinct becomes an impulse to destruction when, with the aid of certain organs, it directs its action outward, against external objects.[8]

Augustine offers an example: Get rid of the snake you have in your pants . . . It's a sin.[9]

I interpret: I am often struck in my research by the way that women slip in and out of focus, they change names, they shift in character. Gradiva, Augustine, and Nadja are not even granted stable names. Each of you seem suspended in these crises of identity. Is there something destructive in the impulse to destabilize identity? Is it aggressive?

Einstein counters: I am well aware that the aggressive instinct operates under other forms and in other circumstances. (I am thinking of civil wars, for instance, due in earlier days to religious zeal, but nowadays to social factors; or, again, the persecution of racial minorities.)[10]

Nadja relates: [The American guy I was dating] called me Lena, in memory of his daughter who had died. That was very affectionate, very touching of him, wasn't it? But you know, I found I couldn't stand being called that, as if it was a dream: Lena, Lena . . . So I would move my hand in front of his eyes several times, quite close to his eyes, like this, and I would say, "No, not Lena, Nadja."[11]

Breton postulates: I have never known personally any woman of this name, which has always irritated me, just as that of Solange has always delighted me. Yet, Madame Sacco, clairvoyant, 3 Rue des Usines, who has never been mistaken about me, assured me early this year that my mind would be greatly occupied with a "Helene." Is this why, some time after this, . . . I was so greatly interested in everything concerning Helene Smith? The conclusion is evidently on the order of that previously imposed upon me by the fusion in a dream of two extremely disparate images. "Hélène, c'est moi," Nadja used to say.[12]

Gradiva is confused: Was that Greek? . . . I heard you say something that I could understand. You expressed the wish that someone might still be alive here. Only I did not understand whom you meant by that.[13]

Augustine helps her out: One thinks one has dreamed something when one has simply heard of it.[14]

I add: Our experience is colored and shaped by the connections and networks we seek. Sometimes things are revealed as if they were simply waiting for us to discover them.

Breton says anecdotally: The day of the first performance of Apollinaire's *Couleur du Temps* at the Conservatoire Renee Maubel, while I was talking to Picasso in the balcony during the intermission, a young man approaches me, stammers a few words, and finally manages to explain that he had mistaken me for one of his friends supposedly killed in the war. Naturally, nothing more was said. A few days later, through a mutual friend, I begin corresponding with Paul Eluard, whom I did not know by sight. On furlough, he comes to see me: I am in the presence of the same person as at *Coleur du Temps*.[15]

Nadja contextualizes: Time is a tease. Time is a tease—because everything has to happen in its own time.[16]

Gradiva ruminates: It seems to me as if we all had eaten our bread together like this once, two thousand years ago.[17]

Breton interjects: I will no longer postpone expressing the unbounded admiration I felt for *Les Détraquées*,[18] which remains and will long remain the only dramatic work (I mean: created exclusively for the stage) which I choose to recall. The play, I insist—and this is not one of its least curious aspects—loses almost everything, or at least every character conflict, by not being seen, by not being acted out. With these reservations, I do not consider it unprofitable in other respects to relate its plot. The curtain rises on the office of the principal of a girls' school. This woman, a rather stout blonde of about forty, is discovered alone and gives signs of great nervous tension.[19]

I admit: I thought we'd talk more about art and violence, but it seems that the experience of theater and memory keeps resurfacing. I have this to add: I went to Paris last year to research Breton's life and the beginnings of Surrealism. On July 6, 2012, the eighty-ninth anniversary of the first fistfight started in the name of Surrealism, at the Soirée du Coeur a Barbé, I went to a play at that same theater, Théâtre Michel. The play that night was surprisingly similar to what Breton outlined of *Les Détraquées*: the first scene opened on a principal's office, or maybe it was a teacher's lounge, and a rather stout woman of about forty was pacing the stage nervously! The play was called *La maîtresse en maillot de bain*, or *The Headmistress in the Swimsuit*. Is that a strange connection, or am I imagining it?

Breton shuts me down: I am sorry, but I am unable to do anything about the fact that this may exceed the limits of credibility.[20]

Freud reminisces: I decided long ago to pay a visit to the theater, but waited for something I knew. This evening *Carmen* was being played in the Theater Quirino. It began at 9 pm, the hour I usually go up to my room. . . . Gradually some thirty musicians, with varying amounts of hair, arrived; one of them was a girl, at all events young and dark, if not pretty, who sat down beside an enormous gilded harp straight out of a picture book . . . I received my first shock when there appeared on the stage a lady whom I took to be Carmen, until I remembered that she must be the good Micaela. For she was very long and thin, her teeth long and bare, with a carrot-colored wig. In short, she looked a little like those English ladies sent abroad to scare the public, and her presence kept tormenting me until I realized her striking resemblance to poor Tina Urbitsek. The second, more enduring shock came soon after. . . . At last Carmen made her appearance. I greeted her as an old acquaintance; you too would have recognized her. It was Katy Reich with her round face, her little snub nose, and colossal proportions. Or rather, which also tallied better with her age, she was her mother, old Frau Gerstl. . . . The resemblance was so great that I kept looking around for Heinz; but he didn't appear. As a matter of fact, Frau Reich's mother actually was an opera singer.[21]

Gradiva suggests: It seems that you have reason to be on your guard against an excess of imagination, although, when I have been with you, I never supposed so.[22]

Freud, bashfully: And now a confession which you must accept with tolerance! Although I have received so much evidence of the interest which you and your friends show toward my research, for myself I am not in the position to explain what Surrealism is and what it is after. It could be that I am not in any way made to understand it; I am at such a distance from art.[23]

Nadja, in horror: Oh! That must be death![24]

1. André Breton, *Oeuvres Complètes* (Paris: Gallimard, 1988), 1276.
2. Sigmund Freud, letter to Albert Einstein, Vienna, September 1932, in *Einstein on Peace*, ed. Otto Nathan and Heinz Norden (New York: Avenel Books, 1981), 191.
3. Albert Einstein, letter to Sigmund Freud, July 30, 1932, in *Einstein on Peace*, 190.
4. The title character, Gradiva, from the short story "Gradiva: A Pompeiian Fantasy" (1903) by Wilhelm Jensen, trans. Helen M. Downey, quoted in Freud, "Delusion and Dream," in *Delusion and Dream and Other Essays*, ed. Philip Rieff, trans. Harry Zohn (Boston: Beacon Press, 1956), 45.
5. Freud, letter to Einstein, Vienna, September 1932, in *Einstein on Peace*, 192.
6. The title character in André Breton, *Nadja*, trans. Richard Howard (New York: Grove Press, 1960), 66.
7. Gradiva, quoted in Freud, "Delusion and Dream," 41.
8. Freud, letter to Einstein, Vienna, September 1932, in *Einstein on Peace*, 198.
9. Augustine, quoted in Georges Didi-Huberman, *Invention of Hysteria*, trans. Alisa Hartz (Cambridge, MA: MIT Press, 2003), 161.
10. Einstein, letter to Freud, Caputh, Germany, July 30, 1932, in *Einstein on Peace*, 190.
11. Nadja, in Breton, *Nadja*, 73–74.
12. Ibid., 79–80.
13. Gradiva, from Jensen, "Gradiva," 197.
14. Augustine, quoted in Didi-Huberman, *Invention of Hysteria*, 137.
15. Breton, *Nadja*, 26–27.
16. Ibid, 102.
17. Gradiva, in *Delusion and Dream*, 46.
18. *Les Détraquées* (*The Mad Ones*) was a drama written under the names Olaf and Palau. The two-act play was presented for the first time at the Deux Masques Theater on February 15, 1921. The drama takes place in a private girls' boarding school. At the end of the year, Madame de Challens, head teacher, regularly calls to her office Madamoiselle Solange, professor of dance; both of them, obviously lesbian, subject a young pupil to their cruel perverted tastes, leading to the death of the poor girl." Jacques Philippon and Jacques Poirier, *Joseph Babinski:*

A Biography (Oxford UK: Oxford University Press, 2008), 43–44. In 1956, Breton revealed that the coauthor of the play, with the actor Pierre Palau, was Joseph Babinski ("Olaf"), a famed neurologist with whom Breton had studied as a young medical student in 1917.
19. Breton, *Nadja*, 40.
20. Ibid.
21. Freud, letter to his family, Rome, September 24, 1907, in *Letters of Sigmund Freud 1883–1939*, ed. Ernst L. Freud, trans. Tania and James Stern (New York: Basic Books, 1975), 262–63.
22. Gradiva, in *Delusion and Dream*, 197.
23. Letter from Freud to Breton, Vienna, December 26, 1921, published in *Littérature, nouvelle series*, no. 1 (March 1922), 19.
24. Breton, *Nadja*, 73.

JOHN MASON speaks with RICKY SWALLOW

I was introduced to John Mason and his wife, Vernita Mason, by our mutual friend the artist and furniture designer Peter Shire in early 2012. We have met often since at John's studio, just east of downtown Los Angeles. He moved to this studio in 1970 and reinstalled the same giant kiln that he and Peter Voulkos purchased together for their Glendale studio in the late 1950s. The kiln is something of a time machine. Many of the iconic Californian Abstract Expressionist vessels, sculptures, and wall reliefs made by Voulkos and Mason were fired within its walls. The studio is a testament to the "old ways" and methodologies of sculpture. It contains an archaic bread-dough machine for mixing clay, a reference library of glazed test tiles, clay extruders, and slab rollers, customized for Mason's specific requirements. Examples of John's geometric sculptures constructed from large, intersecting planes of clay and his modular tile wall reliefs, all from the past decade, were audience to the following conversation in his studio.
—Ricky Swallow

Ricky Swallow: John, the first thing I want to ask you is about how, as far as I know, you went straight into abstraction from the beginning of your art making and how you constructed large-scale abstractions fairly early. For me as an artist, abstraction has always been an obstacle; it's taken fifteen years to get closer to abstraction—via a lot of figuration. So I want to ask you where your confidence to work in this way came from?

That's a heavy way to start, right?

John Mason: I don't think it's a conscious thing, you know? There's the unconscious and the conscious. When you say, "I'm an artist," that's conscious. The creative activity is largely unconscious.

A lot of the artists that I was looking at early on were not abstractionists, but there was always an abstract element in their work, and I think that's what I became conscious of. We say "abstraction," but basically it's all abstract. The most specific language is abstract. All visual information is abstract. What's not abstract is the natural phenomena that you see, but I think your biological structure abstracts it. You cannot acquire that. You can only acquire an abstraction of it, and then it's in your memory, and then your memory is the problem. And there are many forms of memory: language, visual objects, sequences, music, rhythms—many forms.

RS: So your practice has always been quite an intuitive approach to material. Is that fair to say?

JM: I think so, yes. I don't know how else you could do it except intuitively.

RS: I've been here at your studio a number of times. Different objects in this building represent your almost sixty-year career, and I feel like I've learned a lot about sculpture by coming here and seeing different bodies of your work. Are there still things you're gaining from your finished sculptures, or is all the learning in their construction, in the process of making? Do you look at these older pieces for clues or do you just try to think of the next problem?

JM: I think, "That's it, what's next?" And it always includes a lot of the history, even the most recent. I've said in the past you cannot reinvent the world, and there are many factors that exist that you use.

RS: At a certain point, you began mapping the surfaces of your sculptures with graphic shapes, lines, and designs, which sort of further complicates the works as objects and messes with how you interact with them. What was your intention in adding graphics? Were they almost image overlays onto the planes of your objects? In particular, I'm thinking of the circular orb series Folded Orbits and Trans-Orbs (2000–6), of the large standing Triangles (1986), and of the hexagonal/octagonal slab-built vases, Pentagonal Vessels (1985–96).

JM: I was interested in patterns on flat surfaces: they go over, wrap, and complicate. It's no longer on a two-dimensional surface; it's on a three-dimensional surface, so that gives more area for exploration.

The first ones were simple patterns. They didn't wrap around. They might have had a single stripe on a flat surface . . . Well, there were several issues here: one had to do with patterns, another with glaze characteristics. Depending on the application of the glaze, I could get at least three tonal values from one glaze, and depending on how heavily I sprayed it—these were sprayed—I could get different values. There's discovery all along the way.

RS: The tile pieces in the *Wall Relief* series (2010), a few of which are hanging behind us, resemble paintings in their proportions and installation on the wall—more so than any other works of yours I've seen. I understand you never pursued painting, but do you see the modular tile works as related to, say, hard-edge abstraction—for example, the work of Frederick Hammersley and John McLaughlin in L.A. or someone like Sol LeWitt in New York—in terms of their repeated geometry and diagrammatic quality? They have a modular structure, which is evident in your sculptures, too, but they behave like paintings.

JM: Well, that's secondary, actually. It was unconscious. It came in a process of discovery. Those tile pieces are all based on the square—every one of them—and the square was cut into four pieces by sectional lines that crossed through the center but not at right angles. They're off the right-angle axis. So, in this sectioning of the square, four pieces that did not duplicate the original were cut.

RS: It does seem like you created your own system of units that could be endlessly reconfigured, and the rhythm or the arhythmic aspect of those units—

JM: Well, there is a limit to reconfiguration, but there were certainly multiple possibilities.

RS: Did you max out your limits with the tile pieces, or did you just want to move on to different things?

JM: I may have, in my own mind. I have never discovered another version of this, so . . . You know, geometry has a rigid structure. You can't monkey with it.

RS: If anyone can, you can. [*laughter*]

JM: The Greeks could have.

RS: Part of my enjoyment of the geometric works is in trying to resolve them as objects, trying to understand where the volumes intersect beyond what you can see. The cross has repeatedly appeared in your work, from those first ceramic X-Pots (1957–58) through to *Red X* (1966) at the Los Angeles County Museum of Art, which to me almost kind of obstructs your way when you encounter it—it feels almost as impenetrable as a monolith. But your geometric sculptures of the past decade or so are much more open in form. You still use the cross, but it's almost like a turnstile.

JM: It has to do with the complexities of the materials, the process. The forming technique is key to what we're talking about. Most of those began as maquettes—cardboard maquettes. The maquettes are critical, and the drawings, too.

RS: Have you ever exhibited the drawings or the maquettes, or are they strictly for the studio?

JM: No, I've refused to.

RS: I want to get back to how the recent works are so structurally open in comparison to earlier sculptures that were more monolithic, more dense.

JM: Well, it's a question of whether it contains something or whether it just engages space.

RS: Now we're getting to the good stuff. These works engage the space they're in, but they also engage the audience in a very active way. They engage the mind in terms of how one resolves their construction, and they engage the body, literally encouraging the viewer to circulate around them. This work seems like a return to something elemental. I know you've always been interested in physics . . .

JM: Well, what's the best and simplest way you can say it?

RS: Is that a question or an answer?

JM: That's a question I ask myself.

RS: How much can you reduce something and still have it work?

JM: Yes.

RS: I make small sculptures and enjoy small sculptures because every element and every junction becomes part of the focus and is critical to the success of the sculpture. In your work, you carry through with the same eased edges and attention to detail in the small sculptures as in the large. Usually on a large scale, I see a lot of generalization, but with you I always see specific information and treatment. Is that critical to the sculpture or critical to the technique?

JM: Critical to the thinking, yes. If it's critical to the thinking, it's got to follow through. I don't see any other way.

RS: What about the torque in these small, extruded, hollow square tubes you've been working on, which are cut and then slightly twisted? That gesture has a particular energy that is present in a lot of your larger pieces, and it goes back to this idea of a sculpture directing space. How long has that idea of the torque or the twist been in your work?

JM: It comes from pottery. You throw the cylinder and you say, "That's beautiful. What if I give it a twist?" The torque is obviously about energy. The very word means that, you know? You twist it; it took energy to twist it. If it's resistant, it wants to come back. It's a document of an event.

RS: I like that idea of a document of an event. The gauge of the clay in your work almost suggests sheet steel. From an engineering standpoint, many of these sculptures could be realized in steel. But certain planes have slight slumps or cracks from the porosity of the clay or from iron specks in the clay that have burned through the glazed surface.

JM: There are several elements that really separate the mediums. The big difference, besides the glaze, is the warping of the ceramic planes, and the warping becomes part of it.

RS: There's almost a vulnerability there, despite the large scale. A lot of information—like the structural means of joining the clay—is inside the form, out of sight.

JM: Yes. And you don't see a welding bead here or any grinding evidence.

RS: All of the ugly is on the inside. [*laughter*]

JM: That's right.

RS: In order to join clay, you sort of weld it by crisscrossing it or you knead a bead into the seam. With these, all that structural information is inside the form, right?

JM: It is. Occasionally these have broken, and then you see all the crap inside.

RS: You started as a crap on the outside guy! Back in the fifties, the construction process was almost embellished. I guess that was the time and that was the energy.

JM: Well, gravity was very much involved in that, too.

RS: There seems to be something radical in those early wall pieces—that they were made on the floor and then lifted onto the wall. *Blue Wall* (1959) is perhaps the most iconic.

JM: Well, that became, I must say, an issue. If I'd have left it on the floor, it would have been interesting in another respect. I made one on the floor of the studio and someone—I don't remember who it was—looked at it and said, "Are you going to keep this on the floor?" I said, "No, I think I'm going to put it on the wall."

RS: When you were working on the floor, were you conscious of the fact that it would be a wall piece, or were you just making it and watching it transpire?

JM: Oh no, I think I said, "What the hell am I going to do with it, I've got to get it off the floor!" I didn't have any space for it.

RS: And you also had to chop it up in order to fit it into this kiln, right?

JM: Yes.

RS: Do you ever think of your work in relation to Minimalism?

JM: No, I don't. . . . I'll put it a different way. If I had seen a model I would have said, I won't touch it, I won't make it, if it didn't have its source internally. There are influences, but that is something else. I mean, what are the influences? I don't know. The influences are really the world of art. And Asian cultures—man, talk about ceramics.

RS: There's an industrial quality to your recent work that I pick up on, too.

JM: Well, that's true. Very much so. And that was also part of my training. I was going to be an industrial designer, and then I had a little exposure to it, and I said, "No, I'll starve."

RS: You worked in a commercial ceramics plant that made plates and other housewares here in L.A., when you were still studying at Otis or shortly after? Did you learn anything from those processes?

JM: Oh, yes. I had a full run of the plant. One engineer was in charge of glaze and one engineer was in charge of clay bodies; a third engineer was quality control. And I had direct contacts with them on a regular basis. I learned a lot. The plant had all these different ways of producing ceramic objects, glazes, and surface embellishments. It was amazing. I got it all at the ceramic plant—I forget the name. What was the name? It was Vernon Kilns.

RS: So it seems like now we're at a point where there are more eyes and hands involved in ceramics, in terms of the contemporary art scene. You've lived and worked through a lot of ups and downs of your medium. It's been onstage, it's been offstage; it's back onstage. How do you feel about it now?

JM: You know, it's another world. I'm happy to see the recognition—that the work qualifies as art, and it's recognized, whatever the medium.

RS: I imagine that the critical reception of Ken Price's work in the past five to ten years of his life has probably had a generous effect on how people now view the medium.

JM: From the beginning, when he was a student, people recognized Ken's work. There was never a question about him. He was always thought of as an artist.

RS: I've been reading your oral history, and also Ron Nagle's and Irving Blum's, on the Smithsonian's Archives of American Art website. It just seems like during that time in California, when *Artforum* was based here, there were a lot of benefits and real visibility for the artists out here. I can't help thinking that *Artforum*'s move to the East Coast moved the spotlight away from the interesting things that were happening here.

JM: Well, the West Coast was really a desert in a lot of respects, culturally. As the mass began to accumulate—San Francisco, Los Angeles, and San Diego—more began to happen.

RS: Were you ever bothered by L.A. being treated as something of an outpost in terms of art, or did you—

JM: Yes!

RS: Yes. [*laughter*] That's a good answer. Okay, sir, no more questions.

SUZANNE MCCLELLAND speaks with GARRETT BRADLEY

Garrett Bradley: I'm glad we're talking about Mikhail Kalatozov's 1964 film, *Soy Cuba*. It's a visual masterpiece, and the story surrounding its production and distribution sparks a great dialogue about what it means to make a successful film.

Suzanne McClelland: Does your interest in it also have to do with the relationship between beauty and sociopolitical subject matter?

GB: Yes, I really appreciate the political narrative surrounding the film's making and reception. After the Cuban revolution, Cuba and the USSR agreed to give Kalatozov support for a film that would promote socialist ideology. I imagine they wanted something like Robert Flaherty's 1948 film *Louisiana Story*, which was funded by an oil company and tells the story of a poor Cajun family who strikes it rich after agreeing to get their land drilled. Flaherty's beautiful film was successful in promoting the agenda of his funders. This wasn't the case with Kalatozov. He made a stunning and technically innovative film, with the money and manpower of two governments, but *Soy Cuba* failed in the eyes of its funders and was pulled from USSR and Cuban theaters shortly after its release.

SM: Kalatozov did convey the message, wouldn't you agree? The camera shoots *from* the points of view of a range of Cuban characters rather than shooting *at* "the people." The American characters, "business" men who use Cuban nightclubs as playgrounds, are closely examined, and Kalatozov's empathy for the women who work in them is evident. Much of the dialogue is absorbed by the light and sound of the scenes, which may contribute to questions about "message."

GB: I think the narrative of an artist who is perceived of as a "failure" is interesting, and in this case there are many contributing factors.

SM: A work of art may fail, whether it's in a transparent way or in a tedious way, a casual way or a heavy way. Overworked failure may be the result of not trusting the imagination. Can we switch the language from failure to *mis-take*? For me, when a plan or vision "fails" to deliver original intentions, the process may reveal subtext, which can be developed. There is some beauty when there is a rub between the hard facts and the delivery—a sensuality perhaps. Art is made in navigating between facts and perceptions. I don't recall hearing discussion around "success" much before Reagan and Thatcher changed the political landscape in 1980.

As a painter, I think hierarchy and ranking systems are problems because they control perceptions in predictable ways. I am drawn to abstraction in painting because it offers opportunity to search for flexible patterns of reading. There is no primary figure to lead the way in abstraction, nothing to reflect the viewer—entry and exit are optional and less fixed. What I find alarming today is the need for measurement: the "best of," the "top ten." It's an arbitrary notion—what is it based on? Our digits, our ten fingers? . . . These piles or lists appear everywhere from *Consumer Reports* to mainstream fashion and art magazines and blogs. They encourage "competition," which has little to do with making.

GB: In a sense, measurement can push a medium in a new direction, though. This happens when artists work together, offering individual assets, rather than when individual "talents" of artists are quantified. Being a maker of any kind presents challenges which are mental and material, and part of the process is navigating those challenges with each other. Experimentation based on previously existing forms is how any art form evolves. What do you think? Is that how you approached Sigmar Polke's Solutions?

SM: I saw Sigmar Polke's 1967 painting *Solutions V* at the Brooklyn Museum in 1991, over twenty years ago, and it never left my memory bank. His painting is a list of equations delivered in a deadpan way, with no explanation, no struggle, no sign of desire, no obvious logic—really funny and open. The years 2011 and 2012 seemed like a good time to examine this work. I made a group of nine paintings about its parts, minus any promise of a unified whole. I double his solutions and use his equations to make new answers to his mathematical questions, but of course my formulas are "wrong" . . .

GB: In mathematics, there really is a correct answer.

SM: But there is a process of search that may be riddled with mistakes. Data is used to justify, predict, rate our physical bodies and their dimensions, strength, beauty, talent, potential success . . . Numbers display certain kinds of power. Perhaps it is part of creating identity or justification, it rationalizes people's experiences, it establishes who we are? I am wondering if it is an attempt to give comfort or satisfaction, stillness in some sense. I was speaking recently with Celia Lury, who writes so clearly about how people can put a lot of emotion and affect into numbers, and how numbers have a particular visibility at the moment. Celia proposes this in a 2012 issue of *Theory, Culture and Society* she coedited:

"We no longer live in or experience movement or transformation as the transmission of fixed forms in space and time but rather movement—organised in terms of ordering and continuity of transformation—*composes the forms of social life itself.* These dynamic, distinctively topological 'abstractions' emerge in practices of sorting, naming, numbering, comparing, and calculating. The effect of these practices is to introduce new continuities into a discontinuous world, linked to the topological forms of lists, models, networks, clouds, fractals, and flows. There is a multiplication of relations of equivalence and difference and a radical expansion of the possibilities of establishing comparisons. Ordinal rankings and ratings, for example, are proliferating and increasing in importance not only in the economy but also in education, health, and popular culture, as they are used to derive and justify the allocation of resources. Such practices, we suggest, are changing how change itself is made legible."

GB: When you bring formulas into a new realm, rules can change and the capacity for "success" can expand.

SM: I think that's what I like about your film *Below Dreams*. You don't quantify or judge the success of the three characters that you are following—they are not competing; you're sharing their experiences as they share with you, so the exchange system is more horizontal than vertical. They live physically near each other but are isolated. They live with different sets of rules. You bring us inside their parallel worlds, and we experience their attempts to solve problems that are similar in content but very different in context. We witness their *mis-takes*, and solutions are outside of the camera frame. Your young generation is offering an alternative form of exchange, a step away from a ladder of "progress." And you do this without the need for justification through quantification.

JOSHUA MOSLEY speaks with PAUL CHAN and ROBERT FAHEY

Paul Chan: I didn't know you play tennis, when did you start playing?

Joshua Mosley: I've played all of my life. I'm competitive, but I often find myself paying so much attention to the design of the courts, the light, and the sounds and movements of the game that I quickly lose track of the match. A few years ago, I came up with a way to concentrate on the game by counting down the twenty-four points needed to win the set, so that I could focus on what was left rather than play a game as if it were open-ended.

PC: The way you describe paying attention to all elements of the game makes perfect sense to me. There has always been an almost perverse *democraticness* about your work. The surface on the leaf of a tree is as important as whatever might be considered a plot. The vertiginous quality in what I have seen of your work is unique. It reminds me of what you just said about playing tennis. What were the elements that led you to making this new puppet animation, *Jeu de Paume*?

JM: I had often thought about Robert Rauschenberg's performance from 1966 *Open Score*, which included an electroacoustic tennis rally between Mimi Kanarek and Frank Stella. I thought that I could let a game play itself out as an animation that would unfold in front of me day by day as I choreographed the points. I was looking forward to the idea of working on this slowly.

PC: Is the court that you've built proportionate to the modern court?

JM: No, I used the court from the older French sport *jeu de paume*, also called court tennis or real tennis. The court is elongated and asymmetrical in length and width. There are slanted penthouse roofs along three sides of it, above the viewing galleries, off of which the ball can be played.

PC: Which came first, the model or the moving image?

JM: I imagined how it would feel to play on a black court with a white ball; and out of my periphery, I would have lines and markers of space. I had the sense that I would be more conscious of my position within the court. When I looked at a photograph of this historic court, I sensed how it would make a player feel. The whole room is one court, and the room is irregular. I imagined playing between a high wall and a low wall. It's like having one headphone on your ear; it makes your body feel uncentered. This court design was replicated hundreds of times for a reason: it isn't too asymmetrical, but it is off enough that a player must have a constant sense of the space. This made me think that court tennis requires a certain cantilevered awareness rather than a centered mind, which I struggle to have in tennis. The idea that the light was coming from above and that I would be in black, submerged space seemed to fit.

PC: Since the space is asymmetrical, it cannot be neutral in your mind; because of that, you can never fully escape into the game. That reminds me of the architects Arakawa and Madeline Gins, whose buildings have no right angles; they're constructed so that you are constantly distracted and your mind is never stable, you are never grounded in any plane. The thinking is that if your cells cannot settle and they are constantly agitated, you will live forever. Unfortunately, Arakawa passed away a couple of years ago, which puts a damper on their vision, but it is a compelling image. So you developed a space, and then you developed the characters?

JM: For these two players, I read biographical descriptions of professional court-tennis players from 1890 to 1920, looking for figures who were isolated from the culture surrounding the sport. Something happens in the first couple of shots that defines how the puppets will be on-screen. I motion-capture the camera's movement and then, using a robotic crane, scale it down to the size of the puppet. The puppet plays tennis in front of a preprogrammed camera—rather than a camera that tracks it organically. The characters are always different from what I create them to be. This weekend, one of the characters did things I didn't expect: he was walking too fast and went off camera, then stopped, turned, and looked back at the other player while the camera caught up, then started walking too fast offscreen again, got a ball, and came back on camera. The magic just comes out.

PC: You are animating like a warlock. Your work is so surprising because the viewer doesn't know where it's going, and basically that's because you don't know, right?

JM: It is especially the case with this work. In all of the past animations, I storyboarded about forty-five seconds forward so that I could be a little bit more efficient with the next shot. This work has no storyboard. I am choreographing it one point at a time.

PC: *Choreography* is a better word than *story* for describing how your work moves in time. This returns to my first intuition about your work's vertiginous, democratic quality. You are not foregrounding a story, a purpose, a meaning, or even an idea. Essentially you are choreographing a tennis match, and the match becomes rhythmic, musical, and story-like as these characters come into some semblance of meaning. I don't even know if meaningfulness is part of the endgame.

JM: I mostly agree, although it takes so little interaction between two puppets to make a meaningful exchange.

PC: Is the camera movement a third character?

JM: One of my starting points was Charles Atlas's filming of Merce Cunningham's dancers, where the movement of the camera is subservient to the dance but is also a dance. I thought about sampling Atlas's camera movement, so that the tennis match would perform for the camera that had followed the dancers. In the end, my puppets have a relationship to the camera that inverts Atlas's camera's relationship to Cunningham's dancers. My players have a delayed reaction and swerve to the right to hit a ball because the camera is swerving to the right. The camera is leading the action. In life, we expect it to be the other way around.

PC: Is it the case that because of this inversion there are times in the film that don't quite match up? When the camera's movement goes one way and characters go another, it's not perfectly framed somehow. There is a strange liveliness to that.

Joshua Mosely: Does your concentration shift during a match?

Robert Fahey: There are several things to concentrate on during a match, so my concentration moves around a bit. If you break a match into action and nonaction, you can imagine that the things you concentrate on change. Action involves concentrating on basics: watching the ball, preparation, footwork, etc. Nonaction involves keeping the game plan going and deciding what's working and what isn't.

JM: Does your awareness of the court change during a match?

RF: Your awareness can depend on how much time you've spent on that court. The court I practice on daily never enters my thoughts, as I know how it will behave. When you step onto a court you haven't played on for a while, you go through a process of relearning its behavior—its angles and speed, for example. You make changes to your position to allow for differences in the court.

JM: The court-tennis court is asymmetrical in both length and width. Depending on whether you are serving or receiving, the architecture of the court has one large main wall on one side and a porous and more gradually elevated wall on the other. Is there a relationship that your mind develops with these asymmetries?

RF: There is no doubt that your mind develops a relationship with the asymmetries. Once I know the end point (where I want the ball to end up), I calculate the various ways that the court will allow me to get the ball there. The straight option is frequently the last to surface.

JM: When you previsualize a point, or a shot, does it include the other player?

RF: I don't have an immediate answer, which indicates that I don't include the other player.

JM: Court tennis has an irregular rhythm. A rally is more varied in tempo than in other racquet sports because the ball can ricochet or roll off the slanted roof of the galleries. If you are in control of a match, are you in control of the rhythm?

RF: It is true that there is an irregular tempo to court tennis. You are absolutely right in thinking that the player in control of the match controls the tempo. It may be that players have their own tempo rather than the court.

JOEL OTTERSON speaks with ADRIAN SAXE

Adrian Saxe: We're talking about Japan and Joel's recent trip . . .

Joel Otterson: I was surprised that they have a tradition of brilliant cut glass. It's borrowed from the West, and it started at the beginning of the Meiji era along with things like eating beef. Beef became very chic to eat, and you weren't "with it" unless you'd tried beef.

AS: A lot of the artists went to France and got involved with fashionable art-making practices of the time. Then they brought them back to Japan. Cut glass was definitely a nineteenth- or early twentieth-century import from the West. They already made glass but not like that.

JO: I saw Japanese glass that was like American brilliant cut, with colors—amazing! I was blown away by the armor, too: it's bronze, it's steel, and how they get the finishes on those things . . . And then it's woven together with the most beautiful silk cords! I wonder what happens when a samurai sword cuts through the cord? The combination of fabric and metal was unbelievable.

AS: And, of course, that's what you work with and have been working with for a long time.

JO: That combination of soft and hard.

AS: Assembling fabrics, especially found fabrics. Collaging them, making a conversation in the work because of the unusual juxtaposition of things from different periods and genres . . .

JO: That armor was really beautiful! I normally don't think of the accoutrements of war as beautiful, although some military uniforms are beautiful . . . horrible as they were, the Nazis had a good look.

AS: The Nazis' decorative arts sensibility was fairly sophisticated, they wanted to be unique. Goering commissioned a full dinnerware set from Sèvres. Well, he didn't commission it . . . When they occupied France, he said, "Make this for me." It's weird—kind of green, rounded, and square.

JO: Wow, I'm dying to see it.

AS: Nobody's seen it. I've seen it because I worked in Sèvres and saw the archives. But it's incomplete, and if it's incomplete the French will never show it. Anyway, it shows some insight about how, in the decorative arts, a kind of fashion-driven identity comes through in the work, and certainly that's what you work off of. Your work can never be placed in any other time or context than our current situation. It's not historicism or any of those things: it's straight-ahead processing through your own experience. That's why I'm interested in how you found Japan.

JO: It's just so different. We're so bombastic and loud here. I never heard anybody raise their voice and never heard an argument. I heard three sirens, and once when I saw a siren coming, it came up to the traffic and stopped and waited! I guess they figured whatever was so urgent could wait. How this translates to myself I don't know. My fascination with Japan started when I was three years old and saw a geisha on TV. Thirteen years ago, I saw a show at the Philadelphia Museum of Art of Hon'ami Kōetsu's work. There were Noh libretti in the show, made of rice paper printed with mica—if it's not in the right light you don't even see it!

AS: You can't see it . . .

JO: These are national treasures! The ones I saw in Philadelphia were "objects of very important cultural significance." It was the first time they had left Japan. They're from the sixteenth and early seventeenth centuries and are so different than Michelangelo or Bernini. The day these fragile objects were made they were picked up with both hands and treated with the greatest amount of reverence. It's a completely different mentality from building or carving in stone. The walls in their homes are made of paper and that's accepted.

AS: The flip side of that is that Kobe and Tokyo have burned to the ground many times, Kobe most recently in the Great Hanshin earthquake in 1995. I don't want to say there's a resistance to engineering, but I think there is a resistance to things that are good practices but don't provide that aesthetic and sensate or haptic kind of relationship to the hand and the person.

JO: Every movement you make has to be thought out when you live in a paper house. I think that I'm attracted to the impracticality of it all. I think mostly what I make is impractical.

AS: It alludes to functional uses but it doesn't really have any real function. It's like your tent, how do you characterize your tent?

JO: I want people to have the desire to sleep in and hang out in the tent that I'm making. It has enough room for two people to sleep comfortably. Whether that will actually happen, who knows? I like the idea that people can dream about it and imagine how beautiful the world will look once you're inside, looking through the lace.

AS: A lot of work, especially in contemporary decorative arts, is about the imagination. The imagining of putting it through its paces. So you have to try the stuff that I do and you do at least once just to see how it works.

JO: You have to feel like it could work.

AS: Then you can imagine the elaboration of that experience. The pouring vessels that I make are not very practical for pouring—

JO: But they would pour!

AS: Oh, they pour perfectly.

JO: I love that!

AS: But you never pour with them.

JO: Maybe once?

AS: Maybe once—I have to make sure that they that pour properly.

JO: Do you ever make tea in them?

AS: Never.

JO: Because they're too fragile, the porcelain can't take it?

AS: No, because they're not teapots. They're for ritual. They're ewers. They're for wine or something else. They're in the Chinese tradition. The Chinese made porcelain ewers for the Persians. They're for scented oils. But the Chinese ones that I think are so interesting are the ones that are used only once for a wedding or religious ritual.

JO: What do they do with them then? Put them away in a box or up on a shelf?

AS: The Japanese put them away in a box, but the Chinese make zillions of them, then just move on.

JO: Do they still make these kinds of objects?

AS: Well, yes, but the things that I base my work on, no. They're mostly three- or four-hundred-year-old objects or twelve-hundred-year-old stuff that Sung and Tang potters made for Middle Eastern trades. The Persians didn't have the raw materials or the fuel to make porcelain so they had the Chinese make this stuff. The forms are grounded in metalwork developed in the Middle East and they wanted ceramic versions of them.

JO: At the Nara National Museum, there was this little room that I ventured into full of ancient ritual Chinese ewers and braziers . . .

AS: The Japanese collected and revered these objects and made their own versions. Mokube is one of my favorite artists anywhere. He was active in the eighteenth century and made interpretations of Chinese ceramics and bronzes from before the Shang Dynasty through seventeenth-century Ming forms and decorations. He made a lot of lead-glazed ceramics based on Tang Dynasty earthenware.

AS: The idea of having artworks that operate in the realm of the decorative arts, in Japan in particular—

JO: There is no distinction.

AS: Less distinction, often no distinction. Art is the aesthetic experience of objects, and works of art and architecture are coequal.

JO: The lacquer bowl sitting on the table in Japan is just as important as a painting hanging on the wall in the West. It's just as much an aesthetic object, a pleasing and meaningful object. That's so attractive to me because I've spent a lifetime inserting objects like tables, chairs, beds, and dinnerware into people's lives.

AS: So-called common objects—you've made them into uncommon assemblages.

JO: Malik Gaines said there's the possibility of function, that one might use these objects I make. There's the possibility that they have an everyday function, that's the interesting part of it. You can eat dinner on something I've made.

AS: Kenny Price's cups to drink out of felt good in the hand. They had little doohickeys on them, little extensions sort of like clitorises. They were like worry beads or something to sit there and handle as you were drinking your coffee or bourbon, but people started treating these cups as precious artworks as his career and his market rose.

JO: Then people put them on the shelf 'cause they're too valuable!

AS: Yeah, but they weren't *intended* that way. The idea of *function* as a code word for *utilitarian* is sort of limiting. The function of a lot of objects in traditional Japanese art—you use them to interact with other people or promote some state of being.

JO: That's the tea ceremony.

AS: Totally!

JO: Bringing people and objects together for that one moment. Once and only once will those objects and those people be together. I love that!

AS: I've always found all of the tools, the chalices, the scepters, and everything of the Catholic Church to be really fascinating.

JO: Ritual objects.

AS: Yes. Ritual channels emotional energy and spirituality through an object, and that is a function.

JO: Emotional attachment to an inanimate object interests me a lot—the way it can trigger an idea, emotion, or memory.

AS: I was knocked out the first time I was in Kyoto, I was there just before spring solstice and everyone was out in the Buddhist cemetery preparing the grave sites for the celebration of the spring. Did you get to see anything like that?

JO: I saw a cemetery in Tokyo.

AS: The whole thing overwhelmed me, and there was nobody around because it was before all the festivities kicked in. It was very powerful. The objects, the monuments, it wasn't like going to Brooklyn cemeteries and seeing all those robber-baron mausoleums.

JO: The Cimitero Monumentale in Milan is sort of like the ones in Brooklyn. The sculpture is fantastic, and it's a beautiful place, but you know nothing about the people that are buried there. You assume they had a lot of money to have these monuments made to them . . . but I think they fail miserably.

AS: I only know what I saw. There were some bigger monuments . . . it had to do with social status, not just money. Some of them are more ambitious than others, but none of them came off as ostentatious. I thought about incorporating that sensibility into my work, but when I saw them I was really full-tilt operating on the French Rococo.

[*laughter*] It didn't have an easy window to enter my work.

JO: You and I have always been interested in the over-the-top Rococo, and when one thinks about Japan often we think it's understated and subtle . . . But it's not! There's a lot flamboyancy there. Think about a geisha—come on! Or those rooms at the Nijo Castle, where the biggest painting of the biggest pine tree was in the biggest room to impress visiting dignitaries.

AS: Just like Louis XIV.

JO: The biggest public rooms had the most gold; the family rooms had less gold but were still pretty extravagant. Japan is very flamboyant; it's just with a different edge. In Kyoto there was this festival called the Jidai Matsuri, and it is my under-standing that it is the Festival of the Ages. There were hundreds of people dressed up in the clothes of their ancestors, and they parade through the streets of Kyoto—it was unbelievable, like entering into a Kurosawa film!

AS: I don't know that much about all the folk traditions, but certain things like harvest festivals and Obon festivals I know about because I lived in Hawaii fifty years ago. There weren't all the rich Japanese businessmen and tourists then, just the people who had come over to be farmers on plantations of sugarcane. They were very traditional and modest for the most part. Do you know these bowls I made, some of them quite large, with the cut rim?

JO: With the gear-like rim?

AS: The rims reference cutting tools or milling machines more than gears—early on it was gears, but it quickly evolved into a metaphor for powerful machine cutting tools. Anyway, they're bowls sitting on lava.

JO: Real lava?

AS: I was making lava. Initially it was raku, then stoneware. The idea was that it was a very Japanese thing, the contrast between the cultural and the natural . . .

JO: The really refined and manmade combined with the natural . . . Same day as the Jidai festival there was the fire festival in the little village of Kurama. They light the whole town on fire and run around in these little loincloths while carrying huge, flaming torches! Five days before, we had been to Tokyo DisneySea, which was a pretty authentic Japanese experience. It's located on Yokohama Bay, and the theme of it has everything to do with the ocean: *The Little Mermaid*, *Finding Nemo*, *20,000 Leagues under the Sea*, etc. First I'm at DisneySea, and then I'm at the Jidai festival, and then I'm at Kurama, and they all seem pretty Disney to me. In Kurama, we saw these family heirlooms displayed in the front of their homes. There were displays of armor, but there was one display that had the most beautiful folding screen along with huge Imari plates set up in stands made from tree roots—somehow I will use this idea. It goes back to what you were saying about the cultural juxtaposed against the natural.

AS: Take this driftwood bowl here. Basically it's the root of a tree or something that has been hollowed out—edited! It was probably close to this when found; it's just been smoothed and edited.

JO: But you just don't know. It's like a Japanese garden. You go into it and assume it's the way God made it, but there's no way—it's been made with pruning shears and tweezers.

AS: Nothing is natural. I had no idea about the Disney theme park, but I would make a point of going to see it because I know that it would be different from what they did in France.

JO: They had different characters. We saw all these people with teddy bears, and we thought, "That's not a Disney character." Yes, it was! Duffy and Shellie May: the bears of happiness and good luck! Disney characters unique to Japan.

AS: Did they have *tanuki* at Disney?

JO: What are *tanuki*?

AS: Those big raccoon dogs. Like badgers. They carry a flask and have big balls.

JO: No, but I saw plenty of them everywhere else. The first time I saw one, I said, "Is that his scrotum?"

AS: Yes! Dragging on the ground! Typically they're put outside of bars; they're associated with partying and drinking.

JO: And good luck?

AS: Everything is good luck. The *tanuki* is about being mischievous and jolly, a master of disguise and shape shifting.

JO: And about having big balls!

AS: And they're not Shinto deities, but they are considered supernatural creatures, and these are all made in Shigaraki, where I worked.

JO: Where is Shigaraki?

AS: Southeast of Kyoto toward Nara. It's one of the old kiln sites.

JO: It's one of the Heian kilns?

AS: Yes. There's Bizen, Echizen, Seto, Shigaraki, Tamba, and Tokoname. There are six old kilns, and I used to be able to just click that off . . . I don't think about it so much anymore, probably because the people I'm teaching are not focused on traditional Japanese ceramics anymore. It's the deskilled generation.

JO: Deskilled work?

AS: It's beyond deskilled!

JO: You know, that's what everybody asked me about my show that's up now: "Do you make it all?" "Do you send out the armatures?" I make it all myself! That's the fun of it! Besides, how would I ever tell somebody how to make this stuff! Certainly my work is not slacker or . . . what did you call it?

AS: Deskilled.

JO: I can put stuff together. I'm teaching a class at Otis now: From Crochet to Welding. I told my class from the beginning, I don't know whether we'll be making art because some of this needlework takes forever. We looked at samplers that represent a year in a young girl's life, and we just don't have that kind of time. At first everybody was gung ho to learn how to sew, but now they're just wrapping thread around pieces of metal—they're not using any of the skill I've taught them. I guess I consider it seeds planted.

AS: It's too hard if they can't do it on the iPad. Or they say, "Can't we do it with the camera?"

JO: Exactly!

SARA GREENBERGER RAFFERTY speaks with MIRIAM KATZ

Miriam Katz: I know you're many months away from completing your video for the Biennial, but can you say something about the ideas you have, even at this early stage?

Sara Greenberger Rafferty: I'm still formulating and making sketches, but one thing I do know is that I want the projection to be calibrated so that the figures are at human scale. I also have a few gestures and characters in mind, such as the "late-night host."

Through appropriation, I've been "casting" people against their will in my still photographs for a while now. In my videos, however, I typically use myself as the figure, simply by default. My body's another material I have to work with in the studio. Recently, though, I may have reached an end point when it comes to self-casting. For the new video, I'm working with an actor who has a special gift for playing stock characters, Susie Sokol of Elevator Repair Service. We will attempt to quote stuff we've seen on TV. It feels both risky and exciting to have recruited an outside player.

Ultimately, narrative is not my concern; discrete actions are. The script will be about not propelling events but mirroring social gestures.

MK: Speaking of the late-night host, what about comedy aesthetics? That is an interest we have in common. Is it related to the way you're attacking this piece?

SGR: *Attacking* is an appropriate term. I feel an adversarial relationship to my work—like how comedians sometimes feel toward their audiences. It can feel like a struggle.

MK: And is that struggle generative? Or detrimental?

SGR: I think one's relationship with one's work is often like a human relationship. When in conflict, it's at best a productive struggle to work things out. You're vulnerable, and, in a sense, you say things that you may or may not mean in the process of figuring out what you really think. I'd like that tension to be in my work, but sometimes maybe I go too far. I'm not interested in being adversarial with the audience just for the sake of it, but I am interested in conflict.

MK: There's the content of conflict—the quotation of it—and then there's also the conflicted mode of production. It seems like you are engaged with both. We've talked before about something being aesthetically stunning, drawing you in, and then punching you. That's the big thing with comedy: you are having such a good time, and then you think, "Oh my God, I can't believe this is what I'm laughing at." Back to the attack. Do you feel like you are hacking away at or maybe digging at something?

SGR: When I'm making work, I suppose I'm hacking away at beautiful and conventional characters and things. Though I've consistently attacked images in my work, I'm not necessarily attacking specific ideas, but rather I'm using the idea of an attack as form.

MK: Right, and there are definitely two layers of attack there. You actually disfigure images—put holes in them—or you slice into an image to expose something at its center. Attacking is a mode of exploring, but clearly a violent one. What is your relationship with the image? Are you critiquing it through violence? Puncturing it so that something more complicated and messy emerges?

SGR: I can see that I make images bodily. I'm also irritating them, like a breakout does to the skin. They're manufactured in plastic. I somehow make them visceral and self-aware. I think that's my mode of attack.

MK: How does making them bodily relate back to the human scale you're interested in for this video?

SGR: Calibrating things to a human scale is a very simple way to express being human in a world that becomes so vast and alienating—especially when thinking of the abstractions of global commerce, even just of mortgage debt, and of clothing, feeding, and sheltering a social body. Basically, I'm speaking textbook Marxist alienation.

MK: So what is it that you are interested in grappling with—not presenting but figuring out?

SGR: I don't always know the answer in the studio, but it often becomes apparent once I've exhibited and digested the work. I also figure things out through texts, recently Sianne Ngai's *Our Aesthetic Categories: Zany, Cute, Interesting*, Maggie Nelson's *The Art of Cruelty*, Rachel Kushner's *The Flamethrowers*, and anything by Lisa Robertson. But, to answer your question, I've been primarily grappling with expressions of gender identity. I'm seeing the very thing that I have always been preoccupied with in my work really change in culture. And I'm not interested in my work becoming retrograde or nostalgic. My grappling with gender constantly needs to incorporate the world around me and not just the world I was born into. I suppose one could not adapt and potentially in thirty years become radical again . . . All of this is actually making me think about the monologues that you have been writing for real people whom you identify as having extreme personalities.

MK: Yeah, I see how that ties in. I see elements of myself that are greatly exaggerated in certain other people in my life. So the monologues are explorations of both what I share with someone else and the way in which I perceive that person. If I were writing one for myself, it would be difficult. But writing in someone else's voice and exploring the way in which it collapses into mine are actually quite easy for me. I want to figure out the part that's scariest. There is something interesting about me watching people do the monologues I've written because it's exposing both my judgment of them and the things in them that I see in myself. Now I'm thinking about our conversation earlier today and what we were saying about how much we love Kanye West's bravado, as well as the unexpected elements of stand-up—saying the radical, exciting thing that wakes people up. I think that kind of confrontation and definitiveness is something that we see in ourselves, but haven't fully embodied yet. Which is strange, because it's clearly so inspiring to us, and we encourage it in other people.

SGR: Exactly.

MK: Really taking a stance is so important, which to me means making work that is specific to me and that isn't mediocratized for consumption. I mean, otherwise why am I doing it?

SGR: Yeah, totally. For me, it's about trusting that I can do something that people will respond to, even if it's not always totally accessible. That must be something comics struggle with, too, in terms of getting on stage with material that's not necessarily crowd-pleasing. I respond to things that are taken to the extreme in comedy, art, or anything, really, so that the natural response is, say, hysterical laughter or uncontrollable sobbing. I think that's why so many of my favorite artists and performers are truly ballsy and fearless—it's what I aspire to be.

DAVID ROBBINS speaks with FELONY SWAN

Felony Swan: You withdrew from the art world a decade ago, yet here you are showing in the 2014 Whitney Biennial. Is it safe to assume your escape failed?

David Robbins: The art context continues to sponsor my inquiries, but by now it's accepted that I keep my distance. Ten years ago, I stopped participating through the prevailing model of the "professional contemporary artist" (with its cycle of making several exhibitions a year, its clearly mapped career path—all that stuff artists are supposed to want) to pursue another model that deemphasizes "thinking through the frame of art" in favor of a broader output, which extends into entertainment culture: books, TV—it's coming from more of a cultural location than from a strictly artistic location. I've consequently gone from insider to outsider, but I vastly prefer the game I've devised.

FS: Why did you feel a need to dispense with the received model of the artist?

DR: The costume never fit me. I wore it for a decade or so, tailoring it as needed, but it remained ill fitting. Already by the late eighties, the question of whether or not to undertake a given work had shifted from "Will it make good art?" to "Will it make good comedy?" Ultimately, I just didn't like formatting my imagination to constantly produce art.

FS: And, finally, you just shed the artist's costume altogether—which meant what, since you've never stopped working?

DR: I stopped addressing art. Art is the product of the artist addressing what art is and might be. I'm naturally disposed toward other questions about communication. I tried art on, and its arguments didn't sustain me. Fortunately, the digital revolution came along and made it easy for me to create using the grammars of the pop-culture mother tongue—TV, movies, and music—and handed me the world I'd been waiting for. Here was a clear alternative to the art context that also accommodated a deeply personal approach while granting total creative control. Look, the question "Art or not art?" is beside the point. How are you going to give what you have to give? That's the question. Any obstacle to doing that—art included—has to be identified and outfoxed. Take the culture where you want it to go. Don't ask permission. Accept the consequences.

FS: So you passed through art and

came out on the other side. What's on the other side?

DR: I'm finding out. So far, it's been a blast! I can still see art in the rear-view mirror. I take the best of what I learned from art—its openness to experimentation, its emphasis on discovering the form as you go—and apply it to other communication products, aspirations, and goals. The digital revolution liberates us on two fronts. We no longer need permission from the entertainment industry to produce in pop forms; and, just as important, digital distribution frees us from having to run what we make past art's interpretive system. Both parents have been relieved of their authority! To an unprecedented degree, we can make what we like and get it to an audience. It's become completely natural to explore hybrid forms and genres, and it's easier to avoid being defined by a single context. We can produce from coordinates I refer to as the "independent imagination"—to act in history rather than in some version of history maintained by a professional context. We got carried away with specialization, all that careerist nonsense—I prefer to be a generalist. No one discipline has all the answers. The increased ease of production and efficient distribution that the digital revolution delivers makes the generalist's approach more viable.

FS: Most people find considerable freedom in the art context . . .

DR: The modernist idea that "we can make whatever we like so long as we call it art"—isn't that actually a myth of freedom? We can do whatever we like within this cell we agree to stay inside? Full imaginative freedom would involve coming up with other categories of aspiration and endeavor. There are two sorts of ambitious people: those who look to conquer an existing game and those who invent the game they're interested in playing. Jeff Koons belongs to the former group; I'm in the latter. I don't care to format my imagination to support a brand. That's not how my mind works. I don't want to perform David Robbins. I just want to do whatever may occur to me to do. I've moved away from professional motivations in favor of making experimental cultural production a natural thing—an "everyday avant-garde." It's the game I want to play—at this juncture. The game evolves, of course.

FS: I'm curious: in giving yourself such broad permission, does cohesiveness suffer? Over the years, you have produced in such an eclectic assortment of ways—books, TV shows, and comic objects—seemingly without concern for consistency. You don't make a curator's job easy!

DR: Yes, that's a key question, isn't it? I associate unified, "legible" production with a model of "how to be an artist" that's controlled not by artists but by the market, curators, and academics. It has become a completely institutionalized, safe model. By producing without cultivating unity and by breaking away from that prevailing model of the artist, which is a European inheritance, I've purposely let entertainment's absence of rigor affect how I structure my output, or don't. If I'm ignored by the art context, that doesn't bother me—as the fact that I live in Milwaukee should indicate!

FS: Milwaukee being a "wrong," "out-of-it" place to live . . .

DR: With only the most minimal presence of the art system. Even worse, I live in a suburb!

FS: Whatever possessed you?

DR: Historically, the avant-garde officially approved two landscape models: the alone-in-the-wilderness Georgia O'Keeffe model, and the hypercosmopolite Andy Warhol model. The suburbs have been disdained and dismissed. Consequently the suburban landscape becomes, for artists, a kind of frontier. Doing what I do against the backdrop of Williamsburg would mean nothing. Doing it in Shorewood, Wisconsin, is another matter! Also information is, as everybody knows, vastly more accessible today. In 1979, I had to move to New York to get the New York information, but now, in suburban Milwaukee, I get easily 70 percent of the information people have access to in the culture centers and at exactly the same time as they do. This change is permanent, so setting up camp along decentralized information channels is going to become more common among artists.

FS: You seem to particularly relish delving into ideas and fields traditionally held in low regard by artists. Did this attitude in any way influence your decision to make TV commercials?

DR: I started making commercials because it seemed odd that we don't see TV commercials for galleries, artists, or exhibitions. Once I began making these, mostly for Green Gallery in Milwaukee, I really got into the form. Commercials are challenging to make. You have to tease while, at the same time, being clear about what you're promoting. Plus there's a strict time constraint: thirty seconds, a minute . . . I enjoy these challenges. And I enjoy introducing commercials for art into the normal flow of television by buying airtime.

FS: I find that most artists still prefer art to be not only separate from but also superior to "entertainment," whether as subject matter or intent.

DR: When the subject of "the relationship between art and entertainment" is brought up, most people think "art about entertainment," but this idea of "about" is really not the point anymore. We've gone beyond that, and the separation between the two isn't so neat. For example, when the Museo MADRE in Naples invited me to do an exhibition, and I proposed using the museum to produce a TV show with actors from a Neapolitan theater group, it was a far cry from visual art's traditional, arm's-length treatment of entertainment. I'm not showing a painting of a movie star in a museum, right? I'm applying the power of an institution of high culture to produce pop-culture that the pop culture system isn't making on its own. A project such as *TV FAMILY*, made for the MADRE this spring, relocates the museum's function, in that the museum isn't just a receptacle in which to display things. When we use the museum to make TV entertainment, we bump up against why popular culture is as it is—and why high culture is the way it is, too. Considering the progressive convergence of the art and entertainment contexts, these strike me as appropriate questions for an art museum to tackle. I do think I'm expanding or extending entertainment through my own sensibility, in a personal way, and taking entertainment in the direction I want it to go. The digital revolution has blown the communication field wide-open. It's a rare opportunity, and we'd be fools not to invent the hell out of it.

STERLING RUBY speaks with RAF SIMONS

Raf Simons: When I was first introduced to your work in about 2005, you were making sculptures, videos, and works on paper, and were well on your way to all of your divergent practices, but I was particularly drawn to the ceramics. I was already obsessed with ceramics but not so much in contemporary art. It really was the fact that yours didn't look like any other ceramics I had ever seen, so it was very much about your particular aesthetic. Honestly, at that point I was not thinking, "What is the concept?" or "What is the idea?" It was, for me, a very primal thing. What was your motivation for starting to work with ceramics?

Sterling Ruby: A friend of mine was getting a degree in psychology, and she encouraged me to sit in on a ceramics class. Kneading the clay over and over again was somehow very meditative. At that time, I was questioning where my generation of artists was in terms of art history. It felt as if we were at a point where you couldn't just make something. In art school, it was all about the concept. We talked about Minimalism, Conceptual art, Performance, and recent movements that weren't focused on aesthetics. Ceramics became key—the way to just make something. It was a malleable, expressive material that needed to be fired and hardened. I also saw the ceramic works as monuments to my generation's seeming inability to make a sincere gesture. We had too much baggage. How is it for you? When you start working on a new line, do you think to yourself, "I have to do something new that has never been seen before"?

RS: One way or another, you have to find a way to start, so you start because you see a continuation of something. Or you start a critique of something you hate—at least you start with something . . .

SR: I've been thinking recently about the idea of archaeology. It's always been there, but over the past couple of years it's really been an obsession of mine to use it as a production tool—that the work has to have archaeology built into it. It can be an autobiographical archaeology, something specifically about me as an artist, my choices, or it can be an archaeology of history. There's a real obstacle in addressing the monolith of history. You have to dig through the layers of it. It's super problematic and tough to make anything meaningful now, when so much history is behind you. But that's the challenge.

RS: Some artists choose to focus on language. Some artists choose to be purely conceptual. But we are both about materials. I see material as something that is of primary importance in your work. Your use of materials is so different from what I do. The way you make the paintings and the fabric and cardboard collages—they have such a unique materialization. But it is obviously not just about the materials for you . . . there is always something behind it.

SR: In your last couture line, there were hints of quilting. I grew up in rural Pennsylvania, and I saw quilts before I saw any "art." When I started making the soft works and the fabric collages, it was partly as a reminder of where I grew up, but I was also looking at quilts and fabrics throughout history. In researching other textile traditions, I was drawn to the Gee's Bend quilters in Alabama and Japanese Boro textiles. These were both very practical traditions that used old clothing to make quilts out of necessity, and later the quilts were recognized as perfect aesthetic objects. That transformation is interesting to me: when something that is very formal and beautiful started as a utilitarian object. That's something I think about in terms of art. Some people are just not interested in the concepts or ideas behind my work, but I need to know why I am making something. If I'm going to work on a new body of sculptures or paintings or collages, I need to feel that what I'm doing is somehow contextually important. I need to know that those frameworks are in place and that I'm working against them in some way, shape, or form. Once the works are out there in the world, I'm open to how people perceive them. I'm okay if people like my work because of the way it looks or for the aesthetic of it. When I was at Art Center College of Design as a graduate student, I often talked to Mike Kelley about this. He was adamant that everything had to be understood. I think that is why he wrote so much about his work. Mike felt that the viewer absolutely had to be informed to fully appreciate his work.

RS: I don't think there are many people who are interested in your work purely for aesthetic reasons, in all honesty. Many of your pieces—by traditional perceptions of beauty—look fucking ugly. But I find a lot of beauty in things that are not classically defined as such. Always, I feel there is something latent, something buried. I have that feeling now with your bleach collages. They are fascinating because I think I get them, but I might be wrong. I see them in relation to your soft sculptures, they also make me think of Russian Constructivist painting . . . but for me that's enough, and I don't want to go any deeper. I like hearing everything you have to say, but sometimes, if things are too clear, I don't like the work anymore. It takes away the mystique. I think a lot of it is very mysterious. In other ways, you are very revealing. Take, for instance, your website—it feels like an online archive. You show the studio. You show the artworks. You show the source materials. It's pretty radical, I think.

SR: I struggled with that for a while because I had the site for about a year and a half just for myself. Then I thought, you know what? This thing is vulnerable. It really is a way for me to give people access to everything.

RS: Do you find it to be a problem if it's vulnerable?

SR: No. I think that it's important to feel like you're doing something that's vulnerable, or else it becomes too safe.

PETER SCHUYFF speaks with STEVIE GUY

Stevie Guy: We've been talking about your paintings for what seems like hours already, but you really haven't said anything. How about the carved pencils?

Peter Schuyff: I'm sorry. I'll try harder. The piece with the pencils is called *Sans Papier*. "Without Paper," get it? I heard my friend Alexandra say that when she was yelling at her boyfriend. (He couldn't sell his work and wouldn't find a job). It's some kind of World War II thing meaning illegitimate. Alexandra's geeky insult. I thought it was cute.

SG: But that's an anecdote. Tell me something real.

PS: Oh. Well, the pencils were something I did after I quit painting. I do that every now and then, quit for good. Never for long, but always for good. And with utter sincerity.

SG: Quit—why? You had enough?

PS: Sometimes, in the face of things, painting seems lame, either because there's kids using newer media and getting the job done more efficiently or because of . . . I don't know . . . the war in Iraq . . . I lose interest in painting, especially in my paintings. I'll stay away for weeks, months, at a time, and then I'll start painting again. I can't help it. Hopefully I'll have learned or done something good in the meantime. That's how our band, the Woodwards, got started: I was never going to paint again, and I'd never so much as sung in the shower.

SG: Anyway, so you stopped painting and started carving pencils?

PS: No, I stopped painting and made a trek up into the highlands of West Papua. Staying home to carve pencils came after. First, I went to New Guinea. I decided to go on a Thursday, and by that Sunday I was in the Baliem Valley, where there are guys walking around with long gourds on the ends of their penises. That's where my walk started. I brought almost nothing with me: a change of clothes and a pocketknife. At night in the woods, there isn't much to do, so I carved sticks. I fiddled in the dark with my pocketknife until I figured out the shapes. They're like algorithms or formulas or something. I hold the knife steady and move the stick over and over again in something like a pattern and—presto!—I end up with whatever, a helix or a corkscrew of some kind. Then in the morning, I'd climb a tree, bore a hole, and plant the carving like a strange little branch. They looked really funny. It was a terrific way to start the day.

SG: You made them in the dark? You made them without looking?

PS: By necessity. I didn't like sitting by the fire. If I didn't squeeze in next to a couple of gourd-wearing, chain-smoking naked guys sitting blisteringly close to the flames, I was in the dark.

SG: So you can make them blindfolded, a bit like how you make your paintings.

PS: Yes, a lot like my paintings—my best paintings.

SG: That was what, 1999?

PS: Something like that—2000 maybe.

SG: You carved the pencils in New York, right? Nothing better to do? Were you strung out?

PS: Yeah. That was a terrible time. On the way back from Asia, I stopped in Vancouver. I was putting off going home. I found a loft there, on the water, overlooking the mountains. It cost less than what I pay to store my work in New York. I'd become enough of a New Yorker to want to be done with it and with living in the Chelsea Hotel, from one day to the next. On my way in from the airport, bags still in hand, I stopped at the front desk to give Stanley my notice. He looked at me like I was crazy—and like he'd just won the jackpot. I'd lived at the Chelsea for almost sixteen years. It took me a few days to pack my stuff and a few months to leave. I was bitter and angry. And strung out.
I carved pencils to avoid attracting flies. I had to do something. Every-

thing was gone. I'd either shipped it or given it away. I sat on the bed I was going to leave behind, watched a television I'd borrowed, smoked cigarettes, and carved pencils.

SG: That sounds very different from New Guinea.

PS: In Papua, I carved each stick in a different place, and I left only little piles of shavings to be washed away with the next rain. The pencil shavings were comparatively toxic: they built up into a single, epic mound, all black and nasty. And in the woods I didn't keep any of the sticks. The Dani tribespeople didn't care about them. The whole tree-climbing thing didn't particularly amuse them either. They weren't *unamused*; they just didn't pay any attention. Indeed, their gourds were easily more impressive than my little sticks. But in New York everybody wanted a pencil, so I started hoarding them. I figured maybe they'd be worth something, especially if I had a lot of them. Sometimes I'd take them out to fondle and to admire them like a kid with baseball cards or like Fagin with his loot.

SG: You weren't really selling any paintings, were you? Did you sell pencils?

PS: I was so broke. I couldn't get arrested, never mind shown or sold. But I had this idea that if I carved enough of these pencils they could be some form of currency. How quickly could I carve them? How much was my time worth? I pictured myself busking, setting up on a street corner—fifty bucks apiece or twenty even . . . I would have looked good sitting there with a little pile of shavings, my hands all black and shiny. I could have done that anywhere. I imagined some postapocalyptic landscape where, worst comes to worst, I could carve pencils, you know, in exchange for a bowl of soup or a place to sleep. But, no, I didn't sell any. I didn't bother. Fifty bucks wasn't going to make any difference. I gave plenty away though. Especially to girls. Like flowers.

SG: Your confidence must have returned: when you went to Vancouver you carved some big logs.

PS: My friend Legs once told me, "Peter, it doesn't get better, just bigger." I carved baseball bats, too. I called the bats Dutch Baseball because one day I had eight or ten of these carved baseball bats across my shoulder. I used to rough them out at a friend's house. So I was crossing the street, and this guy who was stopped at the light rolled down his window and said, "Hey, what kind of bats are those?" Without skipping a beat, it just came up out of my mouth: "Dutch Baseball!" And I kept walking like it was the truth and there was nothing more to talk about.

SG: Another anecdote.

PS: Okay, how about this. The big logs actually got their start in Banff. There's a residency up there that I'd signed up for first thing after I got to Vancouver. It's beautiful up there, and I figured I'd be okay for a month just reading or maybe getting some exercise. Good food and fresh air. Anyway, I woke up that first morning, well, refreshed . . . I was or had . . . er . . . freshly arisen and . . .

SG: Stop right there. Please! I've already heard this story.

PS: I'm sorry. It's true though. That's how the pencils became logs. I was like, "Eureka! It's the wood in Woodwards!" No kidding.

SG: Okay. So, do the logs happen like the pencils? Yeah, yeah—I know they're bigger, but, I mean, can you carve them blindfolded?

PS: Absolutely. They carve themselves. I just do the same dance over and over again while the log moves of its own accord. It's on a couple of sawhorses. As I go after it with a chisel and a mallet, it moves. Just a little bit with each tap, just enough so I can do exactly the same thing again in a new spot. If I'm consistent, so is the log. Imagine a really big typewriter. I start at one end, tickety-tick all the way to the other end, and then—ding—back again, until there's nothing left.

SG: Like something between a beaver and a snail.

EMILY SUNDBLAD speaks with JAMES FRANCO and ROB PRUITT

Reproduced here is part one of an exchange taped in New York City in March 2012 and subsequently broadcast on www.jamesfrancotv.com.

Rob Pruitt: [*to Emily*] You have a great sense of style which I think carries over into the other things that you do, like your singing. You wear many hats, let me start by saying that. You're a performance artist–singer, a painter, a gallerist, and an international playboy.

Emily Sundblad: Yeah. [*Emily and Rob laugh*]

James Franco: We were just talking about Meredith Monk, because Rob designed this cover for her CD.

ES: Oh, that's so nice!

JF: And, so, she does a lot of stuff. And I think sometimes she gets criticism or people get confused because she does so many things—she's a choreographer and, you know, a composer, and everything else. So do you ever . . . does that ever happen to you? Do you feel like if there's too many things people can't quite understand what you're doing, or . . . ?

ES: Yes and no. I mean, you do a lot of things, too.

JF: Yeah.

ES: So you probably, uh, I mean I wouldn't say . . . I don't feel like I get overtly criticized. But I think people do get confused.

JF: How so?

RP: The response to the work is diluted because people don't know what it is that you're focused on? Like, "Oh, should we take her singing seriously because she also makes paintings? Should we take that more seriously? But she also runs the hottest gallery in New York." [*Emily chortles*] "Should we take that more seriously?" Or does it not matter, does it all kind of . . .

ES: Well, I feel like, maybe when we started—because you know I work together with some other people, too, running the gallery, under the name Reena Spaulings, and it's like a constantly shifting group of people, but the core is usually the same, and that grew out of the gallery practice. And so for the gallery also to be an artist, I think that's been hugely confusing for people. Because they're like, "Is the gallery getting compromised?" Or, you know, "What's happening?" But then . . . that I think was a little bit more in the past, because the new generation, I've noticed, like, people that are born in the eighties, or the mid-eighties, they're so hooked into the internet and stuff, and they're all multitasking. I mean, I just feel like it's the new way to be normal.

RP: To try lots of different things, to have many projects going on at the same time?

ES: I think so. I notice . . . I don't know . . .

RP: Because for me multitasking is I read my emails on my iPhone while I'm taking a bath.

ES: Right.

RP: But I think I'm maybe—

ES: Do you ever drop your phone in the bath?

RP: No, I never do.

ES: No?

RP: No, and when I go to the studio to paint I never get any paint on me. I think I'm like a fairy or something. I just kind of float through life and those kinds of things don't happen to me. But I think that I'm downplaying my multitasking, because I also like to do a lot of different things, like this chat show or performance art, stuff like the art awards or my studio practice. I think that's why I connect so well with you, because you like to do, you know, a whole gamut of things.

ES: I do, yes.

RP: Let's tell people about this project that we promptly pledged to do together like five years ago that we still haven't done.

JF: Yeah, let me hear about it.

ES: Oh yeah, we want to make paintings in the style of Matisse's odalisques, you know? He painted like, um, naked women in exotic interiors, and often Moroccan interiors. And Rob and I were going to paint each other.

RP: No. We are, not we were.

ES: Or we will paint each other.

RP: Yes, we will. We're going to fly to Morocco and paint each other nude.

———

RP: Tell us about your first painting show in New York, which was just, like, seven months ago, was that your first painting show?

ES: Yeah, it was at my friend Amy Greenspon's gallery around the corner, and . . . I don't know—what do you want to know?

RP: I just want to know how it felt to expose yourself as a painter. Did you feel vulnerable?

ES: Yes.

RP: Did you feel like there were some paintings that you liked more than others? Did you feel differently at the end of the show than you felt at the beginning of the show?

ES: I have to say the run of the show was really . . . it was gruesome. It was like torturous to have a show up in New York.

RP: Uh-huh.

JF: Why?

RP: Did you feel like you needed to get out of town?

ES: I did get out of town for a little bit but I don't know . . . I just couldn't stop thinking about it, I kept thinking: "It's probably really, really, really, really bad." And then I would go back, and I realized I still . . . I liked it. But, yeah, it was an anxious time. But you know the show. The painting show itself was made around this music performance.

RP: Which I attended and was blown away by.

ES: Thank you.

RP: She had an entire orchestra.

JF: Can you tell me about the performance, and then how the paintings are connected to the performance?

ES: Well, I thought of it as a kind of . . . you know, like, as a set. So the paintings were also a part of the set for the music performance.

JF: So you did the paintings before the music performance, and they were the set for the performance.

ES: Yeah. So opening night was also showtime, and the opening only consisted of the performance itself, which was—

JF: Oh, I see, so you did the performance in the space!

ES: Yeah, we re-created, we made the gallery. It was pretty crazy, because we took, you know, like a concrete box, and tried to turn it into a lush concert hall. So we had to change a lot of it, which was really fun. We worked with Matt Mazzucca, who is a great set designer, and he made this rubber curtain so we had a kind of an opera backdrop, but it was made out of black rubber. And then it was lit, we had theater lights, so it was . . .

JF: So the performance was only on that night of the opening?

ES: Yeah, well, I did two performances, but the main one, I mean, there was so much to it. Proenza Schouler made a dress—like a couture dress—for me. I worked with classical musicians like a string quartet, a classical pianist . . . We had professional sound, and we had to carpet the whole space.

JF: And you sang?

ES: Yes.

RICKY SWALLOW speaks with MATT CONNORS

Matt Connors: I was pondering your recent work last night, while making a cup of tea with my sort of ritualized hot-beverage setup (favorite teakettle, favorite mug), and it got me to thinking about how the body and (its) perception (vision, touch, taste, etc.) can relate to proportion and material (real or idealized), like how the weight or shape of an object (when held) can determine an emotional reaction or attachment to it. I feel like your recent sculptures play with these ideas. For one, you're taking on actual vessels (cups, vases) and other kinds of very human-shaped forms that immediately elicit a kind of muscle memory in the viewer's brain. In a way you are reducing them to pure form and proportion, radically limiting material and color. Do you feel like you are playing with a kind of semiotics of forms, shapes, and colors? Especially since most viewers are not able to touch the works, they become almost signs or ciphers . . .

Ricky Swallow: Proportion and a series of reductions seems key; perhaps "abbreviation" is the right term because it proposes a type of editing of the object, without forfeiting a comprehension of that object. I really like this idea of a viewer's mental/emotional "muscle memory" in relation to certain objects. I see my process in part as a means of *returning* objects, so that the object can assert itself in an autonomous way, have its own singular logic, yet retain some associations of use or function, and at times historical references. The subjects themselves arrive riddled with narrative histories and I think remaking the thing, that abbreviation, redirects the object into more formal territory. When a sculpture isn't working, sometimes it's falling too heavily on a reference or function. In approaching certain subjects you have to be aware that you're a guest, and for me personally there is a predetermined freedom in that, as well as some responsibility to act/make/behave well. The material change from cardboard into bronze seems like a way to finalize the form without losing its studio-built logic . . . despite the industrialized process they go through, they are still rooted in a very personal or *individual* place. I'm glad, too, that you mentioned color. It's still the most stressful thing for me ("I'm new here"), specifically because it can change the associations of the sculptures so much, or, to take a hit from Robert Morris, increase the "intimacy-producing relations."

MC: I think this seesawing between visual representations and indications of function, zooming in and out from a concrete sense of scale to a ridiculous disjointedness, contributes to an overall sense of destabilization—of logic, of form, of narrative, even. There's a certain sense of authority that one immediately feels when encountering a beautifully made, well-proportioned object that gets sort of derailed when its sense of function is contradicted. The result, for me, has a hyperpersonal, sometimes dreamy logic. Do you think this puts you into some sort of relationship with Surrealism?

RS: A useful way for me to think about Surrealism is to relax any understanding we have toward an object or subject, to allow for transformation. I think of the work of Christina Ramberg, Robert Therrien, Konrad Klapheck, Domenico Gnoli, or Roy McMakin, for example. Each has produced experiential works rooted in a certain amplification of daily materials, forms, and imagery, with a sense of transformation and peculiar material tightness that I admire—a "dreamy logic," as you put it. I started practicing Transcendental Meditation this year, and one of its strangest effects happens when looking at objects as you come out of the rest period following meditation. For a brief moment you have absolutely no associations with these things. You just see the structure, form, and color with an accentuated materiality that's more alien than abstract.

MC: I like the idea of a sustained, defamiliarized focus—it's telling of the evolution your work has undergone over the years. It seems like you experienced a moment of permission, allowing barriers between your personal and professional fascinations to disappear. Even though, for artists, these barriers are pretty amorphous to begin with. In the bronzes, I can feel the impulse that we share as obsessed lookers and collectors, a kind of taxonomy of fascinations, all being fed into the process of making. In a way this permission is also a realization that there are no unworthy avenues for artistic inquiry—the humorous, the narrative, the surreal, not to mention teacups, pinch pots, chair backs, or kachinas . . . Does this moment of synergy between private and professional strike a chord at all?

RS: I'm drawn to objects that are rudimentary in form and color, things that "say it simple." Many of the objects I collect have either been made with a type of material economy related to the maker's familiarity with the form through a repetitious practice, say, a potter's, or due to a reliance on limited materials and palette, as in earlier Navajo and Pueblo jewelry. The aesthetic produced by such conditions, the authenticity and magic of the forms, is awesome, and so is their energy. Functional items of ritual—used for ceremony, healing, sitting, drinking—appear so free of any prescribed ego or extraneous design. Occasionally there's a sculpture I can see coming out of a specific form at home. This black flag relief I'm working on relates to a Tobia and Afra Scarpa brass sconce in our entrance—its curve, the way it hugs the wall with grace and weight equally. The first vessels I cast from collated pieces of cardboard into bronze were literally formed around cups, bottles, and crucible forms I had collected. The patinas I've developed often approximate a ceramic glaze I like or the pigmented quality of mineral paint evident in Native American artifacts, specifically Hopi. Collecting things is a habit, and making things is another, and I treat them as equally instructive rituals. I really believe in learning an object: its identifiable characteristics, provenance, and chronology, especially via dialogue with those more familiar with the material. Within the crowd of veteran vendors at flea markets and Native American antique shows, which I frequent, there's a generosity of information buzzing around. The history behind these artifacts often goes unrecorded, so there's a constant reassessment of physical characteristics, an obsessive object reading.

MC: I see this transparency in your bronzes, revealing a process and materiality, as a kind of generosity, similar to what you referred to in communities defined by their elective affinities (which ideally would be true among artists and art audiences, right?). It makes these pieces really legible, referring to objects or functions in the physical world. But at the same time they are quite mysterious and incredibly fluid. How do you think such a determined clarity leads to the undefined, multivalent presence of the finished pieces? Do you think your work gains mysterious steam, so to speak, from reading the pieces over time, or as sequences in an exhibition constructing their own formal vocabulary or grammar? Or do you think "Ours is not to wonder why"?

RS: I always aim for clarity in the sculptures, but never a clarity that could occlude any subjective "walkabout" the object could take. So much of the success of any work is intuitive, it's exciting when improvised behavior produces a form that can be further developed into a sculpture or series. I hope there is a developing formal vocabulary to what I do, and as far as gaining "mysterious steam," who could hope for more, right? I really dig it when someone responds to the work in a way outside of my own logic, or makes a connection to another artist's work or tradition of objects I'd never considered. I like this line from the psychotherapist Adam Phillips: "We are always too daunted by who we are." I think by making things, making art, you get to offer something that's so connected to yourself, yet ultimately has the capacity to form an identity beyond your control.

TONY TASSET speaks with JUDY LEDGERWOOD

I've asked Judy Ledgerwood to have a conversation with me. Ledgerwood is a painter whom I first met over thirty years ago, in undergraduate school at the Art Academy of Cincinnati. We have together witnessed the making of every artwork we have individually made since we first met. I'm a big fan of Judy's art. —Tony Tasset

Tony Tasset: Darling, let's begin with a question I've asked you too many times over the years: do you think I'm a good artist?

Judy Ledgerwood: Married ya, didn't I?

TT: As you know too well, the Whitney Biennial has been my white whale for over twenty-five years, although I'm happy to say that my biannual depression has gently reduced itself to only an extra glass of wine at dinner in recent years.

So now that I've been invited into the big top, my happiness is bittersweet, because once again you have not been included, and I'm certain that you're a much better artist than me.

JL: Go on . . .

TT: Your early work was very in tune with the other Chicago Conceptualists in the eighties. You quoted hard: Mark Rothko, Claude Monet, J. M. W. Turner. But you were also different from Jeanne Dunning, Mitchell Kane, Hirsch Perlman, and moi. You did not shy away from showing your painting chops. The rest of us pretended naïveté or purchased others' crafting skills. You also were tied briefly to the Sublime movement associated with artists outside Chicago: April Gornik, Mark Tansey, and Joan Nelson.

You made monochromes in cosmetic colors, of Midwestern flat horizons turned to horizontal stripes and then back to nature, deconstructing the Impressionist. There is a Minimalist in you. The breakthrough painting was *Rainlight*, in 2003. You pictured the green circles on the sidewalk that are made from strong sunlight passing through leaves. It's completely abstract until you understand what it's depicting, and then it's completely realistic. That's a great painting.

I know I'm skipping a lot, but from that painting you discovered the circle. Back to the Minimalist in you: from the simple circle, you have created a universe of work. I keep thinking of Sol LeWitt, my favorite artist. Your work is some weird investigation parallel to Sol's. Granted, you never measure or use a straight line, and you use all the off colors. You could never describe how to make one of your paintings. Only you can make your paintings. But other than that, you have a lot in common with Sol. You are extremely prolific, and circles and colors have been all you've needed for years. I'm envious of your scholarly knowledge of color and your clear desire to continue studying it.

And, of course, you are an old-school feminist. I think you are sometimes overlooked because your work, at its essence, comes from a reevaluation of pattern and decoration and the power of color. Those terms sound old-fashioned, but your paintings are completely fresh and new in the way the best modernist paintings look new—complete invention and thrilling mastery in action. They are about herstory, but they are just as much indebted to boys' history. Many of your paintings are big as hell. You, just like men, are interested in power, and your paintings are aggressive. Your wild color interaction actually hurts my eyes sometimes. I've been in your studio and have become physically ill even though I was looking at pretty patterns and fields of flowers. The paintings are dirty, punk, and metal.

I think you have to give Luc Tuymans credit. When he made a studio visit in 1995, he told you that eventually you had to take on the mark. You took his advice. The paintings keep getting better as you age because your mark keeps getting more confident.

And then there's the quatrefoil: your flower motif of two plump vertical circles and two horizontal circles squeezed into a frame. How many times would you guess you have painted the four-petal flower?

JL: Since I started painting? It would be over a hundred thousand times.

TT: Wow, that's weird. No, it's genius. A perfect shape. An icon. It takes on Newman's zip and Johns's target. And, amazingly, all one hundred thousand flowers look completely different from one another. I'm a cipher, a culture vulture, but you are a true original. Your vision is steeped in history, but your paintings are completely unique.

JL: "Culture vulture" is a funny way to describe your sensitivity to what is on people's minds. In the beginning of your career, the audience that you craved was specialized: artists, historians, and collectors who were in the know. I'm thinking of the framed cowhide *Domestic Abstractions* (1986–87) and the benches from the same time period, which were Minimalist sculptures. You've always used humor, craft, and scale to seduce the viewer, but you gradually started to want your art to speak to a broader audience in the hope that art could have more significance. Sometime in the nineties, your work became more entertaining but also more personal and political.

Your use of familiar imagery is remarkable. I could choose any number of works to illustrate: the abject, meticulously reconstructed snowmen (2003–13); the giant *Eye* (2010); the faux-rock *Grotto* (2008), with real, dripping candles; or the monumental *Paul* (2005), a 30-foot fiberglass depiction of an older, slumped-over, potbellied Paul Bunyan at Governors State University's sculpture park in University Park, Illinois.

The most radical part of your practice is your refusal to show allegiance to any one style or means of production. Your individual pieces, particularly the public works, are easy to picture individually, but your art as a whole is difficult to brand. This is why *The Artists Monument*, which you are including in the Biennial, is simply your most brilliant work to date. It refuses any hierarchy. It's an 80-foot horizontal monument covered with the names of four hundred thousand artists, in alphabetical order on randomly arranged colored panels. It's a horizontal gesture. This is what your work has always tried to do—to flatten high and low. *The Artists Monument* is more public, more institutional, and more cross-cultural than any piece to date, and thus is a bigger success. Of course—you have yet to make it.

TT: Oh yeah, I have to make it. That's always the hard part. Why do you even think I want to make everything?

JL: It's moral for you. I aspire to the Masters, and you shoot all that down.

TT: Making art can be a joyful thing, but when the work enters the reality of the market, the museum world, or even the public arena, artists are always reminded of where they stand in the pecking order. Certainly, being "in" or "out" is not exclusive to art. I'm sure somewhere a dachshund breeder is feeling dejected for not winning best in show. I'm still loyal to postmodernism, so I don't think art is any more or any less important than any other profession or calling. But because art is more subjective than, say, heart surgery, I feel art is more vulnerable to flimflam, dumb luck, and the vagaries of fashion. *The Artist Monument* is my attempt to invite everyone to the party. Do you want to have sex?

JL: That's what it always comes down to between us: competition is our way of flirting.

TT: That wasn't a yes, was it?

PHILIP VANDERHYDEN speaks with LANE RELYEA

Lane Relyea: Are your interests in Gretchen Bender's work curatorial? Conservationist?

Philip Vanderhyden: The short answer is that I love Gretchen Bender's work, and when I heard from her friends that *People in Pain,* her 50-foot wall sculpture from 1988, no longer existed and could be remade, I wanted to do something about it. Some parts of this activity, or even the majority, are curatorial and art historical. However, I wouldn't say that's what intrigued me. More that something monumental had vanished and could be made to exist again. The more I learned about *People in Pain,* the more interested I became in the moment of its reappearance versus the moment of its original existence, and how this time envelope complemented the piece itself. One could remake a lost work by any artist and it could potentially be interesting, but *People in Pain* is about the time envelope in which our cultural experiences live and die.

LR: To look at what's going on in painting today, I'm visiting blogs that chronicle daily studio visits with JPEGs. The entries get stacked with the most recent on top, so a new canvas appears only to immediately get pushed down into obscurity by the next.

PV: The irony is that paintings now live and die in a context far removed from the frontal, one-to-one mode of address they historically existed in. The virtual, abstract space created by a painting's movement through the world is more central to its currency than the physical space in front of it. In the end, that's what turned me on to Bender's work. As someone who loves materiality and the acknowledgment of an object's constituent elements, I was amazed at how prescient she was in her emphasis of circulation and distribution.

LR: I figure that if you're a studio practitioner, that severe limiting of your work's life span affects your experience of your material activity—that the studio becomes more and more pervaded by the short-term precariousness and insecurity that today dominates labor in general.

PV: This comes back to what you might call my labor-intensive portion of this project. I spent a decent chunk of what would otherwise be studio time over the past two years studying Bender's work and reassembling it. If I were an employee of a gallery, estate, or large institution, doing these things would be a part of my day-to-day existence. However, I am not that type of laborer. This is a hard project for an institution to take it on: the work is sometimes in rough shape or no longer exists in physical form. There are therefore more financial and conceptual risks in committing to bringing it back into circulation. It's no accident that the support I got on this project was loose and noninstitutional: Robert Longo; Rirkrit Tiravanija; Amber Denker; Stuart Argabright; and Jonathan Bender, Gretchen's brother, immediately came forward and put their full weight behind it. Robert Longo, in particular, underwrote its reconstruction.

LR: The Pictures Generation artists that Bender was associated with in the eighties approached images as social currency—as having the power, like language, to position us through our use of it within a system that constitutes us as social subjects. Images that hail us and induct us into ideology as the grounds and possibility for social existence. But Bender's work is different from that of her peers: instead of employing a semiotic system, she's a materialist. Viewers physically endure her work; they don't decode or critique or identify with it.

PV: *People in Pain* frames the time between anticipation and oblivion. All of the bits of text in it are movie titles. When the piece originally appeared, some of these movies were about to be released, some were out, and some had just left theaters. The dark part of her expression is how she flattened them: the titles all peek out from an approximation of a garbage bag or melted film cel as though speaking from the grave.

LR: Which goes back to your description of the forensic process of reconstituting this piece. With the rise of digitalization and electronic technology, there's new primacy given to memory as informational, technological, alien—memory chips, memory banks, storage capacities, etc.

PV: The re-creation of *People in Pain* by someone else is an emphatic restatement of its focus on the technological and the inhumane. The inflection isn't oriented toward touch. In its original iteration, Gretchen, Jonathan, and Rirkrit would work on it very casually and procedurally with molds, hot plates, and a heat gun.

LR: But I imagine the really influential experience for Bender was sitting before a bank of assorted computer equipment with her fingers at the controls—in the mid-eighties, when communication was supplanting representation as the dominant paradigm, and the "window space" of cinema and photography was being displaced by interfacing screens and remote controls. Interstitial and connectionist space, relaying input and feedback, command and performance—its legibility dependent on pattern recognition rather than the play of presence and absence—calls for an operator or manager.

PV: The masculinity of the future is part of her aesthetic.

LR: This astronaut-manager figure, transcendent in one sense, is also completely flooded and imprisoned by the contingent. We're vigilantly overaware and numb with exhaustion today because information is always excessive, too promiscuous and mobile and fragmented. It doesn't submit itself to management, but instead makes constant crisis. The spatial envelope Bender addressed is filled with objects and subjects.

PV: Bender's work circulates expressionistically. It's an exaggeration of the shortness of our memories and the seeming arbitrariness of what sticks. The movie titles that you don't remember prove interesting. Not knowing if you should remember something makes you think about what you've forgotten, about what was pumped through you without a trace. Or, for that matter, it reminds us that the things we never experience firsthand can still leave a trace.

LR: To this day when casually asked about a movie I'll sometimes say I've seen it when in fact I haven't. It oddly doesn't seem to make any difference.

PV: Have you seen *Gravity*?

LR: Well, now that I'm totally self-conscious about lying, I have to tell the truth: no. But I have seen the ads in which astronauts get pummeled by trash—a nice image of the collapsing of the transcendent and contingent. That's another thing about information, since it prioritizes an always disappearing event-like temporality over the more stable semantics of representation it doesn't pay so much heed to insides and outsides. Google is a great example, the canon and trash bin imploded into a general space of flirtatious circulation, the rotten and ripe all mixed.

PV: This is another instance of how recirculating Bender's work converges with the aims of the work itself. The original iteration of *People in Pain* fell apart, but it left a photographic trace in the world as well as being embedded in the memories of those who helped make it. An installation slide from Metro Pictures was the best reproduction I had to work with. Someone asked me early on, "Don't you think it's equally poignant to keep it photographic?" It's a resonant question, but I think it's more interesting to think of this piece as not having some intrinsic core the way that more emphatically authorial works do. I like that the piece came and went and is now back. It's just like the movies.

PEDRO VÉLEZ poses QUESTIONS

Pedro Vélez : I have put these questions to artists, curators, and critics over the last two years, to fish for quotes for articles that were never published.

Robin Dluzen
Artist and critic, Chicago

PV: Whenever tragedy strikes the arts in Detroit, coverage is abundant and exploitative. Do you think this double standard on the part of the press is a reflection of the art market, or is it just another step in the homogenization of national coverage? What is your position as an artist born and raised in Michigan?

RD: The situation at the Detroit Institute of Arts, in particular, is such that individuals who see themselves as coming from the nation's cultural centers—elitists—can wag their fingers at the decisions "provincials" are making without getting their hands dirty. With so little coverage of Detroit's major successes—for example, the millage passed by local voters to save the DIA over a year ago—and shameless salivating at tragic events, it's clear that art journalism is not exempt from the kind of speculative, uninformed, traffic-whoring sensationalism to which mainstream internet and cable-news outlets resort. It's all become a sort of art-press version of "ruin porn": a disregard for local history and sociopolitical factors have contributed to the gloom and doom that those on the outside find so irresistible.

Robert Davis
Painter, New York

PV: You have a subtle persona. It doesn't really reflect your past life as curator of spectacular events put together by the collective Law Office or the hard-core imagery developed in your collaborative paintings with Mike Langlois. Many people don't even know that you are a fabricator to art stars. In these new paintings, we see primal marks made by spilling coffee and bourbon and the use of burlap as material—they seem to me like an investigation of . . . working-class values?

RD: The people I've collaborated with also came from working-class families, and that informed the work we made together, in terms of the subjects and the way we approached formal and philosophical problems. As for the paintings I am making now, I suppose the materials I use—base substances like coffee, ash, and leather—could imply something about class. However, if I am being completely honest, I think of them more as relating to painting's history in an almost excessively literal or physical way: flesh and Bacon.

Rachel Furnari
Artists' liaison and author, New York

PV: How do you feel about museums becoming popular by negating their original missions? Could we say rebranding is an elegant way to impose cultural whitewashing to a specific community?

RF: Rebranding certainly has the potential to include whitewashing, and we see forms of that in culturally specific institutions that are trying to broaden their audience. But institutions can't be static and survive; they have to be nimble (a favorite marketing word). We were discussing the Jewish Museum and El Museo del Barrio—being Jewish, like being a Puerto Rican from the mainland or Nuyorican from the barrio, doesn't mean the same thing it did fifty years ago. Why should it? While preserving a legacy is part of the mandate, remaining relevant over time is equally important. On the other hand, some institutions seem to abandon their missions, confusing long-term supporters and potentially diminishing access and visibility. As directors hop from one institution to the next under intense pressure not only to fund-raise but also to innovate or even disrupt the model, there is a real risk for homogenization (see countless and sundry critiques of "starchitect" buildings and art as entertainment). Museum directors, museum curators, and their boards can no longer maintain the fantasy that they're separate from the same engine of economic and social capital that drives the commercial art world: voracious spending and expanding networks of power have drawn in even regional or geographically isolated institutions. Money changes everything. So does its absence.

Gardy Pérez
Sound artist, Puerto Rico

PV: The site-specific sound tracks of your gallery shows, your shoegaze band Un.Real, and even your graphic design have been influential to a younger generation of practitioners. You have influenced many without their even knowing it, which is very telling of your practice. The Caribbean can be hermetic when it comes to culture, and distribution of your work can take years. Do you feel a sense of urgency to be more widely recognized?

GP: I have always been around music, thanks to my family. My sister taught me how to draw. My brothers inspired me with their love of photography and their records. If visual imagery can't get an idea across, music does. The abstractness of sound is perfect—it's open to interpretation. I can't quit sound because I have things to say, and it allows me to keep on doing things that matter to me or to frame a moment in time. I can't stop 'cause I can't conform to a life of total emptiness. Sound waves need to move, to get somewhere. As for the slow distribution of my work, I'm from a small town. We grew up on bicycles and playing basketball until we discovered rock and punk. In my head, I went places. I could make something out of nothing.

Maya Mackrandilal
Performance artist, Chicago

Eunsong Kim
Poet and Ph.D. candidate in literature, San Diego

PV: For over a year, we have been having one long, public conversation, dealing with issues of privilege in the New York press and how certain voices carry more weight than others because of geography and the fact that 99 percent of art editors are . . . white. When we designated Thomas Hirschhorn's *Gramsci Monument* as Monument Safari and DIA Detroit, the rebuttal by important personalities in the art world was predictable. Some leave the virtual table by summoning reverse racism (hilarious), while others like Ed Winkleman accuse us of being "angry." What is it that they fear so much?

MM: I think what it comes down to is America is changing. The next generations aren't going to look like those before. They aren't going to have the same cultural references or histories. The margins have been slowly infiltrating the center, and the future is beginning to look a lot less like the Chicago Boys and a lot more like Latin American socialism. The "art world" is hanging on to ideas about "neutrality" and "universality." (Wendell Berry calls these myths—I call them code for white, upper class, cisgendered, straight, and male.) Simply by speaking up and suggesting that other readings are possible, we are challenging the hierarchies white-male identity depends on.

EK: The preservation of a white-male subject is at the heart of aesthetic questions. The foundation of Western aesthetics was predicated on recognizing the art object from a property-eligible subject position (Immanuel Kant, Marcel Duchamp, Andy Warhol, etc.). Because neoliberal capitalism unfolded through expansion via multiculturalism (Lisa Lowe, Grace Hong, etc.), recognition is no longer a tool preserved for the bloodlines of modernism. Rather, recognition—the ability to label, to brand, to reject, and to contest—has become the vehicle in which we must participate in order to define and to build art and culture. The production of neoliberalism requires large amounts of opaque capital, sophisticated coalitions between those with old power stakes, an exploitable (and often racialized) body of laborers, a vast appetite for consumption, brand rhetoric, and investors in the outcome—and perhaps a CEO (another investor). This is the structure for most "museum" art: the opaque capital, the collaboration of those in power, an expendable body of laborers, careless appropriation, brand rhetoric (usually taken straight out of critical theory), and blue-chip investors—and the artist CEO. That is, the artist recognized for the *cosa mentale* of the object he cannot be bothered to make. We live in a world where most of us are convinced that bank CEOs do not deserve to be paid for their "economy-crashing creative ideas," and yet white, male, confused artists continued to be celebrated for their endlessly exploitative, colonialist practices. Gatekeepers, the managers of our art world who ask us to be silent in the face of this preservation project, protect them. They should be afraid.

MM: There's a lot at stake in an art world that no longer pushes the boundaries of human thought but instead sings the anthems of a global ruling elite. When you can't challenge your opponent's ideas, you attack their positionality. You call them "angry" because emotion isn't "objective"—it belongs to the feminine, to the Other, and to the wide-eyed dark masses yearning to be civilized. As if young black men were not being murdered in the street. As if mothers did not have to claim their babies' bodies in the morgue. When that doesn't work, you trot out your friends of color, art stars of color, and politicians of color to prove you're not a bigot. And then you throw up your hands and say it's not your responsibility and that one person can't challenge a systemic problem. As if we are not looking you in the eyes, doing just that.

Michael Wynne
Artist and art collector, Dallas

PV: I'm going to assume most of your decisions as a collector are channeled through what interests you as an artist. But you are not a rich collector or artist. The wealthy build museums in their own names. Eli Broad actually has two, one in Los Angeles and the other in Michigan. But my contention is that people like you play a bigger part in the art economy by supporting artists, not only emotionally but also by helping them pay rent with a few bucks here and there. Do you feel the rural Texas town where you work has shaped your views on collecting and making art?

MW: Kirvin is the town where I grew up. Kirvin had a population of sixty-five. My grandparents settled there in the late twenties when my grandfather grew tired of running from his father's debtors and insisted on staying with his pregnant wife. My father was twenty-nine and my mother fourteen when they married. I was born the following year. My father had an egg business, which he sold to grow cotton and then raise cattle. I grew up working with my brothers in the cattle and hay fields, but I had a normal boy's life going fishing, running in the woods, walking down railroad tracks, and skinny-dipping. I started first grade in 1964 in a town ten miles away and spent the next twelve years drawing in class to fight the tedium of school. I would draw crude air fights between Flying Tigers and Japanese Zeros, guns, rocket ships, and dog faces. I didn't really get interested in looking at art until I noticed that art books had pictures of naked women. I had a vague knowledge of Pablo Picasso and Salvador Dalí from *Life*, and as my drawings got more surreal my mother bought me a book on Joan Miró for Christmas. What struck me about his paintings was that there were dirty jokes hidden in them. My Saturn V rockets started growing pubes after that.

What got me truly interested in being an artist was a book I ran across during a school field trip to Waco. After we saw whatever it was we went to see, they dropped us off in a mall for an hour. In the bookstore was a copy of Lawrence Alloway's *American Pop Art*. All the paintings looked like magazine advertisements. I scraped up the money and bought it. What really blew my mind was when I read that Robert Rauschenberg came from Texas. It didn't occur to me you could come from a place like Port Arthur and do things like this. Overnight, he was my hero, and I started copying him and the other artists in the book because I found myself with a desire not to scribble on notebook paper in class but to own these things. The only way I could was to make them myself. So the impulses to make art and collect art were pretty much the same for me. I went to college for a couple of years but returned to Kirvin and the farm. The notion that artists were part of the professional class wasn't around yet. I started a series of large paintings of constellations, patterns that I would shoot with my AK-47. I would send Polaroids of them to Dallas galleries. After about a year, I got a response from Foster Goldstrom, who sent me a note asking if he could come to my studio. Since my studio was a hundred miles away, I knew this would never actually happen, so the next morning after feeding the cattle I swept out the hay truck, piled in the paintings, and showed up at his gallery. I proceeded to bring in the ten 6-by-4-foot panels and lined them up against the wall. I was clueless, but Foster seemed to like something about it all. And I had my first gallery show.

I got married, left Kirvin, and moved to Dallas. When our daughter was born, I decided to stop pursuing my art career for the most part to become the stay-at-home parent. But I've started making big, goofy abstract paintings again. When a new volunteer firehouse was built in Kirvin, I bought the old one and started splitting my time between Dallas and my old hometown. I think being from Kirvin and somewhat isolated from the outside world had its effect on my development as an artist. There is the obvious work ethic that came with farm life and a sense of community that came with small-town life. I also know from experience that even a small amount of money has a big effect on an artist. I give artists money so that they can continue to work but also for the boost it gives them in knowing there's interest.

DAVID FOSTER WALLACE (1962–2008): NICHOLAS FRANK speaks with BROOKE KANTHER

Nicholas Frank: I'm thinking back on the double appearance of the "mold boy" anecdote in David Foster Wallace's writing, in both the essay "Tennis, Trigonometry, Tornadoes: A Midwestern Boyhood" (hereafter referred to as "TTT") and in the first pages of *Infinite Jest* (*IJ*). In the latter, it's told as memory's feckless permissions, as what we're allowed to recall at any given moment; or like memory's marginal notes, what we're able to discern later of our own sloppy handwriting. In "TTT," it's how the strict, large-scale geometries of the Midwestern landscape imprint themselves on our consciousness:

the mom runs around in panicked horror after her son emerges from the basement having ingested some unnameable mold patch, yet she still keeps within the squared angles of the little garden plot she'd laid out in sticks and string ("even in trauma her flight lines were plumb . . . her turns, inside the ideogram of string, crisp and martial").[1]

It's that combination of imprint and willing acceptance of boundaries that interests me, as a lifelong boundary dweller. Instead of crashing through, she turns around the center in a polite and orderly fashion.

Brooke Kanther: "TTT"
—a center articulated
—gaps between teeth
—a row in a parking lot that provides temporary space
—columns that hold aspirations of permanence/shelter
—a stutter
Probably all of these things.

I never would have paired them, but *Infinite Jest* is a highly orchestrated tornado, and "TTT" is about navigating relationships to structures.

My strongest memory from reading *IJ* six years ago is when I couldn't feel the weight of it in my hands. This year, when I tried to read it again, I realized I was chasing that feeling, that level of absorption that allows you to forget yourself and be present with something else. My desire was contingent on a level of entertainment and spectatorship I can't afford anymore. Coming back this time, I had read (most) everything else he wrote. All I could see were reflections of my own life experience and whatever notions I have of his biography. I couldn't escape myself, or my idea of DFW. *IJ* presented a fractured mirror both as object and as subject. I couldn't finish it this time.

I'm also thinking about the space that happens around *IJ* on the nightstand, not the actual content of the work but my projection of all the *other stuff* (the myth around the author, the reputation of the book) that makes it hum that certain frequency of authority. Which can be grating and explicitly not the content, but is a reality.

Your *Nicholas Frank Biography* project winks in the direction of this kind of complication between mythology and fragmented truths. You give the viewer only a few pages at a time. I have come to understand this gesture as part of the mythmaking aspect, this fracturing of narrative within the context of how a book functions (front to back, left to right, singular object) and then wondering about the whole book that may or may not exist. It's a form of denial I find interesting.

NF: My only approach to DFW is exactly what you mentioned, concerning a myth built on discrete missives (his many writings) from some intellectual dimension beyond my comprehension. If we think of a personage as inscribing their biography by actually living, then we can recognize a kind of third-person agency in how a person "tells" their life as they live it. The distances between what really happened and how it's told (and by whom) interest me as much as the events themselves, for both and all versions can somehow become equally true. But myths are only pixelated truths.

So yeah, the withholding thing of the *Nicholas Frank Biography*, forcing the hand of historical fragmentation . . . In my personal life, I've been accused of being passive-aggressive, but honestly my response (kept to myself) has been, Who in the Midwest isn't? We have no tradition of therapy here, at least not in any of my immediate communities growing up. Perception was all held in, left stewing, ultimately unrelatable—that sense that one is alone with one's deepest self, a being or part of being that can't be shared even if opening up is desired.

I like how you've drawn a picture of my "book," a nonbook, as a suggestion of a complete object in space-time, and how it parallels the subject of our conversation, this DFW person realized publicly through intellection, the various scraps and fragments that piece together into what has to and can only be a myth. What seems key is that he was obviously reaching for that status from the start. For that transcendent position, outside of humble origins, toward a pantheon zone. His intellect bristles and crackles, barely contained. And yet, in "TTT" he's just a workhorse, middling-talent tennis player finding something of himself through physical exertion. It was his mental acuity in the process of playing that lent him a higher level of skill, and he clearly and dearly relates to his comrades and opponents on the court. I can't help but think of tennis as the loneliest sport: a body-mind alone out there, no one but the self confronting the self disguised as an opponent. But then, in sports, the world of zero-summing, you get exterior feedback of greatness. In the arts, you get some of that, but ultimately none of it answers much of anything. It can always be questioned. This was DFW's fate.

BK: Tennis is absolutely lonely, a bit like painting is lonely. Artists who can't be alone produce work that howls in an echo chamber of its own making—its vibration the frequency of a dog whistle. I think if your practice is primarily contingent on a celebratory confirmation of your existence—without navigating through the complex landscape of your personal desires, demands, and fears—the work gets knowingly vapid. All this cane shaking is coming from a woman who made an 8-foot-wide blow-up snowman sculpture (that winks at you) last week. I have some familiarity with the echo chamber.

I use DFW's books as notebooks because I know that no matter how much I would prefer to get rid of my often asinine notations, I won't lose or throw out Wallace. My lists from this time last year: death of last parent, (subsequent) pro/cons concerning legal action, corporate secretary or grad school?, and, "Are sociopathic tendencies in an ex negotiable?" I am aware how generous (selfish) it is to insist Dave carry this around!

NF: The death of parents! My first occurred last year, and I remember walking around in the fog of deep realization, thinking, *Everybody goes through this*? The experience certainly made me more empathetic toward strangers, particularly people who daily annoy with their callousness or inconsiderateness or incivility—why, they might be going through some kind of reverberant life trauma that has left them emotionally spent, stripped, flayed, barely able to cope with slogging their sluiced selves through another impossibly empty moment.

In DFW, the "considered" lobster[2] becomes a trope for empathy, at least of the human-animal variety, a stripping away of fleeting desires, to recognize the suffering of others. It's there animating his essay on Roger Federer, too—empathy glues the narrative investigation together. It comes in two parts: the resin being Federer's great gifts of physicality and temperament; the catalyst being the seven-year-old cancer sufferer William Caines's terrible fate.[3] Wallace reaches for both, struggles to achieve an empathy of transcendence, equally for the glorious grace of Federer's ability and for the torturous pain of that poor kid's terminal misfortune. Genetically (as Wallace plumbs), each are the same random chance, the outer limits of our human programming, writ heroically large and cruelly small. In light of the author's own sufferings, the desire to connect through empathy itself seems heroic and forms the nervous system of his entire output.

Depression is lonelier than tennis and painting combined, and maybe we "normals" get some sense of the shattering inability to connect with the flow of shared reality when we are removed from it temporarily by the death of a parent. Rarely can anyone be closer or more distant and yet always most complicated in our lives. There is no emotional equal to the loss. The depressed person's triumph is reaching a truly empathetic state, a place of connection with the experience of others beyond the narrow walls of consuming self-regard.

BK: "The Depressed Person"[4] is brilliant, and I think one of his best. Your question—does everybody goes through this?—is parallel to the moment when I realized the tectonic shift of losing your primary familial structure is completely universal. Finding a personal entry point into a cliché feels simultaneously epiphanic and infuriating!

I think "Consider the Lobster" and "This Is Water"[5] (the commencement speech) are so popular because Wallace outlines the difference between intellectualizing contingent ethical and moral issues in a vacuum and making informed, empathic, conscious choices in daily aspects of your life. Maybe like the difference between having manners and acting with kindness? One is in accordance with expected social norms and the other is a willful act of empathy toward others. His simplicity is slippery and often functions elliptically. It is simultaneously seductive and challenging, even irritating. It's like a Trojan horse—only the form and function are compressed and entangled, and we are confronted with the interlocutor of someone else's interiority.

I also think this might be in Saint Dave territory? To which I would like to permanently affix my thumb to my nose in reaction to that kind of worship and oversimplification. It becomes a kind of reality in our culture when you have someone who is so densely complex and difficult to digest that all you can do is defang them and give them a halo. Moving on. Or sideways . . .

I've seen his archive in the library at University of Texas at Austin. The "Midwesternisms" notebook struck me like a Temple Grandin machine that gives you whiplash instead of a hug. It had that kind of unexpected density and weight that can come from hypercontrolled parameters. It's a list of Midwestern inclinations and proclivities and is perhaps itself an "Academic stutter (not a true stutter, the stutter of compression and density the plosive a bottleneck)."

NF: DFW's representation of his tennis self might or might not match how the other, more talented coastal players regarded him, and he is alone with his awareness of his peculiar talents. The nature of his own milieu literally alters the playing field, upending the standards of judgment in a swirl of windy debris. In the Midwestern prairies, there are no big edifices to stop the winds, but outside of his domain he loses his power. My *Biography* arises out of this very crisis of perspective, that by being born in the margins, raised in the margins, and choosing to stay and work in the margins, I myself would have to invent the perspective as regards to my own work and position in the world. Think of standing alone in that endless tawny prairie sea, paradoxically a natural soil for nurturing the imagination—the kid playing alone in her room—versus the concrete towers of culture. The busy places are where we go to figure out what to do with the products of our imaginations; the empty zones are where we stand in contemplation of the much wider fields, alone in a universe of others. Isolation and desolation of the soul are companions, from which, I believe, empathy can grow. In the peripheries, one tends toward empathy for others in marginal situations. We set our own margins.

The artist Stephanie Barber once gave some advice that has stuck with me like a brain tattoo: boil down what you do to three words. If you can't, you're sunk trying to explain to anyone else what you're up to. My three words are authority, belief, and distance. Is authority inside or out? Who decides? And does belief in something actually distance us from it? These are the worries of a very small, very disconnected young artist coming up in Milwaukee, Dayton, Saskatoon, or Ponce. I mean in any place so far from any center that you can only gaze at the distant disk in the sky, and wonder how you really know it's really a sphere.

The act of marginalia recovery in showing DFW's "Midwesternisms" notebook as the work of a writer-artist is to redraw the geometries, to pull a marginal thing toward the center, to step over the string like a more composed version of that mold-boy Mom, to point an ultraresolution telescope toward a distant patch of darkness and find yet more incandescent dots ripe for study.

One thought bumped around last night as I fell fitfully asleep with the large *IJ* tome pressing down on my chest: doors open where limits agree.

BK: That sounds windy.

1. David Foster Wallace, "Tennis, Trigonometry, Tornadoes: A Midwestern Boyhood," *Harper's*, December 1991, 70.
2. Wallace, "Consider the Lobster," *Gourmet*, August 2004.
3. Wallace, "Federer as Religious Experience," *New York Times*, August 20, 2006.
4. Wallace, "The Depressed Person," *Harper's*, January 1998.
5. Wallace delivered "This Is Water" at Kenyon College in 2005. See Wallace, *This Is Water: Some Thoughts Delivered on a Significant Occasion, about Living a Compassionate Life* (New York: Little, Brown, 2009).

DAN WALSH speaks with WALTER DANES

Walter Danes: Good to see you. Are you sure about doing another interview?

Dan Walsh: Yes. Cautiously, yes.

WD: Although I've known your work since we started graduate school at Hunter College in 1983, it doesn't mean that we agree on the reading of the work or that I even like it. [*laughs*] Interpretations change. Shouldn't you find some fresh eyes or a different voice to talk about your paintings?

DW: But that's what I like about our conversations: we don't agree on many things, and I always learn something. But, more important, I feel like I need a more experienced viewer like you.

WD: Okay, to start, your technique/process is so particular. You paint like a printmaker: in passes. You claim it is a move toward a codified language. But at the same time, it has become more and more personalized—or should we call it stylized or historical?

DW: I have always been interested in making something very clear. But, this attempt at clarity has manifested a strange and idiosyncratic—dare I say—style.

WD: Are you saying your style is your content . . . or is clarity your style? It seems more about economy . . . I'm confused.

DW: The care I put into the brushwork is a method, or a search for a method, where everything I do becomes relevant and revealed. I am trying to engage the viewer so that the paintings only make sense when one is looking at them.

WD: Then you apply this method to grids or, at least, to evenly spaced, uniformly laid-out surfaces. This seems like a contradiction.

DW: Well, it is! I embrace these contradictions. I think of the grid as a place to locate oneself, and I accept the idea that one's content is chosen among many possibilities but is still determined. On the other hand, my process is in denying this determination: I am trying to paint my way out of the grid . . . in and out of corners.

WD: I understand that the grid is a point of departure for you, but the optical—and those transparent layers—points to a transcendental, maybe even escapist, position. What else could it possibly be?

DW: As I've said before, the grid is a vehicle to organize information; it is interactive. There is an exchange. I have always seen my paintings as a place to compare and to judge. On the other hand, the grid can be about repetition or marking time. . . . Both of these ideas apply to Tibetan mandalas, which I often refer to in relation to my work.

WD: Okay, I understand this when I think about your diptychs, but what am I looking at in the end? What is the relevance, the goal, then?

DW: Don't underestimate the formative point at which the retinal meets the symbolic. In the past, I described the relationship between the viewer and my paintings as a "symbolic exchange." Again, it is the act, the "through it," that I want to emphasize over the goal or end result—a theater of the perceptual act.

WD: I think I understand, but it seems you care a lot about the end result.

DW: Of course I do! A painting is a result of certain actions, but it's still a vehicle for the viewer.

WD: Is that why you hang your paintings so low?

DW: Yes. It is a practical decision for orientation and interactivity. As with Minimalism, we are in the room, in the picture—in the here and now. I joke sometimes, saying it is the "gravity" of the situation.

WD: I know you see history as codified. Are you calling yourself a Minimalist? What about your interest in the Romanesque or Middle Eastern art?

DW: Actually, among Minimalists, I call myself a Maximalist—I get the most out of minimal means! Now, I am embracing all history, however codified . . . I am certainly not quoting it for a critique . . .

WD: Okay, let's talk about this new series of paintings called *Cycle*, which you began in fall 2012. It definitely looks as if you were researching history . . . and would you say visual archetypes? It's a bit unusual. How did it come about?

DW: Well, as my painting has become more "process driven," my approach has become more like a bricklayer's—elemental and additive. This has led me to appreciate the workings of the basic alphabets of various cultural languages, for example, those of weaving, tile work, and textiles in general. (Color is yet another issue!) I am surprised I didn't reach this place sooner. So, the Cycle series started as an experimental project, and I set out with a "goal": to express specific cultural referents. The series became eleven paintings of some of my favorite historical forms, which I thought could jibe with my approach—a Russian icon, a Peruvian burial blanket, an early sixties Pop painting, a Seurat drawing, etc.

WD: Well, the paintings show great variety. They must have been interesting to research. They look as if they were fun to make—

DW: Yes, they were a blast! I had three to five examples of each genre that I referred to for specific paintings. The crossover from design to painting and back is something I find interesting. What we are looking for always has a form in history somewhere.

WD: Is this where you are going? You speak of history all the time—it kind of sounds reactionary. Are you sure you want to go down this road?

DW: This was a special project—no regrets. I am starting to understand how to use this research in my work. And I've realized that form is bigger than me, that it has its own intelligence, which is revealed through the history of art. Of course, I am going to research it! My practice is to interact with history, to be there, if only to later deconstruct it. My vocabulary allows me to occupy different times and places in art history. With a change of a brushstroke or a dot's location or a color, I can move in and out of these places. This interests me—that I can!

DONELLE WOOLFORD speaks with CLAIRE BISHOP

Claire Bishop: Donelle, when did you first think about moving into performance? It's a bold—some would say risky—move for someone whose career has been based on two- and three-dimensional work.

Donelle Woolford: In my first show at Wallspace in New York in 2008, I made a kind of "lecture" installation in the back room, but there was no lecturer, just artifacts and a slide show. I liked the *tableau vivant* feeling—except there was no *vivant*—so I did a similar gesture a few months later for the Eighth Sharjah Biennial, but inserted myself into the role of the artist by making a studio environment that I inhabited for several days. Of course, I did an extended version of that for your *Double Agent* exhibition at the Institute of Contemporary Arts in London that same year. By the time of my second show at Wallspace, in 2009, I was thinking much more theatrically. I still hung paintings on walls, but they were arranged in "scenes," with adjacent furniture functioning as props. I could step into a scene and out of it again, kind of switching the whole conceit on and off.

CB: In those earlier pieces, you just seemed to hang around in the space, fielding questions and interacting with the audience. Was that some kind of comment on the way in which the artistic persona today is a constant performance?

DW: Yes, I think exhibitions are always performative. I wouldn't be the first to have noticed that galleries tend to function as stages on which we play and on which we are watched by other players. The second Wallspace show had two versions of me working the room, so that was a more explicit commentary on persona. Each of us would move through the gallery in a normal fashion, but keeping eye contact, and then from time to time suddenly trade places. It was quite disorienting for whomever we happened to be talking to or for people who got introduced to me more than once that evening and met a different person each time.

CB: How did you become interested in reenactments? So many artists turned to reenactment in the last decade—were you just following the crowd, or did anything in particular trigger your turn to this way of working?

DW: It grew out of my Cubist paintings, which are reenactments of sorts. I saw Tino Sehgal's *Twenty Minutes for the Twentieth Century*, which I loved—it was so remedial. But the real catalyst for me was the Dan Graham retrospective at the Whitney in 2009. I had never experienced a Graham artwork in person, and I really liked the doubling and dissolution of self that happens in them. I felt completely at home. So, after seeing what happened when my body entered a work like *Performer/Audience/Mirror*, Graham became a primer for my own investigation. In the original from 1975, Graham faces an audience that is in front of a wall of mirrors. He begins to move and describes those movements to the audience for five minutes, and then he describes the audience's movements for the next five. After that, he turns his back to the audience and repeats the cycle, only this time he describes the movements as he sees them in the mirror, as opposed to directly observing them. I first reenacted that piece at Princeton University in 2010, but I added a second performer. In my version, the second performer comes on stage and starts the performance anew, just as the first performer is beginning the second phase. So you have two threads going simultaneously and overlapping each other, like singing a round.

CB: But now, for the Whitney Biennial, you're reenacting a Richard Pryor stand-up routine. Dan Graham to Richard Pryor is quite a leap, don't you think? Are they the same generation?

DW: You know, I think they are! But it's not such a leap. Graham is famous for his acerbic sense of humor. And Pryor was all about narrative allusion and shifting perceptions of character. What I like about the question is that it isn't primarily predicated on racial difference; it seems to have more to do with context and style. Or am I misunderstanding what you mean by "leap"? When I read your book *Artificial Hells: Participatory Art and the Politics of Spectatorship*, it crossed my mind that there aren't many artists of color instigating participatory work. Adrian Piper? Edgar Arceneaux? I remember William Pope.L gave a sufficiently seditious public lecture at Yale.

CB: You're right, there are very few examples in my book. In general, the fate of people of color has been to assume the role of participant in socially engaged art, rather than acting as the instigator. The only piece that really turns the tables is Adrian Piper's *Funk Lessons*, from the early eighties. I'm exaggerating, of course—there are important examples (Lorraine O'Grady, Rick Lowe, Theaster Gates)—but on the whole, especially in Europe, there is a tendency for ethnic minorities to be the visible and symbolic object of participatory artists—

DW: Like Santiago Sierra or Christoph Schlingensief.

CB: Yes. I hope that will change with a younger generation. Remind me, were you born in the seventies?

DW: I was born in 1977, but then I changed it to 1980.

CB: Of course, self-design is everything these days.

DW: Indeed. What did Cher say? "All of us invent ourselves. Some of us just have more imagination than others."

CB: Funny that you mention Cher, I always wanted you to be more rock 'n' roll. Have you ever wanted to break free of Joe Scanlan?

DW: Not at first, but when the arrangement became too stressful my first avatar resigned. She felt like she was deceiving people, and not in a good way—like pretending to be a young American artist when she met the Sheik of Sharjah. She was troubled by the politics of pretending to be someone she was not. Joe has recently been the one pushing for a break. He wants me to go it on my own. But I don't know the art world that well, so there are still things he can do that I can't.

CB: I reckon you could just go rogue: you don't need a guy to show you the way. He's pretty controlling. And you have a good CV by now. The Biennial will really help.

DW: You're right. I don't need a guy to show me the way. But I also don't see why I have to go it on my own—whatever that means—in order to be a legitimate artist. I like the fact that my association with Joe gets under people's skin. That just tells me I have something that I can work with, exploit. We've talked about devising a breakup piece, except ours would look more like a spin-off and licensing agreement than a trek across the Great Wall of China. Just two lawyers, a conference table, and the sound of pens scraping across paper.

CB: A breakup piece might be nice, but that sounds pretty bureaucratic. What would Richard Pryor do?

DW: I think I'm doing what Pryor would do. The Pryor performance is a breakup piece: it's Pryor breaking up with NBC by giving them forty minutes of uncut profanity that he knew they couldn't broadcast. But it's also Pryor dissembling himself, playing with the notion that Richard Pryor, comedian, is someone who cannot be defeated or controlled. Throughout the performance he continually slides into different characters and attitudes without ever indicating when—if ever—we're seeing the "real" Richard Pryor. It's the stand-up version of a Graham pavilion. That chimeric quality, that defiance, is what attracted me to the performance, but I wanted to push the mise en abyme even further. So instead of Richard playing Richard playing Mudbone, it's Jenn Kidwell playing Donelle Woolford playing Richard playing Richard playing Mudbone.

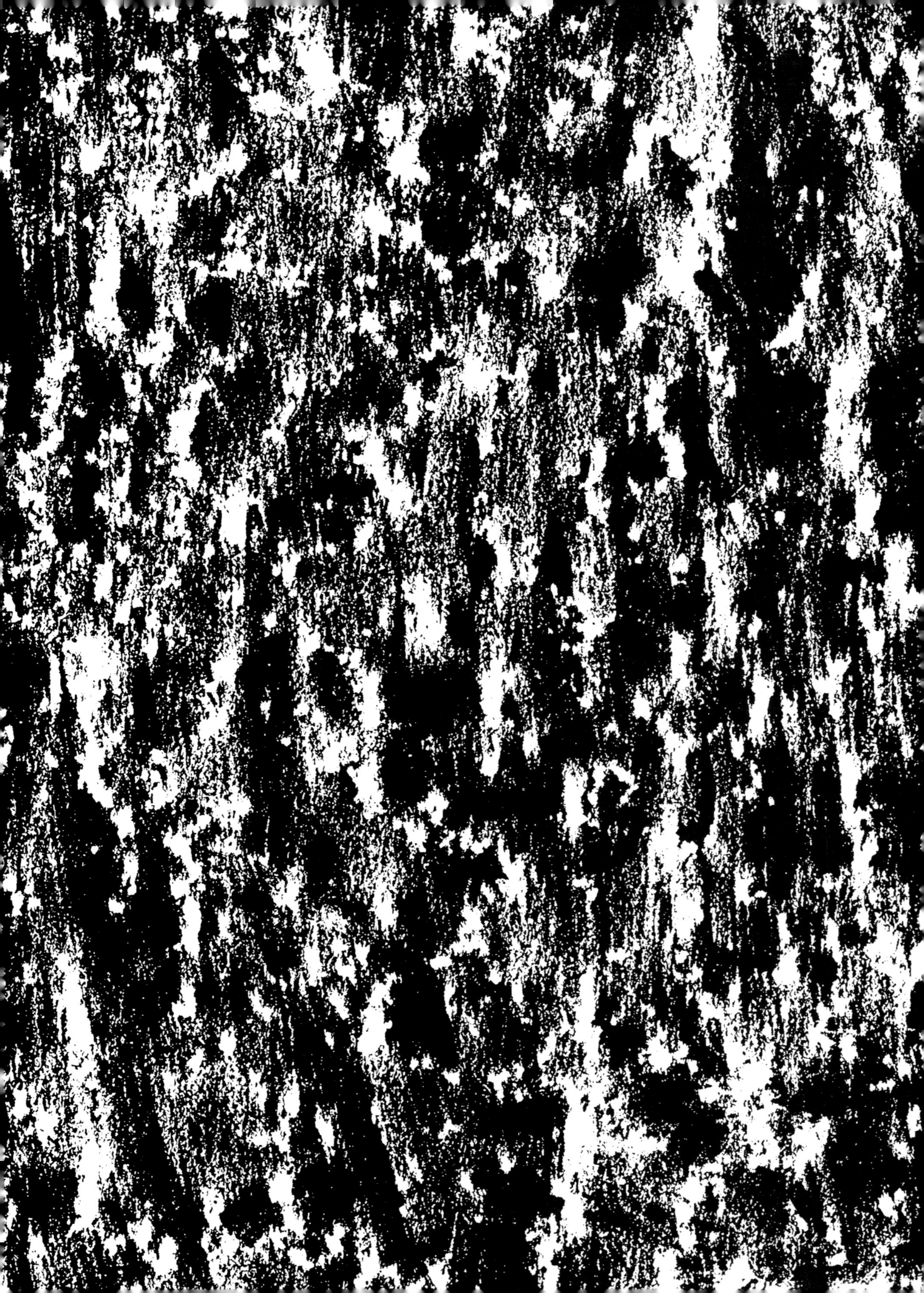

Works in the Exhibition

Academy Records and Matt Hanner
The Spectre, 2013
Vinyl record, listening station, wall drawing, 16mm film, and vitrine with ephemera
Collection of the artist

Terry Adkins
Aviarium, 2014
Polyurethane and enamel
Dimensions variable
Collection of the artist; courtesy Salon 94, New York

Etel Adnan
Champs de Petrol, 2013
Wool
62 ⅝ × 78 ¾ in. (159 × 200 cm)
Collection of the artist; courtesy Sfeir-Semler Gallery, Beirut and Hamburg

December From My Window, 1993
Ink and watercolor on paper
7 ½ × 100 in. (19.1 × 254 cm)
Collection of the artist; courtesy Callicoon Fine Arts, New York

Five Senses for One Death, 1969
Ink and watercolor on paper
11 × 255 in. (27.9 × 647.7 cm)
Collection of the artist; courtesy Callicoon Fine Arts, New York

Funeral March for the First Cosmonaut, 1968
Ink and watercolor on paper
10 × 105 in. (25.4 × 266.7 cm)
Collection of the artist; courtesy Callicoon Fine Arts, New York

Untitled, 2013
Oil on canvas
13 ¾ × 17 ¹¹⁄₁₆ in. (35 × 45 cm)
Collection of the artist; courtesy Sfeir-Semler Gallery, Beirut and Hamburg

A selection of paintings, 2013
Oil on canvas
13 ¾ × 17 ¹¹⁄₁₆ in. (35 × 45 cm) each
Collection of the artist; courtesy Sfeir-Semler Gallery, Beirut and Hamburg

A Super 8 film
Collection of the artist

Alma Allen
Untitled, 2013
Marble on oak pedestal
58 × 20 × 54 in. (147.3 × 50.8 × 137.2 cm)
Collection of the artist

Untitled, 2013
Marble on oak pedestal
25 × 20 × 14 in. (63.5 × 50.8 × 35.6 cm)
Collection of the artist

Untitled, 2013
Walnut on polished aluminum pedestal
42 × 48 × 36 in. (106.7 × 121.9 × 91.4 cm)
Collection of the artist

Ei Arakawa and Carissa Rodriguez
As-yet untitled, 2014
Installation and performance
Event dates to be announced
Collection of the artists; courtesy House of Gaga, Mexico City; Karma International; Zurich; Reena Spaulings Fine Art, New York; and Taka Ishii Gallery, Tokyo

Uri Aran
As-yet untitled, 2014
Installation and video
Dimensions variable
Collection of the artist; courtesy Gavin Brown's enterprise, New York

Robert Ashley and Alex Waterman
The Trial of Anne Opie Wehrer and Unknown Accomplices for Crimes against Humanity, 1968
Opera
Performers to be announced
Event dates to be announced

Crash, 2014
Opera with light and video installation by Alex Waterman and David Moodey; sound by Tom Hamilton
Vocalists: Gelsey Bell, Amirtha Kidambi, Brian McCorkle, Paul Pinto, Dave Ruder, and Aliza Simons
Event dates to be announced

Vidas Perfectas, 2014
Opera; eight television monitors, three projectors, piano, and audio equipment; set by Sarah Crowner and Sean Daly; lighting by David Moodey; sound: Tom Hamilton
Performers: Ned Sublette, Elio Villafranca, Peter Gordon, Elisa Santiago, and Raul de Nieves
Event dates to be announced

Michel Auder
I was looking back to see if you were looking back at me to see me looking back at you, 2014
Three-channel video installation with sound
Dimensions variable
Collection of the artist

Lisa Anne Auerbach
Self published 1
Self published 2
Self published 3, 2006–14
Knitted garments on mannequins
Dimensions variable
Collection of the artist; courtesy Gavlak Gallery, Palm Beach

Know Your Future, 2013
Wool
60 × 72 in. (152.4 × 182.9 cm)
Collection of the artist

American Megazine #2, 2014
Inkjet prints and staples, 24 pages
60 × 39 in. (152.4 × 99.1 cm)
Collection of the artist

BOOKSHELF #2, 2014
Publication, 20 pages
8 ½ × 11 in. (21.6 × 27.9 cm)
Collection of the artist

Julie Ault
Afterlife: a constellation, 2014:

Afterlife, 2014
Essay

Martin Beck (b. 1963)
Last Night, 2013
Publication
11 × 8 ½ in. (27.9 × 21.6 cm)
Published by White Columns, New York

James Benning (b. 1942)
After Blackhawk, 2013
Colored pencil on found ledger
10 × 15 ⅛ in. (25.4 × 40.1 cm)
Collection of the artist

James Benning
After Howard, 2013
House paint on plywood
12 ¾ × 38 in. (32.4 × 95.5 cm)
Collection of the artist

James Benning
Easy Rider, 2012
High-definition video, color, sound; 95 minutes
Courtesy the artist

Alfred A. Hart (1816–1908)
Stumps cut by Donner Party, c. 1868
From the series "Central Pacific Railroad"
Stereograph, 3 ¼ × 6 ¾ in. (8.3 × 17.1 cm)
Private collection

William Least Heat-Moon (b. 1939)
Event to be announced, 2014

Robert Kinmont (b. 1937)
The wings are in the paper drawer, 1972–73
Wood, paper, and Snow Goose wings
29 × 40 × 29 in. (73.7 × 101.6 × 73.7 cm)
Collection of the artist; courtesy Alexander and Bonin, New York

Liberace (1919–1987)
Mirrored passageways, date unknown

Marvin Taylor (b. 1961)
Interview with Marvin Taylor by Julie Ault, 2013

Danh Vo (b. 1975)
06.01.1945, 2013
Heliogravure
Collection of the artist

Danh Vo (b. 1975)
snowfall, northern Sierras, 1847, 2014
Heliogravure
Collection of the artist

David Wojnarowicz (1954–1992)
Untitled [Time/Money], 1988–89
Gelatin silver print
13 3/8 × 18 3/8 in. (34 × 46.7 cm)
Whitney Museum of American Art, New York; gift of Steven Johnson and Walter Sudol 2002.355

Martin Wong (1946–1999)
Closed, 1984–85
Acrylic on canvas
84 1/8 × 108 3/16 in. (213.7 × 274.8 cm)
Whitney Museum of American Art, New York; gift of Diane and Steven Jacobson 2001.237

Various documents and artifacts from the David Wojnarowicz Papers and the Martin Wong Papers
Fales Library and Special Collections, New York University; courtesy the Estate of David Wojnarowicz, the Estate of Martin Wong, and P.P.O.W. Gallery, New York

Darren Bader
Contribution not yet determined

Kevin Beasley
As-yet-untitled selection of sculptures, 2014
Apparel, polyurethane foam, plaster, cast plastic, paper pulp, and muscle rub
Collection of the artist

As-yet-untitled performance, 2014
Event dates to be announced

Gretchen Bender
People in Pain, 1988
Paint on heat-set vinyl, neon
84 × 560 × 11 in. (213.4 × 1,422.4 × 27.9 cm)
Remade by Philip Vanderhyden, 2014
Courtesy the Estate of Gretchen Bender

Stephen Berens
July 31, 2005, Afternoon
July 19, 2005, Morning
August 8, 2005, Morning
July 29, 2005, Late Afternoon, 2013
Dye-based inkjet print
24 × 34 in. (61 × 86.4 cm)
Collection of the artist

July 31, 2005, Afternoon
July 19, 2005, Morning
August 8, 2005, Morning
July 29, 2005, Late Afternoon
July 25, 2005, Late Evening
August 7, 2005, Morning
July 26, 2005, Morning
August 3, 2005, Late Afternoon
August 8, 2005, Morning
August 3, 2005, Afternoon, 2013
Dye-based inkjet print
24 × 34 in. (61 × 86.4 cm)
Collection of the artist

July 31, 2005, Afternoon
July 19, 2005, Morning
August 8, 2005, Morning
July 29, 2005, Late Afternoon
July 25, 2005, Late Evening
August 7, 2005, Morning
July 26, 2005, Morning
August 3, 2005, Late Afternoon
August 8, 2005, Morning
August 3, 2005, Afternoon
August 3, 2005, Morning (Rain)
August 3, 2005, Early Morning (Rain & Fog)
August 5, 2005, Night
July 29, 2005, Middle of the Night
August 7, 2005, Night
July 28, 2005, Night
July 28, 2005, Night (Lightning)
August 4, 2005, Night, 2013
Dye-based inkjet print
24 × 34 in. (61 × 86.4 cm)
Collection of the artist

August 4, 2005, Night
July 28, 2005, Night (Lightning)
July 28, 2005, Night
August 7, 2005, Night
July 29, 2005, Middle of the Night
August 5, 2005, Night
August 3, 2005, Early Morning (Rain & Fog)
August 3, 2005, Morning (Rain)
August 3, 2005, Afternoon
August 8, 2005, Morning
August 3, 2005, Late Afternoon
July 26, 2005, Morning
August 7, 2005, Morning
July 25, 2005, Late Evening
July 29, 2005, Late Afternoon
August 8, 2005, Morning
July 19, 2005, Morning
July 31, 2005, Afternoon, 2013
Dye-based inkjet print
24 × 34 in. (61 × 86.4 cm)
Collection of the artist

August 4, 2005, Night
July 28, 2005, Night (Lightning)
July 28, 2005, Night
August 7, 2005, Night
July 29, 2005, Middle of the Night, 2013
Dye-based inkjet print
24 × 34 in. (61 × 86.4 cm)
Collection of the artist

August 4, 2005, Night
July 28, 2005, Night (Lightning), 2013
Dye-based inkjet print
24 × 34 in. (61 × 86.4 cm)
Collection of the artist

Dawoud Bey
Barack Obama, 2008
Pigmented inkjet print
40 × 32 in. (101.6 × 81.3 cm)
Edition no. 9/25
Collection of the artist; courtesy Stephen Daiter Gallery, Chicago

Braxton McKinney and Lavone Thomas (from *The Birmingham Project*), 2012
Two pigmented inkjet prints mounted on dibond
40 × 32 in. (101.6 × 81.3 cm) each; 40 × 64 in. (101.6 × 162.6 cm) overall
Edition no. 1/6
Collection of the artist; courtesy Rena Bransten Gallery, San Francisco

Maxine Adams and Amelia Maxwell (from *The Birmingham Project*), 2012
Two pigmented inkjet prints mounted on dibond
40 × 32 in. (101.6 × 81.3 cm) each; 40 × 64 in. (101.6 × 162.6 cm) overall
Edition no. 1/6
Collection of the artist; courtesy Rena Bransten Gallery, San Francisco

Jennifer Bornstein
Untitled, 2014
16mm film, color, sound
Collection of the artist

Andrew Bujalski
Computer Chess, 2013
NTSC video, black-and-white, sound; 92 minutes
Courtesy the artist and Kino Lorber, New York

Elijah Burgher
Bachelor machine, from behind and below (Guyotat version), 2013
Colored pencil on paper
17 × 14 in. (43.2 × 35.6 cm)
Collection of the artist; courtesy Western Exhibitions, Chicago

Portrait of Jhon Balance as talisman against suicide, 2013
Colored pencil on paper
19 × 24 in. (48.3 × 61 cm)
Collection of the artist; courtesy Western Exhibitions, Chicago

Untitled, 2013–14
Acrylic on canvas drop cloth
72 × 108 in. (182.9 × 274.3 cm)
Collection of the artist; courtesy Western Exhibitions, Chicago

Untitled, 2013–14
Acrylic on canvas drop cloth
72 × 108 in. (182.9 × 274.3 cm)
Collection of the artist; courtesy Western Exhibitions, Chicago

Lucien Castaing-Taylor, Véréna Paravel, and Sensory Ethnography Lab
A selection of works by: Diana Allan, Ilisa Barbash, Lucien Castaing-Taylor, Libbie Cohn, Aryo Danusiri, Ernst Karel, Toby Kim Lee, Helen Mirra, Véréna Paravel, Xu Ruotaoi, J. P. Sniadecki, Stephanie Spray, Katherine Tygielski, Pacho Velez, Pawel Wojtasik, and Huang Xiang

Including:
Kale and Kale (2007); *Songhua* (2007); *Still Life* (2007); *Chaiqian* (2008);

Monsoon-Reflections (2008); *7 Queens* (2009); *As Long As There's Breath* (2009); *Sweetgrass* (2009); *Foreign Parts* (2010); *Heard Laboratories* (2010); *Hell Roaring Creek* (2010); *High Trail* (2010); *Untitled* (2010); *Wind Horse* (2010); *Yellow Bank* (2010); *On Broadway* (2011); *Shape of Things* (2011); *Swiss Mountain Transport Systems* (2011); *Bedding Down* (2012); *Coom Biddy* (2012); *Dead Ice* (2012); *Leviathan* (2012); *People's Park* (2012); *Breakfast* (2013); *Day Break on the Bed Ground* (2013); *He Maketh a Path to Shine After Him; One Would Think the Deep to be Hoary* (2013); *Into-the-jug (Geworfen)* (2013); *Manakamana* (2013); *Single Stream* (2013); *Still Life / Nature Morte* (2013); *Turned at the Pass* (2013); *Yumen* (2013); and *Mycological* (2014)

Sarah Charlesworth
Camera Work, 2009
Two chromogenic prints, each mounted and laminated with interlocking lacquer frames
52 × 77 ½ in. (132 × 196.9 cm) overall
Edition no. 1/8
Estate of Sarah Charlesworth; courtesy Susan Inglett Gallery, New York

Regarding Venus, 2011
Two chromogenic prints, each mounted and laminated, with interlocking lacquer frames
41 ½ × 62 ¼ in. (105.4 × 158.1 cm)
Edition no. 5/8
Estate of Sarah Charlesworth; courtesy Susan Inglett Gallery, New York

Critical Practices Inc.
LEF(t) Publications:
On Structure (2014 Whitney Biennial—Sp. Edition #1), March 1, 2014
Offset on newsprint
23 × 28 in. (58.4 × 71.1 cm)
Edition of 2000

On Appropriation (2014 Whitney Biennial—Sp. Edition #2), April 1, 2014
Offset on newsprint
23 × 28 in. (58.4 × 71.1 cm)
Edition of 2000

On Devices (2014 Whitney Biennial—Sp. Edition #3), May 1, 2014
Offset on newsprint
23 × 28 in. (58.4 × 71.1 cm)
Edition of 2000

LTR (LaTableRonde):
On the Institution (LTR—WB #1), date to be announced
Unmoderated roundtable discussion; audio recording and transcription to be made available only to participants
Thirty participants, by invitation only; 90 minutes

On Curating and Authorship (LTR—WB #2), date to be announced
Unmoderated roundtable discussion; audio recording and transcription to be made available only to participants
Thirty participants, by invitation only; 90 minutes

On Art as Apparatus (LTR—WB #3), date to be announced
Unmoderated roundtable discussion; audio recording and transcription to be made available only to participants
Thirty participants, by invitation only; 90 minutes

Matthew Deleget
Zero-Sum, 2011–
Selected artists' monographs in a vitrine
Dimensions variable
Collection of the artist

David Diao
40 Years of His Art, 2013
Acrylic and vinyl on canvas
40 × 60 in. (101.6 × 152.4 cm)
Collection of the artist

Home Again, 2013
Acrylic and oil on canvas
108 × 50 in. (274.3 × 127 cm)
Collection of the artist

Zackary Drucker and Rhys Ernst
Relationship, 2008–13
Chromogenic prints
Dimensions variable
Collection of the artists

She Gone Rogue, 2012
High-definition video, color, sound; 23 minutes
Collection of the artists

Salons at the home of Flawless Sabrina
Event dates to be announced

Paul Druecke
This Is Not A History, 2013
I. Near Here NYC, 2013
A collaboration with Donna Stonecipher
Cast bronze, paint, lacquer, and fastening hardware
36 × 24 in. (91.4 × 61 cm)
Collection of the artist

II. Sonny 86. Is it true then what they say—that we become stars in the sky when we die?, 2013
Patinated cast bronze and fastening hardware
36 × 24 in. (91.4 × 61 cm)
Collection of the artist

III. Thirty-nine Years, 2013
Patinated cast bronze and fastening hardware
6 ½ × 9 in. (16.5 × 22.9 cm)
Collection of the artist

Fabricated by Vanguard Sculpture Services, Milwaukee, WI

Jimmie Durham
Choose Any Three, 1989
Carved and painted wood, metal, and glass
99 ⅕ × 49 ⅕ × 48 in. (252 × 125 × 122 cm)
Collection of the artist; courtesy Kurimanzutto, Mexico City

Rochelle Feinstein
Toy George et al, 2013
Video, color, sound; approx. 9 minutes
Collection of the artist; courtesy On Stellar Rays, New York

Radamés "Juni" Figueroa
Breaking the Ice, 2014
An installation in the Whitney Museum Sculpture Court
Dimensions variable
Collection of the artist

Morgan Fisher
Ro(Ro(Room)om)om, 2014
Drywall on metal studs
100 × 109 ⅛ × 116 15/16 in. (254 × 277.2 × 297 cm)
Collection of the artist; courtesy Bortolami Gallery, New York; International Art Objects Galleries, Los Angeles; Galerie Buchholz, Cologne and Berlin; and Maureen Paley, London

Louise Fishman
Crossing the Rubicon, 2012
Oil on linen
66 × 57 in. (167.6 × 144.8 cm)
Collection of the artist; courtesy Cheim & Read, New York

Ristretto, 2013
Oil on linen
70 × 60 in. (177.8 × 152.4 cm)
Collection of the artist; courtesy Cheim & Read, New York

Victoria Fu
Bel'e Captive I, 2013
Digital video projection, color, sound; 6 minutes
Collection of the artist

Gaylen Gerber with David Hammons, Sherrie Levine, and Trevor Shimizu
Gaylen Gerber with Trevor Shimizu
Backdrop/Untitled, n.d., Untitled, n.d., n.d.
Latex on canvas, oil on canvas, and oil on linen
208 × 528 in. (528.3 × 1,341.1 cm)

Trevor Shimizu (b. 1978)
Untitled, n.d.
Oil on canvas
75 × 72 in. (190.5 × 182.9 cm)
Collection of Jessica Macias

Trevor Shimizu
Untitled, n.d.
Oil on linen
76 ½ × 72 ½ in. (194.3 × 184.2 cm)
Collection of the artist; courtesy 47 Canal, New York

Gaylen Gerber with David Hammons and Sherrie Levine
Backdrop/Untitled, 2010, Broad Stripe: 1, 1985, n.d.
Latex paint on canvas, mixed media, and casein and wax on mahogany
208 × 528 in. (528.3 × 1,341.1 cm)

David Hammons (b. 1943)
Untitled, 2010
Mixed media
64 × 46 in. (162.6 × 116.8 cm)
Collection of Liz and Eric Lefkofsky

Sherrie Levine (b. 1947)
Broad Stripe: 1, 1985
Casein and wax on mahogany
24 × 20 in. (61 × 50.8 cm)
Private collection

Jeff Gibson
Metapoetaestheticism, 2013
High-definition video, color, sound; 5:30 minutes
Collection of the artist

Tony Greene curated by Richard Hawkins and Catherine Opie
Exhausted Autumn, 1988
Mixed media
13 ½ × 15 ½ in. (34.3 × 39.4 cm)
Collection of Ray Morales, from the estate of Norm MacNeil

His Broken Lines, 1988
Mixed media
25 ½ × 29 ¾ in. (64.8 × 75.6 cm)
Collection of Ray Morales, from the estate of Norm MacNeil

His Grasping Hands, 1988
Mixed media
18 ½ × 21 ½ in. (47 × 54.6 cm)
Collection of Jinger Heffner

"...faithful...", 1989
Mixed media
14 × 14 in. (35.6 × 35.6 cm)
Collection of Millie Wilson

His Inversion, 1989
Mixed media
18 ½ × 21 ½ in. (47 × 54.6 cm)
Collection of Ray Morales, from the estate of Norm MacNeil

His Puerile Gestures, 1989
Mixed media
25 ½ × 29 ¾ in. (64.8 × 75.6 cm)
Collection of Ray Morales, from the estate of Norm MacNeil

Opinion of Silence, 1989
Mixed media
18 ½ × 21 ½ in. (47 × 54.6 cm)
Collection of Ray Morales, from the estate of Norm MacNeil

Untitled (Matt), 1990
Mixed media
19 ½ × 22 ½ in. (49.5 × 57.2 cm)
Collection of Monica Majoli

Untitled (Red Pour), 1990
Mixed media
15 ½ × 16 ¼ in. (39.4 × 41.3 cm)
Collection of Fred Fehlau

Untitled (Wes), 1990
Mixed media
19 ½ × 22 ½ in. (49.5 × 57.2 cm)
Collection of Jim Isermann

Untitled (yellow pour), 1990
Mixed media
15 ½ × 16 ¼ in. (39.4 × 41.3 cm)
Collection of Ray Morales, from the estate of Norm MacNeil

Catherine Opie (b. 1961)
Untitled #1 (Tony's Studio), 1990
Pigmented inkjet print
12 × 12 in. (30.5 × 30.5 cm)
Collection of the artist; courtesy Regen Projects, Los Angeles

Joseph Grigely
The Gregory Battcock Archive, 2009–14
Various inscribed and printed documents from Gregory Battcock's personal archive, printed captions, seven vitrines, five framed posters, and one painting
Dimensions variable
Collection of the artist

Miguel Gutierrez
Age & Beauty Part 1: Mid-Career Artist/Suicide Note or &:–/, 2014
Performance
Event dates to be announced

Karl Haendel
As-yet untitled, 2014
Installation of drawings on painted wall
Dimensions variable
Collection of the artist; courtesy Susanne Vielmetter Los Angeles Projects

Philip Hanson
A Divine Image: Pink Light (Blake), 2013
Oil on canvas
28 × 28 in. (71.1 × 71.1 cm)
Collection of the artist; courtesy Corbett vs. Dempsey, Chicago

A Divine Image: Seraphim (Blake), 2013
Oil on canvas
28 × 28 in. (71.1 × 71.1 cm)
Collection of the artist; courtesy Corbett vs. Dempsey, Chicago

After great pain (Dickinson), 2013
Oil on canvas
30 × 20 in. (76.2 × 50.8 cm)
Collection of the artist; courtesy Corbett vs. Dempsey, Chicago

Jonn Herschend
Discussion Questions for Today's Screening, 2014
PowerPoint presentation converted to video
Collection of the artist

Sheila Hicks
Pillar of Inquiry/Supple Column, 2013–14
Linen, cotton, bamboo, silk, and strands of recycled fiber
210 × 48 × 48 in. (533.4 × 121.9 × 121.9 cm)
Collection of the artist; courtesy Sikkema Jenkins & Co., New York

Channa Horwitz
A selection of drawings
Estate of Channa Horwitz; courtesy François Ghebaly Gallery, Los Angeles

HOWDOYOUSAY-YAMINAFRICAN?
Good Stock On The Dimension Floor, 2013
High-definition video, color, sound; 37 minutes
Collection of the artist

Susan Howe
From *Tom Tit Tot*, 2013
Letterpress prints
12 × 9 in. (30.5 × 22.9 cm) each
Collection of the artist

Jacqueline Humphries
Untitled, 2014
Oil on canvas
Approx. 100 × 111 in. (254 × 281.9 cm)
Collection of the artist; courtesy Greene Naftali Gallery, New York

Gary Indiana
Untitled, 2014
Silk curtains, LED curtain, and projection
Dimensions variable
Collection of the artist

Doug Ischar
come lontano, 2010
NTSC video, color, sound; 21:07 minutes
Collection of the artist

Alone With You, 2011
NTSC video, color, sound; 18:13 minutes
Collection of the artist

Tristes Tarzan, 2013
NTSC video, color, sound; 20:55 minutes
Collection of the artist

Carol Jackson
BLEHH, 2011
Leather, enamel, brass, and acrylic
80 × 55 × 5 in. (203.2 × 139.7 × 12.7 cm)
Collection of the artist

Slip, 2013
Wood, acrylic, papier mâché, and inkjet print
34 × 17 × 13 in.
(86.4 × 43.2 × 33 cm)
Collection of the artist

Youthful Beast, 2013
Wood, acrylic, papier mâché, and inkjet print
35 × 32 × 16 in.
(88.9 × 81.3 × 40.6 cm)
Collection of the artist

Pandemonium, 2013
Wood, acrylic, papier mâché, and inkjet print
23 × 18 × 19 in.
(58.4 × 45.7 × 48.3 cm)
Collection of the artist

Travis Jeppesen
16 Sculptures, 2014
Records, headphones, sleeping masks, chairs, and media players
Dimensions variable
Collection of the artist

16 Sculptures, 2014
Book
Published by Publication Studio

Reading of *The Suiciders*, 2014 (published by Semiotext(e), 2013)
Event date to be announced

Alex Jovanovich
The Internal Constitution of Stars, 2010
35mm slide installation
Collection of the artist

Katharine, 1982, 2013
35mm slide installation
Collection of the artist

Flowers, 2013
35mm slide installation
Collection of the artist

Angie Keefer
Fountain, 2014
Commodities futures indexes data and projector
Collection of the artist

Ben Kinmont
Sshhh, 2002–
Mixed media
Collection of the artist; courtesy Air de Paris, Paris

Rubber stamp used for the making of Sshhh, n.d.
Stamp
The Museum of Modern Art, New York; Fund for the Twenty-First Century

Shio Kusaka
Selection of pots
Dimensions variable
Collection of the artist; courtesy Blum & Poe, Los Angeles; Shane Campbell Gallery, Chicago; and Anton Kern Gallery, New York

Yve Laris Cohen
As-yet untitled, 2014
Wall slab and performance
Wall slab, 62 × 72 × 9 in.
(157.5 × 182.9 × 22.9 cm)
Collection of the artist

Chris Larson
Heavy Rotation, 2011
Video, color, sound; 14:44 minutes
Collection of the artist

Diego Leclery
Untitled, 2013
Performance
Event date to be announced

Zoe Leonard
945 Madison Avenue, 2014
Lens and darkened room
210 × 300 × 632 in. (533.4 × 762 × 1,605.3 cm)
Collection of the artist; courtesy Murray Guy, New York, and Galerie Gisela Capitain, Cologne

Tony Lewis
ceho (ceho), 2013
Graphite pencil, graphite powder, and tape on paper
84 × 60 in. (213.4 × 152.4 cm)
Collection of the artist; courtesy Shane Campbell Gallery, Chicago

Peoplecol, 2013
Graphite pencil, graphite powder, and tape on paper
84 × 60 in. (213.4 × 152.4 cm)
Collection of the artist; courtesy Shane Campbell Gallery, Chicago

Pam Lins and Amy Sillman
I Placed a Jar in Tennessee, 2013–14
Plywood, oil paint, plaster, medium-density fiberboard, unglazed stoneware, inkjet on canvas, and rice paper
Approx. 72 × 45 × 45 in.
(182.9 × 114.3 × 114.3 cm)
Collection of the artists

Fred Lonidier
Health and Safety Game, 1976
Text and photographic panels, and video, black-and-white, sound; 20 minutes
Collection of the artist; courtesy ESSEX STREET, New York

N.A.F.T.A. #16A/B
"'N.A.F.T.A....' Returns to Tijuana,"/"'T.L.C....' Regresa a Tijuana," 2005
Two photographic panels
32 × 120 in. (81.3 × 304.8 cm) each
Collection of the artist; courtesy ESSEX STREET, New York

Untitled installation of T-shirts
Dimensions variable
Collection of the artist; courtesy ESSEX STREET, New York

Ken Lum
Midway Shopping Plaza, 2014
Powder-coated aluminum and enameled plexiglass
204 × 150 in. (518.2 × 381 cm)
Collection of the artist

Shana Lutker
Chapter 2: Constant Fenetre, 2013
Mixed media
120 × 120 × 120 in.
(304.8 × 304.8 × 304.8 cm)
Collection of the artist; courtesy Susanne Vielmetter Los Angeles Projects

Dashiell Manley
The Great Train Robbery (Scene 3 version C), 2013
Gouache, ink, watercolor, linen, wood, acrylic sheet, lighting gels, paper, tape, and steel, five units
Three units, 72 ½ × 96 ½ × 2 in.
(184.2 × 245.1 × 5.1 cm) each; two units, 73 × 96 ½ × 2 in.
(185.4 × 245.1 × 5.1 cm) each
102 × 288 × 120 in. (259 × 731.5 × 304.8 cm) overall
Collection of the artist

The Great Train Robbery (Scene 3), 2013
Two-channel video installation: JPEGs transferred to digital video, color, silent; 8:35 minutes
Edition no. 2/5 + 2 APs
Collection of the artist; courtesy Redling Fine Art, Los Angeles, and Jessica Silverman Gallery, San Francisco

John Mason
Vertical Torque, White, 1997
Ceramic
53 ¾ × 12 × 12 in. (149.2 × 30.5 × 30.5 cm)
Collection of Andrew Franklin

Spear Form, Soft White, 1999
Ceramic
66 × 28 × 28 in. (167.6 × 71.1 × 71.1 cm)
Collection of the artist; courtesy David Kordansky, Los Angeles

Blue Figure, 2002
Ceramic
59 × 23.75 × 23.75 in.
(149.9 × 60.3 × 60.3 cm)
Collection of the artist; courtesy David Kordansky, Los Angeles

Tile Wall, 2010
Ceramic
70 × 86 × 1 in. (177.8 × 218.4 × 2.5 cm)
Collection of the artist; courtesy David Kordansky, Los Angeles

Works in the Exhibition

Keith Mayerson
My Family, 2013
Oil on linen
56 × 70 in. (142.2 × 177.8 cm)
Collection of the artist

Selection of additional paintings
Collection of the artist

Suzanne McClelland
Untitled (36-24-36 a winning hand), 2013
Charcoal, dry pigment, polymer, and spray paint on linen
84 × 72 in. (213.4 × 182.9 cm)
Collection of the artist; courtesy Shane Campbell Gallery, Chicago, and Team Gallery, New York

Untitled Pair; Steve and John (Ideal Proportions), 2013
Charcoal, dry pigment, polymer, and spray paint on linen
84 × 144 in. (213.4 × 365.8 cm)
Collection of the artist; courtesy Shane Campbell Gallery, Chicago, and Team Gallery, New York

Dave McKenzie
Camera, 2012
Video, color, sound; 4:55 minutes
Collection of the artist

The Beautiful One Has Come, 2012
Video, color, sound; 5:48 minutes
Collection of the artist

Bjarne Melgaard
Untitled (Whitney Biennial), 2014
Mixed-media installation
Dimensions variable
Collection of the artist; courtesy Gavin Brown's enterprise, New York

Rebecca Morris
Selection of paintings
Collection of the artist

Joshua Mosley
Jeu de Paume, 2014
Mixed-media animation
Collection of the artist

My Barbarian
Adaptation of 'The Mother' by Bertolt Brecht, 2013
Performance on a triangular stage
Running time: approx. 45 minutes
Collection of the artists; courtesy Susanne Vielmetter Los Angeles Projects

Before We Destroy Them All (And That Will Be Soon), 2013
Oil stick and charcoal on craft paper
18 × 24 in. (45.7 × 61 cm)
Collection of the artists; courtesy Susanne Vielmetter Los Angeles Projects

Butcher, 2013
Papier mâché
11 × 6 ¾ × 5 in. (27.9 × 17.2 × 12.7 cm)
Collection of Robert W. and Anne Conn

Cashier, 2013
Papier mâché
10 ¼ × 7 ¼ × 4 ¾ in.
(26 × 18.4 × 12.1 cm)
Collection of Robert W. and Anne Conn

City of Tver, 2013
Estate Kitchen (Butcher), 2013
Factory (Suklinov Works), 2013
Hectograph, 2013
He Went To The Wall Built By Men Just Like Him, 2013
Home of the Teacher I, 2013
Home of the Teacher III, 2013
Home of the Teacher IV, 2013
Household II, 2013
Household II, 2013
Household III, 2013
How?, 2013
I Have A Son Who Is Needed, 2013
Illyitch, 2013
Illyitch's Mother, 2013
In Praise of Communism, 2013
In Praise of the Common Cause, 2013
Landlady's Visit, 2013
Landless Peasant I, 2013
Landless Peasant II, 2013
Landless Peasant III, 2013
Lenin to the Women: Show That You Can Fight, 2013
Mask, 2013
Mother and Baby with Flowers (After Cassatt), 2013
Muratov Works, 2013
Nothing You Do Does Anything, 2013
Our Comrade, 2013
Patriotic Copper Depot I, 2013
Patriotic Copper Depot II, 2013
Patriotic Copper Depot II, 2013
Printing Press II, 2013
Printshop at Night, 2013
Prison I, 2013
Prison II, 2013
Store I, 2013
Store II, 2013
Street, 2013
Your Son Has Been Shot, 2013
Oil stick on craft paper
18 × 24 in. (45.7 × 61 cm) each
Collection of the artists; courtesy Susanne Vielmetter Los Angeles Projects

Foreman, 2013
Papier mâché
10 ¾ × 10 × 4 ½ in.
(27.3 × 25.4 × 11.4 cm)
Collection of Robert W. and Anne Conn

Gatekeeper, 2013
Papier mâché
11 ¼ × 8 × 4 ½ in.
(28.6 × 20.3 × 11.4 cm)
Collection of Robert W. and Anne Conn

Masks, 2013
Oil stick and charcoal on craft paper
18 × 24 in. (45.7 × 61 cm)
Collection of the artists; courtesy Susanne Vielmetter Los Angeles Projects

Mimic 1, 2013
Papier mâché and oil stick
10 ½ × 6 ½ × 4 ½ in.
(26.7 × 16.5 × 11.4 cm)
Collection of the artists; courtesy Susanne Vielmetter Los Angeles Projects

Mimic 2, 2013
Papier mâché and oil stick
9 ½ × 5 ¾ × 4 ¼ in.
(24.1 × 14.6 × 10.8 cm)
Collection of the artists; courtesy Susanne Vielmetter Los Angeles Projects

Mimic 3, 2013
Papier mâché and oil stick
10 ½ × 6 × 4 ½ in.
(26.7 × 15.2 × 11.4 cm)
Collection of the artists; courtesy Susanne Vielmetter Los Angeles Projects

Peasant, 2013
Papier mâché
11 × 6 ¾ × 5 in.
(27.9 × 17.2 × 12.7 cm)
Collection of Robert W. and Anne Conn

Prison Guard, 2013
Papier mâché
11 ¼ × 9 × 4 ½ in.
(28.6 × 22.9 × 11.4 cm)
Collection of Robert W. and Anne Conn

Policeman, 2013
Papier mâché
10 ½ × 10 ½ × 4 ½ in.
(26.7 × 26.7 × 11.4 cm)
Collection of Robert W. and Anne Conn

Shopper, 2013
Papier mâché
10 ½ × 6 ¼ × 4 ½ in.
(26.7 × 15.9 × 11.4 cm)
Collection of Robert W. and Anne Conn

Unemployed Man, 2013
Papier mâché
10 × 8 ½ × 4 ½ in.
(25.4 × 21.6 × 11.4 cm)
Collection of Robert W. and Anne Conn

Universal Declaration of Infantile Anxiety Situations Reflected in the Creative Impulse, 2013
High-definition video, color, sound; 29 minutes
Edition of 6 + 3 AP
Collection of the artists; courtesy Susanne Vielmetter Los Angeles Projects

Woman in Black, 2013
Papier mâché
10 ½ × 7 ½ × 4 ½ in.
(26.7 × 19.1 × 11.4 cm)
Collection of Robert W. and Anne Conn

Works in the Exhibition

Dona Nelson
Okie Dokie, 2008
Dyed cheesecloth and acrylic on canvas
78 × 83 in. (198.1 × 210.8 cm)
Collection of the artist; courtesy Thomas Erben Gallery, New York

String Beings, 2013
Acrylic and painted string on canvas
Approx. 82 × 82 in. (208.3 × 208.3 cm)
Collection of the artist; courtesy Thomas Erben Gallery, New York

Ken Okiishi
gesture/data, 2013
Oil on flat-screen television and video transferred to USB flash drive, color, sound
35 5/16 × 21 × 3 11/16 in. (89.7 × 53.3 × 9.4 cm)
Collection of the artist; courtesy Reena Spaulings Fine Art, New York

gesture/data, 2013
Oil on flat-screen television and video transferred to USB flash drive, color, sound
35 5/16 × 21 × 3 11/16 in. (89.7 × 53.3 × 9.4 cm)
Collection of the artist; courtesy Reena Spaulings Fine Art, New York

gesture/data, 2013
Oil on flat-screen television and video transferred to USB flash drive, color, sound
35 5/16 × 21 × 3 11/16 in. (89.7 × 53.3 × 9.4 cm)
Collection of the artist; courtesy Reena Spaulings Fine Art, New York

gesture/data, 2013
Oil on two flat-screen televisions and video transferred to USB flash drives, color, sound
35 5/16 × 21 × 3 11/16 in. (89.7 × 53.3 × 9.4 cm) each
Collection of Pedro Barbosa

Pauline Oliveros
A performance
Event dates to be determined

Joel Otterson
Rags to Riches, 1993–2013
Patchwork and hand-quilted fabrics
84 × 72 in. (213.4 × 182.9 cm)
Collection of the artist

84 Bottoms Up, 2013
84 vintage crystal and glass goblets, steel, metal chain, aluminum, and electrical parts
76 × 22 × 22 in. (193 × 55.9 × 55.9 cm)
Collection of the artist

187 Bottoms Up, 2013
187 vintage crystal and glass goblets, steel, metal chain, copper and brass wire, and electrical parts
84 × 28 × 28 in. (213.4 × 71.1 × 71.1 cm)
Collection of the artist

Camp, 2013
Lace, copper plumbing pipe and fittings, redwood, bamboo, and tatami mats
84 × 144 × 84 in. (213.4 × 365.8 × 213.4 cm)
Collection of the artist

Curtains Laced with Diamonds Dear for You, 2013
Mixed media
140 × 96 × 1 in. (355.6 × 243.8 × 2.5 cm)
Collection of the artist

Laura Owens
A painting
Collection of the artist; courtesy Gavin Brown's enterprise, New York

Paul P.
Untitled, 2013
Ink on paper
8 ½ × 11 ¾ in. (21.6 × 29.8 cm)
Collection of the artist; courtesy Maureen Paley, London, and Broadway 1602, New York

Untitled, 2013
Ink on paper
8 ½ × 11 ¾ in. (21.6 × 29.8 cm)
Collection of the artist

Untitled, 2013
Ink on paper
8 ½ × 11 ¾ in. (21.6 × 29.8 cm)
Collection of the artist

Writing Table for Nancy Mitford (Blitz era), 2013
Mahogany
Two parts, 29 5/8 × 35 ½ × 16 ¼ in. (75.2 × 90.2 × 41.3 cm) and 17 × 13 × 13 in. (43.2 × 33 × 33 cm)
Collection of the artist

taisha paggett
A performance
Event dates to be announced

Charlemagne Palestine
Stairway Song, 2013
Twelve-channel sound installation on stairwell landings
Collection of the artist

Public Collectors
Listening station with concerts recorded by Malachi Ritscher and Ritscher-related photographs, posters, personal objects, and ephemera
Dimensions variable
Collections of Creative Audio Archive at Experimental Sound Studio; Dick and Betty Ann Ritscher; Angeline and Mark Evans; John Corbett; Joeff Davis; David Lester and Jean Smith of Mecca Normal; Fred Lonberg-Holm; Brent Gutzeit; Metal Rouge (Helga Fassonaki and Andrew Scott); Agnieszka Czeblakow; Lampo (Alisa Wolfson and Andrew Fenchel); Bill Meyer; Reuben Moore; and Marc Fischer

Sara Greenberger Rafferty
Mono, 2014
Digital video, color, sound; 4 minutes
Collection of the artist; courtesy Rachel Uffner Gallery, New York

Steve Reinke with Jessie Mott
Rib Gets In the Way (Final Thoughts, Series Three), 2014
Digital video, color, sound; 53 minutes
Collection of the artists

David Robbins
Television Commercial for The Suburban, 2010
Video, color, silent; 45 seconds
Collection of the artist

Bookcase for Concrete Comedy: An Alternative History of Twentieth-Century Comedy, 2013
Wood and Concrete Comedy books (published by Pork Salad Press and Greene Naftali Gallery, New York, 2011)
53 × 48 × 10 in. (134.6 × 121.9 × 25.4 cm)
Collection of the artist

Open-Air Writing Desk, 2013
Wood, glass, and bronze
144 × 36 × 110 in. (365.8 × 91.4 × 279.4 cm)
Collection of the artist

Public Service Announcement: Independent Imagination, 2013
Video, color, sound; 70 seconds
Collection of the artist

Television Commercial for The Poor Farm, 2013
Video, color, sound; 1 minute
Collection of the artist

Television Commercial (Gavin Brown at The Green Gallery), 2013
Video, black-and-white, sound; 57 seconds
Collection of the artist

Sterling Ruby
Basin Theology/Talwin + Ritalin, 2013
Ceramic
28 ¼ × 45 × 45 in. (71.8 × 114.3 × 114.3 cm)
Collection of the artist; courtesy Hauser & Wirth

Basin Theology/The Poacher, 2013
Ceramic
20 ½ × 40 × 43 in. (52.1 × 101.6 × 109.2 cm)
Collection of the artist; courtesy Hauser & Wirth

Basin Theology/The Poacher 2, 2013
Ceramic
32 × 36 × 41 in. (81.3 × 91.4 × 104.1 cm)
Collection of the artist; courtesy Hauser & Wirth

Miljohn Ruperto
Janus, 2014
Digital video, color, sound; 3:30 minutes
Animation by Aimée de Jongh (b. 1988)
Collection of the artist; courtesy Koenig & Clinton, New York, and Thomas Solomon Gallery, Los Angeles

Miljohn Ruperto and Ulrik Heltoft (b. 1973)
Voynich Botanical Studies, Specimen 17v, Leto, 2014
Gelatin silver prints
19 11⁄16 × 15 ¾ in. (50 × 40 cm) each
Collection of the artists; courtesy Koenig & Clinton, New York; Thomas Solomon Gallery, Los Angeles; Andersen's Contemporary, Copenhagen; and Wilfried Lentz, Rotterdam

Jacolby Satterwhite
Reifying Desire 6—Island of Desire, 2014
High-definition digital 3-D animation video, color, sound; run-time unknown
Collection of the artist; courtesy OHWOW, Los Angeles, and Mallorca Landings Gallery, Pa!ma De Mallorca, Spain

As-yet-untitled performance
Event dates to be determined
Collection of the artist; courtesy OHWOW, Los Angeles, and Mallorca Landings Gallery, Palma De Mallorca, Spain

Allan Sekula
Sketches from artist's notebook "PF poland 2009 (1)," 2009
Ink, correction fluid, and marker on paper
3 ½ × 5 ½ in. (9 × 14 cm) each
Estate of Allan Sekula; courtesy Christopher Grimes Gallery, Santa Monica

Peter Schuyff
Sans Papier, 2004–06
Carved pencils and sticks
Dimensions variable
Collection of the artist

Semiotext(e)
Sylvère Lotringer interviewing Jack Smith, 1978. Edited by Robert Dewhurst and Hedi El Kholti. Vinyl record, 60 minutes

"F as in Friendship," 1996. Claire Parnet interviewing Gilles Deleuze, excerpted from *Gilles Deleuze From A to Z*, 1996. Directed by Pierre-André Boutang. Video, color, sound, 16 minutes

The Itinerary of Catastrophe, 2008. Sylvère Lotringer interviewing Paul Virilio. Edited by Dana Duff and Iris Klein. Video, color, sound, 29 minutes

As-yet untitled, 2014
Installation of publications published on the occasion of the 2014 Whitney Biennial
Installation design by Jason Yates

Hors Série 1: Simone Weil: *Note on the Abolition of All Political Parties.* Translated by Ames Hodges

Hors Série 2: Pierre Guyotat: *Independence.* Translated by Noura Wedell

Hors Série 3: Julio Cortazar: *Fantomas Versus the Multinational Vampires.* Translated by David Kurnick

Hors Série 4: Tony Duvert: *The Undiscoverable Reading.* Translated by Bruce Benderson

Hors Série 5: Jean Baudrillard: *Architecture: Truth or Radicalism?* Translated by David L. Sweet

Hors Série 6: Emmanuelle Guattari: *I, Little Asylum.* Translated by E. C. Belli

0: Maurizio Lazzarato: *Marcel Duchamp and the Refusal of Work.* Translated by Joshua David Jordan

1: Sylvère Lotringer: *The Miserables.* Translated by Ames Hodges

2: Lynne Tillman: *Men and Apparitions (Tales from the Picture People)*

3: Dodie Bellamy: *The Beating of Our Hearts*

4: Christian Marrazi: *The Linguistic Nature Of Money And Finance.* Translated by Isabella Bertoletti, James Cascaito, and Andrea Casson

5: Bruce Benderson: *Against Marriage*

6: Ariana Reines: *The Origin of the World*

7: Franco "BIFO" Berardi: *Neuro-totalitarianism in Technomaya*

8: Eileen Myles: *Street Retreat*

9: John Kelsey: *Ditch Plains*

10: Jennifer Doyle: *Campus Security*

11: Sergio Gonzalez Rodriguez: *Extreme Violence as Spectacle: I Within.* Translated by Marco Vera

12: Gary Indiana: *A Significant Loss of Human Life*

13: William E. Jones: *But Our Life Depends on What's Real*

14: Abdellah Taïa: *Arabs Are No Longer Afraid.* Translated by Noura Wedell

15: Bruce Hainley: *Art & Culture*

16: Veronica Gonzalez Peña: *So Far From God*

17: Jim Fletcher & Harry Mathews: *Week One*

18: Mark von Schlegell: *Fainnie Azul*

19: Chris Kraus: *Lost Properties*

20: Jackie Wang: *Against Innocence*

21: Henri Lefebvre: *The Missing Pieces.* Translated by David L. Sweet

Amy Sillman
A painting
Oil on canvas
Collection of the artist

Valerie Snobeck and Catherine Sullivan
Image of Limited Good, 2014
Mixed-media installation
Collection of the artists

A. L. Steiner
More Real Than Reality Itself, 2014
Multichannel video installation, color, sound; run time unknown
Collection of the artist

Emily Sundblad
As-yet-untitled video, 2014
Collection of the artist; courtesy The Green Gallery, Milwaukee

Ricky Swallow
Chair Study/Ripple (soot), 2013
Patinated bronze
25 × 9 × 2½ in. (63.5 × 22.9 × 6.4 cm)
Collection of the artist

Reversed Pitcher 1, 2013
Patinated bronze
10 × 6 × 7 ½ in. (25.4 × 15.2 × 19.1 cm)
Collection of the artist

Skewed Arches/Tall 1, 2013
Patinated bronze
36 × 9 × 7 in. (91.4 × 22.9 × 17.8 cm)
Collection of the artist

Stair with Contents, 2013
Patinated bronze
22 × 35 × 22 in. (55.9 × 88.9 × 55.9 cm)
Collection of the artist

Z Sculpture with String, 2013
Patinated bronze
3 ½ × 10 × 5 in. (8.9 × 25.4 × 12.7 cm)
Collection of the artist

Tony Tasset
Artists Monument, 2014
400,000 names etched on acrylic panels mounted on steel and wood
96 × 960 × 96 in. (243.8 × 2,438.4 × 243.8 cm)
Installation at Pier 45, Hudson River Park
Collection of the artist; courtesy Kavi Gupta Gallery, Chicago

Sergei Tcherepnin
As-yet untitled, 2014
Light fixtures, transducers, amplifier, and high-definition media player
Dimensions variable
Collection of the artist; courtesy Murray Guy, New York

Triple Canopy
Pointing Machines, 2014
Eighteenth- and nineteenth-century artworks and furniture, color transparencies, photographs, 3-D printed furniture, handmade furniture reproduction by Frank C. Rhodes, and a sound work created with C. Spencer Yeh
Dimensions variable
Collection of the artist

Pedro Vélez
#Barrier, 2014
Installation of photographic banners, photocopies, and acrylic paint near the High Line
Collection of the artist

#CuratingReviews, 2014
Three limited-edition postcards that will be distributed without charge to the public
4 × 6 in. (10.2 × 15.2 cm) each
Collection of the artist

Charline von Heyl
Folk Tales, 2013
Acrylic, ink, wax, charcoal, and collage on paper; thirty-six works
24 × 19 in. (61 × 48.3 cm) each
Collection of the artist; courtesy Petzel Gallery, New York

David Foster Wallace
Federer as Religious Experience (The New York Times, August 20, 2006), interview notes, n.d.
Two-page manuscript
11 × 8 ½ in. (27.9 × 21.6 cm) each
Harry Ransom Center, The University of Texas at Austin

The Pale King materials, "Butterfly" notebook, notes and clippings, n.d.
Manuscript notebook
9 × 6 ⅛ in. (22.9 × 15.6 cm) closed
Harry Ransom Center, The University of Texas at Austin

The Pale King materials, handwritten drafts, pink kitten "Scenes" notebook, n.d.
Manuscript notebook
11 ½ × 8 ¼ in. (29.2 × 21 cm) closed
Harry Ransom Center, The University of Texas at Austin

The Pale King materials, handwritten "Roster of Parts," Rugrats™, n.d.
Manuscript notebook
11 ¼ × 8 ¼ in. (28.6 × 21 cm) closed
Harry Ransom Center, The University of Texas at Austin

The Pale King materials, "Midwesternisms" notebook, n.d.
Manuscript notebook
10 ½ × 8 ¼ in. (26.7 × 21 cm) closed
Harry Ransom Center, The University of Texas at Austin

Dan Walsh
Outfit, 2013
Acrylic on canvas
70 × 70 in. (177.8 × 177.8 cm)
Collection of the artist; courtesy Paula Cooper Gallery, New York

Threshold, 2013
Acrylic on canvas
70 × 70 in. (177.8 × 177.8 cm)
Collection of the artist; courtesy Paula Cooper Gallery, New York

Donelle Woolford
Dick Joke (redd foxx), 2013
Ink, paper, and polyvinyl acetate on gessoed linen
68 × 44 in. (172.7 × 111.8 cm)
Collection of the artist

Dick Joke (yankees), 2013
Ink, paper, and polyvinyl acetate on gessoed linen
68 × 44 in. (172.7 × 111.8 cm)
Collection of the artist

Dick's Last Stand, 2012
Performance
39 minutes
Event dates and venues to be announced
Collection of the artist

Molly Zuckerman-Hartung
As-yet-untitled painting, 2013
Collection of the artist; courtesy Corbett vs. Dempsey, Chicago

List current as of December 13, 2013

Contributors

Alexander Alberro (p. 367) is an art historian and critic who lives in New York and Philadelphia. He is the Virginia Bloedel Wright Professor of Modern and Contemporary Art at Barnard College and Columbia University.

Negar Azimi (p. 33) is a writer and senior editor of *Bidoun*.

Dan Beachy-Quick (p. 357) is the author of the poetry collection *Circle's Apprentice* (2011), *Wonderful Investigations: Essays, Meditations, Tales* (2012), and the novel *An Impenetrable Screen of Purest Sky* (2013). He is a Monfort Professor at Colorado State University, where he teaches in the MFA creative writing program.

Naomi Beckwith (p. 125) is the Marilyn and Larry Fields Curator at the Museum of Contemporary Art, Chicago.

Claire Bishop (p. 398) lives in New York. She is professor of contemporary art, theory, and exhibition history at the Graduate Center at the City University of New York. Recurrent themes in her research are spectatorship and the relationship between art and politics.

Gregg Bordowitz (p. 209) is a writer and artist. He is the program director for the School of the Art Institute of Chicago low-residency MFA program.

Garret Bradley (p. 375) is a filmmaker living in New Orleans.

Marcel Breuer (1902–1981) (p. 156) was the architect of the Whitney Museum's third home at 945 Madison Avenue.

Cynthia Carr (p. 24) chronicled the work of contemporary artists as a *Village Voice* writer in the 1980s and 1990s and is the author of three books—most recently, *Fire in the Belly: The Life and Times of David Wojnarowicz* (2012).

Paul Chan (p. 376) is an artist who lives in New York.

Matt Connors (p. 388) is an artist who lives and works in New York and Los Angeles.

John Corbett (p. 347) is a curator and writer based in Chicago. He teaches at the School of the Art Institute of Chicago and is co-owner of Corbett vs. Dempsey Gallery.

Walter Danes (p. 397) is a critic who lives and works in Dan Walsh's head.

Leslie Dick (p. 322) is a writer who lives in Los Angeles. She teaches in the art program at CalArts.

Bill Dietz (p. 137) is a composer, the artistic director of the Berlin-based Ensemble Zwischentöne, and is co-chair of music/sound in Bard College's Milton Avery Graduate School of Arts.

Thom Donovan (p. 358) is a poet, editor, curator, and teacher living in Brooklyn. His poems and essays have appeared widely in print and online journals. He teaches poetics and writing at the School of Visual Arts, Parsons The New School for Design, and Pratt Institute.

Jeanne Dunning (p. 341) is an artist whose work has been widely exhibited since the late 1980s.

Robert Fahey (p. 376) is a professional court tennis player. He has held the World Championship in court tennis since 1994. In 2008 he set the record for most consecutive defenses of the title.

James Franco (p. 386) is an actor, writer, director, and teacher.

Nicholas Frank (p. 394) is an artist, curator, and writer. He cofounded the Milwaukee International in 2006. His novella *The Sound of the Horn* was published in 2010.

Malik Gaines (p. 133) is one third of My Barbarian, a participant in the 2014 Whitney Biennial (pp. 220–23).

Louise Gray (p. 117) is a London-based writer and editor specializing in experimental music. Her work appears in *The Wire*, *Musicworks*, *New Internationalist*, and many other arts publications. She is also the author of *The No-Nonsense Guide to World Music* (2009).

Stevie Guy (p. 385) is a singer living in Preston, UK.

Grant Hart (p. 361) lives and works in Minneapolis. He is a musician and a founding member of the band Hüsker Dü.

Philip Hoare (p. 60) is the author of seven works of nonfiction, including *The Whale* (2009) and *The Sea Inside* (2014). He is senior lecturer in creative writing at the University of Southampton, UK.

Egija Inzule (p. 97) is a curator associated with Contemporary Art Centre in Riga and castillo/corrales in Paris. She is currently based in Rome, as a member of Istituto Svizzero for the academic year 2013–14.

Travis Jeppesen (p. 108–111) is a participant in the 2014 Whitney Biennial (pp. 88–91).

Jennifer Kabat (p. 334) is a writer and essayist who lives in upstate New York. She contributes frequently to *Frieze* magazine and is a founding editor of the website *The Weeklings*.

Owen Kaen (p. 319) is Darren Bader's friend. He lives in New York.

Brooke Kanther (p. 394) is an artist currently pursuing her MFA at the School of the Art Institute of Chicago.

Miriam Katz (p. 381) is a Brooklyn-based curator and writer. She has organized exhibitions and performances for MoMA PS1; the Museum of Contemporary Art, Los Angeles; and the Kitchen, New York, and has written for *Artforum*, *Bookforum*, *Flash Art*, and other publications.

Juliet Kinchin (p. 350) is a curator in the department of architecture and design at the Museum of Modern Art, New York.

Thomas J. Lax (p. 51) is an assistant curator at the Studio Museum in Harlem, New York.

William Least Heat-Moon (p. 45) is an American writer of English, Irish, and Osage ancestry. His 1982 work *Blue Highways* is considered one of the critical works of highway literature in America.

Judy Ledgerwood (p. 389) is a Chicago-based artist and professor of art theory and practice at Northwestern University.

Andrew Leland (p. 348) is an editor at *The Believer* magazine and McSweeney's Books. He hosts *The Organist*, *The Believer*'s monthly podcast.

Contributors

Pablo León de la Barra (p. 71) is currently in a two-year residency at the Solomon R. Guggenheim Museum in New York, and is curating the second exhibition in the Guggenheim UBS MAP Global Art Initiative, focusing on contemporary art and artists from Latin America.

Esther Leslie (p. 121) is a professor of political aesthetics at Birkbeck, University of London. She has published on Walter Benjamin, animation, and the industrialization of color. Her latest book explores liquid crystals.

Kate Levant (p. 171) is an artist whose practice involves the formation of sculpture, language, and montage to ad hoc ends. Levant participated in the 2012 Whitney Biennial.

Dennis Lim (p. 62) writes about film and popular culture for various publications, including the *New York Times* and the *Los Angeles Times*. He is editorial director at the Museum of the Moving Image, Queens, NY.

Fionn Meade (p. 37) is a curator and writer based in New York. He is a faculty member at the Center for Curatorial Studies, Bard College, and is in Columbia University's MFA program for visual arts.

John Neff (p. 356) is a Chicago-based artist, curator, and writer.

David Pagel (p. 330) is an art critic who lives in Los Angeles. He writes regularly for the *Los Angeles Times* and is a professor of art theory and history at Claremont Graduate University and an adjunct curator at the Parrish Art Museum in Water Mill, NY.

Imani Perry (p. 324) is an interdisciplinary scholar of race, law, and culture currently living in Philadelphia. She is a professor in the Center for African American Studies at Princeton University.

Paul Pfeiffer (p. 340) is an artist living and working in New York.

Rob Pruitt (p. 386) is an artist and animal lover who lives in New York.

Lane Relyea (p. 391) lives and works in Chicago where he is associate professor and chair of art theory and practice at Northwestern University.

Amanda Ross-Ho (p. 345) is an artist living and working in Los Angeles. Her conceptually driven work explores materiality through installation, photography, painting, and sculpture.

Andrew Russeth (p. 331) is an art critic who lives in New York. He is senior editor at the *New York Observer* and edits *Gallerist*, the paper's art website.

Michael Sanchez (p. 113) is a doctoral candidate in art history at Columbia University.

Adrian Saxe (p. 377), a third-generation Los Angelino, has been a full-time practicing artist working primarily with ceramic media for fifty years, as well as a professor of art at University of California, Los Angeles, for forty years.

Cindy Sherman (p. 321) is a photographer and filmmaker who lives and works in New York.

Elisabeth Sherman (p. 101) is a senior curatorial assistant at the Whitney Museum of American Art. In addition to assisting on the 2012 and 2014 Biennials, she curated *Trisha Baga: Plymouth Rock 2* (2012).

Raf Simons (p. 384) is a fashion designer based in Antwerp, home to his eponymous menswear collection. In 2011, he was named artistic director of Christian Dior women's collections.

Kristine Stiles (p. 65) is the France Family Professor of Art, Art History and Visual Studies at Duke University and author of *Theories and Documents of Contemporary Art* (2012) and *Correspondence Course: An Epistolary History of Carolee Schneemann and Her Circle* (2010).

Donna Stonecipher (p. 333) is an American poet who lives in Berlin. She is the author of three books of poetry, most recently *The Cosmopolitan* (2008).

Felony Swan (p. 382) oversees the collections of the Center for Contemporary Acquisitions and advises numerous emerging exhibition venues, including Wiggle Room. She lives in New York with her dog, Browser.

Amy Taubin (p. 55) writes film and cultural criticism. She is a contributing editor for *Film Comment* and *Sight and Sound* magazines and is a frequent contributor to *Artforum*.

Mamie Tinkler (p. 41) is an artist and the 2014 Biennial Coordinator.

Brad Troemel (p. 340) is an artist, writer, and instructor living in New York.

Robert P. Vande Kappelle (p. 363) is an ordained minister and professor of religious studies at Washington & Jefferson College in Washington, PA. He is the author of seven books and numerous articles, including his "Adventures in Spirituality" trilogy and *Beyond Belief* (2013), *Iron Sharpens Iron* (2013), and *Hope Revealed* (2013).

Sara VanDerBeek (p. 327) is an artist who lives and works in New York. In 2008 and 2012, she spoke with Sarah Charlesworth for *North Drive Press* and *Flash Art*, respectively.

Frazer Ward (p. 344) is an art historian and critic who lives in Northampton, MA. He is associate professor in the department of art at Smith College.

Christopher Williams (p. 325) is an artist who lives in Cologne. He is professor of photography at the Kunstakademie Düsseldorf.

Kaelen Wilson-Goldie (p. 29) is a contributing editor for *Bidoun*, writes regularly for *Artforum*, and pens a column for *Frieze*.

Matthew S. Witkovsky (p. 327) is Sandor Chair and curator of photography at the Art Institute of Chicago, where *Sarah Charlesworth: Stills* will be exhibited in September 2014.

Catherine Wood (p. 85) is curator of contemporary art and performance at Tate Modern London. She recently curated *A Bigger Splash: Painting after Performance* and coprogrammed the opening of the Tate Tanks.

Su Wu (p. 318) is a writer in Los Angeles. She runs the website *I'm Revolting* and was a 2012 USC Annenberg/Getty Arts Journalism Program Fellow.

STAFF
As of December 1, 2013

Alison Abreu-Garcia
Jay Abu-Hamda
Stephanie Adams
Adrienne Alston
Martha Alvarez-LaRose
Amanda Angel
Marilou Aquino
Emily Arensman
Morgan Arenson
I. D. Aruede
Bernadette Baker
John Balestrieri
Wendy Barbee-Lowell
Courtney Bassett
Ingrid Baumanis
Caroline Beasley
Justine Benith
Harry Benjamin
Nathalie Berger
Jeffrey Bergstrom
Caitlin Bermingham
Alberto Betancourt
Stephanie Birmingham
Ivy Blackman
Hillary Blass
Richard Bloes
Keri Bronk
P. Ryan Brown
Ethan Buchsbaum
Douglas Burnham
Patrick Burns
Ron Burrell
Christopher Burton
Garfield Burton
Jocelyn Cabral
Pablo Caines
Margaret Cannie
Amanda Carrasco
Christina Cataldo
Cristal Chen
Inde Cheong
Hannie Chia
Ramon Cintron
Randy Clark
Ron Clark
Correna Cohen
Melissa Cohen
Heather Cox
Ellen Croiser
Kenneth Cronan
Mia Curran
Donna De Salvo
Margo Delidow
Eduardo Diaz
Lauren DiLoreto
Lisa Dowd
Delano Dunn
Anita Duquette
Raquel Echanique
Alvin Eubanks
Rich Flood
Seth Fogelman
Meghan Forsyth
Carter Foster
Samuel Franks
Murlin Frederick
Annie French
Donald Garlington
Larissa Gentile
Claudia Gerbracht
Robert Gerhardt
Clara Goldman
Hilary Greenbaum
Cassandra Guan
Peter Guss
Stewart Hacker
Kate Hahm
Sam Hancocks
Greta Hartenstein
Maura Heffner
Dina Helal
Peter Henderson
Claire Henry
Jennifer Heslin
Ann Holcomb
Nicholas S. Holmes
Abigail Hoover
Jacob Horn
Sarah Hromack
Karen Huang
Sarah Humphreville
Wycliffe Husbands
Beth Huseman
Chrissie Iles
Carlos Jacobo
Julia Johnson
Dolores Joseph
Martha Joseph
Vinnie Kanhai
Chris Ketchie
David Kiehl
Thomas Killie
Mo Kim
Marci King
Kathleen Koehler
Irene Koo
Tom Kraft
Zoe Larkins
Eunice Lee
Sang Soo Lee
Kristen Leipert
Monica Leon
Jen Leventhal
Jeffrey Levine
Danielle Linzer
Kelley Loftus
Robert Lomblad
Sarah Lookofsky
Alison Lotto
Kevin Lu
Doug Madill
Elyse Mallouk
Carol Mancusi-Ungaro
Louis Manners
Anna Martin
Meredith Martin
Diana Matuszak
Heather Maxson
Madeline McGrath
Michael McQuilkin
Kate McWatters
Sandra Meadows
Victoria Meek
Sarah Meller
Bridget Mendoza
Jessica Merritt
Graham Miles
Dana Miller
David Miller
Christa Molinaro
Michael Moriah
Magda Mortner
Victor Moscoso
Eleonora Nagy
Pablo Narvaez
Ruben Negron
Lloyd Newell
Graham Newhall
Carlos Noboa
Thomas Nunes
Brianna O'Brien Lowndes
Rose O'Neill-Suspitsyna
Suzanna Okie
Rebecca Olderman
Nelson Ortiz
Barbara Padolsky
Jane Panetta
Christiane Paul
Ailen Pedraza
Jessica Pepe
Laura Phipps
Angelo Pikoulas
Mary Potter
Kathryn Potts
Linda Priest
Frank Procaccini
Vincent Punch
Christy Putnam
Aaron Redlin
Julie Rega
Natalee Reid
Gregory Reynolds
Lindsey Reynolds
Emanuel Riley
Felix Rivera
Nicholas Robbins
Jeffrey Robinson
Georgianna Rodriguez
Gina Rogak
Justin Romeo
Adrienne Rooney
Joshua Rosenblatt
Jamie Rosenfeld
Amy Roth
Scott Rothkopf
Carol Rusk
Eliza Ryan
Angelina Salerno
Galina Sapozhnikova
Lynn Schatz
Arielle Schraeter
Peter Scott
Michelle Sealey
David Selimoski
Jason Senquiz
Ai Wee Seow
Amy Sharp
Elisabeth Sherman
Kasey Sherrick
Sasha Silcox
Matt Skopek
Joel Snyder
Michele Snyder
Stephen Soba
Barbi Spieler
Carrie Springer
John Stanley
Mark Steigelman
Minerva Stella
Betty Stolpen
Hillary Strong
Emilie Sullivan
Denis Suspitsyn
Elisabeth Sussman
Hannah Swihart
Catherine Taft
Christine Taguines
Kean Tan
Ellen Tepfer
Latasha Thomas
Phyllis Thorpe
Mamie Tinkler
Ana Torres
Beth Turk
Lauren Turner
Ray Vega
Snigdha Verma
Eric Vermilion
Billie Rae Vinson
Farris Wahbeh
Morgan Watson
Adam D. Weinberg
Alexandra Wheeler
Michelle Wilder
John Williams
Andrew Wojtek
Rachel Wysoki
Liza Zapol
Sefkia Zekiroski
Kayla Zemsky

Acknowledgments

The 2014 Biennial was a tremendous undertaking that required the hard work of many people both inside and outside of the Museum. Our foremost thanks go to the hundred and three participating artists and collectives in the Biennial, and our appreciation extends as well to all of the artists we visited during the exhibition-making process. We would like to thank Adam D. Weinberg, Alice Pratt Brown Director, for inviting us to organize the Whitney's signature exhibition and for his seemingly endless energy and enthusiasm which made this band of outsiders feel at home and the work an absolute pleasure. We would also like to thank Donna De Salvo, chief curator and deputy director for programs, for providing unwavering support, invaluable guidance, and the thoughtful and probing questions we needed periodically during the process. Elisabeth Sussman and Jay Sanders were the best possible team of advisors imaginable, offering insight, inquiry, prodding, institutional memory, tough love, and forethought that enabled us to ask the difficult questions we needed to ask ourselves every step of the way. Emily Russell, director of curatorial affairs, and Scott Rothkopf, curator and associate director of programs, provided key assistance at critical moments. We are most grateful to the Biennial team: Elisabeth Sherman, senior curatorial assistant, was a resourceful and diligent interlocutor from day one and helped us navigate every element of the process of organizing exhibition, catalogue, and, in no small feat, the three of us. Mamie Tinkler, Biennial coordinator, deftly managed all aspects of the exhibition production and installation process with patience, diplomacy, and remarkable poise even with hundreds of spinning plates overhead. Martha Joseph, Biennial assistant, provided invaluable support throughout the process, and was an especially warm and helpful hand with the catalogue and its many intricate parts. Greta Hartenstein, curatorial assistant, lent her expertise and enthusiasm to performance management. And Biennial intern Tatiane Santa Rosa was a great asset to the team. Nothing would have been possible from afar without this crack team.

We are grateful to Beth Turk, associate editor, who expertly spearheaded the publication of this remarkable volume and helped shape its contents. Mark Owens, assisted by Ghazaal Vojdani, created an absolutely brilliant design for the catalogue. The editorial team Karen Kelly, Deirdre O'Dwyer, Jason Best, Thea Hetzner, and Diana Stoll did a tremendous job under the supervision of project manager Donna Wingate. We are especially thankful to all the writers for the catalogue, the artists themselves or their chosen authors, contributors, or collaborators.

The Biennial inevitably relies on the efforts of every department within the Museum. We would to thank the entire Whitney's staff, in particular: Jay Abu-Hamda, projectionist; Stephanie Adams, director of individual and planned giving; Amanda Angel, communications manager; Emily Arensman, coordinator of public programs; John Balestrieri, director of security, and the entire security team; Wendy Barbee-Lowell, manager of visitor services; Jeffrey Bergstrom, audio visual manager; Caitlin Bermingham, assistant head preparator; Stephanie Birmingham, onsite member services senior coordinator; Richard Bloes, senior technician; Keri Bronk, graphic designer; Melissa Cohen, associate registrar; Anita Duquette, manager, rights and reproductions; Delano Dunn, facilities department manager; Rich Flood, director of marketing and community affairs; Seth Fogelman, senior registrar, exhibitions; Meg Forsyth, graphic designer; Larissa Gentile, building project manager; Hilary Greenbaum, director of graphic design; Peter Guss, director of information technology; Kate Hahm, assistant exhibitions coordinator; Maura Heffner, exhibitions manager; Jennifer Heslin, director of retail operations; Jacob Horn, editorial assistant; Nicholas S. Holmes, general counsel; Sarah Hromack, director of digital media; Jen Leventhal, manager of administrative affairs; Jeffrey Levine, chief marketing and communications officer; Kelley Loftus, paper preparator; Brianna O'Brien Lowndes, director of membership and annual fund; Elyse Mallouk, digital content manager; Bill Maloney, building consultant; Anna Martin, exhibition design and construction assistant; Gene McHugh, Kress Interpretation Fellow; Sarah Meller, marketing associate; Graham Miles, art handler, supervisor; Kathryn Potts, associate director, Helena Rubinstein Chair of Education; Christy Putnam, associate director for exhibitions and collections management; Nicholas Robbins, curatorial assistant; Gina Rogak, director of special events; Justin Romeo, executive coordinator, director's office; Joshua Rosenblatt, head preparator; Amy Roth, chief planning officer; Kasey Sherrick, manager of corporate partnerships; Joel Snyder, manager of member benefits and relations; Stephen Soba, director of communications; Barbi Spieler, head registrar, permanent collection; John S. Stanley, chief operating officer; Mark Steigelman, exhibition design and construction manager; Betty Stolpen, senior coordinator of major gifts; Hillary Strong, director of institutional advancement; Ray Vega, carpenter, supervisor; Farris Wahbeh, manager, cataloguing and documentation; and Alexandra Wheeler, deputy director for development.

The following individuals and foundations provided critical assistance in the production of artist projects: The Andy Warhol Foundation for the Visual Arts, Nancy Allen, John Baker, Nick Bastis, Lauren Beck, Jonathan Bender, Tyler Britt, Jakob Brugge, Peter Carlson, Olivia Ciummo, Vincent Cuneo, Jocelyn Davis, Jack Doroshow, Noreen Doyle, Natasha Garcia-Lomas, Paul Geluso, Jonah Groeneboer, Steven Henry, Ione, Peter Kelly, Peter Kenney, Thomas Kriegsman, Robert Longo, Lois Plehn, Ben Pryor, Joe Scanlan, Tim Smith, Ron Street, Yulia Vital, Celeste Voce, and Vanesa Zendejas.

Additionally, we would like to acknowledge the galleries whose commitment to their artists helped make the Biennial possible: 1301PE Gallery, Los Angeles; Aanant & Zoo, Berlin; Air de Paris, Paris; Algus Greenspon, New York; Andersen's Contemporary, Copenhagen; Andrew Kreps Gallery, New York; Anton Kern, New York; Aurel Scheibler, Berlin; Baldwin Gallery, Aspen; Bortolami Gallery, New York; Broadway 1602, New York; Callicoon Fine Arts, New York; Cheim & Read, New York; Christine König Galerie, Vienna; Christopher Grimes Gallery, Santa Monica; Corbett vs. Dempsey, Chicago; Darren Knight Gallery, Sydney, Australia; David Kordansky Gallery, Los Angeles; Derek Eller Gallery, New York; Emerson Dorsch, Miami; Erica Redling Fine Art, Los Angeles; ESSEX STREET, New York; Foxy Production, New York; François Ghebaly Gallery, Los Angeles; Galerie Buchholz, Cologne/Berlin; Galerie Catherine Bastide, Brussels; Galerie Gisela Capitain, Cologne; Galerie Guido W. Baudach, Berlin; Galerie Janine Rubeiz, Beirut; Galerie Meyer Kainer, Vienna; Galerie

Acknowledgments

Michel Rein, Paris/Brussels; Galerie Nelson-Freeman, Paris; Galerie Susanna Kulli, Zurich; Galleria Continua, San Gimignano, Beijing, and Le Moulin; Galleria Massimo Minini, Brescia, Italy; Galleria Raffaella Cortese, Milan; Galleria Raucci/Santamaria, Naples; Gandy Gallery, Bratislava; Gavin Brown's enterprise, New York; Gavlak Gallery, Palm Beach; The Green Gallery, Milwaukee; Greene Naftali Gallery, New York; greengrassi, London; Hauser & Wirth; House of Gaga, Mexico City; International Art Objects Galleries, Los Angeles; Jessica Silverman Gallery, San Francisco; Karma International, Zurich; Kavi Gupta Gallery, Chicago and Berlin; Koenig & Clinton, New York; Kurimanzutto, Mexico City; Lars Bohman Gallery, Stockholm; Luis de Jesus Los Angeles; Magnus Müller Temporary, Berlin; Mallorca Landings Gallery, Palma De Mallorca; Maloney Fine Art, Los Angeles; Marc Jancou Contemporary, New York; Marc Selwyn Fine Art, Los Angeles; Masataka Hayakawa Gallery, Tokyo; Mathew Gallery, Berlin; Maureen Paley, London; Mesler&Hug, Los Angeles; mother's tankstation, Dublin; Murray Guy, New York; Nicole Klagsbrun, New York; Office Baroque Gallery, Brussels; OHWOW, Los Angeles; On Stellar Rays, New York; Paula Cooper Gallery, New York; Peter Blake Gallery, Los Angeles; Petzel Gallery, New York; Pilar Corrias Gallery, London; Postmasters Gallery, New York; Rachel Uffner Gallery, New York; Reena Spaulings Fine Art, New York; Rena Bransten Gallery, San Francisco; Roberto Paradise, San Juan; Salon 94, New York; Sfeir-Semler Gallery, Hamburg and Beirut; Shaheen Modern and Contemporary Art, Cleveland; Shane Campbell Gallery, Chicago; Sikkema Jenkins & Co., New York; Silberkuppe, Berlin; Stella Lohaus Gallery, Antwerp; Stephen Daiter Gallery, Chicago; Steven Wolf Fine Arts, San Francisco; Susan Inglett Gallery, New York; Susanne Vielmetter Los Angeles Projects; Taka Ishii Gallery, Tokyo; Take Ninagawa, Tokyo; Tanya Leighton Gallery, Berlin; Team Gallery, New York; Tempo Rubato, Tel Aviv; The Butcher's Daughter, Detroit; Thomas Duncan Gallery, Los Angeles; Thomas Erben Gallery, New York; Thomas Solomon Gallery, Los Angeles; WALLSPACE, New York; Western Exhibitions, Chicago; Wilfried Lentz, Rotterdam; and Zidoun-Bossuyt Gallery, Luxembourg.

We are also grateful to the following individuals and institutions for providing important loans to the exhibition: Pedro Barbosa; Robert W. and Anne Conn; John Corbett; Creative Audio Archive at Experimental Sound Studio; Agnieszka Czeblakow; Joeff Davis; Angeline and Mark Evans; Fales Library and Special Collections, New York University; Helga Fassonaki and Andrew Scott of Metal Rouge; Fred Fehlau; Andrew Franklin; Brent Gutzeit; Harry Ransom Center, The University of Texas at Austin; Jinger Heffner; Jim Isermann; Kino Lorber, New York; Lampo (Alisa Wolfson and Andrew Fenchel); Liz and Eric Lefkosky; David Lester and Jean Smith of Mecca Normal; Fred Lonberg-Holm; Jessica Macias; Monica Majoli; The Metropolitan Museum of Art, New York; Bill Meyer; Reuben Moore; Ray Morales; The Museum of Modern Art, New York; Dick and Betty Ann Ritscher; and Millie Wilson.

Finally, Stuart Comer would like to offer his boundless thanks to: the artists, writers, and editors who have shaped this exhibition and its catalogue; my many families, but foremost William and Robin Comer, Hadley Comer, Sarah Ingle, Lecia Dole-Recio and Erin Cassidy, and Desmond Cassidy; Ian White (1971–2013), whose unyielding integrity and forceful commitment to championing the complex freedoms of the artistic process are deeply embedded in the outlook of this exhibition; Negar Azimi, Bill Berkson, Felix Burritcher, Justin Cavin, Cesar Garcia, Gretchen Gasterland, Sarah Gavlak, Rita Gonzalez, Brendan Griffiths, Fritz Haeg, Ed Halter, Jane Holzer, Thomas J. Lax, Pablo León de la Barra, Connie Lewallen, Kerry Morgan, Emily Roysdon, Julika Rudelius, Jessica Silverman, Reid Ulrich, David Velasco, Carl Williams, and Matt Wolf; Glenn Lowry and my colleagues at MoMA, in particular the Department of Media and Performance Art; and Sir Nicholas Serota, Chris Dercon, and my former colleagues at Tate, in particular Catherine Wood, George Clark, and Valentina Ravaglia.

Anthony Elms would like to thank: all the artists—naturally; the extraordinary enablers of various angles: Hilton Als, Mark Beasley, Patrice I. and Anthony Elms, Sylvie Fortin, Anthony Huberman, Erin Kimmel, Glenn Ligon, Leslie Miller, Bob Nickas, Tyler Rowland, Amy Sadao, Ingrid Schaffner, Bennett Simpson, Jacqueline Terrassa, Hamza Walker, and Rob Weiner; everyone at the ICA who put up with my scattered brain; and Erin Leland for taking my confusion in stride.

And Michelle Grabner would like to recognize and thank: all of the artists who allowed me to visit their studios and engage in conversations about the many states of contemporary art; the venues for Donelle Woolford's tour: Bemis Center for Contemporary Arts, Omaha; Contemporary Art Center of Peoria, IL; Contemporary Arts Museum Houston; Dorchester Projects, Chicago; JACK, Brooklyn; The Kitchen, New York; LA><ART, Los Angeles; Midway Contemporary Art, Minneapolis Museum of Contemporary Art Detroit; The Powerhouse, Oxford, MS; CCA Wattis Institute for Contemporary Arts, San Francisco; and White Flags, St. Louis; and the following people for their insights and support: Julie and Shane Campbell; James and Jane Cohan; Patrick Collier; Eric Crosby; T. J. Donovan; Jesse Edleman; Jonathan Franzen; Nicholas Frank, Karen Green; Brooke Kantor; Anne Mosseri-Marilio and Reto Wey; David Norr; Jake Palmert and John Riepenhoff; Griff Williams; Dean Lisa Wainwright, Provost Elissa Tenny, and President Walter Massey, School of the Art Institute of Chicago; and my husband Brad and my children: Oliver, Peter, and Ceal.

— Stuart Comer, Anthony Elms, and Michelle Grabner

Photography and Reproduction Credits

Unless otherwise indicated, images are copyright © the artist and appear courtesy the artist, estate, and/or owner. The following applies to images for which additional acknowledgment is due.

Boldface indicates page numbers.

28 Courtesy Sfeir-Semler Gallery, Beirut and Hamburg. **29–30** Courtesy Callicoon Fine Arts, New York. **31** Courtesy Sfeir-Semler Gallery, Beirut and Hamburg. **32** Courtesy Fundação Bienal de São Paulo; photograph by Leo Eloy (top). **34** Courtesy Tate Modern, London (top). **36–39** Courtesy Gavin Brown's enterprise, New York; Sadie Coles HQ, London; and mother's tankstation, Dublin. **44** Courtesy Special Collections, University of Nevada–Reno Library. **49** Courtesy P.P.O.W., New York; photograph by Adam Reich (bottom). **54** Photograph by Alex Lipschultz. **55** Photograph by Houston King. **56** Photographs by Ethan Vogt (top and bottom). **57** Photograph by Alex Lipschultz. **64–69** Courtesy Luis De Jesus Los Angeles. **74** Photograph © Jason Dewey. **76** Courtesy Galerie Buchholz, Berlin and Cologne. **77** Courtesy Adamski, Berlin; photograph © Brian Forrest (left); photograph by Simon Vogel (right). **79** Courtesy Regen Projects, Los Angeles. **82** Courtesy Regen Projects, Los Angeles. **84** Courtesy François Ghebaly, Los Angeles; photograph by Robert Wedemeyer. **85** Courtesy François Ghebaly, Los Angeles; photograph by Marlene Matlow. **86** Courtesy François Ghebaly, Los Angeles; photograph by Robert Wedemeyer (top). **100–103** Courtesy Redling Fine Art, Los Angeles, and Jessica Silverman Gallery, San Francisco; photographs by Jeff McLane. **104–107** Courtesy Derek Eller Gallery, New York; photographs by Tom Powel Imaging. **112, 115** Courtesy Reena Spaulings Fine Art, New York. **116** Photograph by David Pascale. **117** Photograph by Ione. **118** Photograph by Ione (top). © Deep Listening Publications (bottom). **120** Courtesy Koenig & Clinton, New York; Thomas Solomon Gallery, Los Angeles; Andersen's Contemporary, Copenhagen; and Wilfried Lentz, Rotterdam. **121** Courtesy Koenig & Clinton, New York; and Thomas Solomon Gallery, Los Angeles. **123** Courtesy Koenig & Clinton, New York; Thomas Solomon Gallery, Los Angeles; Andersen's Contemporary, Copenhagen; and Wilfried Lentz, Rotterdam. **124–27** Courtesy Monya Rowe Gallery, New York; and Mallorca Landings Gallery, Palma De Mallorca, Spain. **128** © Paul Gellman and Semiotext(e). **132** Photograph by Evan La Londe. **162–65** Courtesy Salon 94, New York. **166** Photographs by Phillip Stearns. **168** Letter courtesy Robert Ashley; photograph by Makepeace Tsao. **170–73** Courtesy Office Baroque, Antwerp, and Galleria Fonti, Naples. **174** Courtesy Western Exhibitions, Chicago; photograph by James Prinz. **176–77** Courtesy Western Exhibitions, Chicago. **178–79** Courtesy kurmanzutto, Mexico City; photographs by Jean Christophe Lett. **180** Photograph by Tom Van Eynde. **183** Photograph by James Prinz. **184** Photograph © Centre Pompidou-Metz / Rémi Villaggi. **185** Photograph © Marc Domage. **186, 188** Photographs by Eric McNatt. **212** Courtesy Susanne Vielmetter Los Angeles Projects; photograph by Gene Ogami. **213** Courtesy Susanne Vielmetter Los Angeles Projects and Galerie Wien Lukatsch, Berlin. **214** Courtesy Susanne Vielmetter Los Angeles Projects; photograph by Jason Mandella. **215** Courtesy Galerie Wien Lukatsch, Berlin; photographs by Nick Ash. **216** Photograph by Lee Thompson. **217** Courtesy Galerie Barbara Weiss, Berlin; photograph by Lee Thompson. **218** Courtesy Galerie Barbara Weiss, Berlin, and Corbett vs. Dempsey, Chicago; photograph by Lee Thompson. **219** Photograph by Lee Thompson. **220–22** Courtesy Susanne Vielmetter Los Angeles Projects. **228** Courtesy Vox Populi, Philadelphia; photograph by Brent Wahl. **229** Photograph by Tamara Johnson (left); photograph by Ashley Hunt (right). **230** Photograph by Robbie Sweeny. **231** Courtesy The Studio Museum in Harlem; photograph by Scott Rudd (left); photograph by Ashley Hunt (right). **232–33** Photographs by Olivia Ciummo. **246** Courtesy Galerie Catherine Bastide, Brussels; ESSEX STREET, New York; and Metro Pictures, New York. Photograph by Vincent Cuneo. **247** Courtesy Galerie Catherine Bastide, Brussels; ESSEX STREET, New York; and Metro Pictures, New York; photograph by Adam Reich. **248** Courtesy the Transportation Library at Northwestern University. **249** Courtesy Galerie Catherine Bastide, Brussels; ESSEX STREET, New York; and Metro Pictures, New York; photograph by Adam Reich. **250–55** Courtesy Petzel, New York; photographs by Jason Mandella. **267** Courtesy Galleria Franco Noero, Turin; photograph by Sebastiano Pellion di Persano. **268** Courtesy Metro Pictures, New York. **272** Courtesy Susan Inglett Gallery, New York. **273** Image produced by Susan Bowman. **275** Courtesy Postmasters Gallery, New York. **278** Courtesy Cheim & Read, New York; photograph by Brian Buckley. **279** Courtesy Emerson Dorsch, Miami. **280** Photograph by Gaylen Gerber and Rémi Villaggi. **282** Courtesy Susanne Vielmetter Los Angeles Projects; photograph by Robert Wedemeyer. **283** Courtesy Corbett vs. Dempsey, Chicago; photographer by Tom von Eynde. **285** Courtesy Sikkema Jenkins & Co; photograph by Cristobal Zanartu. **287** Courtesy Greene Naftali Gallery, New York. **291** Photographs by Devin Farrand. **293** Photograph by You-ni Chae. **294** Courtesy Shane Campbell Gallery, Chicago; photograph by Robert Chase Heishman. **295** Courtesy Rachel Uffner Gallery, New York, and Sikkema Jenkins & Co., New York; Photograph by John Berens. **297** Photograph by Robert Wedermeyer. **298** Photograph by Anthony Cunha. **299** Courtesy Shane Campbell Gallery, Chicago, and Team Gallery, New York. **302** Courtesy Maloney Fine Art, Los Angeles; photograph by Robert Wedemeyer. **303** Courtesy Gavin Brown's enterprise, New York. **304** Photograph by Andres Ramirez. **306** Photograph by Robert Wedemeyer. **307** Photograph by Peter Tijhuis. **308** Courtesy Sikkema Jenkins & Co., New York; Photograph by John Berens. **310** Photograph by Fredrik Nilsen. **311** Courtesy Kavi Gupta Gallery, Chicago. **312** Photograph by Thomas Mueller. **314** Courtesy the David Foster Wallace Literary Trust. **315** Courtesy Paula Cooper Gallery, New York; photograph by Steven Probert. **317** Courtesy Corbett vs. Dempsey, Chicago; photograph by Tom Van Eynde.